Hiking, Biking
Canyonlands
and Vicinity

MW00534009

Featuring: Hiking, Biking, Geology & Archaeology,
and Cowboy, Ranching & Trail Building History

2nd Edition

Michael R. Kelsey

Kelsey Publishing
456 E. 100 N.
Provo, Utah, USA, 84606-3208
Tele: 801-373-3327
Email Address
mkelsey@kelseyguidebooks.com

For the latest list of other books published by Michael R. Kelsey and Kelsey Publishing, a list of current distributors, current email address or important updates on the canyons in this book, go to the **website:**

kelseyguidebooks.com

First Edition May, 1992
Second Edition, April, 2013
Copyright © 1992 & 2013, Michael R. Kelsey
All Rights Reserved
Library of Congress Control Number: 2012920982
ISBN 978-0-944510-29-2

Primary Distributor
All of Michael R. Kelsey's books are sold by this distributor. A list of his titles is in the back of this book. Or go to **kelseyguidebooks.com** for the most up-to-date list of his books currently in print.
Brigham Distributing, 110 South, 800 West, Brigham City, Utah, 84302, Tele. 435-723-6611, Fax 435-723-6644, Website *brighamdistributing.com*, Email *brigdist@sisna.com*.

Most of Kelsey's books are sold by these distributors.
Partners West, 1901 Raymond Avenue, SW, Renton, WA, 98057, Tele. 425-227-8486, Fax 425-204-1448, Email *orders@partners-west.com*, Website *partners-west.com*.
Books West, 18101 East Colfax Avenue, Aurora, Colorado, USA, 80011, Tele. 303-449-5995, or 800-378-4188, Fax 303-449-5951, Website *bookswest.com*.
Treasure Chest Books, 451 N. Bonita Avenue, Tucson, Arizona, USA, 85745, Tele. 520-623-9558, or 800-969-9558, Fax 520-642-5888, Website *treasurechestbooks.com*, Email *info@rionuevo.com*.

Some of Kelsey's books are sold by the following distributors.
Liberty Mountain, 4375 W. 1980 S., Suite 100, Salt Lake City, Utah, 84104, Tele. 800-366-2666 or 801-954-0741, Fax 801-954-0766, Website *libertymountain.com*, Email *sales@libertymountain.com*.
Rincon Publishing, 1913 North Skyline Drive, Orem, Utah, 84097, Tele. 801-377-7657, Fax 801-356-2733, Email *rinconpub@utahtrails.com*, Website *utahtrails.com*
Recreational Equipment, Inc. (R.E.I.), 1700 45th Street East, Sumner, Washington, USA, 98390, Website *rei.com*, Mail Orders Tele. 800-426-4840 (or check at any of their local stores).
Online--Internet: *amazon.com; btol.com; ingrams.com; Bdaltons.com; BarnesandNoble.com*.

For the **UK and Europe**, and the world contact: **Cordee,** 3a De Montfort Street, Leicester, England, UK, LE1 7HD, Tele. Inter+44-116-254-3579, Fax Inter+44-116-247-1176, Website *cordee.co.uk*.

Printed by Press Media, 5600 N. University Avenue, Provo, Utah.
All fotos by the author, unless otherwise stated.
All maps and geology cross sections drawn by the author.

Front Cover

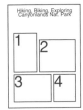

1. The Castle, Ruin Park, Beef Basin
2. Indian Paintings--Pictographs, Clearwater Canyon, Under the Ledge
3. The Doll House, The Maze, Under the Ledge
4. Secret Spire, Spring Canyon Point, Between the Rivers

Back Cover

5. Determination Towers, Mill Canyon, near Monitor & Merrimac
6. The 13 Faces Panel, Horse Canyon, The Needles
7. Corona Arch, Poison Spider Mesa/Bootlegger Canyon, Potash Road
8. Kerby Trail, Lower Little Canyon, Potash Road
9. Indian Paintings--Pictographs, Hell Roaring Canyon
10. Moki House/Cliff Dwellings, Middle Park, Beef Basin

Table of Contents

Acknowledgments

Much of the history in this book is "Oral History". This was obtained from over 80 of the oldest and/or most knowledgeable citizens in the country surrounding Canyonlands National Park. Most of those people lived in Hanksville, Green River, Moab, La Sal or Monticello. All had 2 things in common; most were/are getting along in years, and they lived or worked in the area of Canyonlands and vicinity all or most of their lives and have a personal first-hand knowledge of its history. Most were either ranchers or cowboys, while others were miners or drove team & wagon. They have all contributed to preserving the history of this region which would otherwise have been forgotten. As of 2012, most of these people listed below have passed away.

This listing is in approximately the order of importance for the **1st Edition**. Perhaps the best source was Kenny Allred of Moab, who was a cowboy for years in the Between the Rivers country; also Ned Chaffin, who grew up on the Chaffin Ranch and punched cows in Under the Ledge country; Karl Tangren of Moab, tried to settle on Anderson Bottom, and ran cows along the Colorado River for years; Pearl Biddlecome Marsing Baker, grew up and lived for years on the Robbers Roost Ranch, then Green River; Ray Tibbetts of Moab, remembered lots of stories of his famous father Bill Tibbetts; Chad Moore of Green River, ran cattle on the range west of the Green River north of the Roost country; Kent Johnson of Moab, worked for the Dalton Wells CCC Camp & Grazing Service (fore-runner to the BLM) and helped build many of the access roads in this country; Swanny Kerby, formerly of Moab, ran cows along the Colorado River for years; Buck Tomlinson, lived at the Chaffin Ranch--before the Chaffins, and in Green River; Buster Irvine, grew up in Green River, and once lived on Yokey Bottom; Frank Tidwell, grew up on the Tidwell Ranch and in Green River; Mitch Williams of Moab, whose father first settled on Williams Bottom; Carl Seely helped his family run sheep in Under the Ledge country; Evelyn "Tizzy" Ekker Bingham, lived at Dubinky and later Green River; Lorin Milton, formerly of Green River, who cowboyed in the Tenmile Point area for years; Juni Marsing Barton & Bob Marsing lived on Junes Bottom as children; Illa Mae offered fotos of the Tidwells and John Romjue; Faun Chaffin formerly of the Chaffin Ranch and Green River, ran cows for 25 years in Under the Ledge country; Butch Christensen of Moab, drove equipment to the Indian Creek oil fields; Bill Hatch of Emery, remembered Ray Hatch, his brother, getting shot; Howard Silliman of Green River, whose father helped E.T. Wolverton in Elaterite Basin; Gene Dunham of Green River, knew the later history of the Ruby Ranch; Albert Thayne of Price, remembered the death of Clyde Tidwell; Rusty Musselman, knew about Roy Musselman, wolves and the Dugout Ranch; Paul Moynier of Price, ran sheep in the Under the Ledge country; Verona Murphy Stocks of Moab, helped her father drive cattle up the Murphy Trail in 1918; Angus (Puge) Stocks, built the first roads in The Needles for Al Scorup; Ray Holyoak of Moab, ran cattle on the White Rim; John Scorup of Monticello, knew the Indian Creek country; Crystal, Alex and Joe Tidwell, knew something about alleged murder of Clyde Tidwell; Richard Bedier of Green River, remembered river history; Delmar Titus of the Dugout Ranch, remembered the old homesteads on Indian Creek; Pearl Bliss Buttes lived and worked as a teen ager at the Dugout Ranch in 1912; Erma Wimmer & Bette Wimmer Lang of Crescent Junction and Bobbe Wimmer Kidrick of Salt Lake City, and Duane Wimmer of Moab, all knew some history of the Wimmer, now Rudy Ranch; John Jackson's 3 daughters--Opel Lemon, Alice Olson & Ellesa Jackson Day Ekker; Nick Murphy of Moab, helped built the Shafer Trail Road; George W. Shores, Jr. of Appleton, Wisconsin, remembered his father living at Anvil Bottom and the old Doc Shores Ranch; Bobby Tidwell, lived on the Tidwell Ranch and Bottom for a while as a child; Harold Halverson of Green River, ran cows Between the Rivers; Eric Simonson, told of his father's cabin at Little Valley; Jack & Varna Watterson, lived on McCarty Bottom for a while; Ted Ekker of Green River, knew where most of the trails along the Green River were; John Henry & Prommel Shafer, told about the Shafer Trail; Tex McClatchy, river rat of Moab; Fran & Terby Barnes of Moab, have written many books on the Canyonlands country; Art Secrest of Moab, remembered his father being killed in Shafer Basin; Earline Nelson of Green River and her son Randy still run the farm at Little Valley; Buster Stewart of La Sal, whose father placer mined on the Colorado River during the Depression; Malcom Politano of Green River, knew a little about Jakes Bottom; Rolley Thompson of Green River, whose grandfather lived on the Wheeler (now Ruby) Ranch; LaVern Young of Jerome, Idaho, the last person to live at Dubinky.

Also Murial Smith & Ben Coomer of Green River; Reed Wilson and Kent Frost of Monticello; Barbara Ekker of Hanksville; Jim Hurst, formerly of Green River then Ft. St. John, B.C. Canada; Pudge Ray, Beverly Guire, Sam Taylor, Elsi White, Doloras Shoemaker, Fred Newman and Rudy Higgins of Moab; Louis Thomas of Salt Lake City; Doyle Perkins and Rigbe Wright of Monticello; and Kenny Davis of Thompson; and Paul Moynier of Price.

Also, Jim Braggs, Stan Steck and Gary Cox of the NPS proof-read parts of the manuscript. Also, proof-reading the entire book was Reaola Kelsey Holm and my mother Venetta B. Kelsey.

For the **2nd Edition** of this book here are some new names: Richard Schwarz revealed locations of some interesting places; Zane Taylor (son of Sam) knew stories of his great grandfather, one of the first settlers to Moab; Norma Marsing Bryant lived on Junes Bottom in the early 1930's; Val Dalton ran cows along the Colorado; Tom McCourt of Price wrote about Bill Tibbetts; Clyde Denis, has written about early-day cattle companies and Chesler Park; Vonna Kerby McDougall had info on her father the late Swanny Kerby; La Var Wells of Hanksville knew a little about John Romjue's life; Tera Lyn Allred and Connie Murphy Skelton offered fotos of Kenny Allred's family; Dave Baker of Moab helped built the Kane Creek Road in 1956; Pierre Moynier III of Price told about the Moynier family history and added more to Henry Moynier's death Under the Ledge; also Kathren Seely, Rodney Tangren, Tom Higgenson, Jo Anne Chandler, Neal Dalton, and more stories from Ray Tibbetts, Karl Tangren and Ellesa Jackson Day Ekker. Also, neighbors Laura & Scott Bagshaw helped proof read this 2nd Edition.

The Author

The author was born on March 17, 1943, and experienced his earliest years of life in eastern Utah's Uinta Basin, first on a farm east of Myton, then in or on farms near Roosevelt. In the summer of 1954, the family moved from Roosevelt (and the Great Depression) to Provo where he attended Provo High and Brigham Young University where he earned a BS Degree in Sociology. Shortly thereafter, he discovered that was the wrong subject, so he attended the University of Utah, where he received his Master of Science Degree in Geography (minoring in Geology), finishing classes in June, 1970.

It was then real life began, for on June 9, 1970, he put a pack on his back and started traveling for the first time. Since then he has seen 224 countries (now he can count South Sudan), republics, islands, or island groups. All this wandering has resulted in self-publishing 17 books. Here are his books as of 2013, listed in the order they were first published: *Climber's and Hiker's Guide to the World's Mountains & Volcanos (4th Edition)*; *Utah Mountaineering Guide (3rd Edition)*; *China on Your Own, and Hiking Guide to China's Nine Sacred Mountains (3rd Ed.)* **Out of Print**; *Non-Technical Canyon Hiking Guide to the Colorado Plateau (6th Edition--in **Color**)*; *Hiking and Exploring Utah's San Rafael Swell* (the **4th Edition will be ready by the winter of 2014**); *Hiking and Exploring Utah's Henry Mountains and Robbers Roost (3rd Edition--in **Color**)*; *Hiking and Exploring the Paria River (5th Edition--in **Color**)*; *Hiking and Climbing in the Great Basin National Park (Wheeler Peak, Nevada)* **Out of Print**; *Boater's Guide to Lake Powell (5th Edition--in **Color**)*; *Climbing and Exploring Utah's Mt. Timpanogos* (**Temporarily Out of Print**); *River Guide to Canyonlands National Park & Vicinity (2nd Edition--in **Color**)*; *Hiking, Biking and Exploring Canyonlands National Park & Vicinity (2nd Edition--in **Color**)*; *The Story of Black Rock, Utah*; *Hiking, Climbing and Exploring Western Utah's Jack Watson's Ibex Country*; and *Technical Slot Canyon Guide to the Colorado Plateau (2nd Edition--in **Color**)*.

He also helped his mother, the late Venetta Bond Kelsey, write and publish a book about the one-horse town she was born & raised in, *Life on the Black Rock Desert--A History of Clear Lake, Utah* (**Out of Print, but at some time in the future will be Updated & Reprinted**).

Attention Readers:

Beginning in the winter of 1990, the author started working on 2 books. One was published in June of 1991 and titled, **River Guide to Canyonlands National Park and Vicinity**. It's a guide for river runners, therefore it concentrates on information for those floating down both the Green and Colorado Rivers. The discussion on history and other subjects in that book stays pretty close to the rivers, and includes history of river bottoms & boating, old cattle trails and stories of the cowboys and river men of those days. The **2nd Edition** of that book came out in February, 2012 and is in color.

This book, the 2nd Edition of the **Hiking, Biking and Exploring Canyonlands National Park and Vicinity**, covers some of the same parts of the country as the River Guide, but expands back from the rivers, especially in the areas of Upper Horseshoe Canyon, the Flint Trail, Waterhole Flat and along the Hite Road west of the Green River and Upper Lake Powell. In the Between the Rivers country, this book covers upper Tenmile, Dubinky, the Dalton Wells CCC & Japanese Concentration Camps, Mill, Sevenmile, and Bull Canyons, Courthouse Towers and nearby, Poison Spider Mesa and Grays Pasture, otherwise known to the CNP/NPS as Island in the Sky. Along the east bank of the Colorado River, this book starts with Behind the Rocks and expands to the lower end of Mill Creek east of Moab to include lots of new rock art discoveries. From there it takes you south along the Lockhart Road to The Needles and Upper Salt Creek and other canyons, to the Dugout Ranch and the Rock Art on Indian Creek, and into Beef Basin Country to the south. Also, new to this 2nd Edition is a brief history of Charley Steen and Moab's uranium boom and the story of moonshining in the canyons along with a brief story of John Romjue, the best moonshiner of them all. Also added to this edition is a history of Moab's own Swanny Kerby and his days supplying buckin' horses and bulls to the Professional Rodeo circuit and his eventual induction into the Pro Rodeo Cowboy Hall of Fame.

The emphasis in this book is to show & tell people how to get to special places by coming into the area in cars, 4WD's or mountain bikes. Because these 2 books overlap in places, much of the history is repeated. The areas with repeated information are close to the river. For example, the Devil's Slide Trail is covered in both books, but one describes it from the bottom to the top, the other talks about how to get from the top down. Also repeated is the history of Tidwell Bottom and the story of Clyde Tidwell, Bill Tibbetts & the Range War of 1924-25, and the wild & wooly brothers John Jackson & Bill Hinton.

As in the River Guide, the emphasis is on hiking and local history, including lots of oral history--which in some cases cannot be authenticated. The biggest problem in doing oral history is that 2 people will usually remember a specific event differently. However, much of what one person says has normally been backed up by what someone else said. In almost all cases, several people were asked the same questions, but then the person who was closest to the actual event is (or in some cases, who was the best story teller) usually was the one quoted. Always keep this in mind as you read oral history. In ad-

dition, the author always tried to backup dates & authenticity of events by going through 50 years of the old local newspapers and other sources.

From near the end of **Spring Canyon Point** looking due east with the Green River below. Straight ahead is **Bowknot Bend**, and to the right a little is the narrow ridge separating 2 bends of the river. In the lower left, and barely visible, is the old road running upriver to Hey Joe Canyon and the uranium mine there.

5

Map Symbols

Town or Community	☐ ▫	Stream or Creek, Running Water	∿
Building or Cabin	▫	Large River	⌇
Campground	⋏	Dry Creek Bed or Wash	⌇
Ranger Station, Visitor Center	◤ ⛪	Canyon Narrows	⌇
Airport or Landing Strip	✦✦	Lake, Pond or Stock Pond	⬤ ⋎
Interstate Highway	▬(70)	Waterfall or Dryfall	⇥
US Highway	▬(191)	Spring, Seep or Well	○
Utah State Highway	▬(24)	Canyon Rim, Escarpment	⊓⊓⊤
Road--Maintained	═ ═	Natural Bridge or Arch, Corral	∩ ⊂
Road--4WD	═ ═ ═ ═	Mine, Quarry, Adit or Prospect	↖ ↗
Track--Old Road, Unusable	▬ ▬	Geology Cross Section	⌐¬
Trail--Foot or Horse	▬ ▬ ▬	Pass or Divide	≍
Route--No Trail	• • • • •	Rock Art--Petroglyphs	(PET)
Elevation in Meters	1490	Rock Art--Pictographs	(PIC)
600 Meters	600m	Mile Posts (mp) Markers	135 136
Peak & Prominent Ridge	▬✖▬	Carpark or Trailhead	/P\

Abbreviations

Canyon(s)	-C (C's).	Campground	-CG.
Lake	-L.	Low Range/High Clearance/4WD-	-LR/HC/4WD
River	-R.	Two Wheel Drive Vehicle or Road	-2WD
Creek	-Ck.	Four Wheel Drive Vehicle or Road	-4WD
Peak	-Pk.	High Clearance Vehicle or Road	-HCV
Waterfall, Dryfall, Formation	-F.	Off Road Vehicle	-ORV
Kilometer(s)	-km, kms	All Terrain Vehicle	-ATV
North, North East	-NNE	Spring	-Sp.
South, West South	-SWS	Sandstone	-SS
Piñon/Juniper Forest (Cedars)	-P/J	July 4, 2012	-7/4/2012
Trail Marker, Pile of Rocks	-Cairn	Ruins, Granary	-R, G
Elevation in Meters	-1236	500 Meters	-500m

United States Geological Survey	-USGS
National Park Service	-NPS
Canyonlands National Park	-CNP
Bureau of Land Management	-BLM
(United States) Forest Service	(US) FS
Civilian Conservation Corps	-CCC's
Trails Illustrated/National Geographic maps	-TI/NG
Grand Valley Times, Moab newspaper between 5/30/1896 to 9/5/1919	-GVT
The Times Independent, Moab newspaper from 9/12/1919 to the present	-TI

Metric Conversion Table

1 Centimeter = 0.39 Inch	1 Mile = 1.609 Kilometers	1 Ounce = 28.35 Grams
1 Inch = 2.54 Centimeters	100 Miles = 161 Kilometers	1 Pound = 453 Grams
1 Meter = 39.37 Inches	100 Kilometers = 62.1 miles	1 Quart (US) = 0.946 Liter
1 Foot = 0.3048 Meter/30.5 Cms	1 Liter = 1.056 Quarts (US)	1 Gallon (US) = 3.785 Liters
1 Kilometer = 0.621 Mile	1 Kilogram = 2.205 Pounds	1 Acre = 0.405 Hectare
1 Nautical Mile = 1.852 Kms	1 Metric Ton = 1000 Kgs	1 Hectare = 2.471 Acres
1 Kilometer = 3281 Feet	1 Mile = 1609 Meters	0.1 Mile = 161 Meters
1 Cubic/Liter = 61 Cubic/Inches	50 C/L = 3050 C/I	100 C/L = 6100 C/I

Meters to Feet (Meters x 3.2808 = Feet)

100 m = 328 ft.	2500 m = 8202 ft.	5000 m = 16404 ft.	7500 m = 24606 ft.
500 m = 1640 ft.	3000 m = 9842 ft.	5500 m = 18044 ft.	8000 m = 26246 ft.
1000 m = 3281 ft.	3500 m = 11483 ft.	6000 m = 19686 ft.	8500 m = 27887 ft.
1500 m = 4921 ft.	4000 m = 13124 ft.	6500 m = 21325 ft.	9000 m = 29525 ft.
2000 m = 6562 ft.	4500 m = 14764 ft.	7000 m = 22966 ft.	8848 m = 20029 ft.

Feet to Meters (Feet ÷ 3.2808 = Meters)

1000 ft. = 305 m	9000 ft. = 2743 m	16000 ft. = 4877 m	23000 ft. = 7010 m
2000 ft. = 610 m	10000 ft. = 3048 m	17000 ft. = 5182 m	24000 ft. = 7315 m
3000 ft. = 914 m	11000 ft. = 3353 m	18000 ft. = 5486 m	25000 ft. = 7620 m
4000 ft. = 1219 m	12000 ft. = 3658 m	19000 ft. = 5791 m	26000 ft. = 7925 m
5000 ft. = 1524 m	13000 ft. = 3962 m	20000 ft. = 6096 m	27000 ft. = 8230 m
6000 ft. = 1829 m	14000 ft. = 4268 m	21000 ft. = 6401 m	28000 ft. = 8535 m
7000 ft. = 2134 m	15000 ft. = 4572 m	22000 ft. = 6706 m	29000 ft. = 8839 m
8000 ft. = 2438 m			30000 ft. = 9144 m

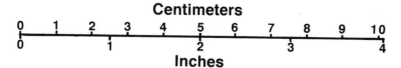

Centimeters / Inches

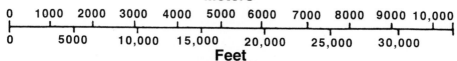

Meters / Feet

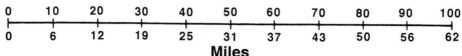

Kilometers / Miles

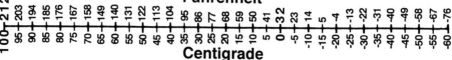

Fahrenheit / Centigrade

Introduction

Local Towns, Facilities, Accommodations

Moab The most important town in this area is Moab. It has a couple of supermarkets, a dozen or so gas stations & convenience stores, a BLM field office, a multiagency visitor center for the National Park Service, BLM and Forest Service located at Center & Main Streets (right in the middle of town) and many restaurants and motels. There are about 9 different campgrounds in the valley, plus many biking and rafting outfitters where you can rent boats, bikes or 4WD's. There's one good place to buy books and maps, that's Back of Beyond Bookstore, plus lots of other specialty outlets in town. Moab has about everything and has become a booming little tourist town and has become known world-wide, especially in the spring, summer and fall seasons.

Here are some Moab Tele. numbers: NPS Headquarters, 2282 SW, Resource Blvd., south Moab Highway 191, 435-259-7164 (or 435-710-2100); Needles Visitor Center, 435-259-4711; Island Visitor Center, 435-259-4712; Hans Flat or Maze Visitor Center, 435-259-2652; Reservations Office for Canyon-lands NP, 435-259-4351; Moab BLM Field Office, 82 East, Dogwood, 435-259-2100; Forest Service Of-fice, 62 East, 100 North, 435-259-7155; and road information at Grand County Roads, 435-259-5308.

Hole in the Rock highway reststop, located on Highway 191 between Moab and Monticello, has a little curio shop, plus a highway rest area & picnic site on the north side of the Hole in the Rock.

Monticello has several gas stations, a couple of small supermarkets, several restaurants and a BLM office, Tele. 435-587-1500; a Forest Service office Tele 435-587-2041; also a new visitor center a block or two south of the main intersection in town where you can buy books & maps. For backcountry road information call San Juan County Roads at 435-587-3230.

Hite on Lake Powell has a ranger station, gas station/convenience store, several motel units, but the marina is no longer there because of low water levels. You can still launch a boat, but the docks were taken downlake to Hall's Marina. It's open year-round, but not a lot is going on there.

Hanksville is west of the region covered in this book but it has about 3 gas stations & convenience stores, a small garage, a couple of motels--campgrounds, and a BLM office, Tele. 435-542-3461. Hollow Mountain gas station and Blondies next door, has some books and maps for sale.

Green River is the second most important town in this area. It's located on I-70 and the Green River. It has half a dozen gas stations, convenience stores, and one small supermarket. Also, there are 3 campgrounds, several rafting outfitters, plus the **Powell Museum and Visitor Center** at the east or Elgin side of the Green River, Tele. 435-564-3427. This is about the only place in Green River to buy books & maps of the area, plus tourist information. It's open 7 days a week year-round.

Crescent Junction has one gas station with the usual goodies for sale. **Thompson** now has nothing but a gas station-convenience store south of town on the freeway. Passenger trains no longer stop there. Both of these places are north of Moab and on or near Interstate Highway 70.

Emergency Kit for Your Car

Before leaving home one of the first things you should be aware of when visiting this region is that some parts are very isolated and remote and a long way from pavement or the nearest garage. It's rec-ommended you take a good running vehicle--one you can depend on. Always have a full tank of fuel--always more than you think you'll need. Also take extra water, food, tools, battery jumper cables, a tow rope or chain, a shovel, tire pump, extra oil and any other item you think might come in handy in an emergency. In recent years and with some improved roads (others are worse than ever), there is more traffic on the back roads around Canyonlands (especially on weekends in the spring and fall), but you'll want to go as well-prepared as possible. A little time spent planning your trip may prevent a bad expe-rience in the long run.

Best Time to Hike, Bike or Explore--Weather and Climate

Most of us have vacations in summer, but generally speaking the best time to visit Canyonlands is in the cooler months of spring or fall. The reason is, most of the areas in this book are low to moderate elevations. Most hikes range from about 1200 to 2000 meters altitude, therefore summer months get pretty warm and uncomfortable. The author generally prefers the time from about mid-March through April (the very best month) and May, then again in the second half of September and October--but he does hike throughout the summer months. The good things about spring are longer days than in fall, and lack of insects. The fall season also has few insects, but the days get very short by late October. Remember, October 21 has the same amount of daylight hours as does February 21; and September 21, the same amount of daylight as on March 21. If you were to camp in late December, you'd have to have a tent on the ground by about 5 pm, then sit there for 5 or 6 hours before bedtime. If you wanted an early morning start you'd have to get up in the dark!

The month with the heaviest precipitation in Canyonlands (CNP) is generally August. Next would be July or September, then October (?). The driest month of the year is normally June. One important thing you want to remember here is the monsoon season. Generally speaking, it begins sometime in July and continues through about mid-September. However, this is a dry desert area for the most part, which isn't the same as the rainy season in the humid tropics. There are still many sunny, dry, hot days, even in August. When you get close to this area, always keep an ear on the radio for the latest local weather forecasts. If you're heading to far-away places with dirt-road access only such as Beef Basin, Lockhart Basin, the White Rim, Dubinky & Tenmile, or anywhere along the west side of the Green River--Upper Lake Powell, and especially into Under the Ledge country, then make sure you get updates on road conditions and be alert to any approaching storms. It's summer cloudbursts which washout back roads! Right after a big storm, some of these back roads are impassable. BLM offices are one place to get updates on road conditions; so are the **road departments in San Juan and Grand Counties**. Their telefone numbers are listed above under Moab & Monticello.

The Insect Season

Over the years the author has found that insects begin to appear in about mid or late May and con-tinue until mid or late summer in most cases. Probably the most bothersome insects in this area are the large **horse flies**. These are often found along some generally dry washes but near seeps with tamarisk, and sometimes cottonwood trees. They're also generally found in areas where cattle come down to waterholes. However, about the only time these flies really bother you is when you're wearing shorts. They always hang around bare legs, so the cure for this problem is simply a pair of long pants.

In early summer you may also be bothered by small **midges, gnats, or no-see-ums**. These aren't found everywhere, but when they find you they'll get in your hair and bite your scalp. June seems to be the worst month for these, and by mid-summer, they seem to disappear (?). Wearing a hat, especially one with a curtain sewn on around the back, will be a deterrent, as will insect repellent put on around the ears and hair.

Mosquitos are almost never a problem. About the only places you'll find mosquitos in this area will be along flooded bottoms of the Green and Colorado Rivers. In years where there has been no big spring floods, you'll find very few if any mosquitos, even along the rivers. Mosquitos breed in swampy places or places with standing water, so if there's been no spring flood, there are normally few if any of these insects. The extra wet year of 2011, brought high water which flooded and pooled behind the natural levis, and it was the worst mosquito year in at least a couple of decades! You may see a few in summer in well-watered canyons, or in canyons after a flash floods and where water has pooled.

Also, what few mosquitos there are in this country, seem to come out mostly at night and are almost never seen in daylight hours. Make sure your tent has mosquito netting and these insects should never be a problem. Incidentally, the author never carries insect repellent anywhere on the Colorado Plateau.

Another possible nuisance is the ordinary **house fly**. Flies come out in daylight hours only and are usually seen only in places which are often used as campsites. If campers would simply keep their campsites clean, no one would ever see these flies.

Drinking Water

Despite what many people think about this so-called desert, there is water of some kind in almost every canyon in this book. The question then arises, what water is safe to drink as is, and what needs to be treated, filtered or boiled?

When it comes to actually drinking the water, old timers used to say; *"if it's clear and it's a fast flowing stream, then it's normally safe to drink."* On all his hikes, the author normally test-drinks water from springs not muddied by cattle, and sometime from small streams which have no sign of cattle or beaver upstream, before he recommends it to other hikers. He has yet to become sick from doing so.

But it's important to choose your drinking water carefully, because it's possible to get an intestinal disorder called **Giardiasis**, caused by the microscopic organism, Giardia lamblia. Early-day fur trappers used to call this ailment *Beaver Fever*. Giardia are carried in the feces of humans and some domestic and wild animals, especially cattle and beaver. The cysts of Giardia may contaminate surface water supplies. The symptoms usually include diarrhea, increased gas, loss of appetite, abdominal cramps, and bloating. It is not life threatening, but it can slow you down and make life miserable.

BLM and national park rangers constantly warn hikers about its deathly possibilities (which is a little overdone in this author's opinion), but they are required by the Public Health Service to make such statements to stay away from lawsuits. Also, since many hikers haven't the experience to determine what water is safe to drink as is, and what is not, here are some tips: If you're on a day-hike, simply carry your own water, which would be from a culinary supply. On backpacking trips, take water directly from a spring source or perhaps from a pothole with clear fresh-looking water which is out of reach of cattle. Or take it from a stream near a spring source free from signs of cattle or beaver. Or boil water for one minute, treat with iodine, or filter. On backpacking trips the author always carries a small bottle of Iodine tablets which can be used in an emergency. In all the author's travels to 224 countries, republics, major islands and island groups and to all corners of the Colorado Plateau, he has used Iodine tablets (or clorox bleach on one trip) maybe half a dozen times to purify water while climbing or hiking.

Remember, in this part of the world the most common carriers of Giardia are cattle and beaver, so when you see signs of either of these animals, take precautions. There are cattle grazing in some of the canyons surrounding Canyonlands NP, which is normally their winter range. In this region, about the only places where beaver are found are along the Green and Colorado Rivers and in the upper end of Lake Powell in Cataract Canyon.

In the end, the very best way to stay away from any health problems caused by drinking water out in the canyons, is to take a good supply of water in your car at all times. On longer trips, the author normally carries 6 to 8 gallon jugs in his car, most of which are kept full of good culinary water.

Equipment for Day-Hikes

For the less-experienced, here's a simple check-list of things you might need for taking a day-hike in or near Canyonlands. These are what the author usually takes: A small to medium sized day-pack, a one liter bottle of water (a lot more on a hot summer day--up to 4 liters), camera, extra batteries, tripod, a short piece of nylon rope or parachute cord, toilet paper, pen & small notebook, map, chapstick, compass, pocket knife, sunscreen, a cap with a *"sun shield" or "cancer curtain"* sewn on around the back, a pair of long pants (for cooler morning temperatures or possibly horse flies or other insects) and a lunch for the longer hikes.

In warmer weather, he normally wears shorts and a "T" shirt; in cooler weather, long pants and a long-sleeved shirt, plus perhaps a jacket and gloves. In cooler weather and with more things to carry, a larger day-pack may be needed.

Equipment for Overnight Hikes

Few people will likely do any backpacking in this region, but there are some good backpacking possibilities mostly in The Maze area and other places west of the Green River. Also, there are some longer hikes requiring overnight camps in The Needles District, especially along Upper Salt Creek. For those with less-experience, here's a list of things the author normally takes on overnight hikes. You'll surely want to add to this list.

A large pack, sleeping bag, sleeping pad (Thermal Rest), tent--with rain sheet, small (kerosene) stove, several lighters (no more matches!), 10m or more of nylon cord or small diameter rope, camera, tripod, extra batteries, one large water jug, a one or 2-liter water bottle, a stitching awl and waxed thread, small pliers, cannister with odds and ends (bandaids, needle & thread, patching kit for sleeping pad, wire, pens, etc.), maps, notebook, reading book, chapstick, compass, toilet paper, pocket knife, rain cover for pack, small alarm clock or watch, tooth brush & tooth paste, face lotion, sunscreen, cap with cancer curtain, soap, headlamp and/or small flashlight, long pants and long sleeved shirt, perhaps a lightweight mini-umbrella in bad weather spells, and maybe a light-weight coat and gloves in cooler weather.

Food usually includes such items as oatmeal or cream of wheat cereal, coffee or chocolate drink, powdered milk, sugar, cookies, crackers, candy, oranges or apples, carrots, Ramen instant noodles, soups, macaroni, canned tuna fish, sardines or chicken, peanuts, instant puddings, bread, margarine, peanut butter and salt & pepper. Also, a plastic eating bowl and cup, spoon, small cooking pot and extra fuel for the stove.

Boots or Shoes

Most hikes discussed here are either in canyons with sandy or gravelly bottoms, along old cattle or sheep trails, or over barren smooth sandstone called **slickrock**. So there's normally no need to wear heavy-duty mountaineering-type boots. Many people, including this writer wear some kind of simple running or athletic shoes. These are light weight and comfortable and seldom if ever cause blisters. Most people have a pair of these in their closet, so there's no need to go out and buy a new pair. But if you do decide to buy a pair for hiking this country, then perhaps the best ones are the new light-weight **trail running shoes**. These are the perfect footwear for Canyonlands, because they are relatively inexpensive, light weight, comfortable and normally don't cause blisters. The only real drawback with trail running or regular running shoes is, they are of lighter construction, and you may have problems walking through cactus patches with them. Next best footwear would be a pair of the new light weight low-cut hiking shoes. Also, here's a tip; don't buy a light-weight running-type shoe with mesh around the toe; or you'll be dumping sand out all day long.

As a backup, consider taking along a pair of half worn-out shoes of some kind which can be used for wading. These might come in handy if you're hiking along Salt Creek or in Horseshoe Canyon. There are small streams in several other canyons, but none are big enough to have to wade through.

Preserving Archaeology Sites

In some places in Canyonlands there are ancient cultural sites such as Anasazi or Fremont cliff dwellings, moki houses or granaries, petroglyph & pictograph (rock art) panels, and flint chip sites. Many of these are accessible and easily destroyed, but others are hidden in hard-to-get-to alcoves, so carry a pair of binoculars on some hikes. Salt Creek is a good example of where some sites are both easily accessible or inaccessible. The author has marked the sites he found on the individual maps.

However, if too many people visit these sites, damage can occur; not so much by vandals or pot hunters, but simply by careless visitors. It's highly unlikely you will ever discover any moki houses which have not already been plundered or studied; and it's true that the simple cliff dwellings you may see will never contribute anything more to our present understanding of the Anasazi people, but regardless of how simple the sites may be, it's important to make as little impact as possible to prevent any deterioration. Many more interested people will follow in your footsteps, so it's important to leave these ancient places as pristine as possible.

Here's a list of things you can do to help preserve Anasazi ruins or moki house as the locals sometimes call them. First, don't climb onto the walls or any part of the structure. Some may seem solid, but in time and with abuse, walls will tumble down. Why not just observe, take pictures, and leave it as is for the next visitor to discover and enjoy. Second, if the ruins are under an overhang approachable via a steep talus slope, try to get there from the side instead of scrambling straight up the talus. Undercutting ruins is a problem for some sites and most damage occurs simply by thoughtless individuals. Third, if mother nature calls and you have to use the toilet please don't do it in or near the ruins. Defecate as far from these sites as possible, and bury it. This is becoming a problem in some places. Fourth, don't touch petroglyphs or pictographs, because it leaves oil from your hands on the walls.

And fifth, keep in mind it is **against Federal law to damage any ancient artifacts**. Part of the Federal law states, *No person may excavate, remove, damage, or otherwise alter or deface any archaeological resource located on public lands or Indian lands unless such activity is pursuant to a permit issued.....* What this is saying is, picking up a potsherd/pottery fragment or corn cob and taking it home is illegal. So is putting your initials on a wall next to some petroglyphs or pictographs.

Take a Good Map

The author has done his best to make the maps in this book as accurate as possible, but these sketch maps are no substitute for a real good USGS topo map. Always buy and use the USGS, BLM or other maps created by private companies of the region you're about to visit. The best maps available are listed under each individual hike or mapped area. All or most of the maps suggested in this book can be bought in Moab, with others available in Green River, Hanksville, Hite and Monticello. More information about individual maps is found in the section below titled, **Maps For Hikers,....**

In recent years, some people are relying on **GPS devices**, but there can be problems with them; one being they use batteries (which can die), they can be dropped & damaged, or simply go kaput. Newer GPS devices can download maps--at a pretty good price, but the screens are small and its impossible to see the bigger picture. So a regular paper map is still the best option for getting around in the backcountry--both for driving to the trailhead, and for hiking.

Off Road Vehicles (ORV's, ATV's and 4WD's)

In recent years with increased traffic of all kinds around Canyonlands and the Colorado Plateau, there's also been a dramatic increase in the number of off road and 4WD vehicles. Since some of these are called *"off road vehicles"*, naturally the owners want to test drive them *"off the road"*. This indiscriminate use and the destruction of public lands has caused a backlash from other people (tree huggers or environmentalists) who want to protect the land, especially lands that are as special as those around Canyonlands. This is the primary reason why there's been a move in recent years to protect the more scenic regions by locking them up into wilderness areas or set aside as national parks. Just one thought for ORV and 4WD owners; it's you who have been using the public lands as test tracks for your noisy toys, and who have caused so much land in recent years to be locked up into wilderness areas and parks. Slowly but surely the BLM, which administers most of the land surrounding Canyonlands NP, is closing off areas formerly destroyed by ORV traffic.

Also, and thank somebody's god, in the past several years the BLM has been busy as beavers installing signs which state something like, *All Vehicles Must Stay on Designated Roads*. You'll see signs like this if you're going into the Between the River country north of Canyonlands, and in the Indian Creek and Lockhart Road area east of the park. So please, just stay on existing roads and there will be no problem. Otherwise those people who love making regulations will soon follow!

Camping on BLM Lands in the Moab Area

Since the 1st Edition of this book came out in 1992, big changes have occurred in Moab and the surrounding countryside. Biggest change is; Moab has become one of the premier outdoor recreation centers in the United States. Recreation includes special routes or drives along 4WD or ATV roads, mountain biking areas many on slickrock, and boating, rafting and canoeing on the Green and Colorado Rivers. Winter with skiing is about the only season and sport not represented. So for most of the year, things are hopping pretty good around Moab. Because of the hoards of people going there, the nearby BLM countryside has become heavily used, especially in the spring and fall seasons. For this reason, the BLM and other entities have created a number of campgrounds/campsites, some of which are undeveloped to some degree, but some of which have a user fee. See the website for the Moab BLM field office at **http://www.blm.gov/ut/ st/en/fo/moab.html** to see all the new camping regulations in the Moab area. Going to this website is the only way to stay current on events in the Moab area.

Briefly, here is what you can expect in some areas. Downstream from Moab along the Colorado River and along the Potash Road, you'll find **3 BLM campgrounds; Jaycee Park, Williams Bottom and Gold Bar Camping Sites** all with dumpsters, toilets and some with tables or varandas. And of course, you have to pay for these, but **none have water** so bring your own. Beyond Potash and going toward the national park, there are some restrictions for people who camp with tents, but for those who sleep in their cars and leave nothing behind (?).

On the other side of the river and along Kane Creek Road, which starts at McDonalds at the south end of Moab, there are 2 campgrounds on public lands; **Kings Bottom and Moonflower Canyon**. When you get inside Kane Springs Canyon, there are walkin campsites at the mouth of both **Spring and Hunters Canyons**. Beyond those, and into the wider part of Kane Springs Canyon below and east of Hurrah Pass, there are 2 new rough camping areas called **The Ledge Camping Area--Loop A & B**. These now, or soon will, have tables, toilets and fire pits, with all sites for a fee.

Besides these BLM sites, there are several campgrounds with similar amenities located on private land on King Bottom. These are found along the paved road between **Moonflower Canyon** and the mouth of **Pritchett Canyon**. Beyond **Hurrah Pass** there are basically no restrictions, but a word to the wise; leave a clean campsite, or somebody will slap more restrictions on us all in that area too!

Going upstream (east) along the Colorado are more organized campgrounds, some privately owned, some on BLM land, but that area is out of the boundaries of this book. In the region north of Moab and into the Between the Rivers country, the BLM has come up with a new way to describe camping there; they call it **DISPERSED CAMPING**.

Here are some brief statements on dispersed camping and other restricted camping areas copied from the website: **http://www.blm.gov/ut/st/en/fo/moab.html**. However, not all of the areas described below are within the scope of this book:

Camping is restricted to **designated sites** *along Highway 313, the Gemini Bridges Road,.... the Mill Canyon Road area..... In addition, camping is restricted to designated sites where Kane Creek Road crosses Kane Creek itself (the Ledges Camping Areas Loops A & B), and at Dripping Springs near Ten Mile Wash. These sites are marked with a brown fiberglass post and a tent symbol. These sites are* **free**, *but campers are required to carry out all garbage, including* **solid human waste**. *Campers are required to possess, set up and use* **portable toilets**. *Campers may not bury, or leave exposed, solid human body waste and soiled toilet paper. The disposal of solid human waste off public land is required. There is no wood cutting allowed. Some sites are summarized below.*

Gemini Bridges Road *- There are 6 campsites located in Bridge Canyon.*

Picture Frame Arch Area *(?)- There are 4 sites located 6 miles [10 kms] from Highway 191.*

Mill Canyon/Cotter Road/Dubinky Road Area *- There are approximately 40 sites located in this area which is north of No Mans Mesa, and Monitor & Merrimac Buttes.*

Kane Creek Crossing *- There are approximately 28 sites located along Kane Creek where the Kane Creek Road crosses the water. These are the new Ledges A & B sites.*

Dripping Spring near Ten Mile Wash *- There are several large campsites on the west side of the road and within the riparian fences.*

There are several areas in which no sites are designated and camping is not allowed. The **Shafer Basin**, *which forms the viewshed of Dead Horse Point State Park and is important bighorn sheep habitat, has no sites.* **Long Canyon** *is subject to extreme flooding and is also bighorn habitat, has no sites.*

No camping *is allowed in the* **Mill Creek** *area immediately east of the city of Moab, or on the* **west side of Spanish [Moab] Valley**. *No camping is allowed within one mile of developed recreation sites in the* **Canyon Rims Recreation Area** *[This would be the Hatch Point country and on the high ground where The Needles & Anticline Overlooks are located].*

Remember, when using free designated sites, you are required to remove all solid human waste from the area. Campers are required to possess, set up, and use **portable toilets**. *Campers may not bury, or leave exposed, solid human body waste and soiled toilet paper. The disposal of solid human waste off public land is required and no wood cutting is allowed. Following these simple rules will ensure that the sites are attractive to future campers.*

If you don't like paying to camp, plan your trip so you overnight as far away from Moab as possible! And leave a clean campsite or more restrictions are sure to follow.

Mountain Bikes

Since the second half of the 1980's, there has been an increase in the use of mountain bikes. Fortunately, these can seldom if ever be ridden off a road or trail, so they aren't as destructive as ORV's, especially ATV's & motorcycles. You simply can't ride them in sandy areas or in dry creek beds. However, if a lot of people start trying to ride them in areas where they're forbidden, then they too will be in the same category as ORV owners. Please keep bikes on established roads or tracks.

In the late 1980's, the author bought a mountain bike which in some places extended the range of his car. He used it only on 4WD-type roads where his cars undercarriage could be damaged. Incidentally, at the time, the author drove a 1981 VW Rabbit Diesel, which was equipped with tires 10% larger than normal. That gave him added ground clearance and it went to a lot of places ordinary cars wouldn't dream of. But, the mtn. bike took over when the car had to be parked.

(For this 2nd Edition, the author used a 2007 Jeep Patriot AWD, which is only half a Jeep. It has a longer wheel base than preferred, no low range gear box, and had only 20 cms (8") of ground clearance;

but 4 Light Truck (LT's) tires 2 sizes bigger than normal were added, and that made clearance 23 cms (9 inches) or more. Most areas in The Maze were about the only places it couldn't go; but the kilomage/mileage is lots better than regular Jeeps. Just looking at the features, it's pretty good as fuel-efficient SUV's go, but Jeep quality is not as good as most other brands (but is getting better).

For those hikers with cars only, a mtn. bike is a cheap way to extend the range of the family car. There are many places in this book where a mtn. bike will save a lot of walking, because you can park your car in a safe place a few kms from the end of a rough 4WD road, and use the bike to reach the trailhead. In some places you can lock up a bike at one end of a canyon or hike, drive to the other end; do the hike, then bike back to the car. This will eliminate backtracking or a lot of road-walking and the need for 2 cars.

Here are some tips for the novice mountain biker. Store your mtn. bike inside your car if you can, rather than on the roof. One bike on the roof will increase fuel consumption about 5-7% on the highway (?). To do this you'll need a bike with a quick-release front hub, and maybe quick-release seat as well. That way one bike can be put in the back of most cars--if it's a hatch-back and you remove the rear seat. One fits inside a VW Rabbit or Golf easily.

Install an under-the-seat carrying bag on the bike and always have a small **tool kit** along. Include in it pliers, special bike wrench, a couple of screw drivers, tire patching kit, small can of chain lubricant like silicone (for longer trips), bike chain repair tool, and a couple of rags--one for hands, one for cleaning the bike chain. You'll also need a tire pump and 2 water bottles mounted on the bike, and an extra bike chain, inner tube and tire in your car.

If you're planning to do day-trips on your bike, then one sack or bag mounted under the seat and one on the handle bars is enough. Put your tools under the seat, your camera and maps in the front bag. You'll also need a small day-pack for your lunch and extra water if it's warmer weather.

Don't take this water advice lightly. Biking all day in warm weather requires more water than hiking! The fatigue factor could be twice as much for biking as well. You'll find yourself totally exhausted at the end of a mtn. biking day of 8-10 hours! Even your arms get a remarkable workout--just hanging on for dear life on some rough roads.

Riding tips. When you're going down into a dry wash, and will have to climb out the other side, be sure to downgear while going down, and certainly before you start climbing. If you try to downgear going uphill and exerting pressure on the pedals, you may break a chain, especially if it's an older one. Lower tire pressure will give you a smoother ride, but higher tire pressure means easier peddling. For someone serious about biking, thorn-proof inner tubes are a very good idea--or required, as are the widest fattest tires money can buy. Many parts of this country have sandy tracks, and the wider the tire, the better. For further tips, see a professional bike dealer or rental agency in Moab. Moab may be the mountain biking capitol of the World!

Some Driving Tips for Back Roads

As you leave the paved highways and head out on gravel or dirt roads, here are some things to keep in mind. First, you should lower the air pressure in your tires. The author normally runs his vehicle on the highways with 38-40 warm lbs. of pressure in his tires. When he leaves the pavement, it's normally lowered to about 25-30 lbs. This does 3 things. First, it gives you a smoother and softer ride. Second, it helps prevent sharp stones from puncturing your tires. And third, it gives you much better traction, whether in sand, snow or mud. This means you'll have to carry at all times a tire gauge and pump of some kind to re-inflate your tires when you get back on pavement. This can be a hand pump, or electric, which runs off the car battery. The electric ones work faster, which means you're more likely to lower the tire pressure in the first place.

If you're driving in sandy areas, lower the pressure in your tires even more, and you can drive through places you would ordinarily get stuck in. This is what drivers of dune or rock buggies do, and they never get stuck (the Rock Buggies going up Pritchett Canyon or along the Amasa Back Trail lower their tire pressure to 5 lbs; but no less than 10 lbs. for radial tires). Simply lower your tire pressure to somewhere between 10 & 15 lbs in your drive tires. This puts more rubber to the road, thus increasing traction. Each person will have to experiment with this technique in order to gain confidence; in the meantime, always carry a shovel and a tow rope, and never over-extend your ability.

Also keep in mind, when you're driving sandy roads, a little rain helps. It makes the sand more firm and you don't sink in as far. However, if storm clouds are coming, and you're in areas with roads made of clay, better high-tail-it back to pavement fast. Clay-based roads become very slick when wet. If you get into a situation with slick wet roads and can't move, simply wait an hour or two, and you can normally drive away OK. If heavy rains come, then you may have to wait overnight for the road to firm-up. This is one of the best reasons to always carry more water and food than you think you'll need. A shovel and tow rope are standard equipment for anyone driving back country roads.

Hiking Times

As you read this book and do the hikes, be aware that the author is a full-time hiker-climber-traveler. If he is hiking a canyon or climbing a mountain he often has a little different type motive in mind, so he usually travels faster than the average person. Be aware of this as you read some descriptions of hikes.

Along with most hikes in this book, the author normally tells his own experience, along with the amount of time it took him to do the hike; then sometimes he estimates the time for the average hiker. Usually there's a small difference. However, as this book comes off the press, he'll be 70 years of age, and taking better fotos is a little more important than sheer speed. Also, instead of putting the time needed in hours, it's sometimes put in terms of half a day or all day. A half-day hike will take about 4 hours, round-trip; a long half-day hike is about 5-6 hours; an easy day-hike, 6-7 hours; a full day means about 8 hours; and a long all-day-hike might take 9 or 10 hours or longer.

Respect the Land

Some people are becoming alarmed at the slow destruction of parts of Canyonlands and the Colorado Plateau and want to lock it up into wilderness areas. Perhaps the main reason for this movement is the overuse and abuse by ORV's. Another reason is the amount of trash left behind by a few thoughtless individuals. Around some more heavily-used campsites and along some roads one can see the sign of the times; the aluminum soda pop and beer cans. Outside the national park, there are very few sites with garbage collection service, so it's up to all of us to pick up our own garbage, and in some cases, the trash of our less-concerned neighbors, and dispose of it properly. The author always arrives home with a bag of trash and aluminum cans that were left behind by other people. Hopefully, all of you will do the same.

Getting and Using a Backcountry Permit for Canyonlands National Park

Here's something you'll just love--more rules and regulations. The control freaks in Canyonlands NP are trying to operate their outfit the same way, as for example, in Great Smokey National Park, which is only a 3-4 hour drive from about 100 million people. As a result, almost no Utahns go to Canyonlands anymore; they prefer to recreate on BLM lands where the breathing is a little easier. Almost all employ- ees for the NPS are from somewhere else--not Utah.

Please go to this website: **nps.gov/cany** for more information, disappointments and all the latest. This is just a sample of what you'll be up against if you want to backpack, or car-camp, in Canyonlands NP. Because of this, the author goes on day-hikes only. Maybe you will too. Here are just a few things more or less **copied from the website just mentioned:**

Notice of Fee Increase

*Effective July 9, 2012, Canyonlands began charging $30 for all overnight backcountry permits and group campsite reservations. Four-wheel-drive day use permits will increase to $10 [for the drive into Horse & Lavender Canyons]. All overnight trips in the backcountry require a permit. In addition, permits are required for horseback riding and four-wheel-drive day use [$10] in Horse and Lavender canyons in the Needles District. **[If you park at the locked gate and walk up Horse or Lavender on a day- trip, you don't need a permit or pay the $10 fee. But if you backpack overnight in either canyon, it will cost you $30 for a backpacking permit. You must also camp 1 1/2 kms from any road.]***

HOW TO OBTAIN A PERMIT

*Backcountry permits are issued seven days a week at **district visitor centers**. Permits can be re- served in advance [see below]. Walk-in permits are only available the day before or the day of a trip. Permits are issued up to one hour before the close of business each day.*

RESERVATIONS

***Reservations** are recommended, but not required. Currently, competition is greatest for White Rim trips during the spring and fall and Needles backpacking trips during spring. For these activities, visitors should apply as early as possible. Campsites and permits not reserved in advance are available on a first-come, first-served basis at district visitor centers.*

***Reservation Office** staff are available by phone to answer questions and assist with trip planning Monday through Friday, 8 a.m. to 12:30 p.m. (Mountain Time), at **435) 259-4351**. When workload per- mits, phones may be answered until 4:00 p.m. Visitors may also email questions [see website].*

Canyonlands is open year-round, *24 hours a day. Each district has its own visitor center with op- erating hours that differ depending on the season.*
Island in the Sky: Tele. 435-259-4712
The visitor center is open daily from 9 a.m. to 4 p.m. with extended hours spring through fall. It will close Thanksgiving Day, Christmas Day, and New Year's Day.
Maze: Tele. 435-259-2652
The Hans Flat [sometimes called The Maze] Ranger Station is open daily from 8 a.m. to 4:30 p.m. It will close Thanksgiving Day, Christmas Day, and New Year's Day.
Needles: Tele. 435-259-4711
The visitor center is open daily February through early December from 9 a.m. to 4 p.m. Closed Thanks- giving Day and for an extended period during the winter.

Campsite Reservations for the White Rim Road

Go to **Map 17**, page 190, Introduction to the Island in the Sky District of Canyonlands, for details.

Horses in Canyonlands National Park

Apparently horses are allowed in Horse and Lavender Canyons in The Needles for day-use only, but you'll need a $10 permit (?). See the website **nps.gov/cany.**

Metrics Spoken Here

As you can see from reading thus far, the metric system of measurement is used almost exclusively in this book. The reason is, when the day comes for the USA to join the rest of the world and change over to metrics, the author won't have to change his books. This writer feels that with a lot of luck, that day may come before he's dead.

In 1975, the US Congress passed a resolution to begin the process of changing over to the metric system. They did this because the USA, Burma, and Brunei were the only countries on earth still using the antiquated British system. This progressive move ended with the Reagan Administration in 1981.

Use the **Metric Conversion Table** on **page 7** for help in the conversion process. It's easy to learn and use once you get started. Just keep a few things in mind; one mile is just over 1 1/2 kms, 2 miles is about 3 kms, and 6 miles is equal to 10 kms. Also, 2000m is about 6600 feet, 100m is about the same as 100 yards. A liter and a quart are roughly the same, and a US gallon jug is 3.78 liters. One pound is 453 grams, and one kilogram is about 2.2 pounds. The author presently stands about 5' 10" tall, or 178 cms, and weighs about 145 lbs, or 66 kgs.

Maps for Hiking, Biking and Touring

As for maps of this area, there are now several series at different scales, and from different sources including the USGS and private companies, to choose from.

One set of USGS maps is at **1:100,000 scale** and they're mostly **metric**. They include--from north to south: *San Rafael Desert, Moab, Hanksville and La Sal.* To cover the very southern part of the re- gion in this book, you'll need just the top part of 2 other metric maps, ***Hite Crossing & Blanding.*** These 6 maps cover all of the country from Green River and Moab to the head of Lake Powell, including all the access roads. These maps are relatively new, having been published by the USGS and the BLM in the 1980's. They have been updated in recent years and for the most part show the roads as they are on the ground today. The USGS & BLM versions of these maps are identical except for colors. On BLM maps, the different colors indicate land ownership: private, BLM, state, Forest Service and National Parks. Even though the elevations on these maps are in **meters**, the little square blocks on each represents one **section**, which is **one square mile**, or 640 acres (250 hectares). So in reality, these metric maps are only half metric.

In 1990, '91 & '92, when this writer was doing the 1st Edition of this book, only part of Utah had the USGS maps or quads at a large **1:24,000** scale completed, so few of those were used at that time. But by 2012, the entire state of Utah was covered by this scale of maps which are often referred to as **7 1/2' quads**. These maps were used often by this writer to update & upgrade this 2nd Edition. Under each mapped area or chapter, the individual map or maps required is listed.

The next set of maps the author used in 1990 were at **1:62,500 scale (15' quads)** and were published by the USGS. These were older maps, most dating from the 1950's, although some were updated. They showed the rivers and canyons very well, but most didn't show the newer roads. These maps are no longer printed, but you may be able to find a few; if so they may be valuable in some ways.

Another set of maps is put out by **Trails Illustrated** which has been bought by **National Geographic (TI/NG)** and are made of plastic. These maps are tearproof and waterproof, but images do wear off in time. There are several maps in this series. One is titled **Canyonlands National Park** and is at appropriately **1:70,000 scale.** It's based on the USGS maps, but it has been updated as far as roads, trails and facilities are concerned. If it's more detail you want, TI/NG also has **3 maps** at about **1:35,000 scale**; they cover each of the 3 districts of Canyonlands, **Island in the Sky, The Maze** and **The Needles**.

In addition to these, TI/NG also has **Moab North**, which covers areas as far north as Green River and I-70, plus Arches National Park. Its scale is 1:70,000. Another one is **Moab South**. It covers the Moab area, both east and west, and parts of eastern Canyonlands NP. Half of it is at 1:70,000 scale, the other side is at 1:35,000. These maps are generally good quality and updated as best as can be, but since TI/NG has a working relationship or sweetheart deal with the NPS, they sometimes leave off some roads; in other words they've been *sanitized by the NPS to some degree to fit their philosophy.* For example, the TI/NG maps don't show the old mining track running southwest between Davis & Lavender Canyons and to the top of Cedar Mesa (in the middle of The Needles District). Contact National Geographic's website **nationalgeographic.com** for more details.

Another company that's making inroads into TI/NG territory, is **Latitude 40°**. They have a plastic map called **Moab West** (Moab East too, but it doesn't cover this area) that covers land north nearly to I-70 and south to Beef Basin. It also shows the Green River, and all of Canyonlands NP, except for the Horseshoe Canyon Unit. This map is at about 1:75,000 scale and its claim to fame is it shows all roads, ATV tracks and trails **designated or sanctioned** by the BLM. It seems to be designed more for the ATV and 4WD recreation crowd, than for hikers. The author used the Moab West map frequently for driving and distance gathering. And of course, Latitude 40° maps aren't sanitized by the NPS like the TI/NG maps are. This map does show that old mining track to the top of Cedar Mesa mentioned above, same as the USGS 7 1/2' quads. Both the TI/NG and Latitude 40° maps show **driving distances** between various points.

Speaking of designated roads, for those of us who scream at the BLM to do something about ATV's and motorcycles running all over creation and destroying this country in the process, it has to be said, that as of 2012, the BLM has been busy erecting signs pointing out designated roads or tracks. Hopefully, those not sanctioned will eventually be blocked off and rehabilitated. The only problem with that big idea is a low budget. Canyonlands NP gets about 10 times the money as the local BLM, but the BLM has about 10 times the amount of territory to look after.

Many, if not most of the maps listed above can be purchased at BLM offices or the multiagency visitor center in the middle of Moab. They can also be found in the **Back of Beyond bookshop (best place)**, and other stores in Moab; especially those businesses catering to the mtn. biking, 4WD'ing and boating crowds. Many are also available in the **Powell Museum** in Green River.

Warning: Don't Blame Me!

Please keep a few things in mind before hiking in the Canyonlands National Park region. This writer has done his best to collect information and present it to readers as accurately as possible. He has drawn maps as carefully as possible, and encourages everyone to buy the USGS topo or the latest privately printed maps suggested for each hike. He has tried to inform hikers that canyons change with every flash flood, and that many of the hikes in this book are in isolated wilderness settings. He's also tried to inform hikers that some hikes or to some regions are for experienced and tough hikers only, while others, and this includes most hikes in this book, are pretty easy even for tourists.

For those who somehow get lost, stranded, or have to spend an unexpected night in a canyon and/or be rescued, all I can say is, I've done my best. The rest is up to you, so don't blame me or this book for your mistakes, lack of attention or preparedness--and yes, and in a few cases, even your stupidity!

Before doing any hike, always stop at the nearest BLM office or NPS visitor center, and get the latest information on road, trail, water, flood or weather conditions & forecast. Also, **tell someone where you're going and when you expect to return.** That way, friends can call for help if you don't return on time. Aron Ralston's epic adventure in Blue John Canyon in the Robbers Roose country just west of Canyonlands is the best example of not telling anyone where you're going (See the movie, **127 Hours**. The book Aron used was the **4th Edition** of this writers Canyon Guide to the Colorado Plateau, and the **bolts** he rappelled from at the end of Upper Blue John were put in by this writer and a friend).

One last thing to keep in mind; in some cases the information in this book is different than in the 1st Edition, and all information in this or any other guidebook can be outdated the minute it goes to press due to floods or policy changes on the part of the BLM or NPS.

Another Warning!

Here are 2 events which should have us all thinking about rules & regs in our national parks, who should carry guns in our gun-happy society, and should **DEATH** be the penalty for anyone parking crooked at a national park trailhead, or for someone sleeping in their car at any trailhead.

In late August of 2012, I found myself near the Willow Flat Campground in the Island District of Canyonlands NP. I had pulled off the paved road near an NPS employees-only road. There's a gate at the beginning of that road which leads to a kind of dumping place for various items of CNP. As I was about ready to go on a short hike, **CNP patrolman Steve Kurtz** pulled up and asked what I was doing; I said I'm getting ready to go on a hike. He said I couldn't park there because it might block trucks from entering their dump site. So I looked to the other side of the road and saw a place for 2-3 cars to park completely out of the way of any traffic. I said, *"Can I park over there?"*, and he said, *"No you have to park in an official parking place so go down the road 300m and park at the campground"*. So I went down there and parked. He followed me to make sure I complied; and to make sure I understood he was the law because he carried a gun & badge. I had parked a little cockeyed, so my car was facing the afternoon sun so I could use a sun screen on my windshield to keep the car cooler so it wouldn't melt my ice so fast. So he said, *"Change the way you're parking, one tire is on a line separating parking spaces and it could cause an accident"*. So I did; and he left and I hiked to Halfdome.

The next morning, I arrived at the Upheaval Dome Trailhead. It was about 7 am, and I ate breakfast before doing a hike. As I was preparing to leave, Officer Kurtz drove up again and said, *"Please change the way you're parking, it's dangerous and could cause an accident"*. I was parked a little cockeyed again so I took up one official parking spot, plus a little extra space at the end of a parking strip. That extra space wasn't an official parking spot, it was simply left over asphalt. My car wasn't on any trail or walkway or blocking traffic in any way--I was simply occupying an official parking place plus I was on a little extra pavement.

Anyway, I explained to him I was parked that way so my car (Jeep Patriot) could face the sun so I could use a sun screen on the windshield to block out the sun, to keep the ice in the cooler from melting as fast. I usually go out for a week at a time, and I like my ice & cold water in hot summer weather.

I asked Kurtz several times how my way of parking could possibly **cause an accident?** He had no answer. The sole reason for this alleged parking violation was that Kurtz wanted all the rubber duckies under his command lined up in a perfect row and if one was out of line just a little, he got paranoid and I ultimately got a parking ticket.

By then it was about 7:30 am and no one else was around. Just Kurtz and I. After about 15 minutes of writing the ticket, he gave it to me and I pushed it through a crack in the window of my car and said something to the effect that now I have the ticket, I'll begin hiking and take care of it later. As I was walking away, Kurtz said, *"Now I'm ordering you to change the way you're parking."*

Before that moment he had been rather polite, but then his entire demür changed, and he had a very determined look on his face and in his eyes. He was also standing there like his next step was to use force. My first thought was; this guy is going to pull out his handgun and shoot!. At first I said, you've already punished me by given me a parking ticket, so why can't I just go on the hike and take care of it later. But he said no, *"Change the way you're parking"*.

So with a potential crisis unfolding, my thoughts instantly went back nearly 2 years to a shooting which took place at the **Poison Spider Trailhead on November 19, 2010.** That trailhead is downriver from Moab about 15 kms (10 miles) along the Potash Road. That shooting involved Brody Young, a state park ranger, and another guy. It seems the guy was sleeping in his car at that trailhead. That carpark has a toilet, but the authorities don't want people camping at trailheads, even if they're just sleeping in their vehicle, and even though the tourist season was long gone.

Anyway, there was an argument of some kind and things escalated, and since both parties had guns, shooting started. Brody Young was shot 9 times but survived; the other guy was also shot, but he got in his vehicle and drove down the river another 20 kms before getting out and walked away. He has never been found but most people think he crawled into a cave, or tried to swim the Colorado River, and died of his wounds. No one knows what happened to him, and no one has heard his version of what happened that night before the shooting started. All we know is what Brody Young has told us.

So, this is what was going through my mind at the time. We were alone and there was no one to witness this event. And Kurtz has a gun. To me, and going back to the determined look on his face, I was afraid this guy was ready to pull his gun and shoot me--because I had parked crooked. No one knows what might have happen then; but I felt my life was in danger--and again, no witnesses. Had I been shot, it would have been Kurtz' word against my body. My story would never have been told.

So I walked back to my car while making the statement, *"Give a guy and gun and a badge and he thinks he's some kind of an f'ing god"*. I then got in my car and left that space altogether, and parked a short distance away, which was a better place anyway--too bad I hadn't noticed that place before. Kurtz drove around the one-way circle and stopped and looked the situation over very carefully and left. I then went on my hike.

Several days later when I returned Moab, I went to NPS headquarters and talked to park superintendent Kate Cannon, and Denny Ziemann. I told them of this experience with Kurtz, but they seemed to have little sympathy for my point of view.

Now the reason I'm making a big deal out of this is, I honestly think Kurtz is not the type of person who should be given a gun & badge. Surely he'll make a good employee some place, but not in law enforcement. Also the National Park Service policy is partly to blame. In my travels around the Colorado Plateau, some Canyonlands NP employees have to be the most protective towards what appears to outsiders to be, *their private reserve*. But it's public land, our park, not theirs. The people in this park set down rules & regs which must be the strictest, and in this case, the most Micky Mouse, in the NPS system. I've never seen anything like this in my life, or in any other park. But can you believe this; backcountry rangers in Grand Canyon NP now carry handguns while hiking!

It also seems to me, that since this rubber ducky wasn't lined up perfectly, it had to somehow be brought into conformity, so Officer Kurtz made up his own interpretation of the law to justify his actions. I'm sure there are codes which govern parking policy, but which are so vaguely written, they can be interpreted in many different ways. The important thing here is, there was absolutely no chance what-so-ever that the way I was parked could possibly cause an accident. Kurtz made that up to justify his own paranoia and *control freak* mentality--something that permeates CNP staff these days.

Looking northeast from an overlook of the **Colorado River**. To the lower left is the **Poison Spider Trailhead**--read the story on page 15. Also left, is the Potash Road and Williams Bottom, and on the other side of the river in the near distance left if King Bottom; and in the far distance is Spanish Valley and Moab. On the right is private land at the mouth of Pritchett Canyon, and Behind the Rocks. In the shadows to the right is the beginning of the Jackson Trail

The **11 Faces** panel in **Horse Canyon** in **The Needles**. Three other images are to the far left and out of sight, but they're pretty faded. These are very similar to, but with blue instead of red colors, to the other Faces panels in or near The Needles District. They are; **3 Faces** on Big Bottom (Map 27, page 283) **4 Faces** in U. Salt Creek, **5 Faces** in Davis Canyon, and **9, 11 & 13 Faces** in Horse Canyon.

Area and Reference/Index Map of Mapped/Hiking Areas

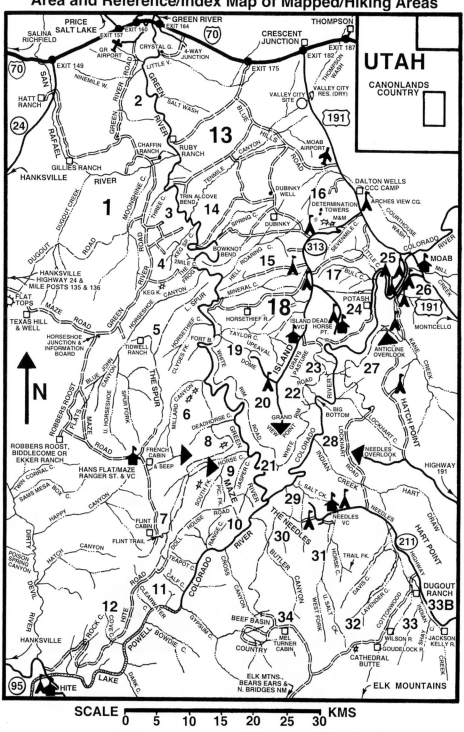

Introduction: West Side of Green River, and Green River Road

Before leaving the town of Green River and heading south on the west side of Labyrinth Canyon, there are a couple of interesting places to see on the east side. The most popular place is **Crystal Geyser**. To get there, drive east out of Green River and across the river bridge as shown on the map. If you haven't done so, be sure and stop at the **Powell River Museum** immediately east of the bridge. They have the **River Museum**, a gift shop that sells books & maps, and a tourist information booth that's open year-round, Tele. 435-564-3427.

Continue east, then south as if you were going to enter the freeway on the east side of town. Instead of getting on Interstate 70, go over the top to the south side. From there, turn left and follow an old bumpy paved road southeast about 3 kms until you come to a **4-Way Junction**. At that point, turn right or south. Soon you'll be on a well-maintained graded dirt road which first runs south, then west toward the river. Just before you reach the river, turn right or northward and soon you'll be at the geyser. You'll know you're there when you see golden brown **mineral terraces** extending down to the river from the bench above. These terraces are the result of mineralization or tufa buildup from the highly mineralized water coming out of the geyser. This geyser is a result of an attempt to drill for oil in the mid-1930's by Glen Ruby, of Ruby Ranch fame.

Now back to the west side of the river heading south. Before beginning any long journey south along the moderately well-traveled **Green River Road**, be sure you have a full tank of fuel (and maybe a little extra), ample food & water supplies and other items you might need for a trip to some very far away places--and the proper maps in hand. The recommended ones for driving this route are the 1:100,000 scale metric **San Rafael Desert & Hanksville** maps. These 2 show almost the entire route from Green River to Lake Powell, and are put out by both the BLM and the USGS. When you get into The Maze District and for all the Under the Ledge country east of the Hans Flat or Maze Ranger Station, other maps are recommended, but they will be discussed under each of the following mapped sections.

Then, from the middle of Green River and at the **Chow Hound** fast food place, drive south 5-6 blocks on **Long Street** to another street running southeast next to the railroad tracks. About 2 short blocks later, turn right or southwest, cross the tracks, and continue on the paved **Airport Road**. Drive **1.2 kms (.7 mile)** and pass under the freeway. See **Map 2** for a good look at the beginning of this trip. Continue southwest toward the airport. At **Km 4.6 (Mile 2.9** from the Chow Hound) turn left or south onto the graded & graveled **Green River Road** (the paved road continues southwest to the airport). The Green River Road is well-maintained by the county. In the north it crosses some clay beds and can be slick when wet, but it's more sandy toward the south so a little moisture doesn't hurt there. This road is good for all cars--in normal conditions.

By driving the Green River Road south, you can visit such places as the west side of Little Valley, McCarty Bottom, Yokey Bottom, Dry Lake Rincon & Bottom and the Chaffin Ranch. These areas close to the Green River are covered in another book by the author titled, *River Guide to Canyonlands National Park and Vicinity, 2nd Edition.* That book came out in 2/2012. The history of the Chaffin Ranch is in that River Guide.

This book begins with short hikes to a couple of rock art panels as seen on **Map 2**. One is near Butterfly Bend of the Green River, the other is west of the Chaffin Ranch near the end of the San Rafael River. From there it's into Moonshine & Three Canyons and Junes Bottom country. Further along, the Green River Road will take you to Upper Horseshoe Canyon, the Hans Flat or Maze Ranger Station, and down the Flint Trail to the Hite Road and Waterhole Flat. Eventually you can end up at Lake Powell near the Hite Marina.

If you're coming from the **Hanksville area**, there's another way to the Green River Road without going all the way to Green River town. Drive along **Highway 24** which runs between I-70 and Hanksville. Between **mile posts 135 & 136** turn east onto the **Maze Road** and drive southeast, then east; then at a major signed intersection called **Horseshoe Junction & Information Board**, veer left or northeast onto the southern end of the Green River Road. This junction is **39.3 kms (24.4 miles)** from Highway 24. If you turn south at that point you'll be heading for the Hans Flat Ranger Station (**Km 73.7/Mile 45.8** from **Highway 24**) on the Maze Road, and the Flint Trail and beyond to Lake Powell, if you choose.

One of the bigger rock art panels in the group of boulders located near **Butterfly Bend** along the Green River.

Area Map 1: Introduction to the West Side of the Green River, and the Green River Road

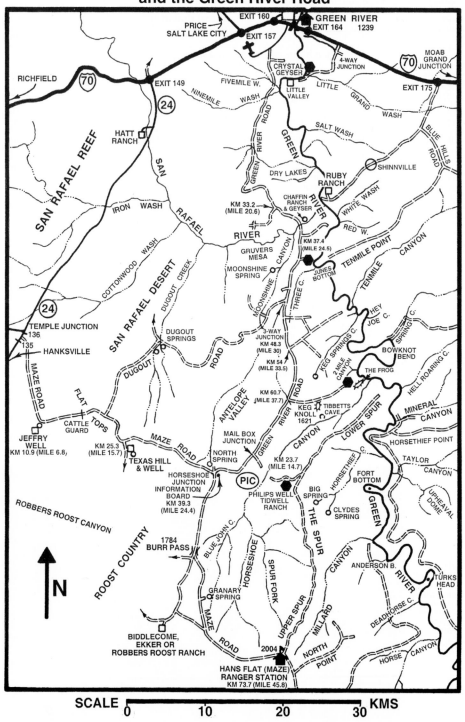

SCALE 0 10 20 30 KMS

Butterfly Bend and the Lower San Rafael River Rock Art Sites

Location & Access If you're driving south out of Green River on the Green River Road heading for Canyonlands NP, here are a couple of rock art sites worth seeing. The first place is very near **Butterfly Bend** on the **Green River**. To get there, start at the **Chow Hound** in the middle of Green River town; drive south 5-6 blocks on Long Street to another street running southeast next to the railroad tracks. About 2 short blocks later, turn right or southwest, cross the tracks, and continue on the paved **Airport Road**. Drive **1.2 kms (.7 mile)** and pass under the freeway. At Km 4.6 (Mile 2.9 from the Chow Hound) turn left or south onto the graded & graveled **Green River Road**. Continue south a short distance to **Km 5.3 (Mile 3.3)** and turn left or east onto a good graded road. Drive this for a little over 2 kms or 1.4 miles until you reach the end of the road which is very near the top of a high ridge and one of the highest points around. Park there which is the trailhead for the hike to the **Butterfly Bend rock art site**.

To reach a couple of panels on the lower San Rafael River, continue south on the **Green River Road**. You'll pass Nine Mile Wash, Horse Bench Reservoir on the right, Dry Lakes Wash & Rincon on the left or east, then as the road is turning east, turn right at **Km 33.2 (Mile 20.6 from the Chow Hound)**. This road is good for cars. At **Km 34.9 (Mile 21.7)** you'll pass 3 round metal livestock **water troughs** (if they're still there?). At **Km 36.6 (Mile 22.7)** turn left and head south. At **Km 37.3 (Mile 23.2)** you'll be on the edge of the plateau and going down a short **steep hill** covered with fist-sized cobblestones. Cars can get down this, and likely back up, but if you have a 2WD car, consider parking there just before the 15m-long steep part. Continuing south; at **Km 38.5 (Mile 23.9)** is a **4-Way Junction**--continue south. Finally you'll come to the end of the road on the rim of the San Rafael River Valley which is **39.5 kms (24.6 miles)** from the Chow Hound. The last 50-60m is a little rough.

Elevations Butterfly Bend Trailhead, 1356m; San Rafael River Rim Trailhead, 1256m.

Water None on either hike, so take your own.

Maps USGS or BLM map San Rafael Desert (1:100,000); BLM road map San Rafael Motorized Route Designations (approximately 1:180,000). This free map from the BLM shows designated roads open to vehicle travel; and Green River, Horse Bench East & Moonshine Wash (1:24,000--7 1/2' quads).

Main Attractions Short hikes to some pretty good petroglyph rock art sites.

Butterfly Bend Rock Art Site From the trailhead, walk east and straight down a steep hillside covered with junk and empty shotgun shells; locals target shoot clay pidgeons here. At the bottom, continue east and look for an old vehicle track. Get on it as it circles around to the east side of the **rounded hill** labeled **4344T** (1324m) on the *Green River 7 1/2' quad*; from there head north, then northeast. After walking about 1300m (.75 mile) you'll be at the top of, and looking down into, a little **cove** only about 250m northwest of **Butterfly Bend** on the river. That little cove, about 100m square, is choked with small to medium-sized boulders and all covered with black desert varnish. Work your way down into these rocks and be observant; the author once counted 14 boulders with some **rock art**. The best half dozen panels are about 1m square, and one boulder has several old cowboy signatures. If you walk down through the cove and across a little flat, you can downclimb over one rim going east toward the river. You'll see at least one more panel on top of a prominent boulder. The author has been there twice, the last time was along the route described. That hike took 1 1/2 hours round-trip.

Lower San Rafael River Rock Art Site From the end of the road, walk almost due east about 75m to a white metal **cross** (this could be gone when you arrive?). From there, again walk almost due east to the last little rim above the river. The author left a **cairn** marking the place where you can look right down on the **1st of 2 panels**. You can see this one from the rim; or downclimb 2m and have a closer look. This panel is just under the rim and faces up 45°. It shows 4 adults holding hands, plus a child and 4 snakes. These snake heads appear to be of rattlers, but this writer has never seen any rattles on any rock art snakes anywhere. From there, if you walk back to the west you'll find an old cattle trail following a bench. Walk this but be looking for an easy way down to the bottom going south, then after just a few meters, walk back east to the base of the cliff until you're under the same ledge with the 1st panel; nearby will be several large boulders. From there look up to see a **2nd panel** under the ledge. This 2nd panel is immediately west and below the 1st. Part of it seems to have been a pictograph at one time. You can see both panels and return in 15 minutes.

The 1st of the 2 rock art panels seen along the **Lower San Rafael River** as shown on **Map 2**. It faces south, is upturned about 45° and can best be seen from the rim.

Map 2, Butterfly Bend & Lower San Rafael River Rock Art Sites

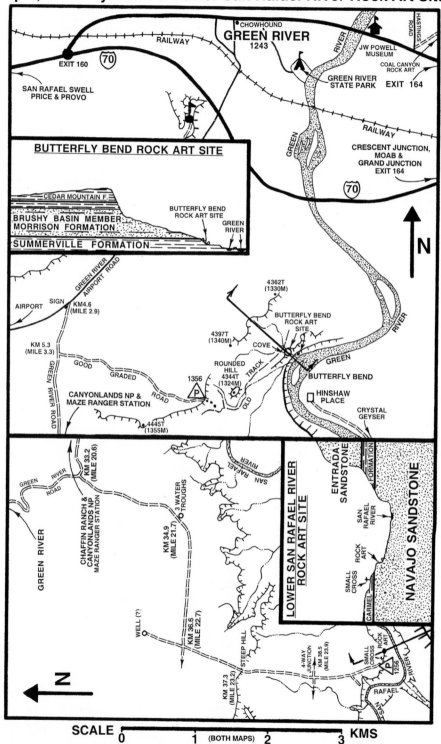

Moonshine & Three Canyons, and Bull & Junes Bottoms

Location & Access This mapped area is roughly 35 to 50 kms (25-30 miles) south of the town of Green River, and on the west side of the Green River. You can get to these parts easiest from Green River (using the Green River Road), the recommended starting point. Or, from the Hanksville area and Highway 24, but that's a longer drive on dirt roads. See **Area Map 1, Introduction to the West Side of the Green River, and the Green River Road**; read the **Introduction:...** with it for how to reach this area.

Elevations The drill hole near lower Three Canyon, 1334m; Moonshine Spring & trailhead for Moonshine Wash, 1402m; the Green River, about 1220m.

Water Take lots of water into this country, but there is good water in several places in Three Canyon, a minor spring behind Junes dugout, and really good water at Moonshine Spring. Water from the Green River must be treated or boiled before using.

Maps USGS or BLM map San Rafael Desert (1:100,000); BLM road map San Rafael Motorized Route Designations (approximately 1:180,000). This free map from the BLM shows designated roads open to vehicle travel; and Moonshine Wash & Tenmile Point (1:24,000--7 1/2' quads).

Main Attractions Two good canyon hikes, a historic sheep bridge over a nice slot, a short hike to Bull Bottom, and Junes Bottom which had a historic homestead.

Bull Bottom and the Bull Bottom Trail

The first place of interest here might be a short walk down the Bull Bottom Trail to Bull Bottom on the Green River. About **37.4 kms (24.5 miles)** south of the **Chow Hound** in Green River, is a side-road heading east. Drive this northeast about 3.5 kms (2.2 miles) to where it ends on the edge of a cliff. This road runs over some clay beds of the Carmel Formation, which is sandwiched in between the Navajo Sandstone below and the Entrada Formation above. It's a pretty good road and normally most cars, driven with care, can make it to or near the canyon rim. Beware of a sandy place or two.

Right at the end of the road is a parking place and a small **fenced enclosure** big enough for half a dozen cows. This enclosure is at the top of the **Bull Bottom Trail**. It leads down a short distance to **Bull Bottom**.

All the old stockmen of the area knew this place by the politically incorrect name of **Nigger Bill Bottom**. **Buck Tomlinson** had this to say about how it got that name: *An old nigger lived in there one winter I was told. That was way back there before my time. That old nigger that lived in there was called Bill, so they called it Nigger Bill Bottom. I think he only lived in there one winter as I remember the story. The Nigger Bill that the canyon was named after was the same one the river bottom was named after.*

The canyon Buck is referring to is **Negro Bill Canyon** northeast of Moab. A brief history on this man comes from the book, ***Grand Memories***, a history of Grand County, Utah: *In the spring of 1877 William Granstaff (Nigger Bill), and Frenchie, a trapper, arrived in Spanish Valley. Frenchie had a burro. Bill had a few head of cows. They were prospecting, but after seeing Spanish Valley, they decided to stay. They took possession of the fort left by the Billings Party. Each lived in half the fort and each claimed half the valley.*

Bill drove his cattle east along the southern edge of the Grand [renamed the Colorado on 7/25/1921] River until he came to a stream of clear mountain water, with grass lining its banks for miles upstream, where he left his cows. This canyon a few miles up the river from Moab is named "Nigger Bill," after this man.

No one is sure who changed the name to Bull Bottom, but the reason is obvious. That drainage near Moab is now officially known as Negro Bill Canyon *(As this book goes to press, there is a movement in Moab to change the name from Negro Bill to **Granstaff Canyon**; which is obviously offensive to some.).*

It was that man who some think this bottom is named after, but he was around a long time ago, so this one could fall into the category of folklore.

The late **Chad Moore** of Green River has known the place for many years and he had this to say about it: *We called it Nigger Bill. I was a grown kid before I got down there. My dad [Andy Moore] when he started, weaned some calves on that bottom. I think Halverson's blasted the trail in there. I don't know, but I always thought that Halverson made all them trails in there and Keg Spring Canyon, but he may not have.*

We didn't know that place because Chaffins used that country. So we never was in there until Chaffins sold out. We knew there was a bottom down there, but it wasn't on our allotment, so I never did go down there.

If we'd run short on feed we'd run cattle on the river bottoms, but we didn't run them there every year. We used to run our bulls on Nigger Bill Bottom; we put 'em in there for 4 or 5 years. Then the BLM told us to get out; that's another guys allotment--that belongs to the

The **Bull Bottom Trail**, looking southwest. Bull Bottom is to the left, and the Green River left of that. Behind the camera is a small wire corral or holding pen.

Map 3, Moonshine & Three Canyons and Bull & Junes Bottoms

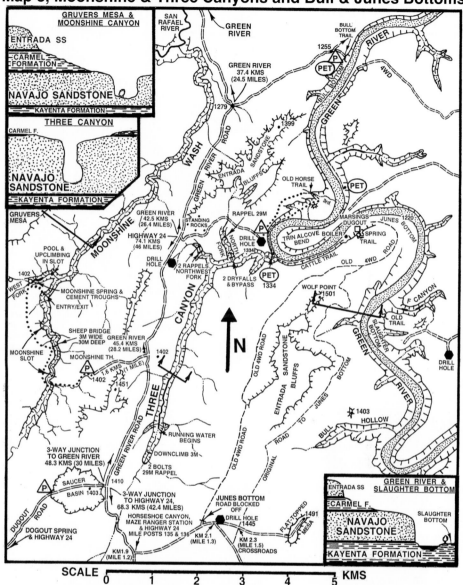

SCALE
0 1 2 3 4 5 KMS

sheep herders [Moyniers out of Price, Utah]. Sheep herders can't get in there, and they can't get any good out of that little ol' bottom, so we put our bulls in there and then when they [BLM] got a little bit rough on us, then we said to hell with you, we're not going to argue with you, so nobody used it for quite a few years. Then some of the guys from here [Green River] sneaked some horses in there. Ol' George Seely, when he was here, he used to run it. The Chaffins put some horses or some cows there sometimes. Since it was close to their ranch everybody figured it belonged to them. Later the Moyniers bought out Chaffins. They didn't want the ranch; all they wanted was [the grazing rights to] Underneath the Ledge. Then every Tom, Dick and Harry took a turn at leasing that ranch. But they couldn't raise nothin' but sand burrs.

Everybody the author talked to about the place said there was moonshining going on there during the prohibition years of about 1919 to 1933. Someone mentioned there was an old moonshiner's dugout down on the bottom somewhere; to that Buck Tomlinson said: *It was damn close to the canyon, that little canyon that goes into the lower end of Nigger Bill Bottom. It was close to the river but near the mouth of that canyon. It was a dugout, kind of a ratty little shelter. I believe ol' **John Romjue** might have made it. I know my dad and John both made moonshine whiskey in there. They'd move around the country; they didn't stay in the same place for very long.*

23

The author never did find that little dugout. It may be hidden by tamarisks now or covered with sand. Tamarisks didn't start coming into this part of the country until sometime around the 1930's.

Here's an interesting hike which will only take an hour or so. Once down on the bottom, walk southwest from the trail about half a km, and you'll come to a break in the wall with a log standing between the main wall and a large boulder. This is obviously an old Indian route, because on the river-side of that boulder are some **petroglyphs**. As you wander around look for more rock art. There is one little short side-canyon which is interesting; and be on the lookout for that old moonshiner's dugout.

Three Canyon & Trin Alcove Bend

Continue south from the turnoff to Bull Bottom. If you're a hiker, one of the best canyon hikes in this book has to be a trip up **Three Canyon**. To get there, drive about **42.5 kms (26.4 miles)** south of Green River and turn left or east onto a little side-road. Drive this eastward for 2.7 kms (1.7 miles) until you come to an old **drill hole site** that's situated on the rim of Labyrinth & Three Canyons. Most cars driven with care can usually make it.

Now there are several ways into Three Canyon, but all except this one is for people who have ropes and know how to use them. With ropes you can enter at the head of the canyon, or by way of 2 short forks near the bottom end of the drainage. One 60m rope will get you down any of the routes. If you're interested, see this writers other book, *Technical Slot Canyon Guide to the Col-*

Top From the mouth of **Three Canyon** looking north with the Green River on the right. On the left or west side of river is a route or trail to Three Canyon. Notice the boats in the inlet and campers in the alcove. **Above** Looking west from above the upper end of **Junes Bottom** toward the mouth of **Three Canyon** (above center). You can barely see the **trail** located on the talus slope to the left.

orado Plateau, 2nd Edition.

But for this book, here's a fun walk-in route. From the drill hole, walk northeast over slickrock staying back a ways from the canyon rim. After about 2 kms, be looking for the **3rd** little drainage running southeast. You may see a cairn or two. Walk down this shallow slickrock drainage and near where it steepens, you'll see that it's been blasted out with dynamite to make a **horse trail**. At that point you'll see more cairns. Once down off the steeper parts, turn right or southwest and walk/route-find toward the lower end of Three Canyon. A little further on, you'll be walking along some narrows ledges just above the river. Deer and maybe big horn sheep use this, and now a few hikers. Soon you'll be at the mouth of Three Canyon (Looking down on this trail from the top, you wouldn't think you can walk this route!).

River runners stop here as it's one of the more popular places to camp (and fill up on good water) on their entire river trip. Near the mouth of this Three Canyon, you can see a couple of big alcoves on either side of the main drainage. In 1869, **John Wesley Powell** named this place **Trin Alcoves and Trin Alcove Bend**, because as seen from various places it appears to be 3 alcoves. Just as you begin to enter Three Canyon, look up to the right at the corner of the drainage and you'll see a very old **rock art panel**. From there, walk on boater's trails into the canyon.

From the bottom to the head of this drainage it's only about 7-8 kms, and can be done round-trip in about half a day; or a little more. The stream in the lower end is small but the water is normally safe to drink. Higher up it's a dry wash in places and the lush vegetation you find near the river disappears. At the extreme upper end it becomes deep and quite narrow; with water in a few places. At the very end is the usual big dryfall you cannot climb. This entire canyon from top to bottom is made of Navajo Sandstone. Plan on taking most of a day to hike down to the mouth of Three Canyon then up to the big dryfall and back.

Some of the more recent history of the Trin Alcove area is tied to Junes Bottom. **Chad Moore** was there as a kid with his family punchin' cows during the 1930's. He remembered that: *Three Canyon is just up the river from Junes. I mean you gotta go to Junes Bottom, then there was a trail upon the hillside and you could walk to Three Canyon. I was ridin' a horse up there one day and the trail slid off with me and I went in the river. They had to reach down and pick me up off the saddle and brang me up the bank. We had to go into Three Canyon for somethin', I think we had some cows in there.*

Junes Bottom will be covered in more detail later, but this old cow trail Chad talks about runs from the mouth of Three Canyon along the river all the way to Junes Bottom. But in times of high water it would be a real bushwhack to get out of the mouth of Three Canyon and onto this trail. This trail likely hasn't been used since the 1940's or '50's for cows, but is still used by deer and/or big horns. From the rim directly above, the trail is clearly visible in most places.

Moonshine Wash

The next place of interest is Moonshine Wash or Canyon. You could enter at the lower north end, but that part isn't very interesting. The best part is in the upper half of the drainage. So if coming from Green River, drive to a point **45.4 kms (28.2 miles)** from the Chow Hound and look for a side-track on the right or west side of the road. From there, drive 1.6 kms (1 mile) to the end of the side-track and the **Moonshine Trailhead** as shown. The author last used this on 5/20/2012, and it's getting more-used but rougher every year. Overall it's not too bad but you'll need a little more clearance than cars, and

Moonshine Spring is in the background left seeping out of the rocks. To the right are the **3 cement tanks** that were used as watering troughs for livestock. Moonshining took place here, but not in these cement tanks; that would have been in metal tanks of some kind with a fire underneath.

AWD/4WD for a couple of steep places. Drive a car about halfway, park, and walk from there.

From the Moonshine Trailhead, walk southwest into the shallow drainage. Follow it about 1 km, then downclimb over a ledge into **Moonshine Wash**; or follow an old sheepwagon road to the right or north a little, then walk into the drainage. Immediately, you'll be at the beginning of the slot. In the slot, you'll find several chokestones and short dropoffs, but anyone who calls him or herself a hiker, should be able to climb up or down these minor obstacles. Near the end of this 1 km-long slot, look up to see an old 3m-long **sheep bridge** about 30m above. Soon after that, the canyon begins to open. After yet another km is a steep scramble up to an **entry/exit** on the left, or west. You can leave the canyon at that point and rim-walk south back to your car, seeing the sheep bridge up close along the way. The lower, or northern 3/4's of Moonshine is confined, but not nearly so deep or interesting as the slot just described.

A short side-trip, would be to climb up from the bottom end of Moonshine's **West Fork** about 600m to find **Moonshine Spring** and **3 cement tanks**. These tanks weren't used for making moonshine whiskey during prohibition days of the 1920's, but moonshining took place nearby in metal vats. John Romjue was the best moonshiner in the business and in these parts, and the most likely suspect.

There are no cattle into this spring today, so it's good drinking water. On 8/26/2010, a week after heavy rains & floods hit the area, the author upclimbed from the lower end of West Fork which involved swimming through 3 pools--but most of the time it's dry, or with little water. From the spring, walk out of the West Fork, then south along the main drainage, seeing the sheep bridge on the way, and return to your car. This is the recommended loop-hike; but if you can't upclimb lower West Fork, you can get to Moonshine Spring via the **entry/exit** mentioned above. This might be the easiest way to the spring because upclimbing the West Fork might be too much for some people--depending on conditions. Plan to take most of a day (a half-day for fast hikers) for this loop-hike. This is a fun hike and the best slot canyon described in this book.

Junes Bottom and the June Marsing Family Ranch

The last place of interest on this map is **Junes Bottom** (The USGS always spells it Junes, not June's!). To get there continue south on the Green River Road until you've reached the south end of Three Canyon as shown on the map. At the **3-Way Junction** shown, which is **48.3 kms (30 miles)** from Green River, reset your **odometer at 0**, then continue south on the Green River Road. After **1.9 kms (1.2 miles)**, veer left or east onto a side-road. Reset your **odometer at 0**. After another **2.1 kms (1.3 miles)** is a **drill hole** by Shell Oil on your left or north (**NOTE**: about 500m before that is where another road used to start which ran out to Junes Bottom, but it's been blocked off because it's a wilderness study area and ATV's have done their best to ruin that possibility). The drill hole site is a good place to park and/or camp, but for now continue east toward a **flat-topped mesa** in the distance. After 300m is a **crossroads**; of these 4 roads, the one you're interested in is the one heading north. This according to **Bob Marsing**, is the original route or road his father June Marsing used to reach Junes Bottom. If it's blocked off, and it will be at some point in time, you can **walk to Junes Bottom in about 2 hours**.

This original road to Junes Bottom was mostly very good for pickups in 5/2012. For most of the way, it runs along the contact point between the white Navajo Sandstone below, and the red Carmel Formation dirt above. Once you're in the area just northeast of **Wolf Point**, either pick your way along the old road (which is impossible to find now!); or just beeline-it north to the canyon rim and route-find down from there. Only near the end of the old road as it runs across slickrock is it visible with several places where June and his family stacked up rocks by hand to make a road grade. Or, at one point, you can

Both pictures are from **Moonshine Wash**. **Left** Going back up and over one of several chokestones in the slot--it's easier than it looks. **Right** The 3m-long sheep bridge over the middle of the slot.

walk down a short drainage to the northwest, and easily downclimb along a trail June made which was a shortcut to the dugout the family lived in for 3 years.

For now, here's a history of Junes Bottom as told by the remaining family members of **June & Edith Marsing**. Originally this was called **Willy's Bottom** (the author was unable to find anyone who knew where the name Willy originated from, but it likely came from someone who tried to settle it during the peach boom around Green River in the years just after 1900). However, ever since June Marsing & family lived there from the spring of 1933 until the spring of 1936, it's been called **Junes Bottom**. Three of June & Edith Marsing's children who lived there were still alive in 2012; from the oldest to youngest they are, **Norma Marsing Bryan** of South Weber, Utah; **Wilma June (Juni) Marsing Barton** of Torrey, Utah; and **Bob Marsing** of Willard, Utah. In addition, Sherma Marsing Eves, a daughter who was born after the Marsing's Green River adventures, helped put together a family history using a couple of small diaries belonging to their parents June & Edith:

To start, here are 2 lines from June's diary: **May 1931**--We were camped on Wolf Point on the edge of Three Canyons and I rode over to Willy's Bottom for the first time. That was when we decided to go there and farm.

All the Marsing children contributed some history for this story: *In the spring of 1932, we moved from Green River down to what is now known as the* **Ruby Ranch**; *in those days we used to call it the* **Wimmer Place**. *Bill Tomlinson, a friend of Junes, had leased the Wimmer Place and he wanted Dad to go down there and run it.* **Grandpa Alma Marsing** *was there and worked with Dad all summer. They had a sharecropping agreement where they were to receive half the hay crop. Dad, who used whatever materials were available, built a contraption that would enable us to bale the hay and move it to storage. That same summer, Dad built a boat using scrap lumber to navigate the river. In September of 1932, Mom took us kids back to Green River so we could go to school.*

The winter of 1932 & '33 was very cold and the river froze solid so Dad and Grandpa Alma moved everything [Model T Ford truck, wagon, horses, cattle, chickens, etc.] just across the river on the ice to the Chaffin property at the confluence of the San Rafael and Green Rivers. Dad tied gunny sacks on the animal's feet so they could cross without slipping and falling. At Christmas time, 1932, Mom and we kids joined Dad and Grandpa at the camp at the Chaffin Place and Mom taught us school for the rest of that year [They stayed in, and/or used, the old **cellar** *just across the Green River from the boat ramp as shown on the map of the Ruby Ranch,* **Area Map 13, Between the Rivers**, *page 139].*

In March of 1933, the ice on the river broke and Grandpa took the boat and camping equipment and supplies down the river and set it all up at Willy's Bottom. At about the same time, our family left the Chaffin Place and moved everything to a ledge above Willy's Bottom and with the aid of ropes, moved what we could, including the family, down to the bottom. Then with pack horses he moved everything else down to the river bottom on a trail. I [Juni] remember that move well because we had a box of chickens in the back of the Model T Ford truck. When we stopped for that one night, Dad set that whole box of chickens over on the side of a hill, and we'd feed and water them in that box--and they laid eggs too. It took us 2 days to move everything down there. That first summer we lived in a boarded-up tent.

At that time **Andy Moore** *had the grazing rights [he would have had a grazing permit from the Grazing Service after the Taylor Grazing Act went into effect in June of 1934] for that area and he gave Dad permission to farm and ranch there. You can't buy ground on that river now, and I guess you couldn't then. So after we set up camp, Dad and Grandpa started building a road so we could get the truck down to*

This is part of the **road to Junes Bottom** that June Marsing and his father Alma built by hand in 1933 & '34. Junes Bottom is straight ahead and to the right.

the river. My brother Bob, who was 3 years of age, had a little wagon, so my sister Juni, who was 6, and myself [Norma] 9 years of age, would fill the wagon with rocks and take it over to help Dad and Grandpa build the dugway [which is still there and can be seen in at least 4 places]. If you didn't know where it went, you couldn't find it.

That summer we lived in a tent, but in the fall of 1933, Mom took us kids back to Green River to attend school. While we were gone Dad and Grandpa built a **dugout** or **rock house** to replace the tent. Dad built it back into the hill and used cottonwood logs covered with dirt for a roof. He rocked-up the front because it was right back in the hill. There was a little spring just behind the dugout in a little canyon but sometimes it would go dry, so we'd go upriver toward Three Canyon for drinking water. There was a lot of poison oak in there and Mom couldn't get around the poison oak--so when she went up there it was in the boat. There was another spring up there too. We'd go up and get water in wooden kegs and throw them in the river and float 'em down to the ranch. We didn't drink the river water.

Bob Marsing was 3 years old when the family first moved to Willy's Bottom. He added more to what Juni & Norma have stated above, but their recollections are a little different especially about where they got their drinking water. Bob remembered: We got our drinking water at Three Canyon most of the time. That was a real good spring. Mostly we just filled the kegs from the small stream there at the mouth of the canyon, or we probably went a little ways up. But there's several springs as I recall in Three Canyon--several places where water comes out--but I think Dad just dug out a place there near the river where it would be deep enough to fill the kegs. We'd fill the kegs and then put 'em in the river. I remember my mother used to swim back, or float down with the kegs. We'd tie these kegs together and that's the way we'd get 'em back down the river, even though there was a good trail from our place to the mouth of Three Canyon.

We kids weren't supposed to get out in the river. There was a bar out in the river in front of our ranch, so when our Mom and Dad weren't lookin'--naturally we were in the river! I [Juni] remember a boat full of tourists going down there one summer, and we were so excited because we hadn't seen people for a long time. We even had a couple from Turkey come down the river and they stayed with us a couple of days. They gave Mom some seeds to a Zanzibar Palm that really grew well.

We were down there for 3 years. I remember I had a cousin down with me and we were about 6 or 7, because we'd go down and stay in the summer. In the fall we kids along with Mother would have to go into Green River for the winter so we kids could go to school.

We had an old Model T Ford truck that we jacked up and hooked one wheel to a pump and pumped water out of the river to irrigate. Dad cleared the bottom and made a ranch out of it.

Some of my [Juni] memories were that we'd take care of Andy Moore's cows; kept them out of the river, because they'd get in the quicksand. Dad would go down with a saddle horse and pull 'em out. He'd get a rope on their horns and drag them out of the mud. He'd let me go and I'd sit on the saddle behind him and when he'd get ready to pull that cow out, he'd tell me to hang on. I remember it because it was so exciting. We'd pull that old cow out with the horse just workin' like heck, then as soon as she got out and to her feet, she'd take after the horse. And Dad had to get the rope off.

We raised the most fabulous gardens you ever saw. Anything we planted, grew. We could raise anything. I can remember riding the horse while we cultivated the corn, and going to sleep while on the horse. We raised corn and watermelons. My brother and I couldn't in any way lift the watermelons, so we'd take his wagon and lean a board up against the side of it and roll the mellons in. We never ate anything but the heart. There was no way to get the produce out [and to market] except back upriver, and you couldn't always do that because in the fall of the year the water would be pretty low.

We used Three Canyon to pasture our cows, and horses were put on **Slaughter Bar [Bottom]** across the river and downstream a ways. There wasn't any tamarisks in there then.

There were quite a few snakes down there. We had an old dog named Toby and every place we kids went that dog was right in front of us. When he'd see a snake, he'd turn around and growl at us, then he'd kill the snake. If it was a rattlesnake, and after they strike a few times, they slow down, then he'd get it right behind the head and give it one flip, and it wouldn't move. That old dog never got bit.

To supplement our income Dad went out on the desert which had lots of wild horses. He'd catch 'em and sell 'em. This was during the 1930's and the Great Depression.

We built our corrals in the oak. Dad would take out some of the trees and leave a little space in the middle. The corrals were up by the house.

Now we were poor, dirt poor. We had the cows and we had the milk. And mother always made bread. Her sister Aunt Ernie [Wells] & children were down in there once, and we simply didn't have enough food to feed everybody. So they made this great big pan of milk gravy for supper. Everybody was going to eat homemade bread and milk gravy for supper. But this lizard came flying from the rafters of the house and it lit right in the pan of gravy. And since they didn't have anything else to eat, Mom just took the lizard out--but she and Aunt Ernie didn't eat!

We had 2 sisters who died young. One sister died before we ever went to Willy's Bottom, she was 5 years old; then another one was just a year old when we moved down on the river and then later she died over in Hanksville when she was 5 [Lois was born March 1, 1932 and died January 9, 1938]. They both died at age 5, but they didn't know each other.

The main reason we left the river was because of poison oak. Dad took Mother to the hospital in Price and was told she was allergic to it and the last spring we were there she was so bad the doctor told Dad if he took her down there again he'd better take a coffin because she wouldn't live if she contacted it again.

My mother's parents, Sam & Minnie Wells, had moved to Hanksville, and in the spring of 1936 we were in Green River for school. Dad had stayed at Willy's Bottom in the winter and in the spring moved us out to Hanksville where I [Norma] finished school. Dad sold some of our stuff to Andy Moore, then Dad & Mom moved to the Cat Ranch in the Henry Mountains. I stayed with my Grandparents in Hanksville while I finished the 8th Grade. Later we all moved to Teasdale so us kids could go to school in Bicknell.

The late Chad Moore [Andy Moore's son] of Green River and the ranch on Texas Hill in the Roost Country, was also down in there at the time and was the same age as the oldest Marsing kids (born in 1925). He remembered a few more things: Ol' June, he run a few head of cattle there on the lower end of the bottom. About halfway down he had a fence across it. He'd use the lower end for his cows. Then when he'd run out of feed there, he'd run 'em up there in Three Canyon. About 8 or 10 head.

I remember they grubbed all the brush and oak off from the bottom, just below where the house is, and made 'em a garden. And I know they took that oak up there and threw it in the boiler to make steam to pump water. I don't think anybody in those days had money to buy gas to pump anything. June didn't even own the boiler. It was **Lilly Denny's**. She probably let June borrow it, or have it, or something. There wasn't any money no place. Her husband probably stole it off from an old oil rig or something. He was an oil man, and he went around to ever' rig there was, after they shut it down, and he'd haul half of it off. That's where he probably got that old boiler.

If you have come down to this bottom via the old road shown on this map, you'll have walked down part of the **old road & dugway** June, his father Alma & family built in 1933 and probably '34. From the last of the constructed part of that old road, walk west about 600m and at the mouth of an obvious little canyon or **alcove** just to the left or south, is the **dugout** June and his Dad built in the fall of 1933. The roof is long gone, but the stone wall in front is still standing. Inside and half buried is an old stove, bedstead and #3 galvanized bath tub. When asked about why they left all that stuff there, Norma said: *I guess the reason we left the stove and bed springs is because Dad was thinking he might go back.* Bob added: *Until the day he died, Dad always wanted to return to the Green River and Willy's Bottom.*

Immediately west of the Marsing dugout is a boulder and part of a little rock wall forming an enclosure. This was the **chicken coop** and it had a roof at one time. On a large flat rock are some Marsing artifacts still there--please leave them there for history's sake. Just to the east of that are the remains of an old **corral** (which wasn't obvious in 2012). Behind the dugout and in the alcove is a little **spring** used by the Marsings, and just above that is a route or **trail** up through the ledges to where they parked their Model T Ford truck when they first went down there. Halfway up are 2 metal shafts or stakes that were drilled into the slickrock and which must have been the foundation of a trail. June likely had a log and maybe some rocks and dirt across there at one time to keep the kids from falling off the ledge down to where the spring is.

If you walk west from the dugout about 300m you'll come to the old **boiler** Lilly Denny gave June. There are also a couple of wheels and an old car axle, plus the **transmission** of June's Model T Ford truck. It has 3 pedals which were used to change gears; when the Model A Fords came out in December, 1927, the transmissions were changed to something like we know today. The boiler site is where they pumped water out of the river. From there you can walk upriver and into Three Canyon along an old game path that June (and likely Andy Moore before him) worked over to make into a cow trail.

Here's what Norma had to say about that trail and a **second little spring** they used to get water from: *There was a spring between Three Canyon and the Marsing Ranch and we built a trail up there from the boiler, and it went all the way up to Three Canyon. The spring is in the* **little alcove** *[about 100m southwest from the old boiler]. My dad went in there and rocked-it-up so animals couldn't get in it, and that's where we got some of our drinking water.* No sign of this is visible today.

About 300m east of the dugout is what appears to be the bed of an **old wagon** and part of a **scraper** of some kind, maybe a Fresno (?). They used to have a corral there.

Looking west at the front of the **Dugout** that June Marsing and his family lived in from sometime in late 1933, until the spring of 1936. The roof is long gone but the front is still pretty much intact. To the upper right is the boulder which formed one wall of the **chicken coop**.

Above The **boiler** that Lilly Denny gave to June Marsing. It was used to somehow supply power to pump water onto Junes Bottom. In the foreground right is what appears to be an axel and transmission from June Marsing's **Model T Ford truck**. Notice the 3 petals in the transmission; they were used to change gears. Model T's first rolled out in 1908. The Model A Fords had a different type of trany, and they first began to be built in December of 1927.

Right This is the interior of **June Marsing's** family **Dugout** looking eastward. The bedstead is still there, and half buried in sand is a cookstove and #3 galvanized bath tub. Near the cottonwood tree in the far background is where the Marsings grew a garden.

Wolf Point Three Canyon Drill Hole Trail Trin Alcove Bend Junes Bottom

Above Aerial view of Trin Alcove, Trin Alcove Bend, **Three Canyon,** Wolf Point and **Junes Bottom** looking south, southwest.

Left This is part of the trail June Marsing built directly above the **Dugout.** This trail was used as a shortcut to Junes Bottom before they finished building the road down to the river and their ranch. Notice the 2 metal rods or stakes drilled into the rock. They were used as anchors for logs and other material to create a safe way for the kids to get up & down to the Dugout.

Wolverton, Keg Spring, Twomile and Lower Horseshoe Canyons; The Frog & Angel Trails, and Tibbetts/Perkins Cave

Location & Access This is the next map south from the area of Moonshine & Three Canyons, and Junes Bottom, and is not far north of the Horseshoe Canyon Unit of Canyonlands National Park. It's also about halfway between the town of Green River and the Hans Flat or Maze Ranger Station. All of this area is reached via the **Green River Road**. Please refer to the **Area Map 1: West of the Green River** for the access routes to this section. The roads on this mapped area are generally good and are well-maintained by county road crews. Since most of these local roads are a little bit sandy, some wet weather usually makes them better for driving.

Elevations The highest point in the area is Keg Knoll, at 1621m; while the Green River at the mouth of Horseshoe Canyon is about 1220m altitude.

Water There are several good springs in the head of Keg Spring Canyon, and running water with beaver & crawfish in the middle parts. Also, there's a good year-round water supply in Horseshoe Canyon. However, take care when drinking from that stream (and Keg Spring Canyon) as there may be beaver around, which carry Giardia. Also the Green River, but you'll have to treat that before drinking.

Maps USGS or BLM map San Rafael Desert (1:100,000); BLM road map San Rafael Motorized Route Designations (approximately 1:180,000). This free map from the BLM shows designated roads open to vehicle travel; and Tenmile Point, Moonshine Wash, Keg Knoll & Bowknot Bend (1:24,000--7 1/2' quads).

Main Attractions Several good viewpoints where you can look down into Labyrinth Canyon of the Green River, at least 8 historic cattle trails, and an interesting old abandoned meander of the Green River known as The Frog.

Wolverton Canyon and Trail

Starting in the north, the first place of interest might be an **overlook** of the Green River and Tenmile Bottom & Canyon, and a hike down to the river via a trail in what this writer calls **Wolverton Canyon**. The trail appears to have been built by a miner named **Edwin T. Wolverton**. This is surely the trail, or one of the trails, that Wolverton built to take copper ore from his claims down to the river.

To get to this **overlook**, drive along the Green River Road until you reach **Lookout Point** (54 kms/33.5 miles from Green River; or 62.6 kms/38.9 miles from Highway 24). This is on top of a big hump and the highest place around. Near this junction is an **old corral** and sheepherders **dugout**. From there, you'll see a good road running northeast. Drive northeast about **8.6 kms (5.3 miles)** to the end of the road. If you're in a 2WD car, beware; the last part of this road runs through sandy country. In 1991, the author made it to the overlook twice in his VW Rabbit, but both times it was in cooler weather and the sand had some moisture in it (by 2012, the county had put a blade on that road and seems much better). If you're there after a long dry spell and driving a car, you could get bogged down in the sand. For this reason it's best to have an AWD/4WD. Mtn. bikes may or may not work. Walk around the point for the best views.

To hike down Wolverton Canyon, drive along this same road about **7.7 kms (4.8 miles)**, or about **800m** short of the end of the road. Park somewhere in that area and walk south and around some Navajo bluffs and into the head of a shallow drainage. Follow it down toward to the east. Soon you'll come to a dropoff. From there, walk along the rim on the south side about 100m and look for a break in the wall which will be the upper-most part of the Wolverton Trail. You'll then walk down the dry wash a ways, then veer to the left or north side of the drainage. At that point the trail will become visible for the first time. It then zig zags down and runs over to the south side of the canyon again, and from there down to the river to the east. The bottom of the trail is wide enough to be a road--it was likely built for wagons. Just south of the mouth of Wolverton Canyon you may see what could have been a workers or cowboy campsite. At the river you could walk south into the lower end of **Keg Spring Canyon**.

To walk from the road to the river and back might take only 2-3 hours round-trip, or longer if you do more exploring. Take water if it's a hot day.

Now a little history on this trail and the nearby bottom at the mouth of Keg Spring Canyon as told by the late **Chad Moore** formerly of Green River:

Here's a scene in about the middle of what this writer calls **Wolverton Canyon**. Shown is the horse trail on the north side of the drainage looking west. In the lower canyon, the trail is on the south side; that's where it looks like a wagon road.

Map 4, Wolverton, Keg Spring, Twomile and Lower Horseshoe Canyons; The Frog & Angel Trails, and Tibbetts/Perkins Cave

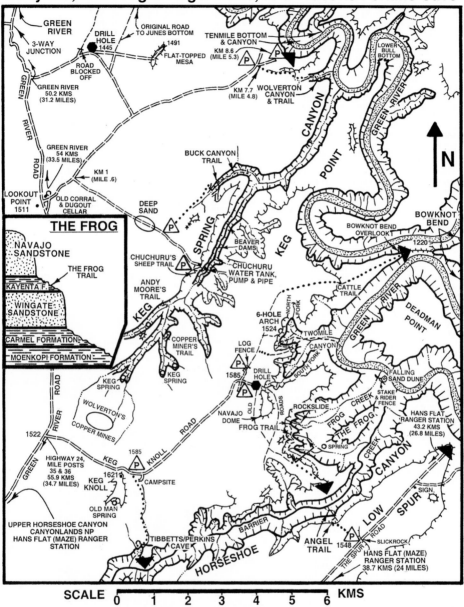

We called it the **Upper Bull Bottom Trail**. We put our bulls down in Keg Canyon and there was a bottom down below Keg; that was the **Big Bull Bottom**. That trail went up that little ol' canyon just as you come on the bottom. I don't know who built the trail, but from the bottom they started to build a wagon road. It's a big trail at the bottom, then it would narrow just to a regular trail. They went in there lookin' for copper. Somebody went in there before my days, and they sacked the ore and took it out that trail on pack horses and they was going to build a wagon road out of there to haul the ore out, but I guess the ore didn't run high enough to justify it and I guess they just dropped it. They never did do much of anything.

E.T. Wolverton (see picture on page 42) testified in the ***Colorado River Bed Case hearings*** in 1929 not long before he died. That court case was to determine whether or not the river was navigable and who owned rights to oil and other minerals under the river bed. And who had the right to collect taxes.

Wolverton stated that in 1903, he and a guy named Kendrick helped to organize the Utah-Nevada Copper Company. Kendrick was the principal stock holder. Wolverton went out on the desert south of the Chaffin Ranch and mostly between Keg Knoll and the upper end of Keg Spring Canyon, and found copper bearing ore in the Carmel Formation. He staked out 8 claims on August 26, 1903. They were recorded in the Wayne County courthouse in Loa 3 weeks later on September 16.

Six of these claims were all bunched together and located, according to Wolverton: *on high ground about 3 miles [5 kms] southwest of Keg Spring and about 1 1/2 miles [2 1/2 kms] north of the monument on Monument Hill.* This was before the country was surveyed, so they used some of the local place names at that time to pinpoint their claims. **Monument Hill** is obviously **Keg Knoll** today. The claims were called Antelope, Bluebell, Emerald, Maybelle, Monarch and Ophir. He also laid out 2 more claims further north. One was *about 9 miles [13 kms] southwest of the mouth of the San Rafael River,* and called the Monitor. Another was *on the north side of Three Canyon and about 5 miles [8 kms] west of Green River.* This claim was called the Kara.

Wolverton used his boat named the **Wilmont**, to carry supplies from Green River down to his ranch (just south of the present-day Ruby Ranch) and to this side-drainage, which we'll call Wolverton Canyon, for lack of a better name. They must have built the trail before any ore was taken out. Then the ore from at least some of the claims was apparently taken on pack horses or mules down to the river and either loaded into the Wilmont or in one of 2 company scows which were built for that purpose. Then they took part of it up to Green River to the railroad, and part was dumped at his ranch. It appears the ore samples taken from the Kara and perhaps the Monitor claim, was taken by wagon to the bank of the Green River and dumped directly across from his ranch. However, the ore from the Monitor could more easily have been taken to this little side-canyon and down to the river and the boats. The ore from the Monument Hill claims could also have been taken down the Twomile Trail, which is discussed later. No one alive today seems to know exactly what route was used to get the ore to the river from the various claims. See the book, *River Guide to Canyonlands National Park and Vicinity,* for more information on the Wolverton Ranch, Wolverton's boats and the Colorado River Bed Case.

Keg Spring Canyon

The next place of interest is **Keg Spring Canyon**, and a minor tributary the Moores called **Buck Canyon**. To get there, first go to **Lookout Point**, then head northeast **1 km (.6 mile)** and turn right and drive southeast down a short but steep hill. After the steep part, it's a fairly good road to the rim of the canyon which is **4.5 kms (2.8 miles)**. However, about halfway to the rim of the canyon you'll come to a short section of wind-blown sand dunes across on the road, so **gear down, rev up and go fast** through this section; an AWD/4WD is recommended for this part. It might be best for cars to be parked there, but if the sand is wet, it can be crossed with a 2WD. A mtn. bike will be handy here for people in cars; or walk the rest of the way.

On the rim of the canyon is a metal tank & watering trough, both of which were likely installed by the **Chuchurus** of Montrose, Colorado. There's also a pipe running south and over the rim. More on this in a moment. From the watering troughs, return up the road for about 200m and turn left. This short piece of road ends about 300-400m from the water tank and near the head of the **Chuchuru Sheep Trail**. Walk down it, first over the Navajo SS, across the Kayenta bench, and finally down through the big Wingate cliffs to the bottom. Once there, turn down-canyon and walk about 100m and you'll find a small cinder block structure which houses an old water pump. This is the pumphouse the Chuchurus used to pump water from the bottom of the canyon to the water tank & troughs on the rim. The pipe is still used today by whoever has the grazing rights, but the pump is located up on top and near the rim.

The Chuchurus were sheepmen who came into the canyons 1945; that's when the Chaffins & Tidwells left this country. This pump house has a date of 1962 on one side, but it's believed they had something there earlier than that. Their idea was to pump water to the sheep on top so they could stay longer in the spring and wouldn't have to trail them down in the canyon for water. When their ewes got heavy with lam in the spring, they couldn't go down in every day for water

Chuchuru's Sheep Trail looking northeast. Notice the Chuchuru's **water tank** on the rim of **Keg Spring Canyon** in the upper middle part of this picture. The road ends at that water tank.

and get back out.

Chad Moore had this to say: *Chuchuru bought out the Tidwells in the spring of 1945, so he could increase his sheep. The Chuchurus didn't come here every year because on this side of the river they had a permit there in Antelope Valley and the only water they had was snow. They could only stay up in that country awhile, then they either had to go to Keg Springs and trail in & out down there, or they had to leave. So it got to the point that it wasn't worth it to them to come over here. Then they sold their permit to Milt Oman of Salt Lake in 1983.*

If you're looking for an interesting hike, walk back up the trail to the Kayenta bench above the Wingate walls. From there walk upcanyon on the bench a couple of kms using old livestock trails. At that point you'll see on your right and up near the canyon rim, a trail built by Chad's father, **Andy Moore**. If you continue straight upcanyon, you'll find several springs, some running water and some short narrows.

If you turn to the left or south from just before you reach **Andy Moore's Trail**, you'll be in the main fork of this drainage. If you walk south you'll come to the head of the canyon and Keg Spring. Actually, there are springs in each of the 3 upper tributaries, and all seem to go by the name **Keg Springs**. About 1 km south of Andy Moore's Trail and on the left or east side, will be a minor drainage. If you walk into it, you'll soon find what Chad Moore called the **Copper Miner's Trail**. This is evidently the route E.T. Wolverton's miners used to get into the canyon bottom to the springs when they worked the copper mines a little to the south. This trail, as well as the other 2 previously mentioned, are washed out a little now, but horses could probably still be taken up or down it.

Now for a hike down Keg Spring Canyon. If you were to walk downstream from Chuchuru's water pump, you'd be in a minor jungle of water-loving plants. In this section you'll find **beaver dams** and a live beaver population, lots of water & ponds, and lots of crawfish or crawdads, as they're known on Lake Powell. If you're there in the warm season and wearing shorts, better have a pair of long pants for the next 3-4 kms because it'll be bushwhacking through reeds & willows most of that way (best to wade right in the water to avoid most brush). Some sections have been reamed-out, likely by the big floods of 10/2006; then the thick vegetation ends at the mouth of **Buck Canyon**.

Here's an alternative way to reach Buck Canyon from about where the sand dunes are on the access road. Park southwest of the dunes about 500m, then head northeast and walk to the head of this short drainage. In it is what remains of an old road, which is totally washed out now. You can use this to get to the lower end of Keg Spring Canyon if you don't like bushwhacking. Or if you come down the main watery drainage, you could use Buck to return to your car. Best to make a loop-hike.

Chad Moore tells a little of the history of this trail in Buck Canyon: *In that canyon there's an old road. My bother Bill done that in the early 1950's, him and some other guys. They went down what we called Buck Canyon, that's a little drainage that runs into Keg Canyon. They took a compressor and a Cat and everything and went down there and was goin' to get some uranium out of there. They had some claims down in the bottom of Keg Spring Canyon, but they never did do any minin'.*

*We used to have a trail down there. I think Chris Halverson built that. I remember when I was a kid, his name was on the wall. But then when my brother and this here uranium outfit went down there and built the road, they just took everything as they went, and filled in the wash to get down there. You could drive a vehicle down there when they got through. My brother was Bill Moore. Dr. Flum, he was a Chiropractor, he came out here and it was his company that my brother was staking claims for and working for and he [Flum] put up the money to do that. Him and his brother was both Chiropractors from back east and they was loaded; they had some money! And they went down on **Lower Bull Bottom** as we called it. That's down canyon from the mouth of Keg Spring Canyon. But they didn't build a road down that far. They finally giv'er up. They just got the road built into Keg Canyon and quit. After a flood went down there the road through Buck Canyon wasn't nearly as good as the old trail we had, because the trail was up on the side a little.*

Going further, Chad again said: *We'd take our bulls in there and*

This is **Keg Spring Canyon** at the end of the **Chuchuru Sheep Trail**. On the left is the **water pipe** that runs from the pools and little **pump house** in the lower part of this picture, up to the **water tank** on the highest part of the canyon rim. See the foto on the opposite page.

shove'em down on the river. That's about as far as we ever went. We never used any of them other river bottoms below Horseshoe Canyon.

Downstream from Buck in Keg Spring Canyon there might be a little water in places, but it's not the jungle you find further upcanyon. About halfway between Buck Canyon and the river is one of several large alcoves and what appears to be some Fremont Indian sites. It's not the typical Anasazi-type cliff dwelling--instead it appears to be just a campsite. Anasazis didn't get this far north.

If you wanted, you could probably walk downcanyon along the river all the way to the mouth of Horseshoe Canyon and beyond, but there would likely be some bushwhacking along the way. Tamarisks have taken over this country up to the high water mark (HWM).

If you walk upcanyon from Chuchuru's pumphouse (some bushwhacking for a short ways) to Keg Springs and visit all the upper tributaries, plan to take at least half a day round-trip. The time will depend on how much exploring you want to do. If you go down Buck Canyon (or the main Keg Spring Canyon drainage) to the river and back, it should take more than half a day, but for some this could be an all-day hike (?). Horses couldn't be taken down Buck Canyon today because of the washed-out road.

Keg Knoll and the Tibbetts--Perkins Cave

The next stop would be **Keg Knoll**. About **6.7 kms (4.2 miles)** south of **Lookout Point** is a graded road running east from the Green River Road. This junction is **55.9 kms (34.7 miles)** from Highway 24. You'll soon come to Keg Knoll. If you want to see the **Wolverton Copper Mining area**, park somewhere just before or northwest of the Knoll, and walk due north on the bench just west of a minor drainage. After about 2 km you'll come to a sandstone rim, which is the lower Entrada. Below this rim are the clay beds of the Carmel Formation. The area marked out by claims is just below the sandstone rim and running east-west. Wolverton staked out 6 claims for the first time in 1903, then in May & June of 1968, the late **Don (Buster) Irvine**, the same guy who used to live on Yokey Bottom on the Green River, restaked the same area and did some assessment work. He took a bulldozer down there and pushed some dirt around for 10, eight hour days, but nothing ever came of the claims. All the claim markers you see there now are his doing's.

The next place of interest is the **Bill Tibbetts--Tom Perkins Cave**. To get there, drive to a point just east of Keg Knoll; this will be between 2.8 & 3.3 kms (1.7 & 2 miles) from the Green River Road. At the fartherest point east is a little road running south 125-150m to a good **campsite**. From that area walk due south along a shallow drainage which is on the east side of the Knoll. As you near the rim of Horseshoe Canyon you'll come to a short slot canyon; at that point turn west. There you'll find yourself between the rim of Horseshoe and some Navajo Sandstone bluffs to the north. As you wander west, be looking north and soon you should see an alcove-type cave facing south. Make you're way into it and you'll find on the ceiling 2 inscriptions put there by 2 accused cattle & horse thieves. The inscriptions read, **"My Home, Bill Tibbetts, Sept. 15, 1924"**, and **"My Home, Tom Perkins, Sept. 15, 1924"**.

Briefly, here's the story of how these names got on the ceiling of this cave. In July, 1924, Tibbetts and Perkins were arrested for stealing cattle somewhere in the Big Flat or Dubinky country out Between the Rivers. They were put in jail, but their attorney advised them to break out if they could. This they did with the help of some relatives. They made their getaway by rowboat down the Colorado River. Later they had a shootout with a sheriff's posse but escaped. They hid out in the area for several months, while at the same time raising hell with the cattle of those who had accused them of cattle rustlin'. It was during the period of time they were running from the local sheriff, they hid out in this cave. Some

Inside the cave that **Bill Tibbetts and Tom Perkins** stayed in while they were on the run from the law. They broke out of the Moab Jail in July, 1924, and spent a little time here. They left their signatures on the ceiling, **"My Home Sept. 15, 1924"**. See a picture of that on page 375.

time later, in the winter of 1924-25, they both took off for Kansas, Oklahoma and New Mexico and spent several years there. Read a more detailed account of this story in the chapter at the end of this book concerning **Tidwell Bottom**, Clyde Tidwell, the Range War of 1924-25, and the John Jackson Story. From the road to this cave and back should only take a couple of hours at most round-trip.

On your way back to your car, you might head for **Old Man Spring**, which is in a little alcove on the south side of Keg Knoll. This spring was probably named after old John Romjue, reputed to be the best moonshiner in the country during Prohibition days of the 1920's. He evidently had a still there at one time. Next to this spring is a cave that was used by Indians; maybe outlaws and cowboys too.

Twomile Canyon & Trail, 6-Hole Arch, and the Bowknot Bend Viewpoint

From Keg Knoll, continue northeast to **Km 7.2 (Mile 4.5** from the Green River Road) to the carpark at **1585m**; see map. This is a good road for most cars and is graded on occasions, but there are a couple of rough places. As you near the end of this road, you'll drop down off the Carmel rim to a wide parking/camping area at the top of the Navajo Sandstone which is about 1 km west of an old **drill hole**. The last 500m of that old road has now been blocked off because that part below the parking place is in a Wilderness Study Area. This WSA includes all of the lower Horseshoe Canyon complex, Twomile and Keg Spring Canyons, plus the Bowknot Bend. From the first parking place, continue north about 400m to where the track disappears on Navajo slickrock. Just beyond the point where the red clays of the Carmel rim give way to the white Navajo slickrock, is where the WSA boundary is located, so park/camp somewhere there on the slickrock.

To reach **6-Hole Arch & Twomile Canyon**, begin walking northeast from where you parked on the edge of the Navajo slickrock. In the past, people have flouted the small WSA sign, and driven on with 4WD's or ATV's, so there is a track you can follow (this was created before the sign & barricade were made). After about 300m is a **log fence** across this track supposedly blocking vehicle traffic--but not quite. About 600-700m from the log fence, you should see a line of rocks across the old track, and to the east, a couple of cairns. Follow these cairns zig zag fashion east toward the rim of Twomile Canyon. After another 500m or so, and as you near the rim, veer left or northeast. Soon you'll see a most unusual arch which has 2 skylights on top where water drains down, and 4 windows opening to the east (originally the author called this 5-Hole Arch, but it has 6). You can enter and wander about.

To get into **Twomile Canyon** from the 6-Hole Arch, return part way back toward the track, but before that, walk cross-country on slickrock for 500-600m and veer eastward and find a way off the bluffs of Navajo Sandstone and down to a flat bench below. From above you can see a trail below. Follow this map carefully and keep in mind, the first place you must go to is the point separating the **North and South Forks** of Twomile Canyon. When you get out to the far eastern end of that point, which is on top of the lowest part of the Navajo, then look left or north, and you should see the beginning of the **Twomile Canyon Trail** cutting down through a crack. It zig zags down a couple of bends, then heads back west along the Kayenta bench. After 300m the trail veers back to the northeast and drops down atop a rockslide covering the Wingate Sandstone. At the bottom of the rockslide & steeper parts, the trail may disappear, but make your way along the dry wash bottom to the river. It appears that about half the traffic on this trail is from boaters on the river. To go to the river and back will take about half a day. You could likely get a horse down this trail, although it's pretty steep and washed out in a place or two. This is one of the most impressive natural arches, trails, canyons, and hikes around.

If you like making loop-hikes rather than backtracking, you could walk from the mouth of Twomile

The **6-Hole Arch** as seen from the front. Formerly, this writer called it 5-Hole Arch, but it does have 4 windows and 2 skylights. Just to the left and out of sight is the remaining window & skylight. This unusual arch is right on the rim of **Twomile Canyon**.

37

Above A good look inside **6-Hole Arch** looking eastward. Fremont Indians likely camped here at some point in time but there's no soot on any part of the ceiling.

Right The beginning of the **Twomile Canyon Trail** just as it starts down through the lowest layer of the Navajo Sandstone. Just a few meters below this are benches of the Kayenta Formation; you can see them on the far side of this short canyon. The buff colored cliffs & domes on the opposite side of this canyon are made of Navajo Sandstone.

downstream along the river to near the mouth of Horseshoes Canyon and the abandoned meander called **The Frog**. Then you could go up the **Frog Trail** and back up to the drill hole and finally back to your car. If you decide to do this long loop-hike, take a lunch & water and plan to take all day; a long day for some.

Before leaving Twomile Canyon, here's a little history about the place. An early-day cow puncher named **Andy Moore** ran cattle for Neil McMillan in this country (mostly on the desert above the river) as a youngster before World War I, then on his own after about 1920. He, according to his son the late Chad Moore of Green River, never was sure who built the trail in the first place. But Chad did have this to say:

From the mouth of Horseshoe, there's a trail up along the river to the mouth of Twomile and then it goes on around the hill and into what they call the Bowknot. At the mouth of Twomile, there's no place for cattle to graze. At one time somebody started a road out of there. They started at the bottom. Now old Wolverton might have done that (?). Once we put some bulls up on the Bowknot, and we'd ride a horse in and out of Twomile, but we never did take any cattle up that trail; it was always too steep.

The author isn't sure if he saw the old road Chad talked about, but it's probably eroded away by now. The possibility that Wolverton built it sounds logical, but no one knows for sure. Since some of his copper mining took place just north of Keg Knoll, it would have been a much shorter and faster way to get ore down to the river through Twomile, than to take it north and northeast and down Wolverton Canyon. It could be that the ore from Wolverton's 2 claims or mines further north may have been taken down Wolverton Canyon just north of the mouth of Keg Spring Canyon; then ore from the Keg Knoll country might have been taken down Twomile (?).

Before leaving the Twomile area here's another hike with a fantastic view. From the **6-Hole Arch carpark** walk along the old track to the northeast toward the **Bowknot Bend Overlook**. When the track ends, continue to route-find northeast on your own. A compass and a better map than this will help to keep you oriented. Soon you'll come to some bluffs in the upper Navajo; walk down any one of several routes to a flat area. Continue east to the next line of Navajo cliffs and to the most-easterly point on that rim. On the northeast side of that protruding point are some piled rocks, and if you look closely, you'll find an old **cattle trail**. The author chased a big buck mule deer down this once. From the bottom of this trail head east to a point overlooking the gap between the river which is the beginning of Bowknot Bend. This is one of the better viewpoints around.

The Frog, Frog Trail, Lower Horseshoe Canyon, and the Angel Trail

Now back to the first of the 2 trailheads above the drill hole. Here's a hike down still another of the many impressive cattle & horse trails in this country. It's called the **Frog Trail**. It runs down into an old abandoned meander or rincon called **The Frog**. The reason it got this name is because it's shaped like a horse's hoof mark. The bottom of the hoof is call a "frog", at least that part which leaves the high place in a hoof mark in the sand or mud; thus the name. It's actually the raised part in the middle of this abandoned meander that's called "The Frog".

To get there, first walk down the now blocked-off road from the carpark to the **drill hole site**. From there, head in a southeast direction around a big **Navajo dome** rock on either side. The trail symbols

Aerial view of the upper part of **Twomile Canyon**. Notice the **6-Hole Arch** right on the rim of the western part of Twomile Canyon. The approximate location of the Twomile Canyon Trail is shown.

39

Looking east from the **Bowknot Bend Overlook**, one of the better viewpoints around. An extra wide angle lens would help to see a bigger part of this scene.

on the map are actually old vehicle tracks. Follow either of these tracks southeast until you reach a point just opposite the **Angel Trail** (see map), then veer left or east and route-find down over the lower Navajo to one of several Kayenta benches below. From there, bench-walk back in a northerly direction following a fading cattle trail in places. When you reach the **3rd little drainage**, the trail descends on top of a big **rockslide** covering the Wingate, which normally forms a big cliff.

Before going further, let's go back up to just before the trail heads down the rockslide. About 75m south of the top of the rockslide and under a Kayenta ledge, is a box of dynamite, some fuses, a sledge hammer, a bit, a long metal rod and a Prince Albert tobacco can with part of a 1940's funny paper inside.

When this trail and the very old dynamite was mentioned to **Pearl Biddlecome Baker**, who grew up on the Robbers Roost Ranch not far from this site, she stated that it's dangerous as hell, especially if it's crystalized. So don't touch it! She went on to tell a story which was told to her by a friend:

This story really happened over in Colorado, to a friend of mine, Dell Aldred. A friend of his had him go out and take over a ranch that he'd just bought. He said that things are kind of run down out there and you've got to shape things up, so he went out with him on the first day and they looked around and in the shop was this box of dynamite that had been there god knows how long. And he said, "you'd better get rid of that first". So Aldred said he would tomorrow.

So the next morning after the round-up crew left, he went out and got this box of dynamite and carefully put it in a bucket. It was so crystallized and dangerous that he was almost afraid to even move it. He was trying to decide what to do with it, so he took it down and across the canyon and put it under a little ledge and was going to shoot it. Now that's the way they got rid of old dynamite in those days. That was the only safe way you could do it.

So just as he got back to the house and got his gun and was ready to shoot this dynamite, a Mexican boy rode up on a roan mule. So Dell put his finger up to his lips and was going to fool the boy. And the boy saw that Dell was looking over in the trees and assumed he was going to shoot a bear or something. So Dell let fly with the rifle and hit that bucket and my god the whole thing blew up, and it blew a tree off the top of the ledge, and the rocks came down nearly to the house. It was a terrible commotion.

Of course when the shot went off, the mule stampeded and threw the kid off and the mule ran for home. And so the kid got up and looked around and says, "My gosh mister, that some gun, where you get him".

The last time this writer saw that dynamite was in 5/2011, and it had all but melted away, so what's left of it is likely harmless (?).

Now back to the hike down the Frog Trail. It's pretty rough getting down over the rockslide, but the trail is there. It will be difficult to get a horse down it today because of washouts. From the bottom of the rockslide, the trail vanishes into the old abandoned meander. From that point you can reach the river by going either right or left around the butte in the middle. If you go right, you'll pass a minor spring in the red Moenkopi ledges as shown on the map, then you'll come to the lower end of **Barrier Creek** which flows through **Horseshoe Canyon**. It disappears in the sand in a place or two, but for the most part it's a flowing stream throughout the lower end of this canyon. *As you near the Green River, you may find some beaver dams and lots of water loving plants. You might consider getting upon the bench on the left (north) side to avoid all the bushwhacking.* The previous 2 sentences were written in 1991

The mostly-melted **dynamite** and trail-building tools under a ledge along the **Frog Trail**. This was likely left there in about 1946 by Andy Moore and his crew.

but in 10/2006, there were some huge floods come down this canyon and the lower end of Horseshoe was cleaned out--in 2011 & '12, it was an easy walk with no bushwhacking and no beaver dams.

Now for a little history of the Frog Trail and another old cow trail that used to come down Horseshoe Canyon. The late Chad Moore and his father Andy Moore may have been the last cattlemen to put cows down in The Frog and to use the Frog Trail. He tells of one experience which probably took place in the winter of 1945-46: *In the 1940's we put a bunch of cattle down on The Frog. That dynamite could be ours, because we had to re-build the trail to get in and out of there. We went right down Horseshoe Canyon with the cattle and it took us a week to get down because we had to shoot some ledges off as high as this ceiling to make a trail there because water had washed them out. But we couldn't get back up that way, so we worked this other trail over [the Frog Trail]. We took 104 head of calves down there with us. This was about 1946, or something like that. I remember my brother was in the service, and another kid was there workin' for us, and my dad--and we put them calves down there and left 'em one winter, right in The Frog. That had been Tidwells country for grazing. Anything in Horseshoe Canyon was Tidwells. Then they sold out in 1944 & '45 [same time as the Chaffins]. After they sold out, we put the calves down there and wintered 'em. But it was such a hassle, that, well, people are too lazy to do that anymore.*

We put the calves in the western part of the rincon [abandoned meander]. It had a little spring or two. Right there where it ends and goes into the river, there's a net wire and **stake & rider fence** *right across the drainage.* (The fence Chad talks about is near the end of **Frog Creek** where it cascades off the Moss Back ledge or bench almost into the Green River. Just south of that dryfall is a **falling sand dune** which allows cattle or people to walk over the ledge. So that fence prevented calves from escaping The Frog pasture; but you can walk down it).

Chad thinks the dynamite was theirs. In explaining the blasting caps and tobacco can he said: *That's what the caps was wrapped in. When you took dynamite some place, you always wrapped the caps in paper and shoved'em in a can. To blast the rock, you'd have to punch a hole first. We used a bit and a sledge hammer. Hit it, and bring it [the bit] up and pour some water in the hole and make mud out of it, then take the end of a stick and pound it so the mud comes out. Clean your hole out, pour more water in it, and do it again. Then you put dynamite in the hole and blast it out.*

Horseshoe Canyon could be one of the better hikes in this book. You can walk all the way up to the middle part which is the detached section or unit of Canyonlands National Park, but it's a long way. That's up where the pictographs are located and you can drive up there to that part of the canyon. But this lower section of the canyon is nice too. It's very deep and wild and all part of a Wilderness Study Area. There's a good supply of water up to very near the park boundary, with lots of possible campsites. The water in this canyon should generally be good to drink as is because there are no more cattle around. However, beaver can pollute the water with Giardia too, but this danger would likely exist only in the lower end of the drainage. The higher up you go, the better the water quality will be. If you see fresh sign of beaver, be careful. Take water from a spring if you can.

Here's another interesting hike for someone interested in historic cattle trails, or for someone who wants to reach the canyon rim for some good views down on The Frog. It's called the **Angel Trail**. Here's what **Frank Tidwell**, formerly of Green River and the Tidwell Ranch, had to say about it:

It's my understanding our family made that trail. I remember Dad telling about it. I never went up it--I just saw it as we rode down Horseshoe Canyon. It was a narrow trail, and they always walked their horses up or down it. To build it, it took a lot of dynamite, and pick and shovel work. I was 15 years old when we left there [1945], and I only remember Dad talking about it. I would guess the last time anybody in the family ever used it was in the early 1930's, because I can't personally remember anybody ever using it. Seems to me it was used more with horses as an access route, rather than taking cattle up and down. (Frank Tidwell is the son of Delbert Tidwell, one of 2 brothers who had a ranch at the old Phillips Petroleum Well further up Horseshoe Canyon near the pictographs).

In 1986, Delbert Tidwell was interviewed by several people from the National Park Service. They were trying to get the history of the Tidwell Ranch located on The Spur. In that interview Delbert made one statement which went like this: *Did you know that up the canyon [Horseshoe] a ways from the mouth, the* **CCC's built** *a trail into the canyon. They built it in about 1936 and had a camp up out of the canyon. We took water to them sometimes.*

The trail he's referring to could have been the one down into The Frog, but if they had a camp up out of the canyon, and the Tidwells took water to them, it seems more likely it would have to be the Angel Trail he's referring to (?). No one the author spoke to could confirm this however. So who ever built the Angel Trail remains a mystery. However, it appears the CCC's built it, then the Tidwells likely did some maintenance work on it at a later time (?). Or it could have been a rough trail started by the Tidwells, then the CCC's made it better (?).

To get to the Angel Trail from the north side, simply walk up Horseshoe Canyon to a point about 4-5 kms above the river. One or 2 kms beyond The Frog, begin looking to the left or south side for a big rockslide coming down from the south covering the Wingate Sandstone wall. At the bottom of this huge slide will be a couple of stone cairns. At that point it's hard to locate a trail, but it's there. Just head straight up the slide and you'll soon run onto it; it's now marked with cairns. At the bottom it zig zags up the crest of the slide, then as you reach the point where 2 slides come together to form the one you just climbed, veer left or east and zig zag up the left-hand or eastern slide. At the top of that rockslide the trail contours to the right or southwest at the top of the Wingate. From there it again zig zags up through the Kayenta benches and finally makes a big jump to get up through the bottom layer of the Navajo Sandstone rim. The top of the trail comes out on the Carmel Formation, and on top of the Lower Spur.

The Angel Trail rises almost exactly 300 vertical meters and is perhaps the steepest and has the highest elevation gain of any cattle trail the author has seen. In this respect it's very similar to the **Devil's Slide Trail**, near the mouth of Millard Canyon. It's a good hike and well-worth the effort. You can also reach this trail from the road running down along the top of **The Spur** from the **Hans Flat** or **Maze Ranger Station**. In the next chapter, this trail will be discussed again, but from the Low Spur down. The Angel Trail is still in pretty good condition and horses could still be walked up or down.

Concerning the history of driving cattle, and trails in Horseshoe Canyon itself, Chad Moore had more to say: *That trail in Horseshoe was there before we got there. It was there even before Tidwells, I think. Ol' Clyde Tidwell might have done it, Delbert's half brother. That used to be the way you went down Underneath the Ledge. Or you could go out there off this Keg Knoll (Frog) Trail into The Frog. Or the Twomile Canyon Trail. That's the only way you could go, then you'd go down the river and in Underneath the Ledge. That's the way Chaffins came out when they sold out in 1945. They came up that way with part of their cattle, because it was dry and they didn't have any water coming across the top. So they brought everything up there so they was near the water, on the river, then they came up Horseshoe Canyon with their cattle to the [Phillips] road. In Horseshoe Canyon you had to blast off the little ledges and fill'em up with rock or something every year because the water would wash'em out. At least there was water in the canyon and along the river coming from clearn down from Underneath the Ledge.*

Chad uses the term **Underneath the Ledge**, to refer to what other local people call **Under the Ledge**. The National Park Service calls a small part of that country **The Maze**.

If you're a long distance hiker and want a challenge, here's one just for you. Head down the Twomile, The Frog or Angel Trail, then walk downriver along the west bank. This part wouldn't be easy even though there used to be a trail along the river for cows, but tamarisks have invaded the river bottoms up to the high water mark. Now it's a big mess to get through; so stay above the HWM.

You could then get out of the canyon via Horsethief Canyon or come up the Devil's Slide Trail, both of which are shown on the next map. From there you could head north along The Spur and drop back down the Angel Trail to get to your car. This would take perhaps 3, 4 or 5 days or maybe a week for a loop hike, depending on which trails and/or routes you use and how tough you are!

L to R Orson Robins (a worker), **E.T. Wolverton**, and Wilmont Wolverton, E.T.'s wife. This foto was taken sometime after 1912; that's when E.T. left the Green River and went to the **Henry Mountains**. He built this cabin on **Crescent Creek** somewhere east of the south end of Mt. Ellen. E.T. is the same guy who built the **Wolverton Mill** which is today behind the BLM office in Hanksville. (Pearl B. Baker Collection)

Above Aerial view of **The Frog** looking northeast. The Green River is at the top left; **Barrier Creek** in **Horseshoe Canyon** is to the right in the green trees.

Left Aerial view of the **Angel Trail.** In the lower right-hand side is **Barrier Creek** in **Horseshoe Canyon.** The bigger cliffs in shadow is the Wingate Sandstone; above that are the Kayenta benches; and the highest rim is the lower part of the Navajo Sandstone. The Angel Trail is shown in its approximate location.

Horseshoe, Horsethief, Big & Clydes Spring Canyons, the Angel, Devils Slide & Deadman Trails, and the Tidwell Ranch

Location & Access This area is just west of the Green River and the middle part of Canyonlands National Park, north of the Hans Flat or Maze Ranger Station and east of the Robbers Roost Ranch and the Roost Country. Get to this area either by driving south out of Green River on the Green River Road--see **Area Map 1: West Side of the Green River** for driving instructions. Or leave **Highway 24** between **mile posts 135 & 136** and head southeast on the **Maze Road** past Jeffery Well, Texas Hill & Well, and finally to where the Green River & Maze Roads meet. That is **Horseshoe Junction & Information Board** which is north of Burr Pass as shown on **Area Map 1**. From that point you can head south to reach the Hans Flat Ranger Station and The Maze District; or head north along the west side of the Green River on the Green River Road. The **Maze Road** coming in from **Highway 24** is well-used & maintained for cars, and this is the **recommended route of approach** to this mapped area.

Elevations Altitudes range from about 1215m along the Green River, to 1629m at the Philipps Well/Tidwell Ranch, and to about 1900m on the higher part of The Spur covered by this map.

Water Carry all the water you'll need in your car! And, possibly at North Spring (after treatment), several seeps near the Great Panel in middle Horseshoe Canyon, throughout lower Horseshoe (good water), several places with good water in Horsethief Canyon and at Big & Clyde's Springs. All other springs shown on this map may be totally dried up and cannot be counted on to have water.

Maps USGS or BLM map Hanksville (1:100,000); Keg Knoll, Bowknot Bend, Sugarloaf Butte and Horsethief Canyon (1:24,000--7 1/2' quads); the plastic Trails Illustrated/National Geographic map Canyonlands National Park (1:70,000); and the eastern part of this area is shown on the plastic Latitude 40° map Moab West (1:75,000).

Main Attractions A couple of deep, wild & isolated canyons, plus the entrenched Green River Gorge, four impressive & historic livestock trails, an old oil well drill site--then ranch, a well-preserved historic moonshiner's still site, and perhaps the best pictograph rock art panel in the world.

Middle Horseshoe Canyon and the Great Gallery of Pictographs

The best way to reach the middle part of Horseshoe Canyon is to leave Highway 24 and drive eastward until you reach a 3-way intersection called **Horseshoe Junction** which is **39.3 kms (24.4 miles)** from Highway 24. See **Area Map 1** for this drive. From there veer left and head east on the **Green River Road**. After another **8.4 kms (5.2 miles)** will be the turnoff to the normal **Westside Trailhead** to Horseshoe Canyon. That turnoff is called the **Mail Box (Junction)**. Now before going further, the junction called the Mail Box has to be explained. The late **Pearl Biddlecome Baker** lived on the Robbers Roost Ranch at the time and she tells this story:

When they put the road across Horseshoe Canyon, Arthur Ekker was working for them, the Phillips outfit, and they liked Arthur very much--he was just a big kid. He was their truck driver. That was when him and Hazel were going together and before they were married. So he used to bring the mail out to the Mail Box which we put up, and leave it for us. The company made trips to Green River almost every day of course when they were drilling over there, so he'd get the mail in Green River and bring it out. That's why it's called the Mail Box. Then we'd run down a couple of times a week and pick up our mail. The mail box itself is long gone, but that junction or corner still has that name hung on it.

From the Mail Box, drive **3 kms (1.9 miles)** south to the west side of the Horseshoe Canyon as shown on this map. For anyone with a car, this is the normal route into the pictograph panels; there used to be a rough place or two along this stretch, but on 6/11/2012, it was all smoothed out and good for any car. Near the lip of the canyon is a large parking area with a BLM installed **toilet**. You can camp at or near this trailhead as it's on BLM land, but please *cleanup your campsite* when you leave; or they'll slap us all with more regulations.

From the trailhead, walk down what was originally an old road built by the **Phillips Petroleum Company** back in 1927 & '28 (mtn. bikes are not allowed). It went down and across the canyon and ended at the **Phillips Well**, which later became the **Tidwell Ranch**. More on those places later.

Not far from the trailhead will be a large **metal tank** and some livestock **watering troughs**. These were installed by the **Chuchurus** from Montrose, Colorado. They came into this country in 1945, just after they bought the grazing rights from the Tidwells. In the years after that, they installed a pump at the bottom of the canyon, and for a short period of time pumped water from the canyon bottom to the rim for their sheep. However, they weren't the first to try to pump water up to the canyon rim.

In a 1986 interview with **Delbert Tidwell**, who was one of the co-owners of the Tidwell Ranch, he told about how they tried to get water from the bottom of Horseshoe up to the rim of the canyon on the west side. In about 1938 or '39, he and his brother Leland salvaged some of the pipe the Phillips Company had left behind when they abandoned their well drilling operations across the canyon at what is known now as the **Tidwell Ranch**. They hauled it to the west side of the canyon. From there they lowered some of it over the cliffs to the bottom to make a vertical pipeline. They bought a small gasoline motor & pump, built a little shelter around it, and hooked it up to the pipe. Then they tried to pump water up to a **small stock pond or reservoir** they had built on the western rim. This wasn't very successful. Later the Chuchurus tried to improve the system, using some of the same equipment, mostly the pipes from the old well, but without a lot of success either.

Here's what the late **Chad Moore** formerly of Green River had to say about it: *The Tidwells put the pipeline there first, then Chuchuru's bought out the Tidwells, so they could increase their sheep herd. The Chuchuru's didn't come here every year because on this side of the river they just had a permit there in Antelope Valley and the only water they had was snow.*

I'll bet that outfit wasn't pumped a hundred hours in all the years it was there. It would have worked if you had a lot of water and if you were going to pump it in the spring of the year or summer time when it wouldn't freeze.

After the Tidwells left, the Chuchuru's moved the troughs down the trail a ways so they wouldn't have to pump it so far. They only done that one year, and after the old man died the boys never did pump it. It just wasn't feasible to pump it up there. They trailed in and out of there a little bit, then finally they said it wasn't worth it. It was cheaper to buy feed in Colorado or somewhere than it was to keep the sheep here after the snow left.

Later interviews of the Tidwells by Gary Cox and others in the NPS, added more to this story. In 1947, the Chuchurus, with aid from the BLM, built a new **pumphouse** at the bottom of the canyon, plus they added the big **water storage tank & troughs** which are located not far from the trailhead. This

Map 5, Horseshoe, Horsethief, Big & Clydes Sp. Canyons, & the Angel, Devils Slide & Deadman Trails, and Tidwell Ranch

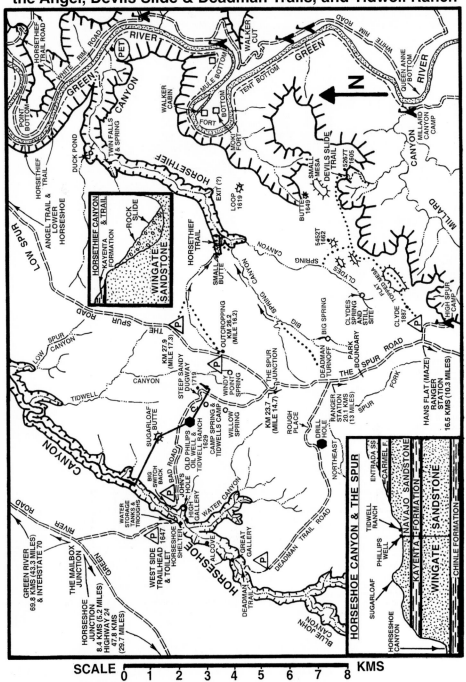

SCALE 0 1 2 3 4 5 6 7 8 KMS

Above The big **water storage tank & watering troughs** that were put in by the Chuchuru's and the BLM in about 1947. These are located near the beginning of the West Side Trail going into Horseshoe Canyon.

Right From the western rim of Horseshoe Canyon looking due east and down into **John's Hole**. This is one of many places **John Romjue** set up a **still** and made moonshine whiskey during Prohibition days of the 1920's and early '30's. The still was located at the bottom of the big dryfall and in the trees which is the green part in this foto.
All the pictographs in Horseshoe Canyon are located to the right of this picture and upcanyon to the south.

replaced the stock pond or reservoir the Tidwells tried to use but without success.

Now more hiking. From the tank & watering troughs, continue down the old road as it turns to the north and drops off the rim to a big sandy slope. At the bottom, the old road crosses to the east side and makes one **big switchback** to reach the eastern rim. Once at the bottom, you could head down-canyon to the northeast. You could do either a day-hike, or take a pack and walk all the way to the Green River (it's almost all on BLM land--and no permit needed). It would likely take most people a couple of days just to reach the river. If you wanted, you could then climb up to the canyon rim via the Twomile, Frog or Angel Trails, then road-walk back to your car. That would be a long hike!

Immediately southeast of where the Philipps Road crosses the canyon bottom, is a short & deep little side-drainage coming into Horseshoe from the east. This is what the Tidwells called **John's Hole**. The name comes from the best moonshine whiskey maker in southeast Utah, **John Romjue**. Read more about him in the back of this book under, **Moonshining in the Canyons During Prohibition Days**. John's sister was Eva Romjue Loughery Tidwell, the mother of Clyde Laughery Tidwell, and Le-land & Delbert Tidwell; these were the people who turned the old Philipps Well into the Tidwell Ranch. Here's what Delbert's daughter **Ila Mae Tidwell Clark** remembered about John's Hole:

That's where John Romjue had a still [during the 1920's and in the Prohibition years] in Horseshoe Canyon. I went down there as a kid and I remember that pipe, and Leland and Dad [Delbert Tidwell] would dig out a pond and we would swim in it. On the hottest summer days it would be oooh so cool. That was where we'd go in the heat of the day and eat lunch and drink the water from the spring. And that's where John made his hooch. I never saw the still; it was gone by then, but my dad and Leland used to talk about the still that John had there and that he had booze buried all over the desert.

We sold the ranch when I was 8 years old [1945]--things were startin' to go down the tube then with the drought and all. Later, John used to live with my grandmother Eva; she was his sister. Then he lived in Price with the Prettyman's [his only daughter married a Prettyman] for a while. I remember John out on the desert before we left the Spur and when we were all living out there for the summers; in the winters we kids would go into town to go to school. It was just too hard to live out there in winter.

Ila Mae's brother **Frank Tidwell** remembered a little more: *That's where Uncle John Romjue had one of his stills and did his moonshining. I remember the still being there when I was about 4 years old [in 1934 and just a year after Prohibition ended]. It was still there. The thing I remember about it espe-cially was the smell of corn and sugar. I remember Leland used to say that it was so damn inaccessible that the law couldn't get there.*

If you walk up the short drainage into John's Hole today, you'll find at the bottom of a big dryfall, a spring up on the green slope a ways. You may hear it dripping. If there's been a flood recently, you'll likely find a pool of water too. But at the bottom of that slope is a piece of metal pipe which was surely used by Romjue to get water down from the spring to his still at the bottom. If you have time, wander about the area and maybe you'll find something else. On the author's last trip, he flushed-out 8 deer.

From John's Hole, most people walk upcanyon (south) and visit **4 pictograph sites**. Also, after less than a km, you'll come to the place where the little **pump house** discussed earlier used to be. All you'll see there now is some of the original pipe standing against the vertical canyon wall to the west--the pump house was taken out in 1997 because is wasn't old enough to be classed as antique--typical of the NPS in Canyonlands NP! Also, there are 3 pictograph panels in this section (**Horseshoe Shelter, High Gallery and Alcove**) and on both sides of the canyon. There are trails to each. However, the very best pictographs are upcanyon to the south about 3-4 kms at what is called the **Great Gallery**. There will be several little seeps or pools of water along the way, maybe even some running water, but usually only in winter & spring, or after heavy rains and floods. If you're just going to see the pictographs,

A wide-angle view of most of the better parts of the **Great Gallery** in **Horseshoe Canyon**. The **Bar-rier Creek rock art style** is in the center & left and was apparently done with the aid of ladders

Above The **Deadman Trail** located about 500m south of the **Great Gallery** in **Horseshoe Canyon**. A lot of blasting was done on this trail indicating it may have been built with government assistance. But it was made with old cables that may have come from the old Philipps Well which later became the Tidwell Ranch. Frank Tidwell Jr. thinks it was made by the Chuchuru's after they bought the grazing rights from the Tidwells in 1945, but no one else this writer talked to could confirm that theory.

Right A small part of the **Great Gallery**, the most southerly panel in Horseshoe Canyon. The painters who did this must have had ladders, or created some kind of scaffolding to get up that high. There are several different kinds of rock art here. The most famous are these red paintings; they are called **Barrier Creek style**. These are nearly identical to those found in Pictograph Fork, Range, Clearwater and Hell Roaring Canyons. There's also a very faded painting in the upper end of the South Fork of Sevenmile Canyon. This writer thinks they could have been painted by the same man or clan, but they can't be dated.

48

then it can be done in a long halfday, maybe 4-6 hours round-trip. Or all day for some.

An alternative for real hikers, would be to head south and upcanyon about 500m from the Great Gallery, and locate the **Deadman Trail** coming down from the east side. You could climb that, then walk cross-country north around the head of Water Canyon, and drop back down into Horseshoe via the old Phillips Road. Still another alternative would be to continue to the upper part of Horseshoe Canyon. This area is better discussed in this writer's other book, *Hiking and Exploring Utah's Henry Mountains and Robbers Roost, 3rd Edition* (the color edition).

Going to The Spur: Clydes Spring & Still Site and The Devils Slide Trail

The next stop in the area of this map might be **The Spur** and the **Devils Slide Trail**. To get there, drive south from **Horseshoe Junction & information board** on the **Maze Road** in the direction of the Hans Flat or Maze Ranger Station. You'll head up over Burr Pass, across Robbers Roost Flats, skirt north of Twin Corral Flats, and finally east to the ranger station (Km 73.7/Mile 45.8 from Highway 24). Be sure to stop there for any last minute information on road, water or trail conditions. They're hooked-up to the internet, so if weather is a problem, ask to see the 24 hour loop from the weather bureau.

From the ranger station/visitor center (open 8am-4:30pm, 7 days a week year-round, Tele. 435-259-2652) head north to The Spur along what is generally called **The Spur Road**. This road is fairly good in most places, but it has some rough places where a HCV is best--4WD isn't really needed along most of this main road. **At Km 19.8 (Mile 12.3)** will be the end of National Park Service (Glen Canyon National Recreation Area--GCNRA) jurisdiction and the end of all the CNP rules & regulations on camping and everything else. North or beyond that, you can camp where you like--*but always leave a clean camp-site*--or the BLM will start slapping rules & regs on their land too!

However, a little ways before that boundary, and **16.5 kms (10.3 miles)** from the ranger station is the turnoff to the CNP campsite called **High Spur**. No one in their right mind would pay $30 to camp down there!; one reason being you'll need a LR/HC/4WD vehicle to get back out! Another reason is, all you have to do is drive anywhere north of the GCNRA boundary & camp for free without reservations!

Anyway, at that junction turn east and drive about 300m and park just before the road goes down a steep hill. To hike to **Devils Slide**, you'll need a good topo map in hand, preferably the **Horsethief Canyon 7 1/2' quad**. From the parking, start walking in a northeast direction along the highest rim of Millard Canyon. After a ways, you'll reach a high point called **Clyde Peak** at 6190' or 1887m; a ways after that will be a small **flat topped mesa**, the highest point around. On the northeast side of that mesa, route-find down to the northeast along a shallow drainage with Navajo bluffs on either side. At the bottom of the steeper part, veer to the east. At about that point, and to reach **Clyde's Spring**, head north & northwest between a couple of little flat topped buttes or small mesas (one has an altitude of **5452T** (1662m). When you reach the rim of **Clydes Spring Canyon**, route-find down in and head up-canyon to the southwest. About 250m before you reach the head of this box canyon, notice the alcove on your left of south side. Up in there is **Clydes Spring**, named after Clyde (Loughery) Tidwell.

Clyde was the half brother to Delbert & Leland Tidwell who were prominent in the history of the Tidwell Ranch which is discussed below. Their common mother was Eva Romjue Loughery Tidwell, and her brother was John Romjue, the moonshiner. Because of that influence, Clyde also got involved in making moonshine whiskey--and this was where he, and surely his Uncle John, had a **still**.

From the bottom of the little drainage coming down from where the spring is set back in, walk through the oak brush on the left side of the creek bed. About halfway to the spring and on the left will be a **platform** made of rocks built into the hillside. On top of that is a pile of cedar (juniper) logs, which appear to have been standing upright in the beginning. It seems as though it was a small 2m square enclosures but without a roof (?). In the middle of that little log pile, are the remains of an old wooden barrel complete with a couple of metal sleeves which held the barrel together. Also on the platform is a metal barrel about 2/3's the size of a 55 gallon drum. This was surely what moonshine whiskey was made in at one time or another. This is a **historic site**, so please leave everything in place.

There's a little trail running from the platform up to the spring and if you watch carefully, you'll see part of an old pipeline. Surely, this was setup to bring water from the spring down to the still site. This writer never did see any remains of any troughs, and according to Frank Tidwell, son of Delbert, it was never a developed spring with a water trough--apparently its flow was never that great--but it sure was isolated!. In 1991, this writer didn't see any water, just wet ground; but in 5/2012, there was enough of a flow that you could get a good drink--but you'd need a small pan or two to catch the dripping water.

Now back to the route running toward the **Devils Slide Trail**. At about where you turned northwest towards Clydes Spring Canyon, look east and in the distance you'll see a couple of high points. The one on the left is a **butte** marked **1649m**, the one on the right a **small mesa**. Head for the south side of the small mesa. When you reach the rim of the Millard & Green River Canyon, just southeast of the little mesa, look for an old camp with tin cans scattered about. This marks the beginning of the Devils Slide Trail. This is almost exactly where the bench mark **5267T** (1605m) is located on the *Horsethief Canyon 7 1/2' quad*. Before hiking down, here's a little history of how and when it was built. The late **Ned Chaffin** (he died on 11/11/2011) helped build it and this is what he had to say:

Now in 1919 when we first came into the country with cattle, Eph Moore and Bill Tibbetts were in Big Water (Elaterite Basin), down in Horse Canyon, around the Millard Canyon Rim, up Millard Canyon, and then they used those first 2 or 3 bottoms just above Millard Canyon, plus Valentine and Anderson Bottoms and all those. They was already there when we moved in.

In the winter of 1932 we went down the Devils Slide onto Anderson. Now the trail that goes to the Devils Slide come right across upper Horsethief Canyon, then southeast. We used to go around another way, and then some sheep herder told us about the Devils Slide, then we started using that trail.

It was the winter of 1934 & '35, that the government sent crews out to build trails, trough-up springs, and etc. in that country. I was out of high school and this was a little part-time thing I did besides taking care of the cattle. I did the packin' for the boys workin' on the Devils Slide Trail. I took my mules and everything and hauled dynamite, drills, bits, sledge hammers, food, tents--the whole bit. And that winter [January 1935] we went there and worked on that trail for about 3 weeks. There was myself, and Dad [Lou Chaffin], Warren Thompson, Vassar Howland, and it seemed to me there was about 6 of us altogether. It wasn't CCC's, but it was a government program--we may have been working for the Grazing Service (?).

We had 3 tents and one of them little sheep herder stoves, like they packed around. Warren Thompson was the cook. Warren was a great bean cook--white beans with lots of garlic in 'em. So we had lots of beans, and then of course it was in the winter time, so we had fresh meat--it would stay frozen.

This is what remains of the **still site** that **Clyde Tidwell** had during the early 1920's. It's located in the upper end **Clydes Spring Canyon**. Clyde died in December, 1925, so everything is getting old.

Looking north at the slopes where the **Devils Slide Trail** is located (the approximate route is shown).

He'd take the old ax out there and chop off a couple of steaks or a roast or whatever. Then of course we had the bakin' powder biscuits. That was our bread that he'd fix in the little oven in the sheep herder's stove. Then we'd have canned food too--whatever comes in cans--corn or beans, vegetables. And rice, we all ate lots of rice in those days. It's easy to pack around and doesn't spoil. Then of course we always had coffee. We melted snow for our water, so I didn't have to haul water to 'em.

We had a lot of those old western novels and we'd take turns reading at night. We'd have one reader-

-that's the way we spent those long winter evenings, was reading by the candle light. One guy would read and the others would listen. All we had was candles. Coal oil lanterns would be to hard to pack, so we didn't use them. For sleeping we just had our old tarps with some quilts in it, and some blankets, the same as when we was cowboyen. We didn't have sleepin' bags. We all wore those old pure-wool long-handled underwear, and I don't ever remember sufferin' much at night, even though we was there in January.

We worked 7 days a week, and it took about 3 weeks for us to build that trail. It was January, with long nights and short days, so we worked from about daylight until it got dark. Ol' Lou Chaffin wouldn't have anybody around who wasn't a good worker, so we all worked pretty hard.

We had dynamite, and of course Dad took care of that. He did all the blasting, but we did very little blasting. He'd drill the holes by hand, with the single jack, and the double jack, then shoot 'em off, and then everything else was with a pick and crowbar and shovel.

I don't think anybody ever put any sheep down it. If they were to go down there, they'd spread out and might start a slide. The sheep herders gave that one a wide berth!

We took cattle up and down it, single file--but it was a bad one. It was one of the worst trails in that country. We went down it with horse and packs all the time. To get cattle down it you'd take your horse and lead one of the cows, then the others would all follow, usually. The first time we put cattle down there, we killed one cow and one calf. She jumped off that one rim there about halfway down, and her calf followed her. And of course that was the end of them.

Before we built the Devils Slide Trail, we would either come down the Flint Trail or the North Trail and drop down into Big Water and come around. Or there's another trail down in from the head of Millard Canyon. I have used it, but it was really out of the way. About the only time we ever used the Millard Canyon Trail would be if we were going to gather stock in Millard Canyon--you'd drop down there because you'd be in the head of the canyon. So if you was there in the summer branding calves, all the stock would be below you. Then you could make an easy drive.

Now for hiking. The trail which zig zags down a broken part of the Wingate Sandstone wall. From the old campsite, walk about 40-50m south to the actual rim. The trail starts by heading down to the right and around the corner going west. It then zig zags down a little, then veers to the left or southeast. At a point about halfway through the Wingate, it contours along a natural bench toward the east. In about the middle of this east-west bench, is debris from a landslide which has come down since the trail was built. There's one big car-sized boulder which would be hard to get a horse around, otherwise a horse would have no trouble walking up or down this trail. After a ways, it then zig zags straight down to the bottom along the top of a big rockslide.

At the bottom of this Wingate slide, which covers most of the Chinle Formation as well, is an old uranium miner's exploration track running both directions. Take the one running to the right or west. After about 350m, it gradually veers to the right or northwest. After another 100m or so, be looking for a large stone cairn on the left. This marks an easy route down through the ledge-forming Moss Back Member of the Chinle Formation. After walking down through it, simply stay in the bottom of the dry creek bed until you reach the **Millard Canyon** drainage, then turn left until you reach the Green River just opposite **Queen Ann Bottom**. Read more about the history of that bottom and Millard Canyon in the next section.

The trail you see on the map, running between Millard and Horsethief Canyons along the river, was an early-day **cattle route** rather than one distinct trail. You could probably walk it today, but tamarisks have overgrown it in places, so walking would have to be above all the brush and the high water mark.

The Deadman Trail

Now continue north along The Spur. To repeat, at Km 19.8 (Mile 12.3) along The Spur Road, you'll leave the GCNRA and enter BLM land, where you can camp where you like without all the NPS permits, reservations and restrictions. Then at **Km 20.1 (Mile 13)** will be a junction. Turn right onto the **Deadman Trail Road** which will require a LR/HC/4WD vehicle to make it all the way to the trailhead; for that reason this is a great place to use a mtn. bike. You can camp anywhere in the area from The Spur Road to the trailhead at Deadman Trail. Not covered here, but the little canyon on the map called the **Northeast Spur Fork**, has several sections of fotogenic slots and ends with a rappel. The head of Big Springs Canyon has some nice technical slots (with rappels) as well. For more information on these, see the author's other books on the **Henry Mountains & Robbers Roost, 3rd Edition**, or the **Technical Slot Canyon Guide to the Colorado Plateau, 2nd Edition**. Both are in color.

Now from the end of the road, the first part of the **Deadman Trail** is across the flats and easy to follow, but as you near the rim of the canyon, it turns to slickrock and you'll have to follow cairns carefully in some places. When you get right to the canyon rim, then it's easy to follow the constructed part of the trail to the bottom.

No one the author talked to knew how it got this name, but surely somebody must have died out there at one time (?). Also, no one was quite sure who may have built it, but since it has some boards and steel cable forming a fence near the top, it's assumed that the Tidwells built it sometime during the 1930's (?); but Frank Tidwell thought it may have been the Chuchurus (?). Or it could have been there before they got to this county, then they rebuilt it later. The boards and cable wouldn't have been available to them until the Phillips Petroleum Co. abandoned their oil well late in 1929. The CCC's could have had a hand in building it, or remodeling it as well, because there was quite a lot of blasting near the top. From the bottom of the trail, walk about 500m north to reach the **Great Gallery**.

Horsethief Canyon & the Horsethief Trail, and Big Spring

One of the more interesting hikes in this book would be down the **Horsethief Trail in Horsethief Canyon** to the Green River. To do this, you could park in any number of places along The Spur Road, but maybe the best landmark to start at in this almost featureless landscape, would be where the **Deadman Trail Road** veers west. A sign marks the junction.

From that point, walk & route-find downhill to the northeast in between 2 upper tributaries of the Big Spring Canyon drainage. After about 1 km, you'll have to look for a route down over the Navajo Sandstone rim, but there are lots of different options to choose from. When you reach the bottom of the drainage (for the most part follow the route shown on the map), head straight down the dry wash bottom of lower **Big Spring Canyon** which runs northeast. About 7-8 kms from the carpark, you'll come to the upper part of Horsethief Canyon. Just before the dry wash drops off the rim, veer left or north, and walk along the rim for about 300m. Then just to the right or east of a **small butte** on the left, and just after you cross a small drainage, you'll walk along a little ledge right on the rim. Immediately around that

Looking due east from the top of the **Horsethief Trail**. To guide cows, there's a short fence at the top made of cables & metal poles. Some old cowboy signatures are on the wall behind the camera.

This is what this writer calls **Twin Falls** located in the lower end of **Horsethief Canyon**. Immediately upcanyon to the left is flowing water; it then falls over 2 limestone layers in the Chinle Formation

corner to the left or north will be the beginning of the **Horsethief Trail**. This is a constructed trail down into the bottom of the canyon. At the very top are some metal poles and cable forming a fence, which was built to keep cattle out of, or down in, the canyon.

There are a couple of other parking places where you could begin a hike to the Horsethief Trail. To reach these, continue north on The Spur Road to **The Spur Junction** at **Km 23.7 (Mile 14.7** from the Hans Flat Ranger Station). You could start there, but you'll have to route-find over 2 ledges before you enter lower Big Spring Canyon. Or turn right and go along The Spur Road to **Km 26.2 (Mile 16.2** and the **outcropping**; or go on to **Km 27.9 (Mile 17.3)**. If you start at either of these points, use your compass and aim for the prominent butte in the distance labelled **Loop 1619** on any map. If going to the Horsethief Trail you must have a **map & compass**. GPS numbers won't help unless you have a map!

Before going further, first a story about this trail and this canyon. The late **Ned Chaffin**, one of the sons of Lou Chaffin of the Chaffin Ranch on the San Rafael River, was down in this part of the country off and on for years running the family's cattle. He tells about a big snow storm in this country during the Christmas holidays of 1931-32, and how the Tidwells had to get some cows down in there and out of the deep snow. He recalls:

Delbert and Leland Tidwell wanted to put some cattle down into Horsethief, to get out of the deep snow, which was about the deepest snow we ever had in that country. So we took 'em over there--and I'll never forget; we was puttin' the cattle down this Horsethief Trail you're talking about, and there was one cow that wouldn't go. And she had long horns. Well, Leland Tidwell was a giant of a man--he was about 6'4" [1.93m] and over 200 lbs [90 kgs]. And he finally got so mad at that cow--we'd get her up there right at the edge of the canyon and she'd break back and run right over us. So finally old Leland grabbed her by one horn and held her, and jumped off his horse, took her over there and shoved her off the first rim, then after that she went on down. We did kill one cow that day puttin' those cows down there. The cattle jammed in and one cow was shoved off a little rim. So we skinned her and hauled her back to the ranch and ate 'er. We just put the cows down in the bottom and let 'em go.

The early history of this trail is somewhat shrouded in mystery, but there are stories that some work was done on it by white men back as early as the 1880's. As the story goes, outlaws would leave the Robbers Roost country just southwest of this mapped area, and go over to the La Sal Mountains east of Moab. They would steal horses there, then run them northwest across the Colorado River, and probably up Sevenmile Canyon to near Big Flats, then west along the Horsethief Point Country south of Mineral Canyon. From there, they built and used a steep trail running down through the Wingate Sandstone cliff (It's now the Horsethief Trail Road). Once on the Green River, they crossed over to Woodruff Bottom, then followed the west bank down to and up Horsethief Canyon. From this trail, they would have headed southwest and around the upper end of Horseshoe Canyon and finally to the Roost just north of today's Robbers Roost, Biddlecome or Ekker Ranch.

Later in time, early-day sheep herders may have done some work on it and used it, but there wasn't much happening in this lonely outpost until the family of **Frank Tidwell** came into the country with horses sometime in the mid or late 1910's. Then they brought cattle in for the first time in 1919 and stayed on until 1945. It was Frank's step-son Clyde Loughery Tidwell, and 2 of his own sons, Delbert & Leland Tidwell, who really built the trail you see here today. Read more of the Tidwell history below.

As you start down the Horsethief Trail, look around on some of the cliffs facing east. You may find some historic cowboy signatures. The author found 2; **Martin Wall, Dec 30, 1900** and **Lila Tidwell, 1920**, but there may be more. This trail zig zags down a big rockslide covering the Wingate wall, and

Frank Tidwell (right) who married **Eva** Romjue Loughery (middle) and is the father of **Delbert** (left) & Leland Tidwell, the ones who ran the Tidwell Ranch on The Spur. This picture from about 1910 is believed to have been taken at **Sunnyside**, which is east of Price and at the base of the Roan Cliffs. (Ila Mae Tidwell Clark Collection)

Above Left
One of the workers on the **Phillips Road**. This place is believed to be on the **big switchback** located on the east side of **Horseshoe Canyon**.

Above Right
The camp for the men building the **Phillips Road**. It appears to be below where the Chuchurus water tank and troughs are today.

Right
Lou Chaffin on the **big switchback** in Horseshoe Canyon.

it's still good enough to walk a horse down today. At the bottom of the trail, you may be walking beside a small stream of good water in the upper part of the canyon where there's lots of greenery. Further down, you'll come to a couple of springs where you could camp and get safe-to-drink water. One good place is at what this writer calls **Twin Falls**; another interesting place is what is shown on this map as the **Duck Pond** (on one trip, the author spooked-up some ducks from that pond).

Immediately before the river, and all the tamarisk, is a big rock on the right with some big horn sheep **petroglyphs**. Beyond that, is an old livestock route going downriver--but don't attempt this today as parts are overgrown with tamarisks.

Just before you reach the river, and on the left, will be signs of the old Horsethief Trail running upon the first little bench above the river. From there you can follow the west bank all the way upstream to Woodruff and Tidwell Bottoms, and to Horseshoe and Twomile Canyons. There is a long and interesting

54

history about Tidwell Bottom, including the death and alleged murder of Clyde Tidwell and the story of Bill Tibbetts and John Jackson, but that part is featured in the back of this book.

Somebody who likes wild country and backpacking challenges could do a loop-hike by walking down Horsethief, up along the Green River, then up the Angel Trail and back to his/her car via The Spur Road. Such a trip would take about 3-4 days, or more. Or if you were to ascend Horseshoe Canyon instead of the Angel Trail to get back to your car, it would take a couple of days longer for the loop-hike. But please keep in mind, the trails along the river were routes for cows, not real trails, and they were seldom used. Also, tamarisks have taken over the river bottoms, so getting around there now is no easy task. You'll have to walk along the hillside above the tamarisks and the high water mark. Also, none of this area is in the national park and you wouldn't need a permit of any kind. .

Now for **Big Spring**, but be sure to read the history of the Tidwell Ranch because these 2 places were more or less tied together. It's not easy to get to this spring, but the **Deadman Turnoff** is as good as any starting point, and it's an easy landmark to find. From there, head northeast as if you were going to the Horsethief Trail, but at the first opportunity, route-find down into the upper more-entrenched parts of **Big Spring Canyon**. Once there, simply walk southwest up the drainage. In the upper end are 2 main forks; walk into the one on the left or east. About 500m into this short fork is Big Spring underneath the big headwall. It has year-round flowing water.

Frank Tidwell Jr., the son of Delbert Tidwell, knew a little about this spring. He states: *We developed that spring. Dad took some pieces of lumber from the Phillips Well and put them on the old pack mule and brought it over there and put a trough together.*

In 1991, the author viewed this spring from the canyon rim and saw no sign of watering troughs, but there was a nice trickle of water in the upper end of the canyon. In 5/2012, which was after a dry winter & spring, he walked into this gorge to find a fair amount of water, so it's a permanent spring source. There was no sign of any troughs, but in the past 70 years or so, they surely have been washed away. Unfortunately, he saw fresh tracks of at least one bull, which didn't quite make it to the spring and didn't pollute the water at the source.

The Phillips Well and Tidwell Ranch

The next stop heading north along The Spur Road is the old **Tidwell Ranch** which is located where the Phillips Petroleum Company drilled a well in the late 1920's. To get there, turn left or west at **The Spur Junction at Km 23.7 (Mile 14.7)** and continue north. As you near the ranch, you'll first be driving along a flat bench formed by the top of the Entrada Sandstone. About 2 kms before the ranch, you'll come to the end of an escarpment. From there, the road heads west down a **steep dugway** which can be very **sandy** after long dry spells. If you have a 2WD, park there on top of the bench, because if you go down you may not get it back up; walk it off first and check it out. In winter when the sand is frozen and/or wet, then a 2WD would surely be able to get back up that steep sandy dugway. Other options would be to walk or ride a mtn. bike from there.

You'll know you're at the Tidwell Ranch when you see a pile of square timbers and a large wooden wheel on your left. But first a little history of the place. It all started in about 1910. That's when Frank Tidwell of Wellington, Utah, sold a herd of about 500 cattle and bought a herd of 400 horses. They kept only 6 cows and one bull. The horses were then scattered all over the country from the coal mining areas of Carbon Country to the San Rafael Desert (west of Horseshoe Canyon). Some may have even ended up on The Spur. Once they got out on the range, they immediately turned wild. Now **Delbert Tidwell,** who was one of Frank's sons, was interviewed by several people from the National Park Service in October of 1986 concerning the history of this ranch. In that interview he stated:

We, that is Dad and some of the boys, started to round up and sell wild horses out at Horseshoe Canyon about 1910. We raised horses for a few years but the market wasn't much good by about 1918. One of the last carloads we sold went to a fish farm up somewhere--didn't get but a few dollars a head for them.

So throughout the years from about 1910 until December of 1918, they ran a small herd of cattle somewhere near Wellington and chased wild horses all over the country. During World War I, the flu epidemic hit the world and Frank Tidwell was one of the casualties. Frank's death on December 24, 1918, put an end to his family's involvement with chasing and selling wild horses. The late great **Pearl Biddlecome Baker** who grew up on the Joe Biddlecome or Robbers Roost Ranch, had a funny story to tell about Frank Tidwell, which illustrates his family's involvement with wild horse flesh. This legendary story probably began floating around after he died, and goes like this:

The Devil was showing somebody around hell one day and there was this great big kettle turned upside down and some fingers was coming out from underneath. One fellow was going to run over there and turn it over and let that poor fellow out, but the Devil said, "Don't do that, that's Frank Tidwell, and if you turn him loose, he'll have hell full of wild horses before morning".

After Frank died, everything changed. The family, which consisted of several boys, made the decision to get rid of the horses and begin to build up a herd of cows. The oldest boy was Clyde (Loughery) Tidwell, a stepson, who we'll hear more about in the back of this book. Clyde was in the army until February of 1919. When he got out, he and Delbert took a couple of horses along with a string of pack donkeys, and went down along the Green River, then up Horsethief Canyon and started rounding up what horses they could find. Most of them were in the area of **Big Spring**. That year they moved most or all of the horses off The Spur and later the same year moved a herd of about 30 cows up to the Big Spring country to replace the horses. The boys involved were Clyde, Delbert and Leland.

Some time after that, Clyde, who was the oldest and who more or less ran the outfit, went to work for Joe Biddlecome over at the Robbers Roost Ranch (Joe was Pearl Biddlecome Baker's father). For his pay he was given one heifer calf a month. This meant the herd increased rapidly.

In the beginning, the way they got upon The Spur, was to go down either the Twomile or Frog Trails, then south down along the Green River to Horsethief Canyon, then up that drainage to the top. At first they camped out under the stars, or leaned a piece of canvas up against a cedar tree, or in caves. Ned Chaffin believes at one time they somehow got a wagon down to Big Spring and set up their base camp there. Big Spring is the most-reliable waterhole on The Spur, so it was likely their main hangout. They also had cows down on the Green River and had a small cabin on what is now called Tidwell Bottom.

Then in the mid-1920's, there was an oil boom throughout southeastern Utah. Geologists thought there might be oil under the middle part of The Spur, because of a small uplift called the Barrier Creek Anticline. So the **Phillips Petroleum Company** wanted to give drilling a try. In the *December 1, 1927, Moab Times-Independent (TI)* newspaper under *"Oil Fields Report"*, it states: *A road contract in-*

The **Frank Tidwell clan**--minus Frank Sr. From L to R, Helen & husband Leland Tidwell; Eva Romjue Loughery Tidwell, Delbert & wife Mary Tidwell (and baby Ila Mae); in front is Bobby, Leland's son, and Frank (Jr.), Delbert's son. In Green River in 1937 or '38.

volving about $15,000 was this week let to Green River parties and work will start at once. Drilling equipment to be moved in as soon as road is completed.

Ned Chaffin also stated: Uncle Art Chaffin [of Hite Ferry fame] and Dad [Lou] took the contract from Phillips Petroleum Company to build that road across upper Horseshoe Canyon. They had a time limit on that road and it seems like it was 100 days. Now I know a couple of old sheep herders like Lou and Art couldn't build nothing, but they built the road and they made it work.

As it turned out they must have started the road work sometime in December of 1927, because in the **January 1, 1928** issue of the **TI**, it stated: Road work progressing nicely, and should be completed within a month. In the **March 1, 1928** issue it states: Water line to camp being laid and other preliminary work under way. Road to well site will be completed within a week, so that heavy equipment can be moved onto location. The **March 8th, TI** issue states: Road to well site completed Thursday [**March 7, 1928**] and heavy equipment now being moved onto location.

Ned Chaffin was there as a young man (born in 1913, died on 11/11/11) and remembered a little about it: At one point near the bottom of the canyon was a big sand dune, and is what they did was cut the road in, then they got a lot of trees and everything and put on there and put on cables and deadmen [anchors] to hold them up. I remember the first truck that went over it was one of old George Franz's Moreland 6-wheelers, and they took it down empty to see if it was going to hold. Of course it held, and it was still there when I left a few years later.

The well was spudded (drilling began) in on **April 18, 1928**. In the **July 12** report, they were down to 716m and in the Coconino Sandstone. By **November 1**, they were at 1082m and still drilling. By **December 13**, they were closed down for repairs. The repairs lasted for more than a month, but by **February 28, 1929**, drilling was again resumed at 1445m. But the deeper they got the more trouble they had. By June, they struck water at about 1524m but they kept on drilling. The last report came in the **October 17, 1929** issue of the **TI**. Part of it read: Abandoned and plugged at 5139 feet [1566m]. after passing through several hundred feet of water formation which could not be cased off.

While the drilling was going on, Ned Chaffin remembered what the place was like, at least part of the time: It seems to me there was a cook shack and 4 or 5 big tents for the guys to stay in. So I'd say they had 18 or 20 men working there. When they shut it down, the buildings weren't worth tearing down and hauling away. My guess is that they just abandoned them.

They finally chopped that old rig down and the only reason they did that was they didn't want it blowing over on somebody. I think the government made 'em do that. Frank Tidwell Jr.'s father, Delbert, told him: they sawed one of the legs, then hooked one of the big Mohrland trucks onto it and toppled it over.

When the Phillips people moved out, they took most of their equipment, but left a lot of other things. In the 1986 interview, Delbert stated: They left everything here and gave us the dining house for our home, which had three rooms and a storage closet..... So from sometime in late 1929 or early 1930 until the spring of 1945, this was where they lived and it became known as the **Tidwell Ranch**.

Frank Tidwell Jr., who was Delbert's son, and who was born in May, 1930, remembered a few things about life on the ranch: My dad and uncle brought down about 30 head of cattle to begin with [1919], then finally they got in excess of 400 when things were really good. They moved their cattle down from around Sunnyside from a range they called the Patmos. They moved them down sometime after my Uncle Clyde Loughery [Tidwell] got out of the army.

Then I think it was 1930 when our family moved down from Wellington to Green River. Then we lived on the ranch full time until I started school in the fall of 1936. We had a home in Green River, and that's where we stayed in the winters after 1936 [so I could go to school].

The house our family [Delbert's] lived in was what had been the kitchen and dining room for the Phillips workers. Then in a cabin below ours is where Leland & Helen stayed. The third building was

This walled-up tent was located at **Camp Spring**, due east of the **Phillips Well & Tidwell Ranch**. The woman is Eva Romjue Loughery Tidwell; the boy on the lower left sleeping is unidentified.

just left vacant, and for storage. Finally is what we did on that was, we cut out the front part of it and made it so we could use it as a garage for our pickup.

Then above the houses was a huge tank. It had been used to store the water which cooled the engine that ran the driller. The water in the tank was pumped up from what we called **Water Canyon**. They run a pipe right down to the bottom end of Water Canyon. It came up from down in Horseshoe up to the rim and to the Phillips Well. It was about a 3 mile-long [5 kms] pipeline.

The Chuchurus moved that tank from the Phillips Well across the canyon for water storage for their sheep. That old cabin which used to be at the beginning of the trail down into Horseshoe Canyon may have been the same house that Leland & Helen used to live in. I saw it in 1973 when I was there. I think maybe Leland's house was torn down, moved and reconstructed over there where the trailhead on the west side of the canyon is now [Somebody burned that old cabin down in about 1989].

Those big square logs you see lying around there now were part of the derrick when they were drilling. They were used to make our corral. Then there was a granary. At one time we bought a bull from Pearl B. Baker, and they named it Old Pearl. And that old devil would get in that granary and eat the oil cake we had in storage. Then dad would have to go get 'im out, and I was afraid he wasn't going to appear again. That old bull wanted that oil cake.

To this **Ned Chaffin** added another story about the granary at the ranch: After they chopped the rig down it just laid out there in the sun for 3 or 4 years, then they decided they was going to build 'em a granary. So they took the boards off the rig and built the granary. Finally they got the roof on it which was kinda rounded without much slope on it. Then they had to nail the sheeting on the roof. Now Delbert had an old broken rig ax, with a short handle--the handle had been broke on it, and they'd thrown it away and he retrieved it and he was up there nailing this sheeting on the roof. He did pretty good for a while, then he hauled off and missed that nail and it bent that nail right around his finger and just smashed that finger just like you'd smash a potato. He come down that old ladder and the blood was just gushing, and he thought he was a stuck hog, and he was a laughin' and a cussin', and using words that a pirate wouldn't use. And he kinda went like this, and standin' there shakin' his head like this and ol' Leland says, "Hey Delbert, has the feelin' come back into it yet". And Delbert said, "Oh you son-of-a-bitch, the feelin' never left it." I was a witness to that, and I really got a charge out of it.

When asked about the frames of the old cars still at the place, **Frank Jr.** continued his story: One was a Chevrolet truck from the late 1920's that they bought from Phillips Petroleum. The other one might be the one old Uncle John [Romjue the moonshiner] had, or it might be a vehicle that the Chuchurus left. I heard the Chuchurus left some vehicle there abandoned.

Our range was on what we called the High Part or **High Spur**. Then there was Horseshoe Canyon and the South Ridge. Also Clydes [Spring] Canyon, Horsethief Canyon, and Salvation and Woodruff Bottoms along the river. We left some cows down there year-round, and we got down them through Horsethief Canyon. On the Horsethief Trail, we did quiet a bit of work on that; and I guess we lost one or 2 horses on it also. Then down in the lower end of Horseshoe Canyon was the Angel Trail. This was one that Dad told about; that was such a dangerous old place. He said they lost one or 2 horses on that one too.

Dad used to tell us about the place and he said it looked like a wheat field when they first came in there, the grass was so tall. He used to tell about how it would strike your stirrups on your saddle horse as you rode along, and then if a cow laid down, it would be lost. That was at about the beginning of the drought, along about 1930, then it just kept drying away, and when we finally sold the cattle--and I know this sounds far-fetched and everything--but I remember it very vividly, where they were eating the cactus along the way to Green River.

It was a fellow by the name of **Jean Chuchuru**, who bought us out. He was a Mexican [more likely a Basque?] from Montrose, Colorado. We sold the range rights for $12,000. That wasn't a bad price in those days and we were willing to take it. I remember we had to make some improvements along the way too, to keep things up. As I understood it, we could sell range rights. To the best of my knowl-

edge, it was the drought that forced us off, and not the government squeezing us off. At least Dad never said anything to me about it. Now that sale was in **November of 1944**, *and then we had until May of 1945 to get all our cattle and everything off the range. It was about* **May 28, 1945** *when we finally got to town with the last herd of cows. [the Chaffins pulled the last of their horses off Anderson Bottom in October, 1945. Read more on that adventure along with Valentine Bottom on page 89]*

When we came in off the range we brought in about 200 head of cattle, and we sold them to a cattle buyer by the name of Sam Boyden. He took them over into Colorado and got'em fattened up. We were really embarrassed; they were so skinny and half starved to death when we brought'em in. After we left the range, Dad bought a farm near Green River from Joy Chiney.

At the Tidwell Ranch today (5/2012), here's what you'll find. Immediately on the south side of the road is a big wooden wheel, which was somehow used in the actual drilling of the well. Also, there's some scrap lumber and several huge square timbers lying there. This is what remains of the old drilling derrick. Then in the first 150m south of that are a couple of old car frames. The first one may have been Uncle John Romjue's, because it looks too old to have been left by the Chuchurus. The one further south is likely the old 1924 Chevrolet the Tidwells bought off the Phillips Company (?). Then just south-west of the second car is a pile of boards from one of the houses including the roof still intact, tin cans, and other odds and ends, including 2 old cook stoves. This is what remains of the driller's camp and what later became one of the Tidwell's homes. The first large pile of boards is what's left of Delbert & Mary's house. Down below that somewhere was Leland & Helen's place. There's nothing there now, which indicates it may have been moved by the Chuchurus over to where the trailhead to Horseshoe Canyon is today on the western rim of the canyon. Just south of the 2nd old car are some timbers from the drilling rig which could have been a holding pen for their riding horses. If you drive back up the road to the east about 500m you'll see off to the south and against a low cliff a cedar post & cable corral; they likely kept some cattle, or maybe horses, there.

When the Phillips outfit was there drilling the well, they got their water from down in Horseshoe Canyon at a seep near the mouth of Water Canyon. They pumped it up to their well & camp through a pipeline. But when the Tidwells moved in they got their drinking water just up the hill at what they called **Camp Spring**. To get there, head back up the road to the southeast. From the big bend of the road which is about 300m of so down from the top of the hill, go south and walk between the main escarpment on the left and a little Entrada slickrock hill on the right. Just south of that little hill is a drainage with a number of very large cedar (juniper) trees. Right there in the middle of half a dozen trees is where their camp was. Frank Tidwell Jr. tells us a little about the camp and the spring:

They had a tent out there with a kind of floor and wooden sides, then the canvas tent itself was stretched over this frame. In the 1930's, the Camp Spring was dug out, and seems like it was cemented off a little bit. Then there was a cellar-type door covering the water box that you could open up to get at the water. We'd drive up there with the pickup and a 50-gallon drum, then 3 or 4 of us would dip water out and someone on the pickup would put it in the barrel. After we got'er filled up, we'd take it down by the ranch house and roll it around until we got it into the right place, then we had a little piece of hose that we'd syphon water into a bucket. Then we took that into the house and that's what we drank from.

Frank had thought Camp Spring was the Tidwells first permanent camp on The Spur, but Ned Chaffin was there in 1926, and couldn't remember any troughs, camp or improvements on the place. Ned believed their first permanent camp was at **Big Spring** over the hill to the east. Delbert Tidwell seems to indicate this too in his own life story. This sounds more reasonable, because Big Spring was/is a good water source and close to Horsethief Canyon, which is where they ran cattle up or down to their river range. A more likely scenario would be that the Tidwells occupied the Camp Spring site while the Phillips people were drilling the well, then moved down to the well site shortly after drilling stopped.

At Camp Spring today is a small pipe which they stuck in the ground to collect water, which flowed down to a wooden box, which must have held water. Nearby can be found some old camp litter.

From the ranch & well site, you can also use the old Phillips Road to get down to the rim of Horseshoe Canyon--but it's about the roughest road you'll ever see--best just to walk. It's about 2 kms from the ranch to the canyon rim. That's as far as you go today because the NPS has blocked off the road to the bottom. But you can walk down that big dugway and into the canyon to see the rock art, Along that wall south of the dugway, is a large alcove with lots of greenery and a spring. This the Tidwells called **John's Hole**, as discussed earlier. Read its history above.

The Angel Trail and the Low Spur Overlooks

The last part of this chapter has to do with the northeastern end of The Spur, which is sometimes called **The Low Spur**. To get there, regress from the Tidwell Ranch until you come to **The Spur Junction**, then turn left or northeast. The first part of the road just north of the Tidwell Ranch turnoff, is over both the Entrada Sandstone and the Carmel beds. There can be some slick places during or right after a heavy rainstorm, but in normal times it's a good road. Further down and to the northeast, The Spur Road runs atop the Navajo Sandstone, and it becomes more sandy. During long dry spells, 2WD's will have a problem in a place or two, so a 4WD/AWD with a little clearance is required--as is a shovel (in 2012 it was kind of a mess in a place or two), otherwise it's generally a good road all the way to the end of The Low Spur which is about **43.2 kms (26.8 miles)** from the Hans Flat Ranger Station--see **Map 4** for a better look at the northeastern end of The Low Spur). If you make it there, you can walk about 1 km in 3 or 4 different directions for some good views overlooking Labyrinth Canyon of the Green River. The best overlook is the one view down on the mouth of Horseshoe Canyon and The Frog. Check with the ranger station for the latest information on this road's condition.

Now for a hike down the **Angel Trail** into the lower end of Horseshoe Canyon. Its history has already been discussed, so to get to it from The Spur Road, stop at a point about **38.7 kms (24 miles)** from the ranger station (see **Map 4** again). At that point you will have passed through the **2nd big flat** and will begin to climb a rounded hump with a little **slickrock** exposed; you can't miss it, it's the only slickrock around. This makes the best parking place and the best landmark. From there, face north, and you'll see a very low indistinct sandy dome-like hump out in front of you at about 10 or 11 o'clock. Walk almost due north and to the right or east of that sandy hump. About 1 km from the road will be the top of the Angel Trail. The place is marked by a stone cairn or pile of rocks, which is just to the southwest of an indentation in the canyon wall which is the top of a short rounded drainage.

The trail first cuts down and to the right or east as it drops off the bottom layer of the Navajo Sandstone with a man-made dugway (see foto on page 61), then it zig zags straight down through the various

Kayenta benches. Finally it cuts back to the right or east on top of the Wingate, then zig zags down to the bottom on a rockslide covering the Wingate. Once you get on this trail, there are cairns to follow. You could walk a horse down this one today, even though a few places have been washed out by floods. At the bottom you could walk downstream to the Green River, checkout the Frog Trail, or head up Horseshoe Canyon.

The **Tidwell Ranch** in 1932-'33. Shown is **Frank Tidwell (Jr.)** (Delbert's son born in 1930) with 2 of the Tidwell trucks and the tarpaper shack in the background. That building was once the kitchen & dining room for well drillers--then the home of Delbert & Mary Tidwell after the Phillips Petroleum people left in late 1929. Tidwells would have moved in sometime in 1930.

Tidwell Ranch again and the same building as above, but showing **Eva Romjue Loughery Tidwell** with the smallest child being **Bobby Tidwell,** the son of Leland & Helen. This was about 1933.

What's left of a coal or wood burning cook stove at the **Tidwell Ranch**. To the left is the stove itself with the oven and cook top. On the right is the **warming oven** which sat on top of the stove on the left side. The stove pipe ran up through the warming oven on top where food was kept warm.

59

The former **Phillips Well**. The capped well is seen on the right in the form of a metal pole. To the left is a big wooden wheel which was used in the drilling operation. Looking northwest, and in the background is **Sugarloaf Butte**. Behind the camera and to the left about 100m is where the drilling crews, then the Tidwells lived.

This is what's left of the home of Delbert & Mary Tidwell at the **Tidwell Ranch**. See the upper foto on **page 59** which shows what it looked like in 1932-'33. Its roof was mostly intact in 5/2012.

This is one of the Tidwells cars--or maybe a small truck--located at the old **Phillips Well**, and later the **Tidwell Ranch**. Nearby is a second frame of a vehicle, that one looks more like a truck.

Near the top of the **Angel Trail** is one of several places where a lot of construction work took place.

Millard and North Trail Canyons, and North Point

Location & Access The area covered by this map is north, northeast and east of the Hans Flat or Maze Ranger Station. To get there, drive along **Highway 24** to a point about halfway between Hanksville and Interstate Highway 70. Just south of Temple Junction and between **mile posts 135 & 136**, turn east onto the **Maze Road** running to The Maze District of Canyonlands National Park. See **Map 1** which shows this entire driving route. The distance from Highway 24 to the **Hans Flat Ranger Station & Visitor Center** (Tele. 435-259-2652) is about **73.7 kms (45.8 miles)**, so have a full tank of fuel plus extra--especially if you intend to do much driving in this region. You can also get to this area by driving south out of Green River on the Green River Road, but you'll drive farther on dirt roads using that route. The Hans Flat Ranger Station has several employees in the warmer half of the year, then a guard or maintenance man living there in winter. It's open year-round.

Elevations About the highest point around is the ranger station or visitor center, which sits at a lofty 2004m. Everything else is below it. Cleopatras Chair is 1987m altitude, and the low point in the region is the Green River at the mouth of Millard Canyon, at about 1210m.

Water Always enter this country carrying lots of water in your vehicle. But if you do need to fill up, do so at French Spring or Seep. It's a year-round spring and the water tastes good, but you'll need a cup to dip it out with. Better purify it first as no one takes care of it any more (the grazing permit has been bought by a conservation group). The author used to stock up there--but no more. For people in cars, just park on or near the Maze Road, then walk down the steep rough track to the spring. The people at the **ranger station have to truck water in, so don't go begging water from them.**

Maps USGS or BLM map Hanksville, and the San Rafael Desert metric map (1:100,000) which shows the entire route from Highway 24; Head Spur, Gordon Flats, Elaterite Basin & Cleopatras Chair (1:24,000--7 1/2' quads); or the plastic Trails Illustrated/National Geographic map Canyonlands National Park (1:70,000), but this map doesn't show The Spur very well.

Main Attractions A couple of very deep & scenic canyons, a couple of historic cattle trails, and several viewpoints looking down into the Under the Ledge Country, often referred to as The Maze District.

The Millard Canyon Trail

There is one very old livestock trail (used mostly by horses) down into Millard Canyon, plus at least one other hiker's route down in not far away. If you combine these 2, you can come up with one of the more scenic loop-hikes around. To start, stop at the ranger station for any last minute information (they're open 8am to 4:30pm daily) then drive north on **The Spur Road**. This is a well-traveled road, but it's seldom maintained and is rough in places. Most high clearance cars can make it down along this road, if driven with care. If you don't want to take a chance with your car, then use a mtn. bike. There aren't too many identifiable land marks along this road, so the best place to stop and park would be at the first road branching off the west; that junction is **5.7 kms (3.5 miles)** north or downhill from the ranger station.

From the road & junction, walk just a little south of due east for about 1 km; then look for a route or trail down through the bottom layer of the Navajo Sandstone rim. At the bottom of this ledge, you'll be on a **Kayenta bench**. From there, bench-walk south. As you walk along you'll see the Navajo wall on your right, and the sheer cliff of the Wingate below on your left. Along this trail, you'll likely see lots of

Looking due north down into Millard **Canyon** from the **viewpoint** on the Maze Road

Map 6, Millard and North Trail Canyons, and North Point

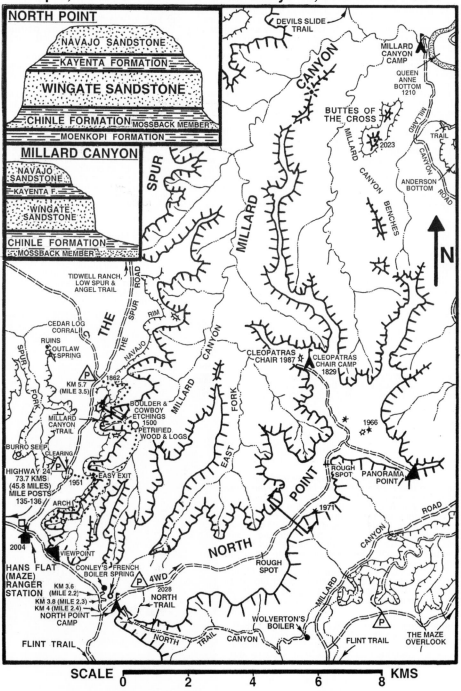

NORTH POINT

NAVAJO SANDSTONE
KAYENTA FORMATION
WINGATE SANDSTONE
CHINLE FORMATION MOSSBACK MEMBER
MOENKOPI FORMATION

MILLARD CANYON

NAVAJO SANDSTONE
KAYENTA F.
WINGATE SANDSTONE
CHINLE FORMATION
MOSSBACK MEMBER

DEVILS SLIDE TRAIL

MILLARD CANYON CAMP
QUEEN ANNE BOTTOM 1210
BUTTES OF THE CROSS
2023
MILLARD CANYON BENCHES
TRAIL
ANDERSON BOTTOM
MILLARD CANYON ROAD

N

THE SPUR

MILLARD CANYON

TIDWELL RANCH, LOW SPUR & ANGEL TRAIL

THE SPUR ROAD

RIM

CEDAR LOG CORRAL
RUINS
OUTLAW SPRING
KM 5.7 (MILE 3.5)
1862
BOULDER & COWBOY ETCHINGS 1500
PETRIFIED WOOD & LOGS

THE NAVAJO

MILLARD CANYON

EAST FORK

CLEOPATRAS CHAIR 1987
CLEOPATRAS CHAIR CAMP 1829

1966

SPUR FORK

MILLARD CANYON TRAIL

BURRO SEEP
CLEARING
HIGHWAY 24, 73.7 KMS (45.8 MILES) MILE POSTS 135-136
1951
EASY EXIT
ARCH

2004
VIEWPOINT
HANS FLAT (MAZE) RANGER STATION
CONLEY'S FRENCH BOILER SPRING
KM 3.6 (MILE 2.2)
KM 3.8 (MILE 2.3)
KM 4 (MILE 2.4)
NORTH POINT CAMP
4WD
2028 NORTH TRAIL

FLINT TRAIL

NORTH POINT

ROUGH SPOT
PANORAMA POINT
1971

NORTH

ROUGH SPOT

WOLVERTON'S BOILER

NORTH TRAIL CANYON

FLINT TRAIL

MILLARD

CANYON ROAD

MILLARD

THE MAZE OVERLOOK

SCALE 0 2 4 6 8 KMS

63

hoof prints of wild burros. More on these later. About 2 1/2 kms from the road, you'll then head northeast down a steep rockslide covering the Wingate wall. This is where the constructed part of the **Millard Canyon Trail** is. Toward the bottom of the rockslide the trail disappears.

As you get down out of the canyon and the land begins to level, look for a large house-size **boulder.** There are a number of old historic **cowboy signatures** on it. East of that boulder is some **petrified wood.** You could walk all the way to the Green River, but that part of the canyon isn't so interesting, and besides, it's a hell of a long walk without water.

For those who have a little adventure in their blood, here's an alternate to returning the same way. Simply head south upcanyon along the dry creek bed. As you near the head of the canyon, you'll see small north facing alcoves with Douglas fir trees clinging to life. This indicates there was a wetter climate here in the past.

Near the head of the canyon, you'll notice it has 3 minor forks or drainages. Make your way into the right-hand or western-most tributary. You'll have to route-find up through some rough country, but anyone can do it. As you near the head of the drainage, be looking for a route up through the Wingate to the Kayenta bench above. Once you get on it, then simply bench-walk back to the north. At one point, you'll walk right under a natural **arch**, then after less than another 2 kms, look west for a route up through a break in the Navajo slickrock above. From there head due west to the road. You should come out to a small **clearing** in the cedar & piñon trees at **1951m.** From there you'd have to walk back to your car; or deposit a mtn. bike there in the trees somewhere, which would make it easier getting to your car. You could begin to hike at the clearing, but the route down from there is not as well-defined.

Since this route involves some route-finding, it's recommended for experienced hikers. You'll also want a better map than this, and should have a compass as well. If you're there in the warm season, carry plenty of water. The loop-hike suggested will take the average Joe most of a day. If you just go down to the cowboy etchings and back up the same way, it'll take about half a day.

History of Millard Canyon

In the beginning, this drainage was called **Miller Canyon**, after **Andy Miller.** Andy was one of the earliest stockmen to run sheep in the **Under the Ledge country**. There's a big flat far to the south of here named after him. Andy Miller, John Boline, Henry Dusseir and Pete Maziet were the first in this country with sheep which may have been as early as 1890, or thereabouts, but surely before 1900.

The late **Pearl Biddlecome Baker** said this about how it started being called Millard Canyon: *When my parents, Joe and Millie Biddlecome, came to the Roost in 1909, we thought it was named for Millard Fillmore, so we called it Millard Canyon. It was named Miller Canyon, but we didn't know that for many, many years. In fact I'm not sure if my mother & father ever knew it. It was probably my father, or our family, who first called it Millard Canyon.*

Pearl, who grew up on the Robbers Roost Ranch west of the upper part of Horseshoe Canyon and the Roost Flats, knew a little about the upper part of Millard Canyon. She tells a funny story about some wild burros that were in that part of the country:

We sometimes used the trail down into Millard Canyon. My dad put calves in there once, but I don't think he used it very much because the trail was so bad. It actually wasn't that good a country and we didn't need it anyway.

There's quite a story about the Millard Canyon burros. Bill Moore took the first burros down on the river. He had horses and burros and I don't know why he took them down there. He took some spotted burros down on the river, and I think Arthur Ekker went down and brought them up. They were in Horseshoe Canyon for a while.

Anyway, Arthur took a little burro over to Hanksville and gave it to Barbara Ekker's kids. And the burro got it into his head that he was a human, because the kids were with him every minute in the summertime. So when they went to school that fall he followed them to school, then he'd stand and bray all day long. So the teacher would call Barbara and said, "Barbara, come down here and get your ass out from in front of our school". So she'd have to go down and bring the burro home.

The guy who brought those mules into the Millard Canyon country was **Bill Moore**, an older brother to **Eph Moore** who is featured in other parts of this book. The late **Kenny Allred** of Moab, who cowboyed for

Bill Moore in his early 20's (?) and in about 1890 (?) He was born in 1872. He was an older brother to Eph Moore. One of his sisters was Amy Moore Tibbetts Allred, the mother of both Bill Tibbetts and Kenny Allred, both of whom contributed to the history of this book. Later in life he had one leg amputated and was called **Peg Leg Moore** after that. This is the man who introduced burros into Millard Canyon; and some of their descendents are still found in upper Horseshoe Canyon and the Roost Country today. Every few years the BLM has to go in there and remove some so they don't overgraze the place--thanks to a federal law.
(Kenny Allred Collection)

many years just across the Green River to the east, remembered a little about this fellow:
I had another uncle, Bill Moore; he was Eph's brother. He rode a horse clearn into Canada when he was a kid. Bill brought them burros into that country. They had quite a pack string, and they took 'em down in there and got'em across the river. They traded 'em from the Indians. They had some pintos and straight colored ones too. I heard Uncle Eph tell that story a lot of times. It was Bill Moore who started that herd of burros in Millard Canyon. I was just 10 or 12 years old [1925 or '27] when I first went down in there, and there was a lot of burros there then. He might have brought them in there around 1920 or something like that (?).

He later broke his leg out there the other side of Dubinky and crawled a couple of miles for help. They had to take his leg off just below the knee. He hung out at Thompson--he never lived here in Moab after he was grown up. Him and another guy swiped some burros or something when they was kids, and anyway they sent him over the road! They made an example out of him--the Mormons did, and he didn't have no use for the Mormons from then on, so he didn't live in Moab. We didn't know him too well. He had a little ranch up there in Floy Canyon [somewhere north of the Floy Siding near Exit 175 on I-70] not far from Thompson and Crescent Junction.

After Bill's leg was amputated, most people just called him **Peg Leg Moore**.

Conley's Oil Well, French Spring, North Point and North Trail Canyon

As you drive southeast from the ranger station on the Maze Road, after about **1.3 km (.8 mile)** you'll come to the **viewpoint** of upper Millard Canyon. Be sure and stop and have a look. The foto you see on page 62 was taken from that place and it's quite a sight. From this viewpoint continue southeast to **Km 3.6 (Mile 2.2)** to see a road to the left or north signposted for **French Cabin**. Follow it 300m or so to a place with a dugout or **cellar** used by early-day sheepmen to store supplies, especially in winter; also an old metal granary, the French Cabin, and **Conley's old boiler**. This boiler was used to help drill for oil back in the early 1920's.

When asked about the origin of this old boiler, **Pearl Biddlecome Baker**, had this to say and how she remembered it: *There was an oil well drilled out there. My father let them have the overflow water out of the troughs. This was the Conley outfit. A guy named **T.C. Conley** used to go back east and raise some money, then hire a bunch of guys and go out and drill on that well. Then he'd run out of money, and the people would finally quit because they weren't getting paid. He'd go into debt every way he could then he'd go back east and raise more money. They tell me, one time he went back east and didn't have any money at all. He had a group of financiers together, and the only thing he could afford for paper were these rolls of wall paper. He tacked it on the wall and drew pictures of his scheme and talked about it. Finally he raised the money and came back to this country and drilled again. Then I think one of the main oil companies finally took it over and did the last drilling on it. Conley almost spent his life out there. He was there all throughout the 1920's.*

When the oil drillers left French Springs, my father [Joe Biddlecome] bought their cabins, and that's what he built the cabins at the Roost out of--other than that first cabin he built of logs.

From this old oil well site, drive along the main road again to **Km 3.8 (Mile 2.3** from the ranger station) where you'll see the road heading left or north to **French Spring**. Drive part way down this very rough track, park and walk to the spring. There you'll see a couple of small water troughs, a big metal tank and another long trough. This used to be the best waterhole in this part of the country, but there's no more cows, so no one maintains the spring any more. You can dip water out slowly, but purify it first.

Pearl B. Baker tells about how this spring got it's name: *Before the turn of the century, there were probably 2 sheep outfits in the Under the Ledge Country which is east of this spring. **John Boline** and **Andy Miller** were apparently the first ones in there. When Joe Biddlecome [Pearl's father] first came to the Roost in 1909, **Henry Dressier** was already down Under the Ledge with sheep. **Pete Maziet** was also there about that time. These mostly French [Basque] sheepmen used the North Trail to get in and out of that lower country and they used this spring or seep as a **supply depot**, and of course as a*

The **boiler** belonging to **T.C. Conley**. To the left less than 100m away are the French cabin, a fallen-down metal granary and a dugout or cellar used by sheepmen in the 1920's and early '30's.

waterhole. *This spring is named after one of those early-day French sheepmen or one of their sheep herders.* (There's at least one dugout or **cellar** in that area and it's between Conley's boiler and the French Cabin & the metal granary. That's where the herder owners left supplies during winter to keep things from freeze. Then the sheep herders would come up from Under the Ledge to restock.)

Only about 150m from the turnoff to French Spring, is the road turning left going to **North Point** at **Km 4 (Mile 2.4)**. A sign there states: *Panorama Point--8 (13 kms), Cleopatra's Chair--9 (14 kms)*. The road going out on this finger of high country is mostly good, but there are 3-4 places which are rough and steep. A LR/HC/4WD is needed because of those rough sections. Some people may have to move some rocks or use a shovel to smooth out some bad spots. In about 1990, the author drove his VW Rabbit with oversized tires out about halfway, then used a mtn. bike to finish the trip; but it was far worse in 2012 and his Jeep Patriot (which is only half a Jeep) only got to about as far as the VW.

At Cleopatra's Chair & campsite, the road is blocked off and you'll have to walk out to the point, which gives you a good view of Millard Canyon. If you go to Panorama Point, you'll have some nice views of upper Horse Canyon and The Maze, with the La Sal Mountains in the background to the northeast.

Now for the hike down the **North Trail** and **North Trail Canyon**. Only about 200m from the Maze Road is the North Point Campsite--but it's better to camp on BLM land 150m west of the ranger station for free! Beyond the campsite, the North Point Road gets rough for a short distance, then at **Km 1.7 (Mile 1.1)**, you'll come to the trailhead parking to the left and a sign, North Trail. For those who don't have a 4WD or mtn. bike to get down into The Maze via the Flint Trail Road, this is the only way in.

The North Trail is fairly well-used, easy to follow and is marked with cairns. After less than a km from the road, you'll drop off the Navajo rim and onto a Kayenta bench. Then it's a bench-walk to the west and to the very head of the canyon where it zig zags down a rockslide covering the Wingate Sandstone. This is the part which has been construction over the years. After another 500m, you'll be walking east down the dry creek bed. The further you go, the more open the canyon is, with the most scenic places back to the west in the upper end.

At the very end of the canyon and about 300m before you reach the Milliard Canyon Road, you'll see a rusty old boiler. This was used by **E.T. Wolverton** (see his picture on page 42) and the Chaffins in 1919, when they attempted to drill for oil there in **Big Water**--which today is called **Elaterite Basin**. The full history on this operation will be discussed in depth in the next section (Map 7) along with the Flint Trail. While there, walk over to the north a ways and to the bottom end of North Trail Canyon's drainage. Look closely, and if it's warm weather, you may notice some oil seeping out of the White Rim Sandstone. This will be coming out of the yellow colored parts of the otherwise white rock. This basin is full of it. In cooler weather, you'll only see yellowish-brown stained rocks.

There's not a lot of history associated with this North Trail. It was called the North Trail, because there was another trail made off the southern part of the Big Ridge down into upper Hatch Canyon. That's called the **South Trail**. Pearl B. Baker stated: *One of the earliest sheepmen down there was* **John Boline**, *he was there before the turn of the century [1900]. It was he who fixed the North Trail, and after he'd come out in the spring of the year, then he'd roll rocks down and make it look like it was impassable so other sheepmen wouldn't know it was possible to get down it. He was one of the first ones to make and use the North Trail.*

In the years before the **Flint Trail** came into being, this was the normal route for sheepmen who took flocks down to Under the Ledge country. After 1919, and improvements on the Flint Trail were made, it was used a little more.

On the left is what is known as the **French Cabin**, to the right is the metal **granary** mentioned above. To the right a ways is a dugout or cellar used by sheepherders, and T.C. Conley's boiler.

This is the **dugout or cellar** located near the **French Cabin**. Sheep herd owners would deposit supplies in this then their herders could collect it when they needed more stuff. Sheep herders were in this country and Under the Ledge only in winter, and supplies stored here wouldn't freeze.

Looking northwest at **Cleopatra's Chair** which is in an eastern fork of upper **Millard Canyon**. There's an official NPS campsite just before you get there, but the road is pretty bad in places.

From the head of **North Trail Canyon**, looking east with **Elaterite Butte** in the distance. According to Pearl Biddlecome Baker, this was the main route from the Robbers Roost Country down to **Under the Ledge** (The Maze). Sheepmen originally built the trail running down this canyon.

This **boiler** belonged to **E.T. Wolverton**. For more about him, read the information under **Map 7**.

Looking south into the upper end of **Millard Canyon**. In the middle skyline would be where the Millard Canyon Viewpoint on the Maze Road is located.

From the very end of the **Low Spur,** looking northwest at the Green River in Labyrinth Canyon. Just below the center of this picture is the **falling sand dune** as shown on **Map 4.** That's right at the bottom end of **Frog Creek**. Just to the left and out of sight is the mouth of **Horseshoe Canyon**.

The Big Ridge: Flint Cabins & Trail, and Lands End Butte

Location & Access This map shows most of the high country southeast of the Hans Flat or Maze Ranger Station. Also shown is part of what all the old timers in this country knew as **Under the Ledge** which refers to all the areas east of the high plateau country where The Spur, North Point, and the Big Ridge are located. Under the Ledge also extends east to the Green & Colorado Rivers down to where the Dirty Devil River now enters Lake Powell.

The best way to this elevated plateau area is leave Highway 24 about halfway between Hanksville & I-70; between **mile posts 135 & 136** turn eastward and drive the **Maze Road** to the ranger station (Tele. 435-259-2652), then south along the Big Ridge. See **Map 1, page 19** for a look at this driving route. Another more difficult way would be to head toward Hite on Highway 95 near the north end of Lake Powell. There you would turn off **Highway 95** between **mile posts 46 & 47** and drive east, then northeast along the **Hite Road** to the 3-Way Junction, then up the Flint Trail. The only problem with this is, you'll need a LR/HC/4WD to get up the Flint. Read more on areas along the Hite Road under **Map 13**.

Elevations Hans Flat or Maze Ranger Station, 2004m; top of Flint Trail, 2097m; the Flint Cabins, 2073m; and Lands End Butte, 2180m.

Water Take all the water you'll need into this country, there's almost none around. Between the Hans Flat or Maze Ranger Station and the top of the Flint Trail, about the only reliable water will be at French Spring, but it's hard to get water there these days because no one is maintaining it. Where to get water Under the Ledge will be discussed in each of the remaining 5 sections.

Maps USGS or BLM map Hanksville (add San Rafael Desert for part of the drive)(1:100,000); Fiddler Butte, Gordon Flats, Elaterite Basin & Clearwater Canyon (1:24,000--7 1/2' quads); or the plastic Trails Illustrated/National Geographic map Canyonlands National Park (1:70,000).

Main Attractions Great viewpoints from several places on top of the Big Ridge, which is also a cool respite in summer, a pair of old historic cabins & trail, and a short hike to the top of Lands End Butte, the highest point in the area.

History of the Flint Cabins & Flint Trail, and Oil Well Drilling in Big Water or Elaterite Basin

From the Hans Flat or Maze Ranger Station and French Spring area, head south along the top of the **Big Ridge** on the **Maze Road**. This road to as far as the top of the Flint Trail is sometimes maintained, so any car can be driven there under normal conditions. At times however, it can become rutted and rough in places. There is some traffic these days, but not as much as before Canyonlands NP hijacked the high part the GCNRA region and began requiring everyone to camp in designated campsites and pay $30 for a camping permit. Best to camp anywhere on BLM land just west of the ranger station and make day trips to these parts; but cleanup your campsite or they'll hijack that area too!

After driving **14.6 kms (9.2 miles)** will be a sign pointing out the **Bagpipe Butte Viewpoint** on the left. Continue south. About **18.2 kms (11.3 miles)** from the visitor center you'll see a side-road running west about 200m to a tree-less little flat which is the **Flint Seep Campsite**. If you want to visit the old **Flint Cabins**, then drive to and park at or near this Flint Campsite. From there, and with compass in hand, set off to the South, Southwest right along the top of a very low hogsback ridge. In 6-8 minutes, or 300-400m, you should see something--either some camp junk and old rusty tin cans, or the **Flint Cabins** (You could also drive down the main road another 200-250m and begin in the big sagebrush covered Flint Flat with a 1950's airstrip, but there's no place to park in that area, so best to park & begin at the Flint Campsite). The cabins are sitting next to a ledge on top of a low hump; one is made of stone

The **Flint Cabins** in **1926**. You're looking north at the eastern side of the cabins. You're also looking at both horses & pack mules belonging to the Chaffins. **Ned Chaffin**, age 13 (born in 1913), is seen to the far right. (Ned Chaffin Collection)

Map 7, The Big Ridge: Flint Cabins & Trail, & Lands End Butte

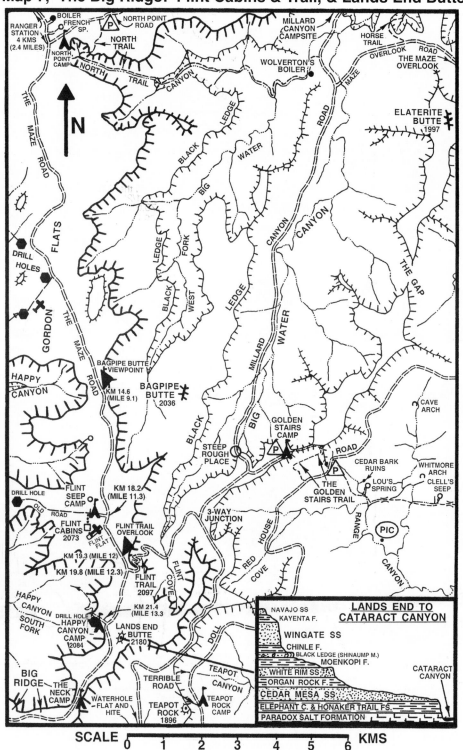

SCALE 0 1 2 3 4 5 6 KMS

This is the **Flint Trail,** which is now a road, as it looked in 2012. It has 3 tight bends or switchbacks forcing all vehicles to backup a time or two just to make the curve. Almost any vehicle can get down it, but only a LR/HC/4WD can make it back up.

This picture shows all 3 of the parts of the **Flint Cabins**. The one on the left is the stone cabin that Wolverton built; the one in the middle is the one with double-log walls, Wolverton also built that one; and on the far right is the stone cabin that Lou & son Faun Chaffin built.

without a roof, the other made of logs, with an extension made of rock. This second cabin was built by **E.T. Wolverton** (see his foto on page 42), and **Lou & Faun Chaffin** (Faun was Lou's oldest son).

Before getting into the history of these cabins, it should be said that in the early 1900's, prospectors had found oil seeps down in a place the old timers called **Big Water**; but today it's called **Elaterite Basin**, about 15 kms north of the bottom of Flint Trail. Oil seeps out of the White Rim Sandstone all over that country. Courthouse records show that some mineral claims were filed as early as 1907 by **E.T. Wolverton, Lou Chaffin, A.I. Anderson** (first to settle & name Anderson Bottom) and others. Later in time Wolverton joined forces with Green River bank clerk, **Bert Silliman**, and they started looking for ways to get money so they could attempt to drill for oil. Silliman worked at the Commonwealth Bank in Green River, so he was in a position to look after finances and solicit money.

So they formed a corporation called the Nequoia Association, or **Nequoia Oil Company**, which filed the claims. There were 114 oil lease claims filed in the courthouse in Loa, the seat of Wayne County. This was sometime in the mid or late 1910's, but after 1912 (That's the year Wolverton stopped boating on the Green River, and soon after abandoned his Riverside Ranch just south of today's Ruby Ranch). The names on the claims were Wolverton's, Bert Silliman's and Bert's father. Bert Silliman sold the stock to people in the mid-west and E.T. Wolverton went out and staked the claims and ran the company in the field. It was sometime in the summer and/or fall of 1919, that Wolverton finally got out to Flint and started building these 2 cabins. This was in preparation for drilling oil down in Elaterite Basin.

Now here's an oral history of these 2 cabins and the oil drilling scheme. The late **Ned Chaffin**, who grew up on the Chaffin Ranch on the lower San Rafael River, was one of the better sources on the subject. He told this writer about his father, **Lou Chaffin**, and older brother **Faun**, and of the time they helped built the cabins, the **Flint Trail**, and how they lowered a drilling outfit down the hillside:

Now I know Dad fooled around gettin' horses for the government a lot during the war, and they wouldn't take him in the service because he had too many mouths to feed. He jobbed around--he mined some and was in the stock business all this life. He worked for the Utah Oil Refining Company off and on for a long time, clearn up into the 1930's. He was always a get-rich-quick man. But he had to feed the kids. He did have some livestock in Loa or Torrey, but he had a lot of horses; in those days you had to have a lot of horses.

He also worked down on the Stanton Dredge [on the Colorado River], in fact, he did the freighting down there for those people, hauling the materials in for 'em. And that's where he got the drilling rig that they used down in Elaterite Basin. He traded the people who owned the Stanton Barge. He traded and went down there and brought it up from the Colorado. Johnny Newby had it over on the east side of the river from the mouth of Halls Creek there somewhere. He brought that drilling rig up out of there just prior to them startin' to drill those wells in Elaterite Basin.

Now Delbert Tidwell told me the first time he ever met my father was when my father [Lou Chaffin], and a bunch of other men, was bringing that little Keystone drilling rig up from the Colorado River up Halls Creek. Delbert and his dad Frank was going down there to do a little placer mining. This means that he was bringing it up sometime before Frank Tidwell died, which was on December 24, 1918. Then we moved from Loa to Green River in 1919, and sometime after that they started drilling the little well down in Big Water.

*Now **Wolverton** built those 2 Flint Cabins [the **stone house** with no roof and the **double-log cabin**]. When he built his log cabin part, he used whatever kind of logs was handy. The pine logs there on the roof that had dirt would get moisture into 'em and they rotted fast. The log cabin part was starting to deteriorate the last time I was there. But the stone cabin addition on the northeast end of Wolverton's cabin that Faun and Dad built last, had all cedar in it. It's a cedar roof and still good [the NPS finally added another roof to the middle section with the double walls].*

The little rock cabin was really nice and had a big window in it. It had a floor and everything. But it finally burned down some time in the 1920's. The story on that was that Ezra Huntsman was camped there with some other guy, and they had a fire in that damn fireplace and the roof caught on fire and it burned down. It burned the roof off, and some rocks had fallen down. Those cabins were the headquarters for Dad and Wolverton while they were drillin' down in Elaterite, and I think they built them before they took the boiler down the Flint; must have been 1919. I know they built that stone addition on there a little later, and before 1921, which was the first year I went down in there. We just called it the Flint Cabin.

When I was there later, the Flint Trail was a good one, because Wolverton did all that work on it. It was probably a game or Indian trail to begin with, maybe an outlaw trail. But when he started, it was a road he was working on at first. He was about halfway down when Dad got there. But they must have done work on it all the way down, because they used it to get back up to their headquarters which was at the Flint Cabins.

Wolverton was starting to build a road down there on the Flint Trail, then when Dad got there he said, "What do we want to built a road for", so of course they had a lot of old cable on the rig, and they had to put out a little mid-night requisition over at that old well at French's Spring to get a little more cable, and they and Dad slid the damn thing off the top on the snow.

Now before going further with Ned Chaffin's story of sliding the drilling outfit down the hillside, it might be best to hear what **Faun Chaffin** had to say. Faun was older, born in 1899 (and lived to be over 100), and was there doing the work; but he was pretty old and starting to forget things when the author spoke to him about it in 1990. However, his information seems to go along with what his younger brother remembers, only in more detail:

Dad said with all this damn snow on the ground, I can snake that outfit down a chunk at a time. So Wolverton said "Let's give'er a try", and good hell it wasn't no time at all before we had it all down there. We started in with wheels and stuff like that from that little old rig and let them down first, and after we once got it slick with that cable there wasn't no trouble. All you had to do was start it down there and she'd go. Somebody would be down at the bottom there and unhook'er, then we'd roll the cable back up. And away we'd go again, and we had it all down there before spring come [spring of 1920].

Now Ned continues with his story: *Now Faun worked down there for more than a year for Wolverton, and I think they only came to town twice, after they actually got to drilling, which must have been in the summer of 1920. You just as well be on Mars as down there in those days. I think they came out to Green River for the 4th or the 24th of July and at Christmas time. And then in the end his check bounced when he got it for his years work. Dad's checks cleared the bank; of course Dad had drawn some along the way to keep the family going, but Faun's check was no good. He got what the owl left on the log-- if you know what I mean.*

Those wells in Elaterite Basin were just little old shallow wells. I would say that they fired up the boiler and they used those scrub cedars and piñon pines for fuel, and in fact they practically denuded the lower end there where they were drilling. They couldn't have been very deep because that little old rig wouldn't drill over 400 feet [120m] at the most. But you see, what they thought they would do is just drill down there and tap it real easy. That's what they had in mind. But if they knew then, what we know now, they would have known the only way to get that oil out of the rock is by retort or heat. (That old boiler is in the lower or bottom end of **North Trail Canyon** about 300m before you reach the Millard Canyon Road. See the previous map which shows how to get there.)

After Wolverton and Silliman went broke--or couldn't get any more money, Wolverton headed for the Henry Mountains and spent the last 9-10 years of his life trying to mine gold on the east slopes of Mt. Pennell. He's the one who built the **water wheel** you'll now see behind the **BLM office in Hanksville.** After the Nequoia Oil Company stopped using the Flint Cabins for the drilling operation, the Chaffins took them over and began using them as a camp and supply depot between the Biddlecome or Robbers Roost Ranch, French Spring and Waterhole Flat in Under the Ledge country.

Ned goes on to say: *We later built that little corral below the Flint Cabins, it wasn't there when Wolverton and Dad was down there in Elaterite Basin drilling. We also had a little carpenter-style blacksmith shop between the corral and the cabins. Dad, Faun and I built that in the early 1920's, because you need a horse corral around your camp. When they were drilling down in Big Water, they had the Flint Cabins as their headquarters. They'd bring all their supplies to the cabins, then they'd take down what they needed. And then after the drilling, we used that as our headquarters for a long time when we were down Under the Ledge. Also, right there in front of the cabins we used to have a little round steel granary; well it wasn't exactly a granary, it was a metal tank that we put a lid on, but it's gone now.*

*At the Flint Cabins, we got water at the **Flint Spring** and then of course we put the trough over at Harness-up Spring and that was primarily the source of our water--because the Flint Spring would dry up in the summers in those dry years. **Harness-up Spring** was a good source of permanent water. It was a mile west of the cabins.*

I remember one story about the Flint Cabins which took place not long before I left that country. George Franz was suppose to meet me over at French Spring with supplies. I left Tidwell's Ranch going to French Spring and he was suppose to have my grain there and everything for my horses when I got there. He wasn't there, so I got under a cedar tree and stayed there the night. The next morning I headed for the Roost at Crow Seep to see what had happened to him, and about halfway over there I saw where he had got stuck in a snow drift and he had dumped my corn and grain off in a pile and left it there, so I put it on my pack mules. By that time it was gettin' late and those winter days are awful short, and I went to Flint. I got to Flint just at dark. I had a little black mule I called Bango. The snow on the level would just touch the bottom of the packs. And when I got to that cabins, I opened the door and there it was nice and dry and the wood box was full of wood. There's nothing in my life that looked as good as that did. There was a stove in the addition cabin, and a fire place in the stone cabin. That must have been in the winter of 1934-35.

Now Mel Marsing, who was Pearl Biddlecome Baker's first husband [and June Marsing's brother], wanted to set up a thing for the sheepherders there at the Roost. Also, remember that we didn't have good roads in them days and we didn't have good vehicles either. So the Roost was an ideal place for the sheepherders to bring their supplies, then the herders who had their sheep down on Waterhole Flat, could leave there, go to the Roost in one day, load up his mules and go back the next morning--2 days. Or if he had to go into the old French Ranch on the lower San Rafael River, it was 2 long days and 3 long days back to Under the Ledge. So a lot of them made a supply depot there at the Roost.

*When Joe Biddlecome died, Mel & Pearl were working for the Texas Company. Dad got Mel the job for him pumping the water from the **Tasker [Jeffery] Well**, over west of the Flat Tops, over to the drilling rig on Texas Hill. They had to have water for drilling. It was his job to pump water and have plenty over there at the Texas Well. There was a little cabin there at the Tasker Well, so he and Pearl stayed there. That's where they lived. So when Joe passed away, Mel and Pearl moved back to the Roost. Mel was a lot more help on starting a store out there and takin' money from sheepherders than he was in punchin' cows. As it turned out, I think he tried to make a few too many extra bucks off those sheepherders, so they moved their supply depot to what was **upper Blue John Spring**. So after they built several granaries, the place became known as **Granary Spring**. They also built cellars in the ground to store food in the winter so it wouldn't freeze. Later, after the drillers went to French's Seep, some of the herders moved their supply depot over there. That's where one boiler is now [also a clapboard cabin, steel granary and at least one cellar].*

Here's what you'll find at the Flint Cabins today; one well-built stone structure without a roof. This is the one Ezra Huntsman accidentally burned down. Look inside and at eye level for, **Nequoia 1919**, carved into one rock. That must be the year it was built. Immediately northeast of that is the log cabin Wolverton built. Notice it's made with a double wall of logs, the only one of it's kind this writer has ever seen. The roof of this cabin was about half caved in 1991, but the GCNRA put a new roof on it in 2005. Now it's dry inside and a good shelter. Attached to it on the northeast end is another square stone addition. This is the part Lou & Faun Chaffin built. The roof on this one is still good, and dry inside. Out in front are scattered debris of various kinds; old #3 bath tubs, bed springs, rusty tin cans, etc.

The next stop before going down the **Flint Trail** is the highest point in the area called **Lands End.** This is actually a small **butte** made of Navajo Sandstone rising above the Kayenta Formation bench, which covers most of the top of Big Ridge. However, the caprock on the 5 x 100m summit is made of limestone which must be a lens within the Navajo.

If you'd like to hike up this easy-to-climb butte, drive south from Flint Flat, and instead of turning left or east to the Flint Trail, continue straight ahead to about **Km 21.4 (Mile 13.3** from the ranger station). At that point a side-road signposted for **Happy Canyon** heads right or west. About 100m along that side-road is the **Happy Canyon Campsite** which is located at an old **drill hole** site. But don't take that road, continue south from the junction another 300m to be a little closer. From wherever you park, walk east 10 minutes to the top for some nice views in all directions.

The **Flint Trail** (the turnoff is **19.8 kms/12.3 miles** from the Hans Flat Ranger Station) is now a road which was built sometime in the early 1950's during the uranium boom. It's very steep and it makes 3 switchbacks. The corners are so tight that all vehicles have to back up a time or two getting around them. The top part of this road is at about **2097m**, which means the snow stays on it into April in some years. It's usually open to traffic by about April 1, and closes down because of snow or ice about November 1. Around the bottom part there are many clay beds which can be slick in wet weather. The condition of the rest of the roads in this region will be covered in each of the 5 remaining sections. Call the Hans Flat/Maze Ranger Station, Tele. 435-259-2652 for the latest information on the Flint Trail.

74

Above This is the inside of the **middle Flint Cabin**, the one with double walls and built by E.T. Wolverton. A new roof was put on by the Glen Canyon National Recreation Area (GCNRA) in 2005 so it's dry & comfortable inside. The new logs put into the roof are made of cedar or juniper, so they will last a long time if the dirt stays on top to protect them.

Left This is the front of the **middle Flint Cabin**, the one made of double logs. It has a new dirt roof which should protect the new logs below for a long time. The door frame is also new, otherwise everything is original--including he bed springs.

On November 8, 1991, the author drove his '81 VW Rabbit Diesel with oversized tires down the Flint without trouble, but had no chance to get back up. Instead, he went south to Waterhole Flat and out to Lake Powell via the **Hite Road**. His VW had oversized tires which helped a lot, but getting back up the Flint Trail Road with a 2WD is impossible, even when it's in good condition. In 2011, his Jeep Patriot with a regular 5 speed transmission couldn't get up it either. Any HC vehicle can get down the Flint, but you need a **LR/HC/4WD** to get back up.

If you have a regular 2WD car and haven't had a lot of experience driving such terrible roads, then consider taking a mtn. bike down this hill. There are several places at the top of the Flint Trail where you can park (but not camp as in the good old days before 1991) under some large piñon-cedar trees. This Under the Ledge country is ideal for using mtn. bikes. Going down the Flint with a mtn. bike is easier and faster than walking down the North Trail with a backpack.

Before leaving the Big Ridge and the Flint Trail areas, one last tragic story has to be told. It has to do with the death of **Honore (Henry) P. Moynier** on **February 11, 1954**. Henry was part of the French family of Moyniers who bought the Chaffin Ranch and their range or grazing rights in the fall of 1944 (they had a year to gather all their stock which was finally taken out at the end of October, 1945). After that time, they had herds of sheep down Under the Ledge until about 1970. The story about Henry's death is best told by Pearl Biddlecome Baker in her book titled, *Rim Flying Canyonlands, with Jim Hurst*. The story went like this as told by Jim:

One day in the early 1950's I was laying tile on the drug store floor right shortly after we bought it, when Leon Moynier came in. He was real excited, said he needed a rescue plane, that his cousin, Henry Moynier, had cut his leg badly and was bleeding terribly. He wanted me to land at the Robbers Roost Ranch [Biddlecome--Ekker Ranch today] as they were going to try to take Henry there where maybe Hazel Ekker could help him. Leon had come on ahead [in one of 2 Dodge Power Wagons the Moyniers had] to get a plane to meet them there, that being the best place to land.

As we took off in the PA-14 he told me that he had burned the motor out of his truck driving in. This accident had happened down Under the Ledge, below the Flint Trail, and that he had come up horseback to where his truck was parked at Flint, got into it and had taken off for Green River. It is over a hundred miles [160 kms] and the roads were not improved like they are today; U-24 was not even surfaced at that time. Beyond it, the road was mostly just two ruts more or less parallel, with sand patches every few miles. He had driven like crazy, and was lucky to get the truck to town before it quit on him.

*The men with Henry [one was Henry's brother, **Marius or "Mias" Moynier**] were to bring him out as carefully as they could to a pickup [2nd Dodge Power Wagon] at Flint, then take him to the Robbers Roost Ranch where Mrs. Arthur Ekker [Pearl's sister Hazel], who had taught First Aid, might be able to help him. By that time, Leon [who was Henry's 1st cousin] should have a plane there and they could take the wounded man to a hospital.*

As we were crossing the road just east of the Texas Well we saw their pickup coming in. We couldn't understand that; they were supposed to wait for us at the Roost. I didn't know what else to do, so I looked around and inspected the road near the Texas Well, and come in and landed the PA-14 just ahead of the pickup.

The Grazing Service [forerunner to the BLM before 1946] signs out there are put up with two angle-iron posts and the sign hangs between them. I didn't see an obstruction, the road was cut down there, with high banks on each side. I landed and went rolling along and lo and behold! there was one of those angle irons sticking up. The sign had been knocked down. I just hooked the navigation light on my right wingtip on the damn thing and we stumbled off the road, ran the nose into the bank, broke up a propellor and busted a wing and the tail.

About that time the pickup came along, and they told us Henry had died so they just came on in. He died just before they got to the Roost; they went on down anyway, but the Ekkers were not at home.

Henry had been skinning out a sheep, slitting down the belly, pulling down on this knife. The blade slipped out of the skin, and because he was exerting considerable pressure, his hand jerked down, and the knife blade went into the upper thigh, cutting the femoral artery.

The fellows at camp didn't know what to do for him. No one knew about pressure points, he was bleeding so terribly and they were all so frightened, but hoping that the blood would stop of itself, as it almost always does. They headed for help, but were just too far away from doctors and hospitals.

See pictures of **Henry & Leon Moynier** on the opposite page; plus read a little history of the Moyniers in this part of the country on page 114. There was another earlier and successful rescue by plane at Waterhole Flat, but that story is discussed later starting on page 127 along with Map 11.

Two trucks belonging to the **Tidwell Clan** crossing what is now the **old San Rafael River Bridge**. The bridge is still there, but half gone and half buried in tamarisks; it's located a short distance east or downstream of the new bridge. These bridges are found just southwest or upstream from the old and now-abandon Chaffin Ranch. The 3 men on the far left are unknown. (Ned Chaffin Collection)

The **Joe Biddlecome family** (minus Joe) at the Biddlecome or Robbers Roost Ranch, 1927. L to R: Hazel Biddlecome, Harold Ekker, Milli Biddlecome holding baby Joe Marsing, **Pearl Biddlecome Marsing** at age 20, Ted Crumb and Arthur Ekker. Pearl was married to Mel Marsing, but he died on 9/13/1929, and she later married Slim Baker; Arthur later married Hazel. (Ned Chaffin Collection)

Honore (Henry) P. Moynier with his pack sting of mules--but he's riding a horse! Henry is the one who died on 2/11/1954 from an accident while skinning a sheep. That story is on the opposite page. Identifiable objects on the mules are #3 galvanized bath tubs and a nose bag. Henry was the one in the family who preferred to be out with the sheep than staying in town.

L to R: **Paul Moynier**, his twin brother **Pierre II,** born in 1912; then **Leon Moynier,** born in 1919. This foto was taken in about 1930. Leon is the one who drove a Power Wagon to Green River to get Jim Hurst to fly out to The Roost to help his double 1st cousin Henry Moynier. (both fotos from Pierre Moynier III Collection)

Under the Ledge: Mouth of Millard Canyon, and Anderson, Valentine & Cabin Bottoms, Turks Head & L. Horse Canyon

Location & Access This mapped area is northeast of the Hans Flat Ranger Station, just west of the Green River and below the high country known as the Big Ridge. Old timers from this region always called this area **Under the Ledge**; the CNP/NPS calls this third of the national park, the **Maze District**.

Be sure you have another map better than this one if you're heading into these parts because the region on this map is about as far from civilization as one can get in America. So whether you're in a HC/4WD or a mtn. bike, make sure everything is running well and you're well-supplied with everything such as fuel, food and water. Don't pass by the **Hans Flat or Maze Ranger Station** without stopping and getting last minute information about road & weather conditions, camping info., etc. Or call ahead at Tele. 435-259-2652 and get everything sorted out. If you have to be towed out of this neck of the woods, it'll cost a small fortune!

Let's begin this section at the bottom of the **Flint Trail**. Most of the time, high clearance (HC) 2WD's can get down the Flint Trail, but you'll need a LR/HC/4WD to get back up, so plan this part of your trip carefully. A couple of kms from the bottom of the Flint Trail, you'll come to a **3-Way Junction** (see Map 7). The road going south is the **Hite Road**, which will take you to **Waterhole Flat**, toward **Hite** on Lake Powell, and **Highway 95**. For the first 6-7 kms south of that 3-Way Junction, the Hite Road is rough in a place or two, but good for regular cars after that.

The road heading northeast at that point will be going north to the **Maze Overlook** and to the mouth of **Millard Canyon**. This is generally known as the **Millard Canyon Road.** Turn northeast and after 1.6 kms (1 mile) will be another intersection. The road veering right will be the one heading to the **Golden Stairs Campsite** (another 1.6 kms/1 mile) and to the top of the **Golden Stairs Trail**. The one heading left or north will be the **Millard Canyon Road**. For now, head north. Soon you'll come to a series of rough ledges as the road heads **down** through the Chinle Formation, the rough part of which is generally known as the Black Ledge. This **steep rough section or place** (see Map 7) lasts for about 1 km and you'll need a LR/HC/4WD to get back up; you may have to smooth it over by using a shovel and throwing rocks off too. At the bottom of this steep rough part is **Elaterite Basin**, but the first stockmen into this country called it **Big Water**. Once you get down in it's generally a good road (a few rough places) all the way to the mouth of Millard Canyon on the Green River. Ask the rangers about any other problems along the way. When you finally reach the area covered on this map the road generally runs along on top the White Rim (Sandstone).

Elevations Top of Flint Trial, 2097m; bottom of Flint Trail, about 1600m; Millard Canyon Road passing near the head of Horse Canyon, about 1500m; mouth of Millard Canyon, about 1210m.

Water Carry all the water you'll need into this country. For hikers, there's a small spring on Anderson Bottom and in Horse Canyon, but Green River water must be treated.

Maps USGS or BLM maps Hanksville & La Sal (1:100,000); Horsethief Canyon, Cleopatras Chair, Turks Head & Elaterite Basin (1:24,000--7 1/2' quads); the best one overall is the plastic Trails Illustrated/National Geographic map Canyonlands National Park (1:70,000); or the plastic Latitude 40° map Moab West (1:75,000).

Main Attractions Historic river bottoms; an old cabin chimney & boat, petroglyphs, pictographs & Anasazi ruins; not to mention some wild & wooly country.

Mouth of Millard Canyon and the Buttes of the Cross

There's not a lot to see at the mouth of **Millard Canyon**. Right where the road ends on the White Rim ledge just above the river, you can look straight across to see **Queen Anne Bottom**, but that will be discussed in another part of this book. There's also a minor rapid right where Millard Canyon empties into the river. This is about the closest thing to real rapids on the Green River between the town of Green River and The Confluence with the Colorado. Also, immediately above the river are some metal stakes in the rock. This is where a cable car was once tied down, which was used during the 1950's uranium boom to transfer supplies across the river.

If you look to the south from the mouth of Millard about 300m will be a couple of cottonwood trees and a nice place to camp with some shade and grass. There's a road heading that way.

The lower end of Millard Canyon is wide-open country and is a little different scenery-wise, than up or downriver. But it's still interesting because there are several free-standing buttes in the valley which in a way resembles Monument Valley. This location actually marks the end of **Labyrinth Canyon** and the beginning of **Stillwater Canyon** to the south. Stillwater ends at The Confluence--or maybe Spanish Bottom (?). It's here at about the mouth of Millard Canyon you can see 2 large buttes to the southwest that have an interesting configuration. It was John W. Powell who gave it a name back on July 17, 1869: *Off to the south we see a butte in the form of a fallen cross. It is several miles away, but it presents no inconspicuous figure on the landscape and must be many hundreds of feet high, probably more than 2,000 [600m]. We note its position on our map and name it* ***"Buttes of the Cross"***.

Actually, it's 2 buttes, one in front of the other. The only place it looks like one butte is at or near the mouth of Millard Canyon. You would have noticed it as you drove in this direction.

For the energetic, you could climb up the **Devils Slide Trail** from this point, instead of coming down from The Spur. To do that, see **Map 5** with **Horsethief Canyon**. Use that description, but in reverse order.

Anderson Bottom

About 3 kms south of, or before you arrive at the mouth of Millard Canyon, you'll cross a minor wash near the base of the Buttes of the Cross. It has no official name, but we'll call it **Anderson Canyon Slot**. Somewhere on the south side of this wash stop and park. Pay attention to this and your other map, because there's a **cattle trail** not far away, which is only one of 2 ways down to **Anderson Bottom**, and to all other river bottoms shown on this map from the north.

The other way down is via Anderson Canyon Slot. It probably has the best slot in the entire White Rim Sandstone. There are several potholes and 6 dropoffs, and most people can get down OK, but one drop near the end is a one-way slide. One person can get down, but not back up. To upclimb that part you'll need about 3 people to first push, then pull the others with a short rope. If going to Anderson Bottom, go down the slot, and come back up the cattle trail.

To find the **Anderson Bottom Trail** from the road, head about due east from where the road crosses Anderson Wash. You'll be walking on the White Rim Sandstone slickrock most of the way. There's no

Map 8, Under the Ledge: Mouth of Millard Canyon, and Anderson, Valentine & Cabin Bottoms, Turks Head & L. Horse C.

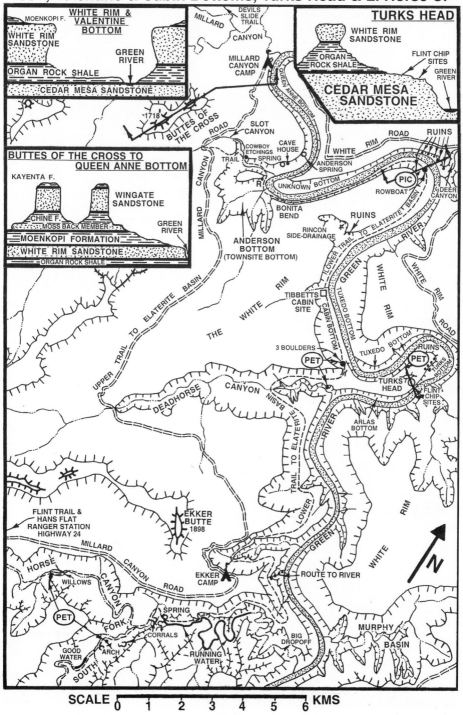

WHITE RIM & VALENTINE BOTTOM

MOENKOPI F.

WHITE RIM SANDSTONE

ORGAN ROCK SHALE

GREEN RIVER

CEDAR MESA SANDSTONE

TURKS HEAD

WHITE RIM SANDSTONE

ORGAN ROCK SHALE

FLINT CHIP SITES

GREEN RIVER

CEDAR MESA SANDSTONE

BUTTES OF THE CROSS TO QUEEN ANNE BOTTOM

KAYENTA F.

WINGATE SANDSTONE

CHINLE F.

MOSS BACK MEMBER

MOENKOPI FORMATION

GREEN RIVER

WHITE RIM SANDSTONE

ORGAN ROCK SHALE

DEVILS SLIDE TRAIL

MILLARD

CANYON

MILLARD CANYON CAMP

QUEEN ANNE BOTTOM

1718

BUTTES OF THE CROSS

ROAD

SLOT CANYON

COWBOY ETCHINGS

CAVE HOUSE

SPRING

TRAIL

R

UNKNOWN BOTTOM

WHITE

RIM

ROAD

RUINS

PIC

ROWBOAT

DEER CANYON

ANDERSON SPRING

BONITA BEND

RUINS

RINCON SIDE-DRAINAGE

GREEN

RIVER

MILLARD

CANYON

ANDERSON BOTTOM (TOWNSITE BOTTOM)

LOWER TRAIL TO ELATERITE BASIN

WHITE

RIM

THE

TIBBETTS CABIN SITE

3 BOULDERS

PET

DEADHORSE

CANYON

BASIN

UPPER TRAIL TO ELATERITE BASIN

CABIN BOTTOM

TUXEDO BOTTOM

TUXEDO BOTTOM

RUINS

PET

TURKS HEAD

TURKS BOTTOM

FLINT CHIP SITES

GREEN

WHITE

RIM

WHITE

RIM

ROAD

RIVER

ARLAS BOTTOM

TRAIL TO ELATERITE BASIN

LOWER

GREEN

RIVER

WHITE

RIM

N

FLINT TRAIL & HANS FLAT RANGER STATION HIGHWAY 24

EKKER BUTTE 1898

EKKER CAMP

ROUTE TO RIVER

MILLARD

CANYON

ROAD

HORSE

CANYON

WILLOWS

FORK

SPRING

CORRALS

PET

GOOD WATER

ARCH

SOUTH

RUNNING WATER

BIG DROPOFF

MURPHY

BASIN

SCALE 0 1 2 3 4 5 6 KMS

79

Buttes of the Cross as seen from the Green River immediately upstream from the mouth of **Millard Canyon**. You can just see the beginning of a good riffle in the water ahead.

Anderson Bottom as seen from the White Rim on the opposite side of the Green River. In the background right are the **2 buttes** which, if seen from the north, resembles a cross; as in **Buttes of the Cross**. The **frog** in the rincon is to the left, and the **2 springs & cave house** to the right.

The lower end of **Anderson Canyon** has one of the best **slot** in this book. The author is wareing knee & elbow pads, but they normally aren't needed in this slot.

sign of a trail out on top, so you'll first have to make you way to the rim of the Anderson Rincon. Once on the rim, look for a shallow drainage just south of where Anderson Slot enters this abandoned meander of the Green River. Walk east into that shallow drainage then as it drops off the rim, ledge-walk to the left or northwest and be looking for Ned Chaffin's signature from 1935. Soon you'll see where the constructed part of the trail heads down to the bottom. Near the bottom is a metal gate which used to keep cows either in or out of Anderson. Karl Tangren put that gate in at the bottom of the trail. He had Glen Holyoak of Moab build it in 1957, then Karl took it down and installed it on the trail.

From the very bottom of the trail, turn right and just across the canyon on the opposite wall will be a panel of **cowboy etchings**; some of these look like cattle brands. This is about 300m from the end of Anderson Slot. From there head south & east out of the canyon and into the flats.

But first a history of Anderson Bottom, which was originally known as **Townsite Bottom**. This river bottom is an abandoned meander or rincon, plus a narrow strip of flat land extending to the northeast, which includes an old field once used by Albert I. Anderson and later in time by Ralph Miller, Bill & Ray Tibbetts, then Karl Tangren.

The first documented visit to this place by a whiteman was John W. Powell on July 17, 1869. On that day the first Powell Expedition named the tight curve of the river **Bonita Bend**. Powell's second expedition passed this way on September 12, 1871. In **F.S. Dellenbaugh's** account in *A Canyon Voyage*, he states: *the bottom lands along the river had evidently been utilized by the aboriginal inhabitants for farming, as fragments of pottery occasionally found indicated their presence here in former days.*

One of the best sources for the early history of the whiteman's use of this bottom is from the testimonies in the **Colorado River Bed Case hearings** which determined who owned the minerals rights under the river beds of the Green & Colorado Rivers. One of those who testified was **Albert Isaac (A.I.) Anderson**. He was 74 years old at the time of the hearings, which were in the 1920s. He explained that he had first arrived in the country in 1908 at Hanksville and had made a quick trip to Elaterite Basin to look for oil. Later that same year he went to Green River and went downstream in boats: *There were four of us in the party and we went from the town of Green River down to the mouth of Miller's Canyon [now called Millard Canyon] with two rowboats..... [They were met there by another group with horses and then went into Elaterite Basin, or as it was called then by sheepherders, "Big Water".]*

I again returned to Green River in January of the next year. My next river trip was from Green River to Townsite Bottom in a rowboat with Bill Coyle and others..... This trip was taken about March, 1909. Later I made the trip from Townsite Bottom upstream to Green River in that rowboat. I would row and tow going upstream.....

On one trip when I went down to Townsite Bottom in a rowboat, I came back with Ross Wheeler in his boat. I [once] made an upstream trip from Townsite Bottom with a man named Ed Prothero. I also took a trip with Mr. Wolverton in his boat the Navajo when we went to the Tuxedo Bottom about 110 miles [177 kms] below the town of Green River.

When asked what he was doing right at Townsite Bottom, he stated: *I didn't homestead a place down on the Green River, but it was my intention to do so when I went there [to Townsite Bottom]. I remained there part of two or three seasons and abandoned it. I just had tents there and planted some stuff. I planted sugar cane and within sixty days it grew ten feet eight inches high [3 1/4m]; when it was pretty well up I put in a stake and measured it and it grew three inches [7 1/2 cms] a day. Everything you planted there was wonderful and had excellent flavor. I raised onions, lettuce, turnips and carrots. Those bottoms were **withdrawn from entry by the government in about 1912**. Before then I had* abandoned the place but would have gone back if anything turned up. However, I couldn't stay down there alone and my sons didn't wish to remain down there.

The seasons Anderson talks about were the summers of 1909, 1910 & 1911. The last time he was in Elaterite Basin was in 1911. No reason could be found in his or anyone else's testimony, which would indicated how this place got the name Townsite Bottom. However, old timers in the country say it was named Townsite by this same Albert I. Anderson, who apparently intended to make a settlement of some kind there. There were a lot of other people going down the river at or near the beginning of the peach boom in Green River and Elgin. So whoever named it Townsite Bottom, likely put the name on it sometime in the period after about 1906 or '07.

The towns of Green River and Elgin (east side of the Green River where the Powell Museum is located) started growing fast at that time, about 1906 & '07, because of promoters going back to the midwest and bringing people out to this country. From the railroad in Green River, they were taken downstream by rivermen such as Wolverton, Oppenheimer, Wimmer, Anderson, Ross and others. At that time there was also a concerted effort by various rivermen and other promoters to get the boating and freight hauling business going between Green River and Moab via the rivers.

About the time Anderson was leaving Townsite Bottom, another young man went down there to have a look around. This was **Henry C. Tasker**, who also testified in the *Colorado River Bed Case hearings*. Part of his testimony concerned the Townsite Bottom area. He went with his family to live in Green River as a boy of 17 in 1911. In the hearings Tasker stated:

In 1912, I made a boat trip to Townsite Bottom with Mr. Wolverton.... I made this trip for the purpose of looking the country over with the idea of running stock there, intending to make Valentine Bottom a permanent camp and run our stock on the west side of the river. My father paid Mr. Wolverton to take me down. I did not return with Mr. Wolverton, but remained down there for about two weeks, using a saddle horse with which to look over the country and then riding my horse back up to Green River..... As a result of my investigation I took some stock in there and remained there for about three years [1912-1915]. During that time I made one other motor trip down there with Mr. Anderson. Mr. Anderson took several loads of supplies down to Townsite Bottom for me and on this one occasion I was with him. Mr. Anderson was paid for the service.

The next people to use Anderson Bottom may have been **Eph (and maybe his brother Bill) Moore**, and their nephew **Bill Tibbetts**. Now Eph Moore was born in 1879 and Bill Tibbetts in 1898. Eph would have been there first and Bill apparently went down to help out as a teenager before World War I. He enlisted in the army in February of 1918 and got out in July of 1919. These 2 cowboys ran cows from Turks Head up along the river to the country north of Millard Canyon; and in Horse Canyon and Big Water or Elaterite Basin. The Moores may have moved cattle in when Henry Tasker pulled out (?).

Ray Tibbetts had a funny story to tell about an experience that happened to his father (Bill Tibbetts) at Anderson Bottom sometime between about 1919 & 1923:

He was tellin' me there was one time at Anderson Bottom, which was when he was down on Tuxedo Bottom trappin' and so on, that they went in there after dark on horseback and he said he could smell sheep all over. And he thought, "My god, there's got to be some sheep here." And so they went down to where Anderson Wash runs into the river, which is where they normally camped, and sure enough there was a herd of sheep there. So that night they gathered up 2 or 3 fat sheep by just feeling 'em, and they hung 'em up in a tree, and skinned 'em out.

Now he said there was a lot of these migratory sheep herds going through the country in them days, from Nevada, or wherever. And this herd had moved into his range and he wasn't going to allow it. Anyway, the next morning he looked out from under his bed tarp and he could see a pair of boots standing out there. So he grabbed his six-shooter and just started shootin' at those boots. And he said that ol' boy hurried out of there and gathered up his sheep and moved them back on top and out of there.

He said these guys were all Basque herders, and none of them could speak English. Dad said a lot of times they'd ride into a sheepherder's camp and drink their wine--they all had wine--then they would encourage them to take their herds and move on. They had quite a squabble at that time, everybody was trying to claim a range and find a place to settle with their cattle or sheep.

While Eph Moore and Tibbetts were on the river bottoms and in Elaterite Basin, the Chaffins were over to the south a ways, then when the Moores moved their cattle operations out, then **George Franz** came in and joined the **Chaffins** along the river bottoms and in Elaterite. The late **Ned Chaffin** recalls bits and pieces of the history of this area, including Anderson Bottom:

Now I know our outfit moved cattle in there in 1919, more to the south, into The Maze and Waterhole Flat and The Cove. Sometimes we did graze Elaterite Basin on account of water. Of course there was already guys by the name of Eph Moore and Bill Tibbetts, out of Moab in there. They come down Between the Rivers and had a boat and swam their horses across the river, then come into there. I don't know when they moved in, but they was there for a long time before we had cattle there.

Eph Moore and the Tibbetts, now there was a family of 'em, they sold out to a guy by the name of George Franz. Now George Franz was very prominent in the oil industry and transportation, and anyway

This is the little one-room cabin the **Chaffins & George Franz** built on **Anderson Bottom** in **1930 or '31.** Billy Hay (left) and Clell Chaffin, in about 1932. This is the cabin Clell Chaffin and his wife Goldie Franz ran to one cold winter night after the Tibbetts Cabin they were staying in on Cabin Bottom burned down. (Ned Chaffin Collection)

he bought part of Eph Moore's range rights out in about 1929 [west side of the Green River]. This was after the Texas Well [located on the Maze Road between Highway 24 & the Hans Flat (Maze) Ranger Station] had been abandoned. It had been abandoned and George Franz got the water rights for that. So Franz moved part of his cattle up in the Elaterite Basin. Maybe that was the early 1930's (?). Now Clell [one of my older brothers] married George Franz's stepdaughter, Goldie Franz. Now he must have married her in the winter of 1931-'32 because that's the winter I worked for George down on the river and I fed the cattle down there on Anderson and Valentine Bottoms. I spent all winter down there. After Clell & Goldie got married, they ran George's cattle operation there until--I think they got a divorce in 1937. Then George hung on for about a year. He got Charley Hanks to run his outfit for 'im and I guess he wasn't satisfied and so on and so forth, and he [George] sold out in about 1939. That was in Elaterite Basin and Under the Ledge. He moved all his cattle out, sold 'em all--all but one cow he gave to me.

At Townsite Bottom, Dad [Lou Chaffin] and George Franz built a little one-roomed **cabin** [see picture on opposite page] out of clapboard lumber. They floated the stuff down the river in a boat, and Billy Hay was with them. They also took one of those steel **Butler granaries** down there in a boat and set it up. Boy, I spent many a lonesome night in that little ol' cabin. They built it up off the ground a little, and it had a little porch where you could throw your packs and saddles. It was located right underneath the point of the frog; on the east side of the frog [the high point in the middle of a rincon that's shaped like a horses hoof print in wet sand or mud] right near the river. The granary was up on the flat, and over near a big rock where we fixed up a corral.

Then when Franz moved out, we moved north into Elaterite Basin, and that made a pretty good little operation. So up until 1939, we were on Waterhole Flat, Ernies Country and The Cove, then after 1939, we were also in Elaterite Basin and more along the river. Altogether, we was in that country from 1919 until October 27, 1944. (But they were still rounding up horses the next year--read more below).

There were several boys in the Chaffin family and Faun was the oldest. He was born in 1898 and lived to be over 100). He spent more time with the cows than any of the other boys. Much of the time he was alone. The late **Kenny Allred** formerly of Moab saw him from across the river on many occasions, but only once did they actually meet face to face. Kenny recalls that experience:

The first time I ever met Faun Chaffin, Buddy [?] and me was camped on Queen Anne Bottom, and we had crossed the river and came around on horseback and down onto Anderson. We then left our horses at Anderson and swam across the river to Queen Anne's. Anyway, the next morning real early we got out of there and swam back across the river and got our horses and headed down there and old Faun and some young fella they had workin' for 'em, was camped there. We seen this young fella comin' out to gather their horses and when he seen us he broke and ran for camp. They had some buckskins [deer], 2 or 3 head laying out there all butchered out. In those days nobody paid much attention to that kind of stuff [poaching]. But they didn't have any idea who we was--coming in there at the break of dawn! That was my first time to meet Faun Chaffin. After that I spoke with him from across the river, but I never got close enough to shake hands with him again. More of the Chaffin's history in the country will be discussed later on.

The old cabin on Anderson is long gone and so is the granary. When Clell and Goldie F. Chaffin were staying in the little cabin on Cabin Bottom sometime in the mid-1930's, it burned down and they lost everything (read more about this on **Cabin Bottom**). So they had to rush up to the cabin on An-

The **cave house** that **Karl Tangren** blasted out of the wall at **Anderson Bottom**. This was built in about **1958**. The original purpose was to make a place to live in, but after Karl left and the national park came in, it was used as a storage place for the CNP/NPS. They still have stuff/junk in there.

derson Bottom, stayed one night, then headed out to get more supplies.

After the Chaffins left Under the Ledge in 1944-'45, the French sheepmen, the **Moyniers, Leon & Pierre** out of Price, Utah, moved in with sheep. It's not clear just where they ran their sheep, but it was mostly south of the Flint Trail and in Ernies Country, Andy Miller Flat and Waterhole Flat. But they likely used some of the river bottoms at times as well.

The next people who made an attempt to do anything on Anderson Bottom was **Ralph Miller** and his son-in-law **Ray Tibbetts** of Moab. They went in there in 1955 and hoped to live there and build a ranch. Ray tells a little about some of his experiences on Anderson Bottom:

When we were there Dad said [Albert I.] Anderson settled Anderson Bottom and his old ditches were still there. Those are the ditches he put in. In fact we put our ditches on the same line as he'd run his. We were there before Karl Tangren went down. My wife didn't want to go down and wouldn't go, and we had our new baby and I mean that sucker was out in the woods.

*There was a **cabin** [that the Chaffins & George Franz built in 1930 or '31] right on the edge of the river. We picked that up and put it on a trailer and took it over to the north and put it under that ledge, and we kept our saddles and stuff like that in it. But when I was back down there with the park service, and that was after 10 years or better, there wasn't anything there that I recognized other than Karl had shot out some rooms and they had a few things back in there, but they burned and cleaned up ever' damn thing else.*

*I developed a **spring** there. I took a shovel up there and made a cut all the way down clearn to bedrock and I hit a mud seam. So I went and got me a big long tamarisk and started shovin' it back in there and pretty quick that water started running out. Later I got a compressor and shot back in there with dynamite and created a nice tank of water and piped it right down to where we had our tent house.*

*Now the old **Anderson Spring**, it was maybe a 100 yards [90m--actually closer to 150m] to the northeast from where Karl later shot that hole in there, and there was a little spring come out on the same mud seam and it was only about 10 foot [3m] off the ground and it dripped into a barrel and it was always full of water. That's where an old tent and all the old camps used to be. There was a few prospectors that camped at Anderson and they landed an airplane in there too. My dad was one of 'em and they camped where the old Anderson Spring was. Well, when we went there, there was still the signs of a tent; it had just caved in and there was 2 barrels of canned goods there, and that was left by these prospectors. My dad and 2 guys had this airplane, Fred Frazier and Harold Provancho, so they made that their camp. When we got there, we ate a few of the cans but not too many, because they was gettin' a little age on 'em.*

In 2011, Ray told this writer that in 1955, and as he and his father-in-law, Ralph Miller, were trying to get something going down on Anderson Bottom, that he was given a couple of different barges by **Monte Mason**, the oil man who drilled for oil down on MGM Bottom (the Discovery Well site) in the 1950's & '60's. They took the barges down there to be used as a ferry. They took the compressor and shot all their equipment across the river with those. But later, the first barge was either untied and let loose by somebody, or high water took it away. The second boat was also lost. Ray also said: *The worst thing about Anderson Bottom was, you had to cross that river when you got down there.*

After Miller and Tibbetts had a try at it and gave up, **Karl Tangren** of Moab moved in. His story of Anderson Bottom went like this:

It was Ralph Miller who went to the state land board and leased Anderson Bottom. Anderson, Fawn Chaffin and Moore's were there before. They were just there grazing--it was open range in those days. And when the Taylor Grazing Act came into effect [July 27, 1934] them sheepmen out of Price and Wellington [Moyniers] got their permits [1944-'45] for the country in down Under the Ledge. That's from down the Flint Trail and up to Millard Canyon and all that country, so nobody did anything with it for years, other than for them sheep coming in there.

The State come in later years and said, everything back to the possible high water mark is State land. Then they started issuing them leases. Old Bill Tibbetts, that's Kenny Allred's half brother, had been all over that country and his son Ray had married Ralph Miller's daughter. Ralph was always wantin' to get in the cow business, so Bill took them to Anderson Bottom. He showed 'im around and Ralph Miller went through the process with the state land board and got a lease on it. That was in about the mid-1950's. Ralph Miller is the one who had the money and actually leased it. Ray's dad Bill knew the country, so they went down there and they was going to build a big cattle ranch. Ray was going to run it. But it never panned out. Ray's wife wouldn't go down there and live, and Ray said he wasn't going down there alone, so Miller ended up putting it up for sale.

Ralph Miller had that for 2 years and they had cleared it and leveled it and made the ditches and everything. The summer before I went there he had it all planted to corn, and then he went in there in August sometime and broadcast winter wheat, and then melon seed and squash seed--I seen banana squash that long, and big old hubbard squash one man couldn't pack. And it was growing all out there in the field corn, and that corn was as high as this ceilin' and a lot of those stocks had 2 big ol' ears on 'em. The Chaffins had put a steel granary there so they picked just enough corn to fill that steel granary, then they just went out on the range and brought about 50 head of steers & heifers that they was goin' ship and they run in there all winter. And they come out of there in March lookin' just like they'd come out of a feed lot. Man they was grain fed! But them ol' cows was eatin' that corn and spillin' a lot of it so they went over to Grand Junction and bought 60 head of hogs and turned them in there with 'em, along with about 60 head of old ewes, and that whole outfit wintered right there on Anderson Bottom.

*So I ended up buying his lease and whatever stuff he had down there. They had the pump there, and I bought that. I had about 100 acres [40 hectares]. We bought that in **February of 1958**. He had that old tractor and a little equipment, and some horses and 212 head of cattle. My brother bought the cattle and I bought the lease and ranch and stuff. Then I run the cattle for my brother on shares. He bought 212 cows and I had another 50 cows I threw in with 'em. Then my 2 other brothers who lived in Provo, had another 50 head of cattle running up there around Mule Bottom and up through the mouth of Horseshoe Canyon.*

*When I first went to Anderson Bottom we took a compressor down there and we shot through them ledges [to make that **cave house**]. Also, we went down to the river and fixed it so we could pull our barge in there in low water and load or unload cattle. When we went in there, we planted about 20 acres [8 hectares] into pasture, right there from the wash back toward the house. Then we cross-fenced it and all that upper end we planted into hay one year.*

I had a hired man down there and he was irrigating and takin' care of it, and I was working out at the [Atlas] mill in Moab. The only time I got down there was on weekends. One year just before the Friendship Cruise, somebody came to me and wanted me to haul 6 barrels of gas down there for 'em so they'd

Left The **spring** that Ray Tibbetts started, then Karl Tangren blasted out to create a box-like **tank** that's hidden in the middle of this picture. The pipe is still there. **Right** About 60m to the right of the spring is the **cave house**, and about 150m beyond that is **Anderson Spring** which is shown here.

Just below center is the **metal gate** that Karl Tangren put in at the lower end of the Anderson Bottom Trail. From the gate, the trail runs up the ramp to the upper right, then contours left or south before running west along the bottom of a shallow drainage. Anderson Canyon Slot is to the right.

85

have extra gas. At the time, I was working the afternoon shift out at the mill, so I got up early that morning and loaded the 6 drums of gas in my pickup and took off for Anderson and got there and unloaded it and got in the boat and went across the river to see how old Reese Bradford was doing, and when I got over there he said "I'm quitin'". So he got his suit case and he rode back to town with me.

And that old hay and oats was up and all ready to cut. I had figured to cut it that weekend, but old Reese quit, so that weekend I and some other guys went to Anderson and got our horses and went out on the rim and rode for a couple of days and gathered about 60-70 head of cattle and brought 'em in there in that field and they summered there. So we never did put up a spear of hay and never replanted it. We just let it die. That's the only time I every planted a crop there; because I just didn't have the time to take care of it. But we did keep that 20-25 acres [8-10 hectares] of pasture out in front of the house. Every time we'd go down there we'd start the pump and get the water to runnin' out onto the pasture, so it was always good pasture for our saddle horses and then I had about 50 head of sheep that I'd run in it in the summer time. We had the pasture fenced from the rincon. The sheep just run in the pasture in summer and then in the winter we'd wean the lambs and kick the ewes out there in the big rincon to the southwest. They wintered right in the rincon.

Back to Reese Bradford: He came up here from California and stayed there about a year at Anderson Bottom for me. I had a tent house there in front of the spring, but I guess later the Park Service went in there and took it out. It had a floor and we boarded up 4 feet [1.25m] and put a tent over it. Then we piped the water out of the spring and we had a sink and running water. It was good water when we were there. We hauled a compressor over there on the barge and just mined it out, just like you'd drill in a mine. Just drilled in there and blasted it, and mucked it out. Anyway, that's where Bradford stayed.

Karl then told about an experience during the **1st year** of the **Friendship Cruise**. He and Kenny Allred were on Mule Bottom [the bottom just west and across the river from Hardscrabble Campsite] hunting for a lost cow. At that same time there was a bunch of guys across the river at Hardscrabble Bottom trying to launch a boat where a seismograph crew had built a little road down to the river. They were going to take supplies on down to Anderson Bottom to prepare for the big boating (the annual Friendship Cruise) event the next day. George Burk had a new boat with a new 100 hp Mercury outboard on it. Bates Wilson, who later became the first superintendent of Canyonlands National Park, was there too along with a bunch of other guys. Karl tells what happened next:

And when they backed that boat down into the water, they didn't unload it, and it just sank. It had too much of a load in it and it just sunk right there on the trailer--brand new 100 hp engine!

Then their stuff started floatin' out of the boat and takin' off downriver. And right on that corner was a big eddy. And old Bates had got excited and jumped in and was trying to save some of his stuff. And that old eddy would grab him and swing him out in the river and then it would suck him back in. Some of those guys on shore had an old chain they had things tied down with, and they picked that up and threw that to old Bates.

Finally, I and ol' Kenny over on Mule Bottom, heard somebody over there a hollering help, help! So we run over there and jumped in our boat and came across the river and picked Bates up in the boat. After that we got in the boat and went on down the river to Fort Bottom and picked up everything we could find floatin'. We came back up there and pulled their boat out and loaded everything. I took Kenny

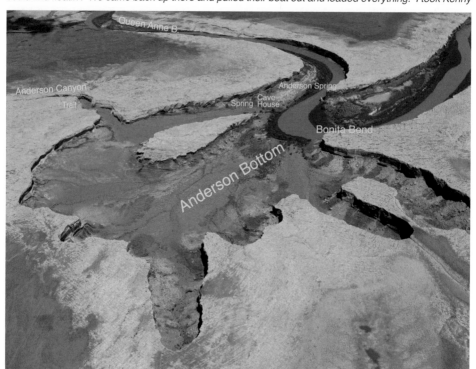

Anderson Bottom as seen from above. In the upper left is **Anderson Canyon & Slot**, to the right is Bonita Bend, in the middle is the Anderson Rincon. At one time it was known as **Townsite Bottom**.

86

back up to Mineral Bottom--he live up there then--and finally I went back and picked up those 3 guys and towed their boat on down to Anderson Bottom. That was the **first Friendship Cruise,** and it was in **1958**. The steaks were all under water, but when we got down there we barbecued 'em anyway.

That was the time I sat there all night long and talked to Bates Wilson about buying Anderson Bottom from Miller. And never once did he ever say, "Karl you ought to back off because I'm going to draw a line across this property and make this a national park". He sat there all night long listening to my dreams of what I was going to do with the place.

It seems like it was 1964 that I had to move things off. They had written me letters and I'd talked to old Bates in the office, and I'd tried to get him to bring that boundary line back here to this corner which would give me my property. And he wouldn't do it. He's the one who drew this original proposal--him and ol' Frank Moss [Utah Senator] and Stewart Udall--who was the Secretary of the Interior then, and they took it up to the President. In all I was on the Green River about 8 years.

Here's what Karl said about what was there in the way of man-made structures when he got there: The only wooden building that was there when I bought it from Miller was a little one-room **cabin** [that Chaffins and George Franz built in 1930-'31] and they had moved it about 200 yards [180m] west from where the spring [and Karl's cave house] is now.

Miners had been there before Miller and built a tent house and it had a wooden floor and wooden sides up about 4 feet [1.25m] and then a tent stretched out over the top of it. That's what Miller was usin' for a home when I got there and that's all we ever used while we was there. That was just below the spring. And that cabin was down along that ledge about 200 yards [180m]. We used it for a chicken coop and we built a fence from right there to the river and fenced that bottom off so we could keep the sheep and the saddle horses in there on that pasture. Miller and Tibbetts was usin' it for a chicken coop when we got there so we just kept usin' it for that too.

That **steel granary** [that the Chaffins assembled in 1930 or '31] was there when the Millers was there, and it was still there when I bought it from them. But Kenny Allred and Dutch Gerhard were employed by the park and after they run me out of there, they told me that they went down there with a bunch of kids, like the park gets in the summer time, and they dismantled that steel granary and I had a corral with 8 foot [2 1/2m] slabs--that was slab lumber, and they torn all that down and dug big holes and put it in and buried it. That granary was put together by bolts and they're in sections. They were called Butler Granaries.

Here are the things to see at Anderson Bottom today. If you need water, the **spring** is a possible place to stock up. It's on the north side of the rincon--see map. The NPS has let it deteriorate--and probably wouldn't recommend you drink the water--but nothing can get up there to contaminate it except for birds or other people! You have to climb up to it from the pipe that's still standing up down under the trees; that's where Miller & Tibbetts, and Karl had their tent house. About 60m east of the pipe and spring is where Karl Tangren blasted a **cave house** out of the solid rock and put a metal door on the front. The NPS used to store their portable toilets there, which were used only during the Friendship Cruise, which is still held on the Memorial Day weekend (now days many people take 4 days, or more, to do the cruise). About another 150m north of the cave house or storeroom is Anderson Spring. It still has dripping water and if you have a pan or two, you could collect enough to camp with.

On the northeast corner of the hump or frog in the middle of the rincon, and up a little on the south side, is an **Anasazi granary**, but it's not much to look at. On the south side of Anderson Bottom, you'll find a grove of cottonwood trees and a large slab of cement [in 8/2011 that whole section was smothered with tamarisk--good luck finding it!]. Karl Tangren says that for the first 2-3 years of the Friendship Cruise, they would go down to Anderson, build some fires and have a steak fry on the Saturday night of Memorial Day Weekend. Many people would camp there too, then finish the cruise the next day. But one problem they had was, it would sometimes get too windy and if a big sand twister came in at the wrong time, it would cover everything with sand. Finally they decided to pour a cement floor that they could dance on, as well as offer shelter and a better place for the annual steak fry. So the people who ran the cruise, the Chamber of Commerce of Green River & Moab, gave Tangren $200 to pour a slab of cement, and to do the steak fry. They poured a 20 x 20m slab of cement with bolts placed around the outside. Then they built a detachable roof to go over it. This offered shade and it kept the sand from blowing in. After the Cruise, they would take it down each year and store it over by the spring. Read more on **The Friendship Cruise** in the author's other book, ***River Guide to Canyonlands National Park and Vicinity, 2nd Edition***. It came out in 2/2011.

Valentine Bottom

From the southeastern side of Anderson Bottom and right where the cliff comes down almost to the river, and directly across from Unknown Bottom, is a bench running all the way from Anderson to the next wide spot along the river called **Valentine Bottom**. Running along that slope is an old cattle trail, some of which may still be visible. This is one of the more visible parts of an old stockman's trail which begins in the north around Twomile Canyon, The Frog and the lower end of Horseshoe Canyon, and runs south along the west bank of the Green River all the way past Deadhorse Canyon, into the middle section of Horse Canyon and ending in Elaterite Basin. Normally the only place you'll see any sign of this long trail is where it climbs up over ledges or is squeezed in between the river and a cliff. Karl Tangren used to call this part running from Anderson south into Horse Canyon, the **Lower Trail** to Elaterite Basin.

After walking about 3 1/2 kms from Anderson, you'll come to Valentine Bottom. It got its name from the first family who tried to settle there. Some sources have suggested they were attempting to build a hunting lodge of some kind (?). The very best place to learn about this family is from several testimonies from the ***Colorado River Bed Case hearings*** of 1929. Cass Hite's brother, **Homer J. Hite**, stated in part of his testimony:

I made a trip on the Green River either in 1892 or 1893...... I had a flat boat.....and I made the trip in August. I made the trip to help a settler named **Valentine** down the river to Valentines Bottom. We were two days going to Wheeler's ranch. We took two milk cows on the boat. We had to unload them because we could not get across the bar near the railway bridge at Greenriver, and we drove them to Wheeler's ranch. We loaded them again, and just below Wheeler's ranch struck again and took the cows off and they were driven 20 or 30 miles [30 to 45 kms] down the river, where we camped and loaded the cattle and they went on down to their location.

.....The persons who comprised the family of Valentines was, Mr. Valentine, his son, three daughters and two grand-daughters. One grand-daughter was about twelve and the other was about seven.....The women and children were in row boats. We used the largest flat bottom boat for the purpose of carrying the household goods and equipment and supplies, and we rode the cows part of the way in it. The row boats followed the big boat.

I made arrangements with the Wheeler boys to meet me at my point of destination with horses. The boats that were taken down were kept by Mr. Valentine for his own use down there.

Joe Ross was another witness in the **Colorado River Bed Case hearings** and part of his testimony went like this:

I was on the river in September, 1893. The purpose of that trip was to bring the Valentine family to Greenriver. I went down the river in a rather large row boat..... There were four besides myself on the trip coming up..... We were about 7 days going to Wimmer's ranch [at the time it was the Wheeler Ranch, but it's now called the Ruby Ranch]. We did not go to Greenriver because we were loaded too heavy to go up over the swift water in the gravel rapids. We got to Wimmer's ranch by rowing with two sets of oars at times and towing with ropes. From Wimmer's ranch the party proceeded to Greenriver by wagon and I rowed and towed the boat up to Greenriver.

The Valentines had been living at Valentine's Bottom for about a year, from September one year to September the next. They got their supplies from Greenriver. Their son would come out with a boat and take supplies in to them by boat. He would come to Greenriver from Valentine's Bottom and go back in a boat.

Joe Ross ended up marrying one of the Valentine girls. Her name was Ella, and she too testified in the same hearings. She stated that: after leaving Valentines Bottom we went to Greenriver and I have lived there most of the time since 1893 until 1915.

No one alive today is sure about what the Valentine's lived in while on the river. However, in the **June 4, 1893** issue of **The Denver Republic**, it ran an article by Lute H. Johnson. He was a newspaper man who was invited to go downriver on the steamboat **Major Powell**. This was the first steamboat on the Green or Colorado River in this part of the country. Read more about the Major Powell in the author's other book, **River Guide to Canyonlands National Park and Vicinity, 2nd Edition.** In that article by Johnson, nothing is mentioned about the Valentines, but it does show a sketch of their camp. It clearly shows a log cabin and a large tent beside it and several people standing around.

The author walked all around that bottom, and couldn't find anything in the way of a cabin or ruins of a cabin. Ned Chaffin camped on Valentine Bottom for several months in the winter of 1931-32, and he was all over the bottom too. He said he never saw anything that might indicate the location of their cabin or camp. It surely burned down with no sign left of its location.

About halfway between the cliffs on the west and the river on the east (see map) is an old **rowboat**. It's located on what was in the past, the old river bank. Below it to the northeast, the ground is much lower, indicating the river may have been right there when this old boat was dragged to its final resting place. In 2012, the sides of the boat were still standing, but the bottom was totally rotted away. On one side there were large letters reading U S ---?. It's about 3 1/2-m long and a meter wide. It's old, but it may, or may not have belonged to the Valentines (?). It more likely was brought there by George Franz and the Chaffins in about 1930 when they brought material to build a cabin and steel granary downriver in boats. They also used a rowboat to get to Deer Canyon--read more below.

One last interesting thing to see on Valentines are some **ruins** and a very fine **pictograph panel**. From where the old rowboat is, walk southwest about 300m. As you walk, look at the cliff in front of you. High up, and at the contact point between the White Rim Sandstone above, and the Organ Rock Shale below, will be one very visible **Anasazi granary**. Head for that. As you near, it will be obvious that part of the ledge where that

The **rowboat** on **Valentine Bottom**. It's possible it could have belonged to the Valentines which dates back to 1892-'93; but that's a long time ago. But more likely it was brought there by the Chaffins in about 1930 (?). It surely was the boat the Chaffins used to get to Deer Canyon to rope deer, as described in the story told on the opposite page.

granary sits has peeled off. When you get right up under the cliff, you'll be able to see the remnants of another granary and in between the two, a small panel of **pictographs**. You'll now need a long ladder to view these up close. You can however get a little closer by walking to the north a short distance, then climb straight up part of the lower wall. This will put you on the same ledge as the granaries, but you can't get out to the pictographs. At the farthest point you can go on that ledge are some **cowboy signatures**. *Ned Chaffin and Bill Wells were there, as was L.H. Green on Sept. 11, [19]07*. Green was one of the men who operated the steam powered pump at Little Valley south of Green River when the peach boom was just getting started.

Just across the river to the north and northeast of the wide part of Valentine Bottom are a number of small **Anasazi granaries** and other **ruins**. The only way you can get there is by boat, but if you have a pair of binoculars, you can see them rather well from Valentine.

Just across the river to the east of the wide part of Valentine Bottom is a little short side-canyon coming in from the north and east. None of the maps have named it, but the Chaffin's hung the name **Deer Canyon** on it. Chaffins called it that because they could go over there any time and poach a deer. Also, Ned Chaffin remembered at least 3 deer being roped in there. It's a box canyon so the cowboys had an advantage. He also stated that a good horse is much faster than, and will run right over, a deer. He said that his brother Clell and an old Texas cowboy roped one each there in the early 1930's. Then in 1940, when they were down there during the annual deer hunt, Faun Chaffin roped another one. He has movie pictures to prove that stunt.

Regarding **Deer Canyon**, roping deer and the **Chaffins selling out**, here are some short quotes from the diary of **Edwin MG Seely** that was printed in a Seely family newsletter, **A Legacy of Love** for *May, 2008* (edited by Montel & Katherine Seely). Edwin, who from Mt. Pleasant, either volunteered or got roped into going out for a week to help Lou, Faun & Clell Chaffin roundup the last of their horses after they sold out **October 27, 1944**. They had a year to roundup all their livestock, both cattle and horses. Part of that diary went like this:

10/26/1945: ....I was not too thrilled over this trip with some of the Chaffin family down "Under the Ledge."....Lou Chaffin was 72 years old. He had a glass eye and was kinda tight (didn't talk much). We traveled 50 miles of San Rafael Desert [in a pickup]. At sundown we were met by his two sons, Clel and Faun, with 3 pack mules and 10 riding horses. We had a dutch oven evening meal there in the sand. 10/27/1945: ....Chaffins had sold out and they were just gathering their horses. The cattle had been moved out a while ago.... 10/28/1945: The four of us rode up River to Deer Canyon. We went across the Green River in a boat they had in the willows, the horses swimming behind us. I drove the deer out of the bushes toward them. Faun roped a 5-point buck; I shot a two-point buck. This was their last annual affair of roping deer during deer season--because they were selling out to the French family [the Moyniers of Price]. We went back across the river in the boat and packed the two deer to camp in the dark. 10/29/1945: We went to their cabin and steel granary (which they had floated down the Green River from the town of Green River), and a corral made with heavy iron cable. We branded a couple of horses. We kicked five horses across the river, and Clel and I drove a cow, calf, and a bull up the Ledge trail--the 1100-foot [335m] cliff [believed to be the North Trail]... We were late getting back to camp--and so tired. I ate too much supper. I drank water from the river. They just drank beer and wine. I'll look back upon this trip later as a good experience. 10/30/1945: ....We had 49 head of horses, mules and a couple of jackasses going out. We left a band of donkeys. It was a full day, trailing them out..... And I was cussing myself for getting in on a deal like this--which, by the way, had no pay attached. 10/31/1945: The father, Lou Chaffin was in the pickup, and Faun and I were with the horses. I rode across 25 miles [40 kms] of San Rafael desert on a rough-gaited horse with a thrown shoe. I was plenty shook up when we reached the ranch which is another 25 miles from Green River. The Chaffins are going to round up more horses in the area. They decided to drive to Green River for the night..... 11/1/1945: No one the Chaffins approached would go back out to help them for a couple of days. I sat on my bedroll and waited for the 2 a.m. bus [back to Mt. Pleasant].....

It seemed that poor town boy Edwin Seely bailed out early on this one. In this day and age, few people are willing to work as hard as the Chaffins and other ranchers did just to make an honest living!

If you walk south, then southeast along the west bank of the Green River from the widest part of Valentines, you'll see a short **side-canyon** (with **rincon**) coming in from the right (along the way, be on the lookout for an old corral the Chaffins used in the early 1930's. It will be up against the cliff before you reach the little side-canyon). This would be considered the lower end of Valentine Bottom. Walk northwest toward the mouth of this little side-drainage; once there, look to the right. Not far away you'll see **2 little alcoves** facing southeast near the corner of the wall. Nestled high above and on some nar-

row ledges in the Organ Rock Shale will be about 3 well-preserved structures, maybe more. The people who made these must have used log ladders and ropes to get up there, because it'll take a tough climber to get to them now. Just

Dave Lee & Faun Chaffin at 11am on October 21, 1939. This picture was taken on **Valentine Bottom**, but the 3 deer were likely shot in **Deer Canyon** (?) across the river to the east.

This picture was taken on **Valentine Bottom** but the deer was shot across the river in Deer Canyon in October, 1940. From L to R: Faun Chaffin, Loren Milton and Herb Webber.

around the corner from these ruins is a very small rincon, which seems a little out of place--it certainly wasn't the river that made it.

Those ruins near the mouth of that little rincon (see foto below) must be the place **Karl Tangren** talked about one day with the author: *I never was interested in seeing those **moki houses** but my one brother was. If you go down toward the lower end of Valentine Bottom there's a little canyon, and there's a pinnacle out in the middle with a big balanced White Rim rock sittin' on top of it. There's a moki house there and you can see it from the river. And one day my brother said, "We're goin' to get up there where nobody's ever been before". So we hauled aluminum ladders down there on a boat and wired 'em together and 2 or 3 of us held 'em and my younger brother climbed up. And he got up there and got in that moki house and says, "Oh shit, we're just a 100 years too late". He pulled out a Prince Albert tobacco can and it had a note in it. It listed the people who had been there back in the 1880's, and 1900! That can is probably still there.*

That's the only moki house I ever attempted to get into until I started doin' trail rides and takin' people out, and then they was payin' me to take 'em out and show 'em these things. I wasn't huntin' cows then, I was gettin' paid for showin' 'em where the moki houses were.

Cabin Bottom

As you walk south from the lower end of Valentine, the river comes over close to the canyon wall. The old trail will be visible there. Soon you'll come to the next little wide place along the west bank of the river. This is called **Cabin Bottom**. As it begins to widen, you'll come to a large grove of cottonwood trees. There are several shaded campsites there and it's a favorite overnight spot for boaters. In about the middle of the grove, you'll see a **chimney** standing by itself, but as of 2012, an old dead cottonwood tree has collapsed and took out part of the chimney structure. The cabin was burned down long ago. Nearby are some parts of an old corral still standing.

Few people seem aware of this cabin or chimney. After asking many people, several were found who knew something about its history. One was Ray Tibbetts. He wasn't

Here are **2 small moki houses**, (more likely granaries) in 2 little alcoves located at the corner of the little **side-drainage** and **Valentine Bottom** as shown on the map. These are the ruins that Karl Tangren talked about above. Getting up to these sites would be a good climb for the best rock climbers today.

90

even born when this cabin was originally built or burned down, but his dad, Bill Tibbetts, told him about it: *The cabin there on what you call Cabin Bottom was built by my dad, he and a guy named Loren Dalton. They made it out of cottonwood logs. That was shortly after World War I. They was trappin' and messin' around down there; him and Loren Dalton and a guy by the name of Al Portus. I don't know either one of them, but I've heard him tell about it. They spent a lot of time trappin' and workin' on the river. A fireplace would have been the only means of heat in any of them cabins. That far down, nobody had stoves or anything. They spent the winters there.* Because of who made it, we'll call this the **Tibbetts Cabin.**

Another story is by the late **Pearl B. Baker**, the gal who grew up on the Robbers Roost Ranch. In a 1961 magazine article (Sorry the name of the magazine has been lost), she states that the Robbers Roost gang--the Wild Bunch--built a cabin on Cabin Bottom in the 1880's, when they were hiding out in the canyons. They apparently ran horses in Horse Canyon to the south. She said the cabin was filled with nice furniture, including an overstuffed chair. However, she also states that Sheriff Joe Bush burned the cabin down in about 1900. It's possible such a cabin was built there and occupied by the Wild

Above One of **3 large boulders** southeast of the **Tibbetts Cabin Chimney** that are covered with rock art. This one is the best: 3 sides are covered with petroglyphs. In the background and to the left a little is **Turks Head**, one of the more prominent landmarks around. Left of it and nearer the river are several Anasazi moki houses & granaries.

Left This is what's left of the cabin **Bill Tibbetts** built on **Cabin Bottom**. It was likely built in the late 1910's or early 1920's, and before the Range War of 1924-'25. It burned down in the winter of 1935-'36 on a cold night. Ned Chaffin's brother Clell and his wife Goldie Franz were staying in it when it burned down. Read the entire story on page 92.

Bunch, but it couldn't have been this particular cabin because **Ned Chaffin** was almost an eye witness to its burning down. Ned is the son of Lou Chaffin who settled on the Chaffin Ranch on the lower San Rafael River in 1929. The family ran cattle on these river bottoms and throughout Under the Ledge from 1919 until October, 1945. He is one of those who called this place Cabin Bottom, and this is what he had to say:

Now that cabin on Cabin Bottom must not have been too old, and it was made out of willow logs--it wasn't made out of cottonwoods like most other cabins in the country. Then willows were thrown on top and then red clay off those hills was put on the top to shed off the moisture. It may have looked like hell if you'd go there in summertime, but it looked like the Taj Mahal when we moved into it in winter.

My brother, Clell Chaffin and his wife Goldie Franz was staying there and they had a bunch of cattle down there they were taking care of in the winter. One day, they went out to take care of the cattle, and when they were riding back to the cabin they could see smoke, and they got home about dark and the cabin had burned down. It had to have been before the winter of 1936-'37, because that was the winter they got divorced. The fire burned up everything including all their clothes; they didn't have nothin' left. So with everything burned up, they just gathered up their horses and went up to Anderson Bottom and stayed that night in the little cabin there. From there they had to go out and get re-supplied. It must have burned down in the winter of 1935-'36.

The Lower Trail to Horse Canyon and Elaterite Basin

At the southern end of Cabin Bottom, the trail follows along on top of the Cedar Mesa Sandstone Formation. At that point the beds are rising to the south, so as you walk south you'll be slowly gaining elevation. Further south, the canyons, bluffs, pinnacles and spires of The Maze, and The Needles across the river, are made of this same Cedar Mesa Sandstone.

There were 2 trails running between the mouth of Millard Canyon or Anderson Bottom, and Elaterite Basin formerly known as Big Water. **Karl Tangren** says: *We just called the trail on top of the White Rim the **Upper Trail**, and the trail running into Horse Canyon below the White Rim [on top of Cedar Mesa Formation] the **Lower Trail** to Horse Canyon or Elaterite Basin.* The Upper Trail he speaks of is about where the Millard Canyon Road now runs; that's from Elaterite Basin to the mouth of Millard Canyon. The Lower Trail runs north from Elaterite Basin into a main or west fork of Horse Canyon; then down that canyon and out upon a bench on the north side of the drainage. It then follows that same bench as it slopes down to the north to Cabin, Valentine and finally to Anderson Bottoms. From there it leaves Anderson Rincon in the northwest corner, rather than following the river to the mouth of Millard Canyon.

From the area just south or downriver from the old Bill Tibbetts Cabin site, the trail becomes more visible. The reason is, the boaters who camp at Cabin Bottom, walk south to some rock art not far away. At one point the Lower Trail passes between **3 large boulders**, all of which are covered with **petro-glyphs**. This is some of the best rock art found along the river. The presence of these etchings indicates this was a much-used trail for hundreds of years. It was used by native aborigines to get to or from the river bottoms to the higher country to the south and west.

Turks Head & Turks Bottom

Just after you walk past the boulders with petroglyphs, you'll reach the corner of Deadhorse Canyon. Before going further, you should take a short side-trip to the very prominent landmark known as **Turks Head**. From the main route simply walk northeast across the land bridge between a large gooseneck bend of the Green River. After about 3 kms, you'll come to Turks Head.

The top part of Turks Head is a remnant of White Rim Sandstone. Just below that are benches of Organ Rock Shale. On this bench south of the high part are lots of chert (flint) lenses, which arise in the lower part of the Organ Rock Formation. Because of the presence of so much chert, this is one of the biggest **flint chip sites** around. Everywhere you look there are piles of man-made flint chips. Chert with a square shape is natural, but anything that's flat, smooth and has sharp edges, could only have been created by man--either Anasazi or Fremont Indians; or maybe the Archaic Indians (?).

You'll find some **rock art**, small storage **granaries** and **habitation structures** there as well. They're located northeast of the highest part of Turks Head, and down at or near the edge of **Turks Bottom**. To get there, simply bench-walk along the southeast side of Turks Head in a northeasterly direction. These sandstone benches gradually slope down. Soon you'll be able to make your way off the rim and down to the bottom below. Once you get down on the flat, then walk southwest along the base of the ledges. As you walk along, you'll find a number of granaries at different levels. Some are right at ground level, while others are found up higher on some ledges. There's at least one panel of **petroglyphs** too. Arrive in the morning hours for best fotos of these ruins. The presence of these half dozen or so granaries in-dicates Turks Bottom was used as a farming area by the Anasazis.

Arla's Bottom and Deadhorse & Horse Canyons

As you walk along the neck of land between Turks Head and the mouth of Deadhorse Canyon, you'll see a long narrow river bottom just to the south. This is what the Chaffin's called **Arlas Bottom**. **Ned Chaffin** said: *the name comes from George Franz's wife, whose name was Arla, and that's where we'd keep our bulls in winter. This would have been during some of the years between 1930 until 1944.* This is also the last place on the river going downstream where cattle were grazed. Downstream from there, the canyon begins to close in and there are no more *"bottoms"* until you get to Spanish Bottom, which is about 8 kms below The Confluence.

From the Turks Head area, walk along the bench into **Deadhorse Canyon**. You'll be on this same bench just below the White Rim all the way. After 2-3 kms, you'll be able to cross the dry wash and begin walking east again. When asked about how this canyon got its name, none of the old timers really had a good answer. Ned Chaffin said he always understood that one or more horses died of thirst while standing on the point high above the river on the south side of Deadhorse Canyon. He claims that: *a horse when he gets real thirsty, will stand and look at that water and won't make any effort to head the canyon and go around and down a trail.* Kenny Allred wasn't sure of the story of the horses being mesmerized by the water below. He thought they probably just got out there after a rainstorm when water was plentiful in the potholes, then as the tanks slowly dried up, it left them to die of thirst.

As you leave Deadhorse Canyon, you'll continue along this slowly rising bench to the south and southeast. Between Deadhorse and Horse Canyon are a couple of short side-canyons, but you simply follow along on the bench around the head of each. In most places you won't see the trail that's shown on the map. Only where the bench is constricted will you see anything resembling a trail. Also, at one

Above Aerial view of **Valentine Bottom** looking southwest. Anderson Bottom is in the upper right, Deer Canyon comes in from the bottom. Notice the white layer of rock which caps the land above the river; that's the White Rim Sandstone.

Left This is the same large boulder as seen on page 91 with all the **rock art**, but in the background here is **Candlestick Tower**.

93

point, not far northeast from the **Ekker Campsite** above, will be a short drainage with a **route to the river.** If you were backpacking along the Lower Trail, this would give you chance to get down to water.

Finally you'll pass around a corner and be able to look down into the lower end of **Horse Canyon.** If you continue around to the west on the bench above Horse Canyon, it will slowly become more narrow. Finally the trail drops off the bench you've been following for so long. At that point you can see several places where someone has done some trail construction. As the trail drops down, you'll follow it into the drainage to the south and to the small stream which flows through the lower end of the canyon. There are no more cattle (or beaver) in this canyon so the water should normally be good to drink as is.

If you were to walk downcanyon, you would eventually come to a **big dropoff** and perhaps an Olympic-sized pool below. This is about 1 km above the river, which means you can't get to the river from inside Horse Canyon. If you walk upcanyon instead, and after about 2 kms, you'll see on the south side a small corral in a tiny natural alcove in the rocks, then a small but impressive cave in the wall, and nearby a panel of petroglyphs. Not far away is where the water begins to flow in Horse Canyon (no matter how dry the drought, there should be some water in Horse Canyon).

Not far beyond where the water starts to flow will be the confluence of **Horse Canyon** and the **South Fork.** Just before the actual junction and on the east side of the canyon will be another indentation in the canyon wall. Near the mouth of it is another old **brush corral** made out of cedar trees just laid on their sides in the sand. Some people think this may date back to the outlaw days (?).

Pearl Biddlecome Baker wrote a magazine article in 1961, part of which centered on Horse Canyon. Here is one paragraph from her story: *While they never had a boat on the river, the Robbers Roosters left their mark on the banks. In the 1880's sometime, they built and furnished a cabin on Cabin Bottom, furnished it lavishly if one can judge by parts of overstuffed sets still lying around the site. They had used Horse Canyon ten miles [16 kms] down the river for a horse pasture for some time, and some pretty fancy horseflesh grazed among the rocks of this canyon. Joe Bush burned the cabin some time about 1900 and the boys had then been long gone. They left three mares in Horse Canyon, however--an old bay mare and two matched gray fillies three or four years old, in about 1905. Tom Baker from Bicknell went in and brought out the horses, making a trail out of the head of the canyon, and turned the two gray mares in for $75.00 on his grocery bill to James Smith. Smith took them to Richfield where they brought a fantastic price, and then sold for a still higher sum for a matched carriage team in Salt Lake City. L.M. [Lou] Chaffin bought the bay mare and two of his best saddle horses; Shine and Hawk, were her colts.* Go back to Cabin Bottom for an explanation on the cabin that Joe Bush may have burned down.

Karl Tangren thought those 2 old cedar brush corrals shown on the map might have been built by the outlaws because they were really old when he saw them in the 1950's. But that's pure conjecture on his part. These corrals are indeed old, and made of cedar trees just laid out on the ground. There's supposed to be a good panel of cowboy signatures in the area of this second corral, but the author never found it. Down closer to the lower corral, he did find one cowboy etching which read, *W.C.A. Aug. 28, 1920.*

If you walk south up the South Fork, you'd enter what is called The Maze, but that will be discussed with the next map. If you end up going all the way to the upper end of **Horse Canyon**, you'll find one good panel of **petroglyphs** on a wall near the dry creek bed with willows about 4 kms from the confluence of Horse & South Fork. There you'll find the initials *Levi Jensen March 30, 1910.*

Up near the head of Horse Canyon, and shown on the next map, will be a constructed **trail** to the top of the White Rim. That trail exits the canyon at a point where the oil sands have broken down the White Rim. This may have been built by Tom Baker (?), or probably even earlier if the outlaw stories are true. That trail can be more easily reached from the road running out to The Maze Overlook and will be discussed with the next map.

If you decide to do a long hike along this old Lower Trail, from Anderson Bottom to the trail leaving upper Horse Canyon, you could leave one vehicle or a mtn. bike at the head of the trail in upper Horse, then drive to the Anderson Bottom Trail and begin walking there--or vise versa. From there you could see all the sites discussed in this chapter and return to your other vehicle or mtn. bike and return to Anderson. Such a trip should be done in the spring or fall only with cooler temperatures, and could take from 2-4 days, depending on how fast you walk and how much exploring you want to do. Take a filter or purification tablets so you can use river water between Anderson Bottom and Horse Canyon. This will eliminate carrying a lot of water.

The author has been to all these sites, mostly by boat, because he never had the vehicle which could handle the handful of places that requires a LR/HC/4WD. He did make it to the mouth of Millard Canyon by mtn. bike once.

One of several small granaries between the butte known as **Turks Head** and the river bottom to the northeast.

From the air looking southwest at **Turks Head**. In the distance is the snow-capped Henry Mountains.

Looking southwest at **Turks Head** in the upper left. Here are 2 granaries, both in tiny nukes.

Above Two **Anasazi moki houses** or dwellings located on the northeast corner of the gooseneck bend which is **Turks Head** and the Turks Head Bottom. These are just up a few meters from the bottom where the people would have farmed.

Right This small panel of rock art is located about 300-400m up **Deadhorse Canyon** from the river.

The lower end of the **South Fork of Horse Canyon** shown as **Good Water** in the lower left-hand side of **Map 8**. **Ekker Butte** dominates the skyline directly north of this watery scene. The jagged-looking upper part of this butte is made of the Wingate Sandstone.

Just beyond **The Wall** and along the first or southern part of the **Chocolate Drops Ridge**, are several **pinnacles**. None of these have names, but they are remnants of the Organ Rock Formation which sits on top of the Cedar Mesa SS, same as in the Land of Standing Rocks. See **Map 9,** page 99.

The Maze: Horse Canyon and 2 South Forks, and Jasper, Shot & Water Canyons

Location & Access The term **The Maze** or **Maze District** is popularly used to describe that part of Canyonlands National Park west of the Green and Colorado Rivers. However, The Maze is actually a much smaller region. The Maze itself is shown on this map and it basically consists of **South & Pictograph Forks of Horse Canyon, Jasper, Shot & Water Canyons**, and the **Land of Standing Rocks**. This country truely is a maze and is one of the more scenic attractions in America. Be sure to have the **MAPS** recommend below, before venturing into this *maze of canyons*.

There are several ways into this country. First, you can come in from Highway 24 north of Hanksville and pass by the Hans Flat or Maze Ranger Station and then to the bottom of the **Flint Trail** (see previous maps on how to get there) make your way to the **3-Way Junction** (see **Maps 1 & 7**); which is the intersection of **The Maze, Hite and Millard Canyon Roads**. If you turn north, you'll descend into **Elaterite Basin**, then will head northeast to end at the **Maze Overlook**, one of the more popular destinations in this region--a distance of 19.6 km (12.2 miles). You'll need a LR/HC/4WD vehicle or a mtn. bike to get down and back up the **steep rough place** at the head of Elaterite Basin (see Map 7).

Or if you head south from there on the **Hite Road**, you'll contour around some cliffs while driving atop some clay beds of the Chinle Formation. After about 7-8 kms, you'll drop off the Black Ledge and end at Waterhole Flat and **Waterhole Junction**--a distance of 11.3 kms (7 miles). At that point you can head west to Sunset Pass & Hatch Canyon; south to Highway 95, Lake Powell & Hite on a good graded road; or head northeast toward the Land of Standing Rocks, Ernies Country and the Doll House. The last little junction near the end of the road at the Doll House is just above Spanish Bottom is 31.1 kms (19.3 miles) from Waterhole Junction--and the road going there is definitely for LR/HC/4WD's only. There are some **terrible rough spots** beginning just before the Teapot Rock Campsite, plus lots of **deep sand** out beyond the Land of Standing Rocks, which is at it's worst after a long dry spell. This road is generally called the **Doll House Road**

Another way into this region is to drive along Highway 95 between Hite & Hanksville, and to a point between **mile posts 46 & 47**. From there drive along the **Hite Road** heading east, then northeast to Waterhole Flat/Junction (53.8 kms/33.4 miles) and beyond.

The last way in would be to drive into **The Needles District** of Canyonlands NP on the east side of the Colorado River to the **Elephant Hill Trailhead**. From there you could walk west and down Red Lake Canyon to the river opposite Spanish Bottom, put your pack on an inner tube, air mattress or one of the new **packrafting light weight boats** (1.5 Kgs) from Alpacka (**alpackaraft.com**), and float & paddle across. By doing this you could get into this mapped area without a 4WD vehicle or driving many kms of rough roads. This is however recommended only for the experienced backpacker and during August or September--if you're going to have your body actually in the cold water. The reason is, if you're swimming, the water would be too high, fast & cold in spring & early summer, too cold in October. The author did this on a 3 day backpack on October 11, 12, and 13, in 1990. He swam the river in the middle part of the day each time and it was during a warm spell, otherwise that would be too late in the season for swimming! Or take a wetsuit if swimming; or **best to use a packraft** from Alpacka so you're not in the water. This would allow you to cross the Colorado anytime of the year.

One more way into this country, and maybe the easiest, is to **boat** or float down the Green River and hike up Water or Powell's Canyons; or stop at Spanish Bottom and hike into the area from there. There's also a way into lower Horse Canyon from the Green River, but that's described better in the book, *River Guide to Canyonlands National Park and Vicinity, 2nd Edition.*

Elevations Chimney Rock, 1696m; Maze Overlook, 1585m; Spanish Bottom, about 1200m.

Water The only spring at or near any of these roads is at Big Water in Elaterite Basin, but it has a bitter taste, and is not recommended for drinking. There are however a number of seasonal seeps or springs in each canyon, as shown on the map. Lower **South Fork**, has running water in one place before it hits the main fork of **Horse Canyon**, then just upcanyon (south) from the bottom of the trail coming down from the Maze Overlook, there's one generally good spring and a little running water (?). There may be seeps in the lower end of **Pictograph Fork**, plus a number of seasonal seeps up both of these upper forks of Horse Canyon. If backpacking, get the latest water report from the ranger station.

There is no reliable water in **Shot**, but there's a good spring in the lower end of the upper part of **Water Canyon**. In lower Water Canyon there is a series of small waterfalls near the trail going down to the river. Some of the minor seeps shown on this map may be dry at times. The lower end of **Horse Canyon**, above the **Big Dropoff**, has year-round running water. There are no cattle or beaver in any of these canyons, so the water should be good to drink as is--but try to take it at the spring source.

Maps USGS or BLM map Hanksville & La Sal (1:100,000); Elaterite Basin, Cleopatras Chair, Turks Head & Spanish Bottom (1:24,000--7 1/2' quads); the plastic Trails Illustrated/National Geographic map Canyonlands National Park (1:70,000); or the plastic Latitude 40° map Moab West (1:75,000).

Main Attractions Some of the best scenery in the world, wild canyons, historic cattle trails, petroglyphs, and the Harvest Scene, perhaps the second best pictograph panel in this country.

Best Time to Hike or Visit Spring or Fall. March, April, May, September and October.

Author's Experiences Over a period of 23 years or so, he has walked every trail in every canyon on this map, and in some cases several times. Lower Horse, Pictograph, Jasper (closed since the 1st Edition of this book came out in 1991!), Shot and Water Canyons were all hiked from his boat on the Green and Colorado Rivers. Later, he biked down the Flint Trail to the Maze Overlook one morning in 2 hours, 45 min., then hiked down into South Fork and up Horse Canyon to the trail out, then road-walked back to the Maze Overlook that same afternoon in about 6 hours. The next morning he hiked up to the head of South Fork, then cross-country to and down Pictograph Fork, then back to the Maze Overlook in 7 hours. That afternoon, he biked back up the Flint Trail to his car in another 3 hours. That was a very long and tiresome day! And not recommended. Nor can you do something like that today because of over regulation on the part of the NPS/CNP.

In 2011, he came up Water from the river, returned via Shot, all in 7 3/4 hours. He parked his Jeep Patriot near Teapot Rock, rode a mtn. bike to the Doll House, hiked out to the overlook of both the Green & Colorado Rivers, returned the same way in 11 1/2 hours. He biked to the Chocolate Drop TH, walked along the ridge, down to the Harvest Scene, up Pictograph to Chimney Rock and back; 11 1/4 hours. He biked from the steep rough place on the Millard Canyon Road down to the Maze Overlook, went down to the Harvest Scene, and back in 8 1/4 hours. In 2012, he again biked along the Millard Canyon Road to the Horse Canyon horse trail, walked down Horse, up South Fork to the Maze Overlook and

Map 9, The Maze: Horse Canyon and 2 South Forks, and Jasper, Shot & Water Canyons

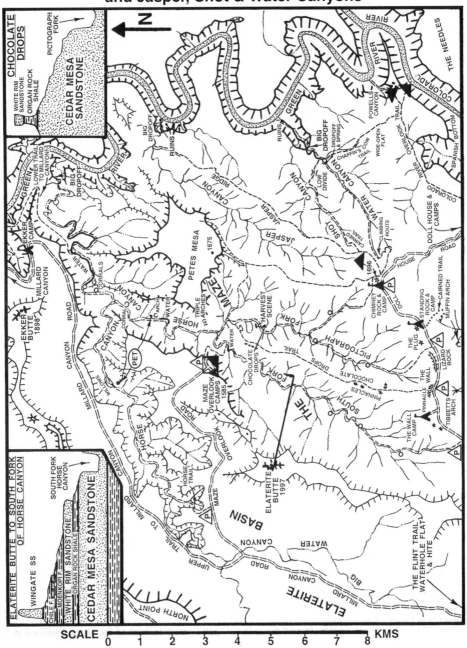

back to his Patriot in 9 hours. There were many hikes up from Spanish Bottom and his boat that aren't worth mentioning.

Hikes from the Maze Overlook

Hikes available from The Maze Overlook Campsite & Trailhead would be down into **South Fork**, then north down to Horse Canyon. If you went downcanyon from there, you could make it to within 1 km of the Green River, before being stopped by a **big dropoff**. Lots of nice campsites down there and there should be water. In the lower part of Horse Canyon are a couple of old corrals and at least one panel of petroglyphs and a number of old cowboy inscriptions as well (the author saw these in 1991, but not in 2011 or '12--so look around where the corrals are). You could also take the Lower Trail to Anderson Bottom which is discussed in the previous chapter.

If you were to go west up the main fork of **Horse Canyon**, you'd be in a totally dry and uninspiring drainage, but there is a **petrograph panel,** with cowboy signatures nearby. One reads, *Levi Jensen March 30, 1910.* At the upper end is a constructed **horse trail** which zig zags up through a break in the White Rim Sandstone. The sandstone wall is yellow in color at that point, indicating it's been saturated by oil--that's the reason for the breakdown of the cliff. From near the top of this trail, road-walk back to your vehicle or mtn. bike at the Maze Overlook.

This map shows a trail in the bottom of each canyon, but there's really no trail except where there's a shortcut across a meander; you mostly just walk up or down the dry creek bed. The trails you will see are very old cow trails, or trails recently made by hikers.

Hikes from the Land of Standing Rocks

In the **Land of Standing Rocks** are 4 trailheads, 2 of which are at the heads of **South Fork & Pictograph Forks.** You could park a LR/HC/4WD or mtn. bike at either of these, walk down one canyon and loop back up the other and road-walk back up to your wheels. That would be a day-hike for most people. Be sure you park at the trailheads--which are a little hard to located sometimes--so you'll be on the trail right from the beginning. Otherwise it will be difficult for beginners to located the trail down into either of these canyons. In each canyon, the trail from the road to the bottom of the drainage is marked by stone cairns (small piles of rocks), so be alert for these, especially over slickrock. These are hikers routes only and were never built to take cows, sheep or horses to the canyon bottoms. These are deep and moderately narrow canyons, so there are only a few places you can enter.

A 3rd trailhead begins at the south end of **Chocolate Drop Ridge** and right on the north side of the road. This trailhead is marked with cairns, and the cairned trail heads north between an **unnamed pinnacle** and **The Wall (see map).** The trail stays right on the hump between South & Pictograph Forks while passing several more **pinnacles**. In the north end, you'll pass just below and east of the **Chocolate Drops,** then head northeast following cairns down onto a point, then into a minor drainage to the lower end of Pictograph Fork. There are 2 exposed downclimbs on this steep route that will make some people nervous, so one person in each group should have a little climbing experience. Also, take a short rope (5m) just in case. Upclimbing will feel safer if you want to do this in reverse order.

The 4th trailhead at **Chimney Rock** is by far the most popular starting point for hikers. From this one parking place, you can walk to all of the canyons shown on this map. However, Horse Canyon and South Fork are best reached from the Maze Overlook. Chimney Rock Trailhead is the starting point for 4 trails. One trail heads northwest from Chimney Rock and takes you down into a southeast drainage of **Pictograph Fork** on a hiker's trail.

A 2nd trail heads north along the east side of Chimney Rock. It runs along the slickrock ridgetop between Pictograph Fork & Jasper Canyons. Near the base of **Petes Mesa**, one trail veers left or west and drops down into Pictograph Fork and toward the Maze Overlook. Both of these routes down into Pictograph Fork are well-used because there are some hikers going down to view the **Harvest Scene pictograph panel**. The other trail runs north along the east side of Petes Mesa. After a couple of kms, it then zig zags up to the top of the Mesa. There appears to be no constructed trail to the top of Petes Mesa, but hikers can get up there easily.

A 3rd trail from Chimney Rock runs northeast. After about 1 km, there used to be a trail branching off to the left or west. This went down into the head of **Jasper Canyon**, but Jasper is now **officially closed.** There were never any sheep or cattle in Jasper, and there is likely no cheatgrass there as there is in other nearby canyons; subsequently the NPS worries you'll carry cheat grass seeds in your socks and leave them there. Never mind that wind, birds, coyotes, deer and big horn sheep can do the same. However in about this same location as where the trail once took off into the head of the canyon, is a viewpoint where you can look straight down the barrel of Jasper's upper end. This is one of the better foto stops around. This view is better than any you'll get going down inside the canyon anyway.

Now continue north along the ridge between Jasper & Shot Canyons. This is a slickrock route almost all the way and marked with small stone cairns. As you near the lower end of Jasper, you'll walk down a slope with several minor ledges and into a shallow drainage as shown on the map. Soon you'll be in the bottom end of Jasper.

If you're looking for a nice view of the Green River, turn right or east at the bottom of Jasper, and head downcanyon. After 1 km or so, you'll come to a **big dropoff**. In the past, anyone who called him or herself a climber could downclimb a wall to reach the river, but sometime after 1991, part of that route fell off--or was pushed by the NPS (?) and it's no longer climbable. In 8/2011, the author came up to that wall from the river, and found it wasn't fit for anyone but the gutsiest of climbers. There are still 3 Anasazi ruins near the river but..... So forget going to the river, but enjoy the view.

Now back to near Chimney Rock and the trail running down into upper **Shot Canyon**. From the turnoff to fotograph Jasper, continue north for another 200m or so, and you'll see another cairned trail heading eastward, then down into the upper end of **Shot Canyon**. Be sure to follow the cairns carefully at the upper end of this trail as it's a little hard to follow. Halfway to the bottom of the canyon you'll see where a trail has been constructed. No one knows who built it, but the late **Ned Chaffin**, who grew up on the Chaffin Ranch tells us a little about this trail into upper Shot Canyon:

I tried to find a way into upper Shot Canyon, and so did Pete Maziet, the old French sheepman. Once I saw that rock buildup [trail] from the bottom in upper Shot Canyon, but I didn't check it out then. So the next time, which was another year or so before I had an occasion to go back there, my brother Clell said he'd take the pack horses and go around the other way--go around the long way to get into Water and Shot Canyons--and I'd go there and try and find a way down. I had a hell of a time finding that trail. I was about ready to give up and go back around when I found it. I was ridin' old Smoky mule and of course he could climb a tree, and we made it down alright but that was pretty scary. I know Dad never knew about that trail or we would have used it, so I know he didn't know about it. He'd been all over that country afoot and on horseback.

So we never advertised the trail was there and never let anybody know that we found it and we never used it with our stock. We didn't want the sheep herders to know you could get off into those canyons that quick with their sheep, because we was afraid they'd eat it [the grass] off for us. I think it was some old cow thief's trail. If a sheep herder had built it, then Pete Maziet and some of the other sheep herders would have known about it. But nobody knew about it. That trail was really a secret. I think it was an

Above The top of the **Horse Trail** in the upper end of **Horse Canyon.** This may have been built by the Robbers Roosters, but more likely it was first built by the earliest sheep-herders like Pete Maziet, Andy Miller, John Boline or Henry Dussier.

Left One of the more fotogenic places on the trail that runs east and down into the **South Fork of Horse Canyon** from the **Maze Over-look**.

old outlaw trail or something that was built there as an escape route out of Shot or Water Canyons. That's what I think because before we shot the trail from Water Canyon into Shot Canyon, you could still go over that pass between the two.

Shot Canyon isn't used too much but the upper part is very scenic. As you walk downcanyon you may see cowboy inscriptions on a wall under an overhang to the left or west, and a Fremont Indian campsite under a ledge. As you near the lower end of the canyon, be sure to follow the cairns carefully, because the trail then goes up over a **low divide** to the east and down into lower Water Canyon. Just over the pass and on the Water Canyon side, is a part that's been constructed. **Ned Chaffin** knew about that and here's what he had to say about it:

Dad and Riter Ekker [of Hanksville] and I shot that trail from Water Canyon into Shot Canyon. That was on the hump between the two down near the bottom end. I'm going to say it was before we bought the ranch in 1929, maybe it was 1928. I think it was the summer of 1928, and hotter than hell. You see, the springs in Shot Canyon was just wet weather seeps; so when it's real dry and you need 'em bad, they're dry, so we put that trail up over there in the hopes that cattle would come in to Water Canyon and trail over into Shot Canyon to eat the feed out of it, because there was a lot of feed in that little canyon at that time.

Let me tell you a story about that trail into Shot Canyon. Dad had quit smoking, and he had a pair of these old cowboy saddle bags that he had kept his tobacco in. Anyway, he had quit smoking, but he had a can of Prince Albert [tobacco] in these saddle bags. So one day Riter and I stole his tobacco, and we had gone out to have a smoke, then we'd usually put the tobacco back. One day Dad came in and was cussin' the world and said, "god I'm going to start smokin' again". And I thought oh, oh, because we had his tobacco can hid that day. So he looked in his saddle bags and couldn't find it. Finally we had to confess that we'd stolen his tobacco. Boy, did he raise hell, because he didn't want any of us to smoke cigarittes. He called anyone who was sorry and didn't amount to anything, "a god damn cigarette smokin' son of a bitch". That was his favorite saying. He said, "When you get ready to smoke, come to me and I'll buy you a pipe, because you're not smokin' them damn cigarittes."

Now back to the Chimney Rock Trailhead. A 4th faint trail, but which isn't on any NPS map, and which they don't want you to know about, heads east and maybe south a little--kinda parallel to the road. This trail or route is the one into **Water Canyon**, but it was never a cattle or sheep trail, just a hikers route only. It slowly turns toward the northeast (or you could walk east on the road for 10 minutes, then head north), then drops down off one ledge and heads back to the west on the first bench below the rim. When you're not too far from Chimney Rock you'll come to another ledge you'll have to get over. In 8/2011, the author upclimbed this steep part by standing on **3 logs**, shaped like an upsidedown Y and leaning against the wall. It worked, but was rickety as hell! because it was made of 3 separate logs! If you're using this **climbing route**, best to have one person who has climbed a little, and have him/her help less-experienced friends down perhaps with a short rope. Then those below can help the last person down if necessary. It's climbable with sticky rubber soled shoes, but a little tricky.

From the bottom of this log route, walk west 75m or so and downclimb another short vertical part, but there are lots of hand & foot holds. Below that it's a walkout. Once in the bottom, follow the one trail right down the dry creek bed. Near the bottom end of the drainage will be a **dropoff** and a good **spring** underneath it. This is the beginning of the little stream in lower Water Canyon. Not far below this ledge & spring, will be a cairned trail to the west and into Shot Canyon. Watch carefully for it.

If you continue down Water Canyon, you'll soon come to another **big dropoff**; this time it's a **waterfall**. The trail runs to the right or east of this waterfall, and then switchbacks down the lower end of the canyon to the river. This part is now being used a lot by river runners. Along the way will be tiny waterfalls, springs and pools.

Now back to the dropoff & spring in Water Canyon. Just below this spring, a minor drainage comes in from the southeast and another trail heads up that way. Follow the cairns and/or trail. Further up, you may see still another part which was constructed by Lou Chaffin, his son Ned, and Riter Ekker in the mid-1920's, maybe 1928. It was via this trail they brought their cattle into Water & Shot Canyons. Once you get out of the canyon you'll be walking in a big **wide-open flat**. After a while you'll come to the **junction** with the **Colorado River Overlook Trail**. It you go left or northeast, you'll soon come to the Colorado River Overlook. The view there is worth the effort. From this overlook, head north & westerly and you'll soon be at the head of a short drainage heading down to the lower Green River. We'll call this **Powells Canyon.** You'll have to look for it, but there's now a cairned trail going down this short steep drainage--and the further down you go, the better the trail becomes. That's because it's used mostly by river runners. The first white men to have climbed up this canyon were several members of **John W. Powell's 2nd River Expedition of 1871.** It was September 16 that year they climbed up this canyon and looked down at the Green River from above. If the one-armed Powell could do it, anyone can climb up or down this drainage. You can also make your way to the rim and view The Confluence of the Green and Colorado Rivers, another view worth the effort.

Now back to the junction in the wide-open flat. If you walk southwest on this Colorado River Overlook Trail, you'll come to where this trail ends--or rather begins--just a little ways from the end of the Spanish Bottom Trail or **Doll House Road**. From there road-walk back to Chimney Rock (see the Map 10 which shows the southern part of that trail).

Here are some times for the average hiker. Making a loop down into and out of Pictograph Fork is a one day hike. Some may be able to climb upon Petes Mesa, along with a loop-hike of Pictograph Fork in one longer day. A hike along Jasper Ridge to the overlook of the Green River and back will be an easy day-hike. Going down Shot or Water to the river and back up the other will be a day-hike for most. Going down Water, then up and over to the Colorado River Overlook and down to the Green via Powells Canyon and back via the Colorado River Overlook Trail will be a long day for serious hikers. Read about the hikes (& times) this writer took in this region on the first page of this chapter.

Above From the south-east corner of the **Chocolate Drops**, we see them and **Ekker Butte** in the distance to the north. Almost due east of these is the **Harvest Scene Pictograph Panel** which is shown to the left. It's located in the lower end of Pictograph Fork of Horse Canyon.

Left This is the biggest part of the **Harvest Scene** panel in the lower end of Pictograph Fork. Be there around noon or mid-day for the best fotos. This panel extends for nearly 100m along the base of this south facing Cedar Mesa Sandstone wall. Some of these paintings are the most-intricate of any this writer has seen.

Left Standing Rock, read sign. One campsite in The Maze District is located here. **Right** This is known as **Chimney Rock**. It's both a campsite and a trailhead to several destinations in the area.

From the **Maze Overlook** looking southeast. Shown is the lower end of the **South Fork of Horse Canyon** along with the Chocolate Drops. Also, to the far right background is **Standing Rock**.

Above Left This is what this writer calls **Triple Arches** located just north of where Pictograph Fork enters the **South Fork of Horse Canyon**. There are 2 arches (maybe bridges?) at the top and one bridge below.

Above Right This is the man-made part of the trail in upper **Shot Canyon**. No one alive in the 1990's knew who may have built it, but it wasn't Chaffins or Pete Maziet.

Left From a viewpoint at the head of **Jasper Canyon** you'll have the best look at this fotogenic drainage.

The Fins, Ernies Country, Cataract & Range Canyons, and The Golden Stairs & Spanish Trails

Location & Access Featured here is that part of **Cataract Canyon** between **Spanish Bottom** and the end of **Teapot Canyon**, which is near upper end of Lake Powell. This is the only part left of what was once (maybe still is?) one of the best white water rivers in America. Also included is the area just south of The Maze, called **The Fins**. This place is criss-crossed with eroded fins of Cedar Mesa Sandstone, which includes 3 main drainages, plus a couple of **springs** and about a dozen natural **arches**. There are also several old trails, 2 of which go down to the Colorado River near Spanish Bottom.

You can get to this mapped area by driving from Highway 24 on The Maze Road to the Hans Flat or Maze Ranger Station, then down the **Flint Trail** with a stock HC/SUV or mtn. bike. From the **3-Way Junction** where The Maze, Millard Canyon and Hite Roads meet, turn left and head northeast until you come to the **The Golden Stairs Trailhead & Campsite**. Near that campsite is one ledge where you may have to do a little road work by hand or shovel to get to the trailhead if driving a stock SUV.

Or if you want to get into The Fins, Land of Standing Rocks or the Doll House area, drive south from the 3-Way Junction on the Hite Road until you come to the **Waterhole Junction** (see Map 11) where the Doll House Road leaves the Hite Road. From there drive northeasterly to get to any of the trailheads on this map (from Teapot Rock you'll need a LR/HC/4WD, mtn. bike, or walk). You can also leave **Highway 95** between **mile posts 46 & 47**, and drive the Hite Road northeast to Waterhole Flat and beyond. See **Maps 11 & 12** for a look at the Hite Road.

Get into The Fins by starting at **The Fins Trailhead** at the west end of the **Fins Trail**; or continue to the **Standing Rock Campsite** for a way into the head of **Sweet Alice Canyon**; or get to the **Doll House Campsite #3** at the east end of the Fins Trail. If you're heading for Spanish Bottom, then follow the road to **The Doll House Campsites #1 & #2**. This would be the best place to start a hike down **Cataract Canyon**.

Elevations Top of Flint Trail, 2097m; Land of Standing Rocks, about 1650m; Spanish Bottom, about 1200m; and the high water mark (HWM) of Lake Powell, 1128m.

Water Always carry all the water you'll need for your trip in your vehicle. Also, at Lou's Spring, normally at Clell's Seep (?), and the Colorado River--which must be treated before use.

Maps USGS or BLM maps Hanksville & La Sal (1:100,000); Elaterite Basin, Spanish Bottom, Teapot Rock, and maybe a little of Cross Canyon (1:24,000--7 1/2' quads); or maybe the best single map is the plastic Trails Illustrated/National Geographic map, Canyonlands National Park (1:70,000); or the plastic Latitude 40° map Moab West (1:75,000).

Main Attractions One of the great canyons of the world, incredible geology & scenery in The Fins, many natural arches and one very good pictograph panel.

Author's Experience He once rode a mtn bike down the Flint Trail and left it at the top of The Golden Stairs Trail. That took 30 minutes. Then he walked as far as Clell's Seep and returned, then biked back up the Flint Trail to his car and camp (This was in 1991 and before the NPS hijacked the high country and requiring everyone to camp only in their designated sites and pay $30 for the privilege!). Round-trip, 8 hours 10 min. Another time, he hiked from his boat on Spanish Bottom, up the Spanish Trail to an overlook on the rim of Cataract, then up Sweet Alice Canyon to Standing Rock, and back by road and trail to the river in a little over 6 hours.

Other trips in 1990-'92; he drove into The Needles west of the river and parked at Elephant Hill Trailhead. He only had a VW Rabbit at the time. He walked down Red Lake Canyon to the river, put his pack on an **inner tube** and **swam across**. He later camped at the mouth of Surprise Canyon. Next day he hiked downriver to the mouth of Sand Tank Canyon, then up to the rim of Cataract to the Sunken Valley, and back down to his camp via the Spanish Trail. Just under 10 hours. The 3rd day, he explored Surprise Valley via Surprise Canyon, then packed up and walked along the river to Spanish Bottom where he re-swam the Colorado River and returned to Elephant Hill in just over 8 hours. This was October 11, 12, & 13, 1990. Each swim across the river was at mid-day to minimize hypothermia. The crossing was about 75-90m wide, and he floated downstream about 125m each time in the process. If doing such a stunt, best to stay out of the water by using an air mattress or a one person inflatable. Checkout (**alpackaraft.com**) for a look at their **packraft** which weighs only about 1.5 Kgs--about the same weight as an air mattress; but this will keep you out of the water.

In 2011 & '12, he parked at the Golden Stairs TH, walked down the Golden Stairs, continued along The Fins Trail to Sand Tank & Sweet Alice Canyons, saw Whitmore Arch, and back; 8 hours. Next time, he did the same thing but got to Sweet Alice Canyon, visited Muffin Arch & others, exited the upper end and road-walked back to his Jeep Patriot at Golden Stairs TH; 10 3/4 hours. Next day, he went down Range Canyon past the big **pictograph panel** to an overlook of Cataract Canyon and back; 8 1/3 hours.

The Golden Stairs Trail

There's an official **NPS/CNP campsite** in the piñon/juniper trees at the beginning of **The Golden Stairs Trail**. But first a short history of this old trail as told by the late **Ned Chaffin**: *They called it the Golden Stairs on account of some of those steps was built with that formation of sandstone that has a yellow color to it. When it rains and the sun shines on it just right, it does look like gold. I think everybody who was down there did some work on that trail. That was a miserable trail too; long & steep.*

From the campsite, locate the beginning of the trail and walk due east. After a short distance, you'll cross a narrow neck of rock, which is the Moss Back (formerly the Shinarump) Member of the Chinle Formation. Just beyond that, the trail begins to zig zag down through the ledges to the south. Soon it comes to a wider bench, then turns west. Contour on this bench to the west about 1 km; then the trail zig zags straight down again and veers southeast. Just before this trail reaches the Doll House Road, it runs along a shallow dry wash. Where it reaches the road it's marked by a large cairn.

From there, road-walk northeast about 1 km to a point just east of a prominent rock called **Woman & Child** as shown on the map. On the right or east side of the road is a trailhead & 4WD parking but there's no sign there, so keep eyes open. This is the beginning of **The Fins Trail**. This trail wanders east through the southern part of The Fins and ends near the end of the Doll House Road. This is the normal route into the southern parts of Range, Sand Tank & Sweet Alice Canyons.

The Fins Trail is well-used, is well-marked by cairns and at first heads southeast. Soon it drops down into the head of a little north fork of **Range Canyon**. Follow the cairns carefully, especially over slickrock. When you reach the dry creek bed of the little north fork, the first thing to see will be a phony Indian structure. To get there, turn north into this first drainage. When the dry wash turns west, look for a way

Map 10, The Fins, Ernies Country, Cataract & Range Canyons, and The Golden Stairs & Spanish Trails

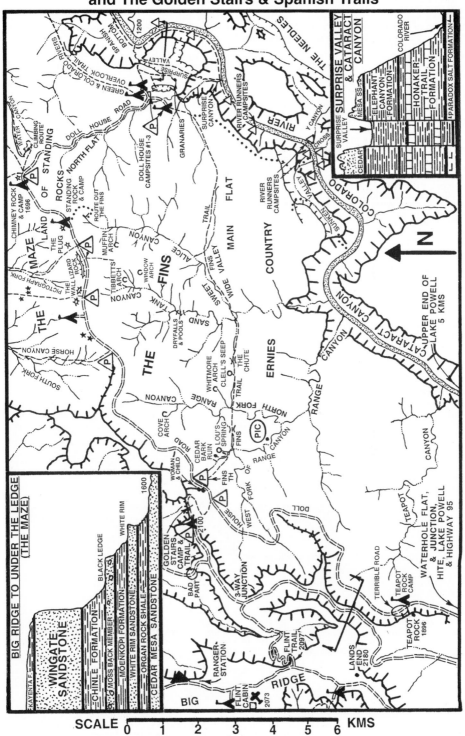

SCALE 0 1 2 3 4 5 6 KMS

upon the next level or slickrock bench. Walk east about 100-150m and inside a small alcove with a wet spot in the back, will be what appears to be an Anasazi shelter. After mentioning this in the 1st Edition of this book, someone wrote saying it was built by palefaced moki Indians--in other words, white folk! Next time there, the author looked it over more carefully and concluded it was indeed as phony as a $3 bill. It's simply not built the same way as the real McCoys! But this one is covered with poles, then a deep pile of cedar bark on top of that which the roof--no Anasazi or Fremont structure was ever built that way. Let's just call this the **Cedar Bark Ruin**.

Now back to **The Fins Trail**. About 50m below where this trail hits the bottom of the little north fork, one path heads east, then north into the minor drainage just east of where the Cedar Bark Ruin is found. Follow that branch trail north to where it ends under a large overhang. Under that is **Lou's Spring**. The late **Ned Chaffin** helped troughed-up this one and he remembers how it got that name:

That's Lou's Spring. That was the official government name applied to that spring. This was another of the projects the government did. They troughed that spring up and I hauled those troughs and everything in there on mules. The guy that was in charge of that government outfit--he had to hang a name on all those places. He said, "We'll just call this Lou's Spring, for your old man". That sure was good water and a good place to camp.

At Lou's Spring today, you'll find a couple of watering troughs full of good water at least 99% of the time. This spring has a much better flow than Clell's Seep. There's also a large steel barrel and a few old odds & ends of antique camp junk lying around. This was one of the favorite campsites for the Chaffins when they were in this country between 1919 and 1944-'45. This spring is completely overhung and the trough has a log frame around it to keep cows out of the spring source. You could camp at Lou's Spring without a tent, but don't camp too close or you'll keep other critters from getting a drink; remember, their lives depend on that water.

Now back again to The Fins Trail. From Lou's Spring, it will follow the dry wash south a ways, then where the main **West Fork of Range Canyon** enters from the west, the The Fins Trail heads due east and will be marked at that point with cairns on a little meter-high slickrock ledge. From there it runs into a little side-drainage. But before leaving Range Canyon, let's take a 1 km-side-trip downstream to see another great panel of **pictographs**. After 1 km, and as you're heading east in the dry wash, look northeast and in the middle of a crescent-shaped bowl of cliffs about 125-150m away, will be the panel. It's hard to see from the dry wash, but binoculars would help; so would following this and the USGS map you should be carrying. The paintings are red and the left hand side is more visible than the right side. Once there, and to get up close, you'll have to climb upon the ledge the painters used. These paintings resemble very closely in style of those found in Pictograph Fork, Horseshoe (Great Gallery), Clearwater and Hell Roaring Canyons (maybe in the South Fork of Sevenmile Canyon too?). One theory is, they were painted by the same guy or same clan--but apparently they can't date the pigment very good. From the paintings, and on the same trip, you could also continue downcanyon to an overlook of Cataract Canyon. From the Golden Stairs TH, this would be an all-day hike down and back up.

Now The Fins Trail again. From the West Fork of Range Canyon the trail heads due east into a side-drainage. After another km, you'll be in the bottom of the **North Fork of Range Canyon**. You could go up that drainage to see **Whitmore Arch**, or continue east. After 800-900m, look for another trail branching off to the left or north toward **Clell's Seep**; this will be 250-300m before or west of **The Chute**. Once again **Ned Chaffin** remembered how these 2 places got their names:

*Now some people called that Clell's Seep. We used to have a drift fence there at that little divide to control the cows. We called that **The Chute**. This was in the early 1930's after Roosevelt came in; this was one of his projects. It may have been the winter of 1934 & '35. I think it was a range improvement*

The **Cedar Bark Ruins** or Moki House. This appears to have been built by palefaced moki Indians, because it's constructed differently; and the roof is one of a kind.

Above The best part of the **Range Canyon Pictograph Panel**. You have to climb up about 4m to reach the ledge the painters used to create this masterpiece. There's more red paint to the right, but it's faded pretty bad. The style of these images is identical to those found in the Great Gallery, the Harvest Scene, and in Clearwater & Hell Roaring Canyons indicating it could have been the same man or clan who did them all. Unfortunately, archaeologists can't date the paint accurately, so at this point in time, we can only guess if the same person or clan did all 4 of the panels mentioned above.

Left Whitmore Arch located in the North Fork of **Range Canyon**.

Lou's Spring, located in a little north fork of **Range Canyon**. It was named after Lou Chaffin, the father of Ned Chaffin. There should always be water dripping into these troughs.

Clell's Seep has less of a flow than Lou's Spring, but normally there's water in these 2 troughs. This was named after one of the sons of Lou Chaffin.

deal that the Federal government put on. That's what they did, built trails and troughed-up springs. This was all done as part of the same project, with the Devil's Slide Trail. We did the spring there in The Chute [Clell's Seep], Lou's Spring, and the Twin Pipes Spring up on Big Ridge. I think this project was to fix up something new, instead of renovating old trails and springs.

Clell's Seep is under an overhang. A **leach line pipe** (a pipe with holes on one side to allow water in, then it flows out the other end into a trough) has been put under the dirt embankment and a small watering trough placed nearby. When the author was there the first time, which was at the end of a 4 year drought, and again in the spring of 2012, the trough was full of moss and the water still very good. It should be good to drink as is and although the flow is very little--there should be water in the trough most of the time (some time after 1991, someone wrote saying it was dry!). If going that way, call the Hans Flat Ranger Station (Tele. 435-259-2652) for an update on whether or not it has water. If camping in this area, do so back from the spring a ways because other hikers & animals depend on it as well.

From The Chute, follow the cairned trail down into **Sand Tank Canyon**. The Chaffins called this main drainage Sand Tank, because there are at least 3 big potholes or pourover pools up there right in the drainage. Whenever they didn't have water in them, then it had lots of sand around, thus the name Sand Tank Canyon. Walk up this canyon about 2 1/2 kms to find the 3 pouroffs & possible pools and maybe the best place to take fotos of The Fins.

About where the The Fins Trail crosses Sand Tank Canyon, another major drainage enters from the northeast. **Ned Chaffin** explains how it got its name:

One time we was down in that country helping some other people do some survey and geology work. It was T.C. Conley [he drilled near French Spring, and the Dubinky Well], and Mr. Prommel, who was in charge of the geological work. And we was camped way up in this canyon near a big water tank there. And Dad [Lou Chaffin] went up to get us some water and he was singin' that old folk song, "Do you Re-member Sweet Alice Ben Bolt". Anyway, Dad was the world's worst singer, and when we got through with our work that night and we was all around the campfire--it was one of those evenings when the wind came up, and of course we was camped by these big old cedar trees, and the wind was kinda moaning through 'em--and the fellas got to talking about the wind moaning through the trees and old man Prommel said, "That sounds just like Lou Chaffin singin' Sweet Alice Ben Bolt". So that's why we named it Sweet Alice Canyon.

These 2 canyons make up the heart of The Fins and there's lots to see in the area. There are several arches, but only 2 are named; **Tibbetts Arch** is up near the head of Sand Tank Canyon, while **Muffin Arch** is in the upper part of Sweet Alice. The 7 1/2' quads show several others, plus there are others not shown on any map. Tibbetts Arch was surely named after Bill Tibbetts, who was involved in punchin' cows in this country along with his uncle Eph Moore.

If you'd like an alternate way in or out of The Fins, then walk into the head of Sweet Alice Canyon and nearly to the end of an upper northeast fork, then look for cairns marking a route heading southeast into a rounded bowl-like drainage. Walk up this along an emerging trail marked with cairns. Near the top, veer right or west, then once on the 2nd to the highest bench, head left or east. From there you'll see Lizard Rock, The Plug and Standing Rock to the northwest. Route-find around the head of the drainage and up to the road on the south side of those buttes. From there, road-walk to where ever your vehicle is.

This is as close as you can get to the heart of **The Fins**. Below is one of the **Dryfalls & Pools** shown on the map. In drier times, this pool would turn to sand, thus the name **Sand Tank Canyon**.

Now back to the Fins Trail. After leaving Sand Tank & Sweet Alice Canyons, the trail heads east through **Wide Valley** and across **Main Flat** and the upper part of **Surprise Canyon** dry wash. Soon after that it ends on the Doll House Road and near **Doll House Campsite #3**.

Next stop will be the **Doll House**. This is in an area of standing rocks and early-day sheepmen and the Chaffins always referred to these rocks as **The Sentinels**. Just before you arrive at the trail heading for Spanish Bottom, you'll come to a dry wash and a sign on the left or north, pointing out the beginning of the **Colorado River Overlook Trail**. This trail heads north skirting to the west and north of Spanish Bottom and ending at an overlook of the Colorado River. See the previous map for the conclusion of this trail and the other destinations you can reach by using this route.

The Spanish Trail and Surprise Valley

Just before you arrive at the **Doll House Campsites #1 & #2**, there will be a parking place for Jeepers on the left. On the right will be the beginning of the **trail** which ends on the Colorado River at **Spanish Bottom** (see foto below). From there to the river it's about 3 kms. The trail is well-used, by people driving into this area and by boaters hiking up from the river. It begins to zig zag down the canyon wall, then about 1/3 the way down, it steepens and you'll notice some construction of the trail. People usually refer to this short section as **The Stairs**. Just beyond that will be a wall on your right which has a number of old cowboy and rivermen's signatures.

After the etchings, the trail continues to zig zag down a minor ridge to Spanish Bottom. However, there's an interesting side-trip you can take beginning about 2/3's the way down. This is a seldom-used trail heading south and up into **Surprise Valley**. There may be a cairn or two to mark the trail junction. At the beginning of the Surprise Valley Trail, it's washed out a lot, but it's easy to follow as it too is marked with cairns. After about 300m or so, you will enter a sunken or graben valley, created by the dissolving away of salts in the underlying formations. When asked about who built this trail, **Ned Chaffin** said:

At that time, there were 2 ways you could get in there. Before you get up to where those steps are, you can turn off to the left [south] and go up through that--we called it the Sunken Valley. They [NPS] called it Surprise Valley because there's no outlet to it, and the water runs down a hole in the ground. We primarily built that trail into Surprise Valley, but there wasn't too much to it. I would think we were the first to build that trail, because it was a lot easier way to get down into Spanish Bottom than down those steps with cattle. It seems to me that Faun, Clell and I did that in the early 1920's. I was born in 1913, and I made my first trip down there the year of the big rain, that was in 1921. So I was 8 years of age.

Once you get into Surprise Valley, you'll find vertical walls on either side and lots of tumbleweeds on the valley floor. This is very similar to the sunken valleys you find in The Needles country across the river to the east. The trail continues to the south end, then it zig zags down the steep canyon wall to the bottom of a short side-canyon we'll call **Surprise Canyon** (for lack of a better name). Once in the bottom of this short canyon, the trail disappears, but you can easily walk on down to the river. **Ned Chaffin** had this to say about the trail down into this canyon:

There was no trail down out of Surprise Valley [at the south end] when we were there. That's been built since, because there wasn't any use having 2 trails into such a small area. We did have one old

These are some of the more-fotographed parts in The Maze called **The Doll House**; but early-day cattlemen called these **The Sentinels**. Behind the camera is a parking place for LR/HC/4WD's.

On the west side of **Surprise Valley**, and near the rim, are these **granaries**. They're in a tiny alcove facing north. Getting there is easy; start at the **trailhead for Spanish Bottom** and follow the signs to the east and southeast. From the trailhead it should take 1 or 1 1/2 hours for the trip. See **Map 10.**

From the rim of Surprise Valley and along the trail to the **granaries** shown above, looking southeast into **Surprise Valley**. You can see some trails running into the 2 arms of this sunken graben.

An old color slide from **October 11, 1990**. The author actually swam from the lower end of Red Lake Canyon across the Colorado River to Spanish Bottom floating his pack on this inner tube. It was midday; but don't try this at home, the water was oooh so cold! Instead, and if you want to get across the Colorado, buy and use one of the new fangled **packrafts** from **alpackaraft.com**.

cow that would walk all the way down to the river for a drink, then she'd walk back up to Surprise Valley. I don't think it could have been over grazed because there was no water there.

If the Chaffins didn't build this trail and if it wasn't there during their days in Under the Ledge, then it may have been built by the **Moyniers** sheep outfit out of Price. They bought the Chaffin Ranch and their grazing rights in 1944 & '45; then in about 1970 sold the Chaffin Ranch land to Keon Jenson, and just sold the sheep and got out of the business entirely. After that, no one ever took sheep or cattle down to the northern parts of Under the Ledge. One reason for that was, part of that area was by then a national park. In addition, all grazing permits in CNP territory were withdrawn on June 30,1975.

Here's a brief history of the Moynier family as told by **Pierre Moynier III** of Price: *There were 2 Moynier brothers that came from France and a town called La Mont near the Gap. They came here in the late 1800's and went to Bakersfield, California first, then come up here to the Price area and got into the sheep business. Their names were **Pierre and Honore (Henry) Moynier**. Then there were 2 girls who came from the same town in France, so the 2 brothers ended up marrying the 2 sisters when they got here. Then my grandma's sister died right after she had her last baby. So my grandma ended up raising all the children of both families--she had 11 children, and the oldest one was like 10 years old at the time. She lived down here on Carbon Avenue in Price.....*

Henry, the one who died in The Roost, was from the other family [read the story of how he died on page 76]. These families were double 1st cousin's [and literally raised together]. But anyway, Henry never came to town; he lived at the sheep camps year-round. In the summer he'd go up on the summer range in the spring, then in the winter he'd go down on the desert [or Under the Ledge].

Leon and Uncle Mias [Marius], Henry's full brother, was down Under the Ledge when Henry cut himself, then Leon took off and got in his Dodge Power Wagon and raced to Green River to get help. My Uncle Mias was coming back in the other Power Wagon and driving slow with Henry in the back.

My dad Pierre II and his 2 brothers, Paul and Leon, run the sheep and were the ones who bought the Chaffin Ranch and grazing permits. Even though the 3 brothers were in the sheep [business] together, it was just Pierre and Leon who actually bought the Chaffin [Ranch land]. Our family hung onto, and we still have today, the mineral rights at the old Chaffin Ranch.

History of Spanish Bottom

Spanish Bottom is a large and relatively flat area covering about 50 hectares, or 120 acres. It's like a big round hole in the ground. The reason it's so large and has a roundish shape is because of the underlying geologic beds. Around the end of **Lower Red Lake Canyon** is the center of an uplifted area called the **Prommel Dome**. The rocks exposed on the east side of the river and on both sides of Lower Red Lake Canyon's mouth, belong to the Paradox Salt Formation. Because it's made out of various salts which were originally way underground, it's generally felt that structures like this are created by the dissolving away of underlying salts, leaving features like Spanish Bottom. Anyway, Spanish Bottom, or **Cataract Bottom** as it was originally called, is a prominent feature situated at the head of Cataract Canyon and only about 1 1/2 kms above the first rapids. Because it's above the rapids, and because any kind of boat can get down to it, it's a popular place. There are several good campsites on the west side, but you may have some competition from boaters. The spot that's occupied almost every night during the warmest 6 months of the year is the one at the lower end of the bottom where the river turns east. Please don't camp there--it's unofficially reserved for rafters.

This bottom has some interesting history. Not counting the Native Americans, the first people who may have seen this valley (?), were the Spaniards. Many of the old timers living in this part of the country insist that it's called Spanish Bottom and the Spanish Trail because it was a variant of the Old Spanish Trail. Now the Old Spanish Trail came north from Santa Fe to Cortez, Colorado, then to near

Monticello, Utah before turning north. Then across Dry Valley to Moab, across the Colorado, and north-west to where the town of Green River is today. From there it went westward, but looped around to the north end of the San Rafael Swell. Finally it went west up Salina Canyon and on to California.

Bert J. Silliman of Green River believed he had found a variant to this trail before he died. He called it the **"Bears Ears Trail"**. It went around south of the Abajo or Blue Mountains, through the Bear Ears near Natural Bridges NM, north across the Elk Mountains and down one of the canyons into The Needles District. Then down Red Lake Canyon to the river and crossed Spanish Bottom. The next land mark would have been the Land of Standing Rocks, then south to Waterhole Flat, west to Sunset Pass, down Hatch Canyon to the Dirty Devil River, up Poison Spring Canyon, across the Burr Desert to Temple Mountain, up and over Sinbad Country, then joined the main route west of the San Rafael Swell. If in-deed this route was ever taken, it would have been with pack horses only, because the country is rough as hell. That's probably why few people outside this area believe the Spaniards or Mexicans ever used it. There also seems to be no documented evidence to prove it. This writer hasn't the proper words to describe how ridiculous the idea of this route is.

Many people however believe it was used a little later by outlaws & horse thieves like Butch Cassidy. They may have used it in the 1880's and up to about 1900. The late **Pearl B. Baker** tells one story of several outlaws crossing the river with a herd of stolen cattle in her book, ***The Wild Bunch at Robbers Roost.*** They were taking them from western Utah to the mines in Colorado, and evidently lost half the herd in the first cataract. It seems a possibility that outlaws did some of the first construction work on the upper part of the Spanish Trail as it leaves Spanish Bottom.

By about 1890 or shortly after, there were sheep & cattlemen, and prospectors going into this country from both sides, particularly on the west bank. In the meantime, boaters were beginning to visit Spanish Bottom. **John W. Powell** was there in 1869 & 1871, then in 1889, the **Stanton Expedition** passed this way. They surveyed the Colorado River Gorge with the dream of placing a water-grade railroad right down along the river from Colorado to California. They later lost part of their group, including the number one financier, to rapids in Marble Canyon. That project didn't go very far, but Stanton always insisted it could be done.

Perhaps the next group who visited this region was the **Best Expedition**. **William H. Edwards** told of his experience with this group in the ***Colorado River Bed Case hearings*** of 1929. He stated that in 1891: *The company by which I was then employed was known as the Grand Canyon Mining Company and our purpose was to find a lost mine, supposed to be located in the lower part of the canyon..... The expedition left Green River, Utah, about July 14..... This party had two boats and 8 men.....*
After losing one of their boats in the 13th rapids in Cataract Canyon: *We let the men who had been riding in that boat walk where they could and would ferry them across from one bank to the other at places, until we came to Narrow Canyon, where we had to go through part way with all eight men in the one boat.*

In 1890, **B.S. Ross** of Rawlins, Wyoming, had gone to Green River by train then went down to Span-ish Bottom in a rowboat. On that trip, he began to think about the possibility of running tourists down the Green River to Spanish Bottom. That would be a good place to finish a cruise because it was above the first cataract and surely could be handled by a simple steamboat. So, joined by several friends, he organized the Green, Grand and Colorado River Navigation Company in the fall of 1890. The intent was to run tourists down to a hotel they would build on Spanish Bottom.

That winter, they purchased a small steam powered launch in Chicago and had it shipped to Green River by rail. It was launched at Green River in mid-August, 1891 and was named the ***Major Powell***. It measured about 2 1/2 x 11m, had a canvas top, and two 6 hp steam engines which turned twin screws. On its first run, Ross was joined by a couple of journalists, who it was hoped, would give some publicity to the venture. As it turned out, the boat sat far too deep in the water, and both the propeller screws were broken off in the gravel bars just below the town of Green River.

The next year, 1892, Ross hired one of the Wheeler brothers from the Wheeler Ranch (now the Ruby Ranch), to help fix the Major Powell so it could be taken downriver. At first they put heavy metal shields around the propellers to protect them from rocks. Then they set out on **April 15, 1892**. The water was high at the time so they had little trouble moving downstream. At Spanish Bottom they looked around for a site for the hotel they proposed to build. Finally they got back up to the Wheeler Ranch, but the swifter spring runoff made the going upstream very slow. Their coal was nearly exhausted, so they put the boat on shore and left it. They returned to Green River by team & wagon.

William H. Edwards again testified in the River Bed hearings and told what happened the next year: *My trip down the Colorado was in the **spring of 1893**. I was in charge of the party and we thought there were a lot of tourists who would like to see the Colorado River from the upper end and we figured that we could possibly operate a boat from Green River down to the junction of the two rivers and take tourists down there, so we organized a Denver company. We leased a steam launch that had been abandoned at Wheeler's ranch and made an attempt to see what we could do with the river. This boat had been abandoned in 1891 [actually '92] and was known as the "Major Powell".*
I got a small boat in Green River and came down to Wheeler's ranch in the later part of February or first of March. I came by water and part by ice, the river being still frozen up there at the time. I dragged my boat over the ice and examined the Major Powell and returned to Denver. With two companions I came back to Wheeler's ranch and we repaired the Major Powell and got her into the water and started down river..... The boat had been built originally for coal and had then been changed so it would burn wood. We spent a good many hours getting wood for the boat and would run as far as we could with the wood and then cut another load and go on until that gave out..... This trip was made in March or April, 1893.

In **Crampton's** study of historic sites in Glen Canyon, he found an inscription left behind by this group. He described the location like this: *At the extreme southern tip of the flat at Spanish Bottom, and located on the northwest face of a big talus block of sandstone, is the following inscription in light paint: "1st Steamer, Major Powell, May 24--93, H. Edwards, H. F. Howard".* The author was never able to locate this inscription in 3 tries. It might be too faded to read now (?).

In 1901, a **Joe Ross**, the same guy who helped the Valentines get out of Valentine Bottom in 1893, was also involved in a second venture to build a sanatorium or tourist resort on Spanish Bottom. He testified in the *Hearings* that: *In 1901, I made a trip from Greenriver to the head of Cataract Canyon with a surveying party who intended to build a sanatorium at the Cataract Bottoms. We had an ordinary row boat,.....and it was in July.* This was his first trip of the season.

Later in the year he made a 2nd trip: *I was engineer on the **Undine** on it's first trip on the river. It had a regular stern-wheel engine, coal burning. We started down the river with the Undine in August,*

1901. We had a crew of 7 or 8..... About halfway between Greenriver and the mouth of the San Rafael we struck a rock in the river and broke a hole in the bottom of the boat. We had to beach the boat and repair it. After we patched it we started down again..... Frank Summerall of Denver intended to establish a sanatorium there..... We camped at the head of the cataracts for several days.....

Later that season, on November 22, 1901, the Undine began another trip from Green River to "Cataract Bottom", then went on to Moab. It seems at that time the Summeril's (there are 2 different spellings of this same name) were very hopeful of putting in the sanatorium the following spring and of hauling freight. **The Times-Independent** newspaper of Moab reported that: *Mr. Summeril assured us that he would have two steamers running between Green river and Cataract canyon in the spring, as a tourist route, and that it lay with the people of this place whether the line extended to here or not, he says that if the merchants here will guarantee him their freight he will put on a line of boats between Green river and Moab, we hope the businessmen are enough alive to their own interests and the interest of the valley to do this..... Mr. Summeril says that he can make the run from Green River Station to Moab in 18 hours, and carry freight for 25 per cent less than it can be hauled by wagon.*

Summeril was obviously over-confident and still didn't understand the Green & Colorado Rivers. As it turned out, he was in Moab again the following May (1902) and on the 23rd, they headed up the Colorado from Moab. About 13 kms upstream from the ferry, and at Big Bend, the **Undine** hit a rock and overturned in a riffle. The several people on board were lucky to get out of the river alive. That accident ended all hopes of freighting on the rivers and of building a sanatorium at Spanish Bottom. Read more on the history of boating in the book, **River Guide to Canyonlands National Park and Vicinity, 2nd Edition.**

From that time on there were countless parties heading downriver by boat. Some were miners, others were government surveyors, others were just out for adventure, but no one attempted to build a ranch or hunting lodge or anything else on what Edwards and others called **Cataract Bottom**. But the stockmen did go there with their sheep or cattle. Who may have gotten there first is a mystery. Pearl B. Baker believes there were sheepmen in there sometime in the 1890's. She states a couple of the earliest were **Andy Miller and John Boline**. Also, there were other Frenchmen or perhaps Basques like big **Henry Dusseir and Pete Maziet** who had sheep.

Later on and not long after 1900, perhaps by the mid-1910's or thereabouts, the Moore family of Moab was in Under the Ledge. The one who spent most of his time there was **Eph Moore**. The family ran cows mostly in Big Water or Elaterite Basin, Horse Canyon and along the river bottoms from the mouth of Millard Canyon on down to Cabin Bottom. They may have been to Spanish Bottom.

Sometime before World War I, the **Seely family** of Castle Dale, south of Price, brought sheep into Under the Ledge, but they stayed mostly to the south of The Maze area. Beginning in 1919 the Chaffin family moved in and in the beginning ran cows mostly in Waterhole Flat and Ernies Country, and apparently on down to Spanish Bottom. Lou was the father and L.M. Chaffin & Sons Cattle Company was the outfit's name. Lou was from the Loa and Torrey area of Wayne County and had been a miner down in Glen Canyon beginning in about 1888. He knew the river well, and had been down to Spanish Bottom before 1900. Since he was aware of the grazing possibilities, it's assumed the Chaffins were the first people to run cattle on Spanish Bottom. However, the sheep men surely beat them there.

Ned Chaffin, one of Lou's younger boys remembers a little bit of what his father told him: *Dad came up that trail before the turn of the century and that trail was there. Dad walked from Spanish Bottom to the mouth of the Dirty Devil. You see, they had heard about these oil sands [in Big Water or Elaterite Basin]. These guys were explorers, and he walked from Spanish Bottom and through The Maze and Waterhole Flat and along where the Hite Road is now. And he said then big stones was there on the trail at that time. We took cattle down there all the time, to Spanish Bottom. Once in a while it'd get so dry on top that we'd take 'em down there to get a drink of water. But normally we liked to keep that for winter range because there was lots of box brush on Spanish Bottom; in fact it was covered with box brush. It was a wonderful place to put cattle in the winter because of the feed and because of the weather too. We probably had 100 or 150 head of cattle Under the Ledge most of the time.*

Before and during the time the Chaffins were there, migratory sheep herds were also in the country. But according the Ned Chaffin, they didn't bother to take sheep down to the river and Spanish Bottom, at least when the Chaffins were there and as far as he knew. Apparently it was just too far down and back up for sheep, and the size of the area was too small to worry about. When the Chaffins left Under the Ledge in 1944-'45, the Moyniers took their place. The only reason the Moyniers bought the Chaffin Ranch on the San Rafael River, was to have commensurate private property so they could run their sheep on the public domain in Under the Ledge.

The only permanent man-made structure on either side of the river was a corral with a deep bed of manure on the north side of the dry creek bed where Lower Red Lake Canyon enters the Colorado. This was on the east side of the river. One of the Chaffins once told C. Gregory Crampton about it, but when he went there in about 1960, Crampton could never locate it. Other than this, the only other known structure to have been built on Spanish Bottom, was by the NPS. They erected a little cabin on the east side of the river to store emergency rescue equipment, but it was there for only 4 years.

Cataract Canyon

Spanish Bottom is a great place to begin hiking and in more than one direction. One hike would be to walk along a faint trail all the way north to **The Confluence**. There are occasionally hikers and boaters out walking this route. From there you could likely continue up along the banks of the Green River then walk up and out of the gorge via Powells Canyon, as described in the previous chapter. The author hasn't done this, but surely it can be done (?).

However, the best hike in the area might be down **Cataract Canyon**. You can actually walk on either side of the river from Spanish Bottom all the way to the upper end of Lake Powell. The distance is only about 19-20 kms, at least to the high water mark (HWM) of the lake.

Before Lake Powell came to be, you could actually walk all the way down to Hite in Glen Canyon, but in some places it must not have been easy. Several people did it in the early days, but the time of year and water levels must have played a role. **E.T. Wolverton** walked through Cataract Canyon once. Here's how he described it in the **Colorado River Bed Case hearings** of 1929:

I have been on foot along the bank of the river through Cataract Canyon to the mouth of the Dirty Devil River. At one place, about ten miles [16 kms] below the first cataract, and at another place, possibly twenty miles [32 kms] below the first cataract where the canyon is very narrow, we were compelled to make a detour. You can always get along the bank of the river there because there is a little talus that is not disturbed lying along the stream. See a picture of E.T. Wolverton on page 42.

There are a number of stories of various people, including miners, who lost boats in Cataract Canyon, then had to walk out. In the *October 30, 1924,* issue of *The Times-Independent* of Moab, a story was told of 2 men who ended up walking back to Moab after they crashed their boat in the canyon about 48 kms below The Confluence. Part of that article states: *A harrowing experience from hunger and exposure was related by Drew Stubbs of Bingham and Ray Rose of Ogden, who staggered into Moab Monday after fighting for their lives for 7 days in the Colorado river canyon, where they were stranded when their boat was dashed to pieces on the rocks of the treacherous cataracts of the lower river.*

Left without provisions, the men fought their way up the river to Moab, a journey of 115 miles [185 kms]. In spite of extreme hunger and exhaustion, they managed to make progress up the river canyon by crawling over cliffs, wading along the banks of the stream, sometimes swimming, sometimes worming their way through the underbrush along the shore. After 6 days of the most gruelling kind of experience, when it seemed that they had reached the limit of their endurance, they arrived at the hunting camp of R.C. Clark, J.T. Leaming and Virgil Baldwin, some twelve miles below Moab. Here they were given food and shown the trail to Moab.......

To begin hiking down Cataract Canyon, walk along a good trail down to the first rapids which is about 1 km downstream from the last campsite on Spanish Bottom. From there the trail comes and goes. Near any of the good campsites along the way are trails going in each direction, up and downriver; but for the most part, you just walk along the river above the HWM. In Cataract Canyon there are very few tamarisks or willows and the appearance is different than in Labyrinth or Stillwater Canyons. In some places near the river you'll find an abundance of driftwood; sometimes stacked in huge piles. You'll also find a number of sandy beaches, some of which can make good campsites. There are other places, especially at or near the mouths of canyons, which have cottonwood trees for shade. In all, there are quite a few good campsites in Cataract Canyon and on either side of the river. On this map, the little campsite symbols shown are official campsites for boaters, so watch where you drop a tent. Boaters have a system of reserving campsites in a log book placed on the east side of the Colorado halfway between The Confluence and Spanish Bottom.

Between the first cataract and Lake Powell's HWM there are about 25 rapids and very few places to reach the canyon rim on the west. However, about mid-way along Cataract, and up above the rim, is a little sunken or graben valley. It's labeled **Sunken Valley** on the map. This is not visible from the river, but you can climb up to it from either end. A good topo map will show it, but you should be able to figure out a route up from either end by using this map. The first route up begins just downstream and across the river from the mouth of **Cross and Y Canyons**. Just climb up a steep gully. The other way up to this hidden valley begins about 2 kms upriver from the mouth of what the Chaffins called **Sand Tank Canyon.**

One good day-hike from the trailhead above Spanish Bottom, would be to walk down to the river via the Spanish Trail, then go downstream to Surprise Canyon, up it and along the trail in Surprise Valley and back to the trailhead. You could also backpack down Cataract to the lake or even further down. Surely you could make it to the mouth of Easter Pasture Canyon, then walk up it and exit at Waterhole Flat, which is featured on the next map. This would be a long hike, maybe 3-4 days, depending on how many vehicles you have and where you park.

You could also return to the canyon rim via one of the 2 routes up to the Sunken Valley. From there you could make your way to The Fins Trail and perhaps even the trailhead at the beginning of The Golden Stairs. There are lots of hiking possibilities here.

This is the trail running between **Shot Canyon** running up to the left; and **Water Canyon** draining down to the right. The Chaffins, including Lou the father, his son Ned, and Riter Ekker built this trail in about 1928 as described in the previous chapter, page 102.

117

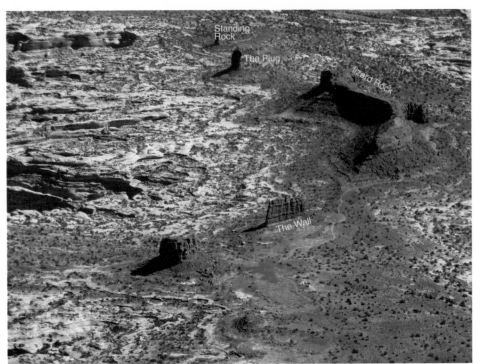

The **Land of Standing Rocks** as seen from the air and looking northeast. Chimney Rock is just out of sight in the upper left hand corner of this foto.

Pictograph Fork, Chocolate Drops and South Fork of Horse Canyon as seen from above and looking southwest. The **Harvest Scene** is to the left, and the route from the Chocolate Drops down into Pictograph Fork is dead center. See **Map 9**.

Looking north down into the head of **Powells Canyon** and the Green River. See previous chapter & **Map 9**. The La Sal Mountains are in the upper right and in the far distance.

Looking northeast down into **Cataract Canyon**. This picture was taken from the rim of the lower end of **Range Canyon**. Notice the gravel bar in the lower right; that's what washed out of Range Canyon.

Waterhole Flat Country: The Chaffins & Seelys, and the Air Rescue of Carl Seely

Location & Access The **Waterhole Flat Country** is located due south of the Flint Trail and southwest of the Land of Standing Rocks. The easiest way to reach this large flat area is to drive along **Highway 95** in the area north of Hite. Between the bridges spanning the Colorado River (now upper Lake Powell) and the lower Dirty Devil River, and between **mile posts 46 & 47**, turn east onto the **Hite Road** (See Map 12). The Hite Road runs northwest through Andy Miller Flats to Waterhole Flat and beyond. From **Waterhole Junction** shown on this map (Km 53.6/Mile 33.3 from Highway 95), you can head for Sunset Pass, the Flint Trail, Millard Canyon; or the Land of Standing Rocks, the Doll House & Spanish Bottom.

The Hite Road is graded all the way to Waterhole Junction but with an occasional rough place, then it slowly deteriorates. Some people classify the Hite Road for 4WD's, but it's better than that. Any higher clearance car can make it to Waterhole Flat & Junction, if driven with care, and in normal conditions. As with any dirt road, you don't want to be there during or after heavy rains. People with lower clearance cars may have to stop in a place or two and throw rocks off the road, or fill in a low place now and then with a shovel. In 1990 & '91, the author went to Waterhole Flat 3 times with his VW Rabbit and never had any problems but that car was equipped with over-sized tires.

Elevations Ocean Point Overlook, 1785m; Chaffin's Camp, 1610m, Waterhole Junction, 1677m; and Lake Powell at the high water mark, 1128m.

Water There's a former stock pond just east of Chaffin's Camp but it will only have water after good rains; so don't bet your life on finding water there! If it has water, you'd need to treat it. Cottonwood Spring may or may not have enough water for a drink; it's the dripping kind. Red Point Spring, which is down in the canyon, is likely a year-round source (?), but it seldom has a flow. The springs in the middle part of Easter Pasture Canyon are there all the time, but a long hike away.

Maps USGS or BLM map Hanksville, and Hite Crossing (1:100,000) for driving there along the Hite Road; Clearwater Canyon & Teapot Rock (1:24,000--7 1/2' quads); or the plastic Trails Illustrated/National Geographic map Canyonlands National Park (1:70,000).

Main Attractions Several hikes to viewpoints on the rim of Cataract Canyon, one interesting route to the bottom of Cataract Canyon, Anasazi ruins, some of the best pictograph panels around, and historic cowboy and/or outlaw etchings.

Best Time to Hike Spring or Fall. March, April, May, September or October.

Author's Experience By 1991, he had been here on 3 different trips by road, and has walked to Ocean Point on 3 other trips from the upper end of Lake Powell. Since then, he's been down Clearwater Canyon with ropes twice and came out Easter Pasture Canyon. He's also passed through the area several other times in 2011 & '12, and has taken one or more hikes to all sights featured on this map.

Waterhole Flat and Chaffin's Camp

Let's begin this chapter at the former **Chaffin's Camp** at the southern end of Waterhole Flat. To get there, drive **51.4 kms (31.9 miles)** from Highway 95 and veer right or east onto a side-road as shown. Continue southeast for **2.1 kms (1.3 miles)** to a place between a **stock pond** and a **stockade-type corral**. This is the place where the Chaffin family built a camp which they used from about 1920 or '21, until 1944 & '45. The late **Ned Chaffin** was there first in 1921 when he was only 8 years old. He remembers this about the place:

When we were in that country, I guess you'd say our headquarters was at Flint [Flint Cabins near the

While on vacation from California in 1938, **Ned Chaffin** is trying to rope a riding horse inside the stockade-type corral at **Chaffin's Camp**. (Ned Chaffin Collection)

Map 11, Waterhole Flat Country: The Chaffins & Seelys, and the Air Rescue of Carl Seely

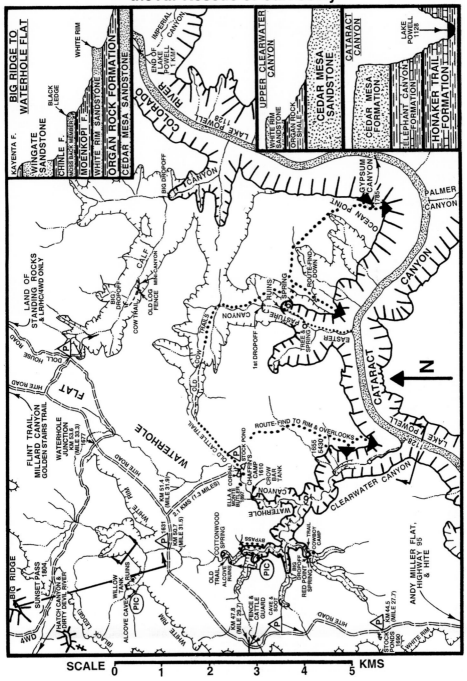

Chaffin's Camp. Left, is the **stockade-type corral** and some old signatures; to the right above the vehicle is the **stock pond**, both were built by the Chaffins in about 1922. The **Chaffin's campsite** is at the far right side of this picture and in front of the SUV.

top of the Flint Trail], the old cabin there, and that's where we'd bring our supplies; then of course we'd pack everything from there. But there at Waterhole Flat was our primary stopping place in the Under the Ledge country. Chaffins were the first and probably the only people to take cattle down in the Under the Ledge country. Of course there was Eph Moore who had cattle in Elaterite Basin and at Anderson Bottom, etc.

Faun, Clell and I, Ned Chaffin, built that stockade-type corral there at the Chaffin Camp. I'm guessin' now, but I think it was built in **1922**. That was the first corral we built. That was the year I was 9 years old. I was down in that country the year before. But somebody has burned down part of it. You see, we used to have a wing there on that corral, so you could herd the stock into it, and it was also a great place for rabbits to stay--with all that brush and logs and all. Dad never would let us kill and eat those rabbits, because he always thought that if somebody come there and was hungry, they could get 'em some rocks and catch them rabbits and have some food.

Faun, Clell, Gay and I made the original Waterhole Flat dam & pond there. We made that after we built the corral. It was sometime in the early 1920's, I think **1922**. The seep over at our camp was just a wet spot, but we got up in there and cleaned the thing out, then went over to Cottonwood Spring and got a bunch of that old red clay and kinda clayed it in there and we put that little half-trough there, and it would make you enough water to water your saddle horse and enough water for camp.

From the stockade-type corral (upright poles), look to the southeast about 125m, and next to a ledge and under some oversized cedar (juniper) trees, will be what's left of **Chaffin's old cow camp**. There's still a flat spot and part of a wooden frame where their tent was placed. Nearby is a small **trough** full of leaves--but no water in 6/2012. Also some old tin cans and what's left of a stove. About 150m northeast from the camp is the old dam & stock pond. It may or may not have water in it, but you'd have to treat it good before using. Just east of that in the upper part of a little drainage, will be some **cottonwood trees** and possibly some little pools of fresh water. Just above that will be some potholes in the slickrock. Maybe some water there too (?). After a long dry spell, there's no water anywhere!

Right behind the corral and on the wall will be some old **cowboy etchings**. But for more real old cowboy & outlaw signatures, walk west down the drainage. After about 300m, look to the right or north, and in a little side-drainage coming in from the north, will be an overhang and some signatures reading: *Ella Butler, 1897; M.R. Butler, 1897 Placerville C.; and Geo. E. Felton 1897.* Some Wild West historians believe Ella and her husband Monte R. Butler may have spent the winter of 1896 & '97 there with the Wild Bunch before Butch & Sundance made tracks for South America.

Monte Butler was apparently a well-know rustler & horse thief in the Indian Creek country during the 1880's & '90, according the research done by Clyde Denis who wrote about Chesler Park in the **Autumn 2010 issue of Canyon Legacy** (buy at Moab's Museum). Butler Wash which drains the country between Beef Basin and The Needles area carries his name.

The late **Pearl Biddlecome Baker**, the gal who grew up on the Robbers Roost Ranch east of Hanksville, once stated that **Ella Butler** was the first woman to be down Under the Ledge. She was the gal who married Jack Moore, and who later nursed J.B. Buhr of the Granite Ranch in the Henry Mountains, back to health. That story is told in the author's book on the **Henry Mountains and Robbers Roost.**

If you continue southwest along the dry wash from the corral and the Butler signatures about 1 km, you'll come to several potholes and maybe some fresh water. The last pothole just before the bottom drops out of Waterhole Canyon was called **Crowbar Tank** by the Chaffins. **Ned Chaffin** recalls an experience they had there one day:

We went down there and took dynamite and fixed it to where you could get livestock down there to the water. Now this was before we built the pond up above. Now this had to be in the very early 1920's. I was just real young. And while working there, I always remember when Clell let the crowbar get away from him and it went down over that big dropoff, and Faun was madder than hell, and really chewed him out and hard-twisted 'im. A hard-twist is when old Joe Biddlecome or Faun Chaffin, or who ever, takes his hard twist rope and doubles it, and lays it down over your weathers! They'd throw you in jail for that now, but I'll tell ya, it sure does wake a guy up. Clell was just a kid at that time. Clell was movin' this rock that we'd just dynamited out, and we had a perfect dump--all you had to do was push it over that ledge and it'd go down 400 or 500 feet [120 to 150m]. And as the rock went, it hit the crowbar someway, and it jerked it out of Clells hands. It's a good thing he didn't try to hang onto it or he might have gone over too. Anyway, that's how we named it Crowbar Tank.

Calf & Clearwater Canyons: Indian Ruins, Caves, Springs and Pictographs

There are several hikes in this area, mostly to scattered caves, Indian ruins and rock art sites. To start, begin at **Waterhole Junction**. From there, take the road running toward the Land of Standing Rocks and the Doll House Road. It first heads south, then quickly veers northeast. After **2.4 kms (1.5 miles)**, you'll see a side-road coming in from the left--it's actually a shortcut that allows people coming down the Flint Trail heading for The Maze area. Park under the big cedar trees in front of you. From that 2WD parking place you can walk south into the upper drainage of **Calf Canyon**. After walking about 2 1/2 kms you'll come to a big dropoff or dryfall. To get down into the middle valley of Calf Canyon, keep to the right or south side. After another 400m, you'll start down a mini side-drainage that runs parallel to, and 75m from, the main canyon. Start down a **natural trail** leading to the bottom. Halfway down this mini canyon will be a bunch of **logs** laid out forming a **fence** which kept calves in the bottom. This was built by the Chaffins during their stay in the country. They used to put young calves down in this middle part of Calf Canyon to wean them from their mothers. Further on and as you reach the junction of the 2 major tributaries of upper Calf, you may see a cave of some kind just as you turn the corner and begin to head north. Somewhere in that area is a pictograph or petroglyph panel Ned Chaffin mentioned once, but this writer never found it. Look for it on some south facing wall or boulder.

Before going to the ruins at Willow Tank, and Cottonwood & Sidewalk Springs, first a little history of an **archeological expedition** which came to this country in the summers of 1929 & '30. **Ned Chaffin** was there and he remembered this:

*It was called the **Emmerson--Claflin Expedition**. Those guys must have furnished the money, and it came out of the **Peabody Museum** back at Harvard University in Cambridge Massachusetts. The gentleman who headed the expedition was Henry Booker Roberts. He was workin' on his doctorate at the time. I worked for 'em in 1929 & '30.*

The first year, in 1929, all we did was reconnoiter--we didn't do a hell of a lot of diggin'. They was camped there at Waterhole Flat and it was after dark, and we was going to camp at Point of the Rocks. When we saw their fire down there, we went on down and they was there. And Roberts asked Faun if I could go with 'em because they wanted someone who really knew the country. They had my good friend Les McDougal from Hanksville with 'em and Faun said I could go with 'em but we had to get the cows branded, so the next day we branded the calves, and when we came back that night Les McDougal was gone. They had laid him off and sent him back to Hanksville. Faun was madder than hell because he didn't want McDougal to lose his job just because I was going to help 'em for a few days. But anyway, we reconnoitered there after we got our calves branded--took us a couple of days. And this was all just goin' and lookin' and seein' what was there. We didn't do any diggin'.

The 2nd year when he came back is when we actually went into the caves and in a scientific manner excavated them. There was Dave Rust--he furnished the mules, and of course was the offi-

This **old log fence** is located along the **cow trail** into the middle part of **Calf Canyon**.

Above On Map 11, these are shown as **Ruins**; and they're on the east side of the drainage just below **Willow Tank**. It looks more like a well-used Fremont Indian campsite than a place that was lived in on a regular basis--or by Anasazi Indians.

Right This tiny **rock art painting** is less than the length of a pen and very intricate. These are found in the **alcove cave** shown on the opposite page (and on Map 11).

Rock Art

The **alcove cave** which holds 2 miniature rock art paintings, one of which is shown on the opposite page. They are just to the left of the words, **Rock Art** seen in this picture.

cial guide of the party. There was Ned Chaffin, I was the mule wrangler and the unofficial guide. There was Henry Booker Roberts who headed up the Expedition. There was also Rand Gordon, James Dennison, and Donald Scott, Jr., all students from Harvard University.

The first thing we did that year [1930], we went over to **Sidewalk Spring**. As you stand there at the dryfall at Sidewalk Spring, you start down the canyon and on the righthand (?) side there's a cave right back in there just a little ways from the spring about 50 yards [45m], and it's kinda hard to see because there's some big rocks out in front of it. And we dug in there and that's where we found an Indian robe, and some very interesting artifacts. Then we went over and investigated the one near **Cottonwood Spring**. We must have spent about a week there; I would say 5 or 6 days anyway. There was 6 of us in the party, and of course I had to take care of the mules. Then we moved up to the **Willow Tank** and did those.

To get to **Willow Tank**, start in the bottom of the drainage where the Hite Road crosses upper Clearwater Canyon. That's **50.7 kms (31.5 miles)** from Highway 95. Park at the crossing, then walk north in the bottom of the dry creek bed. After about 450m, turn left or west and walk along the bottom of a little side-drainage. After another 850-900m, and about 175m from the big dryfall ahead, will be 2 alcoves on either side with **Fremont or Archaic campsites**. This writer found 1 pottery fragment in each, which means the Anasazi may have been in the area at one time--or perhaps their influence (?).

The first will be on your right or east. It has several **old structures** (not moki houses, just low walls), lots of **flint chips** and what appears to be Ned Chaffin's initials *"NLC 34"*. If that's his, it would have been in put in 4 years after the archeologists were there.

The ruins on the left or west side of the canyon, will be in a prominent oval-shaped **cave** or alcove located right on the face of the White Rim Sandstone cliff. You'll have to climb to get there, but there are now 3 tiny moki toe steps. Inside, there is a **low walled camp shelter** and scraps of **wood** up to several thousand years old (if they're from the Archaic people). There are also 3 small **miniature pictographs** on the back wall. These are only about 12-15 cms (6-7") high, but very intricately painted. Please don't touch these. These sites weren't Anasazi, but either Fremont or Archaic instead. Just up the canyon from both of these sites, and under the White Rim will be what the Chaffins called **Willow Tank**. The only time you'll find water there will be right after a flood. Nothing to see there.

Now back to the parking place on the Hite Road; from there, walk downcanyon the dry creek bed of upper **Clearwater Canyon** about 2 kms. At that point will be a 7-8m dropoff and several **cottonwood trees** in the narrows below. If you skirt to the right about 125m, you'll come to an **old trail** allowing you down in. This was built by Joe Biddlecome (of the Robbers Roost Ranch, and Pearl's father) and Lou, Faun & Clell Chaffin in the early 1920's. Near the trees will be what the Chaffins called **Cottonwood Spring**. On several trips, the author didn't find enough water there to get a drink, as the drips are pretty slow.

From the bottom of the trail into Cottonwood Spring, walk downcanyon about 175m. Right where it turns to the left is an big overhang or **alcove** on the right. If you climb up behind all the rocks in front, you'll see a couple of **fire pits, storage bins or ruins** of some kind (see foto on page 126), and the initials: *Ned Chaffin Aug. 17th 1930*. High on the wall and back to the east 15m or so, will be some very much **eroded pictographs** similar to those in Horseshoe Canyon and in the Barrier Creek style.

From this alcove cave, continue downcanyon. After another 500m, will be the first of 6 rappels if you're going down Clearwater Canyon. But for now, walk along a bench on the right or west side of the 40m deep narrows. Roughly 100m from where it first drops off, climb up 5-6m onto the next little bench above to find an emerging hiker's trail weaving through boulders. After another 50m or so, look ahead

Above This is the alcove about 175m below **Cottonwood Spring.** There are a couple of rock-lined holes or boxes; they may have been milling bins, but there was little if any farming in this area and no sign of metatas in this cave. There are some pretty good **pictographs** on the wall above and behind the camera.

Right Cottonwood Spring. Not much water here; you'd need a bucket or two to catch the drops.

another 350m and you can see another **pictograph panel** on a smooth wall facing east. Walk there to see one of the neatest & best preserved panels around. See foto on page 130. These are strikingly similar to the red paintings at the Grand Gallery, the Harvest Scene, and in Range & Hell Roaring Canyons. Because they're all so close together, this writer believes all these could have been painted by the same person, or at least the same clan; but archeologists apparently can't date them with consistency. While there, look directly across the canyon to the east to see a route back down to the bottom of Clearwater bypassing the possible 1st rappel mentioned above. This panel and that route down indicate the aborigines who lived here must have spent a lot of time in Clearwater Canyon.

From Clearwater Canyon walk back to your car and drive southwest on the Hite Road to the area west of what this writer once called **Sidewalk Spring**. But first, there's a problem with locating this place. It seems this writer was there in 1990 or '91 (?), but when he went back down to what he thought was the right drainage in 6/2012, he found nothing that resembled what was described in the 1st Edition of this book. The sad part of this story is, this writer had a casual conversation with Ned Chaffin in the spring of 2011 about this part of the country, and was told that his brother Clell had done some blasting there and that it was a good spring. Then Ned died on 11/11/2011--and this writer still has a million questions to ask! Ned was the last person alive who knew anything about the early history of this country--and now he's taken all those memories with him.

So, the **apparent (?)** starting place is **47.8 kms (29.7 miles)** from Highway 95. That's an easy place to find, because it has a **fence & cattle guard**, and a **sign**. North of that, you have to have reservations and pay $30 to camp where they want you to; south of that sign, camp anywhere you damn well please--but don't leave a mess or ride ATV's everywhere, or the CNP outfit will slap restrictions on that country too!

Here's what the author wrote in the 1st Edition regarding Sidewalk Spring. *From the road, just walk down the drainage bottom about 1 km. From the first dropoff with water probably below, walk left and look for a way down in. Only about 300 meters below the dropoff will be a cave on the left or north side. Not much to see there.* If anybody finds anything that resembles this, or what Ned Chaffin described above, please contact the author.

Another drainage that doesn't have a good spring is south of the fence & cattle guard about 1.3 kms. Park right in the obvious dry wash and head downcanyon. After about 800m is a dropoff into a narrows, but no spring or sign of blasting. About 125m below that and on the left or west is an alcove where the canyon turns eastward. In that Fremont or Archaic era **cave** are flint chips and a fair amount of **soot** from campfires on the ceiling. Nothing of interest is in the canyon below that.

Another interesting hike in this area would be to park just below the **stock ponds** at **1690m** as shown on the map. This is **44.5 kms (27.7 miles)** from Highway 95. Walk right down the drainage. Stay to the right when you reach the first dropoff. Further on, you'll come to another dropoff, and a route on the left or north leading down to a cave Indians used on the right which is where the Chaffin's had another camp. Just below this is a **big dropoff** and pools & spring and water below. This appears to be what Ned called **Red Point Spring**. Downclimb to it from the right or southeast side of the canyon.

Easter Pasture Canyon and the Hike to Ocean Point & Lake Powell

For the more adventurous, 2 of the best hikes on this map would be down **Easter Pasture Canyon** to Upper Lake Powell, and/or to an overlook of Cataract Canyon at **Ocean Point**. To get to these places, drive to and park at or just north of **Chaffin's Camp**, a distance of 2.1 kms (1.3 miles) from the Hite Road. From there, walk northeast about 1 1/2 kms and get down into the upper part of Easter Pasture on a trail the Chaffins, and a few cows built. Faun Chaffin named this drainage Easter Pasture Canyon because he got down there for the first time on an Easter Sunday sometime in the early 1920's.

About a km into the shallow upper end of this drainage, scan the south facing wall to the north. There's a small granary there somewhere, but this writer has yet to find it. Farther along and after you begin to walk south, the canyon slowly deepens. About 5 kms from Chaffin's Camp you'll come to the **1st dropoff**. This is the first of 2 in the canyon. From there skirt to the left or east side of the drainage and contour along one level or bench in a southerly direction. Soon you'll be one bench above and to the east of the 2nd dropoff.

From this 2nd dropoff you have an option. If you work your way down over some ledges, you'll come to a permanent **spring** and an Anasazi ruins or moki house just to the west of the spring and immediately under the 2nd dropoff. If you continue downcanyon, you'll eventually make it to Lake Powell. There are several places in this canyon where water appears and runs for a short distance, but it's all in the upper half of the lower part of Easter Pasture Canyon.

From this part of Lake Powell, you probably could, in times of low water, walk along the mud flats all the way upcanyon to Spanish Bottom and The Confluence. Any difficulty you might have would be near the mouth of Easter Pasture. This would be an exciting hike for the adventurous person. Another slightly less challenging hike would be to walk from the mouth of Easter Pasture, along the HWM and just above the tamarisks to the west, and into the mouth of Clearwater Canyon (which has a nice year-round stream). This writer has been down the entire length of Clearwater twice using ropes and came up and out via Easter Pasture. It was done in 2 days the first time; one long day the 2nd. See this writer's other book, *Technical Slot Canyon Guide to the Colorado Plateau, 2nd Edition* for details.

Now back to the 2nd dropoff with the spring & ruins. From there, route-find up through several ledges to the east until you arrive on top of the plateau. From there, you could walk south to a great viewpoint looking west to **Clearwater Canyon**, straight down on the mouth of Easter Pasture, or southeast up Cataract and Palmer Canyons; or just wander east, then southeast in the direction of **Ocean Point**. Be sure to stay at the head of 2 minor drainages which drain south. Once you get to Ocean Point, you'll have several overlooks to choose from. Looking south will be **Palmer Canyon,** while to the southeast will be the mouth of **Gypsum Canyon**. You can also see a long way north into the bottom of Cataract Canyon. From that point the lake is about 675m below (over 2200 feet). This is probably the best place to look down into Cataract Canyon.

Another very good place to see into this super gorge is from a place high above the mouth of Clearwater Canyon. Get there by walking southeast, then south from Chaffin's Camp. See the approximate route on the map.

Sheepmen Under the Ledge and the Air Rescue of Carl Seely

The following comes from an interview with the late **Carl Seely**. He grew up in Castle Dale, Utah, then lived in Meeker, Colorado in summer, and Mesa, Arizona in winter for several years. He comes from a family of livestock men, and this is how he remembered his days in the **Waterhole Flat** and **Under the Ledge:**

The first time I was Under the Ledge was in 1931. My father and his brother were there earlier. They had been there a number of years before I came into the scene. I don't think my dad was ever down there, but he had men who took sheep down there. His brother was kinda the guy who took care of the range operation, and my father was the wheeler-dealer and trader, and run the business end of it. My dad's name was **Hyrum** or **Hy Seely**. His brother's name was **Karl**, the same as mine, except they spelled his name with a K. They must have been there before World War I, but I don't know how long.

There was a period of time from about 1924 to 1930, when I was kind of off the scene, when I went to the University of Utah, and went on a [LDS] mission, so there was a period of about 6 years that I wasn't around.

We run sheep all over down there **Under the Ledge**. We had about 10,000 sheep. We had 4 herds of about 2500 in each herd. That was a normal size winter herd. Then in the summer time when they had lambs, they'd split 'em, and with the lambs you'd still have about 2500. When I first came into the picture in 1931, one of the Basque sheepmen from Price, **Pete Maziet**, ran sheep down there in Ernies Country (**Pete's Mesa** east of the Maze Overlook carries his name). I knew Pete Maziet. I think the first year I was down there was about the last year he was. In fact that's one reason I went in there, I had talked to Pete, and he said he was pulling out and that you might as well have it. We had lots of sheep, so when he moved out, we moved in. So we had the whole thing to ourselves then. My uncle **Karl Seely**, he had one herd of sheep, and my father had a herd, they each had about 2500 sheep. And **Quince Crawford** always had a herd of sheep there too, about 2500. Between us we covered all that country with 4 herds.

You could go down Under the Ledge about anytime with 2 or 3 herds, because you always had water for those, but if you put more than that, you'd have to wait until you got snow. We would usually take sheep down there about the first of December, usually it would snow a little then. We would just trail the sheep from Castle Dale out there. We'd go down with a couple of herds of sheep in late November, because there was some water. Taking them out of the area depended on the season and water too. In the spring after the snow would melt, you'd have to start a herd or two out, but then you could always leave a herd or two in 'till later in areas where there was a little water. We'd bring 'em out usually in March. We usually spent some time out on the Big Desert [San Rafael Desert] and around the Roost.

We usually took the sheep down what we called the **North Trail**. I don't think we ever took sheep down the Flint Trail--that I know of. Then we'd usually bring in one or 2 bands of sheep in through Hanksville and down what they called North Wash and the Dirty Devil River into **Happy Canyon**. We always had a herd in Happy Canyon.

Pearl Biddlecome Baker knew the sheepmen, because they all used to come in there [Robbers Roost Ranch] for their supplies. Pearl never did have a store but she used to board us when the camp movers went out with supplies. She'd always put us up overnight and feed us.

We had 2 granaries there at the Roost Ranch, then later we moved them over to what they call **Granary Spring**. I instituted that and developed the spring. It was just a little seep, and I did quite a little work on it, then we moved the granaries over there from the Roost. Later some of the other sheepmen had their granaries there too; there must have been 5 or 6 there then. I also built a cellar there to keep stuff from freezing in winter. We'd have to bring food out there for the sheepherders and sometimes they wouldn't get there right when you thought they would, so we'd leave it there. We had a truck, and that was an ordeal--it used to take us 5 or 6 hours from Green River and it was only about 60 miles [100 kms]. We didn't have very good roads in those days.

I remember at one time there were 25 herds of sheep that got their supplies out of the Roost. It must have been in about the mid-1930's. I think we all overgrazed it, but if there was a place that wasn't overgrazed, it was that Under the Ledge country, because it was a difficult place to get into and get out of. I think most people didn't want to buck it down there. You were down there where only a young buck would dare try it. Some of the older guys didn't want to be so far from home.

To get from the Robbers Roost to the far end of that country would take us 3 days--I'm speaking now of the camp movers. The first night we'd usually go to the **Flint Cabin**. That was a regular stop. That corral at Flint has been constructed since I was there [it's nowhere to be found now, 2012]. We always turned our horses loose at night with hobbles on 'em. Then if you were going around to **Waterhole Flat**, you could make that the next day, but if you were going further around to **Andy Miller Flats**, it would take you the better part of another day to make it. The main reason for that was that your mules would be loaded so heavy that they'd get tired and would only go on a walk. We used pack mules.

We'd have 5 mules, and then what we called the **"bell mare"**. The camp mover would usually ride the mare, and for some reason, these mules would stay around with a mare [female] where they wouldn't with a horse. Then we'd have a couple of saddle horses for the sheepherders, so usually you'd have 8 animals. And we always had 2 sheep herders together down there then.

We'd turn the mules and horses loose at night so they could feed, then we'd feed 'em some oats. We'd put a big bell on the mare, then you could hear 'em, because they might be a mile or 2 away by the next morning. The mules would always go with the mare, so when you heard the bell ring, you'd know which way to go to get 'em.

At my sheep camp, I just had an old tent set up, an 8' x 10' [2 1/2 x 3m], and a little portable camp stove. Then I'd roll my bed in the tarp and tie it up in a cedar tree or some where so that mice wouldn't get into it. Then sometimes I'd just carry a bed roll and throw it under a pine or cedar tree--I've done that a lot of times. We'd usually have a tarp because that was pretty waterproof. We put that both under and over us, then they'd usually come with little clips on the sides so you could fold them over and roll 'em up.

We'd try to put one good bell on about every hundred sheep too, and for the same reason. Some sheep would stay together in a herd, others would spread out. It would depend on the breed of sheep. We used to run pretty much **Rambulet sheep** and they have the herd instinct pretty strong. They had a tendency to stay together. When they moved, they stayed just far enough apart to feed. But in later years we bred 'em so they were a little looser wool and they got so they didn't have quite the herd instinct as strong; they had a tendency to spread out more.

When I was a kid, the Tidwells used to have shearing crews of 40 or 50 men. And I guess that paid better money than anything else. So in the spring of the year somebody who could shear sheep and wanted to make a little money, would join one of those crews and shear sheep. At that **mountain shearing corral in Price** they used to shear about 125,000 sheep there ever spring. **Thompson** was another shipping point and they had a big **shearing corral** there too. I've sheared sheep there at Thompson.

128

A sheep shearer gets paid by the head. They used to shear with blades, the hand shearers, and I've seen some of those guys shear 100 sheep in 8 hours. You had to be pretty good to do that many. And a good shearer with a power shearer can shear 125 head in a day. But the best shears I ever saw were the blades. Of course they had to keep those shears sharp and then you could hardly feel them cutting.

We always sheared before lambing. We used to start to **lamb** from the **10th to the 20th of May**. You always wanted your sheep sheared before then; if you could. If you didn't, the wool would get around the ewe's bag and tits, and the lambs would get ahold of a lock of wool and couldn't reach the tit so they'd starve to death. So we always liked to get 'em sheared before lambing. The **shearing** time normally ran from about **April 15** until the **10th of May**. We used to put the bucks with the ewes on Christmas day and that would make 'em lamb on the 20th of May. I think the gestation period is 5 months, lacking 5 days.

I was down in that country from 1931 until about 1940. The last time I was there was when they flew me out. I was on **Waterhole Flat**, and I had a spike camp there. You see, we had 5 herds of sheep down there then, and sometimes I couldn't make it to one of the other camps so I just set up a temporary camp there where I had a bed and could cook something to eat if I got caught there alone. So that's where I was. Well anyway, I got a bad cold and it settled in my ear and I got a mastoid infection and pneumonia and boy I really got sick! This was along just before **Christmas in 1940**.

So anyway, one of my own men came by and I had him bring me some Vicks. He was at one of the other camps. And then I really got sick, my face and ear swelled up, and I think I must have been out of my head. One of my own men had told **Faun Chaffin** that I was ill, so he came by one night about sundown. I couldn't get out of bed. He wanted to do something for me, and I said, "I can't ride out of here and I sure can't walk, so we might have to get an airplane in here some way if we can. That's the only way I'll ever get out of here."

So there was a fellow named **Eddy Drapula**. He was in Grand Junction and was kind of a bush pilot. I'd heard or read something about him, so I said, "Maybe if we can get a hold of him, maybe he'll come in here with a small plane". So Faun said, "I've been riding all day with these horses, but if you'll let me take your 2 fresh saddle horses I'll ride to the Roost tonight, then I'll take your pickup and go to Green River to a telefone and try to get that guy out here". So that's what he did. He rode all night and they got a hold of this guy on the telefone, I don't know who did that, I guess my wife who was in Green River. The pilot said he'd try, so he came to Green River and picked up Faun, and Faun came back with him to where I was camped. He had to show the pilot where to go.

So in the mean time, one of my own men had come around to see how I was, because they knew I was ill. He happened to be there when the airplane and Faun came back and they cleared some brush out of the way and fixed a little runway to where they thought this plane could land. There were 5 guys there when the plane landed. They was Bill Patton, Clyde Wareham, Faun Chaffin, Eddy Drapula the pilot, and of course me, Carl Seely.

Since I couldn't walk, they had to pack me into the airplane; I remember that. Then he flew me into Price to the hospital. It was just a little tiny plane, and I guess the pilot had put in all the fuel he could to get out there. But as I remember, he had to drain some of the fuel out there, because he didn't know if he could lift off. Then of course Faun got out and I got in. As it turned out, he was so short of fuel, he had to stop in Green River and get more in order to make it to Price.

At Green River, someone, perhaps one of the French sheepmen, I think it was one of the Moyniers, had heard that I was out there and coming in, and they met me at Green River and went into town and told my wife. I had a home in Green River at the time. When I first got to the hospital my head was all swelled up, and I remember the first thing they did was to take an X-ray of that, then came in with a knife and lanced this ear and puss just shot out of there. I got some relief after that. I also had pneumonia, so I stayed in the hospital several days. About the only antibiotic they had then was sulfa and they gave me that. And I took too much, because for a month or so after that I broke out all over.

So anyway, I give old Faun Chaffin and Eddy Drapula credit for saving my life, otherwise I'd never have got out of there. I also doubt anyone else would have tried to land a plane in that country.

One of **Carl Seely's** fotos. It shows **Carl's camp** with the wall tent he describes on the opposite page, plus horses and mules all with nose bags eating oats for breakfast. It was taken at what he called **Meeting House Hill at Water Hole Flat Under the Ledge.** This writer still isn't 100% sure where Meeting House Hill is, but sheepmen always camp on a high place so they can watch the herd.

Above This is the rock art panel in the upper end of **Clearwater Canyon**. It might be the best preserved of all the Barrier Canyon style rock art around the Green River area. It has lots of resemblance to the art work at the Great Gallery & the Harvest Scene, and in Range & Hell Roaring Canyons. This panel was likely seen for the first time by white people after about the year 2000; that's when hikers starting going down Clearwater Canyon using ropes. From the end of the canyon, they walked northeast along the edge of Lake Powell and left Cataract Canyon via **Easter Pasture Canyon.**

Right From **Ocean Point** looking northward up **Cataract Canyon**. There are several rapids shown here, which is just above the mouth of Gypsum Canyon. This picture was taken in July of 2007 when Lake Powell was at a low point. When the lake is at or near its HWM, these rapids are under the surface of the lake.

Above Spanish Bottom as seen from about halfway up/down the trail to the Doll House on the west side of the Colorado River. You're looking northeast at the lower end of Red Lake Canyon just a little right of center.

Left This is believed to be **Red Point Spring** in a little westside tributary of upper **Clearwater Canyon**. Water seeps out from above, and is found in small pools in the lower left part of this foto.

The Hite Road: The Block and Cove Spring, and Ned's Hole and Rock Canyon

Location & Access The area on this map shows the **Hite Road** from where it leaves **Highway 95**, between **mile posts 46 & 47**, all the way to just before you reach Waterhole Flat. You can approach this country from The Hans Flat (Maze) Ranger Station and the Flint Trail too, but the Hite Road going to this area is just a short drive from Hite and the nearest gas station.

The **Hite Road** is generally very good, as graded county roads are, but it's best to have some kind of higher clearance vehicle. Most spots are smooth and it's graded all the way to **Waterhole Junction**, but if you're driving a car, there are a few rough places, where you may have to stop and throw rocks off the road. Be sure to take a shovel too just in case.

Elevations South Block, about 2070m; Cove Spring, 1646m; beginning of Hite Road near Highway 95, 1220m; and Lake Powell at the high water mark (HWM), 1128m.

Water Cove Spring and the spring at Ned's Hole were bone dry in 6/2012, but you might get water from potholes in lower Rock Canyon. In other words, take lots of water because there's none there.

Maps USGS or BLM map Hite Crossing (1:100,000); Sewing Machine, Fiddler Butte, Clearwater Canyon & Bowdie Canyon West (1:24,000--7 1/2' quads).

Main Attractions A hike to the top of the South Block; some pretty good narrows in Rock Canyon, and a possible way down into Cataract Canyon.

Best Time to Hike or Visit Spring or Fall. March, April, May, September and October are best.

Bowdie & Cataract Canyon Overlooks

For those interested in having a look down into Cataract Canyon in the upper end of Lake Powell, here's a pretty good way. From between **mile posts 146 & 147** on Highway 95, turn east onto the **Hite Road**. This is the same road that runs on to Waterhole Flat & Junction. After **42.3 kms (26.3 miles)**, will be a side-road running east and downhill for another 1.2 kms (.8 mile). Along the way, will be **2 stock ponds** on the left or north, and just before the end of that road are a couple of rough places, but cars can go most of the way. You won't have a good look into Cataract Canyon from the end of the road, so walk & route-find downhill and over 2 ledges to get a better look at where **Bowdie Canyon** empties into Cataract and the upper end of Lake Powell.

A little farther south down the Hite Road, and at about **Km 41.3 (Mile 25.6)** can be the beginning point for a cross-country hike to another place on the rim of Cataract Canyon and a possible way down. See the approximate route on the map. It'll take some looking around, but there's an indentation in the wall about 2 kms uplake from the mouth of **Cove Canyon**. The author once came up to that point from his boat on the lake, and while he didn't reach the actual rim, it appeared that a route exists to the top. But he hasn't gotten there from the road. There doesn't seem to be any landmarks, so you'll just have to look for the one spot to hopefully get down. Better take a short rope too, if you want to try to get to the lake. Once off the rim, you could walk along a bench about halfway down, and enter the lower portion of Cove Canyon; or you could get down to the shore of Lake Powell. If the water levels are real

This picture was taken about 1 km below the end of the road going to the **Bowdie/Cataract Canyon Overlook**. Upper right is **Bowdie Canyon** draining into upper Lake Powell from the east.

Map 12, The Hite Road: The Block and Cove Spring, and Ned's Hole and Rock Canyon

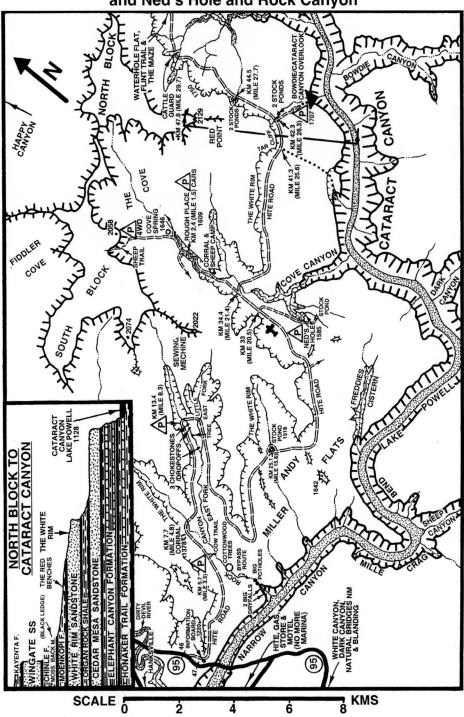

SCALE 0 2 4 6 8 KMS

The old **sheep camp** (or wagon), minus wheels, which is parked next to the **corral** in the middle part of **Cove Canyon**. These rigs were big enough to sleep 2 people, plus they were equipped with a dining table, cupboards and stove. Some newer models have solar panels and a small B+W TV.

low, like they were throughout the 2000's, then you could walk up or down canyon quite a ways on the alluvial or mud benches on either side of the lake/river. You could spend just 2 or 3 hours there, or all day.

The Cove, Cove Spring and the Sheep Trail to the top of the South Block

As you drive around the middle part of **Cove Canyon**, you'll come to where a side-road (**34.4 kms/21.4 miles** from Highway 95) heads north into a shallow drainage above. This is generally known as **The Cove**. If you drive this track, you'll soon come to an old **corral** and next to it, an dilapidated **sheep camp**. See the picture above. This is a special wagon that some sheepherder lived in while herding sheep in this country; and all sheep camps look alike. Further along to the north are some camping places. The best ones are where the White Rim Canyon constricts. Finally this old track heads northwest up and out of the shallow canyon to the bench formed by the White Rim Sandstone. That part of the road is for HCV vehicles. About **1.6 kms (1 mile)** above the 1st rough place and off to the right or northeast will be **Cove Spring**. You can't see it from the road, but the author left a large stone **cairn** where you can park and walk 250m down to the spring--which was bone dry on 6/2/2012! But there are several troughs, tanks and plastic pipes scattered about.

At one time back in the 1930's, **Carl Seely** (read his story is the previous chapter along with Waterhole Flat) had this spring fixed up with tanks, troughs or tubs to collect water, but it's been allowed to deteriorate and now it would be hard to get a safe drink--even if there is water to be found.

If you're up for what could be an interesting hike, walk, mtn. bike or drive a HCV along the pretty good road that this writer didn't see or use in 1991. It runs past Cove Spring heading northwest. About 1.5 kms past the spring the road ends abruptly with the **South Block**, the southern-most extension of the **Big Ridge** to the north, in front of you. From there, walk west along a faint trail. It runs a little to the left or west and eventually into the shallow but obvious drainage coming down from the top. Going up, stay well to the right or north of the drainage bottom, and up closer to the wall on right; that's where the trail is found. The higher you go, the more visible the trail is. Cairns mark the way.

Carl Seely, who once grazed sheep up there, said somewhere on the western rim of this mesa are some rim-top Indian ruins and nearby some rather large natural tanks or potholes. These would be on the upper part of this map somewhere. Expect to take about half a day to reach the mesa top and return; or a lot longer if you look for the ruins. This mesa or plateau is rather flat, so you will need the 7 1/2' quads. To find your way back to the trail, this is the best place to use a GPS; but you still must have a map & compass! The author parked at the 1st rough place, and walked to the rim and returned, including hunting for Cove Spring, in 3 1/3 hours.

Ned's Hole

Another short hike to an interesting place would be to what got the name **Ned's Hole** hung on it. This place is named for the late **Ned Chaffin**, the cowboy who did some work on a spring there. He told about the place and how the 7, #3 galvanized steel bath tubs got down there:

I stole those #3 tubs from Carl Seely. He had a lot of tubs up at Cove Spring to water his sheep in. So we borrowed some tubs, only a couple of 'em, because there wasn't much water down there. We camped there a lot--a good place to camp. It had just enough water for camp and you might water a saddle horse or two. This was throughout the time we were down in that country.

To get there, drive along the Hite Road to a point **33 kms (20.5 miles)** from Highway 95. This is just less than a mile (1 1/2 kms) south of the turnoff to The Cove. At that point turn east onto a side-road which soon heads south. Drive about **1.4 kms or .9 mile**, and turn left or east into some cedar trees-- a good place to camp. From there, walk due east a short distance to the rim of a shallow drainage. Find a way down in and continue east to an overhang about 200m from the parking place. Under the overhang will be a minor seep and next to it, 7 of the old #3 sized galvanized tubs (the exact same kind this writer bathed in until 1954!). They're in good condition, because there never was enough water to fill them and they stay dry under the overhang. They were placed there sometime in the early 1930's.

Also, you'll see where Ned rigged 3 short pieces of what appear to be parts of a rain gutter up against the wall under the seam where the water seeps out. This was to catch water and divert it a meter away to a cement tank set at ground level. From it, he had a pipe coming out of one corner hoping to divert water to one of the tubs. They must have had more water then than there was on 6/2/2012, because there wasn't enough water on that day to get a drink! A lot of work for very small return! Getting to and seeing this place would only take a few minutes from where you park.

Rock Canyon

If you're interested in a slot canyon with pretty good narrows, then **Rock Canyon** might work. There are many places you can enter, but here are 3 of the best. About **5.7 kms (3.5 miles)** from Highway 95, turn east onto a very short road; drive 35m and park. From there, walk southeast roughly 300m to the first rim of the shallow Rock Canyon. Two cairns mark routes off this rim, then walk east another 200m and look for scuff marks of horse and/or cows hoofs going down slickrock. At the bottom, someone has recently used a power handsaw to make steps for cows. From there turn back to the west below the 2nd bench to find a bunch of weathered bones of at least 4 cows (yours truely carried away 2 heads!). From there get into the drainage and walk southward downcanyon. All the little black rocks you see in this drainage bottom are pieces of petrified wood from the Chinle Formation further upcanyon.

The further you go, the deeper it gets. After a km or so, you'll see a bunch a **cottonwood trees**; after about 2 kms, will be a couple of dropoffs into some narrows below. At that point, get up on the left or north side and bench-walk around another 400m; this is the **bypass trail or route** on the map. Then downclimb 20m in a steep raven to the narrows below. Continue downcanyon (passing a couple of big potholes or pools) about another 800-900m to find a 35-40m dropoff into an impressive narrow gorge. From there, again bench-walk to the right or west side and thread your way through boulders to an overlook of the lower end of Rock Canyon and Lake Powell in **Narrow Canyon**. Near the lake is another dropoff of about 35-40m. The author did this hike from the road and returned in 2 3/4 hours in 6/2012.

Now back to where you entered the canyon bottom. If you go upcanyon, you should be able to go as far as a big dropoff in about the middle part of the East Fork of Rock Canyon; that will stop you, and you'll need a rope to get down it if coming down from the upper end.

Here's another starting point for another short hike. Go to the upper end of the **East Fork of Rock Canyon** and park. This will be **13.4 kms (8.3 miles)** from Highway 95. Get into the shallow drainage and head downcanyon. After about 400m will be a chokestone & dropoff; anyone worth their salt can

downclimb this. After another 200m is another chokestone; downclimb it on the right and into a short fairly deep slot; and maybe a pool (?). Continue for another km to a 3rd downclimb. Just after that an upper **little east fork** enters on the left or east side. You could go up that, or head downcanyon. Lots of choices. This short hike took the author about 1 hour.

Just to the east of the lower end of Rock Canyon are 2 short drainages cutting deep into the Cedar Mesa Sandstone. The author hasn't seen either of these, but it's certain you'll find some good but short narrows, dry-falls, probably potholes and some big rappels. This is the same sandstone formation which White Canyon cuts down through in its lower end, and where the Black Hole is located. That's just across the lake to the south of this mapped area. See the author's other book, *Non-Technical Canyon Hiking Guide to the Colorado Plateau, 6nd Edition* for more information on that hike.

One last hike in this area you might be interested in, is to walk from the Hite Road to **Freddies Cistern**. Only with a rope can you get all the way down to Lake Powell--but only if the lake is really high can you reach water. Not so interesting.

In the lower end of **Rock Canyon** are some pretty good, but very short narrows and/or slots. You can walk around this part, but if you're properly equipped, you just slide in swim a little, then walk out. But check the situation out first from the rim.

Above Looking northwest at the watering troughs at **Cove Spring**. The spring is located up the drainage to the left, but it was bone dry in the summer of 2012. Also in the upper left, and in the far distance, is the open drainage where the **sheep trail** to the top of the **South Block** is located.

Right The narrows in the upper end of the **East Fork of Rock Canyon**. This place is below the 2 upper chokestones.

Above Under an over-hang known as **Ned's Hole.** These **#3 galvanized bath tubs** were brought down from Cove Spring in the early 1930's, but there was never enough water from this little spring to fill one. To the far right at the bottom of the wall is the spring or seep that Ned Chaffin tried to develop.

Left The first of 2 big dropoffs or dryfalls in the lower end of **Rock Canyon**. This is a drop of about 35-40m. Notice the pool at the bottom.

Trin Alcove Bend, Tenmile, Hey Joe and Spring Canyons and Bowknot Bend, and the History of Dubinky & Well

Location & Access The region covered here lies between the Green River and the area around the Moab Airport and Highway 191. The high country east of the Green River and north of Canyonlands NP is generally known as **Dubinky country**; whereas anything near Tenmile Canyon or Point is often called **Tenmile country**. Lesser-used names for parts of this region would be the Spring Canyon Point, Deadman Point or Mineral Point areas.

Map 13 shows much of the country **Between the Rivers**, a name used frequently by old timers who grew up in this area before the uranium mining boom of the 1950's. Use **Maps 13 & 14** in this book, and the **Latitude 40° Moab West** map, or the **TI/NG map Moab North** to find your way around. One important access route to look for is the **Blue Hills Road**. It runs from new mile post & **Exit 175** on I-70, southeast to near mile post 143 on **Highway 191**, which is just south of the Moab Airport. From along this road you can turn southwest and drive to the Ruby Ranch, Tenmile Point & Canyon, onto the Dubinky Road, and/or to Brink Spring, a good source of drinking water.

Taking **Tenmile Point Road** will allow you access to Placer Bottom, Trin Alcove Bend, Tenmile & F Canyons, and Slaughter Bottom. By turning off the Blue Hills Road and taking the **Dubinky Road** south, you'll have access to the Dubinky country, plus Spring Canyon & Point, another road into Tenmile Canyon from the south, and to Deadman Point. You can also turn off paved **Highway 313** running up **Sevenmile Canyon** to Deadhorse Point and the Island in the Sky District of Canyonlands NP; and onto the Dubinky Road (right at mile post 14), which takes you to Hell Roaring & Spring Canyons and Deadman Point, the Mineral Point Road, and Mineral Bottom Road.

Here's a list of main roads and their condition from North to South. Blue Hills Road is good for all vehicles but it can be slick in places during wet weather. Ruby Ranch Road is very good for all traffic. Tenmile Point Road is good for cars all the way to Trin Alcove Bend and to Tenmile Point. Spring Canyon Point Road has been graded all the way to the end where an old drill hole is found; it's normally good for cars--if driven with care. The Spring Canyon Road is a little steep in places (it's almost a twin to the Horsethief Road going down to the Mineral Bottom boat ramp), but good for cars down to the Green River. Deadman Point Road is ungraded and a HC vehicle is needed. The Mineral Point Road was once graded to a drill hole site and is good for cars to a point, but toward the end, its been allowed to deteriorate (as of 2012). The Mineral Bottom (or Horsethief Point) Road is a very good & well-used county road and good for all cars. See **Maps 13, 14 & 15** for a better look at this section.

Before venturing into the back roads of this region, remember to have a full tank of fuel and extra food, water, tow rope, tools, etc, to be able to handle any emergency. The Dubinky, Spring Canyon, Mineral Bottom and Blue Hills Roads are graded and fairly heavily used with a fair amount of traffic in the warmer 8 months of the year, but others here are less-used. If you get stuck or have a breakdown, it could be a long walk for help and a long wait. Individual roads will be discussed in more detail below.

Elevations Dubinky Well, 1614m; Dubinky, 1593m; Halverson's former cabin site & Dripping Spring, 1329m; the Green River at Bowknot Bend, about 1210m.

Water There's good water at Dripping Spring, but you'll have to catch it in a pan or bucket. Also in parts of Tenmile Canyon, but cattle are there in the winter months, November to April or May. There's good water in **upper Spring Canyon**, both running and directly from springs. There will not be water at Dubinky Well, it's broke down for good. **Brink Spring** is still alive and well at the water trough below the old stone cabin. Also, there's usually some live water in **F Canyon** (see Map 14). And, possibly at Deadman Springs and the upper end of Hell Roaring Canyon near Jewell Tibbetts Arch.

Maps (Needed to cover Map 13) USGS or BLM maps San Rafael Desert and Moab (1:100,000); Dee Pass, Merrimac Butte, Jug Rock, Tenmile Point, Bowknot Bend, Mineral Canyon & The Knoll (1:24,000--7 1/2' quads); the plastic Trails Illustrated/National Geographic (TI/NG) Moab North (mostly at 1:70,000); or the plastic Latitude 40° map **Moab West** (1:75,000).

Main Attractions About 5 roads leading to viewpoints of the Green River Gorge, several canyons with interesting hikes & historic trails, some rock art, and an old historic ranch & well called Dubinky.

Tenmile Point: Placer Bottom, Trin Alcove Pt, F Canyon & Slaughter Bottom

Refer to **Map 14**. The best way into the northern Tenmile Canyon country is to drive along the **Blue Hills Road**. From I-70, drive south & southeast **13.2 kms (8.2 miles)** from Exit 175; that junction will be the beginning of the **Tenmile Point Road**. Or drive **21.9 kms (13.6 miles)** northwest from Highway 191 on the same Blue Hills Road. Be aware that parts of the Blue Hills Road runs over clay beds and can be slick in wet weather. Inquire at the visitor center in Moab (or see a **range con** [conservationist] guy at Moab's BLM office on Dogwood Street), or at any of the mtn. biking outfitters in Moab about its condition before heading that way.

The good graded **Tenmile Point Road** is sandy for most of its length but not a problem most of the time, even for cars--but an SUV is recommended. However, after a long dry spell, it may have deep, dry sand in places, so if you have a 2WD, gear down, rev up and drive fast for a ways; and take a shovel. The author drove out to the end of this road several times over the years in a VW Rabbit and Jeep Patriot, and had no trouble.

For some nice views and a good hike to **Trin Alcove Bend**, drive along Tenmile Point Road for **20.5 kms (12.7 miles)**. This puts you at the end of the graded road and at the eastern part of Trin Alcove Point. From there walk SSW a couple of kms over mostly slickrock to find a way down off the point to Trin Alcove Bottom across from the mouth of **Three Canyon**. Immediately south and across the river from Trin Alcove Point is **Junes Bottom**. Along the way, you'll have some good views down on it.

If you're in that area, you might visit **Placer Bottom** which is just upriver from Trin Alcove Bend. Drive **17.7 kms (11 miles)** from the Blue Hills Road and turn right or north and drive as far as your vehicle will allow. There's now an ATV/Motor Cycle track going all the way to just across the river from Bull Bottom which is on the other side; then south to Placer Bottom. At the far southern end of Placer is a small **rock art** panel and mining debris (not shown). There's also a little canyon nearby draining into the river, but on the author's last trip, a gang of about 15 motorcyclists were in the process of heading through it from bottom to top--laying waste to the riparian vegetation--and the BLM lets them do it!

Almost at the very end of the Tenmile Point Road is an old **drill hole site** marked **1341m (21.3 kms/13.2 miles** from the Blue Hills Road). Most cars can get there, but it's rough after that. You could park there or nearby and walk south or west to view the Green River.

Or you could walk down the **Slaughter Bottom Trail** to Slaughter Bottom along the Green River. To

Area Map 13, Between the Rivers

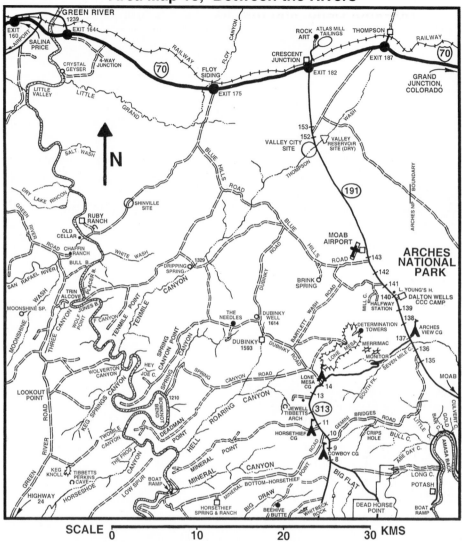

SCALE 0 ——— 10 ——— 20 ——— 30 KMS

do that, backup a ways from the drill hole, and head northwest on a passable track as far as possible. Most SUV's can be driven 1 km or little more on this track and be at the rim of a short little canyon. Park there and walk north around the head of this little drainage to between it and **F Canyon**; then continue west to the rim where you look down on the south end of **Slaughter Bottom** and the river. At that point, look for a break in the cliffs and the only place around where a trail could be built going to the bottom. Evidence of a constructed trail exists in 3 places. Walk down this trail to the river, and up F Canyon, which has some water and several places in the upper end where you can exit and return to your car.

The late **Loren Milton**, formerly from Green River, states this bottom got its name because somebody was down in there and had slaughtered some cows. Someone also used to make moonshine whiskey there during Prohibition days of the 1920's. They may have used water from F Canyon, because there seems to be a year-round source there. At the head of F Canyon there's an old rock fence across the drainage which kept cattle either in or out of the canyon.

Tenmile Canyon, Halverson's Cabin site, Dripping Spring & an old Dugout

Now to Tenmile Canyon. To reach the upper part, leave the Blue Hills Road in the same place as discussed above, which is **13.2 kms (8.2 miles)** from I-70 and Exit 175. From that junction, drive southwest on the Tenmile Point Road for **8.8 kms (5.4 miles)** and turn south onto another graded road. After about **2.6 kms (1.6 miles)** you'll be at the bottom of Tenmile Canyon, which at that point is a shallow & sandy drainage. If you have a 2WD, you may have to gear down & rev up to get across some deep

139

Aerial view of **Bowknot Bend**, Spring & Hey Joe Canyons, and Spring Canyon & Deadman Points.

Left If you go up **Hey Joe Canyon** a ways, you'll find a bunch of old mining equipment like this. It should be there a while too because no one can get up there with a vehicle that can carry it away.
Right Art Murray and his wife Muriel in the 1940's (?). (Jim Buckley foto).

Map 14, Trin Alcove Bend, Tenmile, Hey Joe and Spring Canyons and Bowknot Bend, & the History of Dubinky & Well

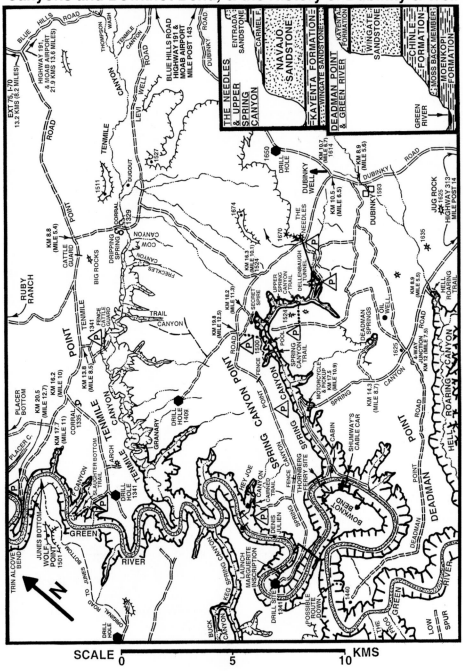

Above Part of a con-structed section of the old horse trail running down to **Slaughter Bottom**. This whole thing is immediately south of the mouth of **F Canyon.**

Right From the air looking westward down on **Trin Al-cove Bend** and the **Green River**. On the left and in the center is Junes Bottom. In the upper left part of this foto is **Three Canyon** which drains into Trin Alcove Bend. The story of Junes Bottom is told in the chapter along with Map 3 and start-ing on **page 26.**

Three Canyon

Trin Alcove Bend & Point

Trail & Spring

Junes   Bottom

sandy places, but in the cooler half of the year, there's normally a little water there, so the sand shouldn't be a problem then.

Now you can reach this same place by driving along **Highway 313** to the head of Sevenmile Canyon to **mile post 14** and turn northwest onto the **Spring Canyon/Dubinky (Well) Road**. After **2.4 kms (1.5 miles)** veer right or northward onto the Dubinky Road. Continue along this very good graded county road for **10.5 kms (6.5 miles)** and turn left or west onto the **Spring Canyon Point Road** which takes you to and beyond a big butte called **The Needles**, which is at **Km 13.8 (Mile 8.5)**. Continue west to **Km 16.3 (Mile 10.1)** and veer northwest & north and continue down a pretty good road another 6.9 kms (4.3 miles) before turning left or west another 1.4 kms or .8 mile to reach the bottom of Tenmile.

Here's what you'll find as the road crosses upper Tenmile Canyon. Just to the east under some **big cottonwood trees** is an **old corral**, built by Loren Milton and used by the Halverson's of Green River. Also, if you look about due west, you'll see some low cliffs with some sap springs and water running down the slickrock face. Part of this is **Dripping Spring**. To get there, walk that way through small sapling trees and look for a way onto the bench to the right. There's one cow trail. Once on that bench, which was the original level of the drainage before floods wiped out the bottom of the canyon, turn left and walk to the Dripping Spring. See picture on page 44. You'll find good water there, but it's hard to catch as it seeps or flows down the slickrock.

While on that same bench, if you walk north a little, you'll see another little corral or **holding pen** and nearby, the charred remains of what used to be a cabin built by Harold Halverson. Next to it is the foundation of a second cabin, but that has been hauled away. Not much to look at there anymore.

Here's what the late **Harold Halverson** of Green River had to say about those cabins, Dripping Spring and the cattle the family ran out there for years:

We run our cattle all over out there southeast of the Green River--on Tenmile and Spring Points, and in Tenmile Canyon. We went out there in about 1929. There was nobody in that Tenmile Canyon country when we went in there. Riordan and Patterson had a few cows drift in there, but that's all. My dad was named Chris Halverson, and my older brother was Alton. Alton was the real cow puncher. He was always out there, but we'd go out when he needed help.

We always had about 300 head of cows. We fed some of 'em here in Green River in winter. The BLM wouldn't let us run all of 'em out there the year-round. The most cows we could have out there was about 200 head. There's water in the bottom of Tenmile, but it kinda dries up in really hot weather. All them little canyons coming into Tenmile has water in 'em so there's plenty of water for cows. In those days we'd just drive'em into town.

The Dripping Spring just comes out of a ledge, and they'd get a bucket to catch the water--it drips down in that bucket--for drinkin', that's all. It's not a place for cows to get a drink. That was our camping place before we built the cabins. The spring is under an overhang, and the moss gathers on that ledge, then it drips into a bucket. It's good water.

There's 2 cabins down there [Harold was interviewed in 1991, and the cabins were gone by 2012]. I guess the first one was built in the fall of 1942, and the second one was built in the spring of 1943. The first one was for hay and grain and the second one was for a bunkhouse. At that time we were goin' down there with a pack outfit [horses or mules], until after the Second World War, then we got a

Looking northeast down into **Tenmile Canyon** near the **corral**, which is near **Dripping Spring**. This picture was taken in early March, 2012, before the Cottonwood trees had turned green. The Entrada Sandstone mesa in the background has an altitude of 1511m.

Above Looking almost due east at the big butte that's commonly known as **The Needles**. In the background to the right are the **La Sal Mountains**. About 3 kms on the other side of The Needles is the Dubinky Well.

Left Dripping Spring located about 250m west of the road (& corral) which crosses the middle part of Tenmile Canyon. See the picture showing the road crossing Tenmile & corral, on page 143; it's to the left of that foto.

jeep in 1946 or '47--along in there. There wasn't nothin' out there before the Second World War. You could go out there all summer and never see a man, then they got them 4WD's and now everybody's runnin' everwhere.

We had 2 corrals out there. One was built after 1943, along with the cabins. That pole corral where we branded the calves, why it was built by Loren Milton. It was after the second war. It was in about 1947 or '48, I'm not sure. I put the gas stove in that cabin when my brother passed away. He died in 1964. I put it there in about 1965 or '66. Alton was the guy who did most of the cow punchin', and I did the farming.

We used to have the cabins down there in under the cottonwood trees. Then Alton come in here one fall and got me, and he says, "You'll have to come out there, we're goin' to lose them cabins." So I went out there and jacked 'em up and put skids under 'em and he went over to the Ruby Ranch where they was workin' on that manganese and got a guy with a Cat to come over there. It was just a little ol' Caterpillar. He pulled 'em out of there and put 'em up where they're at now. They were close to the creek bed, and the flood waters were caving the bank off. They was just around the corner from the Drippin' Spring. This could have been in the early 1950's. My dad died in 1950 and it was after he died [that we moved the cabins]. The corral next to the cabins was built later.

We used that range up until I sold it to Gene Dunham. That was in about 1971 or '72..... He put the range rights on with the **Ruby Ranch**. When we had it, our range rights was tied in with this farm up here. You always had to have some private land to go along with the grazing rights on the public domain.

144

In the lower end of **Tenmile Canyon** is this **granary**, plus another ruin in the upper right background.

As for hiking, downcanyon is a possibility, but it's a long way to the river along a meandering stream channel complete with a 4WD/ATV/motorcycle track. That upper part isn't much to look at and the scenery isn't that great; so best to forget that part. If you'd like to reach the Green River and the best part of Tenmile Canyon, here's what you do. From the Blue Hills Road, drive southwest along the Tenmile Point Road for **13.8 kms (8.5 miles)** and turn left of southeast. Drive downhill about 500m (.3 mile) and turn right or west (at a point marked **1341m** on **Map 14**). Continue about another 500m and veer left or southeast again and head down into the middle part of Tenmile. This last part of the road gets pretty rough, so you'll need some clearance. After still another 500m or so, you'll come to a **fence & cattle guard**. From there 4WD's, ATV's and motorcycles continue along this road and into the bottom of the drainage, but you can walk south to the right and use an old cattle trail to make a shortcut.

Once into this canyon, you'll find a 4WD road all the way up to Dripping Spring, and down to within about 4 kms of the Green River. From there motorcycles and ATV's have made it all the way, but really rough terrain keeps full-sized vehicles out. The scenery in the lower part is pretty good, but noisy vehicles have ruined this canyon for hikers. Along the way, the author didn't find any rock art, and only a small Fremont **granary**, so it's not a good place to look for that kind of stuff. Had the Anasazi gotten this far north, they likely would have farmed it.

There's one last possible hike upcanyon from Halverson's Corral to an **old dugout**. The author looked for this in 2012, but he walked north from the **Levi Well Road** to the south as shown, and didn't find it. It may just be hiding, or it may have been washed away in the 22+ years since he found it. This is an old dugout few people know about. In the first edition of this book, the author stated: *From the corral, walk up Tenmile Creek bed. There may be running water, but you can easily keep feet dry. Stay on the right or south side. You'll pass one little gully coming in from the south, but keep going. When you reach the point where you'll have to wade, get upon the bench on the south side, and walk 200-300m until you reach the next drainage on the right or south. Get down into it and walk up this little shallow canyon another 300m or so, then get upon the bank on your left. From there walk northeast until you come to the 3rd drainage entering the main canyon from the south. About 150m up from Tenmile in this 3rd drainage, will be a little dugout up on the rim.* Or try walking north from the Levi Well Road. If you find it, please contact this writer.

In 1991, this dugout was covered with old logs and bark from cottonwood trees. It appeared to have been dug right down in the ground, then erosion came later to expose one end to the gully. There was a hole in the one corner of the roof and a ladder leading out. In one corner was an old bed and next to it was where a fireplace once was. There was also an old stove inside. No one the author talked to in 1990 & '91, knew when it was built, or who made it, but it was long ago.

Dubinky and Dubinky Well

In between the Green River and Highway 191 linking Crescent Junction and Moab, is a moderately high hump-like plateau. Sitting on top of this hump is a well with a windmill called the **Dubinky Well;** and just down the road a ways is an old ranch called **Dubinky**. The whole area on this hump is often referred to as Dubinky country. The name comes from a man named **Dubinky Anderson**, whose father Albert I. Anderson attempted to settle on Anderson or Townsite Bottom along the Green River.

Here's a little history of the place. It appears there were 4 different families who lived at Dubinky full time before it was abandoned in the late 1950's. It all started sometime around 1920 or thereabouts, no one knows for sure. A guy by the name of Dubinky Anderson was living with his father Albert at a place called **Valley City**. That site is 9-10 kms south of **Crescent Junction** in the area of today's **mile post 152.** The Andersons were involved in the freighting business and apparently owned a truck at

This foto is from a November, 1991 color slide and shows the old **dugout** northeast of **Dripping Spring**. The author failed to locate it in 2012; it was either hilding, or it's been washed away. If you find it, please contact the author at kelseyguidebooks.com.

about this time. They were also likely involved in making moonshine whiskey. Albert I. Anderson was arrested for bootlegging (selling or distributing it) whiskey in April of 1922. They were living at Valley City at the time (One year later, in May of 1923, Albert was arrested for moonshining again at his ranch at Little Valley south of Green River and sentenced to 6 months in jail and fined $100). These tidbits of information come from old Moab newspapers.

It's not known where they may have had a still in the Valley City area, but the late **Kenny Allred** and others believed Dubinky Anderson had a moonshine still there at what is now called Dubinky. Here's what Kenny recalls from the days when he was a young cowboy:

The first time I was there was when I was about 12 years old [1927], and I can remember them 2 dugouts. We come up that Hell Roarin' Trail with a bunch of steers and was goin' to the railroad at Thompson. We stayed at Dubinky that night and I remember them dugouts being there then. Then a guy by the name of Art Ekker bought some permits and he moved over there to this Dubinky place where the spring is in the wash. You had to dig a hole in the wash to get any water out.

Nobody was living there in 1927 and it was called Dubinky then. This old guy by the name of Dubinky Anderson came in here and I don't know what he done in the country beside building the dugouts, but he must have had a few head of cattle or something. I never did hear much of what his history was, but some say he was moonshining. He built the dugouts first, then Art Ekker reinforced 'em with railroad ties. They was getting in pretty bad shape at one time and I know he fixed 'em up. He hauled ties from out there at Thompson. You used to be able to get them railroad ties real easy. They'd tear'em out and you could just go out and get'em. Ekker went in there in about 1931, or maybe a little earlier than that. I went through there in about 1931 lookin' for horses, and he was established then.

Evelyn "Tissey" Ekker Bingham, who is the oldest daughter of **Art & Hazel Ekker**, grew up as a child at Dubinky. She was pretty small at the time but remembered a few things:

When Joe Biddlecome over at the Robbers Roost Ranch died, that left the Roost in thirds, [the Mother] Millie, [and daughters] Pearl and Hazel. And Hazel went to Colorado Springs to college, and she and Daddy were married on the 15 of February of 1931. When Joe died, Pearl was married to Mel Marsing, then he died, so Pearl had the two little boys, Jack and Joe Marsing [both were adopted later by Slim Baker, Pearl's 2nd husband]. That's when she was running the Roost. About that time, Daddy [Art] worked for Pearl over there. Then my parents bought the Patterson & Riordan range rights on the Dubinky side. They were apparently living at Dubinky when I was born in 1932. Eddy Jo was born in Salt Lake in December of 1931, but I'm not sure if my folks were living at Dubinky at the time (?).

*The first place they moved into was the **dugout** house. It would have been between the **Tie House** and the **cellar**. I don't know who built the dugout or anything about it, but I do remember the story that when Mother and Dad went there to live, there was a dead calf in that dugout. Apparently the mother cow had gotten back in there for shelter. They moved this dead calf out and moved in themselves.*

I remember when we children were learning to walk. The floor of the dugout was made of rock and very uneven. So it was very difficult for us to walk in that little house. There was a door and one window. Inside, on the south side there was a wood burning stove and a few cupboards. At the west end was the big double bed. There were water buckets by the doorway and that was about all we had--one room. It may have been about 12 x 12 feet [4x4m]. It was rocked up on the east and it had a lean-to attached to the front. There were 2 poles set up and a pole across the top and branches put up for shade. In summer time we had our water buckets out there. When the sun got up to about 10 or 11 o'-clock then we had shade. That dugout had been just dug back into the hill.

The cellar, if I remember right, had rock all the way around the front on the east, but a wood frame all the way around the door. At that time there weren't railroad ties in either the cellar or the dugout

Above On the left is the **Tie House,** and to the right must be the **Dugout** the Ekkers lived in first (?). The cellar must have been to the right of the Dugout. The Tie House was built in about 1936, but has since burned down. The Dugout, or what ever building it is on the right, is still there. (Connie Murphy Skelton Collection)

Left This is **Art & Hazel Biddlecome Ekker**, and their 2 oldest children, Eddy Joe & Evelyn (Tissey) on the doorstep of the **Tie House** at **Dubinky**. This picture was taken in about 1938, or within the last year they were at Dubinky. Hazel was Pearl Biddlecome's sister. (Evelyn "Tissey" Ekker Bingham Collection)

house. After we built the tie house, then the hired men slept in the **dugout**. We called it the **bunkhouse** then.

The cellar I remember was cool and the floor was cool wet sand--and that's where we kept all the bottled fruit and potatoes and things like that. We used to go to Grand Junction generally twice a year and buy the supplies for the year. And the flour and sugar and things like that we kept over across the wash in the **garage**. The fresh vegetables, like carrots and potatoes, we kept in the cellar.

I remember when we built the **tie house**--Eddy Jo thinks it was **1936**. I went back in the fall of 1970 with my dad and the size was so different--very small. The tie house was there in 1970. It had two bedrooms across the back, and one bedroom opened up into the other. Then there was one big room across the front. The kitchen was on the south end, and the living room was on the north. In the far north end, there was a couch that Daddy had made, and it had iron arms on it. It was a box with 3 bins in it, with large pillows across the back and cushions to sit on. And the radio was there in the northwest corner. There were big windows on the east. There was an outside door on the south and another on the east side. The front yard was made of red clay and it was rocked up to keep the wash from coming up and it faced east.

One of the things I remember very vividly when we lived there was the **chicken coop** made out of railroad ties [the garage and chicken coop are still standing on the east side of Dubinky Wash--2012]. Mother loved the chickens. It was such a lonely place, she loved anything that was alive. Your animals, that's what you communicated with--more or less. She also had guinea hens and at one time had a peacock or two. They were so important to her.

I remember this little platform after we built the tie house, where they had rocked it up to keep the wash from undermining the house, there was a little yard there, and in the summer time Mother & Daddy always slept outside. There was an old set of springs out there and we covered it with a tarp.

I remember very vividly as a child the shear terror I had that the coyotes would get me, because I wasn't a lot bigger than a chicken. I can remember we'd hear the coyotes howl out in the sandhills on the east side and then Daddy would lift his head and aim his 30-30 over the pillow and lie there in bed as he waited for the coyotes to come and try to get the chickens. This was just at dawn. And he'd blast the coyotes away from those chickens. In a child's mind that is very memorable. I was terrified.

Later on we had a battery-powered radio, but to get to Green River to get the batteries charged was a real problem. So we had a little windmill that we charged the batteries with. Because of that, we didn't turn the radio on much, except for the news. We had some candles and some kerosene lanterns for light, and often times the men would come in and eat and then, if there were men helping, often times the evenings were spent with a game of sluff, and then they would visit and tell each other of their experiences of the day.

At that time we never did really hire anybody, so someone would just get his room and board and a little spending money and he would be happy to spend the winter with us. This was during the Depression days of the 1930's. Dad was the 3rd of 9 boys in this family, and more often than not one of his brothers would be with us. Tom Cottrell was also with us a great deal. Tom was very quiet, and sometimes for weeks he didn't talk. Before we built the tie house, the men would sleep across the wash in the garage.

We didn't have water in the house when we were there. I can remember walking down to the wash with a bucket to fill. We didn't have any tank on the hill then. That came later with someone else. The water shortage was so great that I remember Mother melted snow in the winter time to wash with, and the rinse water was always saved for the horses to drink--water was so scarce.

That country by the house was open and the weather was very severe, so Daddy used to take the cattle down onto the river bottoms. We spent much of the winters down there. Now down on the river we lived in a tent, and we had candles, and a tiny little stove. When we were down there the hazard to the cattle were mud holes. They would be weak from the cold winters, and there were places where they would go out and water, and if it was gravelly and rocky they were safe, but often times where a wash came down at the mouth of those washes was clay mud and they'd get stuck in there.

We used the **Hell Roaring Trail** mostly, when we went down into Mineral and Hell Roaring Canyons to get to the river. I remember there were people who went with us who were just horrified going down the Hell Roarin' Trail.

We little kids used to ride with our parents on front of the saddles on pillows. They'd lay a pillow across the saddle horn and that would make it level and even. And very early we were taught, if the cattle got to running or if there was some kind of problem, they'd just drop us and then they'd come back and pick us up when the cattle had settled down.

When Eddy Jo started school in the fall of 1936, he stayed with Millie [Hazel and Pearl Biddlecome Baker's mother, Tissey's grandmother] in Green River. So she would put him on the freight line that went between Green River and Moab. We would go out to the main road and wait for him and he'd spend the weekend at Dubinky with us. Then on Sunday we'd go out to the road and he'd ride the freight truck back to Green River for another week of school. Grandmother would take him off the truck in Green River. Eddy Jo was only 5 years old that December.

When the Taylor Grazing Act came in [signed by FDR on July 27, 1934], Daddy was forced to have what they called **commensurate property** before he could run cows on the public domain. They had to have a qualifying ranch of some sort, so they had to lease a place in Moab for their commensurate property [in times of drought or when changing from summer to winter range on the public domain, the cattle had to be put on the private or commensurate property for a month or two each year]. They leased that from Patterson & Riordan. We left there in 1939 and went over and lived at the Roost. I was 7 years old.

One reason the Ekkers left Dubinky, was that Hazel's sister Pearl was selling the Robbers Roost Ranch and leaving the area with her second husband Slim Baker (her first husband Mel Marsing, died September 13, 1929. Mel & Pearl are buried side-by-side in the Elgin cemetery located on the east side of the Green River and north of the JW Powell Museum). They went to Oregon and bought a dairy ranch. Another lesser reason was they were constantly fighting with the Grazing Service (forerunner to the BLM) over their grazing rights. In 1937, they were apparently given a permit for 88 cows, but it was alleged that Art ran about 250 head in the Dubinky & Big Flat Country just to the south. The case was taken to court on May 6, 1938, where they pleaded guilty. They were fined $130, which represented the approximate grazing fee that the parties would have paid on the livestock had they been regularly licenced **(Moab's Times Independent (TI) 5/12/38)**. The whole thing was an argument over how many cows could be grazed and for how long on the public domain, and how many were supposed to remain on their rented commensurate property in Moab.

In was about June 1, 1939 that Pearl B. Baker sold the Roost Ranch to Art & Hazel Ekker. They moved their cattle over there in the fall of 1939 by fording the Green River near the mouth of the San Rafael where Glen Ruby had his ranch at the time. That has since been known as the **Ruby Ranch**.

The next owner of the Dubinky Ranch, or rather the grazing rights in that allotment (Dubinky was never private property) was **Cecil Thompson**. But he never did live there. After he bought the grazing rights, he ran cattle in that country, and his cowboy for 8 out of about 12 years was **Kenny Allred** and his family from Moab. Here's what Kenny had to say about the place and the **loco weed** problem:

Cec Thompson bought out Art Ekker's grazing rights when Art moved back to the Roost. All he ac-

Looking east at **Dubinky**. Left is apparently the cellar (?), and in the background is the garage, and behind it, the chicken coop & corral. **Dubinky Wash** is in the middle--it's also the road getting there.

tually bought was that old cabin over there on that school section at Dubinky. I lived there for several years while workin' for Cec. That was before I moved to Horsethief [Ranch]. Cecil Thompson was kind of a business man. He owned a big interest in that Moab Garage, then they later turned it into Garrett Freight Company.

I spent several years in that tie house. It was warm in winter; when I stayed there I had a little wood stove, kinda long, the kind they used to have in them days. I burnt a little coal and wood in there. I lived there with my first wife [Babe]. We didn't have any trouble staying warm in there, it was real nice. They had mud in between the ties. It was a good tight building.

Old Dubinky Anderson built those 2 little dugouts [one is gone, one is still there?], then when Ekker moved in, he built a pretty nice house out of railroad ties. He built part of them corrals across the wash too. Ekker built the steel cable corral. The old cedar corral was probably built by Dubinky Anderson, because it was there before Ekker ever was. Art Ekker had that little seep fixed up and cemented up and then he had one of these old hand pumps on the dang thing and he'd water 25 head of horses there. He had all kinds of saddle horses around there too. But we hauled our water from the Dubinky Well--that was real good water. The water in the wash was just a little alkali.

In that Sevenmile & Dubinky country, lots of horses died from that old **loco weed**. They'd just get so crazy and they didn't know which way was away from 'em. They'd just walk in a circle. They'll get under a tree and walk a circle around that damn tree, until they died; fall over dead--choke to death. I lost 2 or 3 nice horses--well actually I traded 'em to ol' Karl Tangren--I don't know what he done with 'em--but he knew the shape they was in. It was fish-bait price I got out of 'em. I had one little pinto mare that was a real nice little animal, and I brought her in here to Moab and leased a pasture. I heard that if you got'em on some green feed and kept 'em there, they sometimes got better.

That loco is terrible stuff, and if they get to eatin' it, they won't eat nothin' else. I had some of old Cecil's horses there and they got on it one fall and I took 'em up to the corral at Dubinky and just kept 'em there in the corral and fed 'em hay and grain for a month or two. But about a week after I took 'em off the range, they begin to act just like a guy comin' off from a bad drunk--got shaky and spooky--everything would spook 'em. So I kept 'em in there 'till they got over that and then I turned this one little brown horse out, and I watched him, and he never stuck his head down to take a bite of grass 'till he got back down to that damn loco weed. And I brought 'im back; he never did entirely get over that loco.

Out there where I was, the cows didn't seem to bother it--or it didn't seem to bother the cows! That was just a big problem with horses in that country. It grows up and gets green, and of course they're huntin' green stuff, and as soon as they get to eatin' it a while, then they don't want nothin' else, just that old loco. It looks a lot like an alfalfa plant, only it spreads out more than standing straight up. It's got a purple flower--there's 2 or 3 kinds of it they tell me--but I only know this one that looks like alfalfa.

Kenny Allred left Dubinky in about 1953, and bought the **Horsethief Ranch**, not far to the south near the Mineral Bottom Road on Horsethief Point. The next people to live at Dubinky was the family of **La Vern Young**, who was living in Idaho in 1991. Here's what he remembered about the place:

I moved there about the time Kenny Allred moved out. Kenny had worked for Cecil Thompson, and I was driving truck for Moab Transportation. Then Cecil asked me to run his cows for 'im. I got married in 1949, then I worked there around Moab for about 4 or 5 years, then I went out there to Dubinky and worked for Cecil.

I built that **cistern** behind the house after I'd been there a year or two. I dug that hole and cemented it up, and run that pipe into the house. Then we hauled water from where ever we could get it. Sometimes we got it at the Dubinky Well, but the best place to get it was down there at **Brink Spring**. At that time it wasn't a really good road out there.

I know a time or two we were snowed in, or the road had washed out in those summer thunder

Dubinky again, this time looking west apparently at the cellar (?). The dugout must have been to the left of it, then the Tie House was sitting to the far left and out of sight.

storms. One time I had to leave my truck at Brink Spring, and ride a horse up to Dubinky. It was a week before we got out, and before they ran a patrol around there.

I had a horse fall through that dugout [Ekker's **bunkhouse?**] closest to the house. It had been covered with dirt so we done away with it. That other dugout we just used as a **cellar** [it's still there in 2012]. It was made out of ties when we were there.

Those washers [washing machines] sitting there [they were gone in 2012] had gas engines on 'em. We could do [wash clothes] some of the stuff there pretty good, but those washing machines were so hard to keep going it was easier to just go into Moab to do our washing.

One time we set a trap to catch a rat, and we caught a skunk instead. We had it tied to the kids bed in the back room. That house wasn't too air tight. We heard the trap go off and rattle around, so I got up out of bed and struck a match to look under the kids bed, then I just got the trap by the chain and led the skunk outside. It never did make a smell in the house. The next morning I followed it's tracks and shot it and got the trap back.

The BLM had that well north of Dubinky. It used to be the sheepmen would come in there in the winter and the cattle stayed year-long. But the sheepmen, when they'd leave, they'd try to destroy all the water supply, because they wanted those cattle out of there. They would try to tear that well up when they left. So the BLM had to kinda watch that. It had a motor on it and a pump-jack, then also a windmill. The way those sheepmen would tear it up was to turn the motor and the windmill on together and then drive off and leave it--and of course that would tear it up. So it got to where I'd take the motor off from it and take it down to camp and keep it when the windmill was hooked up, then when I needed, I'd put the motor on, then climb up on top and unhook the windmill. The motor was a Model A Ford motor I think--or an old 4 cylinder engine anyway.

We used to run cattle out there from Thompson down to that country by Deadhorse Point, and out onto Gray's Pasture. There's a spring just south of **The Neck** that was troughed-up by the **CCC's** [Civilian Conservation Corps]. Everything out there had to be carried from The Neck either by horseback or by hand.

When they built that road up Sevenmile, and on to Deadhorse Point, that shortened our drive from Dubinky to Moab a lot. They put that road up Sevenmile while we were at Dubinky. They built a good enough grade that you could take your truck up and they put quite a lot of shale on the dugway part. After they got that road finished, then we used it to go to town. I would say it was in about 1954 or '55 when they built it.

I had 2 little boys when we first moved out there, Larry and Mickey. Then our daughter Donna was born in 1955, and I was there then. I think the oldest boy was about 4 years old when we went there so it was about 1953 or '54 when we moved to Dubinky.

Then Clark was born while we lived over on **Courthouse Wash**, over near Dalton Wells. We lived up the road about half a mile [800m] from Dalton Wells. I built the house. You'll notice a row of trees right along Courthouse Wash, just above Dalton Wells. There's just a cement foundation there now [the foundation is still there as of 2012 but hard to see. It's about 50m from the highway. See **Map 13**].

We left Dubinky probably in 1956. We had lived there full time and it was our home but when the kids started to go to school, then we moved over on the upper Courthouse Wash. That house had been bought by an old feller by the name of Ray. It was Sog Shafer's father in law, if I'm not mistaken. He had 320 acres [128 hectares], and had started that house, then we bought him out. I finished building the house and then Mrs. Wimmer [who lived at Crescent Junction] used to work in Moab and she'd pick

The **Dubinky Well** complex looking eastward toward the snow-capped La Sal Mountains in the distance. This well is not working today so don't expect to find water there.

up the oldest boy and haul him to school every day.

I worked for Cecil Thompson for a while after I moved down on Courthouse Wash, but then I moved to Price in 1960 and Cec sold his operation about the same time. Nobody ever lived at Dubinky after we left.

When we were there at Dubinky, we'd stand the kids up next to the door jam and mark how tall they were, then put a notch in the door and write their names to the side of it--and their age. I flew right over the little tie house in about 1977 or '78, and it was still there then. Then some time in the late 1980's, we drove out there to steal that board with the marks on it, but it had **burned down** [the tie house].

Here's how to get to Dubinky. First, drive along Highway 191 north of Moab. Between **mile posts 136 & 137**, turn west and drive up Sevenmile Canyon along **Highway 313**. Right at **mile post 14**, turn northwest and drive down the Spring Canyon/Dubinky Road for 2.4 kms (1.5 miles) and veer right or northwest onto the Dubinky Road. Drive to the bottom of Dubinky Wash which is **8.9 kms (5.6 miles)** from Highway 313. If you have a 2WD, best to park there on the main road and walk south 300m to the Dubinky Ranch; with a 4WD, continue down the sandy wash to the same place.

East of the dry wash is the old **garage** or storage shed and what appears to be the old **chicken coop**, both made out of railroad ties. Just to the west of that, and across the dry wash, is the old **cellar**. This is made of railroad ties, but it was originally made of rock, and was used as the cellar by everyone who lived there. Just south of the cellar is a flat spot, with an old pipe sticking up out of the ground. The pipe comes from the water **cistern** located just up the hill a ways, which La Vern Young made in the mid-1950's. This is where the **tie house** used to be before burning down sometime in the early 1980's (?). What everyone who lived there called the dugout, is apparently missing.

Moving along now from Dubinky. Continue along the Dubinky Well Road to the north. About 3 kms from Dubinky will be the **Dubinky Well** which is **10.7 kms (6.7 miles)** from Highway 313. What you see there today are **3 water storage tanks** (2 metal, 1 cement), a **windmill** & tower, a motor storage shed, and some metal **watering troughs**. Here's a little history of this well.

The drilling of Dubinky Well was part of a range improvement program, part of which was carried out by the **Dalton Wells CCC Camp**. Their projects included troughing-up springs, building water wells, and building roads, fences and water storage dams out on the public domain. This well was drilled in conjunction with other Dalton Wells CCC projects. Drilling started about January 1, 1937. The driller hired to do the work was **C.M. Conway**. The progress on this well and others was reported in the **Moab TI**, under *Dalton Wells CCC Camp Activities*. For **January 14, 1937** the paper states:

Work has been started on the Dubinky Well at Dubinky Wash under Driller C.M. Conway. Mr. Conway reports drilling operations advancing very rapidly and that about 180 feet [55m] of hole has been completed to date. One week later, they had to stop and exchange a motor, but they were already down to about 100m depth.

The **February 4, 1937** issue of the *TI* stated: Water has been brought in by Driller Conway at the Dubinky Well this week. This water was struck at a depth of 585 feet [180m] and came up to a depth of about 30 feet [9m]. Mr. Conway will start running the tubing in this well immediately.

A week later: Foreman Del Young and crew have started to erect the equipment at the Dubinky Well which Driller Conway completed drilling last week. This well will be equipped with a large windmill, a 7000 gallon [26450 liter] storage tank and a series of metal watering troughs. All of this was completed by about **March 1, 1937**.

Dubinky Well has been shut down for several years do to bad plumbing, and the BLM has no plans to re-drill or maintain the facility. Today, you'll find a historic marker which includes a sketch of the plumbing of the well. **Notice: there is no water available at Dubinky or Dubinky Well today.**

Spring Canyon Point, U. Spring Canyon Trails & Route down Hey Joe Canyon

Some of the better views down into the Green River Gorge can be found along the north side of Spring Canyon. This section is known as **Spring Canyon Point**. To get there, start at **mile post 14** on Highway 313, the road running up to Dead Horse Point & Canyonlands NP. Turn westward and drive northwest on the **Dubinky Road**. After 10.5 kms (6.5 miles) turn left or west onto the **Spring Canyon Point Road** (that junction is 300m south of the Dubinky Well) which is a good, graded, well-maintained county road. At **Km 13.8 (Mile 8.5)**, you'll come to a very prominent **Entrada Sandstone** rock or butte called **The Needles**. Surrounding this tower are numerous possible campsites and large boulders with cowboy etchings. On one boulder a 1907 date exists. There might be others even older. This is an interesting place to visit.

Before moving on to Spring Canyon Point, here's an interesting side-trip. Right from **The Needles**, you can drive a HC/4WD, mtn. bike or walk southwesterly along a rough and/or sandy track to a place called **Dellenbough Tunnel**. See Map 14. It's about 2.7 kms (1.7 miles) to the end of that road. From there, follow a cairned trail west down into a drainage. There you'll see where flash flood waters have created a virtual tunnel for about 35-40m. The reason for the tunnel is, there's a soft place in the Navajo Sandstone which resembles a cavity in your teeth and over time has dissolved away the softer material making the tunnel. You can walk through it to the other side to see where flood waters fall into upper Spring Canyon. Interesting place, and you can fotograph The Needles to the northeast.

Now back on the Spring Canyon Point Road. Just west of The Needles, the first side-track to the right heads north down into upper Tenmile Canyon. This track is sandy and definitely for 4WD's. The main graded Spring Canyon Point Road continues west past a turnoff to the right **(Km 16.3 (Mile 10.1)** and the main road down into Tenmile Canyon--but veer left at that junction. At **Km 18.2 (Mile 11.3)** is a side-road to the left; this makes a loop to the south to the **Secret Spire**, then back to the main road to the west. This side-road is for HCV's, but you can walk or mtn. bike from either end of the loop and fotograph the spire; a trip well-worth taking. Continue west on the main graded road. At **Km 19.8 (Mile 12.5)** is another junction; this is the west end of the Secret Spire Loop-Road. Near the west end of this loop-road is the best place to park if going into **Spring Canyon**.

Now for a good hike into upper Spring Canyon. From near the western end of this Secret Spire Loop-Road, and with a compass in hand, head **southeast**, or toward a large hump of dome rocks you'll see off in the distance. After walking about 1 km down a **sandy slope**, look for an easy route over a Navajo rim to a Kayenta bench below. This Kayenta bench contours all along the lip of upper Spring Canyon. Once on this bench and the rim of the canyon, bench-walk southwesterly (downcanyon) about another km along a mostly winter-time **cow trail**. Soon you'll come to an indentation in the wall, or a very short steep side-drainage. Head down into this side-drainage to the west side and soon you'll find a constructed cow trail leading down into the canyon bottom. This is the **northern end** of the **Spring**

Above Looking through **Dellenbaugh Tunnel**. Dead center in this foto, is literally, *the light at the end of the tunnel*, which is about 35-40m away. Flood waters from a minor drainage, gradually ate away at a soft place in the Navajo Sandstone and it became a tunnel. This whole thing reminded this writer of a cavity in our teeth.

Right The **Secret Spire** makes a nice foto op no matter what time of day it is.

Canyon Trail. The late **Loren Milton** tells us a little about this place:

There's a trail towards the upper end of Spring Canyon and on the Spring Canyon Point side; that's the west side. If going up the canyon watch close and it's on your left. It went up through a natural fault, and I did blasting--I was one old cowboy that could handle powder; a lot of 'em couldn't. They didn't understand dynamite. I could drill and blast. I blasted on there for Alton Halverson. That trail was made early on; Alton don't even know who made it originally. That trail was made years ago, and there's quite a little bit of rock work done in the upper end of it. I did blasting on rocks that got in the way later. That was after I got out of the army in 1945. It was sometime between 1946 and '48--the late 1940's. I put in 7 or 8 shots on that trail. I had to drill 'em in by hand. We drilled with a single jack hammer. It's a hammer which weighs about 3 or 4 lbs [1 1/2 kgs]. Then you had a drill that you kept twisting with each hit from the hammer. Then you blew or washed out the dust and put your shot in and touch'er off. That trail was the only way into Spring Canyon for us.

This trail actually zig zags down a **rockslide** covering the big Wingate Sandstone walls. At a point in about the middle of this trail, and on a wall next to it is an old inscription *LW 3/9/[19]07*. Look around, there might be others. You could surely walk a horse down this trail today, but it's washed out pretty bad in a place or two. In the bottom of the canyon there's a small year-round flowing stream which should be good for drinking. From the bottom of the trail walk upcanyon. After about 1 km, you'll come to a **pool** below a little cascade. Wade through the pool and climb up the sloping mossy waterfall. Above this are several other minor falls, but anyone should be able to scramble around these. After another km of this, you'll be up through the Wingate, and on or near a Kayenta bench above. From there you can turn left and bench-walk back along the Kayenta (toward Secret Spire) and exit the canyon along the same **cow trail** you used earlier to reach the **northern end** of the Spring Canyon Trail. In the past, cows used to walk along this bench into the upper end of the canyon, but they don't seem to go that far any more. Along this cow trail going back out, are several little side-drainages with **good spring water** in each (cows are there in winter, so purify it then).

Before going back to the northern end of the trail, continue up Spring Canyon to the east to a point about 3 or 3 1/2 kms above where you entered the canyon bottom. Follow this map carefully to find the **southern end** of the **Spring Canyon Trail**. It zig zags up to the southwest along the Navajo Sandstone wall to the canyon rim. You can exit the gorge there, then walk northwest along the rim, or along a 4WD track, to view upper Spring Canyon from the south side. Or, if you have a HC/4WD, you can start there and walk into the canyon; this trail begins near the sandstone bluff labelled **1524m** on this map and about 1 1/2 kms southeast from the end of the vehicle track.

To get back to your car to the north, walk north in the drainage toward Secret Spire, then southwesterly along the Kayenta to the **sandy slope** you came down on earlier, then head up to the northwest and back to the west end of the Secret Spire Loop-Road. This is a nice hike, but you'll be wading a little in the bottom of the canyon and you'll need 6-8 hours to walk from rim to rim and return. It would be easy to make this a full-day hike. This is the best hike on this map and in this region.

Southwest of upper Spring Canyon, the Spring Canyon Point Road is a little rough in places, but it's graded right to the old **drill site** marked **1341** at **Km 32.7 (Mile 20.3)** from Highway 313. In 3/2012, this road was good for any car driven with care. Once you get down near the end, there are a number of viewpoints to see the Green River from. Each will require a short walk from the road.

Here's one last hike from Spring Canyon Point & Road. If you stop at **Km 27.7 (Mile 17.2)** from

Part of the northern end of the upper **Spring Canyon cattle trail**. Before the Halversons, there were Taylors, John Jackson and Riordan & Pattersons; some of them may have built this trail.

Highway 313, you'll find a rough track running northwest to the rim of **Hey Joe Canyon**. There's one bad spot on this track, otherwise it's pretty good for ordinary SUV's. Or walk or ride a mtn. bike 1 km to the rim of Hey Joe. From where the road reaches the first low rim, walk right a little to see some cairns marking a route north down just to the right of a shallow drainage. When you reach the first big ledges, again look for cairns to the right or east of the dry water course and follow a line of cairns north, then east a little and around a corner, then route-find north again down steep slickrock to the bottom of Hey Joe Canyon. There was a lot of uranium taken out of this canyon in the 1950's and there's still some old mining machinery down there. Read more below about the history of mining in this area.

Lower Spring Canyon, Bowknot Bend and Hey Joe Canyon & Mine

To get down into the **lower Spring Canyon and to Bowknot Bend**, start at **mile post 14** on Highway 313. From there drive northwesterly on the Spring Canyon Road for **2.4 kms (1.5 miles)**, but go straight ahead instead of veering to the right toward Dubinky. At this point you'll be on the **Spring Canyon Road** heading west. At **Km 12 (Mile 7.5)** will be a **4-Way Junction**; the one heading left goes down along Deadman Point. But for now continue straight ahead to the west.

Just after you begin going down near the rim of Spring Canyon, be looking for a turnout on the left in the bottom of a shallow drainage just before the road turns to the right and contours along the upper wall of the canyon; this will be about **17.5 kms (10.9 miles)** from the highway. At that point walk a few meters to the left and look straight down over a dryfall in the drainage; about halfway down the Wingate cliff, will be an old pickup and motorcycle sitting on a little bench. Then Moab *Times-Independent* editor, the late **Sam Taylor** knew how they got down there. Here's what he had to say about it:

In the early 1950's Uranium Boom, Excalibur Uranium Corporation, owned the Sevenmile Uranium mines and a number of others in this area. They had staked 600 or 700 claims down on the Green River, on both sides, and were actively mining a few mines. They had rigged a cable and put a ferry boat on the river and took equipment across, some of which is still there.

*Anyway, I went down there with my brother-in-law, who was an executive with the Western Development Company, which absorbed Excalibur for a period of time. The price of uranium was low at the time and the prospects of future contracts were dim, and they were in the process of closing out those uranium mines in the vicinity of **Bowknot Bend**. They had made the decision at that time to pull all the equipment they could out, store it here in Moab, advertise it and see if they couldn't sell it. They wanted out of the mining business and they were simply pulling that stuff out of there on jerry-rigged trailer hitches and up near the top this one time, the trailer hitch broke and things went over the side, and the story I'm told is they got out of their vehicles, looked over the rim and said, "so much for that", and just got back in their rig and left. They didn't try to salvage or anything like that; just left it there. The pickup wasn't being driven, it was being towed. The motorcycle was probably in the back of the pickup. This must have been about 1958 or '59--the late 1950's.*

From where you see the pickup & motorcycle at the bottom of the dryfall, drive your car or mtn. bike down the fairly steep road to the canyon bottom. In 3/2012, this was a good road maintained by the county with the same steepness as the Horsethief Trail Road going down to the Mineral Bottom boat ramp. There's one tight bend, but any car can handle it.

When you reach the bottom, you could park near the stream crossing, and walk upcanyon to the trails, springs and waterfalls already described. From there, it's an easy hour's walk up to where the northern end of the **Spring Canyon Trail** enters/exits the drainage. You can do this as a day-hike or backpack with lots of good water available.

This is the **pickup and motorcycle** that Sam Taylor talked about above and on the next page. Gradually, flood waters will bury these relics of the Uranium Boom.

Continue driving down Spring Canyon. Just above the mouth of the drainage and the river, cross the dry creek bed to the left and drive another 300m or so to a grove of cottonwood trees and look around for what's left of a little log **cabin**. Lots of people have speculated over the years as to who first built it, but the late **Chad Moore** of Green River had the answer:

It was my dad [Andy Moore], his brother and my uncle Bunk Moore, who ran horses in that country, who built that cabin. Alton Halverson told me that. I went out there to help Alt move some cattle one day and he took me over there and showed me that cabin in the mouth of Spring Canyon. Loren Milton formerly of Green River also stated that Alton Halverson told him it was Andy Moore's outfit who built it when they were on the east side of the river for a while. This must go back to World War I days or so.

The late **Buck Tomlinson**, whose family used to live at the Chaffin Ranch before the Chaffins, and later at what is now the Ruby Ranch, punched cows for various people in the 1930's before leaving the country. He recalled an experience he had with that little cabin at the mouth of the canyon like this:

I come up there one night and it was the 17th of January, about 1934, and I had left Anderson Bottom and I got there that night. It was way after dark, and I finally got a fire goin' and I took the roof off that cabin and built a fire out of it. I was 18 years old then. My horse was give-out and so was I, and there was about 8 inches [20 cms] of snow and god I don't know how cold it was but it was cold enough to suit me. There had been a flood down there and swept the place clean and there was snow on the ground and no place to go and I had 4 lousy matches, but I finally got a fire a goin'!

When **Kenny Allred** heard this story he had doubts as to whether anyone, or any horse, could make such a trip in one day (?). In 1991, that cabin had another roof, and on top of the logs were some flat stones apparently used to act as shingles. But by 2012, the roof and most of the logs were nowhere to be found; they were likely used as firewood! Not much to see there today.

There's an old uranium miner's road heading south along the east side of the Green River from the mouth of Spring Canyon. About **1.2 kms (.7 mile)** from the dry creek bed turnoff will be some **cables** from the **Shumway Ferry**; read more below. If you continue south to about Km 2.4 (mile 1.5) the road will be washed out, but motorcycles are sometimes going a little further, but you can walk or possibly ride a mtn. bike downstream nearly to where Horseshoe Canyon reaches the Green River from the other side. There are a number of old uranium prospects or adits along the way but apparently not much in the way of mining.

Now back to those cables just mentioned. There used to be an old cable stretched across the river with an ore bucket hanging down about halfway across. The cable is gone now, but **Karl Tangren** of Moab knew a little about that cable car and what he called the **Shumway Ferry or Cable Car**:

*Now that cable across the river below the mouth of Spring Canyon was put there by **Ray Shumway** and his boys. This was after our metal barge got loose down there at Anderson Bottom and it went down the river and some guys caught it down there before it got to The Confluence and tied it up. And ol' Ray come to me and said, "I'm going to start minin' and I can use that barge". And I says, "Go get it and you can have it".*

That barge is the one we built here in Moab and we used it on this river [Colorado], then we took it down to The Confluence and up to Anderson Bottom. It was all made out of metal. So Shumway went and got it and he brought it back up there and he put a little cable across the river and just pulled that boat (ferry) across--he never put power or nothin' on it, he just put his equipment on it and pulled it across with a cable. This was during the early 1950's when this happened.

Read more about Karl Tangren and his attempt to built a ranch in the part on **Anderson Bottom**.

Not much left of the little **old cabin** in lower **Spring Canyon**. In 1991, it had a partial roof, but it appears someone thought more about a warm fire than an historic artifact.

The **Launch Marguerite Inscription** is located about halfway between the mouth of Spring Canyon and the Hey Joe Mine. It's been there a long time, but it's not showing its age.

From the mouth of Spring Canyon there's another old mining road running upstream along the river to the mouth of **Hey Joe Canyon**. From the mouth of Spring Canyon to the end of the road in Hey Joe Canyon is about **14.5 kms (9 miles)**. It's a pretty good road in places, but there are lots of washouts, plus tamarisks are now crowding in which will scratch the hell out of any vehicle or rider. As of 2012, this was for gutsy ATV, motorcycle & mtn. bike riders only--or walk. 4WD's likely can't/won't make it. For this reason, hikers may choose to go to Hey Joe Canyon via a cairned trail on Spring Canyon Point discussed earlier. This writer gave up with his mtn. bike on this old road; but he had been there in his boat in 2011, and in 2012, he walked down into Hey Joe from the rim.

About 500m upriver from the mouth of Spring Canyon is the east-side base for the **old ferry site** which used to take mining equipment across the river to the mines on the inside part of **Bowknot Bend**. This ferry is shown on the old 1:62,500 scale (15') USGS maps. This must have been where the late **Buster Irvine** formerly of Green River was working with his bulldozer in the 1950's. He had a few words to say about an event there:

I enlarged the road down through Spring Canyon and to Hey Joe. I think it was about in the mid-1950's. I was working for an outfit out of Nevada makin' a road so they could haul uranium out of there. They wanted me to go across the river and do some assessment work, and they wanted to take my Cat across on their barge--which I wouldn't do. So they hired someone else to do it, and the Cat is still down there in the river somewhere--somebody else's Cat! I didn't like the set-up they had for going across the river.

This also appears to be what **Karl Tangren** called the **Thornberg Ferry**. Here's what Karl remembered about this old uranium mining site and ferry:

*A guy named Vance Thornberg from over in Grand Junction was a contractor and he built roads and stuff. And his brother Garth was a dentist, and they come over here in the uranium days [early 1950's] and they bought the Sevenmile Mines just as you're starting up Sevenmile Canyon [where you turn west from Highway 191 going to Canyonlands NP & Deadhorse Point]. They bought them from Nick Murphy and Gordon Babble. Anyway, they started **Thornberg Mining**, and they was mining there, and then they went over on the **Bowknot** and staked a lot of claims. They went down there and since he was a contractor, he brought his heavy equipment and shot that road off of Deadman Point down into **Spring Canyon**, then he went down to the river and built this ferryboat site. They stretched a big cable across the river just above the mouth of Spring Canyon. It was about 2 inches [5 cms] in diameter, and then he built this big barge; it was like a section of bridge with tall sides, and it had a V8 Ford engine in it. Then on the big cable he had shivs with 4 other smaller cables going down to the barge. Those 4 cables held the barge to the big cable. Then there was a little cable about as big as your thumb that was tied off and went out to the transmission and it had a big pulley deal on it and it just had a wrap around it and it went to the other side of the river and tied up so when you kicked that motor in gear, that system would pull the barge across the river. And when you came back you'd stick'er in reverse and it'd pull you back.*

Now they hauled ore with that ferry Thornbergs built. I was workin' for Thornberg Mining out here in the mines for 2 years and when they started producin' ore at Bowknot, I took the job of drivin' truck. We'd go down to the Bowknot when they'd get ore and I'd go across on that ferryboat, load 15 ton of ore on that truck, drive it back on the boat and come across the river and pull'er up out of Spring Canyon and take it to Monticello.

But then later, there was some local boaters goin' down there and a drinkin' and a party'in, and in high water somebody had cut that barge loose--and I don't know who done that--but the cable was still dangling across the river. And in high water them guys came down around the bend and damn near run into that cable. *So sometime later they went down there with a cuttin' torch and cut the big cable.*

From the old ferry site, the road running upriver really deteriorates and is sandy in places. This makes it hard for mtn. bikes, especially when the sand is dry. As you continue around the next big gooseneck bend, and begin going east, beware of an old historic site about 30m above the road. This is the **Launch Marguerite Inscription**. You'll know you're near, when you come to the first tamarisks overhanging the road. Stop there by a boulder and look straight up at a trail. It'll be about 50m away and under a big overhang. The letters are about a meter high, facing north and are painted on the rocks with black paint. It's dated **9/11/1909**, and was put there by **Tom Wimmer** when he took a group of passengers and friends down the river. In much smaller letters underneath "Marguerite", are the names of all the passengers on the boat. They include: *Sambo the dog, A. Tanner, E. Tanner, L. Tanner, Bill Tanner, and T. Wimmer, S. Wimmer, A. Wimmer, L. Wimmer, M. Wimmer, and E. Wimmer.*

The Launch Marguerite was owned by Tom Wimmer, who owned the Wimmer Ranch (today it's known as the Ruby Ranch--read about its history in the author's other book, *River Guide to Canyon-lands*) at the time. Here is part of his testimony in the *Colorado River Bed Case hearings* which took place in 1929: *After I bought my ranch downstream from Greenriver, I got a boat of my own. It was built by Mr. Wolverton and it was called the* **"Marguerite"**. *It was 33 feet long and approximately 7 or 8 feet wide [10 x 2 1/2m]. It had a sternwheel at one time, a propellor at another time, and side and sternwheels at another time. As originally constructed had a sternwheel, seven feet [2m] in diameter. It was propelled by a gas engine. The Marguerite was built either in 1906 or 1907 and I took my last trip in it in 1915......The last time I saw the Marguerite it was tied above the bridge at Greenriver. The name of the boat comes from one of Wimmer's daughters.*

About 3 kms upstream from the boater's signatures, and just as the road steepens and goes up over and around a little dugway, will be one of **Denis Julien's inscriptions**. When you reach the high point of this little dugway, stop and leave your bike. Climb down the steep slope the easiest way and over a ledge going toward the river. About 10m below the road and about 10m upstream from where you probably climbed down, and under a ledge just above the high water mark, will be these words, *"D. Julien 16 Mai 1836"*.

Denis Julien has been the subject of great speculation over the years. According to **Hoffman** and his Arches book, Julien was probably born in the first half of the 1770's somewhere in Canada. His family's ancestral homeland was France, but members migrated to Ireland, then to Canada, and later in time some went south to the USA. Records at a cathedral in St. Louis, Missouri, indicate he had an Indian wife named Catherine, and three children. A daughter born in 1793 was named Marie Josephine. Two sons were named Pierre Paschal and Etienne. They were all born and baptized in the years around 1800. Denis became an American citizen in 1805, and had a licence to trap in Missouri in 1816 & '17.

In 1825, he got into a scrap at Ft. Atkinson on the Missouri River and shot and wounded a man, but may not have been tried or punished (?). In the late 1820's he is thought to have been in New Mexico, then in 1828, his name pops up in association with the Reed Trading Post at the junction of the Uintah and Whiterocks Rivers in the Uinta Basin northeast of present-day Roosevelt, Utah. He was apparently a partner with the principal owner of the post, William Reed. Other partners were James Reed and Augustus Archambeau. Near the trading post was an inscription by Julien dated 1831. This is the first of 8 known etchings Julien made in eastern Utah. He left 5 along the Green River, 2 along the Colorado River, and one inside Arches NP. The one in Arches is dated *June 9, 1844*, when he must have been over 70 years of age. Researchers have never been able to track him down from there, so the speculation continues. His only real claim to fame was his habit of carving his name into sandstone walls.

About 2 kms north of the Julien Inscription will be the mouth of **Hey Joe Canyon**. About halfway up this short drainage is what's left of the **Hey Joe Mine** and **mining camp**. You can ride a mtn. bike up the road on the south side of the canyon and to the mine site.

The Hey Joe operated in the 1950's and was one of the better producers in the area. It has one main tunnel with a number of other adits or test prospects around. There was one old cabin (it's gone now--2012), and several pieces of equipment and old vehicles scattered around. If you hike upcanyon, you can scramble up to the rim to the south and to the end of an old track as discussed earlier. Apparently, some mtn. bikers are coming down this route carrying their bikes, then biking along the river and up the Spring Canyon Road and back to wherever. A challenging all-day adventure, but a 2nd vehicle would make it a shorter day-trip.

Just south of where the dry creek bed enters the river at the mouth of Hey Joe, is an old Caterpillar sitting on the bench and just below it, an ore bin and a mine tunnel angling down away from the river. The late **Gene Dunham** of Green River recalled a tragedy which took place there in the late 1950's:
There's an inclined tunnel that goes down and there's a bunch of equipment down there under water. Jake Fesh was operatin' in that mine and his partner got killed. This was in about 1959 or 1960. They had to pump the water out all the time, even though the shaft was inclined away from the river. That was Columbia Uranium who operated that mine.
Jake Fesh was workin' for Columbia and they lit a round for blasting, and they didn't cut their fuses long enough, because one went off before they got the last one lit. And that other guy was lightin' the fuses and Jake had his back turned and he got shot full of rock, but he managed to pull this other guy out of there back around the first bend in the tunnel--but he was dead. Jake was shot up but survived.

Deadman Springs and Deadman Point

Now back to the Spring Canyon Road. Once out of Spring Canyon and back up the road a ways, is **Deadman Springs**. The turnoff along the main road is **14.3 kms (8.7 miles)** from **mile post 14** on Highway 313. There's a rough road leading to it, so a HC/4WD or mtn. bike is required there. From the Spring Canyon Road it's **2.4 kms (1.5 miles)** to 2 big dryfalls, alcoves and springs below. The main spring is surrounded by tamarisks. Not far away to the east is a another dryfall, cottonwood trees and a minor spring. There's usually water there in both springs, but don't bet your life on it; it could dry up in a long dry spell. This could make a possible campsite, but the road getting there is kinda rough.

Now back to the junction of the Spring Canyon and Deadman Point Roads, **12 kms (7.5 miles)** from Highway 313. From there you can head southwest along the north rim of Hell Roaring Canyon and out to the end of **Deadman Point**. This road was never graded, is rough in places, and sandy in a couple of spots, but the author drove down in it in his VW Rabbit in 1991 to within 1 km of the final crossroads very near the end of the point. He took a mtn. bike from there. He got to about the same place in 2012 in his Jeep Patriot (which is only half a Jeep!). With some shovel work, he could have made it to the very end of each road; but this is a great place for a mtn. bike too. There are many places to stop, take a short hike, and find good views down into the Green River gorge below. From or near the end of the road, you can look right up Horseshoe Canyon and The Frog on the opposite side of the river.

Right at the very end of the road and the point, there might be a way down to the river. See **Map 14**. When the author was on the other side of the river and walking down to the viewpoint of Bowknot Bend, he saw what appeared to be a route for a unaided hiker or climber to get down to the river. It's in the middle of the 3 little alcove-like canyons coming off the very end of Deadman Point. If this route does go, it's surely the only one around.

When asked how Deadman Point got its name, none of the old timers around seemed to know. But there was an incident which happened on the rim of Hell Roaring Canyon which may have been the event which gave it this name. The story was told in the Moab *TI* for **January 13, 1927**:

Domingo Yrueta, a Spanish Basque sheepherder in the employ of Jean Chuchuru was instantly killed Tuesday of last week on the desert 47 miles [76 kms] southwest of Valley City, when he fell from a ledge about 100 feet [30m] high. Yrueta was hunting for lost sheep and had climbed out on the brink of a cliff to look over into a canyon known as "Hell Roaring" canyon. He lost his footing on the icy rocks and plunged to his death. He sustained a broken neck, broken leg and other injuries.

The accident occurred Tuesday. The campmover and other employees of Chuchuru thought, when Yrueta did not return to camp that day, that he had become insane and was wandering about the desert.

They were afraid to hunt for him until Saturday, when a neighboring sheepman visited there camp and led in the search for the missing herder. They found his body about a mile [1 1/2 kms] from camp..... Yrueta has three brothers, who were notified of his death. Two of them arrived this week, and the body was shipped to Winnemucca, Nevada, for burial.

Right Junk and old mining equipment around the former mining camp in the lower end of **Hey Joe Canyon.**

Below A late-**1940's pickup truck** located about half a km inside **Hey Joe Canyon.**

Above Right at the mouth of **Hey Joe Canyon** is this 1950's Caterpillar tractor. Nearby is the inclined mine tunnel where one miner was killed in a blasting accident.

Left One of 2 alcoves which have either a little running water or seeps. This is known as **Deadman Spring**. But it seems, the main spring is to the left or north, and next to a small stock pond, but this one was the only one with water in the spring of 2012.

Tibbetts Arch, Hell Roaring & Mineral Canyons & Mineral Point

Location & Access The 2 canyons on this map plus Mineral Point are located west of Moab, immediate west of the upper end of Sevenmile Canyon and Highway 313, and north of the Island in the Sky District of Canyonlands National Park. Both canyons drain into the Green River just before it flows into the national park.

The normal way to get to this area is to drive along Highway 191 between Crescent Junction & Moab; between **mile posts 136 & 137** turn west onto **Highway 313** which runs up **Sevenmile Canyon** to Dead Horse Point & Canyonlands NP. Once in the high country, the 2 main roads you'll be using are the Dubinky & Spring Canyon Road, and the Mineral Bottom (or Horsethief Point) Road. These are well-maintained county roads and good for all cars, but during or right after heavy rains, they could be a mess because parts of each run through areas with clay beds. Read more below.

Elevations The Knoll, 1925m; Horsethief Ranch, 1560m; Mineral Bottom boat ramp, 1210m.

Water Take your own, there's none available in this area. Otherwise, only in the Green River, which must be treated before drinking. Don't expect to get water at the Horsethief Ranch; they have a gate and barking dogs and it's private property.

Maps USGS or BLM maps San Rafael Desert & Moab (1:100,000); The Knoll, Mineral Canyon and a small part of Dubinky Wash & The Jug (1:24,000--7 1/2' quads); the plastic Trails Illustrated/National Geographic maps Moab North & Moab South (1:70,000); or the plastic Latitude 40° map Moab West (1:75,000).

Main Attractions Historic cattle trail, an arch, good rock art panel & one of Denis Julien's inscriptions.

The Hell Roaring Trail & Crawling Route into Upper Hell Roaring Canyon

Before getting into either canyon, here's a short fun hike to an overlook of **Jewell Tibbetts Arch**, formerly known simple as Hell Roaring Arch. It's located in the far upper end of Hell Roaring Canyon. To get there, drive along Highway 313 north of Canyonlands NP. Near **mile post 13**, and in the middle of a big flat, turn west onto an ungraded, but pretty good road. Drive about 1.2 kms (.7 mile) and stop where a little side-road turns left or south. Park on the main road and walk through a gate then after 75m you'll find the old **Hell Roaring water well** and a great **big log** that's been hollowed out and made into a watering trough. Nearby is the cement footing where the well was drilled by C.H. Conway, who was working under the direction of the Dalton Wells CCC Camp. This would likely have been drilled in 1936 or '37 since Conley was in the area and drilled the Dubinky Well in the first 3 months of 1937. This well hasn't produced water in many years.

From the Hell Roaring water well, continue west and stop at another **fence & gate** that's **2.4 kms (1.5 miles)** from the highway. Cars, driven with care can reach this trailhead. This carpark has an information board with maps explaining the trail running out to the rim of the canyon. From there, walk through a skinny hiker's gate and follow the road & cairns for a ways, then, again following the cairns, head southwest on the **arch trail**. This one-way walk is only about 1 km and you'll end up on the lip of upper Hell Roaring Canyon directly opposite and above Jewell Tibbetts Arch. Return the same way, or continue around on a loop back to your car. Be there in the morning hours for a sun-lit view of the arch. The author took a bunch of pictures, most with a tripod, and the trip lasted 1 hour.

To reach the upper end of Hell Roaring and an historic cattle trail, proceed to **mile post 14** on Highway 313 and turn northwest onto the **Spring Canyon/Dubinky Road**. After **2.4 kms (1.5 miles)** continue straight ahead on the Spring Canyon Road--not to the right which takes you to Dubinky. Proceed west to **Km 6 (Mile 3.7)** where you'll come to a **cattle guard & fence**; and just beyond that, a side-road

Left **Wooden water trough** made out of a hollowed log at the **Hell Roaring water well**. **Right** From the overlook, **Jewell Tibbetts Arch** can be seen. Be there in the morning hours for this shot.

Map 15, Jewell Tibbetts Arch, Hell Roaring and Mineral Canyons, and Mineral Point

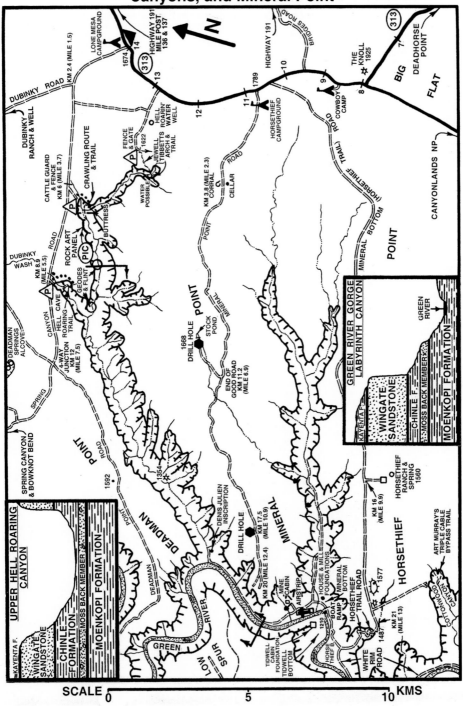

161

heading southwest. If you drive this side-road about 400m, you'll come to a possible campsite which is near the beginning of the **Crawling Route & Trail** into upper Hell Roaring Canyon. To do that, cross over to the east side of the fence & dry wash, then rim-walk south to a kind of **buttress** or butte which separates the main canyon with this little side-drainage. Near that buttress, route-find down to the north, then **crawl** east along a ledge a short distance, then downclimb a little and walk along a hiker-made trail to the bottom. If using this route, an interesting hike would be to head upcanyon to see the **Jewell Tibbetts Arch**, the same one discussed above, but this time from inside the canyon. There's a good chance you'll find a little **water** in the upper end of this drainage. If it's afternoon, go to the west side.

There's a **rock art panel** near this route in, so to see it, continue downcanyon in the main drainage. About 1 km from the Crawling Route, look right or northwest to see a big shallow alcove more than 200m long. Right in the middle of it, and barely visible from the dry wash, is a red painted pictograph with one image bigger than life-sized. It has lots of similarities to the red painting in **Pictograph Fork**, and in **Range, Clearwater & South Fork of Sevenmile Canyon** and the **Great Gallery in Horseshoe Canyon**. They may have been made by the same person or clan, but they can't test the pigments for age because all that's left is mineral matter. At both ends of this big alcove are crude shelters and flint chips indicating they were campsites for either the Archaic or Fremont peoples. In the west end of the shallow alcove is another semi-separate alcove cave with another small rock art panel painted red.

To make a nice loop hike in this area, continue west on the Spring Canyon Road to **Dubinky Wash** at **Km 8.9 (Mile 5.5)** from Highway 313. This is the end of upper Dubinky Wash just before it drops into Hell Roaring Canyon. Park there on the slickrock and walk about 400-500m south along the east side of the canyon rim to the start of the **Hell Roaring Trail** as shown on the map.

None of the old cowboys the author talked to knew who might have originally built this trail, but there were some sheep in the country at or just after about 1900. One of the sheep herders, most of whom were Basques, may have started it, but it may also have been built by one of the early cattlemen from Moab. The Taylors may have been the first ones out there, but no one today can remember much about them. The earliest ones that anyone alive today (2012) can remember were Snyder, Jackson, Patterson and Riordan (they were part of the Moab Establishment in The Range War of 1924-'25; read more about them in the back of this book under the Tidwell Bottom, Bill Tibbetts & John Jackson stories). It could have been one of these men who first blasted this trail out of the Wingate Sandstone. It makes a big loop down on top of the sloping Wingate slickrock. Holes were drilled in the sandstone, pipes put in with logs, then rocks and dirt put on top of the logs. You can still walk a horse up or down it today--but maybe not ride it.

Later, in about 1931, **Arthur & Hazel Ekker** bought the grazing rights for this area from Riordon & Patterson and established a ranch on Dubinky Wash (read their story in the previous chapter). One of their hired hands was the late **Lorin Milton**, a cowboy from Green River. He remembered working on the trail this way:

I worked on that trail for Arthur Ekker. He was at Dubinky. Arthur was using it and it had to be worked over. He lined me up out there before the war [World War II] just after I got out of high school. He and Hazel had to go to Salt Lake or somewhere, so we worked on that trail for 4 days, then we re-gathered his country around Dubinky, and got the weaner calves that we had missed from an earlier round-up. So we had about 15 head of calves, and we kept one cow with 'em.

There's a little [brush] corral at the head of that trail. Because that trail's so bad, you gotta have a corral there so you can whip'em off. You can't drive nothing off without a corral right there and we had

Left The **Jewell Tibbetts Arch** as seen from inside the upper end of a little west fork of **Hell Roaring Canyon**. For this shot, be there in the afternoon. **Right** This is where everyone gets on hands & knees; thus the name **Crawling Route** into the upper end of Hell Roaring Canyon.

Holding
Pen

Above The **Hell Roaring Trail** running down into the upper end of Hell Roaring Canyon. It starts on the left in what used to be a small brush **"holding pen"**. From there it drops down a little, then runs along a bench in shadows before cutting down across the slickrock toward the bottom center of this picture.

Left The best of 2 **rock art paintings** near the upper end of **Hell Roaring Canyon.** Another smaller panel is located to the west or left of this in a 2nd little alcove which was also a camping place.

a hell of a time. We kept one cow that had been there before to be the leader, and down they went. Ooooh, that trail was a son of a bitch. Of all the trails I've had cattle on, that one at the head of Hell Roarin' was one of the worst. We worked on that trail late in the fall, November, 1936 or '37. We'd already weaned and shipped and drove the weaners to Thompson. Then came back and worked on that trail for 4 days, then we gathered the county when he got back and got all the stragglers we'd missed, and weand'em right there at the corral at the head of that trail.

Here's an idea for a short day-hike. Walk down the Hell Roaring Trail, see an alcove **cave** which was an Archaic or Fremont Indian camping place, then into the main canyon. Once there, turn left or east and head upcanyon. But, just as you're rounding that corner, observe along a wide area on that bench, a bunch of **geodes & chert**, and **flint chips**. This is where Indians of one age or another would have stopped to craft some arrowheads or other needed tools. There's another smaller site upcanyon.

Continue upcanyon to view the rock art described above--it's a neat place. From there head east again and round the corner where the Crawling Route is, but walk upcanyon heading southeast. After about 2 1/2 kms, you'll come to a fork in the drainage; go either way depending on the time of day to get fotos of the **Jewell Tibbetts Arch**. There should be some good water in that area. Return downcanyon and turn right at the corner and follow a hiker's trail up to the bottom of the cliffs and the **Crawling Route** out of the canyon. Once out, road-walk about 3 kms back to your car. This suggested trip took the author 5 1/2 hours.

The lower end of the canyon really isn't that interesting. This upper part is better. Read more below about the lower end of this canyon.

Mineral Point

There's not a lot to see on **Mineral Point**, but a fair number of 4-wheelers or ATV's use the place as a test track. Mtn. bikers can also use it, but some parts are a little sandy. To get there, drive along Highway 313 to near **mile post 11**, and turn west at the signs stating the **Horsethief Campground**. Drive a very good road a short distance to the campground, but keep heading west. This one main road to Mineral Point eventually leads to **2 drill hole** sites and the rim of Labyrinth Canyon for good views looking down on the Green River.

At **Km 3.8 (Mile 2.3)** is a **corral** on the right or north and a sheepman's **cellar** on the left. In the 1910's, 20's & '30's, this was used by sheep herd owners to store supplies for their sheepmen during their winter stay in this area. Being underground, nothing would freeze. At **Km 11.2 (Mile 6.9)** the better graded road ends and all tracks beyond that are a little rougher. Also at that point, you can turn right or north and after 1.6 kms (1 mile) you'll be at a **drill hole** site and an old **stock pond**.

Or if you continue west from where the graded or **good road** ends, you'll eventually come to another **drill hole** site at **Km 17.5 (Mile 10.9)**. From there to the end of Mineral Point at **Km 20 (Mile 12.4)** is still a pretty good road. To reach that point all you need is a HCV. Walk a short distance to a viewpoint. There are many other roads on Mineral Point, but there's really not a lot to see in this area, except down into Hell Roaring or Mineral Canyons.

Horsethief Point: Horsethief Ranch, and the Horsethief Trail & Road

Next stop will be **Horsethief Point** along what is now called the **Mineral Bottom Road**. To get there, drive along Highway 313 to halfway between **mile posts 10 & 11**, then turn southwest onto the Mineral Bottom Road. After **16 kms (9.9 miles)** is a turnoff to the left and a side-road running south 800m to the **Horsethief Ranch**. Someone is there all the time, plus 3-4 barking dogs, so forget about going there!

Overlooking the **Horsethief Ranch** just south of the Horsethief Road.

Here's a brief history of that ranch; it was first begun by a guy named **Art Murray** in about 1929 or '30 after he bought the cows and grazing rights from **Eph Moore** (read more about Eph in the back of this book under the Tidwell Bottom and the Range War of 1924-25). Art started building a cabin at a spring that Bill Tibbetts and 9 year-old Kenny Allred first found and developed in 1924. The Murrays lived there until the early 1950's (probably 1953), but Art had so many arguments with the Grazing Service, then the BLM, he gave up and eventually escaped to Canada.

The late **Kenny Allred** and his wife moved in there in 1953. Then when their kids got to school age, they had to move to Moab and sold it to his half brother, **Bill Tibbetts**. In 1965, Tibbetts sold out to **Mac & Alice McKinney**. McKinney was the second superintendent of Arches N.P. The next owners were **Nancy & Dick Eckert**. They bought it in 1973, and were there until 1981; that's when **Michael Behrendt** bought it and he still owns it. He sort of makes Aspen, Colorado his home, but is more often out sailing a yacht around the world--or so they say (?). He has hired hands to live there and watch out for the place. Behrendt is also the author of a little book on the history of the ranch titled, *Horse Thief Ranch--an Oral History*. Some dates in that book are a little different from this writer's sources, but if spending time in this part of the country, you should read it. Buy it at Back of Beyond Bookshop in Moab.

Next stop will be the **Horsethief Trail**. This is/was an old horse trail dating back before 1900. Stories persist that horse thieves would steal horses over on the La Sal Mountains east of Moab, or from farmers around Moab, then drive them north across the Colorado and up Moab & Sevenmile Canyons. From on top, they would head southwest to and along Horsethief Point to where the steepest part of the trail dropped off the Wingate Sandstone ledges. That part was on a very steep talus slope where some trail construction took place. While the entire length of the way is called the Horsethief Trail, this steep place has always been the most famous part. It was always a difficult and dangerous place for animals to get up or down.

From this steep part, it went down across Horsethief Bottom and crossed the river to Woodruff Bottom. Once on the west side of the Green River, it followed the west bank down across Woodruff and Saddle Horse Bottoms, and up **Horsethief Canyon**. At the head of that impressive gorge is another constructed part of this trail. It then went up and out onto **The Spur** and over to the Robbers Roost country west of upper Horseshoe Canyon. Horsethief Canyon and that part of the trail is discussed along with **Map 5**.

Kenny Allred ran cows in this country for years and he remembered: *When I was just a little kid the old Horsethief was a washed out trail. When Art Murray bought our rights (Eph Moore's sister was Kenny's mother) and moved in there [the Horsethief Ranch in about 1930], he fixed that trail up. He had to put in a--we called it a bridge--but it was a big ramp timbered up, and put rocks and stuff on it. It was quite a ledge. It was about a 10 foot [3m] ledge that he had to build up. Then when they put their road off, why they shot that off. So it's not there any more.*

Today as you drop off Horsethief Point, you'll be driving down what is still called the **Horsethief Trail Road**. At the time this road was built, the late **Kent Johnson** of Moab worked for the Grazing Service, which was the forerunner to today's BLM. He was in charge of overseeing the building of many access roads in Grand and San Juan County just at the beginning of World War II. He supervised the building of this road which drops off the high country and zig zags down through the Wingate Sandstone and

Aerial view of the **switchbacks** of the **Horsethief Trail Road** looking southeast.

Chinle Formations. Here's how he remembered the planning & construction: *There was an old wagon road down on Horsethief Point, but we worked our pickup down to the Horsethief Trail. Pres Linford was there, and we argued about the cost of building the road down. We figured it would cost $50,000 for the first mile [1.6 kms] and $10,000 for the next half mile [800 m]. They [Bureau of Public Roads] also gave me $450 a mile for the 15 miles [24 kms] on top of Horsethief Point.*

We had that road finished before I went into the service in February, 1944. So that road must have been built in about 1943. We couldn't follow the trail because it was too steep, so we had to switchback. We would drill little holes out on the [Wingate] slickrock, and stick a pole out there; then you could go out and drill some bigger holes and shoot that; then you could drill down with a jackhammer. Then you'd shoot that off, and pretty soon it was wide enough for a Cat to go around it. The total cost of putting the road down the old Horsethief Trail was $60,000. That must have been in about 1943, because they were pulling ore out of Mineral Canyon before I went into the service. At that time, they brought it up to the top of the hill in small dump trucks, then reloaded it into big Diesel trucks. At first we weren't allowed to put in any culverts, because of the war effort [and steel shortage]. Those came in later.

This road was primarily put down there to go up Mineral Canyon where there were some uranium claims. But in fact, we went clearn up to the mouth of Hell Roarin' Canyon, but Hell Roarin' didn't show much mineralization. We also went down the Green River and went up Taylor Canyon, because Norm Hettman and Buck Taylor and a few of 'em had claims up there that were kinda promising.

There's a parking place at the top of this steep road, and many people stop and park and/or camp there, or just look down at the road with all the switchbacks. This is **21 kms (13 miles)** from Highway 313. It was totally washed out in the late summer of 2010, but was rebuilt in the winter of 2010-11 and reopened on March 31, 2011. It still doesn't have metal culverts, but cement pourovers instead. Under normal conditions, any car can make it up or down. In doing the book, ***River Guide to Canyonlands NP and Vicinity,*** the author drove up & down this Horsethief Trail Road with his boat & trailer. That was with both a 1981 VW Rabbit Diesel and a 2002 VW Golf Diesel towing a 4 1/2m-long (14 ft.) aluminum boat & trailer--so it's not too steep--but it was 1st gear all the way up.

Mineral Canyon

When you finally get down the steep part of the Horsethief Trail, the **White Rim Road** turns left and runs downriver. The White Rim country will be covered later. From that junction, continue straight ahead to the northeast about another 1 1/2 kms (to **Km 24.9/Mile 15.5** from Highway 313). There on your left will be the **Mineral Canyon boat ramp**, complete with a good toilet. There are many places to camp in the area.

From the boat ramp, continue northeast toward the mouth of Mineral Canyon; after about 350m, you'll come to the **foundations** of a building on the right. **Kenny Allred** knew this place well: *There used to be an old mill and a house there. They built a mill, but they never did get it set up and a runnin'. Then when the company broke up, they give me $200 a month to watch it. It was good money for doin' nothin'. I was livin' out there anyway, so we moved into that little house, and lived there all of one summer and one winter. I ended up buying the house then traded it to a guy and he was going to tear it up and move it out, but he went down there and worked about 2 or 3 days, and then all of a sudden the damn thing caught on fire--but he had it insured. He collected $3500 on it. There's some cement work still there.*

Gay and Bob Tibbetts was the carpenters down there. They was workin' for this company. Kent Johnson was in on that mill too. He's the one who got me the watchman job. This must have been in the late 1950's, and the boom was kind of over and it was startin' to cool off. They didn't have no ore down there to speak of, and I think it was just a promotion deal to start with. When they went out of business, the mill and everything was all taken apart and sold. I kinda bought the whole works there after they left.

Kent Johnson remembered a few more things about this place: *That mill at the mouth of Mineral Canyon was owned by old Dell Webb [later he owned many resorts in the west]. He formed a company there, and he give me some stock in it. We had a bunch of them Short Creek people up there, and they was having their homes raided down on **Short Creek** while these guys was in the canyon down there. And you couldn't get'em off the radio--they had to listen to the action. They drove me nuts.*

(Short Creek was the name of the polygamist colony on the Utah-Arizona border raided on July 26, 1953 by 102 State police and Arizona National Guardsmen; they hauled off about 400 men, women & children. The place is now called Hilldale, Utah, and Colorado City, Arizona. Locals always called that event, "The Raid". Warren Jeffs, who is now in prison for life, later became the leader of that group.)

Mineral Canyon is the starting point for many boaters going down the Green and up the Colorado River. The **boat dock** was first built by Kenny Allred of Moab. He told this writer: *Right there at that old tree where you put in, I put the first boat dock in there with an old Cat I had down in there when I was doing some mining work. That was right at the first of the uranium boom--about 1951 or '52.*

Mineral Canyon is another rather long drainage, and it's got a pretty good road up to about its halfway point. That'll discourage some people, but it's an interesting canyon higher up. In the summers of 1990 & 2011, that road was good enough for cars. If you drive up there and stop at the end of the good road, you can continue on a mtn. bike a little further. Finally you can hike to the upper end. If you do go up, you'll find many small miner's test pits, adits or prospects along the way. They're all dug in the **Moss Back Member of the Chinle Formation**. There were about 15 claims staked out in this canyon, mostly between 1951 & '53. The first claims were filed on by Moab men such as Kenny Allred, Bill Tibbetts, Kent Johnson and Felix Murphy. But apparently very little actual mining ever took place. There are signs of old Cat tracks or exploration roads running all the way upcanyon, most of which are now faded away. One of the best places to view this canyon is from the rim. As you driving along the Mineral Bottom Road, stop and walk about 1 km to one of several overlooks in the upper end of the canyon.

Lower Hell Roaring Canyon

From the mouth of Mineral Canyon, start driving up along the Green River. Immediately on your left will be a short **airstrip**, then just above that will be an old **mine** and **mine cabin** on your right with several old junk trucks lying around. **Kenny Allred** remembered a story about that place: *There was a company there by the name of Airborne Prospectors. It was doctors and lawyers from Grand Junction who owned that, and Marlow Smith and me leased it from them when they quit mining it themselves. I was workin' for 'em when they quit minin' it. It got so dangerous in there where the ore* was, it kept cavin' in, and they came down in there and took a look at it one day, and said, "Mov'er out--we're quitin', before somebody gets killed." But there was a lot more ore found there in different places later. Those Airborne Prospectors owned claims on that whole bench.

If you arrive in dry conditions, you can drive a car up along the river about 2 kms toward the mouth of **Hell Roaring Canyon**. But there are rockslides and tamarisks taking over the place, so it's too rough even for 4WD's. That old road is now used by some ATV's, motorcycles, mtn. bikers and hikers.

At the bottom end of Hell Roarin' Canyon and maybe 300m from the river on the south side of the dry creek bed, is an historic site worth seeing. This is the best known and most-easily accessible of all the inscriptions made by the fur trapper named **Denis Julien**. This particular etching reads: ***D. Julien 1836 3 Mai***. See the picture below. To the right of this is a boat with a sail and a round wheel-like etching, perhaps the sun (?).

To find it, drive/walk upcanyon about 300m from the river. At an old parking place, look up to the south about 30m from the road. It's there on some smooth rocks under an overhang maybe 10m above the road. Nearby are several places where others have left there marks as well. One of the best is that left by the Wolvertons. It reads: *"E.T. Wolverton, Mart. Baker, N.E. Wolverton 7/1/1905"*. The "N." stands for Norville Wolverton, one of E.T.'s sons. In 2011, the author failed to see this one.

There's a road heading upcanyon, but it soon peters out. It's a long and tiresome hike to walk all the way from the bottom, so it's recommended you use the Hell Roarin' Trail or the Crawling Route to reach the more interesting upper end. At one time there must have been a cattle trail upstream along the river on the east bank, but there was never a road built there.

Left Looking north from at the mouth of **Mineral Canyon** (the canyon is to the right--the Green River is to the left). Shown here is the foundation of one of the buildings that Kenny Allred mentioned above.

Below The **Denis Julien Inscription** at the mouth of **Hell Roaring Canyon**. It states: May 3, 1836.

Lone Mesa, Determination Towers, Sevenmile & Mill Canyons, the History of the Courthouse Stage Stations, and the Dalton Wells CCC & Japanese Concentration Camp

Location & Access This map shows some interesting red rock country between Highway 191, Sevenmile Canyon, Dubinky and the Moab Airport. This whole area is about 15 kms (10 miles) north of Moab. The rocks are titled down to the north and there are several mesas, buttes and pinnacles in the area. The most prominent formation featured here is the Entrada Sandstone. All the big rose-red colored cliffs are made of the Entrada. Immediately below it is the Navajo Sandstone, with the Carmel apparently missing in at least some of this area (?).

There's not a lot of hiking here, but the place is crawling with 4WD's, ATV's & mtn. bikers. There are several historic sites in the area, which are some of the featured places to visit in this area. The one main access road is **Highway 191**, running between Moab, and Crescent Junction & Interstate 70. Another paved road is the one leaving 191 and running west up Sevenmile Canyon ending at Canyonlands NP & Dead Horse Point; that's State **Highway 313**. On the west is the **Dubinky Road**, to the north is the **Blue Hills Road** (both graded county roads), which runs between Highway 191 (mile post 143) and I-70 at **mile post & Exit 173**. Right after heavy rains or snow, stay away from these last two roads. The Blue Hills Road runs across clay beds and parts can be especially slick when wet. The Dubinky Road can be slick in some lower sections, but it runs through mostly sandy country which means it's better with a little moisture. Read more below for each destination.

Elevations From about 1674m at the junction of the Dubinky Road & Highway 313, down to 1379m where Highway 313 in Sevenmile Canyon meets Highway 191.

Water Best waterhole in the entire country is at **Brink Spring**. There's a swampy spring at the Halfway Stage Station; and Mill Canyon has a small stream that would be drinkable at its source--if there are no cows around (cattle graze there in winter). Don't expect to find water at Dubinky, Dubinky Well or Dalton Wells. There's a small commercial campground, store & gas station (Arches View) near the junction of Highways 313 & 191.

Maps USGS or BLM map Moab (1:100,000); Merrimac Butte & Jug Rock (1:24,000--7 1/2' quads); the plastic Trails Illustrated/National Geographic map Moab North (1:70,000); or the plastic Latitude 40° map Moab West (1:75,000).

Main Attractions Attractive red rock Entrada buttes, mesas & spires, historic copper mine & mill site, historic stage coach stations, the site of a CCC & Japanese concentration camp, and several rock art sites in Sevenmile Canyon.

Brink Spring

Best way to reach **Brink Spring** is to drive along Highway 191 to near **mile post 143** just south of the Moab Airport, and turn west onto the **Blue Hills Road**. Drive west **5.8 kms (3.6 miles)** and turn left or south. Drive along a slightly rough road for 1.9 kms (1.2 miles) until you see a watering trough, then a large metal water storage tank on a hill, and above that, an old stone cabin hidden in brush. It'll be a little green spot on the hillside and the road going to it is generally good for cars but bumpy. This spring has now been troughed-up, with a pipe running from the spring source down past the metal storage tank to the first watering trough you come to. It's great water, and you can camp anywhere nearby.

Just up the road from the tank is a one-room stone cabin out in the middle of a big sagebrush and willow patch. None of the old timers the author talked to had any idea who may have created this first, but it may go back to the late 1800's (?). No one can say for sure, but it's likely this was an important stopping place on the Old Spanish Trail as it ran from what is now the Moab area toward Green River. The Blue Hills Road runs along a natural route between these 2 towns with Brink Spring nearby.

Brink Spring is on one of the mtn. biking routes. There are more routes to the south than are shown on this map, but which are shown on the 2 plastic recreational maps listed above. Apparently there are some slickrock routes up there too. Some of the biking outfitters in

About 300m below **Brink Spring** is this water trough for cattle. It has a good flow, about like a slow flowing garden hose; and you can catch the water before it reaches the trough itself.

Map 16, Lone Mesa, Determination Towers, Sevenmile & Mill Canyons, the History of the Courthouse Stage Stations, and the Dalton Wells CCC & Japanese Concentration Camp

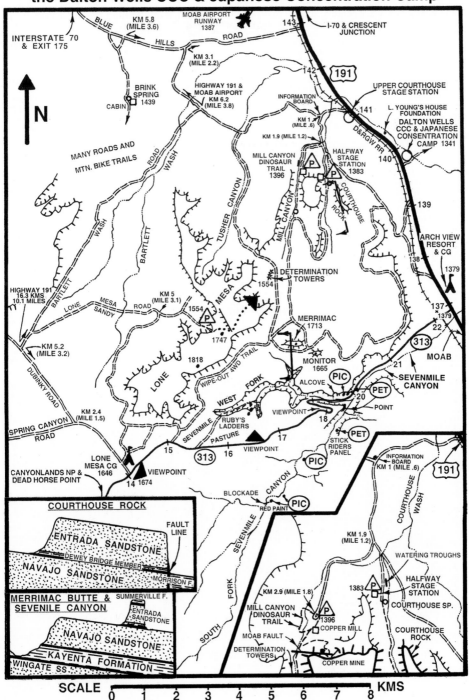

INTERSTATE 70 & EXIT 175

KM 5.8 (MILE 3.6)

BLUE HILLS ROAD

MOAB AIRPORT RUNWAY 1387

143

I-70 & CRESCENT JUNCTION

KM 3.1 (MILE 2.2)

142

191

N

BRINK SPRING 1439

CABIN

HIGHWAY 191 & MOAB AIRPORT KM 6.2 (MILE 3.8)

INFORMATION BOARD

141

UPPER COURTHOUSE STAGE STATION

L. YOUNG'S HOUSE FOUNDATION

D&RGW RR

DALTON WELLS CCC & JAPANESE CONSENTATION CAMP 1341

KM 1 (MILE .6)

KM 1.9 (MILE 1.2)

MANY ROADS AND MTN. BIKE TRAILS

ROAD WASH

TUSHER CANYON

MILL CANYON DINOSAUR TRAIL 1396

MILL CANYON

HALFWAY STAGE STATION 1383

P

P

140

COURTHOUSE ROCK

139

BARTLETT WASH

138

ARCH VIEW RESORT & CG

1379

DETERMINATION TOWERS

1554

HIGHWAY 191 16.3 KMS 10.1 MILES

LONE MESA SANDY ROAD

KM 5 (MILE 3.1)

1554

MESA

MERRIMAC 1713

137

1379

22

313

MOAB

P

1747

LONE

1818

WIPE-OUT 4WD TRAIL

FORK

MONITOR 1665

ALCOVE

PIC

21

20

PET

SEVENMILE CANYON

KM 5.2 (MILE 3.2)

DUBINKY ROAD

KM 2.4 (MILE 1.5)

WEST

SEVENMILE

PASTURE

VIEWPOINT

RUBY'S LADDERS

VIEWPOINT

17

18

POINT

PET

STICK RIDERS PANEL

INFORMATION BOARD KM 1 (MILE .6)

191

SPRING CANYON ROAD

LONE MESA CG 1646

15

313

16

VIEWPOINT

PIC

COURTHOUSE WASH

CANYONLANDS NP & DEAD HORSE POINT

VIEWPOINT

14 1674

BLOCKADE

SEVENMILE CANYON

RED PAINT

PIC

KM 1.9 (MILE 1.2)

WATERING TROUGHS

FORK

SOUTH

KM 2.9 (MILE 1.8)

1383

HALFWAY STAGE STATION

P

COURTHOUSE SP.

MILL CANYON DINOSAUR TRAIL

1396

COPPER MILL

P

COURTHOUSE ROCK

MOAB FAULT

DETERMINATION TOWERS

COPPER MINE

COURTHOUSE ROCK

FAULT LINE

ENTRADA SANDSTONE

DEWEY BRIDGE MEMBER

NAVAJO SANDSTONE

MORRISON F.

SUMMERVILLE F.

MERRIMAC BUTTE & SEVENILE CANYON

ENTRADA SANDSTONE

NAVAJO SANDSTONE

KAYENTA FORMATION

WINGATE SS

SCALE 0 1 2 3 4 5 6 7 8 KMS

169

Moab take their clients past Brink Spring and into the country to the south.

Mill Canyon Dinosaur Trail, Copper Mines & Copper Mill Site

To reach these interesting historic sites, drive along Highway 191 to a point just north of **mile post 141**. From there, turn west, cross the railroad tracks and continue along a dry wash. **One km (.6 mile)** from the highway, you'll come to a large parking place and a **BLM information board** pointing out the interesting sites to the south. From there, head south past another parking area to a road junction at **Km 1.9 (Mile 1.2)**; to the left is the Halfway Stage Station, but for now turn right and drive along a wash bottom with a little running water; follow this road to a trailhead parking in the lower end of **Mill Canyon** at **Km 2.9 (Mile 1.8** from the highway). Most of the time an ordinary car can make it to this place. This parking is at the beginning of the **Dinosaur Trail** and the sites of an old **copper mine & mill**.

At this trailhead at the mouth of Mill Canyon is a trail register and an information board. This sign shows the route of the **Dinosaur Trail**, and there's a small box which sometimes has BLM handouts with written information and a map explaining the site. One handout states:

The Dinosaur Trail is a bold experiment--an outdoor paleontological museum. There are no guards or fences here. You, the visitor, are the protector of this valuable resource. Only you assure that this fragile legacy is preserved so those who follow may see, learn, and enjoy. It is illegal to remove, deface, or destroy improvements, artifacts, rocks, fossils, animals, and plants. Leave only footprints--take only pictures.

From the carpark, walk west on the trail into the bottom of the wash, then up to the ledge on the opposite side. This is only about 100m from the parking place. From there walk south just above the dry wash, which is the lower end of Mill Canyon. There are 15 sites where dinosaur bones are exposed to full view in the rocks of the Brushy Basin Member of the **Morrison Formation**.

After walking maybe 250-300m, you'll be at the end of the Dinosaur Trail and can then either return the same way; or walk east down across the small stream to a former road, now a trail. Before returning to your vehicle from there, you might as well visit another historic site which is the remains of an **old copper mill** and mining area. From the creek, walk upon the east-side bench and look for the remains of an old stone structure. This is what's left of the copper mill. Now a little history of the place, most of which comes from old issues of the original Moab newspaper, *The Grand Valley Times (GVT)*.

On **May 30, 1896**, a man by the name of J.N. Corbin began operating a weekly newspaper in Moab. It's obvious by reading this paper that Corbin is a promoter and did everything he could to promote mining, tourism, boating and freighting on the Green & Colorado Rivers during the years he owned and operated The Grand Valley Times. Keep this in mind as you read the following articles.

The first we know of any mining possibilities in the Courthouse Rock area was mentioned in the **9/9/1898 issue**: *Jeremiah Hatch has discovered a led of manganese ore near the Court House rock and has taken an outfit there to sink a shaft on it. We are just beginning to hear of the mineral resources of this section.*

The first we hear about copper was in the **3/17/1899** issue: *COPPER ON THE DESERT: F.B. Hammond and Jerry Hatch have been out this week examining a copper prospect near the court house rock spring on the Thompson road.* This Hammond fellow was formerly the manager of the Bluff Cattle Pool out of Bluff, Utah, and later he owned a general mercantile store in Moab before 1896 and extending for many years after that. Two weeks later, in the **3/31/1899** paper it stated: *At the Court House rock....., Mr. Young has opened a fine copper vein. Next week we will have more to say of this new district which bids fair to be of so much importance.*

This is what remains of the building which housed the so-called **copper processing plant** in **Mill Canyon**. To the left is a pile of coal, to the right and up the hill is at least one mine adit or prospect.

The next we see anything written about copper at Courthouse is in the **9/1/1899** issue. It seems that during the summer, Hammond, Hatch and others had formed a company: *Twenty sacks of ore from the Evergreen copper property, lately discovered near Court House rock, have been taken to Thompson for shipment as a test of the ore. Parties who have visited the place pronounced this prospect one of the best in the district.* Four weeks later the paper stated: *The new copper strike near Court House rock, is proving to be the best yet this season. The vein has been opened over a mile from the original discovery showing its continuity....*

The **10/6/1899** issue stated: *The shipment of ore from the claims of Hammond et al., at Court House rock amounting to about 1600 pound [700 kg.] sent as a test netted the owners $29 over all expenses.*

F.B. Hammond had miners working there during the winter, then in the **3/23/1900** issue it states: *.....commenced taking out a carload of ore from his copper property near court house rock. They have 20 or more tons of the ore now on the dump.* These shipments were sent to Salt Lake City by train. By **8/23/1901**: *Reports from those who have visited the mining property on which Frank Dixon and others are sinking a shaft near Court House rock, is to the effect that a very fine showing of copper ore is being made. The shaft is now down 60 feet [20 m].* Frank Dixon and the other miners must have been working for Hammond (?).

By the fall of 1901, there was enough promising copper ore along a fault line that Hammond and his partners decided to install a **copper processing plant** on the site as a kind of experiment. Shipping low grade ore from Moab to Salt Lake City being out of the question. By **11/15/1901**: *A car of machinery reached Thompson the first of the week for a copper extraction plant that is to be erected at the Court House Station on the Thompson & Moab road. This is being financed by Salt Lake parties.*

By **12/6/1901**: *Another carload of machinery arrived at Thompson, the first of the week, for the copper plant at Court House. The company expects to have their plant running inside of 90 days, and is the first plant of the kind in this section......* **12/27/1901**: *Mr. M.B. Pope, one of the gentlemen who have a lease and bond on the Hammond Copper claims at Court House, spent Christmas in Moab..... Work was suspended on the Copper plant during the holidays, but will be resumed right after the 1st, and will be completed in a month or six weeks.....*

By **3/7/1902**: *The Clara Copper company have their bleaching plant at Court House running.* It's not known what took place during the next year, but it must not have been high enough grade copper ore, or the experimental processing plant they installed didn't work as well as they hoped. The next newspaper article about the place was on **2/6/1903**: *F.A. Manville left Tuesday for Court House to attach the property of the Clara Copper Mining Co. for the payment of delinquent taxes.* It appears they had financial problems as well.

There were other miners in the immediate area working the summer of 1903, then by **9/4/1903**: *F. B. Hammond returned this week from his trip to Salt Lake. While there Mr. Hammond saw some of his Court House ore tested by a new patented process, the invention of a young California professor. A 5 ton plant is in operation there [Salt Lake] which handles silver and copper ore cheaply and with the addition of another acid, gold can be extracted.*

By **10/9/1903**, an article originating in the *Salt Lake Mining Review*, stated among other things that the American Metal Extraction Company was planning to install a 200 ton plant using the leaching method at the Clara Mines at Court House. That method was supposed to extract 95% to 97% of the copper from the ore. It would cost $40,000 and be ready by the end of 1903. That same article went on to say: *Last year a mill was erected at the property to handle the ores by a modified Gardener process, but it was found that the cost was too great to think of applying it to a 5 or 6 percent copper*

This is the one main adit or prospect for copper located just uphill and south of the old **mill site** seen on the opposite page. Copper is concentrated along a fault line, but there's not much here.

ore like that of the Clara.

Soon after that and in the **11/6/1903** paper it states: *Prof. Frederick Laist, head chemist of the American Metal Extraction Co., and Mr. Hudson Smith, a director of the company, registered at the Maxwell [Hotel] today. They have just inspected the mining prospects at "Court House Rock" and go on to visit the Big Indian and Lisbon country. Their company has a copper extraction process that it is claimed will successfully treat the ore of this section. They are looking for development that will justify the erection of a mill.* Many years later, Charley Steen discovered high grade uranium ore in the same area as the Big Indian Mine. Read more about Charley in the back of this book on page 366.

This was the last anything was mentioned about the Courthouse Copper District. It's assumed that when these men from American Metals had a good look at the Big Indian Country located directly south of the La Sal Mountains, the decision was made to install the plant there rather than near Courthouse Rock. It's also assumed that what you see in the lower end of Mill Canyon today is what remains of the small plant that was erected in the winter of 1901 & '02 and worked for a short time only in 1902.

What you actually see there today is what looks like the back wall of a **stone building**. There is also the remains of a pile of coal nearby, but not much else. It appears that in more recent years there have been other miners in the area taking another look at the possibilities. To locate one of the mines, get upon the more-recently-made **bulldozer track** just above the copper mill, and walk uphill on it. When it gets steep and just after the road ends, continue up the slope on a trail. There is one place that appears to have been an old mine shaft, but it hardly went in or down for 20m as suggested in the one article. It's assumed that one reason for locating the plant there was to take advantage of the year-round water supply in Mill Creek just a few meters away.

Upper and Lower Courthouse Stagecoach Stations

From the old copper mill site, walk north back to your car and drive back to the other road running south directly toward **Courthouse Rock** and the remains of the original **Upper Courthouse Stagecoach Station**. Some have called this the **Halfway Stage Station** because it was about halfway between Thompson and Moab. Cars should be able to get there, but crossing the sandy creek bottom along the way may be difficult, so gear down, rev up, and drive fast for a short distance; or park just before the small stream and walk or ride a mtn. bike 300m or so to the old station site.

When you arrive, there will be a number of cottonwood trees, some springs and some **watering troughs** on the left; and a **5-sided stone structure** without a roof on the right or west. A large sign gives a little history of the place. Before moving on to its history, remember this is the upper station site, as opposed to another station down below to the east next to today's highway. The lower station, usually just called the **Courthouse Station**, was in the Upper Courthouse Wash near where **mile post 141** is now on Highway 191. Immediately west of that mile post and within the first 100m south of the white post along the railroad tracks marked **17**, will be where the lower station once was. When reading about the history of either of these stations you must keep both of these sites in mind.

Most of the information about these sites comes from Moab's first newspaper, *The Grand Valley Times (GVT)*, which ran from May 30, 1896 until September of 1919. After that it was called *The Times-Independent (TI)*.

Keep in mind, the first railroad was put through this region in 1883. It ran east-west through Thompson and Green River. Before that, there were very few people living anywhere in eastern Utah. The coming of the railroad brought about the first real boom to Moab. At first, they must have been using an old trail between Moab and Thompson, but in time a road gradually developed. Sometime later a stage line would have been introduced, but there was no record of when that first got started, at least in the Moab paper (there's a 13 year gap here). The first mention of a road running between the railway at Thompson and Moab was in the **2/19/1897** paper. It was J.N. Corbin editorializing trying to get county commissioners to improve the route: *The present road to Thompson has not one feature on which permanency can be claimed. It is a long disagreeable haul away from water. It has no settlements along it and none possible for some years to come at best.*

It appears from this that no buildings existed at that time, but there were a few springs in the area as there are today. In the **7/2/1897** issue, Corbin states: *The board of county commissioners returned yesterday.... and have found there is no route over which a road could be built to avoid the round about way via Court House rock. They came back disgusted with the whole route and that no amount of work would make a good road in that direction.*

The normal route between Moab and Thompson at the time was down along Courthouse Wash where the highway is today. The worst part, which was very sandy, was right there at or near mile post 141. Old timers in Moab insist that in the early days the sand at that point was so deep, it forced heavily loaded wagons to go up and around to the west and to a spring just north and downhill from **Courthouse Rock**. This was where they used to camp when they were running from Thompson to Moab with wagons fully loaded and before a good road was established. Before about 1897, there apparently wasn't any kind of a halfway house or stage station established at either the upper or lower site, but people must have been thinking about it. With the coming of J.N. Corbin and his newspaper which promoted the country, it must have been about this time, the late 1890's, that more traffic was using the route. Evidence of that was an ad in the **8/6/1897** paper stating: *Court House Springs. Meals At All Hours. Hay and Grain. M.E. Morland, Prop.* It's not known what kind of a building was established at that time, or whether it was the upper or lower site; but in the **9/10/1897** issue it stated: *Monte Morland, has sold out his business at Court House Springs.....* The only spring around was at the upper station site.

By **October, 1898**, there was an ad featuring the *Moab-Thompson Stage Line*, Jeremiah Hatch Jr., *Proprietor*. It was a daily run except for Sundays, and they would have stopped for a lunch break and for watering horses. No mention is made of the facilities, but there must have been a house of some kind and corrals, perhaps at both places. This stage line was operated by the same person who first discovered manganese and copper in Mill Canyon.

The sandy place along the normal route was so bad and slowed traffic so much that by **2/1899**, the call went out for volunteers from Moab to help out. J.P. Miller was the country road commissioner. There were at least 14 prominent local men who took their teams out to Courthouse and donated 6 days of their time. In addition there was another dozen or so who went out for 2 days of volunteer work.

The first time the paper mentions any permanent buildings going up out there was in the **12/22/1899** issue: *J.W. Hayes is erecting a substantial station house at the lower springs at Court House rock and will have complete accommodation for passengers and teams. The house is being built of stone, A.M.*

Stocks and J.A. Elmer are doing the work. By **9/1/1901**, a Jasper Hayes died, and the statement is made: *Mr. Hayes has been for a number of years keeping the lower court house station on the Thompson road.* By **December, 1901**, the telefone line went through the Lower Courthouse Station, which accommodated the copper miners in the area.

By **6/6/1902** the paper stated: *The Court House Wash, that has given so much trouble in the past, will no longer interrupt traffic in that direction. The county let the contract to D.A. Johnson and the work of building a road around the wash has just been completed.*

This statement indicates they were serious about fixing the road once and for all so a detour up and around the wash wasn't needed. The making of this road, which was built up high on the west bank of Courthouse Wash just south of the lower station, must have taken traffic and business away from the upper station.

By **12/11/1903**, this statement was made: *The upper "Court House rock" station on the Thompson road has been abandoned. The stage [is now] going by the lower road. "Aunt Sally" Thompson who made the upper station famous as an eating house has moved to Moab.* It appears this is the last time the upper station at Courthouse Rock was used as a stage coach or halfway station by freighters. It appears likely the upper station was built sometime in the 1890's and abandoned late in 1903. With the improved road, all traffic then must have been down along the bottom of the wash.

By **12/18/1903**, a John Daniels took over the lower courthouse station, but by the first of **April, 1904**, Augustus Stewart moved his family in and took over the eating house at the station. He only stayed there for 3 months. After this time nothing is mentioned until **2/19/1909**: *Geo. F. Perkins and wife have severed their connection with the Court House eating station, which they had been operating for the past year..... Edward Perigen will operate the Court House station.*

The late **Kent Johnson** of Moab remembered the place when he was just a boy: *There used to be a woman out there and she cooked for the freighters. We called her Raggedy Ann. Her last name was Trout, it may have been Tom Trout's daughter. She was up at Upper Courthouse. She charged $.35 for a meal. She had kind of a little dining room there, and then she had a bedroom behind that. It didn't amount to a hell of a lot. They lived pretty hard lives. She just slept in the back. They had the kitchen and a few tables and a counter and they had a corral and water troughs there. I did ride the freight wagons when she was there but I was just a small kid. I was born in 1915, so she was there in about 1920 or '25.*

By **September 10, 1925** we know **John Jackson** and his second wife **Sinda** were living there along the wash, but they had nothing to do with the Courthouse Station. It may have been closed down at that time (?). The Jacksons were running cattle in the area. That was the time when Mrs. Evelyn Standifird's car rolled over right at the station and she was killed. It was Sinda Jackson who helped pull her and others from the car. This was billed as the first highway fatality in southeastern Utah.

It's believed the Courthouse facilities were pretty much closed down by sometime in the 1920's. The reason was, the roads were gradually improved and trucks took the place of the team & wagons for hauling freight from Thompson to Moab. From then on, there was no need for any kind of rest stop.

If you go to the lower station site, stop at mile post 141. Walk across the road to the west and look along the railway tracks south of the **post with 17** on it. There are still some old watering troughs and a well covered with cement. Everything's pretty much gone now, because in about 1963 the railway

The sign on the left summerizes the history of the **Halfway Stage Station.** In the earlier years, it was here they stopped because of the spring nearby; this site is located just downhill and north of **Courthouse Rock**. To the left less than 100m away are the springs & 1930's water troughs. Later, the stage station was moved down to where **mile post 141** is located on Highway 191.

173

went through to Potash and completely covered the site where the stone buildings once were. The highway completely covered the site where John Jackson lived as well.

There's not a lot of hiking in this area because of many 4WD roads, as shown on the map. Because it's close to Moab, these roads are used a lot by 4WD's, ATV's, motorcycles and mtn. bikers today. Many bikers are brought out by outfitters from Moab. One obvious route is up **Mill Canyon**. It has a little water in the lower end on a year-round basis, but by 2012, that former road south or uphill from the copper mill was closed to motor vehicles so mtn. biking and hiking are presently your only options there.

Determination Towers, Lone Mesa and the Monitor & Merrimac

Here's a great hike the author took on 3/8/2012. He headed south uphill from the Dinosaur Trail parking lot along Mill Creek, then walked a little cross-country to the west and to the best foto stop in the area, the **Determination Towers**. From there, and walking on HC/4WD roads, he circled to the south of **Monitor & Merrimac Buttes**, then back almost the same way. That walk took 3 1/4 hours. This is a sandy area, so mtn bikes don't help much.

Or, if you'd like another look at Determination Towers from the top of **Lone Mesa**, here's what you do. Drive up Sevenmile Canyon on Highway 313 to **mile post 14** and turn right or northwest onto the combined **Dubinky/Spring Canyon Road**. Drive this for **2.4 kms (1.5 miles)** and turn right or northeast onto the Dubinky Road. At **Km 5.2 (Mile 3.2** from the highway) turn right again onto the **Bartlett Wash Road**. Set your odometer at 0. After another 300-400m or so, veer to the right and onto the **Lone Mesa Road**. This one is very sandy in most places, but the author went both ways on this track in his Jeep Patriot AWD in the very dry spring of 2012 and did fine--just keep up RPM's & speed in the deeper sandier parts. Continuing, drive downhill and northeast until the junction at **Km 5 (Mile 3.1)** and turn left or east. At **Km 5.7 (Mile 3.5)**, and at elevation **1554m**, turn right or southerly. Continue to the end of the road at **Km 6.5 (Mile 4.1)** and park on top of the hill--if you can get up that last part.

From there, walk southeasterly and down a short distance, then uphill into the obvious steep drainage. A trail of sorts is starting to develop so follow that. Once on top of Lone Mesa, veer left, or northeast, and route-find up over **2 ledges**, then continue downhill to the end of a point or until you have a good look down on the Determination Towers. Return the same way. Back on the road, drive as fast as conditions allow to get up the sandier sections. If you don't trust your vehicle, or your skills for driving in deep sand, then walk from the Bartlett Wash Road. The author drove almost to the end of the road, then made it to the overlook shown, and back in about 2 hours. A mtn. bike won't help here.

Another 4WD, then hike or biking route, would be to head up the track immediately east of Courthouse Rock and end up at the 2 famous buttes called **Monitor & Merrimac**. In 1991, the author drove his VW Rabbit almost to Monitor Butte before getting stuck in deep sand. That road south from the Halfway Station is now closed to all motor vehicles--but you could walk or ride a mtn. bike that way. Or you could go up Tusher and come down Mill Canyon. This would be with a mtn. bike. But again, this is sandy country and bikes won't do well!

Sevenmile Canyon: Rock Art Sites and Ruby's Ladders

Sevenmile Canyon is the drainage where paved Highway 313 now runs up to Dead Horse Point and the northern part of Canyonlands NP. In the lower sections, there are a number of rock art panels

Aerial view looking southwest at **Determination Towers** and **Lone Mesa**. The Mill Canyon Trailhead is located to the right downhill, while Lone Mesa is in the upper left.

located near the junction of the **West and South Forks** and just west of **mile post 20**. About 200m west of mp 20 is a small parking place on the north side of the highway. Immediately north of that is a petroglyph panel which looks like large **square big horn sheep**. About 100m west of that is what some are calling **Intestine Man**; its painted on, has some very small intricate designs, and is under an overhang. Crawl upon a ledge for a closeup view. This isn't big, but it's interesting and worth the stop.

About 300m west of Intestine Man, is a prominent **alcove** facing north. Inside it are a number of large rocks with grooves--it seems someone was sharpening sticks or arrows or something (?). Also, directly south of the little parking place and on the **point** between the West & South Forks, are several small panels stretching over about 100m in length.

Or if you round that corner between the 2 forks, and walk (you can also drive, but in soft sand!) southwest up the South Fork about 1 km and on the left side and on the side of a little drainage alcove facing east, will be another small (1 square meter) but interesting petroglyph panel this writer is calling **stick riders**. On it, some humans look like they're riding stick horse like small children sometimes do today.

If you continue up the South Fork of Sevenmile, you will eventually find 3 more small panels as shown on the map. These are all pictographs and are on your left as you walk upcanyon. These aren't so interesting, but the last one is the best. It's faded **red** paint of some kind and has a similar look to the big panel found in **Hell Roaring, Range, Clearwater, Pictograph Fork and Horseshoe Canyons.** Just below that panel and in the canyon bottom is a **blockade** stopping motor vehicles from going further.

Higher up Highway 313 are 3 viewpoints; one is right at mile post 18, another is between mile posts 16 & 17, the other is near mile post 14. If you stop at either of these places, you'll have a good look at the **Merrimac & Monitor Buttes** across the canyon to the north.

There's one more interesting thing to see in this area, that being an old trail and **wooden ladders** down into the **West Fork** of Sevenmile Canyon. The late **Kenny Allred** cowboyed there during the 1930's & 40's and here's what he remembered:

Glen Ruby put that outfit in there. He was an oil man, and he built that original road off there into upper Sevenmile and Sevenmile Pasture. Ruby came out and got me one day and we walked down in there and found a spring; then he put a pump down there and pumped water. There was no road down in there at all before that. Is what he was trying to do was to get water to drill with, instead of goin' clearn out of the country. So he built this road from the Dubinky Road down into Sevenmile Pasture and to where the ladders and pipe are now. They hung a pipe on the cable to take the weight off the pipe. Somebody's taken the pipe out now I guess. Then in later years when the county decided to build a road, they started right there and built it on down into lower Sevenmile. He put that in there shortly after I went to work for Cecil Thompson. I suppose those ladders and things were put in there in about 1940. The Ruby Ranch along the Green River was named after Glen Ruby.

Glen Ruby became well know in this country because it was he who attempted to drill for oil south of the town of Green River and right on the east bank of the river starting in **September, 1935**, but all he got was a lot of CO_2 gas. Today it's called **Crystal Geyser**. That story is told in this writers other book, *River Guide to Canyonlands National Park & Vicinity*.

To get to **Ruby's Ladders**, look for a side-road running northeast from Highway 313 about halfway between **mile posts 15 & 16**. It's a pretty good road and it's only about 1 km from pavement to the end. Park at the end of this road where you see the cable and look to the left for a little trail going over the rim to the north. Go down a ways to find a steep crack where several sections of wooden ladders used to be; but as of 2012, the ladders had collapsed and are lying on the slope below. However, with

 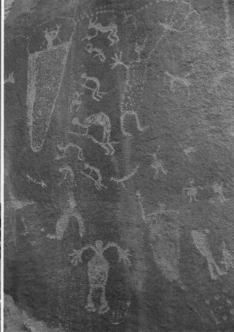

Left Looking southwest at the **Determination Towers**; see another foto on the opposite page. **Right** The **Stick Riders Panel** in the lower end of **South Fork of Sevenmile Canyon**.

care you can downclimb this crack. From where the ladders are sitting, turn left and follow a faint trail down to another ledge where you'll find a **2nd ladder**. See fotos below. This looks a bit unsafe, so best to use another route just to the left or left of that. Once over that ledge, head downcanyon on a hiker's trail. It leads down to a spring and a possible large pourover pool.

If you'd like to do a short loop-hike, use the Ruby's Ladders route to enter the canyon, then walk downcanyon to the first little drainage coming in from the right or south side. You can route-find up it which the author did in 2012. Or walk a little further east and head south up a larger drainage. That's where you'll find an old cow trail which allows access to the rim. Kenny Allred used to maintain that trail, but didn't know who built it originally. It was old the first time he saw it. The cows had to use the trail but you can walk in or out of the upper canyon along many different routes.

Dalton Wells CCC & Japanese Concentration Camp

Next stop might be the **Dalton Wells CCC Camp**. This historic site is on the east side of Highway 191 about halfway between **mile posts 139 & 140**. It was where a couple of cottonwood trees are now growing. Right where you turn off the highway going east, is a parking place and a **plaque** commemorating the site. Also there are 2 cement abutments on each side of the entrance way. But first the history of this camp, some of which comes from old Moab *Times Independent* newspapers.

There were several CCC camps in this part of Utah. They were in Moab, Dry Valley, near Arches National Park and at Green River. The one that stayed the longest was this one, and the local newspaper had a weekly feature titled, *Dalton Wells CCC Notes*. Here are some excerpts from the **3/31/1938** issue (and one other source) which reviewed the camp's history up to that point:

On March 31, 1933, Franklin D. Roosevelt signed the Emergency Conservation Work Act which soon created the Civilian Conservation Corps (CCC's).

Then on April 15, 1933, FDR approved a bill and the **Civilian Conservation Corps** *became a new organization of the federal government..... Range improvement work running into the hundreds of thousands of dollars in value has been accomplished by the Dalton Wells CCC camp, No. DG-32, since its establishment in the* **fall of 1935** *[DG means* **Division of Grazing** *the forerunner to today's* **BLM***]. Construction of reservoirs, development of springs and water holes, drilling of wells, installation of pipe lines, construction of truck trails and stock trails, erection of bridges, posting of driveways, construction of holding corrals and drift fences, and extermination of rodents and poisonous plants have been the major work projects of the camp.*

Early in the **summer of 1935***, two men, representing the division of grazing and the war department of the United States government met with a group of civic-minded people of Moab. Their object was to locate a site for the erection of a CCC camp in Grand county that would meet the rather strict requirements insisted upon by army officials.*

*After visiting several possible sites the group tentatively selected a site 14 miles [22 kms] northwest of Moab on a sagebrush flat and near a previously dug well that was to supply the water for the camp. The well, however required a great amount of cleaning, pumping and general improvement before the final approval for the camp could be secured [***Neal Dalton*** of Moab, who was born in 1934, told this writer that his father Earl, and uncle Newell "Legs" Dalton had someone dig a well there next to Courthouse Wash in the early 1930's. It was dug to water cows. That was apparently the original well at Dalton Wells].*

Left Looking down the first crack holding one of **Glen Ruby's ladders** in **U. Sevenmile Canyon**; in this case they have fallen down the slope a ways. **Right** The 2nd ladder installed by Glen Ruby.

On **July 9, 1935**, an advanced cadre of two reserve officers and 15 enrollees from Moon Lake camp in Duchesne country arrived to begin construction of Dalton Wells camp. Within the week, materials began to arrive at the site and a few weeks later, actual construction was started by local carpenters and men of the advanced cadre.

The camp was reported completed and ready for occupancy on **October 20, 1935**, and the first CCC Company moved in **October 25, 1935**.

Some of the projects this camp did in the immediate area were: the Dubinky Well Road and the road to and across Big Flat and on to Grays Pasture (which is now known as Island in the Sky); the Government or Gooseberry Trail leading off Grays Pasture; the Dubinky & Hell Roaring Wells (C.N. Conway was the driller), and countless water storage dams or stock ponds. These are just a few of the projects which were mentioned in the newspaper over the next half dozen years.

The late **Kent Johnson** formerly of Moab was one of the workers. He was one of the LEM's, or Local Experienced Men. He started working at the Green River camp, then was transferred to Dalton Wells rather late in time. Here are some of the things he remembered about the place:

As you came in the approach road, the Grazing Service office was the one on the left-hand side. Next was the mess hall straight ahead, then on the right-hand side of the driveway were the barracks. The were just like old army barracks. They had a door going in and then it was just a long hallway, and they'd put their single bunks in rows. They usually had 150 men in most of the camps. If I remember correctly, they had 5 barracks at Dalton Wells.

*They also had truck stalls for their crew trucks east of the barracks. They had dump trucks. Then clearn down at the south end was the repair shop. It kind of set out alone. They had to repair their own vehicles in there. To the northwest is an old **rock & cement water tank**. They pumped water from the well with gas engines, and they used that tank for storage. Then later on they pumped water with electricity. That rock tank was one of their projects, and it was really built for stock watering. It has a little stock trough next to it now. They also had an elevated metal water tank so they could have running water in their kitchen and showers. Their showers and restrooms weren't in the barracks, they were in a separate building east of the barracks. They had showers and the water came out of that steel tank.*

They had the big old wood or coal burning ranges in their kitchen. The cooks were mostly just regular enrollees. They had a Mess Sargent and he was an army guy.

The way those CCC camps worked, the military; the army, was in charge of the men, and in the daytime, they released them to the technical agency, whether is was Forest Service, Park Service or Grazing Service--which is the BLM now. They were building roads, reservoirs, and troughing springs. C.N. Conway drilled a lot of the wells, so the CCC's didn't do those. Then at night the military boys would take 'em back and they were under military jurisdiction.

The military had the Company Commander and the First Sargent. The First Sargent was one of the enrollees, and of course they had their Supply Sargent, and Mess Sargent and the whole ball of wax. It was set up just like the army. The CCC workers had to get their passes to come to town, just like in the military.

*Ya see, I worked at the Green River camp first, then when they closed it, I transferred out here to Dalton Wells in **July, 1941**. And some of the men at Green River also transferred here.*

The army had to release the workers I had in the shop everyday. I worked in the shop repairing trucks. Of course, while we were in camp, they'd go eat company chow. If they were out in the field they had to make their lunches. Then when it come quitin' time, they just went back to their barracks. Then we who were local workers at the camp just went back to our own homes or families.

The CCC's was kind of a relief program, as well as developing the country. This original road up to the Arches was built by the CCC's. Their camp was up here on Mill Creek Drive just above old Moab.

The site of the **Dalton Wells CCC Camp** in winter looking west. The author is standing on a slab of cement that may have been the showers & restrooms building. To the right of this is the water well.

At the Green River CCC camp, most of them guys was out of Kentucky. I'm not so sure about where those guys came from who were at Dalton Wells. When I transferred from Green River to Dalton Wells, they were in the process of closing down a lot of the camps, and I lost all my crew pretty soon after that. The CCC's were made up of kids out on the streets with no jobs. They weren't delinquents normally-- we had some damn good kids there. I had some good kids in my shop--very conscientious and really wanted to learn. Those kids in the shop with me were learning how to do things, that was part of my job. I was to maintain the equipment, their trucks and everything else, so I had CCC boys helpin' me do that.

They also had a camp doctor, and a chaplin, and they had an education man out there too; he was responsible for classes, and one thing and another. They had different classes for 'em, but that was under the army's jurisdiction, and I don't remember what their schedule was. We had 'em just during the work hours 8 am to 5 pm, 5 days a week. The foreman of the crews, who were local people, didn't live at the camps. A lot of them were stockmen. They'd haul these kids out, and none of 'em knew how to drive a bulldozer, or move dirt or anything. I ended up going out on a lot of those projects and teachin" the kids how to drive a Cat.

Now when they first started the C's, and this camp up here in Moab, there was a lot of married men went in there from right here in town. But as it developed, they ended up bringing in mostly teenagers.

They finally closed the Dalton Wells camp and a guy by the name of Lester Walker was caretaker out there. It was closed or abandoned for about a year then they brought in the Japanese. The Japanese weren't allowed to come to town or anything--they were prisoners! They never did erect barbed wire fences around the place, but they had the guards.

After the camp finally closed down for good then they hauled it away. Some of it went up here where the BLM office is now [this was right at the beginning of the Sand Flats Road and cemetery--but those old CCC buildings are gone now]. We moved the repair shop out there and set it up behind the main office. Then we moved one of the barracks in there for storage. There's even one of the office buildings that was from the camp, but they moved that after I went in the service in February of 1944. And they're still there [in 1991]. You see, they built those buildings in sections, so you could tear 'em down. Now what happened to the rest of the camp I don't know.

At the time we moved those building out there, the Grazing Service didn't have their own offices, they rented offices in different places around town. Eventually they moved their offices out there to where the BLM office is now but that was after the war [they're now on Dogwood Street]

Bette Wimmer Lang and her husband of Crescent Junction, remembered the old metal water storage tank at Dalton Wells. They bought it in about 1950 or '51, and had it hauled to Crescent. They used it for years at their service station.

In the **November 27, 1941** issue of the *TI*, it had a story about closing the camp down: *The Dalton Wells CCC camp, DG-32, one of the oldest and most successful CCC units of the grazing service, ended its career Wednesday [November 25, 1941] when the 151 enrollees were moved to the Dry Valley camp south of Moab.*

This was less than 2 weeks before the bombing of Pearl Harbor on **December 7, 1841**. On **February 19, 1942**, President Franklin D. Roosevelt signed **Executive Order 9066**, which authorized the US military to exclude people from designated areas. This order was used to relocate and intern American residents of Japanese ancestry who were living on the West Coast, a majority of who were native-born US citizens.

Then on **March 18, 1942,** President Roosevelt signed an executive order authorizing the War Relocation Authority, which was put in charge of interning Japanese-American, with Milton S. Eisenhower (younger brother of Dwight D. Eisenhower) as its director.

By **late March 1942**, there were Japanese-Americans being detained inland away from the West Coast. As it turned out there were a number of large camps built to accommodate these people. And as you might expect, not all of these folks were happy to be locked up in concentration camps. Some of the protesters were sent to Dalton Wells on **January 11, 1943**. The 1/14/1943 paper mentions that event:

The first contingent of Japanese for the Dalton Wells relocation center arrived Monday from Manzanar, Calif. The Japanese, 16 in number, were accompanied by 16 soldiers and two officers.

The Dalton Wells camp will be used for impounding those Japanese who cause friction in the large relocation centers throughout the country and refuse to observe the rules of community life in those centers. It is understood that the first contingent for Dalton Wells contains the ringleaders in the recent riot between Japanese groups at the large Manzanar center.

The Japanese at Dalton Wells will be kept under close guard at all times and will not be permitted to leave the camp. Two officers are in charge of the 16 military police who will maintain order and discipline at the center.

As it turned out they weren't in this camp for long. The **May 6, 1943** issue of the *TI* mentioned this as they left: *The Japanese evacuees who had been located at the Dalton Wells CCC camp were moved last week to Leupp, near Winslow, Ariz., where there are better housing facilities. Thirty-nine Japs, 25 soldiers and six guards made the transfer. The local men who accompanied the Japanese to Leupp, and will be employed there, are Bert Turner, maintenance foreman, and Ruben Allen, A.N. Ray and George Reeves, civilian guards.* It was the **first part May 1943** when they left and the camp was closed for good after that.

From a recent issue of the Provo Daily Herald under **"Today in History"**, it states: *On **February 19, 1976,*** calling the issuing of Executive Order 9066 "a sad day in American history," President Gerald R. Ford issued a proclamation confirming that the order had been terminated with the formal cessation of hostilities of World War II.

It's OK to visit the Dalton Wells camp site today, but as you enter, there will be some fenced land on the left and right as you drive east on the Dalton Well Road (this is on a State Section and someone has leased part of that land). Just as you enter, there's a parking place and a plaque with a brief history of the CCC camp, and the Japanese Concentration center. Beyond that, drive (or walk) east to the 3-4 cottonwood trees between these 2 leased plots and park there. Just east of the trees will be a couple of cement platforms, one with a chimney. Just to the north will be the well itself, but it's fenced in. To the northwest and inside a fenced part is the rock & cement water storage tank. It has some watering troughs for cows next to it. It's still in remarkably good condition after all these years. It was likely built in September or October of 1935. See the picture on the next page.

Top Courthouse Stagecoach Station located along Upper Courthouse Wash. The date on this foto is 1907. It's completely gone now and the Potash Railway runs directly over where these buildings once stood. (Dan O'Laurie Museum, Moab Collection)

Middle The **Division of Grazing CCC Office**, Camp DG 32. Upon entering the Dalton Wells CCC Camp, this building would have been on your left. (Dan O'Laurie Museum, Moab Collection)

Below This is the **cement & rock water tank** you can still see at the **Dalton Wells CCC Camp.** It was built to hold water for livestock and there are still some water troughs around the side of it today.

179

Culvert, Gold Bar, Little, Abe Day and Bull Canyons, Gemini Bridges, and the History of Building the Potash Road

Location & Access The canyons on this map are close to Moab and have become popular with 4WD's, ATV's, motorcycles, mtn. bikers and even hikers in recent years. There are basically 3 ways to enter this region. First, drive north out of Moab in the direction of Crescent Junction & I-70. About 2 kms west of the Colorado River bridge, and near **mile post 130**, turn left or south onto the **Potash Road** and head downstream along the Colorado River until you reach the lower end of **Culvert, Gold Bar, Little or Abe Day Canyons**. Using this approach will put you at the bottom of each drainage.

To get up on top of the plateau, you could continue downstream along the river and turn west between **mile post 1 & 2** (next to Jug Handle Arch) and drive up **Long Canyon** to reach the Big Flat country, but there is **one very bad place** along the upper part of that road. That's up near the top below the last big switchback. Under normal conditions, a very HC vehicle can make it **down** Long Canyon, but getting back up would be impossible except for a **LR/HC/4WD with oversized tires**. Just below that bad place is a **tunnel** created by a fallen block of Wingate Sandstone the size of a large trailer house, but all vehicles except for a pickup with camper can pass under it. Except for these 2 problems, it's a pretty good graded road up to that big rock. For most people, forget this route!

The 2nd, and one of the normal ways into this region, would be to drive north out of Moab on Highway 191 past the entrance to Arches National Park and to between **mile posts 135 & 136**. From there turn west onto a graded county road signposted for **Gemini Bridges**. The **Gemini Bridges Road** running south and up into Little Canyon is normally very good, but the lower northern end is rougher than the upper western section. If driving a car, just go a little slow in places. This road is constantly being up-graded by the county and was in really good conditions as of 6/2012.

However, if your goal is Bull Canyon and/or **Gemini Bridges**, the most popular destination in this mapped area, then the 3rd and **best way** there would be to continue north on Highway 191 to between **mile posts 136 & 137** and turn west onto paved **Highway 313** running up Sevenmile Canyon to Dead Horse Point and the northern part of Canyonlands National Park. Halfway between **mile posts 9 & 10** on Highway 313, turn east at the sign and onto the southwestern end of the **Gemini Bridges Road**. Drive down this well-maintained road right to Gemini Bridges Trailhead. Read more on the road into Bull Canyon and to Gemini Bridges from the drainage below on the following pages. Most other roads in this area are for HC/4WD's.

Elevations About 1220m along the Colorado River; Gemini Bridges, 1573m, upper end of Gemini Bridges Road, 1829m; Big Flat, about 1840m; and Abe Day Canyon carpark/trailhead, 1780m.

Water Running water flows in the lowest km in Abe Day Canyon. There's also an outside water tap at Canyonlands National Park, Island in the Sky Visitor Center, and there is small amounts of free water at Dead Horse State Park--after you pay an entrance fee of $10 for each car.

Maps USGS or BLM map Moab (1:100,000); Gold Bar Canyon, The Knoll, and a little part of Merrimac Butte & Jug Rock (1:24,000--7 1/2' quads); the plastic Trails Illustrated/National Geographic maps Moab North & Moab South--unfortunately, both maps are needed for parts of this area (1:70,000); or the best is the plastic Latitude 40° map Moab West (1:75,000).

Main Attractions Interesting geology and deep canyons in this uplifted region; and the double-spanned Gemini Bridges. The main road is good for cars and this area is popular because it's close to Moab.

Culvert, Gold Bar Arch, Little, & Abe Day Canyons from the Potash Road

First stop here is near **mile post 5** on the **Potash Road** (Bowtie & Corona Arches will be covered with Map 24), which is near the mouth of **Culvert Canyon**. The best parking will be about 200m north-west of the Gold Bar Rec Site, and 100m from **mile post 5**; park in a little nook between the highway and the **metal culvert**. To start, walk north through a nearby culvert under the railroad tracks to reach this canyon--thus the name. Once inside Culvert Canyon, walk upstream on a now-well-used hiker's trail. About 500m from the culvert, will be the first of 2 dryfalls (separated by 150m or so) and perhaps pools; pass both on the right or east side. About 100m beyond the 2nd dryfall, scramble upon a low bench on the left or west side and begin to follow cairns and an emerging hiker's trail north along the prominent Kayenta Bench. After about 800m on this trail, you'll see a 2nd trail coming up to it on the right--this is another route to Gold Bar Arch, but it's a little more complicated to describe.

From where the 2 trails/routes meet, follow the one cairned trail generally northwest and up through a notch in the left skyline and into the **East Fork of Gold Bar Canyon**. Soon you'll arrive at **Gold Bar Arch**. There's a vehicle track leading into upper Gold Bar Canyon and not too far from this arch, but it's for LR/HC/4WD's or other ORV's including mtn. bikes--but it's very rough.

Gold Bar Canyon is west of Culvert, but it's choked with tamarisk in the lower end and doesn't appear to be a fun hike. But an interesting short hike would be into the lower end of **Little Canyon** and to the old **Kerby Trail**. Little Canyon has a big dryfall about 500m up from the river. Near the head of this short box canyon is an old trail built by **Omer Secrest** who was working for the late **Swanny Kerby** at the time. Most old timers refer to it as the Kerby Trail. Swanny Kerby, whose life story is told in the back of this book on page 357, remembered how this trail got built:

It was in the mouth of Little Canyon. You see in the old days we'd have to go up Moab Canyon to near the mouth of Sevenmile Canyon, then go up a trail to the south to the head of Little Canyon. In them early days there wasn't a trail along the river and you never could go down Little Canyon because of that dropoff, that's why we built the trail. Before we built that trail, you'd have to come into the top end of Little Canyon from the north and from near the mouth of Sevenmile Canyon, then west up around Arth's Pasture, and south past The Knoll and Big Flat and down the Shafer Trail. That was the only way you could get into the Shafer Basin country in those days. So I hired Omer Secrest to build that trail. It must have been built sometime in the late 1940's.

The late **Kenny Allred** adds more to this old trail's history: *Omer Secrest built that for Kerby and he pretty much did it alone. I went in there a time or two with Swanny. I didn't help build it, but I've used it. There's a little place there you have to take the saddle off your horse to get around it, or under it. That trail was so rough, ol' Swanny give it up--after he killed a bull or two on it.*

To see this old trail today, stop at a little parking place right where Little Canyon dry wash runs underneath the highway & railroad. That's just downriver or southwest from **mile post 4**. From there, walk down to where the dry wash enters the river, then walk north **under** the highway and railroad tracks in one of 3 large culverts. This puts you in the sandy dry wash coming out of Little Canyon. Stay in the dry wash, otherwise it's a real bushwhack.

Map 17, Culvert, Gold Bar, Little, Abe Day and Bull Canyons, Gemini Bridges, and the History of Building the Potash Road

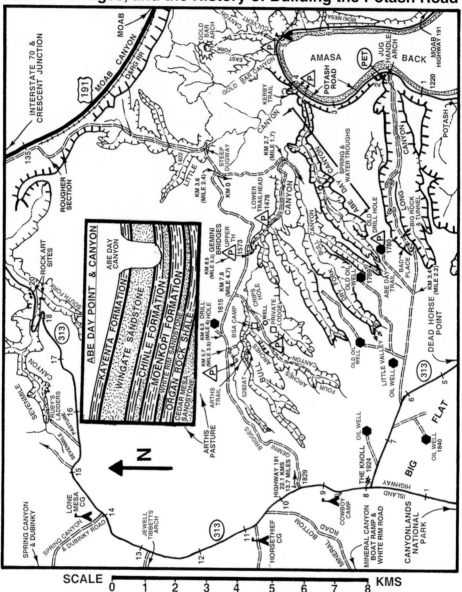

SCALE
0 1 2 3 4 5 6 7 8 KMS

About 250m from the highway and on your left or west side, is a big **rockslide**. Scramble up on it the easiest way possible; there are several little trails. As you climb up, you'll see the main trail running along the base of the canyon wall. At the bottom of the constructed part, you'll now have to climb up on all-4's to get started, then it's along a cat-walk or rim from there up to the top of the first big ledge. About halfway along this trail is a large boulder separated from the wall, with an etching that reads: *My Grandpa Omer Secrest in the 1940's bilt this Horse Trail [by] Butch Tangren.* This was put there in memory of Omer Secrest who died in a fall from high cliffs west of Dead Horse Point in early January, 1952. That story is told starting on page 233 along with **Map 23**.

It just so happens that Butch Tangren is the son of **Karl Tangren**, and he adds a little more to this Kerby Trail story: *Swanny Kerby had my father-in-law, Omer Secrest, build that trail after he went into the Rodeo business. So he had Omer go down there in his boat [this was before the real Potash Road was built in 1962-63] and went up there to shoot that trail and fix it so you could slide a horse down off from it, but a horse can't climb back out--it's too steep. That trail was built in 1947 or '48.*

181

Left Hiking up **Culvert Canyon** will get you to **Gold Bar Arch** which is located in the upper **East Fork** of Gold Bar Canyon. **Right** About 300m inside the lower end of **Little Canyon** is the **Kerby Trail**. Just beyond the author (in red T shirt), is the boulder with the inscription by Butch Tangren.

Next stop would be a hike up from the bottom end of **Abe Day Canyon**. Stop and park about halfway between **mile posts 3 & 4** along the Potash Road. Walk across the railway tracks and through a gate built for hikers only--no vehicles of any kind allowed through it! There used to be an old 1950's road into Abe Day, but it's blocked off now and the lower end of the canyon is totally overgrown with willows & tamarisks. There's a foot trail there now, so just follow it. After 200m or so, you'll have to get up on the left or south side of the canyon wall and walk along a little hiker-made trail to avoid bushwhacking in a jungle. Do this for about 300m, then get back down in the drainage bottom and for the most part walk along the old mining track from there on.

There will likely be some running water in the lower km which should be good to drink as is, because there are no more cattle or beaver around. After about 2 kms, turn right and walk a short distance to where Bull Canyon drops down into Abe Day. This is a big dryfall which you cannot climb.

Back in the main canyon now and going up, you'll pass several little springs, then a little farther up will be an old **water trough** right on the road. From there, look straight up on the north side of the canyon wall and you'll see a spring and more old **watering troughs**. **Kenny Allred** had this to say about the place and the trail out the upper end of the canyon:

Now Abe Day put them waterin' troughs in; and he made that trail off in the head of that canyon too. That was back during the 1930's, when they was doin' drought relief projects. He fixed up that spring because he was gettin' paid for it. The government was payin' him for doin' it. He only had 4 or 5 old cows--he was a bootlegger in the 1920's. He had a still set up down at the mouth of that canyon--of course there wasn't any railroad or highway down there at that time. It was really hemmed in--you come in from the upper end and that was the only way you could get in. Or you swam or used a boat.

I located claims all over that country during the 1950's uranium boom, me and some of my buddies. Then later on, we traded them to the outfit that put that road in there.

From that little trough, just head upcanyon 'till the road ends, then find and follow an old cattle trail to the head of the canyon where you can exit on **Abe Day's old cow trail**. Read about it below.

The History of Building the Potash Road

In the authors other book, **River Guide to Canyonlands**, he included a short history of the Potash Road, but after that he had several more discussions with Karl Tangren of Moab. Karl was there in the early 1950's working for Monte Mason who was drilling for oil near where the Potash Boat Ramp is today. Here's what he remembered about the first road being built part-way down the Colorado:

*It was **Monte Mason**, the guy who drilled the oil wells--he built the first road down the river, but it was a **low water** affair. With high runoff, some places were under water. This was after 1951, because I worked there in '51, the year I got married, and there was no road there then--everything that went downriver then was by boat. It was in the mid-1950's he built the first road down to just before the **Gold Bar**, and when I and my brother-in-law Art Secrest were running boats there--in about 1954 or '55.*

For a year or two when we boated equipment down to the oil well, we had trucks bring stuff to near Gold Bar, then we loaded it on the barge and went on to the well. Then in 1962, the state went in there and started building that new highway; they started it and the railroad at the same time. And when they got there to the Gold Bar, the guys building the railroad shot all that ledge off to put the rails up there,

From the top of the **Abe Day Trail**, looking down to the first big switchback. From there it makes another switchback, crosses the dry creek bed, and continues downcanyon on the east side.

and that filled in the river, and then the highway workers came in and built right on that rock. Before that, the river used to come in right against that ledge--you couldn't even walk around there before that.

I know they was there in 1962 because I was workin' out at the [Atlas] mill. I seen the first charge they ever put in the railway tunnel. We was all out at the mill workin' and they said they was goin' set'er off and we stood out there in the yard and watched that first charge.

The Shafer Trail Road was built first in 1952, but when they started sinking the shaft for Potash, the company that had the contract shot that road down **Long Canyon** so they could bring equipment and supplies in to start building the Potash mill; that was before they built the highway down the river. Before that everything went down by boat. The company named Harrison International was down in there and they might have been the ones who built that road in Long Canyon (?). Potash was [started in February of 1961] and I think the railroad and highway was started in 1962. But the road down Long Canyon was built a year or two before that, about 1960.

Here's more from an **internet website**: The Utah State Road Commission approved a new State Route 279 in 1960, connecting US 160 [now 191] northwest of Moab with Dead Horse Point State Park. The route would follow the right bank of the Colorado River to [Abe] Day Canyon, where it would climb to the southwest onto the plateau containing the park. Within the park, an existing roadway, then its primary access road, would become part of SR 279. The state legislature approved this highway in 1961. Later that year, the commission added a second route—State Route 278 that would continue south alongside the river from SR 279 to the Grand–San Juan County line. However, when it approved the addition in 1963, the legislature made it part of SR 279, renumbering the spur to the park through Day Canyon as SR 278. In addition, the south end of SR 279 was changed to Potash, a point north of the county line where the Texas Gulf Sulphur Company was building a potash plant. SR 279 was built in 1962–'63 to service the Cane Creek potash mine and processing plant, but the road through Day Canyon was never constructed. In 1975, the legislature deleted SR 278 in favor of a new **SR 313**, which followed the existing county road to Dead Horse Point through **Sevenmile Canyon**.

Upper Abe Day Canyon and Abe's Cow Trail from <u>Big Flat</u>

Another way to see the old cow trail built by Abe Day, would be to make your way to the Big Flat country above and come in from there. Drive north from Moab then west into Sevenmile Canyon on Highway 313; just past **mile post 8** turn left or east going toward Dead Horse Point State Park. Drive west to between **mile posts 6 & 7** and veer left going east off from the Dead Horse Point Road. Drive due east on a good graded road for **3.4 kms (2.2 miles)** and turn left of northeast onto an old oil driller's road that hasn't been maintained in a while and drive another **1.6 kms (1 mile)** and stop at an old **drill hole** site. You'll need a little higher clearance for the last 150-200m.

From the drill hole, walk due west from the west side of this big clearing. It's only about 200m to the rim of upper **Abe Day Canyon**. At that point, look across the canyon to see the trail zig zagging down on the west side of the upper-most drainage. Then walk around the upper end and down the constructed trail, which was built in the mid or late 1930's and is still in pretty good condition. A horse could be taken down it today, but it's been washed out pretty bad in a place or two. Return the same way.

There are some viewpoints into the upper end of **Dry Fork of Bull Canyon**, plus another unnamed fork in the area of **Little Valley**. There are also 3 working oil wells (as of 2012), and at least 2 that are shut down in this area and on Big Flat. Follow this map to the overlooks.

Bull Canyon, Arth's Cow Trail, Crips Hole, Gemini Bridges and Little Canyon

From between **mile posts 9 & 10** on Highway 313, turn east and drive along the upper end of the **Gemini Bridges Road**. In 2012, this was a good road for all cars, but like all other graded county roads in the area, it can be slick & muddy in places right after any good rainstorm. Just follow this main road which has signposts at each junction pointing the way to Gemini Bridges and other places of interest.

Here's an interesting side-trip before getting to the bridges. Drive to a point **5.7 kms (3.5 miles)** from the Highway 313 and turn right where 2 roads branch off to the south; take the one on the right or west and drive another 400m until you reach the **Magnificent 7 Bull Run Mtn. Bike Trail**. Park there and walk south about 200m. At that point you'll be the north rim of **Bull Canyon**. Look around and about 200m due west of elevation **5282AT** (1610m) on *The Knoll 7 1/2' quad*, will be **Arthur Taylor's cow trail** running off the rim and into upper **Bull Canyon**. Parts of this historic trail have had steps hacked out with a pick, plus there are a couple of places where holes were drilled, pipes inserted, then logs, rocks & dirt put on top. Read a little of Arth's history below

Here's another side-trip before getting to the bridges. After driving **7.6 kms (4.7 miles)** on the **Gemini Bridges Road**, will be a junction; turn right at the sign stating *Four Arches Trail*. Drive along this graded road into **Crips Hole** (read about Crispen Taylor below). In what used to be a pretty little valley surrounded by colorful Wingate SS walls & pinnacles, now has a **private lodge** with permanent buildings, a gate & fences; plus a Boy Scout **(BSA) camp** nearby (they have tents there for about 90 days of each year). One professional scouter told this writer that both entities were leasing the land and that it was still a State Section--not private land. But the building would belong to someone besides the State of Utah. **Commentary:** To this writer it seems the State of Utah should horse trade State Sections for BLM land closer to civilization where people live, rather than in the middle of a wild scenic area. Most native-born Utahns *can't look at hobbles and can't stand fences, so don't fence us out!* There's got to be a better way to handle and/or sell State Sections to gain revenue for public schools.

Here's a little history of **Arthur (Arth) & Crispin (Crip) Taylor** from the book, ***Grand Memories***, Daughters of Utah Pioneers (DUP) history of Grand County: *Crispin Taylor [for whom **Crips Hole** is named] was the first cattleman to bring stock to Grand County. With two of his nephews, he brought a small herd to Spanish [Moab] Valley in 1875. The Ute Indians were still very hostile and thwarted the Taylor's first attempt to establish a foothold. The Taylors managed to escape but the Indians kept their cattle..... The first successful attempt to begin stock raising in Grand County was made by the Taylor family. In 1879 several members of the Taylor family, came to Moab Valley--then known as Little Grand Valley (The Colorado above The Confluence was called the Grand River until July, 1921).*

About 2 years later another attempt to settle in Spanish Valley was made by **Norman Taylor**, the patriarch of all Taylors in Moab today: *The Norman Taylor family left Little Salt Creek, Juab County, Utah, October 10, 1881, for Moab, arriving on October 30, 1881, after a hard twenty-day trip.....*

The caravan was led by Norman Taylor, an experienced wagonmaster. Norman brought his two families, first wife, Lurana, and nine children, and his second wife, Lydia, and seven children. Among others

Shown here is part of the upper, more-wide-open end of **Little Canyon**. Looking north down on part of the **Gemini Bridges Road** from what is shown on the map as **Steep Dugway**. Beyond the rocks & pinnacles in the upper part of this picture, the road goes downhill to Highway 191.

in the caravan were Mr. and Mrs. Lester Taylor and five children; Mr. and Mrs. Buddy Taylor and one child; Arthur A. Taylor [for whom **Arth's Pasture** is named] accompanied by his bride of one day, Sena Jensen Taylor; and John H. Shafer who was returning to Moab bringing his wife Mary. John and Mary and Arthur and Sena had a double wedding the day before leaving for Moab and the journey to Moab was their honeymoon. In all there were fourteen wagons and a herd of livestock to begin ranching operations. From this start the Taylors became one of the largest cattle operators in Grand County. Later on, Arth Taylor got credit for bringing the first sheep into the Moab country in **August, 1895**.

Now back to Crips Hole. If you drive southwest about 1 km past the private lodge and into the biggest tributary, you'll see on the cliffs to the right or west, 2 of the 4 arches that are apparently in that area. This writer was in a hurry, and just saw 2, both of which closely resembles Jug Handle Arch down on the Colorado next to the mouth of Long Canyon. An ATV trail runs up the drainage.

Now back on the Gemini Bridges Road. About **8.9 kms (5.5 miles)** from Highway 313, turn right or south and continue another 100m and park at the **Upper Trailhead**. From there walk along a good trail about 300m to the top of **Gemini Bridges**. This is actually 2 arches with a 3-4m gap between. This is an interesting place but you can't really get a good picture of the arches from the rim; but you can from inside the canyon below.

To get into Bull Canyon and to the bottom of Gemini Bridges, continue northeastward from the **Upper Trailhead** (set **odometer at 0**) along the Gemini Bridges Road. After another **3.6 kms (2.4 miles)**, turn right or south (set you **odometer at 0** again) and drive down along the 4WD **Bull Canyon Road** for **2.7 kms (1.7 miles)** and turn right or westward and begin driving up the dry creek bed of **Bull Canyon**. Now, for this last part you'll need a HCV as the terrain is partly sand & gravel, partly rough patches with large cobblestones (this is not a good place for mtn. bikes). Continue up Bull Canyon dry creek bed until you're **5.3 kms (3.3 miles)** from the Gemini Bridges Road. There on the right will be the **Lower Trailhead** for Gemini Bridges. On this map it's labeled 1478m. From there, walk another 800m to the bottom of the these twin bridges. Be there in the morning for the best light.

Now back on the Gemini Bridges Road. Instead of returning the same way to Highway 313, might as well continue north down into the head of **Little Canyon**. There's a **steep**, but well-graded **dugway** leading down into this drainage from the west side, and from that steep part you'll have a great fotogenic view north into a flat-bottomed section of Upper Little Canyon surrounded by buttes & spires of the Wingate Sandstone. From the bottom of that steep dugway, a HC/4WD road heads eastward toward Gold Bar Canyon, but one part of that road stopped the author's Jeep Patriot cold in its tracks (Patriots are only a shirttail relative of real Jeeps). Once into that drainage, you can walk to Gold Bar Arch, something this writer has yet to do from the upper end.

From that pretty little valley in Upper Little Canyon, continue north, but there is a side-drainage or two that might be worth while looking at. From there continue north to Highway 191. The lower part of that road is a little **rougher** than the upper parts as mentioned earlier, but cars can make it all the way.

Here's a little story that took place somewhere in **Upper Little Canyon**, as told by **Ray Tibbetts** the son of the well-known & alleged cow thief Bill Tibbetts of Moab. This event took place before the Potash Road was constructed, 3-4 years before the trail in the lower canyon was built, and near the end of the Great Depression:

This one deer hunting trip we took was a family outing with Dad and all of my brothers. I was about 10 years old, so it was in the early 1940's and during the 2nd World War and everything was rationed and it was at the end of the Depression, so going out hunting deer was part of our livelihood.

Anyway, they've got a road into Upper Little Canyon now, but back then there was just a horse trail. So we drove as far as we could up along what is now the Gemini Bridges Road then walked up there and we found deer in a box canyon. We shot a couple of deer and cut'em up and I carried the guns and my brothers and Dad carried the meat back. But we had to get down that upper trail with a herd of bulls in one part of the canyon and the car was down in the bottom. But anyway, them bulls put us up on one of them big rocks--and they just stayed there and pawed the ground, and them damn bulls was blowin' snot and blood, and finally Dad took his 30-30 and shot one of 'em through the horns. And god, it almost knock him flat as a pancake and when he got up he was shakin' his head, then they went a stampedin' away, and we was able to get the hell out of there. Those bulls were old Swanny Kerby's rodeo stock he had fenced in there.

In those days, most of the time we didn't have 2 nickels to rub together, but I don't ever remember eat'in as good as when we was on the farm. Besides that venison, we had fresh pork, and Dad would even cure some of it--he was good at that. We had an adobe house in the back that had real cold water run into it and we kept milk real fresh and cold in there. And you could also hang hams up and other

meat and keep it good until you could either eat it, or can it. Mom canned lots of meat and all the corn, and we had a good garden, and she would make pumpkin pie out of sweet potatos or pumpkins. We was poor, but it was good times.

To sum things up, this country is heavily used by ATV's, 4WD'ers and mtn. bikers. Hikers will have to settle for short hikes into the heads of these canyons. It's rather scenic however, which is partly the result of the sloping Wingate Sandstone, as seen in the geology cross-section.

Looking west across upper **Abe Day Canyon** at the trail Abe Day built in the 1930's. It starts in the upper left, runs down to the right, then down again to the left.

Left Norman Taylor, considered the patriarch of all/most Taylors in the Moab area. Members of his tribe were likely the first people to put cattle onto the Big Flat country. (Connie Murphy Skelton foto)
Right The huge boulder that fell on the road in upper **Long Canyon**. It's created a virtual tunnel.

The best place to get a good view of **Gemini Bridges** is from the canyon below. It's actually 2 bridges spaced close together. Notice the person standing under the bridges in the background.

Above Left This is the bottom of the constructed part of the **Kerby Trail** in the lower end of **Little Canyon**. Most of the rocks that were here have vanished, so you have to climb on all-4's to get up.

Above Right
One of 2 watering troughs **Abe Day** build in **Abe Day Canyon** back in the 1930's. There's a minor spring up the slope a ways to the left. Water from that spring gravity-flowed in a steel pipe down to this trough, and to a second one just below and out of sight on the right. That's the one you'll see next to the old mining road if you walk up or down Abe Day Canyon.

Left From the top of **Arth's Trail** looking southwest into the upper end of **Bull Canyon**. This trail cuts down to the left, then makes a turn going behind the camera, then straight down to the dry wash.

Introduction to the Island in the Sky: Dead Horse Point State Park, Grays Pasture and The White Rim Road

Location & Access Featured here is the northern third of Canyonlands National Park; CNP calls this **Island in the Sky**, or just the **Island**. However, since the late 1800's, or early 1900's, all the high country south of **The Neck** was known locally as **Grays Pasture**. The story of how it got that name is told below. This is an introduction to a part of an even larger region known locally as **Between the Rivers**.

There are 2 main ways to enter this district. The most popular and most-used route goes like this: drive north out of Moab on Highway 191. Drive past Arches NP and up Moab Canyon in the direction of Crescent Junction and I-70. Between **mile posts 136 & 137** (very near the **Arches View Resort**), turn left or west onto **Highway 313** which is signposted for Dead Horse Point and Canyonlands NP. This paved road goes west up Sevenmile Canyon, then south to The Knoll and Big Flat as shown on Map 18. At **The Knoll** & **mile post 8**, turn left or east toward Dead Horse Point State Park; or continue straight ahead (south) for Canyonlands. It's a good paved road all the way to both destinations.

A 2nd way into these parts would be to drive north out of Moab, cross the Colorado River, then near **mile post 130**, turn left or south onto the **Potash Road**. This is paved all the way to Potash, a distance of 25 kms (15.2 miles). From there, continue south about 2 more kms until the pavement ends at a cattle guard and turnoff to the **Potash Boat Ramp**. From there the generally good & graded Potash Road continues westward to the **Potash evaporation ponds**, and **Shafer Canyon**. When you reach Shafer Canyon (and just inside the national park), the Potash Road runs along the bottom of the dry wash and you'll need a HC/4WD for that short section; and the NPS will never fix it because they can't control traffic there.

The **Potash Road** ends at a **3-Way Junction**; climbing to the west and ending on top is the **Shafer Trail Road**, or just the **Shafer Road**. It's graded and that section is normally good for cars. Also beginning at the 3-Way Junction is the **White Rim Road** which heads south and circles around the Island and ends/begins below the steep switchbacks at the bottom of the Horsethief Trail part of the **Mineral Bottom Road**. For this book we'll call that intersection, the **T-Junction**.

To get on the western end of the **White Rim Road**, turn off **Highway 313** between **mile posts 10 & 11**, and drive southwest down the **Mineral Bottom (or Horsethief Trail) Road**. After **23.7 kms (14.7 miles)**, and at the bottom of the steep switchbacks of the Horsethief Trail, and at the T-Junction, turn left or west onto the western end of the White Rim Road.

To get to the eastern end of the **White Rim Road** the normal way, drive Highway 313 in the direction of the Island Visitor Center, but turn left or east onto the top of the Shafer Trail Road which is only 250m south of the **pay booth**; that turnoff is also about 2 kms north of the visitor center. Drive down the Shafer Trail Road **8.8 kms (5.4 miles)** to the **3-Way Junction** mentioned above. That junction marks the beginning of the eastern end of the White Rim Road.

Elevations The Confluence of the Green & Colorado Rivers, about 1200m; White Rim Road, from about 1220-1500m; Island Visitor Center, 1789m; Gray's Pasture, 1800-1900m.

Water Take all the water you'll need into this area. However, there is some water at Dead Horse Point State Park, but they have to truck it in from Moab, and you have to pay a $10 entrance fee to get in. On the south side of Island Visitor Center, there is now an outdoor **water fountain**, but they too have to truck all their water up from Moab too. What few springs there are in the area will be discussed later.

Maps USGS or BLM maps Hanksville & La Sal (1:100,000); Mineral Canyon, The Knoll, Gold Bar Canyon, Shafer Basin, Musselman Arch, Upheaval Dome, Horsethief Canyon, Turks Head, Monument Basin, The Loop & Spanish Bottom (1:24,000--7 1/2' quads); the plastic Trails Illustrated/National Geographic map, Canyonlands National Park (1:70,000); or the plastic Latitude 40° map Moab West (1:75,000). This is the best one if driving or hiking south from **Beehive Butte or Whitbeck Rock**.

Main Attractions The best views looking down on the Colorado River anywhere at Dead Horse Point, and other nearby lookouts; 7 livestock trails down off the Island and onto the White Rim country; the 4WD White Rim Road; and Upheaval Dome, an old and eroded meteor impact or salt dome crater (?).

Dead Horse Point State Park

Dead Horse Point State Park is managed by the Utah Division of Parks & Recreation and is a fee-use area ($10 a car in 2012, and national park or senior passes don't help!). It was officially designated a state park on December 18, 1959. Since then the roads have gradually improved and better facilities built. From the most southerly point in this park, you'll have one of the best views down on the Colorado River seen anywhere. If you're spending time in the area, you shouldn't miss this one and it's open year-round.

Here are the facilities and services available at Dead Horse Point: They have a visitor center with an information desk and gift shop which sells books, post cards, souvenirs & snacks. They also have a campground with restrooms, covered picnic tables, electrical hookups and a sewage dump station. Their water is hauled from Moab, so please conserve. Reservations may be made in advance, otherwise, overnight camping is on a first-come, first-served basis. For updated information call 435-259-2614; or see their website: **stateparks.utah.gov/parks/dead-horse**.

This park also has a shaded pavilion at the overlook, barbecue grills, 13 picnic sites, drinking water, restrooms, and paved & primitive hiking trails. There is no public telefone service (If you subscribe to Verizon and the La Sal Mountains are visible, you should be able to get a connection; maybe others too?), but gas, lodging and restaurants are available in Moab, about 52 kms away. The road to Dead Horse Point is now paved all the way.

There are a number of stories about how **Dead Horse Point** got its name, but they're all pretty much the same. The old timers in this part of the country used to chase wild horses in this upland region west of Moab. The Taylor family was more involved than any other. They used to chase wild horses onto this point, then build a fence across the narrow neck of land separating the main plateau and Dead Horse Point itself. That way they could capture horses easily. The story goes on to say someone forgot to pull down the make-shift brush fence, or forgot to return in time; and a band of horses couldn't get out and they choked to death while gazing down on the Colorado River 600m below. There are several variations of this story.

Grays Pasture and the White Rim Road

The original name for all of this high mesa or plateau was **Grays Pasture**. Here's what the late

Map 18, Introduction to the Island in the Sky: Dead Horse Point State Park, Grays Pasture and the White Rim Road

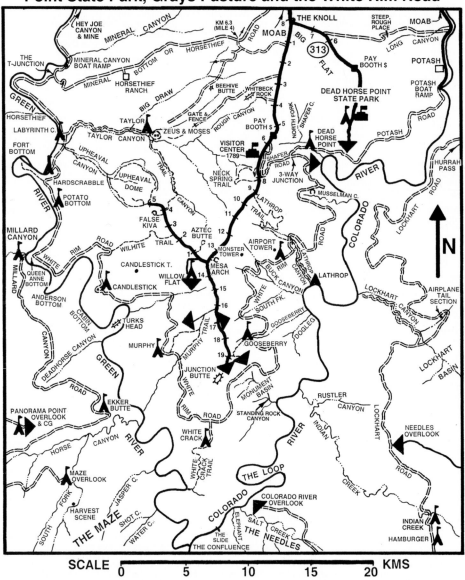

SCALE 0   5   10   15   20 KMS

Kenny Allred of Moab had to say about this name:

   Don Taylor told me at one time they had an old stud they called Gray. They was kinda new to the country and this old stud and his band of mares had disappeared south of Big Flat somewheres and they finally found him down past [south of] The Neck. He'd got across that neck and got down in there, so they called it Gray's Pasture. And that was the first time they got into that country. That was Don Taylor who told me, that's DL's grandad. He was about the oldest Taylor in this country at the time. That must have happened at about the turn of the century [1900] or thereabouts.

   All the older natives of Moab still know and call this high country **Between the Rivers;** and south of **The Neck** by it's original name, **Grays Pasture**. On USGS maps, the name Grays Pasture is attached, but only to the big park-like grassy flat or meadow just south of The Neck. You'll be parking in the middle of it if you hike down the Lathrop Trail. The name Island in the Sky came much later and was introduced by outsiders or move-ins who forgot to ask the locals what the names were of various places.

   Just a few kms inside the boundaries of Canyonlands, you'll come to the **Island Visitor Center**. It's open from 9am to 4pm daily in the off-season (winter). During the busier months of April through October, it's open from 8am to 6pm. They sell maps, books & post cards. Water used to be scare here, but

189

in recent years, the NPS has installed an outside drinking fountain there, so you can now fill a water bottle. But please bring all the water you'll need for your trip from Moab. The reason is, water at that drinking fountain and for the employee housing just west over the hill, is **trucked in from Moab**.

If you're going to any part of this section of Canyonlands, you should stop here first, regardless. They will have all the latest information on the White Rim Road, trails, springs, weather forecasts, etc. There is no food or gasoline for sale there, but they do have their telefones hooked up to the Moab exchange, 435-259-4712. They also have a pay fone, but for cards only. Verizon cellfones work there.

If you intend to drive south on the paved road to Grandview Point or to Upheaval Dome, there's not much to worry about or explain here. Each area to the south will be covered in more detail on the next 5 maps. However, if you're considering driving and camping along the **White Rim Road**, here are some things you should know about camping there. The following is from the website: **nps.gov/cany**, or more specifically, **nps.gov/cany/planyourvisit/whiterimroad.htm**.

Permits are required for all *overnight* trips along the White Rim. During the spring and fall, demand for permits frequently exceeds the number available. If you plan to visit Canyonlands during peak season, it is recommended that you make reservations well in advance.

Drive Carefully Towing charges are very expensive. Visitors caught in the backcountry with disabled vehicles can expect towing fees in excess of US$1,000.

The White Rim Road has long rocky stretches [southwestern section mostly], deep sand, and little shade. Bring at least [4 liters] of water per person, per day--more if you'll be active [more in summer too!]. Plan for a minimum of 10-12 hours of driving.

Campsites Bicyclists and four-wheel drivers must stay in designated campsites. Twenty individual campsites are arranged in 10 camping areas. Toilets are provided at each site. When there is more than one site at a location, they are generally positioned to be out of earshot and, as much as possible, sight of each other. Each campsite will accommodate up to 15 people and 3 vehicles.

Here are the locations of campsites along the White Rim Road: **Labyrinth, Taylor, Hardscrabble Bottom, Potato Bottom, Candlestick, Murphy Hogback, White Crack, Gooseberry, Airport Tower and Shafer Canyon**.

The busiest time on the White Rim, and the times when it's hardest to get reservations, are in the months of April, May and October. Anytime other than these months, you can usually just walk into the Island Visitor Center and pick up a permit for the campsite of your choice. The only problem with car camping in CNP is it'll cost you **$30**. Most people camping there are outfitters escorting mtn. bikers.

To apply for *reservations,* go to this website: **nps.gov/cany/planyourvisit/backcountrypermits.htm**. Here's the address of the national park in Moab: Canyonlands National Park, 2282 SW Resource Blvd., Moab, Utah, 84532. Reservation Office (Backcountry Information), 435-259-4351. Call in from 8am to 12:30pm, Monday through Friday. Here's a list of the visitor centers in Canyonlands: Island in the Sky Visitor Center, Tele. 435-259-4712; The Needles Visitor Center, Tele. 435-259-4711; Hans Flat (Maze) Visitor Center, Tele. 435-259-2652.

If having to make reservations months in advance isn't your cup of tea, you could write a complaint to the same address above, and to the park superintendent. For years the NPS has had the same number of campsites on the White Rim. The only thing that's being done differently now than 23 years ago, is they now require you to make a decision months in advance as to when you want to make the visit. They refuse to build more or bigger campsites to accommodate more visitors. Because of all the restrictions, almost no one from Utah goes there anymore. The locals generally cuss the NPS/CNP.

One major reason why the campsites are full in the spring or fall, is that local mountain bike outfitters in Moab are making reservations way in advance, thus locking up lots of campsites. If you come to this part of the country and have a hard time getting a campsite on the White Rim, then consider writing an email complaining about this situation. Park policies are dictated by just a small handful of people. Your complaint may not be welcome, but the NPS policy is usually based on people's complaints. Letters add up.

Another alternative to camping on the White Rim, is to camp (or sleep in your car) on BLM land outside the park boundary, then drive in from either end of the loop, do a hike or get your fotos, and return the same way. If you want to camp outside the park near Big Flat, drive along one of several side-roads **1 mile (1 1/2 kms) from the highway.** Or do the entire loop, which is a long all-day trip from Moab. If starting & ending your trip in Moab, you won't have time to do any long distance hikes. But the advantage is, **THERE IS NO PERMIT NEEDED FOR DAY-TRIPS ON THE WHITE RIM ROAD.**

Here's more information on the White Rim and the road making the loop. If you start at the visitor center, and drive north to between mile posts 10 & 11, then turn west onto the Mineral Bottom Road, and make the complete White Rim Loop returning via the Shafer Trail, it will be 159 kms, or 99 miles. So have your **fuel tank full** and always take extra fuel, water, food, tools, etc. A good policy is to be well-prepared for any problems.

This White Rim Road gets its name because for the most part it runs along the top of the White Rim Sandstone which is so prominently exposed near the road. In most places, this road is good enough for any vehicle, but there are several bad spots which make it a HC/4WD road. Most bad spots are between the north side of Hardscrabble Hill and go to nearly the turnoff to the White Crack; in other words it's the western and southwestern section. Steeper sections include the south side of **Hardscrabble Hill**, long known as the **Walker Cut**; and on both sides of the **Murphy Hogback**. If it weren't for these steep and/or rough spots, any 2WD HCV could make it.

In 1991, the author had a VW Rabbit with oversized tires. He went up & down the Shafer Trail and all along the Potash Road, and got to as far as the White Crack turnoff. He also made it along the west side of the White Rim Road to the top of the Walker Cut and the trailhead to Fort Bottom. In 5/2012, he did the complete loop in his Jeep Patriot with oversized tires (with about 23 cms/9" of clearance) and no low range gearbox or transfer case. He never scraped bottom, and he did fine on all the short steep pitches, but when you come to a steep part, gear down and rev up. AWD/4WD are pretty much required in just a few places. The NPS/CNP actually does a little maintenance on this road.

The view from **Dead Horse Point** looking southwest. The big bend of the Colorado River is called **The Goose Neck**. The road at the bottom is the **Potash Road** and it runs west up to the Island.

Another view from **Dead Horse Point** looking east at the Potash Road, Potash Evaporation Ponds, the warped beds of the Cane (Kane) Creek Anticline and the La Sal Mountains in the background.

Upheaval Dome & Canyon, and Taylor, Trail & Murray Canyons, & Hikes to Alcove & Holeman Springs, and False Kiva and Fort Bottom Ruins

Location & Access This map covers the area between the Green River and the Island Visitor Center. There are 2 ways to get here. To reach the higher mesa or plateau country use Highway 313 to reach the Island Visitor Center, then drive south and follow the signs to the **Upheaval Dome or Alcove Spring Trailhead**. This is a paved road all the way at altitudes between 1800-1900m. This road will get you to the head of Trail Canyon and the Alcove Spring Trail, and Upheaval Dome. Upheaval Dome is believed to be either an ancient meteor impact crater, or a salt dome; and it may be the number one destination in Canyonlands NP.

You can also drive to the river and the mouth of Upheaval & Taylor Canyons via the **Mineral Bottom Road** on Horsethief Point and the western end of the White Rim Road. To do that, turn west off Highway 313 between **mile posts 10 & 11** onto the good & graded Mineral Bottom Road. From the end of Horsethief Point, drive down the Horsethief Trail to Horsethief Bottom. At the bottom of the switchbacks is a **T-Junction** which is **23.7 kms (14.7 miles)** from Highway 313. If you turn right, you'll end up in Mineral Canyon with lots of campsites; but if you turn left, that is the start of the **White Rim Road**. Set your **odometer at 0**. From there, drive west then south along the Green River to as far as **Labyrinth Campsite** at Km 10.5 (**Mile 6.5** from the T-Junction) on Upheaval Bottom. This part can be done with a car--if road conditions are normal. Going a little farther, some cars with higher clearance might be driven up the south side of **Hardscrabble Hill** and to the trailhead to Fort Bottom, but it's a little rough going up that north-side slope. Nothing but a 4WD vehicle should go down the south side of Hardscrabble and the **Walker Cut**, because you'll never get back up!

The entire road running south along the east bank of the Green River is generally referred to as the White Rim Road, even though the White Rim Sandstone isn't exposed until just south of the Potato Bottom Campsite.

Elevations Upheaval Bottom, about 1210m; Upheaval Dome Trailhead, 1721m.

Water Take all you'll need for your trip, but you now can get some water at the **outdoor fountain** at the visitor center but which is transported in a tanker truck from Moab. You could use the Green River water--after treatment. There should be water just below Alcove Spring, and there's normally water in the Syncline Valley on the northwest side of Upheaval Dome. There may be good water in Cottonwood Canyon northeast of the Dome. Holeman Spring has a good discharge and a year-round flow.

Maps USGS or BLM map La Sal (1:100,000); Upheaval Dome & Horsethief Canyon (1:24,000--7 1/2' quads); the plastic Trails Illustrated/National Geographic map, Canyonlands National Park (1:70,000); or the plastic Latitude 40° map Moab West (1:75,000)--this is the best map to have if you're heading south from Beehive Butte or Whitbeck Rock toward a viewpoint of Zeus & Moses.

Main Attractions Upheaval Dome, Mark Walker's Cabin & Moki Fort ruins at Fort Bottom, Alcove Spring & Trail, Art Murray's trail out of Murray Canyon, False Kiva Ruins, and the hike to Holeman Spring.

Upheaval Dome: Salt Dome or Meteor Impact Crater (?)

Before hiking in this area, here are some of the theories of what caused the circular feature called **Upheaval Dome**. The following is a summation from writings of 2 geologists, Peter Huntoon and Eugene Shoemaker.

The Upheaval Dome of the Island in the Sky of Canyonlands NP is a fascinating geologic structure that has inspired a number of theories which try to explain its origin. It has been described: (1) As a **salt dome**, caused by the upward movement of salt; (2) As a **laccolith**, a mass of rock overlying intruding lava; (3) And as a **cryptovolcanic explosion feature**, a crater associated with a volcanic eruption; (40 However, a more recent new hypothesis is that Upheaval Dome is a **meteorite impact structure**.

The rocks exposed inside the Dome include (from the bottom to the top): The White Rim, Moenkopi & Chinle Formations, Wingate Sandstone, Kayenta Formation then the Navajo Sandstone. At the bottom there are clastic dikes composed of crushed grains of quartzs derived from the White Rim Sandstone. One geology map also shows a little Organ Rock Formation as well right in the bottom of the crater.

Studies of the area in 1983, revealed several pieces of evidence which points a finger directly at a meteor impact crater. That study showed there were faults surrounding the crater which had not been discovered in earlier surveys. A thorough survey of the deformation was done, and it showed rocks were disturbed or deformed in a circle of about 5 kms in diameter. In the bottom of the crater, grains of sand from the White Rim Sandstone were found to be much smaller than those taken from the White Rim elsewhere. The shape of these grains was much different as well, and when compared to sandstone inside and adjacent to Meteor Crater in Arizona, it was found to be very similar. Because of these and other evidence only college-professor-type geologists can understand, the conclusion is that it's a meteor impact crater.

Here's a scenario behind this theory--which is still just a theory. A meteor 500m in diameter hit this part of the country about 60 million years ago. At the time, this land was at a much lower elevation, perhaps near sea level. It scored a direct hit, coming straight down from above. The initial crater is believed to have been about 1.3 kms deep and the original disturbed zone was 9-10 kms in diameter. It's believed that about 2 kms, or 2000m of rock have since been eroded away from the impact area. Any evidence of a meteor is therefore long gone. This was much earlier than the beginning of the entrenched course of the Colorado River, which is estimated to have begun about 5 million years ago. With time and all the erosion having taken place, all we see today are the roots of the original impact structure.

But there is one thing this writer wonders about. If it were an impact structure, why aren't the exposed strata--mainly the Navajo, Kayenta and Wingate formations--broken or fractured with lots of cracks everywhere? As seen from the Holeman Spring side, these formations are warped pretty good, but with no visible cracks. This indicates a very slow warping over millions of years, something like you would get if it was a salt dome feature. Or maybe it was a combination of impact crater, then salt dome forces kicked in (?) This whole thing is still a theory. See the geology cross-section on the map.

<u>From Island in the Sky:</u> Upheaval Dome & Canyon, the Alcove Spring Trail to Zeus & Moses, False Kiva Ruins and the hike to Holeman Spring

For a hike to the rim of the Upheaval Dome Cater, drive to the parking lot at the very end of the paved

Map 19, Upheaval Dome & Canyon, and Taylor, Trail & Murray Canyons, & Hikes to Alcove & Holeman Springs, and False Kiva and Fort Bottom Ruins

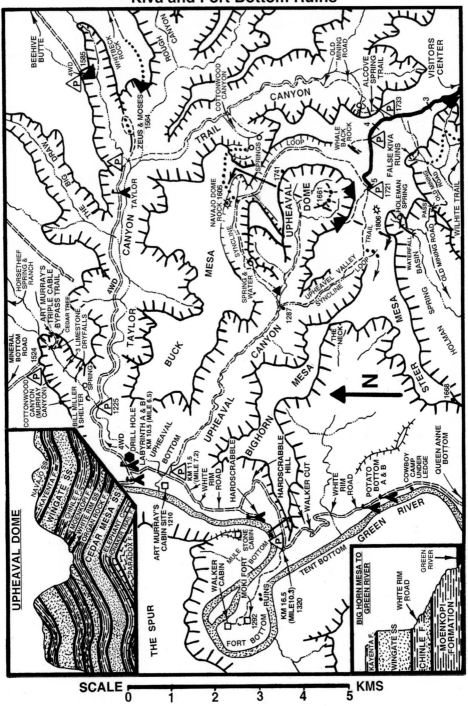

SCALE

0   1   2   3   4   5 KMS

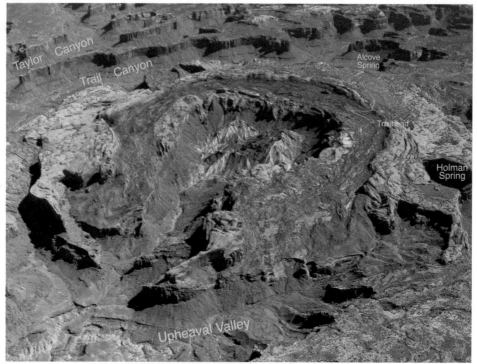

Aerial view of **Upheaval Dome** looking due east.

highway (right at **mile post 5**--from the junction near Mesa Arch). From the Upheaval Dome Trailhead, follow the signs up the **Upheaval Dome Trail.** It's only 500m & 1.3 kms to the top and 2 different over-looks, and can be walked in 15-20 minutes by anyone. This may be the most popular hike in Canyon-lands, and is short enough that you won't need to take water.

For energetic people, leave the trail at the top and walk north along the eastern crater rim. After about 1 km, look for a route down into the center of the crater. There's no real trail, but one may be de-veloping. It's steep until you reach the bottom, then it's an easy walk along the dry creek bed and out a signposted trail to the west. If you try this, better take some water, and perhaps plan to return to the trailhead via one of 2 other trails. These are the trails circling Upheaval Dome.

If you'd like a longer hike, perhaps lasting a long half day, or a full day, and which is about 13.3 kms total, then taking the **Syncline Loop Trail** around the perimeter of the Dome might be just for you. It doesn't matter which way you go, but for this description, we'll go north from the trailhead and do it counter-clockwise. Just follow the signs or cairns--this is an NPS trail.

The Syncline Loop Trail first follows a dry wash which is in one of the circular valleys around and within the Dome. There are some cottonwood trees and maybe a little water in a valley on the north side of the crater as the trail heads west. Then the trail zig zag down through a big rockslide to the bot-tom of a valley where **water should exist** year-round. From there, the loop trail runs south down to ap-parently the only official campsite in the area near where the side-trail heading east into the middle of the Dome takes off. A little below that, the trail running west toward to the Green River takes off down **Upheaval Canyon**. The last part of the loop, circles southeast, then east up a series of steep switch-backs and back to the trailhead.

For someone who wants a longer all-day hike, you could also walk from the Dome down to the **Green River** through **Upheaval Canyon to Upheaval Bottom**. Basically, from just west of the Dome, the trail follows the dry creek bed all the way down. However, if the weather is good and the roads are dry, most cars can be driven down to the mouth of Upheaval Canyon; so it'll be easier and faster if you drive down, then do Murray Canyon and the Fort Bottom hike from the road along the river.

Here are several variations for someone who really enjoys hiking to out-of-the-way places. Try a hike to **Bighorn Mesa.** Begin by walking west from the **Upheaval Dome Trailhead**, then about 300m after the trail begins to zig zags down the steep slope, turn left and route-find southeast, south then west for a ways before starting to climb up the slope to the west. Once you reach the same height of the mesa top, head for the narrow **neck** between Steer and Bighorn Mesas. In the early days this was a place where local herdsmen could shoot their buck real easy. One person would hide close to this narrow neck of land which is only about 3m wide, while others would go out on Bighorn and drive deer in that direction. If deer did come that way they were easy targets.

From there you can walk out to the end of Bighorn Mesa and have some excellent views down on the Green River, Hardscrabble Hill and Fort Bottom. The author once did this hike from the Upheaval Dome Trailhead and back in 5 hours. Some hikers will want most of a day. You could also walk to the end of **Steer Mesa** for some views looking south.

Here's another interesting hike for someone experienced in route-finding on the Colorado Plateau. Walk north from the Dome Trailhead on the Syncline Loop Trail. About a quarter of the way around the Crater, you'll come to a place where you can walk up a gentle slope to the north and up on the east end

Above The alcove holding **Alcove Spring** as seen after walking about 500m from the Alcove Spring Trailhead. There's a little drinking water from this spring, but it's in the short, steep canyon below the green part seen here.

Left If you walk down to and past Alcove Spring, then northward in **Trail Canyon**, you'll eventually come to these rock pinnacles called, **Zeus & Moses.** Another way to gain access and see these, is to come in from Whitbeck Rock or Beehive Butte as discussed on the next page. You can also get there by driving, mtn. biking or walking up Taylor

of **Buck Mesa**. Aim for the **Navajo dome rock** shown at **1605m**, then turn east and head for the Kayenta bench which curves around to the right below the higher Navajo wall, also on the right. Soon, the Kayenta bench tilts down to the south as a result of the warped rocks of Upheaval. This is on the outer fringes of the Dome. It dips down into a little side-drainage called **Cottonwood Canyon**. In places you can see an old trail, but don't waste time looking for it; just route-find down this inclined bench or ramp to the bottom. From there walk out the lower end into **Trail Canyon**. **Ray Tibbetts** of Moab knows a little about this canyon and the old trail from his locally-famous outlaw father, **Bill Tibbetts**:

That's an old outlaw trail, and Dad said they called that place Cottonwood Canyon, because there was a bunch of cottonwoods there. There's also an old outlaw camp back in a cave. There used to be a bunch of old boxes and stuff in there--you could tell it'd been used a lot, and it was close to that spring. My dad said a lot of the outlaws used that as a hidin' place. On horseback the trail was a good escape route. They could take a bunch of stock out on Buck Mesa, then they could herd 'em off into Trail Canyon too.

You might also camp in the lower part of Cottonwood Canyon as there appears to be a year-round spring or seep in 2 different places. From Cottonwood, you could walk up Trail Canyon and get on the **Alcove Spring Trail** and return to your car at Upheaval. This would be a fun hike lasting all day.

If you want a short hike try the spectacular trail down to **Alcove Spring**. There's a marked trailhead parking place on the highway between **mile posts 3 & 4** about 2 kms below the Upheaval Dome Trailhead. From there a good trail follows a 1950's bulldozer track made by **Nat Knight** (According to Ray Tibbetts, he drove a Cat from Alcove Spring all the way down to the mouth of Taylor Canyon) down the steep slope. It's only about 2 kms to the alcove & spring (water is not found in the alcove, but down the drainage another 50-75m instead). Below the alcove, the same Cat track zig zags down an extremely steep slope to the bottom of Trail Canyon. Backpackers occasionally hike down there and into the maze of drainages of upper Taylor Canyon. One destination would be several pinnacles going by the names of **Zeus & Moses** at the junction of Trail & Taylor Canyons, as shown on the map.

Here's another way to reach a couple of overlooks of Zeus & Moses from the canyon rim and from the north. One way is to drive south from Highway 313 and the turnoff to Dead Horse Point toward the Island Visitor Center. Between **mile posts 2 & 3**, turn west onto a pretty good side-road that heads southwest along the northwest flanks of **Whitbeck Rock**. See **Map 18**. You'll need a 4WD with more clearance than a car, or a mtn bike, for this trip. Drive the most-used track southwest past Whitbeck Rock until you come to the CNP boundary with a walk-through **gate & fence**. For this you must have the Latitude 40° map **Moab West**. From that gate walk southwest along an older track that eventually veers west. When that ends, continue west to the canyon rim and a place to view Zeus & Moses.

Here's another way to this area just north of Zeus & Moses. Drive along Highway 313 in the direction of Canyonlands, but between **mile posts 10 & 11**, turn westward onto the **Mineral Bottom** (or Horsethief Point) **Road**. After **6.3 kms (4 miles)**, turn left of south, and following Map 18 and the Latitude 40° map Moab West, head southwest. At one point, it runs just west of the prominent landmark called **Beehive Butte**. Continue southwest to near the rim of the canyon near Zeus & Moses.

Here's something the author did; he parked near Whitbeck Rock, walked southwest to the overlook first mentioned above, then headed cross-country for fotos of Zeus & Moses, and got on the 2nd road discussed above, walked to Beehive Butte (saw several **basque sheepherder signatures**, one reading: Jose Giarellno, En (January) 14, 1906), and finally back to his car. That loop-hike took 4 1/3 hours.

Now back to the Alcove Spring hike. In the upper end of Trail Canyon, you walk along the old road/trail, but further along you walk right in the dry creek bed. This Alcove Spring Trail dates back to the early years of settlement in this country. The late **Kenny Allred** didn't know when it was first built or who built it (surely one of the Taylors), but he used it in the 1920's. One story he tells went like this:

*There was a bull in there at the head of Taylor Canyon that one time belonged to the Dick Tidwell bunch, and they had a $10 reward on it. And ol' **Swanny Kerby** wanted that $10--and $10 was a lot of money then. This was during the Depression in the 1930's. And so we got that bull clean up that dang Taylor Canyon Trail [by Alcove Spring]--and somebody had put a fence up right at the top of the trail, and when that bull hit that fence, he come back over us and ol' Swanny roped 'im. He was ridin' a little ol' pinto horse that wasn't only about that high; and that bull sure jerked that little horse around. It was right on the hill side too. Ya see, we were going to bring that bull to town here. That was a long ol' ways to earn $10, but old Swanny wanted that $10!*

About halfway between the Alcove Spring and Upheaval Dome Trailheads is a parking place and a beginners trail going to a big hump of Navajo Sandstone that looks like a whale's back. It's called the **Whale Rock and Whale Rock Trail**. This is a good short hike for children and anyone who wants a short walk over genuine slickrock.

Another hike from along the Upheaval Dome Road is to the **False Kiva Ruins**. Park at the **Alcove Spring Trailhead**, which is between **mile posts 3 & 4**. From the parking, walk south along the paved road about 250m to find what appears to be an old livestockman's road/track heading westward. Follow this; it's getting to be a good trail although it's not on any official maps (but the secret is out!). After about 1 km, veer right or north and head down a kind of ramp into a big alcove. At one point you'll pass right under the ruins, then the trail doubles back--stay on the trail--don't shortcut.

What you'll find there is a round rock feature about 5m in diameter. One of the first people to discover it must have thought it was an Anasazi Kiva--but it's not--this site is on the northern fringe of Anasazi territory. It was surely built by what we now call Fremont or Archaic Indians, and it could have been a ceremonial thing, or just a wind shelter and/or simple campsite (?). Due south and in the distance is the fotogenic **Candlestick Tower**.

The last hike on this map from the Island is to **Holeman Spring**; but this would be for the more adventurous hikers. This spring is located due south of Upheaval Dome, but at the bottom of a big enclosed Navajo Sandstone enclosure. This spring seeps out of the contact point at the bottom of the Navajo Sandstone and the top of the more impervious Kayenta Formation below. This is a good spring with a year-round flow. The best way of approach is via the **Wilhite Trail**, which is discussed in more detail in the next chapter.

First, go to **Map 20**, to see the very beginning of the Wilhite Trail which is near **mile post 2** on the road to Upheaval Dome. Follow this trail across the mesa top for nearly 2 kms, then it zig zags down a big **rockslide** covering the Wingate Sandstone wall. At the bottom of the rockslide, instead of staying on the Wilhite which veers to the left or west, veer to the right staying on top of the prominent bench which is the **Moss Back Member** of the Chinle Formation, and where uranium is found in this country. Route-find north then westerly to a point directly below the False Kiva Ruins. Immediately after crossing a drainage, you'll find the end of an old mining exploration track; follow it southwesterly for about 1 km,

The **False Kiva Ruins** located just southeast of Upheaval Dome. In the upper right is **Candlestick Tower**, and beyond that in the far distance to the right is **Ekker Butte**.

then it turns abruptly north and goes uphill over a **pass**. On the other side, it angles down to the left or west then splits; one branch continues west toward the White Rim Road, the other heads down to the north to the little stream coming from Holeman Spring. When you get there, you'll find a 7-8m-high **waterfall**. From there, and beginning next to a huge boulder, an old faded **livestock trail** begins and runs uphill on the east side of the stream. This trail likely dates from the late 1930's or early '40's (?). After a ways it disappears. From there you'll have to scramble up a steep slope and around a dryfall on the left in order to reach Holeman Spring itself.

You could also reach this same area with a good map and from the **White Rim Road** to the west, but you'd need a 4WD vehicle and some time running around on dusty, bumpy roads. Coming down from the top with all paved roads seems the best all-around way to reach this spring for most people.

Here's a little history on the man for which this spring is named. **Karl Tangren** of Moab is about the only one left who remembered **John Holeman**:

When Art Murray run cattle in that country there wasn't many sheep in there. But then he left in the early 1950's [1953]; that's when John Holeman got Murray's grazing permit but he took sheep in there. [According to Kenny Allred, some of these sheepmen were on the White Rim part in the late 1930's and early '40's]. At about that same time, John Alise came in, along with Howard Lathrop over on the Colorado River side. Then there was another sheepman named Jim Brown; he come in there and went out on Deer Flats south of Upheaval Dome--stayed up on top--didn't go down on the White Rim, that's all [what they used to call] Deer Flats out on [Grandview Point].

John Holeman was a sheepman out of Montrose, Colorado. He wintered sheep down in that White Rim country back in the 1940's, '50's and into the early '60's. When I was in the truckin' business, I used to haul a lot of water for John Holeman. He had a [grazing] permit that come out onto the Big Flat, Taylor Canyon, Fort Bottom and on the White Rim some, then on down into the blues around the airport when they was shearin'. During the spring seasons I had to haul a lot of water for 'im.

It may have been John Holeman who constructed that livestock trail seen below Holeman Spring today, but he came into that country about half century after the first livestock, both horses and cattle, were first introduced there. It seems odd that his name was put on the spring because others must have known about it before his time (?).

From White Rim Road: Murray's Cabin, Canyon & Trail, & Upheaval Bottom

At the Labyrinth Campsite (formerly Upheaval Bottom Campsite) just north of Upheaval Bottom, is a road junction; to the left is a HC/4WD road running up Taylor Canyon. With the right vehicle, you can drive up this sandy drainage but higher up near the Taylor Canyon Campsite, it's very sandy and may be for LR/HC/4WD's only.

The first place of interest would be what this writer has in the past called **Murray Canyon**--but one old timer from Moab thought it was called **Cottonwood Canyon (?)**. But it could be he was getting this short drainage mixed up with the other Cottonwood Canyon just north of Upheaval Dome (?). But regardless, it's the first major side-drainage on the left or north as you're going up Taylor Canyon. This has an unusual trail-of-sorts out the upper end that was built and used by **Art Murray** (mostly by one of his hired hands, Kenny Allred), thus the name of the canyon and the trail. Art Murray is the cow man who bought out Eph Moore's grazing rights on Horsethief Point in 1929, and later began what would

Left Looking up and to the northeast at the enclosure holding **Holeman Spring**. The spring is just out of site in the upper right. Water seeps out of the contact point between the Navajo SS above, and the Kayenta Formation beds below. **Right** At the bottom of the steep part below **Holeman Spring**, is this little **waterfall** which should exist year-round. Below this, the water soon goes underground.

later be called Horsethief Ranch just a couple of kms north of the upper end of this canyon.

Here's how to get there. From the carpark at the beginning of the Taylor Canyon Road **(Km 10.5/Mile 6.5 from the T-Junction)**, walk up **Taylor Canyon** about 2 kms (drive only with the right vehicle!), then turn left into Murray Canyon. Along the way, you'll pass a miner's shelter on the left, a spring or seep, and 3 low limestone lens & dropoffs. Just below the **3rd dropoff**, veer right and begin climbing while looking for a trail heading up toward the first alcove or indentation in the canyon wall to the right or east of the main drainage. The higher you go the more visible this trail becomes and the better the chances are that you can see it. Head straight up toward the wall at the top. When you arrive at the base of the wall, and just north of a lone **cedar tree**, will be the beginning of **Art Murray's Triple Cable By-Pass Trail**. But first a little history on it, as related by the late **Kenny Allred**:

Ya, I've been up and down that trail, you damn rights, and it raises you're hair I'll tell ya. We used to pack our horses and come up to under that ledge, then climb that damn trail and cable up over that ledge and it was a pretty shaky deal! The first time, I know I got kinda shook-up, 'cause I was hangin' out there on that cable and not knowin' which way to go. Murray wasn't there to show me how to do it. It wasn't so bad after you've done it once or twice. But the first time, I got down there and I couldn't get back up and couldn't get down. I thought I was a gonner!

Later, I took my wife over it several times. We stayed down there on the Green River in the winter time. Art Murray would come out and bring us supplies and just leave 'em there at the cabin at the mouth of Taylor and Upheaval Canyons. But if we needed more supplies, we'd take our horses into that canyon and leave 'em. We had the bottom fenced at the mouth of Murray [or Cottonwood] Canyon, then we could just turn our horses loose. Then we'd walk on over to the cabin [Horsethief Ranch] and stay overnight and the next day we'd pack what ever we had on our backs and go back down the trail.

Murray hadn't had that trail in there very long when I got down there 'cause the cables hadn't worn down into the rocks. The first time I was over it you couldn't see it, then later you could see where the cable was wearing into the rocks just hangin' there. I was about 19 when I went back out there, about 1933 [Kenny was born in 1915], or somewhere along in there. It must have been built in the early 1930's. Art Murray didn't even have his place completed there then--the cabin and things. I helped him finish up. As far as the trail is concerned, it was a long time before he left the country that we stopped using it. He got cut down to a little bunch of cattle, and he was fightin' with the BLM.

Now to climb this unusual trail. Don't bother to look for the first of 3 cables until you get up the zig zag trail and to the cedar tree (the cable hangs down just north of that tree). It's a small cable--about 1 cm in diameter--and you can't see it until you get right to it. You can climb the first pitch without the cable, but it should still be solid and safe enough if you want to use it. This first little climb is near vertical and up about 5m. Then you turn left and ledge-walk about 10m 'till you come to the 2nd cable, which you can hang onto as you pass a narrow part of the ledge. It's anchored by a pair of old rusty horseknip- pers! You can climb this with or without the cable, but the ledge appears ready to fall off; in fact, looking at 1991 fotos, and comparing those with what this writer found in 2012, it appears that part of that ledge has fallen off! This writer decided against doing that part in 2012! But it can be done.

After the 2nd cable, bench-walk on around to the west another 30-40m. Easy walking. Then you'll come to the end of the bench and a big rock. Climb up on it, and you'll see the 3rd cable dangling down. This is the scary part Kenny talked about. If you slip here it's a 30-40m vertical fall! You can also do

Left The beginning of **Art Murray's Triple Cable Bypass Trail**. Holding the cable in one hand adds a little security to this first pitch. The 2nd cable is just to the left out of sight. **Right** The 3rd pitch of **Art Murray's Trail**. The author threw a rope down from the top for added security. The cable, barely visible, is anchored to a log in a crack (upper right) that's been there since the early 1930's!

this pitch without the cable, but it will help. This cable is thin too, and hard to hang onto, but it seemed to be well-anchored by a small cedar log in a crack in 2012; but it's been there since the early 1930's! Once you get up this one dangerous part, then climb a crack to the top (easy). Coming down is more dangerous than going up, so unless you do a lot of this sort of thing, it might be best not to try to go up this last part. There's no place to go on top anyway. The thing that makes this last part so scary and dangerous is the exposure--if you fall, you're finished! This entire trail is for **experienced hikers only**, especially the last part. For this last part, in 2012, the author drove to near the head of this canyon, tied a rope off and went down from the top--which seemed a lot safer for a 69-year-old! To reach the top of this trail, see **Map 15** for a better look at the road getting there.

Next stop along the White Rim Road would be the **Upheaval Canyon Trailhead**. From the Labyrinth Campsite, drive south on a good road, then comes the crossing of the dry sandy creek bed of Taylor & Upheaval Canyons. Best to have a 4WD for this because if the sand is really dry, getting stuck is real easy, especially with a 2WD and an inexperienced driver. Whichever kind of vehicle you have, and to make this 100m-long crossing, gear down, rev up, and go like hell until you climb up and out the other side. Right there on the left is the **trailhead & parking** if you want to walk up Upheaval Canyon **(Km 11.5/Mile 7.2** from the **T-Junction)**.

Here's another possible short walk. From the trailhead, walk west following the dry wash toward the river. About 200m from the road, look for a couple of burned cottonwood trees on the left. Underneath those dead trees you may find the burned remains of the Murray Cabin (the author looked for this on 5/6/2012, but couldn't find hide nor hair of it! A fire burned up 29 acres (12 hectors) on this bottom on 4/20-21/2004 and took out this historic cabin). Look for any sign of this cabin, but it appears nothing will be found, except for maybe an old stove (?). **Kenny Allred** of Moab, cowboyed for Art Murray for about 10 years, roughly from the early 1930's to the early 1940's. He tells about the cabin:

It was made of big ol' logs, and I lived in that thing. Art Murray built that one. Right next to it is an old corral. He built that the year I went to work for him. That would have been in the early 1930's. You see, we sold the remnants of our cattle [Eph & his sister Amy Moore Allred--Kenny's mother] and our ranch to him [Art Murray in about 1929]. That's how he got in there.

That cabin was well-hidden even way back in them days. In those days there was trails through there, with the cattle comin' in to water. It was mostly willows in those days; it's all tamarack [tamarisk] now. I remember them old river bottoms was just covered with tamarack, and them old cows--that was during the drought times, and there wasn't much feed--and those cows would go out on those river bottoms and stay for 2 or 3 days, and they'd eat young tamarack.

Kenny Allred stayed in this cabin off and on for several years. When asked about that, he described how he lived there and in his cow camps along the river:

Murray's Cabin had one of them little cook stoves. It had an oven in it, and legs, it was a pretty nice little ol' stove. He had an old bedstead of some kind in it too. We spent part of the winters there, but as long as we had cattle there, then we'd move. When we'd move the cattle, then we'd move with 'em.

Food was pretty much the same all the time. For breakfast, we'd [Kenny and his first wife Babe] generally eat cereal, or maybe beef. That one winter we ate good beef about all winter--breakfast, dinner and supper! I never did pack a lunch or anything, unless somebody was with me. Then it would generally be a bacon and egg sandwich. Or you maybe packed some canned meat of some kind.

The cabin on **Upheaval Bottom** built by **Art Murray** in about 1933. This foto from an old color slide was taken in 1990. Unfortunately, fire burned up 29 acres (12 hecters) on Upheaval Bottom on 4/20-21/2004 and took out this historic cabin. Look around, you might find the remains of the old stove.

We had one of them little sourdough jugs, then you just rolled your flour sack down and made a little round spot there and made your bread right in the top of your flour sack--then you'd tied the flour sack back up when ya got through. Then you'd add a little water back in your sourdough jug and put some more flour in there and mix it up. You always had enough of that sourdough left in there to keep it workin'. If you used it twice a day, it was a lot better than if you used it once a day. And if you used it only every 2 or 3 days, it wasn't near as good as if it was used real regular. If we was camped out, we cooked in a dutch oven or in a frying pan, but if we were in the cabin, then you'd cook it in the oven. For supper, you always had some bread and beef, and you always had some Kero syrup or something like that. That ol' Kero syrup was about the main thing it seemed like--for our sweetenin'--unless you had some jam or something you'd brought from town.

When we camped in winter, we generally found a ledge or we'd fix up a wickiup. Now down there on Fort Bottom, we fished 3 or 4 big old planks out of the river and made a lean-to, and we spent the biggest end of one winter right there. You'd build a fire right out in front of it and it would throw that heat back inside, and you'd make your bed back in there. And you kept your grain and everything there. There was quite a lot of room in the dang thing. We never did stay in the cabin on Fort Bottom that Mark Walker built--I don't think it was ever finished. As I remember, there was no sign of dobbin between the logs.

If we was where we could, we'd always gather a few cedar boughs to throw under the bed. Now down on the river one time, we made a regular bedstead out of willows--got some logs, and put them willows across it, and tacked them down. Of course we took a bunch of shingle nails in there on purpose to do that. And it wasn't too bad. It sure beat sleepin' on the ground. For sleeping, we had just a bunch of ol' blankets. In them days, there wasn't such a thing as a sleeping bag--as far as I knew. We had an old feather tick too, which was a pretty good outfit to pack around. It was lighter, and pretty warm. I don't ever remember having any problems at night gettin' cold, even in winter.

You always had 2 or 3 pack horses--you had to--to pack all your stuff. Sometimes we'd put hobbles on the horses at night, but sometimes on them river bottoms where they couldn't go anywhere--like on Fort Bottom--I'd just go out with a nose bag [filled with oats] the next morning and holler and they'd generally come in. If they didn't come in, then we'd be in trouble! Oh, I've taken some long ol' walks out on top. I walked from Horsethief over to that Hell Roarin' drift fence one morning before breakfast--then rode back bareback. That's about 15 miles [24 kms] each way!

I read a lot of shoot-em-up magazines and books--whatever you could get. We was pretty easy to please in them days. I've laid out and read by a campfire many nights, so it's a wonder I have any eyes left! We had a lamp in that Murray Cabin on Upheaval Bottom, a coal oil [kerosene] lamp, with a wick. Then we got one of them Aladdin lamps. It burned coal oil, but it had one of them round wicks, and it gave out a lot more light. Then later on, we finally got one of them gas lanterns; that was out at the Horsethief Ranch place.

Kenny also remembered an interesting story of an event which took place in the lower end of Taylor Canyon. It seems there used to be wild burros in there at one time:

We run horses down in there on the White Rim all the time. I had a whole herd of horses when I was a kid. Everybody who had a horse they didn't need, they gave it to me, because I was the kid of the outfit. And one time we went down there with Arnold Holyoak; he was another old cowboy and horse trader. He went with us on a trip down there, and it would have been in the late 1920's. And he caught

Left Looking almost due north we see **Eph Moore** with a string of pack mules traversing **Hardscrabble Hill**. In the upper right, but below the point with ledges, is **Upheaval Bottom**; and on the left is **Mule Bottom**. (Ray Tibbetts Collection). **Right Mark Walker** in about 1900 (born in 1866). He's the one who built the **"Outlaw Cabin"** on **Fort Bottom**. (Kenny Allred Collection)

'im a burro. Taylor Canyon at that time had a bunch of wild burros in it, and that's the main reason he went down there was to get one of them burros. Anyway, we got that burro and got it about halfway home and it just laid down on 'im and that was the end of that--we couldn't get that thing to get up, so we just let 'im go. We caught him in Taylor Canyon. I believe it was an old prospector by the name of Turner who originally left them burros in there. (This could have been Hy Turner, brother of Mel Turner who built the cabin in House Park in the Beef Basin country. Hy lived on Williams Bottom in the early 1900's.)

Hardscrabble Hill, Fort Bottom, and the Mark Walker Cabin

Driving south from Upheaval Bottom, you'll soon come to the turnoff to another small official campsite called **Hardscrabble Bottom (Km 13.8/Mile 8.6)**. The TI/NG map shows 2 separate campsite there, A & B. For those, turn to the right, and they're down by the river. From that turnoff, the White Rim Road heads left or east and steepens as you climb up what has long been called **Hardscrabble Hill**. It got the name because the original trail was so steep and difficult to climb. The road now runs along in about the same location as the trail which is along one of the higher benches of the Chinle Formation. Better have a little clearance and AWD/4WD to get up this road, but conditions will change. After a hard climb, then some contouring, you'll come to a level section and a wide place in the road. Turn right and park at the trailhead to **Fort Bottom (Km 16.5/Mile 10.3)**. From the parking lot, follow an old road, then foot trail, running northwest out to the point as shown on the map. Right on top of the end of the low ridge in the middle of Fort Bottom is what old timers used to call the **Moki Fort**. It's a 2-story Anasazi rock structure which is obviously well-built to have lasted this long. Look around on top for more ruins, and a granary on the west side just below the Moss Back ledge. The fort is apparently where Anasazi Indians stayed when they farmed Fort Bottom perhaps 700-800 years ago. This appears to be the farthest north of any Anasazi habitation site in Canyonlands NP and Utah.

But there are more ruins on Fort Bottom. They're located about due south of the Moki Fort. To get to these, walk down the trail on the north side of the butte, and instead of walking to the log cabin, first head to the left and walk all the way around to the south side of the butte the fort is located on. When you get to the south side, walk east & southeast right along the base of the cliff. You'll eventually come to a minor ruin which is mostly destroyed, then a little humped-up alluvial flood plain at the bottom end of a little drainage. Next to that under a minor ledge is an **old feed trough** that's still in good condition; it was surely built by Art Murray's cowboy, Kenny Allred in the 1930's. Then just southeast of that is another **moki house**.

Or, from the Moki Fort, walk north on a trail that ends at the **Walker Cabin**. This trail is used mostly by river runners who walk from their camp near the cabin to the fort. This little cabin is about 75m from the river. It's made of logs, has a rock fireplace, part of a roof, but the veranda or lean-to on the north side has fallen down; and **the NPS refuses to restore or take measures to preserve it!** (On 12/4/2012, Chris Goetze of CNP, told this writer it's NPS policy not to rebuild things like this! But, if a replica roof were put on; willows, logs and clay dirt, the cabin would remain dry and could last 1000 years! If you feel strongly about this sort of thing, complain!) Otherwise it's in rather good condition except most of the roof is gone, which was made of logs & willows with dirt on top of them. Everybody calls it the **Outlaw Cabin**, but it may or may not have ever been used by outlaws. When asked who might have made it, **Kenny Allred** said:

Mark Walker got credit for building that cabin on Fort Bottom. It's been there since early this century [1900's] or before, because when I was just a kid it was an old cabin. It looked about the same then as the last time I was there. I haven't been there for 25 years [this was a 1991 interview]. It had a pretty good roof on it the last time I was there. Walker and his relatives was in there, evidently before the Taylors was out on top. They run cattle up and down the Green River. It was really before anybody else's time in there. He raised a family and there's still relatives around here. My wife is his granddaughter.

Mark Walker's family history is in the book, **Grand Memories**, but more is told of his life in various newspaper articles and his obituary which was in **The Times-Independent** for **March 26, 1942**. It seems that Mark Walker was born in 1866 near Salt Lake City. He married Augusta Taylor in 1884 and moved to Moab to be near his parents. They were part of the Taylor family who appear to have been the first settlers with cattle in the Moab country. Because he was a carpenter by trade, he built his own home in Moab soon after arriving. The fact that he was a carpenter, and his wife's parents one of the Taylors, they may have been the very first people to run cattle down along the Green River and up on Big Flat. This is good circumstantial evidence that he was the one who built the *"Outlaw Cabin"* on Fort Bottom. That cabin is so well built, it couldn't have been built by just any old cowpoke.

In the 1890's, and for many years, Mark was a justice of the peace in Moab. He also built many of the early homes in Moab before he moved to Idaho for 2 years in 1905 & '06; an educated guess is, he built this cabin before he moved to Idaho (?). For several years after the Idaho trip, he lived in Castleton, east of Moab, where he operated a store and post office. He returned to Moab in 1922 where he remained until he died in March of 1942.

In a 1973 NPS interview, **Leland Tidwell** talked about using this cabin once: *I stayed at that cabin on Fort Bottom in 1921. Clyde [Tidwell] and I went down to see how our horses were doing and found they had been stolen. They had crossed on the ice, so we did too. There had been a little snow but we managed to track them onto Fort Bottom. It was just getting dark and Clyde, said, "What shall we do? Shall we go back or try to stay here?" I said we might as well stay there. I had a small ax run down in the ring on my saddle, so we dragged up some logs and cut them up and built a fire in the fireplace. The cabin was clean. It had a table and a couple of benches in it and we built a good fire and put the benches along the wall and sort of leaned back and went to sleep as best we could. The next morning we took our horses and followed the tracks around until we could see they had been driven out of the country. We met Eph Moore and he said he could get our horses back for us, and he did. Bill Tibbetts had stolen them and Eph made him bring them back. They drowned one, I think, crossing them back over the river and Eph gave us another horse, a little roan.*

Before leaving the cabin, look carefully on some of the logs and you might see some historic signatures. Some date back to the 1910's (?).

Now back to the Fort Bottom Trailhead and driving south on the White Rim Road. After **800m (.5 mile)** you'll come to a **steep dugway**. This will be the end of the line for 2WD's, as this hill is likely too steep to get back up. It's 4WD country from there on (If coming up this part, shift to your lowest gear and rev up--the author's Jeep Patriot with 5-speed trany did fine). This steep hill drops off down through the Moss Back Member of the Chinle Formation, the same platform the Moki Fort is located on. **Kenny Allred** said this used to be an old **cow trail** before they put the road in there in the 1950's:

*They called that the **Walker Cut** when I was a kid. That trail went down steep, and it was more of a cut than it is now. It was probably 8 feet [2 1/2m] wide just shot right down through that Shinarump [now called the Moss Back] ledge. The trail got shot away when the road went down. The trail must have been done with dynamite; it had to have been shot out of there. It was my wife's grandad, **Mark Walker** and his folks who built it, the same guy who built the cabin down on Fort Bottom. That may have been fixed not long after the turn of the century [1900] (?).*

Potato Bottom and the White Rim Road

If you have a 4WD or mtn. bike, you can continue south from the top of Hardscrabble Hill and the Walker Cut. The next stop will be **Potato Bottom**. No one seems to know where this name came from, but in the early 1900's, there were a number of people who tried settling most of the Green River bottoms. Someone may have tried to settle this one too, maybe even grew a few potatoes (?). Near the river there is another official NPS campsite, but in 2 parts, A & B (**about Km 20/Mile 12.5** from the T-Junction). A little ways south of the campsites, a low, white sandstone bench is seen emerging and begins to rise to the south. This is the first time you'll see the **White Rim Sandstone** formation. As you continue south, you'll see this same prominent bench and ledge slowly rising higher and higher above the river. The **White Rim Road** runs along on top of this formation all the way around Gray's Pasture and/or Island in the Sky.

At about the point where you begin to see the White Rim rise, which is just above the bend in the river, is an old **cowboy camp**. It's nestled underneath the ledge about 300m south of the most-southerly part of the 2 campsites. **Kenny Allred** once again tells us about this place:

Right where Potato Bottom meets the White Rim, there's a ledge. We used to camp under there-- and the last time I was there, there was an old trunk still underneath it. Ol' Art Murray packed that trunk in there just to keep groceries and things in. I guess he did, it was there when I went to work for him in about 1933. It's quite an overhang, and we had to fight through the brush to get to it. We had a trail cut out through the ol' willows so we could water our horses. That's what we were drinkin' too, was river water. It was a pretty good place to stay 'cause the rain couldn't get to you. When I first went in there the tamaracks [tamarisks] was just starting to come. Out on them sand bars they come up pretty thick. There was also a lot of iron brush in there too; I don't know what the real name for that was. It has a little ol' blue berry on it that's bitter. They grow ever which way and they're sure hard to get through. We run horses down there on the White Rim all the time. It was before Art Murray came in there, when I used it the first time.

That trunk was still there in 1991, but in 2011 & '12, this writer didn't have the time or energy or desire to fight through the brush from the river or the road to get there. You'll have to be very determined to get there today because of all the tamarisks and other brush.

Above Right on top of the hill in the middle of **Fort Bottom**, is what is usually called the **Moki Fort**. It's a 2-story structure and for sure was built by Anasazi Indians; either as a dwelling and/or lookout.

Left On the south side of the peninsula which is **Fort Bottom**, are several ruins of **moki houses** like this one. These are at the bottom of the cliffs and next to the flat lands.

This cabin on Fort Bottom wasn't really an **Outlaw Cabin**; instead it was constructed by **Mark Walker** as a shelter or line cabin for cattlemen. Mark's wife was a Taylor, and the Taylors were the first people to bring cattle to Moab. In 1990, it had a partial roof, but NPS policy is to not restore or reconstruct anything! With a dirt roof, and just a little TLC, the logs in this cabin would last 1000 years.

From near the **Moki Fort**, looking southeast with Potato Bottom on the far left in the distance. This was August, 2011, after high water in the Green River overflowed into oxbow lakes on Fort Bottom, making it the worst mosquito year since 1986.

If you get upon the little hill behind **Mesa Arch**, you'll have a good view of the arch, **Monster & Airport** Towers and the snow-capped **La Sal Mountains** in the far background.

A good picture of **Kenny Allred** on the **left**. It was likely taken in the late 1940's or early '50's, with a late 1940's/early '50's car behind. The other 3 people are unidentified, but some old-timers remember the guy on the right being around Moab in this time period. (Connie Murphy Skelton Collection)

Green River Overlook & Halfdome Hike, and the Wilhite, Murphy, Grandview Point & Junction Butte, Gooseberry, Aztec Butte and Mesa Arch Trails

Location & Access Featured on this map is the southern half of the high country Between the Rivers known as Island in the Sky or Gray's Pasture. This part is just southeast of Upheaval Dome and includes the southern extension of this eroded mesa called **Grand View Point**. This map also includes much of the southwestern half of the **White Rim Road** which runs along the White Rim. The White Rim is an intermediate level between the Green & Colorado Rivers, and the high ground on top of the plateau.

By far the easiest way to get to the trails featured here is to drive the paved road running south from the Island Visitor Center. This highway is kept open year-round. It allows access for any car to all the trails featured here, but you can also do the some hikes from along the White Rim Road--which is a lot harder to get to; and you'll need a 4WD. The trails featured here will be discussed individually below.

Elevations Trailhead for False Kiva Ruins (same as for Alcove Spring Trailhead), 1733m; Wilhite Trailhead, 1778m; Aztec Butte, 1924m; Willow Flat Campground, 1859m; Murphy Trailhead, 1902m; Grand View Point Overlook, 1914m; Junction Butte, 1951m; Murphy Hogback Campsites, 1609m; and Gooseberry Campsite, 1458m.

Water Take all the water you'll need for your trip, regardless if you're on the mesa top or on the White Rim, but in recent years the CNP has installed an outside **water tap** at the visitor center. There may or may not be water at Murphy Spring so don't bet your life on finding it there.

Maps USGS or BLM map La Sal (1:100,000); Upheaval Dome, Musselman Arch, Turks Head & Monument Basin (1:24,000--7 1/2' quads); the plastic Trails Illustrated/National Geographic map Canyonlands National Park (1:70,000); or the plastic Latitude 40° map Moab West (1:75,000).

Main Attractions Three exciting cattle or sheep trails, and another steep route down off the mesa to the White Rim and Junction Butte; and some of the finest views seen anywhere, especially looking down at Monument Basin and from under Mesa Arch looking at the often snow-capped La Sal Mountains.

From Grand View Point: Mesa Arch, Aztec Butte, Halfdome & the Green River Overlook

As you drive into this mapped area from the Island Visitor Center, the first place of interest would be the trailhead and short hike to **Mesa Arch**. This is between the camouflaged **mile posts 13 & 14**, and about 600m north of the junction of the roads heading for Upheaval Dome and Grand View Point.

This short loop-trail is about 1 km round-trip. It can be hiked in about 20 minutes or less, and without taking any water or lunch. Mesa Arch, created out of the Navajo Sandstone, is on the very rim of the mesa and it arches up, allowing you to see under it. Off in the distance are the La Sal Mountains which are snow covered about half the time. Below you 400m will be the White Rim and Buck Canyon. The best part of this short hike it to fotograph this arch, with Washer Woman Arch & Monster Towers, and the snow-capped mountains in the background.

Next stop might be the **Willow Flat Campground** and the **Green River Overlook**. To get there, drive west from just beyond the Mesa Arch parking in the direction of Upheaval Dome; but after about

One of the more interesting views around is under **Mesa Arch**. The 2 spires you see in the middle distance is Washer Woman Arch & Monster Tower, then Airport Tower, and finally the La Sal Mtns.

Map 20, Green River Overlook & Halfdome Hike, and the Wilhite, Murphy, Grandview Point & Junction Butte, Gooseberry, Aztec Butte and Mesa Arch Trails

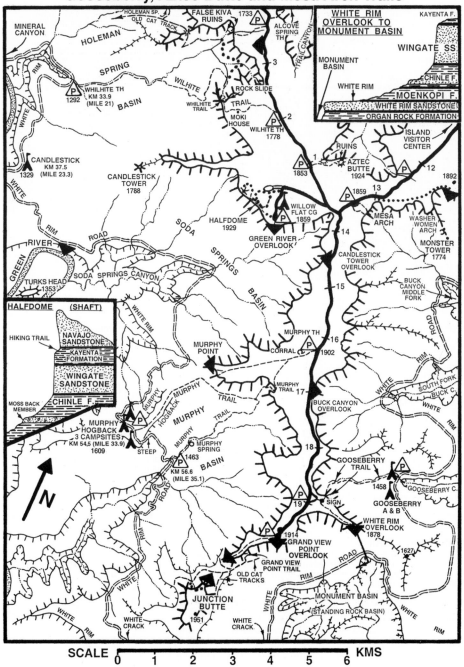

SCALE 0 1 2 3 4 5 6 KMS

Left Looking northwest at the southwest face of **Halfdome (or Shaft)**. A hiker's trail is developing along the top of the Kayenta bench; walk along that for some spectacular views. Or you can climb to the top from the north side. **Right** The **ruins** of a **moki house** on the north side of **Aztec Butte**.

500m from the junction, turn left or south and follow the signs to the campground & overlook. This campground has toilets, picnic tables, but **no water** even though you pay a fee for camping. Just south of the campground is the overlook of the Green River, Soda Springs Basin, and Turks Head.

Here's an interesting short hike that begins at the **Green River Overlook**. If you walk (no trail) due west from the parking lot about 300m, you'll come to a narrow bench made of talus from the Navajo Sandstone which rests on top of the highest Kayenta bench. From there you'll have a good look west at **Candlestick Tower**. Plus, if you walk west on this bench, you'll come to a place that's less than 10m wide. At that point, and going straight up and slightly overhung, is a Navajo Sandstone bluff that looks similar to **Halfdome** in Yosemite NP. On the *Latitude 40°* and the *Upheaval Dome 7 1/2'* maps, this is called **Shaft** and is listed at 1929m (6329'). But the name Halfdome seems more appropriate because it looks just like a big dome cut in half with one vertical face. From the top of Halfdome to the bottom of the Chinle Formation in Soda Springs Basin, it's nearly 500 vertical meters. You can also circle around to the northwest and climb to the top for an even better view. Or you can circle around to the northwest side of another little flat-topped butte west of Halfdome, and climb it for another view looking east.

The next stop is a short hike to the top of **Aztec Butte**. The trailhead is less than 1 km past the turnoff to Willow Flat Campground and just before **mile post 1**. This hike is only about 2 kms, round-trip, and will take less than an hour. The trail run southeast around one little butte, then zig zags up the south side of Aztec Butte. It ends on the top of a remnant butte of Navajo Sandstone, capped with limestone. After you've seen the views from on top, head for the north side. Locate one of several ways down about 3m off the rim to a narrow bench, veer left or west and walk along a trail on the north side. There are several small natural caves under a ledge and 1 genuine **Indian ruin** (plus a couple made by palefaced mokis). This is a short, well-used, and interesting hike.

The Wilhite Trail

About halfway between Aztec Butte and the Upheaval Dome Trailhead, and near **mile post 2**, is the beginning of the **Wilhite Trail**, which runs down to Holeman Spring Basin and the White Rim Road. Few people around Moab seemed to know much about who built this trail and when. The late **Kenny Allred** formerly of Moab remembered a few things though:

*The sheepmen built that one winter. That was after I went to work for Murray [in 1933]. Murray and those sheepmen had lots of arguments over grazing. **Jim Brown**, a guy from Montrose, Colorado, run sheep down in there about that time. It might have been in the late 1930's, or 1940 when they built that. They built it after Murray stopped using that area, and fightin' over the White Rim country, so much.*

From the trailhead parking, the trail heads off in a westerly direction across the mesa top and is marked with stone cairns. It's easy to follow and part of it is along an old livestockman's road (**Kent Johnson** bulldozed that road to the top of the Wilhite Trail in **1942** while working for the Grazing Service. Read more about the 1st roads in this district on **page 230**). After about 1 km, you'll drop down over a minor ledge with a small storage **granary** or moki house underneath next to the trail. It may be a Fremont Indian structure (?). After walking another km, you'll come to the top of the Wilhite Trail (the end of that old road is nearby). It got this name because right at the beginning of the constructed part of the trail, is a boulder with Wilhite Trail painted on it--but in 2012, it was so faded, you couldn't read it. No one knows if he was a sheepherder or someone who just helped build the trail (?).

The Wilhite zig zags down a big **rockslide** covering the Wingate Sandstone Formation. It seems to

Above This **moki house** or maybe a granary is found along the **Wilhite Trail**; it seems to have been made by real moki Indians (?). It's likely an Anasazi structure (?).

Left From above looking southeast and down at the switchbacks along the **Wilhite Trail**. It zig zags down on top of a big **rockslide** covering what at one time was a Wingate Sandstone cliff.

Above Aerial view of **Monument Basin** looking west toward the south end of Grand View Point. Before the Uranium Boom came to Moab in the 1950's, this was known to early-day cattlemen as **Standing Rock Basin**. And the drainage or canyon leading out of it in the lower left-hand corner of this picture was called **Standing Rock Canyon**. Bill Tibbetts & Tom Perkins had a shootout with the Sheriff of Moab in the middle of the night at the mouth of this canyon on July 29, 1924.

Right Halfway down the steep part of the **Murphy Trail** is this little wooden bridge (standing on it). Nearby on the cliff face are some old signatures, one being from 1917, which is likely the year the Murphys built it.

have had work done on it in the late 1980's, because it was in better condition in 1990 than in 1985; in 2012, it was in even better shape. When you reach the bottom of the steep part, the trail is used less, but there are still some cairns marking the route all the way to the White Rim Road.

Further along, it curves around one buttress and heads south on top of the Moss Back Member of the Chinle, then finally drops down through this barrier and heads down the dry wash to the **White Rim Road**. It's about 9.8 kms from road to road, nearly 20 kms round-trip. It would take most people most of a day to do this hike round-trip. If you go all the way to the White Rim Road, take plenty of water, especially if it's a hot summer day. It's not recommended you do this in summer however. Most people are happy just to reach the bottom of the constructed part of the trail and return.

Also shown here is part of the route to **Holeman Spring**, which is discussed along with **Map 19** in the previous chapter. If you hike to, or close to, Holeman Spring and return, it will likely take most of a day for the average person.

The Murphy Trail

About 5 kms south of the turnoff to Upheaval Dome (and just south of **mile post 16**) and in about the middle of Grand View Point, is a turnoff to the right or southwest. About 75m away is the trailhead parking for hiking to **Murphy Point**, and the beginning of the **Murphy Trail**. This parking is in the middle of a big grassy park-like meadow and there are cars parked there all the time.

Before hiking, here's a little history of the family who built this cattle trail. The late **Verona Murphy Stocks**, formerly of Moab, and who was born in 1905, helped her father bring cattle up the Murphy Trail once, and she remembered more about it than anyone. Here's her story:

When my father worked for other people, he was usually paid in cattle; normally 2 cows a month. That's how he built up his herd. When grandfather died in July, 1916, my father sold everything in Blanding and moved here to Moab and lived in his father's house. Then they bought the South Mesa Ranch [Wilson Mesa] from Tangrens in late August, 1916. The Tangrens also sold their winter range out on the White Rim under Monument Point [another name for Grand View Point]. That's why we put cows out there.

Dad had cash to invest in the Murphy Brothers Cattle Co., because he had sold everything in Blanding. Uncle Felix didn't put any money in and didn't like to ride, so he wasn't part of the company. Vic, Tom, Jack, Otho, and Will (Verona's father)--5 brothers were in the company. The brand was 7M; Seven Murphy's.

After they bought the grazing rights from Tangrens, Dad and his brothers built the Murphy Trail. Dad also helped build the Shafer Trail, because he used it sometimes. He didn't want to take his cows all the way around to the Shafer Trail, so he built the new one. They built it mostly during one winter. It was during the First World War when they built it, in about 1917 or 1918. It was 1918, when the Murphy brothers first put cattle on the White Rim below Monument Point.

I was 13 when I first went down there, that was in 1918. In that year, they sold some of the cattle and started buying sheep. They paid $20 for each ewe, then the price when down to $2 a head. The price for cattle fell in 1919 or '20 too. They had both sheep and cattle, then the prices fell. At one time we had over 1000 head of cattle.

We had to leave some of the cows there the first year, because some were ready for calving. Then my two sisters helped Dad bring up the second herd. That was about 300 head. That's all I remember about us going down into that country. It was about 1919 or '20 we lost everything--the South Mesa Ranch and the grazing out under Monument Point. We only had cattle down there for a couple of years, and that was it.

Kenny Allred had more to say about the Murphy brothers, and why they went out of business; read more under the next chapter on the **White Crack Trail** and **Map 21**, starting on page 218.

Now for the hike. The first part of the trail is an old livestockman's road, then after about 1 km, it splits; one trail runs out to **Murphy Point**, the other veers left or south and continues to the edge of the plateau where it begins to zig zags down a rockslide covering the Wingate Sandstone wall. Near the bottom of the steepest part, a kind of ramp or bridge, made out of boards, was built to cross a gap in the wall (see foto). In the area of this ramp, look at the wall for old cowboy etchings. There's one dating from 1917, perhaps the year the trail was made (?). Below that you'll come to the Chinle clay beds, then not far below that the trail splits; one part heads down the dry creek bed, while the other follows an old 1950's miner's Cat track. This one contours along the Chinle, then heads southwest along the **Murphy Hogback** and ends at the campsites with the same name which is located on the White Rim Road.

About the only possible water close to the White Rim Road is in the lower part of Murphy Wash just above the road. It may be there year-round, but **not guaranteed**. At one time, one of the sheep herders tried to develop the spring. You may see some plastic tubing and a metal tank in the drainage bottom.

To hike down to the bottom of the steep part of the trail and back would only take a couple of hours; but to go to the road and back, would be 5-6 hours, or more for some. From the trailhead on top to the White Rim Road is 7.5 kms via the wash; 7.7 kms via the hogback route. The author once walked down to the road and back in about 3 1/2 hours. Take plenty of water if it's warm weather. This trail faces the south and it can be very warm coming back up.

The White Rim Overlook and the Government or Gooseberry Trail

The next 2 hikes begin at the picnic site near **mile post 19**. Park on the far eastern side of the paved loop road; that's where the trail running out to the **White Rim Overlook** begins. From this trailhead walk due east along the top of a narrow finger of land jutting out almost into space. It's about 1.3 kms to the point, but the scenery is well worth the walk. If you face southeast, you'll be looking directly down into **Monument Basin**. It may be the best viewpoint in the park and is one of the most-fotographed scenes in Canyonlands. It'll take about an hour or less to do this hike round-trip.

The other trail was called the **Government Trail** by old timers in Moab, because it was built by a government relief program, but the NPS seems to have changed it to **Gooseberry Trail**. **Kenny Allred** knew a little about this one:

I've always heard it was called the Government Trail, because them guys was workin' for the government. They run some pipe off from there and to some kind of a spring down below. The last I heard, that pipe is still up that hillside (?). That was when the WPA's [Works Progress Administration began April 4, 1935 by FDR] was operating back in the late 1930's, maybe 1940. They had a project which was the same as the WPA where they was fixin' up these water holes.

To hike down this good trail, begin at the same trailhead as the hike to the White Rim Overlook, but just after you start walking east, you'll veer left at the **sign**, and drop down off the rim going north. This trail also zig zags down a very steep rockslide covering the Wingate. It's well-built and in good condition. At the bottom of the steepest part, it then more or less follows the dry creek bed down to where it ends at the **White Rim Road**, a distance of 4.3 kms. Nearby is the **Gooseberry Campsites A & B**.

This trail faces north, so it doesn't seem so hot as the Murphy, but take plenty of water anyway if it's a hot day. It's a fast and east hike. The author was racing the setting sun on one of his trips and made the round-trip hike in 1 hour, 38 minutes. You'll likely want 2-3 hours, or more round-trip.

Grand View or Monument Basin Trail and the route up Junction Butte

The last hike featured on this map is down off the end of **Grand View Point**. It's easy to get there, just drive south on the Island Highway to the very end and park. This is another vista called the **Grand View Point Overlook**. At the viewpoint, locate the trail running southwest. This was once a rough old road that was bulldozed in by Kent Johnson of Moab in 1942, but it's been converted to a trail. To located the beginning of what is known as either the **Grand View or Monument Basin Trail**, walk to the very end of Grand View Point, enjoy the scene there and look at the old mining tracks located between Grand View Point and **Junction Butte**, then back-track about 300m toward the parking lot.

At about that point, head for the east side of the rim looking for a steep ramp heading down to the northeast. There may be stone cairns at the beginning of this very steep route down through the Wingate cliff. CNP is not advertising it because it's so steep and has some exposure near the bottom end. Sometime in the 1990's, a girl got down there and probably developed a case of vertigo, and had to be rescued. For this reason, **this is for more experienced hikers only!**

In the beginning, the trail follows a moderately steep ramp down parallel to the main wall in a northeast direction, then at the bottom of this ramp the route turns 180° to the right or south. From there on down it's a matter of route-finding. It's not an often used route, but will likely have some cairns marking the way. At several places, you'll want to use your hands, but other than that, it's just a steep scramble down slickrock to the bottom--but with a **big drop** on one side! Near the bottom, several steps have been cut. Inexperienced hikers without an experienced leader, will feel uneasy on parts of this route.

When you reach the talus slope below, this hiker's trail veers southwest toward **Junction Butte**. After a ways, you can use an old mining exploration track from the 1950's; be sure to view the route from the end of Grand View Point Trail first before doing this hike; that will help you sort out the way. If you wish, you can follow one of these tracks down to the White Rim Road and to the lip of **Monument Basin**. Or you can look for another old track running west, then southwest along the western side of Junction Butte. When you reach the canyon-like northwest face of this butte, head straight up the steep slope. There's no trail, but a few hikers are using it to reach the top of this lone standing butte. About halfway up, will be a steeper section with 5-6 pitches that may challenge beginner hikers, so each group should have one member who thinks he/she is a rock climber. The picture shows the most difficult pitch; it has a log and a pile of flat rocks. If this isn't to your liking, there's another 7m climb up a crack about 12-15m to the left or north. Coming down that crack is almost like downclimbing 2 ladders about half a meter apart; because there's lots of hand & foot holds. Once on top, head northeast for different views looking back to the north at Grand View Point and Monument Basin.

There's no water on this route and it should take the average hiker from 4-6 hours to walk from the Grand View Point Trailhead to the top of Junction Butte and back. The author did it round-trip in about 3 hours once; but 4 hours the last time while taking lots of fotos with a tripod.

From the White Rim Road

Now let's take up the White Rim Road route from Potato Bottom on the previous map. After leaving that bottom, you'll start a gradual climb to the south along a broad bench known as the White Rim. This is on top of the White Rim Sandstone. After about 5 or 6 kms, you'll come to the last Green River bottom accessible from this road. It's called **Queen Anne Bottom**. There's a little side-road off to the right or west you can use to reach this bottom, and although you can drive down there to some trees and shade, the NPS has not bothered to make this an official campsite. Apparently it's illegal to camp there, at least if you come by road with a 4WD.

Queen Anne Bottom has some history associated with it. When asked how it got this name, **Ray Tibbetts (son of Bill Tibbetts**, the famous alleged horsethief) said this:

All I know about Queen Anne Bottom is there was somebody by the name of Anne who was there. And they called her Queen Anne. She's the one who settled on it. Dad said she was quite the old gal, and she lived there by herself. She lived there only a couple of years; in fact Dad said she was there when he first got back from the war, right after World War I [1919], then shortly after that she packed up and moved out. When I went down there a few years ago, I couldn't see any sign of her setup. Dad said she used to have a camp right there in those cottonwoods where you'd first come down off the hill [where the road is]. Just a camp, and that's how 90% of them river bottom settler's outfits were. It was a short lived deal in the late 1910's.

Kenny Allred added a few more things that his older half-brother, Bill Tibbetts had told him:

Bill Tibbetts told me this story about Queen Anne Bottom. Some woman who they called Anne, had this boat and she called it the Queen Anne. That bottom was evidently her headquarters, and as I understood it, she was going to haul goods and stuff in there for these other homesteaders, and run this boat. But I guess it was so big that it wouldn't go most of the time, the river got too small for it in the dry season. This would have been back in the early 1920's or the teens. Probably would have been in the teens, 'cause Bill was in there with my uncle Eph Moore at the time.

Ray Tibbetts is quite a story teller, and he told a story about his dad, Bill Tibbetts, part of which took place on Queen Anne Bottom. This happened sometime after he got home from the war in 1919, and before the range war of 1924 & '25:

*Dad and **Eph Moore** were camped over in Elaterite Basin runnin' cows, and one day Uncle Eph said, "Bill, I've got to go to town". It was in early spring, and they were gettin' low on supplies and Dad said, "Alright, you go ahead and I'll take care of things here. How soon you going to be back?", and Eph said, "About 2 weeks".*

Well, at that time you had to go from there, about 20 miles [32 kms] north, then you'd cross the ford where Millard Canyon dumps into the river just above Queen Anne Bottom. That was a natural ford. Anyway, he left and Dad said, "Uncle Eph didn't come back and didn't come back, and my supplies were gettin' low". By that time he wasn't even makin' good gravy. And Dad said, "I was really worried about Eph by that time, I thought maybe something had happened to him". He said it was getting later

Above From the very end of Grand View Point, looking south at **Junction Butte**. It's called that because it's near the Confluence of the Green & Colorado Rivers. The route to the top starts in middle center and runs along one of the old uranium roads to the right or west. Then the track heads south; but you climb uphill in the sunlit part of the northwest face. Higher up is a little climbing as seen on page 215.

Left This is the ramp at the beginning of the **Grand View or Monument Basin Trail** as it starts down the cliff face. Looking northeast with the La Sal Mountains in the background. At the bottom of this ramp, the trail or route cuts back in the opposite direction before it reaches the talus slope below. **This trail or route is for experienced hikers only.**

213

in the spring and the water in the river was gettin' pretty high, so he rode up and he was a little bit leery about crossing the river with his horse, so he made 'em a raft--just a bunch of logs tied together. And he put his saddle and all of his stuff on it and he just pushed off, and in crossing he came out at Queen Anne Bottom.

Now they had an old camp out there at that time. So he looked around and they had a few horses and stuff there and he was able to catch one of them with his oat bag and it was a big old gray horse that they was pasturing for some of the Lances. And he said he hadn't been ridden in years. And finally he got'im caught and put the saddle on 'im, then got on and started headin' fer town. And when he got to the top of the hill, about where that road comes down in there, that old horse turned around and went to buckin'; and he bucked all the way down through that iron brush and all the willows.

Now that iron brush is tough. Dad said, "When he quit buckin', the only things I had on was my boots and my belt". He said, "I lost my hat, and my shirt and pants was totally tore off". So he went back up and found his hat, and he was just able to hold enough rags on 'im to keep from sun burning himself real bad.

So he said he rode out and got to the top of that trail at the head of Holeman Basin [must have been an early version of the Wilhite Trail]. He got out on top and one of the Taylors, Lauren Taylor, was camped up there with some cows. And he woke 'im up that morning when he got there. And he shook him and said, "Lauren look". And god, Lauren went clearn to the bottom of his sleepin' bag. Of course Dad was scratched all over, and he had these whickers and that hat on and no clothes. And it scared Lauren when he came out of the bag and woke up. Dad said, "God Lauren, it's Bill Tibbetts, and I need to talk to you". And finally he came out of his bedroll. Well he said, "What do you need", and Dad said, "I need some clothes. Have you got a pair of Levis or something?" Lauren said, "No, the only pair I've got are the ones I got on. But I threw a pair of old Levis away last year over at this other camp"; wherever that was.

So Dad went over and those pants had laid out in the sun all year, and they were bleached white on one side--and they were basically wore out when they were thrown away. Anyway, he said they were better than not having any, although they were too short and too tight for 'im. So he used them to come on to town with. And of course, with those clothes, nobody knew him when he got to town. He found out Uncle Eph had come to town and was just home prunin' his trees and wasn't in any big hurry to get back.

Eph Moore was one of the more important early-day cattlemen in this part of the country. He ran cattle on both sides of the Green River in these parts. He was born June 21, 1879, in Bennington, Idaho. When he was just a boy the family moved to Moab, and was one of the first families into this country. He eventually became well-educated, having gone to college at BYU. He served 5 LDS church missions altogether. He sheared sheep at one time and had a farm in Blanding during the 1910's. He also got into the cattle business. **Kenny Allred** remembered a little bit about his uncle this way:

My mother and Eph were sister & brother. Now Eph's dad was a Mormon bishop over in Castle Valley at one time and I know Eph went on several church missions. As far back as I can remember, he lived here in Moab. And he had a few Indian cattle he'd traded for; now he may have traded for them down in Blanding before he moved up here. I can remember one old steer that had the darndest set of horns you ever saw. And it sure would have been nice to have had it mounted. They was big old rawboned steers--they must have been Texas Longhorns.

Eph stayed out there along the river, and when Bill Tibbetts came back from runnin' away from the law in 1930, Eph had a few cattle. And he talked my mother into selling her cattle and buying sheep. So we bought 1000 head of yearlin' sheep and took out there on that desert and summered 'em--out there on Gray's Pasture and Big Flat, and in that country. So I think Eph sold the majority of his cattle at the same time we sold ours [1929]. We may have taken 'em in the same drive, I don't remember now. Ya see, Eph had cattle on both sides of the river, he had a little bunch on the other side of the river and a little bunch over here. He may have sold part of his cattle to George Franz, because it would have been quite a job to run those cows over here and across the river.

Then after that, in the 1930's, he kinda got mixed up in church work and done a little farmin' here in the valley. This place right here where the bowling alley is now, was his and his sister's [Aunt Lona]. She had been married, and divorced. That was my grandpa's place originally. My Aunt Lona took care of them when they got old and down, so when they died, she got the place--and Uncle Eph just run it for her. He stayed there and run that place for years. [Not far south of the Moores farm, was a place all the old timers called **Moores Pasture**. That was named after Eph's father who used to run cows up there to graze part of the time. Today that place is now called **Hidden Valley** and it will be discussed later in this book with Map 26]

Then he bought up quite a bunch of horses at one time. The county gathered up all the horses in the country and sold 'em to get 'em off the range and get some tax money or something; and he bought about 100 head of them mares. I think he only gave something like $10 a head for 'em. I remember when $100 would have bought about any saddle horse in the country. And he bought a stud and he was going to go into the horse business, but when he took 'em back out there on the desert, why they just went like flies! They all went back to their old stompin' grounds--so he had horses everywheres! Gettin' 'em together was the next thing.

This was before Taylor Grazing came in [7/27/1934], so it must have been in the early 1930's. I know he still had a few horses around when Taylor Grazing came in. I did gather up a few for him. But they were hard to catch. I lowered the boom on the last of them Tenmile broncs out there. They kept gettin' my saddle horses--so I got 'em in a tight spot and shot 'em--about 7 head of 'em. That's a hell of a thing to brag about, but they sure ruin a lot of good saddle horses--them old broomtails. They'll take your horses then you can't catch 'em. Your saddle horses will get just as wild as the wild ones when they get together.

I don't know just how it started, but I think Eph was on one of his church missions and he got to visitin' with this girl. Now this was before my time and it must have been on one of his earlier missions. He was just a young guy then. But anyway, he was supposed to go up there somewhere in Idaho and marry her. So he rode a horse all the way up there, and when he got there, she was out to a dance with somebody else. So he just saddled up and rode away, came home. Them oldtimers didn't think too much about takin' a long time to ride a horse some place. So he never did get married.

Eph Moore died in May of 1950 at the age of 71.

During the 1950's Uranium Boom, the White Rim Road was put in before the road down the Flint Trail was. **Karl Tangren** mentioned the mining era and Queen Anne Bottom:

When I got there the miners had already built a road off onto Queen Anne Bottom. That's where they had their camp, and they had a trolley across the river. They were exploring for uranium west of the river, and Queen Anne Bottom was a good place to transfer supplies. You can still see where they had the cable car strung up on the west side, but on Queen Anne, it's too overgrown to do much looking around. There is some evidence of them being there under the White Rim cliffs across from the mouth of Millard Canyon.

At the lower end of this bottom is the east-side location of Karl Tangren's **ferry site**. He had a cable strung up there across the river and a kind of barge to take supplies across to his place on Anderson Bottom just downstream a ways. He had that set up in the mid to late 1950's until 1964. When the national park came to be in 1964, the ferry site and Anderson Bottom were both abandoned. Read more on **Anderson Bottom** along with **Map 8**. Or, read more details of Karl's ferry in this writer's other book, ***River Guide to Canyonlands National Park and Vicinity, 2nd Edition.***

The next stop along the White Rim Road might be the lower trailhead for the **Wilhite Trail** located **33.9 kms (21 miles)** from the T-Junction--which is the beginning of the White Rim Road. However, overall, it's better to do this hike and all the other livestock trails reaching the White Rim Road, from the top of the mesa and the paved road, rather than walking up from the bottom.

After the Wilhite Trail the next place of interest will be the **Candlestick Campsite (Km 37.5/Mile 23.3)**. Due east of this is **Candlestick Tower**, for which this campsite is named. This is one of the better foto stops on the west side of the Island. From Candlestick, continue south on a pretty good stretch of road around a big bend of the river called **Turks Head and Turks Bottom**. A viewpoint there would be at about **Km 41.8/Mile 26**. There's a bunch of Anasazi ruins & rock art there, but with no access from the White Rim Road.

After Turks Head, you'll come to the next officially designated campsites on top of **Murphy Hogback & Trailhead (Km 54.5/Mile 33.9)**. Three campsites are located there along with some cedar (juniper) trees. To get upon this flat-top ridge, you'll have to go up a steep & slightly rough section of road that covers about 1 km. We're all lucky now because in the summer of 2011, a Jeep tipped over somewhere near the top which prompted CNP to start a little road repair & maintenance. They fixed the top of that part so any SUV with reasonably good ground clearance can get up it. It's the same on the south side, a little steep but smoother than before--but still for AWD/4WD's only. From the Murphy Hogback, you could hike up the Murphy Trail, but most people prefer to hike from the top down. Access at the top is much easier, and cooler!

Going south again. At **Km 56.6 (Mile 35.1)** is the other Murphy Trail which runs down the dry wash. After this trailhead, there are several short steep places heading south but nothing really worth mentioning. When you reach the area at roughly **Km 57/Mile 35**, the road returns back down to the White Rim after running higher up and on a series of benches for 10-12 kms (6-7 miles).

Next point of interest on the White Rim Road will be the turnoff to the White Crack Trail & Campsite. This will be at **Km 67.2/Mile 41.8 from the T-Junction**. From that point turn south at the sign stating, *Whitecrack Campground, 2.2 kms--1.4 miles*. The next map covers that country.

Since the White Crack is roughly halfway around the White Rim, and since the starting point until now has been the **T-Junction** on the northwest end of the White Rim Road, it's been decided to begin counting kilomage/mileage on the eastern part of the White Rim from the **3-Way Junction** which is the starting point for this road in the northeast. That junction is 21.3 kms (13.2 miles) up from the Potash Boat Ramp along the Potash Road; or 8.8 kms (5.4 miles) down the Shafer Trail Road from the paved highway on top near the pay booth and visitor center.

A short distance below the top of **Junction Butte** is this difficult pitch. From this position, and for the final move, turn slowly and sit on a little flat place; at that point you're up safely. Or to the left 12-15m, is a 7m-high crack you can climb easily; it has lots of foot & hand holds.

Above Right Eph Moore on Hardscrabble Hill with a nice buck. It's believed this picture was taken in the early 1920's (?). (Ray Tibbetts Collection)

Above Left Bill Tibbetts on a raft crossing the Green River in the early 1920's, and before the range war. (Ray Tibbetts Collection)

Middle Eph Moore with sheep on his ranch in Moab in the 1930's (?). (Ray Tibbetts Collection)

Right This is **Will Murphy,** Verona Murphy Stocks' father and the one most-responsible for building the **Murphy Trail**. Will's boys are--oldest to youngest: Felix Grundy Murphy, Nicoles Joseph Murphy and Raymond Murphy in about 1916. (Connie Murphy Skelton Collection)

John (Sog) **Shafer** in the 1940's or early 50's (?). He was the one person most-responsible for the making of the **Shafer Trail**. Read the history of the building of the Shafer Trail Road starting on **page 232**. (Prommel Shafer Collection)

The big pinnacle on the left is **Monster Tower**. In the middle is the pinnacle with **Washer Woman Arch**, but no arch can be seen from this angle. This scene is from the overlook shown on **Map 20** which is near the elevation marked **1892m**. To get to that place, you should be able to park at mile post 13 with a bunch of old cedar trees stacked around--if not, park at the Mesa Arch Trailhead.

The White Crack Trail and the Confluence Overlook, and the Lathrop Sheep Trail into Monument Basin

Location & Access Shown on this map is the extreme southern part of Between the Rivers country, the White Rim & White Rim Road, and a small part of the southern tip of Grand View Point. Featured here will be an **old cattle trail** known as the **White Crack**, and several different routes and a **sheep trail** into the bottom of **Monument Basin**.

There are 2 ways to drive into this country. If you have a low slung car and can't drive on rough roads, you could drive the paved highway south from the Island Visitor Center to Grand View Point. From there you could backpack down from the **Grand View Point Trail**. Only problem with this is, distances are great and you have no wheels when you hit the White Rim Road. Also, coming down that so-called trail would be a little difficult & slow with a big pack. The other way would be to drive south along the eastern side of the White Rim Road, the part south of the **3-Way Junction**, and the Shafer Trail & Canyon and Potash Road. Any HC/2WD vehicle can normally make it to this mapped area OK using that route east of Grand View Point. In 1990 & '91, the author twice drove to the White Crack Campsite in his VW Rabbit which had oversized tires. Still another alternative is to use a mtn. bike. If you're using a bike, then you could probably get by with just a backcountry camping permit; if indeed the CNP allows that sort of thing. That may uncomplicate the camping permit end of this trip. Talk to someone at the reservations desk about options; Tele. 435-259-4351 between 8am-12 noon, M-F.

Elevations Grand View Point Overlook, 1914m; White Rim Road, averages about 1500m; bottom of Monument Basin, about 1300m; The Confluence of the Green & Colorado, about 1200m.

Water Basically none--**take your own!** There is however, a little seep at the head of Stove Canyon, the Dripping Spring in the drainage below Monument Basin in Standing Rock Canyon, and the Green River but you must treat that.

Maps USGS or BLM map La Sal (1:100,000); Monument Basin & Turks Head (1:24,000--7 1/2' quads); the plastic Trails Illustrated/National Geographic map Canyonlands National Park (1:70,000); or the plastic Latitude 40° map Moab West (1:75,000).

Main Attractions Three interesting routes down into Monument Basin, and a great hike down the White Crack Trail to an overlook at The Confluence of the Green & Colorado Rivers. Also, a trail down to the lower Green River through Stove Canyon.

The White Crack Trail: to The Confluence Overlook & the Green River

From the extreme southern end of the White Rim Road will be a sign pointing the way to the **White Crack Campsite**. This place will be at **Km 67.2 (Mile 41.8)** from the **T-Junction** near the mouth of Mineral Canyon; or **50.6 kms (31.4 miles)** from the **3-Way Junction** in Shafer Canyon. This 2.4 km (1.2 mile) side-track is less used than the main road, but it's still good, although a little sandy in places.

Just south of the White Crack Campsite is a cleft in the rim of the White Rim Sandstone. This is called the **White Crack**. First a little history on this old cow trail. The late **Kenny Allred** formerly of Moab seemed to know more about it than anyone, and this is part of what he said about it:

When I was just a kid the Murphy Trail [and the White Crack Trail] was built. My brother, Bill Tibbetts--that's Ray's dad--went with 'em [the Murphy brothers] when they took the first cattle there, and they took 'em clearn down in there. They took a bunch off into that country through the White Crack. When they put them cattle down there I think

Looking northwest at the very top of the **White Crack Trail** where it cuts down through the White Rim Sandstone. In the beginning, it was just a narrow crack and an Indian route; then the Murphys made it a cattle trail, and later the uranium miners blasted out a road down to the airstrip seen on the map.

Map 21, The White Crack Trail and the Confluence Overlook, and the Lathrop Sheep Trail into Monument Basin

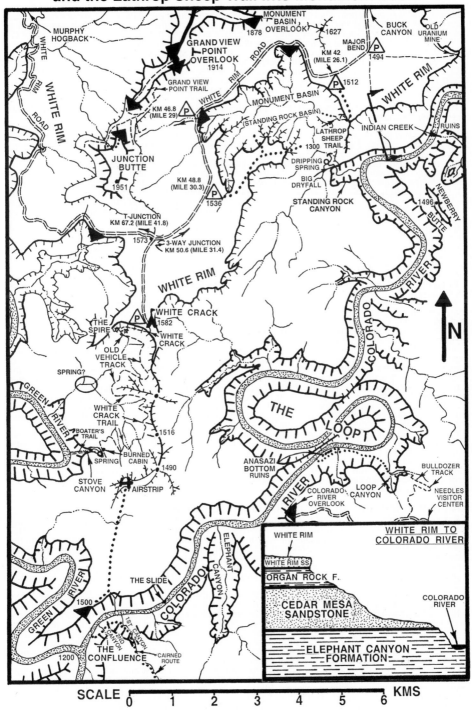

MURPHY HOGBACK

WHITE RIM

MONUMENT BASIN OVERLOOK 1878

GRAND VIEW POINT OVERLOOK 1914

GRAND VIEW POINT TRAIL

1627

KM 42 (MILE 26.1)

BUCK CANYON

OLD URANIUM MINE

MAJOR BEND P 1494

WHITE RIM

WHITE RIM ROAD

WHITE RIM ROAD

KM 46.8 (MILE 29) P

P 1512

MONUMENT BASIN

(STANDING ROCK BASIN)

LATHROP SHEEP TRAIL

INDIAN CREEK

RUINS

JUNCTION BUTTE

1951

KM 48.8 (MILE 30.3)

P 1536

DRIPPING SPRING

BIG DRYFALL

STANDING ROCK CANYON

1300

NEWBERRY BUTTE

1496

T-JUNCTION KM 67.2 (MILE 41.8)

1573

3-WAY JUNCTION KM 50.6 (MILE 31.4)

WHITE RIM

COLORADO RIVER

N

THE SPIRE

P WHITE CRACK 1582

WHITE CRACK

OLD VEHICLE TRACK

SPRING?

WHITE CRACK TRAIL

THE LOOP

GREEN RIVER

BOATER'S TRAIL

1516

SPRING

BURNED CABIN

STOVE CANYON

AIRSTRIP

1490

ANASAZI BOTTOM RUINS

COLORADO RIVER OVERLOOK

LOOP CANYON

BULLDOZER TRACK

NEEDLES VISITOR CENTER

COLORADO RIVER

THE SLIDE

ELEPHANT CANYON

GREEN RIVER

1500

1200

THE CONFLUENCE

1ST CANYON GRAND CANYON

CAIRNED ROUTE

WHITE RIM TO COLORADO RIVER

WHITE RIM

WHITE RIM SS

ORGAN ROCK F.

CEDAR MESA SANDSTONE

COLORADO RIVER

ELEPHANT CANYON FORMATION

SCALE 0 1 2 3 4 5 6 KMS

they just worked that trail over by hand, I don't believe they had any blasting powder. Bill Tibbetts was with 'em and Doc Tangren, he's dead now. He was Karl Tangren's uncle.

Well, the Murphy's took cattle down in there, and they built that trail as they went. And then they lost a bunch of them cattle that winter; they choked to death. They put 'em in there after a rainstorm, and there was water everwheres. There's a spring down in there, but them cattle didn't know where it was, because they could get water anywheres when they first went in there. The Murphys came back to town and didn't get back out there like they should have done and they lost a lot of cows. Fact of the matter was, I think that's what broke'em. They went out of the cow business a year or two after that. My brother [Bill Tibbetts] always told me that's what broke the Murphys.

The Murphys just built a trail down through there, and it was real rough. But when this Uranium Boom come in, that was about 1950, that's when they put the road down through there into that country [about 1954]. It was a uranium outfit. They was a takin' boats up and down the river, and going under that White Crack there, and comin' out that way and haulin' stuff in. Just a promotion outfit I think. There was quite a lot of that goin' on at the time.

Another man who knows something about the area around the White Crack is **Karl Tangren** of Moab. This is what he added to Kenny's story:

Grandma Durham was down in there in the early 1950's when the Uranium Boom hit, and they went there and staked that country along the lower Green. They boated down [to Stove Canyon], then they could walk out. Grover Perriman was one of them. They would boat down the Colorado and up the Green, because it was a lot easier than going around by jeep on the White Rim. They built that road off from the White Rim down to what they called the White Crack, and out to those mining claims.

Originally, there was an old horse trail there and my Uncle Clarence Tangren and Tom Murphy helped build it. When the Murphys run cattle in that country, my Uncle Clarence tells about Tom Murphy finding that crack--and they called it the White Crack--because it was just a crack which went down through the White Rim. They said there was an old Indian trail running off through there when they first seen it. So they shot and widened it and built-up a trail so they could put cattle down into that country Between the Rivers. This must have been in [about 1918]. [The Murphy Trail which comes off Grays Pasture--Island in the Sky--was built in about 1917 & '18]. They used to go out in that country in the snow, and when it would melt, it would fill lots of potholes in the slickrock. But those potholes dry up, and the only live water in the country was that little seep. Right in that vicinity somewhere is a canyon coming out of these red rims, and there's live [running] water in there. After you come down off the White Crack, then break out to the right, then just off from the Green River there's a canyon. There's enough live water to water a dozen cattle.

Read more oral history of this country and the late **Verona Murphy Stocks'** story about her father Will Murphy and the Murphy Trail on page 211.

Today the old cow trail is gone, replaced by a uranium miner's road, which is just a washed-out track today, and no wheeled vehicles are allowed down it. This means no mtn. bikes either; but it makes a great hiking trail. Once you get down off the White Rim, this track more of less contours at about the same elevation around a lot of little side-drainages. Some parts of this track runs across slickrock, so pay attention to the route. The old road ends at the airstrip shown on the map.

Just before you reach the airstrip, and down in a little canyon, is where the miners once had a camp. They used to have a **cabin** there, but it was burned down sometime in the 1980's. Nearby is a stack of pipes and 3 old metal bedsteads or army-style cots. If you'd like to reach the Green River, start at the old camp and walk southeast along the upper end of a little entrenched drainage to its head, then once on the southwest side of this drainage, look for a hiker's trail going down into the head of what this writer calls **Stove Canyon**; so called because at the very bottom near the river, is an old stove apparently brought there in the 1950's. Once in the bottom of this little drainage you may find water in the upper end. From there, climb down over one ledge then use a good boater's trail to reach the river. There's a good campsite at the river if you're interested.

If you'd like to see The Confluence from the north, then continue south on the old track from the old camp. Once you reach the airstrip, then just route-find across the flats just a little east of due south. Further on, angle a little to the southwest and you should come to one of many spots where you can look down at where the rivers meet. If you go all the way to the overlook, take water and a lunch and plan to take all day. Some may want 8-10 hours round-trip. Twice the author hiked from the river and his boat up to the White Crack; then another time he hiked down to The Confluence Overlook from the White Crack in about 6 hours round-trip.

Routes into Monument Basin (Formerly known as Standing Rock Basin)

Before going further, it must be noted that the original name for **Monument Basin** was **Standing Rock Basin**. That's the name all the old cattlemen and sheepherders called it in the early 1900's. This goes back at least to, or maybe before the Murphys built the Murphy Trail off the top and down to the White Rim in 1917 & '18. Also, the canyon draining out of it was always known as **Standing Rock Canyon**. If you go to page 374 and read the story of **Bill Tibbetts**, it was there at the mouth of Standing Rock Canyon that Sheriff Murphy caught up with Bill and cohort Tom Perkins after they broke out of jail on **July 30, 1924**. This information about Standing Rock Basin & Canyon comes from Karl Tangren of Moab.

There are a couple of routes into Monument Basin from the south and here's how to get there. From the turnoff to the White Crack you'll be heading northeast. After a couple of kms and at about **Km 48.8 (Mile 30.3** from the **3-Way Junction in Shafer Canyon)** look for a wide place in the road to park. There used to be an old vehicle track running out that way, but it's difficult to find so it's best just to walk cross-country from the main road with a map & compass in hand. From where you park, head due east for 500m or so, then veer ENE. After less than 2 kms from the road, you'll be at about where that old track ends. From there, you could walk north and route-find a way down. This may or may not go for some people. Getting off the White Rim itself will be the hardest part. Look for a break in the cliff.

Or, if you continue east about another km from the end of that track instead, you may find a few tracks leading down a minor little canyon. There's one ledge that will stop some hikers. It's easy to get down; the problem will be getting back up. Take a rope to hopefully solve that problem. You can also build a pile of rocks to stand on. The author tied a rope to a tree just in case, but managed to get back up without it. Once you get down the steep part, veer north and ledge-walk until you find a way down off another series of minor ledges. This will take a little route-finding. If this isn't for you, you may want to use the third and easiest way down into Monument Basin from the east side.

But before driving all the way around Monument Basin, you might consider hiking up to the southern tip of **Grand View Point** on the trail described in the previous chapter with **Map 20**, and perhaps to the top of **Junction Butte**. Park on the west side of the 'Basin where a minor drainage comes down from the west. This will be at about **Km 46.8 (Mile 29,** from the 3-Way Junction). From there walk more or less due west up along the dry wash, but be looking for an old miners exploration track. One of those old tracks will get upon the bench between Grand View Point and Junction Butte. From there follow other fading old mining exploration tracks in either direction to climb up either of your destinations. Climb Junction Butte from a route up the northwest face as described in the previous chapter.

The last hike here will be down the **Lathrop Sheep Trail** into Monument Basin from the east side. The man who developed this is the same sheepman from Colorado who built the Lathrop Trail down off the mesa into Lathrop Canyon.

This trail was built in the 1940's to take Lathrop's sheep to the bottom of Monument Basin. To get there, drive to the northeastern part of the 'Basin and park somewhere along the road, preferable on slickrock. One place will be at about **Km 42 (Mile 26.1)**; then walk in a southern direction not far from the rim of the Monument Basin. After about 2 1/2 kms, you'll come to the edge of the White Rim with a narrow point of rocks extending south. Right where the White Rim narrows to virtually nothing, look on the west side for a route down in a crack heading back 180° to the north. On this writer's last visit in 2011, there were a couple of cairns marking the upper part. It may be a little difficult at first to see a trail, but a trail is visible further on. From the top, you'll be walking down in toward the north, then after a ways, you'll see where the trail zig zags down a sandy & rocky slope facing west. At the bottom of the steep part, the trail disappears, but you can simply walk north into the main part of Monument Basin. The author has been to the bottom of Monument Basin 3 times using different routes.

Incidentally, there's a **big dryfall** about 500m up from the river, which will prevent you from walking all the way downcanyon to the Colorado. There's also a real good **dripping spring** under one ledge in the lower end of the drainage not far above the big dryfall. That's the only reliable water in this area and big horn sheep use it all the time; in fact, the author met a small herd there on his last trip.

This is **the spire** (see map) you'll see about 400-500m below the top of the original **White Crack**. Look closely to the middle right, and the middle of this picture, and you'll see the former uranium mining road put in sometime in the early to mid-1950's. It makes a good trail today so it's an easy walk down to **Stove Canyon** and the former **miner's cabin**.

This is all that's left of an old **miner's cabin** which was located at the head of what this writer calls, **Stove Canyon**. You can see the upper shallow end of Stove Canyon on the right. In the distance, and in the upper middle part of this picture, is the road running up to the top of a hill and an airstrip.

From near the site of the old miner's cabin (see picture above), you'll have a good look down into the **Green River Gorge.** Looking west at **Stove Canyon** in the bottom left part of this picture, **Elaterite Butte** is to the upper left, and **Ekker Butte** is in the upper right-hand corner.

Above This picture was taken from the old trail down to **The Confluence** of the **Green** (middle right) and the **Colorado Rivers** (coming in from the bottom right). That former trail which is in The Needle District, is now just a cairned route, and is best shown on the lower left-hand side of **Map 21**.

Left This is what this writer calls **Dripping Spring**; it's located in the lower end of **Standing Rock Canyon** which drains Monument Basin (formerly known as Standing Rock Basin). Water drips off several ledges and should have good running water year-round. You can get down to this level by walking along the rim in the upper left, and route-find down a natural break in the ledges. That's the way big horn sheep get down to this water.

The 1973 Airplane Crash, and Dogleg, Gooseberry, Buck and Lower Lathrop Canyons

Location & Access The canyons featured on this map are below the White Rim and all drain eastward into the Colorado River. They're also just east of Grand View Point and Mesa Arch. The **best way** to get to this part of the White Rim is to drive down the **Shafter Trail Road** from the mesa top to the **3-Way Junction** (see Maps 18 & 23) marked with a public **toilet**, then continue east straight ahead on the beginning of the **White Rim Road**. Or, drive southwest from Potash on the **Potash Road** into Shafer Canyon (this has a couple of very rough places and you'll need a HC/4WD to go up that section), then at the 3-Way Junction turn left or east onto the beginning of the White Rim Road.

Elevations Airport Tower, 1772m; White Rim Road, 1400-1500m, Colorado River, about 1210m.

Water Take all the water you'll need because there's none on the White Rim. However, there may be some spring water in Buck, Gooseberry & Dogleg Canyons as shown and described on the map. You can now get water at an **outside fountain** at the Island Visitor Center, your last place to fill up.

Maps USGS or BLM map La Sal (1:100,000); Monument Basin & Musselman Arch (1:24,000--7 1/2' quads); the plastic Trails Illustrated/National Geographic map Canyonlands National Park (1:70,000); or the plastic Latitude 40° map Moab West (1:75,000).

Main Attractions Here-to-fore seldom-visited canyons, a closeup look at Monument Basin, an airplane crash site and nearby uranium mines, and a chance to see desert big horn sheep.

The 1973 Airplane Crash and Dogleg Canyon

To get close to a **1973 airplane crash site** and nearby uranium mines, make your way to the area just east of the northern parts of Monument Basin. At a **major bend** in the road which is at **Km 41.1(Mile 25.2** from the **3-Way Junction)** stop and park. This will be in the middle of a great big flat area. At that point you may see an old faded vehicle track heading due south. This is the remains of an old 1950's Uranium Boom road, of which there are many in this region. The White Rim Road is one of them; but it's the only one that hasn't been blocked off.

Just east of this major bend, is where a **plane crashed** on May 19, 1973. First, a little history of the event. Here's what *The Times-Independent* of Moab had to say about it in the *May 24, 1973* paper:

A tragic plane crash in Canyonlands National Park on Saturday, May 19, took the lives of three Park Service employees and owner of Canyonlands Aviation, Dick Smith.

National Park Service officials reported that pilot Dick Smith took off about 6:30 a.m. with park employees John Ebersole, a seasonal ranger; Bill Cooper, a research biologist; and Charles Hansen, an expert on Desert Bighorn Sheep from Las Vegas; on a search for bands of Desert Bighorn within the National Park boundaries.

When the men failed to return by mid-afternoon, a search was begun by David Minor, District Ranger at Needles; Fred Eyman, a pilot working at Canyonlands Resort and Rick Simmons, a volunteer working for the Park Service. The wreckage of the Cessna Super 185 was spotted near a portion of the White Rim trail at about 5:40 p.m. and San Juan County Sheriff Rigby Wright, along with National Park Service officials left by ground shortly after. They reached the craft about dark and discovered the four bodies shortly after sunrise on Sunday. They reported that all four were apparently killed instantly.

The late **Tex McClatchy**, the former river rat from Moab, was a friend of Dick Smith. He said they took off from Canyonlands Resort in The Needles, which is now called **Needles Outpost**. They were rim-flying low very near the White Rim escarpment and most probably hit a sudden down-draft, as there were some thunder storms in the area during the night. The plane burned, and some of it is undoubtedly still there. The people who got to the wreckage used a route something like that shown on the map.

Former sheriff **Rigby Wright** told this writer: *they came down an* **old track** *to a* **uranium mine**, *then turned south a ways. The wreckage is at the head of the little canyon just northwest of the west end of Sheep Bottom and south of the head of Sheep Canyon. It's on the most level place around, indicating Smith may have tried to stall the plane on a level spot.*

To get to this crash site, which likely will not be visible, walk due south from the **major bend** on a barely visible old mining track; after about 250-300m you should be on a long narrow section of **slickrock**. At the north end of that, look for an old rusty tin can with stones on it, and another small cairn just to the left or east which is on another old track. Walk due east on this **2nd track** for about 2 kms. At that point you should be at or near the lip of the plateau and the White Rim. Continue to follow the same track as it runs along the top of a finger or peninsula of land jutting northeast. By staying on this old track, you'll zig zag down the north side of this promontory and end up at 2 parts of an **old open-pit uranium mine** in the Organ Rock Formation--this is the only place this writer has seen uranium mines in that particular formation.

From this old mine site, contour south and southwest for another km or so. Somewhere in that area is the crash site. You'd likely have to be right on it to see it, something the author hasn't done yet. According to Rigby Wright, it was burned up real bad and so were the passengers. He said Smith's body was outside the plane and wasn't killed instantly--as he had reported the gruesome scene to the press.

Now back on the White Rim Road. If you're looking for an easy route down to the Colorado River, there's one in **Dogleg Canyon**. Walk northeast from the **major bend** as shown on the map (there may be an old vehicle track there, but the author didn't notice one in 2011). When you reach the edge of the White Rim, look for the head of a canyon running almost due north. Before going down, look for desert big horn sheep; there's quite a few in this area, especially at the head of Sheep Canyon.

Once you find the top of this drainage, route-find in and head north downcanyon. About halfway down you'll come to a minor **spring** or seep and maybe a trickle of water. How much water there is will depend on the season, but it seems to be a year-round source (?). About halfway down the second half of the *"dogleg"* is a wet spot under a **ledge**; it was a spring in 1991, but just a damp place in 2011. After another km or so you'll be at the river. If you like, walk north along a bench upriver another km to the bottom end of **Gooseberry Canyon**. Right at the mouth of Gooseberry is an old **corral** or **holding pen** built and used by Karl Tangren in the early 1950's.

If you walk up Gooseberry about 1 km, you'll come to real good spring under an overhang. **Karl Tangren** of Moab used to have a camp in this area when they ran cattle there before it became a national park. You can't climb this ledge, but you can regress about 100m, and climb up on a little bench on the north side. From there you can walk all the way upcanyon. Not much to see there, but there may be a spring or a little more water (?). That spring in the lower end of Gooseberry is the best one on this map.

In the past, you could have walked up along the river into the lower end of Buck Canyon on an old

Map 22, The 1973 Airlane Crash, and Dogleg, Gooseberry, Buck and Lower Lathrop Canyons

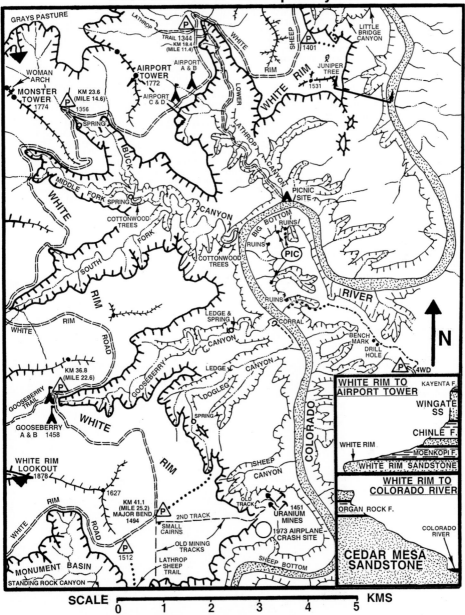

cattle trail, but it's overgrown with tamarisks now, so this is not a good idea. Cattle did it in the 1950's but that was before the tamarisk invasion.

Buck and Lower Lathrop Canyons

Going north now from the route to Dogleg Canyon, you'll first come to the **Gooseberry Campsites A & B** at **Km 37.3 (Mile 23.2 from the 3-Way Junction)** and 450m beyond, the beginning (or end) of the **Gooseberry (Government) Trail** at **Km 36.8 (Mile 22.6)**. Most people prefer to hike this one from the top down because of better road conditions on Grand View Point.

From Gooseberry, continue north around the South and Middle Forks of Buck Canyon. Then finally you'll come to the **North Fork** of **Buck Canyon** at **Km 23.6 (Mile 14.6)**. It was there a very rough spot existed in 1991, but that's been fixed and it's no longer an issue. If you park right there next to the dry creek bed, you can literally walk right down the canyon bottom. If the campsite permits are gone when you arrive, you could get a backcountry camping permit, and walk down this canyon a ways and camp (?). Ask someone at the backcountry desk if that's still possible (?).

Going down Buck Canyon now. After about 350m, you'll likely find a small **spring**, but this depends on the season. It may dry up after a long dry spell. Further downcanyon, and just below the confluence of the North & Middle Fork of Buck, will be another small **spring** that appears to be permanent. There may be running water there in winter, or soon after a storm & flood. Nearby are lots of cottonwood trees. From there, you can walk all the way down to the Colorado River.

When asked how this canyon got it's name, **Karl Tangren** said: *Old Howard Lathrop put his buck sheep in there. He'd pull his bucks out of the herd when he wintered down on the White Rim. There was a trail in then and he had a fence across the mouth, so they couldn't get out of that canyon. He'd pull them out of the herd after the breeding season, and put 'em in Buck Canyon until they were ready to move out of there in the spring. This happened during the 1940's & early '50's when Lathrop was herding sheep in that part of the country.*

Driving north again, you'll pass the campsites at **Airport A, B, C & D** about 800m apart, and at about **Km 20.2 (Mile 12.5)**. From either of these campsites, you'll have some nice views of **Airport Tower** just to the northwest. Next point of interest going north would be **Lower Lathrop Canyon**. The turnoff to the lower canyon is at **Km 18.4 (Mile 11.4)**, and it's signposted for **4WD's only**. In the past, the worst part of this road was right where it cuts down through the White Rim Sandstone. It used to be steep and rough and most 2WD's couldn't make it back up! It's better now. It's also sandy in places in the lower end. Right where the canyon empties into the Colorado River, is the **Lathrop Picnic Site**.

Just north of that turnoff 150m is the end (or beginning) of the **Lathrop Trail** which heads toward the mesa above. That hike coming down the Lathrop Trail will be discussed with the next map, but the lower end of this canyon, not far from the White Rim Road, is perhaps the most spectacular site in the park. About 45 minutes walking from the White Rim Road, will put you where the highest mines are located, and in the deepest and most-impressive part of this canyon.

This canyon was named after **Howard Lathrop**, who first came into this country with sheep in the late 1930's or early '40's. He probably had a trail down into the lower end to the river, but the road was built sometime after 1953 by the uranium miners who had mines up in the canyon above the White Rim Road (see Map 23). They built the road so they could drive down to the river to get water for their mining operations above. Howard Lathrop's sheep and grazing permits in this country were bought by the French Basque Martin Etchart in 1955, and all grazing permits were withdrawn in 1978--that's when all the livestock grazing in this part of the park ended.

In the lower half of **Dog-leg Canyon** is this dropoff or **ledge**. In 1990, it had enough water to get a drink, but in the dry summer of 2012, it was just a wet spot.

Above From the end of the finger or peninsula of land near the **1973 plane crash site**, looking northeast and down at one of 2 small open pit **uranium mines**. **Sheep Canyon** is in the near distance to the left, while the Colorado River is in the middle background. The plateau in the upper right is **Hatch Point**.

Left The nice year-round **spring** in lower **Gooseberry Canyon** that's under a ledge.

The Neck Spring & Lathrop Trails, the Shafer Trail Road, and Shafer, Musselman & Little Bridge Canyons

Location & Access The 3 minor canyons and 2 sheep trails on this map are near the **Island Visitor Center.** If your destination is some place on this map, then it's best to stop at the visitor center first; get the latest word on road and trail conditions, then go from there. The trailhead for the **Neck Spring Loop Trail** is the **Shafer Canyon Overlook** located about 1 km south of the visitor center and immediately north of **The Neck**. The parking place for hiking down the **Lathrop Trail** is just up the road from **mile post 9** and in the northern part of **Grays Pasture**. Look for the little **butte** just east of the trailhead.

The road that replaced the old **Shafer Trail** begins about 2 kms north of the visitor center and between the **pay booth & mile post 6**. It zig zags down the South Fork of Shafer Canyon to the east to intersect the White Rim & Potash Roads. For this book, we'll call that the **3-Way Junction**. All the dirt roads on this map are for HC cars & pickups. The worst part of any road on this map is where the Potash Road runs along the bottom of Shafer Canyon. You'll need a HC/4WD for that part. You can also reach this eastern part of the White Rim Road via Potash to the east and the **Potash Road**--but that one section of road is terrible, and the NPS will never fix it! Best to reach the White Rim Road from the top and visitor center. The Shafer Trail Road is generally good for cars down to the 3-Way Junction.

Elevations Visitor center, at a cool 1789m; Shafer Canyon Overlook & parking for Neck Spring Trail, 1768m; Lathrop Trail parking, 1829m; Musselman Arch, 1403m; Colorado River, about 1210m.

Water Bring all the water you'll need for your trip, but there is an **outside tap** at the visitor center; but they have to haul it up from Moab! There's also a spring or two in lower Musselman Canyon but the amount of flow will depend on the season. There are also several springs along the Neck Spring Trail.

Maps USGS or BLM map La Sal (1:100,000); Musselman Arch (1:24,000--7 1/2' quad); the plastic Trails Illustrated/National Geographic map, Canyonlands National Park (1:70,000); or the plastic Latitude 40° map Moab West (1:75,000).

Main Attractions In summer it's cooler on top of Grays Pasture than in most other locations in this region; a couple of maintained trails, one of which goes down to the White Rim; at least 3 places to hike down to the Colorado River.

From Grays Pasture Plateau: The Neck Spring Loop Trail

The first hike here starts about 1 km south of the visitor center. Park on the east side of the highway at the **Shafer Trail Overlook**. The **Neck Spring Loop Trail** starts there, then crosses the highway to the west, drops down through a couple of Navajo ledges and turns south. This is a good marked trail and has moderate use.

To the south will be several alcoves and inside each will be a small spring with lots of greenery, including gamble oak Some of these springs may dry up in summer or in periods of drought, but 3 have been troughed-up for sheep or cattle. The troughs you see there were put in sometime in the late 1930's by a government program to improve grazing on the public domain; read more below. From **Neck Spring**, the trail heads in a westerly direction along the top of a Kayenta bench. Further on, the trail heads south toward **Cabin Spring**. Along the way, you'll see the remains of an old cabin--more below.

From near where the cabin remains are, the trail climbs upon the Navajo bench to the west, then heads south. To visit Cabin Spring, you'd have to stay down in the drainage. Immediately above Cabin Spring and on the bench or rim above, will be more old **water troughs**. At one time, the water was

First stop from the trailhead on the **Neck Spring Trail** are these former water troughs. USGS maps show Neck Spring in the drainage south of this alcove. It too has old watering troughs.

Map 23, The Neck Spring & Lathrop Trails, the Shafer Trail Road, and Shafer, Musselman & Little Bridge Canyons

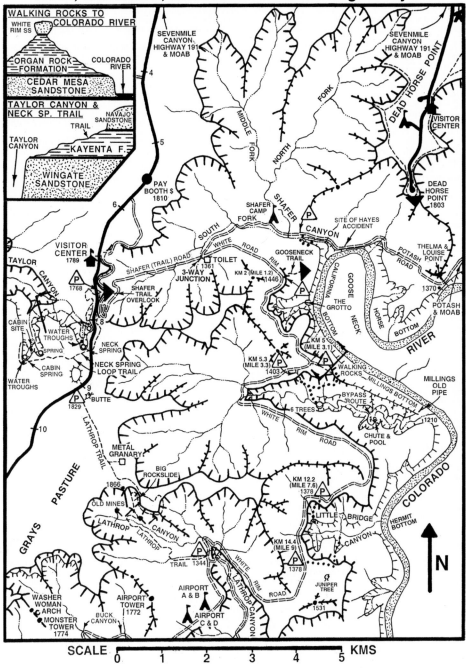

WALKING ROCKS TO COLORADO RIVER
WHITE RIM SS
ORGAN ROCK FORMATION
COLORADO RIVER
CEDAR MESA SANDSTONE
TAYLOR CANYON & NECK SP. TRAIL
NAVAJO SANDSTONE
TRAIL
TAYLOR CANYON
KAYENTA F.
WINGATE SANDSTONE

SEVENMILE CANYON HIGHWAY 191 & MOAB

SEVENMILE CANYON HIGHWAY 191 & MOAB

DEAD HORSE POINT

VISITOR CENTER

MIDDLE FORK

NORTH FORK

SHAFER

DEAD HORSE POINT 1803

PAY BOOTH $ 1810

SHAFER CAMP FORK

CANYON

SITE OF HAYES ACCIDENT

SOUTH FORK

WHITE RIM ROAD

GOOSENECK TRAIL

THELMA & LOUISE POINT

POTASH ROAD

VISITOR CENTER 1789

SHAFER (TRAIL) ROAD

TOILET

3-WAY JUNCTION 1361

KM 2 (MILE 1.2) 1446

CALIFORNIA BOTTOM

GOOSE NECK

1370

POTASH & MOAB

TAYLOR CANYON

P 1768

SHAFER TRAIL OVERLOOK

THE GROTTO

HORSE BOTTOM

RIVER

CABIN SITE

WATER TROUGHS

SPRING

NECK SPRING

NECK SPRING LOOP TRAIL

KM 5.3 (MILE 3.3) 1403

KM 5 (MILE 3.1)

P

P

WALKING ROCKS

MILLINGS BOTTOM

MILLINGS OLD PIPE

CABIN SPRING

WATER TROUGHS

BUTTE 1829

BYPASS ROUTE

6 TREES

WHITE RIM ROAD

CHUTE & POOL

1210

LATHROP TRAIL

METAL GRANARY

BIG ROCKSLIDE

KM 12.2 (MILE 7.6) 1378

P

COLORADO

GRAYS PASTURE

1866

OLD MINES

LATHROP CANYON

LATHROP

LITTLE BRIDGE

HERMIT BOTTOM

KM 14.4 (MILE 9) 1378

LITTLE BRIDGE CANYON

P

WASHER WOMAN ARCH

MONSTER TOWER 1774

BUCK CANYON

AIRPORT TOWER 1772

AIRPORT A & B

TRAIL 1344

WHITE RIM ROAD

LATHROP CANYON

AIRPORT C & D

JUNIPER TREE

1531

N

SCALE 0 1 2 3 4 5 KMS

pumped up from Cabin Spring to the flats above. Just east of the troughs are some remains of that pumping operation. From there the trail heads east to the highway. From the highway, you can road-walk back to your car; or stay on the trail which is on the east side of the paved road. Part of the trail runs along an old road, perhaps the remains of the original track used by livestockmen.

The Neck Spring Trail makes a 9.3 km loop-hike and there should be water at a couple of the springs, although it may be hard to get to. Best to take you own. Most people will want about half a day for this loop, but it can be done in as little as 2 1/4 hours; this was the author's time in 4/2012, but he stopped for a lot of fotos.

Now back to the little cabin below Cabin Spring. The late **Kenny Allred** of Moab was in that country with cattle from the mid-1920's until into the 1960's, and here's what he remembered about Neck and Cabin Springs and the little half-built cabin there:

It was Deb Taylor who told me about that cabin. It's made out of quakin' aspen. He cut 'em right out of that little alcove in there where that water is. Deb built that cabin back in my time, but he never did finish it. All he done was stuck up the walls, and he just kinda used it for a corral to keep his stuff in. He had an old trunk in there, I remember that, but he didn't even have a roof on top of it. It probably dates back to about the late 1920's when it was built. He was kind of a funny feller, he might of been 3 or 4 years buildin' it. There used to be one quaky left in there and the damn bank was about to cave off and get in there last time I was there.

*About those troughs above **Cabin Spring**, the sheepmen brought them in there and set 'em up and put a pump in. There's a spring down underneath right in the head of that little alcove. They had a pump in there for years. Then after the Park Service moved in, they went in and took that pump out.*

*Now those troughs at **Neck Spring** was put in by the government during the 1930's, and they were something like the WPA--a drought relief program--or something like that. Those up on the top above Cabin Spring was put in maybe as late as **1945**. They only used it a couple of years. The sheepmen got to where they wasn't crowdin' it so much after the Grazing Service came in there and they quit fightin' over that country as much. They began to be a little more slack about usin' that country than they was before. Before, they were tryin' everything in the world to choke the cattlemen out. Those troughs above Cabin Spring was put in quite a little while after the Taylor Grazing went in (7/27/1934).*

If you look closely at a good topo map of this area, you'll notice there's a very narrow gap between the head of Shafer Canyon to the east, and the upper end of Taylor Canyon on the west. Where it narrows to almost nothing it's called **The Neck**. Everything to the south of that has always been known locally as **Grays Pasture**--but the new-comers to this country began calling it Island in the Sky. It seems they forgot to ask the locals if they had a name for that area. Ever since about 1900, there was a horse trail across this gap, but it was much later when a road was first put across. The late **Kent Johnson** of Moab, who worked for the Dalton Wells CCC Camp starting in late **July, 1941**, told this writer about the first road across The Neck:

*Orson (Snick) Dalton was workin' for me out at Dalton Wells CCC Camp, and he took a Cat out there to fix up the trail across The Neck just south of the visitor center. When the CCC's finished those reservoirs on Big Flat, he took a Cat across The Neck. He was the first guy to take a Caterpillar across there. This was in **September of 1941**. Then later on when I was with the Grazing Service before I went into the war, I pushed a road across so you could travel it with a pickup. I went across The Neck and south down past the Murphy Trail, then on down to where you could look off **Grand View Point**. Just a bulldozer road and I was on the Caterpillar myself. I would say this was in about 1942. Then I came back and pushed the road over toward **Upheaval Dome**. The reason I did that, was that **John Allise** wanted me to build him a road off there some place so he could get down to his sheep herd. After I pushed that road over there, you could get a pickup over to the head of the **Wilhite Trail**. Then I walked that country huntin' for a way down. Allise wanted a road down off the rim, but it would have cost too much. At the time I built that road across Grays Pasture, I was being paid by the **Grazing Service** [in 1946 it became the BLM] and John Allise had his sheep down below the Murphy Trail. He just turned 'em loose down on the White Rim.*

The Lathrop Trail from Grays Pasture

About 3 kms south of The Neck, and just west of **mile post 9**, will be the trailhead parking place for the **Lathrop Trail**. There's a sign and an obvious parking place. From there at 1829m altitude, you walk southeast across the grassy parkland known as **Grays Pasture**, and along what used to be an old road used by sheepherders, most by **Howard Lathrop**, for whom this trail was named. After 2 kms, you'll see a metal structure on the left (somewhere in that area is an old drill hole site as well). It was a **granary** used for storing supplies for Lathrop's sheepherders down on the White Rim. About a km beyond the granary, the trail reaches slickrock and begins to wander around; but it's a well-used cairned trail so you can't get lost. Soon you'll drop off the Navajo Sandstone ledges onto one of the Kayenta benches below. Once there, the trail first contours south, then west into the upper end of Lathrop Canyon. Finally, the trail zig zags down over a big **rockslide** covering the Wingate Sandstone (which normally forms a big cliff in this part of the country). At the bottom, the trail disappears, but you then follow the stone cairns along a 1950's uranium **miner's track**. It's in that part at about where the old trail ends, and you get on the old mining roads, the scenery is at its best--and the canyon at its deepest. Be on the lookout for old uranium mine tunnels; there are several in the area, but they've all been blocked off to public access (apparently because of poisonous gases?). This trail takes you down to the White Rim Road, to the beginning of lower Lathrop Canyon, and to the Colorado River along a 4WD road.

If your plans are to get to the White Rim Road, then be sure to take water and a lunch. It took the author about 4 1/2 hours round-trip once, but you'll likely want most of a day for this trip. In 5/2012, the author came up from the White Rim Road to where the trail climbs up the big rockslide, saw a couple of mines, took a lot of picture and returned in 1 2/3 hours.

Now a little history of how this trail came to be. **Kent Johnson** and his father had cattle in this country (below the Island or Grays Pasture) for years long before the park came to be, and he remembered a few things about it and some of the sheepmen in this country:

*We originally bought the permits for Shafer Basin country from the **Shafer Brothers**. That was John Shafer, who was called **Sog**, and his brother **Frank**. This was along in the early 1930's. That was for under the Big Flat ledge, along the river, and clearn up along that canyon. We called it the Shafer Basin.*

*Now my dad [Wash Johnson] died February 14, 1941, and it was just a year or two after that, probably 1942 or '43, that I rounded up the cattle and shipped 'em, and sold the permits to **Jim Brown**. It was within a couple of weeks that Brown lost a bunch of his sheep. They must have got to eating the red*

Looking west into the head of **Lathrop Canyon** from the Lathrop Trail, part of which runs along the highest bench formed by the Kayenta Formation.

Looking across **lower Lathrop Canyon** with the White Rim running horizonal across the middle of this picture. Looking west with **Airport Tower** to the upper left, the **road** into Lathrop to the right, and upper Lathrop Canyon to the far right and just out of sight.

clay down there--for salt no doubt. They had a salt deficiency and it killed about half of his sheep. That about wiped Brown out, so he ended up selling out to **Howard Lathrop** (and cattleman **Herman Rowe**) from [Montrose], Colorado. Howard Lathrop and John Allise and all them Colorado sheepmen moved in there in the **early 1940's** (read more about the history cattle in Shafer Basin on **page 264)**.

After Lathrop got the permits, and got down in there onto the White Rim, he made this trail down that canyon. Otherwise in order to get supplies down to his camp on the White Rim, he had to go clearn around and down the Shafer; so the trail in Lathrop Canyon was a lot shorter. I would say it was built sometime in the **mid-1940's**. I don't know when Lathrop left [1955--read more below], but those Colorado sheepmen sort of fizzled away about 20 years ago [this interview was in 1991].

Lathrop and Allise liked it down there on the White Rim because there were no coyotes. Ya see, there's no rabbits or anything for coyotes to eat; so if they didn't follow the sheep down, there just wasn't any coyotes.

To get more accurate dates for grazing permits, etc, one of the old sheepmen was contacted in 12/2012. That was **Martin Etchart** from Montrose, Colorado. He was 87, and still didn't speak English too well, but here's what he remembered about his sheepherding days in what is now Canyonlands NP:

I was 21 years old when I came here in 1947 from Europe; I am French Basque sheepman. And John Allise, he had 3000 sheep and I started workin' for him, and I work 8 1/2 years for John Allise. I think I bought Lathrop [permit] in 1955; I bought his grazing permit and sheep and everything. I bought Howard Lathrop [grazing permit] before I was married. I bought John Allise [permit] too, in 1965. We took sheep out there every year.

John Holeman, he had permit on top; Big Flat and Dead Horse Point. John Holeman, he was my neighbor. Howard Lathrop, he had permit on top too--Big Flat, big beautiful place, you know. Brink Spring, that was Howard Lathrop spring too [for grazing]. That good spring, you bet! On Grand View Point was John Allise permit. Mineral Point, that used to be Jim Brown permit.

In 1978 [NPS/CNP records show all grazing permits expired June 30, 1975], they kick all those sheep out of there, and cows too. We were 6 or 7 sheepmen, and everyone of them dead--I'm only one alive. The rest of sheepmen all dead. My wife, she pass away in 1998.

I had Lathrop and John Allise permits, and I lost all those permits! They [NPS & BLM] gave us nothing! They just take it away, the permits. When we bought 'em [from] government, we had to pay, but they never pay us nothing!

History of the Shafer Trail Road

Normally getting up or down the **Shafer Trail Road** isn't a problem, but be sure to check on its condition before leaving the Island Visitor Center; or inquire at the visitor center in the middle of Moab. Before moving on, first a little history about this famous livestock trail and later road.

The man most responsible for the Shafer Trail and of course its name was **John (Sog) Shafer** (see foto on page 217). According to one of Sog's sons, **Prommel Shafer** and his wife Clara, this is how that road came to be:

Now what Sog told me, it was an Indian trail before he started using it. He said that people from Robbers Roost were using it also. He told me the only thing he ever did was clear off the brush so the cattle could get by more easily. As far as improving it any, other than moving a few rocks and clearing the brush, he didn't make any improvements. There was already a trail there, an Indian or game trail.

John Sog Shafer was born in 1894 and was married in 1920. He was 26 years old

From the **Shafer Trail Overlook** you'll have some nice views of various parts of the **Shafer Trail Road**. Here, you're looking nearly due south at the upper switchbacks of this now-famous road. This is the part that requires some maintenance after every big storm.

when he got married, and he built the trail before he was married. It must have been completed before 1918, because the Murphy Brothers took cattle up it that year. It appears it may have been built sometime in the late 1910's, perhaps at about the same time John Jackson sold his grazing rights to what was later called the Shafer Basin country, because of an impending divorce, which was the summer of 1917.

For years it was used by Sog and Frank Shafer who wintered cattle down in Shafer Basin, and summered them up on the Big Flat country. Later it was used by sheepmen heading down on the White Rim. Still later, uranium miners establish mining claims down in what is now called upper Lathrop Canyon and in Shafer Basin, so they began looking for ways to get the ore out. It was in the **summer and fall of 1952** when the road construction took place. Part of the story is told in **The Times Independent (TI)** newspaper of Moab from **July to September, 1952**.

As far as the construction of the road is concerned, **Nick Murphy** was the only one alive in 1992 who actually worked on the project. It was Murphy who was elected construction manager for the project, with **D.H. Shields** as secretary & treasurer. This is how **Nick** told the story:

Now what started the Shafer Trail Road Project was an oil well outfit down the river which was run by **Monte Mason**. The guy doing the drilling at the time was Chet Smith. This was in the 1940's, and was in the area of the old Shafer Wells [believed to be near the Frank Shafer Well No. 1, the first oil well in the area]. One time my brother Felix and someone else walked down from the head of the Shafer Trail, and Chet Smith put my jeep on a barge and we went down the river. They came from one side and we went in from the other. We met probably halfway down. All I ever asked my brother was, can we do it? And he said yes. That was the beginning of the Shafer Trail Road Project. This would have been during the first week of **July, 1952**.

But before that, I went in the service, and after I got home, me and a friend went prospecting. You couldn't sell a pound of uranium anywhere then, but we prospected for over a year anyway. My brother, he'd been prospecting and located what was called the **Mile High Group** of claims just west of where the Potash plant is today. Now a whole group of people located claims all the way down along the White Rim and up to Mineral Canyon. Finally the Metals Reserves was formed--in other words, the Atomic Energy Commission, and we could sell ore again.

When we finally started the road, Nate Knight and Norm Hettman worked for me. I hired Nate Knight--he was my cousin--and I put probably $25,000 of my own money into that road. My occupation at the time was a miner, and I had my own Cats and equipment to build the road with. Nate Knight had his own Cat too.

After we started it, about August 1, 1952, we finished the road in about 3 months. It was finished sometime in October, 1952. There was **Bud Mertz, Nate Knight, Norm Hettman, Bill Tibbetts, and myself Nick Murphy**--that's all there was. After we came down the Shafer Trail, we built the road over to the claims west of Potash. The first road up along the river, from Moab to Potash, was put in about a year later [cobbled together in 1953 or '54, but was useable only when the Colorado had low water; a more usable version was completed in 1963]. After the [Shafer] road was built, we took ore out up the Shafer in a small single-axle truck. At the top of the Shafer, there was a bin set up, and drivers would dump ore there, then the bigger trucks took it to the warehouse. The big trucks took the ore out along the Dubinky Road. The Sevenmile Canyon Road came a year or two later.

Then **Nate Knight** built the road down to the confluence of the 2 rivers. That was the **eastern half of the White Rim Road**. There was an engineer who had a mining operation down there. He had some claims and was mining, and that's why the White Rim Road was built.

D.H. Shields was the secretary of the operation. He kept track of the money. You see, there was a lot of money put into that Shafer Trail by local businesses. The oil well company put up so much money, and other businesses put up more, but the big uranium companies wouldn't put up any money--said it couldn't be done! And so we just went around and got donations from businesses and the oil company.

Later the Atomic Energy Commission spent about 2 years trying to get me to relinquish any right I had on that road. I was a little angry at them anyway, because they wouldn't put up any money for the road's construction. Then finally I thought well, OK, and I did sign a release. Then they spent quite a lot of money on the road upgrading it; but it's right where we put it. They did that 2 or 3 years after we built the original road [in 1955 or '56]. The uranium hauling stopped when the Atomic Energy Commission quit buying ore. The main boom lasted only 3 or 4 years.

If you're coming from Potash and along the Potash Road, you may have an opportunity to reach the Colorado River right at the bottom end of Shafer Canyon. The lower part of this canyon for about one km is boxed in by cliffs, but if you stop and walk around to the south side of the boxed-in part, you can climb down through a crack in the limestone rim and into the lower end and to the Colorado.

On the ledge immediately east of the mouth of Shafer Canyon, is an overlook right on the Potash Road. There was once a tragic accident right there on these cliffs. It seems that 59 year-old **Ed Hayes** of Moab fell to his death there in late August, 1967. The **August 28, 1967**, issue of **TI** carried the story: Mr. Hayes, a lifetime resident of the area, was employed as driver for Ottinger Tours. He was conducting a tour of the White Rim country for a group of midwestern tourists, and while posing for photographs at the high point overlooking the Colorado river canyon, apparently slipped on loose rocks and plunged some 500 feet to his death.

Here's the story of another tragic accident that happened to **Omer Secrest** of Moab somewhere in the upper North Fork of **Shafer Canyon** as told by **Karl Tangren**. The story was also told in the **January 10, 1952** issue of the **TI** of Moab:

Omer had 2 boys, **Art** and **Ervine**, and one daughter Patsy; and I married Patsy. They was mining up in the North Fork of the Shafer Canyon, and there was no roads down in that country in them days, but they built a trail off the high rim and down a ways into the North Fork. They had to go down over them ledges on ropes, but then they started stringin' some cable; they was gonna build'em a tramway from the mine up to the top so they pull the ore up in a bucket on a cable.

And Omer was down there that day and they let the big cable down over the ledge, and since he was an oil field man and knew how to splice cable and stuff, he went down to the bottom and the 2 boys stayed up on top and lowered that cable. He got it and drug it down to their mine and it went a round a big rock and he spliced it together and everthing, and then he was comin' up out of there that night about 5 o'clock. They said he was comin' up over a ledge and he had about a 50 foot [15m] stretch on a rope--they had to grab it and go hand over hand. And that youngest boy Ervine went down to meet his dad; and Art, he started cookin' supper. Ervine said he got right down about where you had to go off the rim and down over that ledge on that 50 foot rope that ya had to climb hand over hand. And he said, he heard his Dad comin' up that rope, then all at once he heard him let out a holler and then he

From just below the **White Rim**, looking up at some of the features known as **Walking Rocks**. Similar places exit all around the White Rim, but this is one of the better places to see them up close.

Musselman Arch as seen from below and from inside upper **Musselman Canyon**. Seen from above and from near the trailhead, it's not as impressive as this scene.

never heard no more. He must have had a heart attack, I always figured, that made him turn loose of that rope.

He fell down and they don't know how high he was on that rope, but he went down and hit a little ledge that was about 4 foot [1.25m] wide but he didn't stop there. He went off about another 50 feet [15m] and that's where he stopped. So one kid come to town and got us and I loaded 7 head of horses in a new Ford pickup and about everybody in Moab went out there that night to help.

We got out there at the head of the Shafer Trail about 2 o'clock in the morning. **Swanny Kerby** was with us, and **Kenny Allred**--he was livin' out there at Dubinky then, and my brother Ed, and a kid named Tom Burr. Anyway, when we got out to the Shafer Trail, I loaded Tom on a little gray mare, and I got Dr. Temple on another horse and I got on behind 'im to hold 'im on, and Swanny took the lead rope and down the trail we went--he took the lead and led my horse and I was holdin' Dr. Temple, and that's the way we went down.

We went down the Shafer Trail before the road was there; it was still just the old horse trail in them days, and I don't think we had any lights. I remember it was snowin' real lite, and it was a moonlit night, but ever once in a while the clouds would part and the moon would kinda come out a little, and I remember them ol' rocks were slick. And the horses would slip and hit on them ol' rocks and they'd just slide and off we'd go onto to the next one. We stayed on horseback all the way down. Swanny, he knew the country and knew the trails so he took the lead.

Anyway, we got down there and after we got on the White Rim we had to climb clearn up under the Wingate, so we was stumblin' around them rocks in the dark. When we got up there we didn't dare try to move 'em 'till it got daylight, so as soon as it broke daylight we loaded Omer on a stretcher and brought 'im down out of there. We brought 'im down to the White Rim [just north and down a ways from where the 3-Way Junction and toilet are today] on foot to get 'im down over them rocks. We had to hand 'im down with 6 guys, then we'd get down and hand 'im down to another 6, and finally brought 'im down to the White Rim.

Then in the mean time ol' **Puge Stocks** had a little T Craft airplane and he had flown down to Hite because there had been a seismograph crew and oil company here, and they had a helicopter, but they'd moved on down to Hite, so Puge went down there and talked them guys into bringin' that helicopter back up. So they did, and they got there about the time we got Omer down on the White Rim; we loaded him and Dr. Temple in the helicopter and they brought 'em to town. At that time he was still alive--he never did gain consciousnesss but he was still alive. And they said they lite right in front of the hospital which was right there on Main Street in them days. And they said they got 'im in there and cleaned 'im up and had 'im in bed in about 45 minutes, then he died. He never did regain consciousness. That was **January 5th, 1952.**

This event happen 6 months before the Shafer Trail Road was begun, and about 9 month before it was completed.

Along the White Rim Road South

Now to the intersection we'll call the **3-way Junction,** where the Shafer, Potash and White Rim Roads meet. That intersection is **8.7 kms (5.4 miles)** down from the junction with the main Island Highway; and **21.7 kms (13.5 miles)** from the cattle guard & turnoff to the Potash Boat Ramp and along the Potash Road.

Set your **odometer at 0** at the **3-way Junction.** The first part of the White Rim Road runs east and is quite good and any car can make it to the **Goose Neck Trail** at **Km 2 (Mile 1.2).** There's a sign and pull-out on the left for parking (marked **1446m** on the map). A walk of roughly 500m puts you at the **Goose Neck Overlook** of the Colorado River. It's one of the better viewpoints around for a closeup look at the Colorado directly below, and Dead Horse Point to the upper left or northeast. Be there from mid-day to early afternoon for the best fotos.

Moving south; at **Km 5 (Mile 3.1)** will be another side-road running southeast. This takes you to what is called the **Walking Rocks.** This is where the White Rim pinches out into a narrow finger between the Colorado River and Musselman Canyon. Out toward the very tip of this point, cracks have developed in the White Rim Sandstone, and erosion has left several pinnacles standing free. They're capped with the White Rim with red clay beds of the Organ Rock Formation below. Walking across these is like hopping across stepping stones placed in a stream--thus the name Walking Rocks. There are actually many places in this country and along the White Rim that have a similar look.

From the end of this point and the Walking Rocks, you can get down into Musselman Canyon, under Musselman Arch, and down to the Colorado River. At one time Karl Tangren of Moab built a trail down off this point and into the middle part of this canyon and actually took a few cows down there. Look for his old faded trail on the Colorado River side of the ridge. First, route-find down off the White Rim, then head southeast and around the point. From there you can bench-walk west on the same level all the way to a point right under **Musselman Arch.** This short trip involves some route-finding.

Or, route-find your way down over several ledges to the bottom of **Musselman Canyon.** There doesn't seem to be any trail there, but you should reach the bottom where there are at least **6 cottonwood trees** and perhaps a minor seep. From there walk downcanyon. After another 2 kms or so, you may come to a little running water, then an 8m-long chute and a water or dryfall; below that perhaps a pool. In drier times, there will be no pool, so you could downclimb the chute and be on your way. Or, with a pool, backup about 100m, walk east over a little ridge to find a **bypass route** where you can downclimb a couple of minor ledges and get back in the drainage below the **chute & pool.** From the water/dryfall, it's maybe another 3 kms to the river. Easy walking.

Near the Colorado, and just before arriving at the tamarisks on the river's edge, turn left or north, and walk to the lower end of what the Tangrens have called **Millings Bottom.** This is an easy walk with no bushwhacking. About 500m from the lower end of the Musselman Canyon are about a dozen pieces of heavy iron pipe about half a meter in diameter. Near the river's edge is a boater's camp. Karl Tangren tells us in the early 1950's an attempt was made to build a ranch here. The man's name was **Jack (Beans) Milling.** This is the same *"Beans"* who squatted on Tidwell Bottom on the Green River in the early 1940's, and who later worked for Swanny Kerby in the early 1950's at Alfalfa Bottom further upstream. Again, **Karl Tangren** seems to know more about Beans Milling than anyone. This is what he had to say about him on this river bottom:

I knew him real good. After he came from the Green River, he came over to the Colorado. He came over on what we called **Hermit Bottom,** downriver a ways. It never had a name until Jack Milling came there, but he planted maybe 50 to 100 fruit trees on that bottom. Ol' Milling, he lived under a ledge, and

If you're hiking in **Mussel-man Canyon**, you might downclimb/upclimb this **chute** if there's just a small pool at the bottom. Otherwise, there's an alternative **bypass route** around this minor obstacle behind and to the right of where the camera is sitting.

he had a barrel of beans. He was great on them beans! When he first hit the country, he was over there on the Tidwell Bottom. The Tidwells and Kenny Allred used to pack beans into him. Years later Kenny and I went over there and found them beans; there was 3 or 4 barrels of 'em. We just called him Beans, but I found out later his name was Jack Milling. It was during the Second World War, so everybody figured he was a draft dodger. He was probably about 30 years old when I first knew him.

Ol' Jack Milling left this country right after World War II, and went to the Uinta Basin, or somewhere and herded sheep. He was gone for several years, then he came back to this country and went to work for Joe Wheeler upon the mesa. While he was workin' up there for Joe, he took a cow, or heifer--wasn't very big, and a black saddle mare, and a team of bay work mares--small work mares, and he built this old boat out of old quaky logs and tin. He bent the tin around the logs and put a V-8 Ford engine in it and he'd load 2 of those horses at a time and that's when he went down the river and landed on that **Milling's Bottom.** He never did go back to the Hermit Bottom where he was originally. When he landed on this place, we called it the "Milling's Bottom".

On the upper end he built a little cabin, then later somebody came along and burnt it down [after he left]. He got the lumber from these old oil wells up under Hurrah Pass [the Prommel Well No. 1]. He went up there with the team of horses and built him a sled, then he loaded it full of lumber and skidded it down to the river and loaded it on his boat, then took it down there to build that cabin. He also hauled some big pipe down there and it's still laying out across the bottom where he pumped water into it and he had 4 or 5 acres [2 hectares] of alfalfa hay growing there at one time. This was in the early 1950's, sometime before I went to Anderson Bottom.

He then went someplace and bought a bunch of Holstein calves, 8 or 10; then took 'em down there and put 'em on that bottom. Then he built trails out of that place out onto the limestone ledge, then he come down around and into a little canyon we called **Shady Canyon** [on today's maps it's called **Little Bridge Canyon**]. It was right across from Hermit Bottom. He was grazing all that country in between there. He's the one who built the trails along that area. When he was ready to leave, why the calves had grown up and had calves, and he come in to my dad's cafe and traded that whole outfit to my dad; range delivery. Dad said he wouldn't buy 'em unless he put 'em up on Horse Bottom; there's horse trails come into it. So Jack built a trail off of Milling's Bottom up along that ledge and up past Shafer Canyon. Anyway, he put the cows onto Horse Bottom and my dad and I went down and got 'em, and trailed them around and loaded them into a truck and hauled them up the Shafer Trail and out.

When Beans left there, he got in the mining boom; decided he was going to make some of that minin' money, and he got more out in the public. That's why we always thought he was dodging the draft back in the 1940's--because in that time period he stayed down on the river by himself. After the war was over and the Uranium Boom started, then he started coming out into the public. He'd come to town and people got to know him. He ended up staking a lot of claims across from Dead Horse Point.

Now back to the Walking Rocks Trailhead. From there drive west down the road to **Km 5.3 (Mile 3.3)** and turn left at the sign on the road to **Musselman Arch**; it's only about 100m from the main road to the parking place. This is a rather thin arch made out of the White Rim Sandstone. When the late **Kenny Allred** was asked what he knew about the naming of this arch, he growled back:

Ya, I know all about that damn Musselman Arch and it makes me mad every time I think about it. Oh, he was a guy that owned this Musselman Ranch and he took a bunch of dudes down there. A lot

236

of people knew where that arch was for years and years before he did. But when he went down and "discovered it" then they named it after him.

It happened probably in about the early 1940's and all the cowboys and sheepmen in the country knew about that arch. That's why everybody was insulted when they named it the Musselman Arch. Musselman owned the Pack Creek Ranch at the time. He was tryin' to make a dude ranch out of it. They took dudes out on several trips down on that White Rim.

The late **Swanny Kerby** of rodeo stock fame, remembered more details about the *"discovery"* of this arch: *Musselman Arch came to light because of a dentist, a Dr. Williams [not Doc Williams of Williams Bottom fame] in Moab. I was in there getting my teeth fixed one day and he was interested in these arches and other wild country down there. And he asked me if I knew of any arches. So I knew about this arch and told him about it, and he asked if I'd take him down there. So with horses, Dr. Williams and his wife and me and my wife went down in there. We went out to Big Flat and down the Shafer Trail and when we got there we took some pictures of it. Then somehow* **Ross Musselman** *talked to Williams about that arch. So old Ross came around, and he told me he wanted to take some dudes down there, and would I show him where it's at. So he got this party of 5 or 6 people and I took 'em down there to the arch. Musselman didn't know any more than the man in the moon where this arch was because he'd never been there--he'd just seen the pictures. The next thing I knew it was named Musselman Arch--because I suppose he brought it to light to the outside world with his pictures.*

Next stop going south would be what all the maps now show as **Little Bridge Canyon**. Local cattlemen, or at least the Tangrens, knew it as **Shady Canyon;** likely because it's so short & deep. This drainage will be just around the point south from Musselman Canyon. This area is devoid of real landmarks so you'll have to pay close attention to your topo map, compass and your odometer if you're interested in getting down into this little canyon. To start, drive to a point about **12. 2 kms (7.6 miles)** from the **3-Way Junction** and park. This will be near the northwest part of Little Bridge Canyon. See map. From there, walk southwest maybe 300m to the rim of a northwest fork of the canyon. Look for a couple of cairns which mark the only way off the White Rim in that area. It takes a little climbing to get down the first part, then walk to the right or northwest immediately under the White Rim. After about 200m, scramble down a rockslide covering some ledges. Once at the bottom, walk right down the dry stream channel. There will be a couple of downclimbs further on, but they're easy walking. You can walk all the way to the river on a trail made by boaters. In 2012, the author first searched for, finally found, then headed down to the main fork and back in 1 1/3 hours

There's a second way into Little Bridge Canyon. Drive south around the head of this drainage and to about **Km 14.4 (Mile 9)** and park. From there walk due east about 800m. That should put you on the south rim of the drainage, and about 300m north of a lone cedar **(juniper)** tree. Walk the rim to find 2-3 places where you can get down through the White Rim, then scramble down past what appears to be big horn sheep trails, but you just go straight down the easiest way possible. This takes you down to the main fork and to the river as well. In 2012, this writer made it down into the main fork and back out in another 1 1/3 hours. He could have gone down to the river and back in 2 or 2 1/2 hours.

Next point of interest going south will be Lathrop Canyon and the Lathrop Canyon Trail, but that's in the previous chapter along with **Map 22**.

From the end of the **Goose Neck Trail** you see **Dead Horse Point** in the upper left; the Colorado River and the Goose Neck in the lower right; and the Potash Road in about the middle running left to right, or west to east. The cliff in the middle is where **Ed Hayes** fell and died in late August, 1967.

Goose Neck O.

Above From the cliffs above the Colorado about where **Ed Hayes** fell & died, looking west up to the **Goose Neck Overlook**. It's just below where the words are written on this foto. Also seen here is the mouth of **Shafer Canyon** to the right. Just below the center of this foto, you can see where floods have washed sand & rocks into the river. In the far upper right you can see about where the **Shafer Trail (& Canyon) Overlook** is located on the rim of the plateau.

Right This is what the Tangrens called **Millings Bottom**. Looking west at a bunch of pipe brought there by **Jack "Beans" Milling** to irrigate parts of this river bottom. Jack welded 7-8m-long sections together to form a pipeline, then pumped water from the river onto the flats.

Above From the **White Rim Road** looking due east at the **Candlestick Campsite** & toilet. In the background center is **Candlestick Tower**, and to the right of that and just above the roof of the restroom, is what this writer calls **Halfdome**. To the right of that is the Green River Overlook. See **Map 20.**

Left Looking nearly due west at the **Airport Tower**. In the middle of this picture is the lower end of **Lathrop Canyon**, while to the left of the lower part of Airport Tower is **Monster Tower & Washer Woman Arch & Pinnacle**. Part of the **White Rim Road** is seen in the bottom foreground.

Potash, Oil Wells, and Hikes to Alfalfa, Tunnel, Oil Well and Horse Bottoms; and Thelma & Louise Point

Location & Access This map shows **Potash** and its evaporation ponds, and several short hikes to the Colorado River rim or bottoms east of the Island Visitor Center. The best way to get here is to drive north out of Moab on Highway 191. On the north side of the river and near **mile post 130**, turn left or south onto the paved **Potash Road** running downstream along the Colorado River. Drive to and past Potash and to the end of the paved road & a **cattle guard** (which is where you turn left to reach the **Potash Boat Ramp**), a distance of 25.9 kms (16.7 miles). From the Potash Boat Ramp turnoff & cattle guard (**set odometer at 0**), continue westward on the graded Potash Road. Beyond the Potash evaporation ponds, the road deteriorates a little, but it's still good for almost all vehicles (it has one rough section). Further along, the Potash Road continues west into Shafer Canyon, but about where it leaves the left-hand side of this map, it's for HC/4WD's only--and the CNP will never fix it! If you continue west you'll eventually reach the **3-Way Junction**, White Rim Road, the Shafer (Trail) Road, and the Island in the Sky, if you choose.
Elevations Dead Horse Point, 1803m; Potash, 1219m; Potash Road at Thelma & Louise Point, 1370m.
Water None around, except in the river, so take all the water you'll need.
Maps USGS or BLM map La Sal (1:100,000); Shafer Basin (1:24,000--7 1/2' quad); the plastic Trails Illustrated/National Geographic maps Canyonlands National Park and/or Moab South (1:70,000); or the plastic Latitude 40° map Moab West (1:75,000).
Main Attractions High cliffs on the horizon including Dead Horse Point, historic oil well sites, short hikes to several river bottoms, petrified wood/logs, pretty good road for cars and the site of the last seconds of the movie, **Thelma & Louise** at what is now called **Thelma & Louise Point**.

History of Potash and Potash Mining

Potash is a large potash mining complex owned & operated now by **Moab Salt, LLC** (formerly Texas Gulf Sulphur). Years ago, Texas Gulf determined that one of the biggest deposits of potash in the world lay beneath this area. But the potash industry didn't come along until after the 1950's Uranium Boom and since then has replaced uranium as one of the primary mining operations in the region. It all started in February of 1961. That's when the $45 million mining and milling installation was began at Potash.

In the beginning, all supplies for this operation were taken down the Colorado River by boat, with some coming down the Shafer Trail and Long Canyon Roads. About the time operations started, the same company put the road down **Long Canyon**; that according to Karl Tangren, was in 1960 or '61. At that time, it was a better road than the Shafer Trail. The beginning of a road along the river from Moab was started in the mid-1950's by Monte Mason, but it was useable only in times of low water. The Potash Road of today wasn't built until 1962-63; and at the same time, the D & RGW Railroad began work on a 58-km-long spur line from Crescent Junction. That was completed in 1964. Read more history of the Potash Road along with **Map 17**.

In the beginning, there were mine shafts and tunnels blasted out below Potash, and mining was done in the conventional way. About the time the operation was starting to roll, there was a terrible accident. It happened on **August 27, 1963**. Briefly, there were 25 miners working underground at about the 826m level. There was an explosion which trapped them all. Two miners were rescued about 24 hours later. Five men, seeing they couldn't get out the main tunnel, retreated a ways and built 3 barricades in a side tunnel they were in to keep the smoke out. They broke into a water line carrying Colorado River water, which helped them stay alive. They were rescued about 50 hours after the explosion. The other 18 miners were killed and brought out later. Aside from several coal mining disasters in Carbon County, this was one of the worst mining accidents in Utah history.

In about 1968, mine profits began to drop quickly which resulted in a change in the mining procedure. The decision was made to convert from conventional to solution mining. This change-over began in 1970. In the **November 19, 1970** issue of **The Times Independent (TI)** one article stated: *Following a several month period of cleaning equipment out of Texas Gulf Sulphur potash mine at Cane Creek, company personnel this week began pumping the first water down the hole, in preparation for solution mining. Production of potash at the Moab operation, under new solution mining methods, is planned to begin in mid-1971.*

As one might expect, there were delays. In the **January 13, 1972** issue of the **TI** it stated: *Harvest of potash salts is expected to begin within sixty days from newly-completed solar evaporation ponds at the Cane Creek operation of Texas Gulf Sulphur Company, it was stated this week by R.L. Curfman, general manager at the facility.*

For a period of thirty to sixty days, the mill operation, which has been shut down for one and a half years, will operate at about half-capacity, Mr. Curfman stated, with full production planned for sometime around the first of May [1972].

Transportation of the salts deposited in the ponds to the mill, some 3 1/2 miles [5 1/2 kms] away, will be done by slurry lines. The large self-loading scrapers will harvest the salts from the ponds; will deposit them in one of three slurry pits in the pond area, and there they will be mixed with a brine solution which has been recirculated back to that area from the mill to form a 50% slurry solution. The slurry, after arriving at the mill, will be stored in large tanks constructed for that purpose, and then will go into the milling process. From that point on, there are no changes in the operation over the established conventional mining process.

History of Oil Drilling: Cane Creek Anticline and the Frank Shafer Well No. 1

The paved part of the **Potash Road** ends about 2 kms south of Potash. At that point is a cattle guard and a turnoff to the left leading to the **Potash Boat Ramp** about 300m away where most boats going down the Colorado River are launched. Another 2 kms or so beyond the boat ramp turnoff (and on the unpaved part of the Potash Road), and on top of the Cane (Kane) Creek Anticline bench is a little sideroad running to the east. It ends near the rim of the canyon, and directly below is the first oil producing well in this part of the country. It was called the **Frank Shafer Well No. 1** originally, then in later years, it was generally referred to as the **Discovery Well**. To get down to this historic site, walk along the rim of this short canyon caused by the uplift known as the **Cane Creek Anticline**. Soon you'll come to an old and eroded vehicle track heading down to the south paralleling the river. Today this is too rough for any vehicle. Walk down this dugway to the short narrow bottom.

Map 24, Potash, Oil Wells, and Hikes to Alfalfa, Tunnel, Oil Well and Horse Bottoms; and Thelma & Louise Point

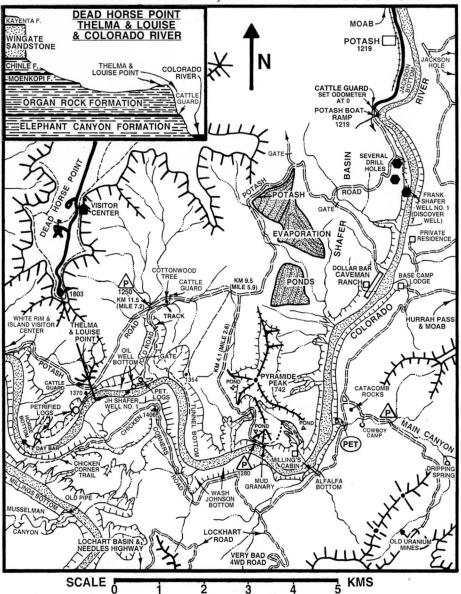

DEAD HORSE POINT THELMA & LOUISE & COLORADO RIVER

KAYENTA F.
WINGATE SANDSTONE
CHINLE F.
MOENKOPI F.
ORGAN ROCK FORMATION
ELEPHANT CANYON FORMATION

THELMA & LOUISE POINT
COLORADO RIVER
CATTLE GUARD

N

MOAB
POTASH 1219
JACKSON HOLE

CATTLE GUARD SET ODOMETER AT 0
POTASH BOAT RAMP 1219

GATE

BASIN

SEVERAL DRILL HOLES

FRANK SHAFER WELL NO. 1 (DISCOVER WELL)

POTASH
POTASH
ROAD
GATE

SHAFER

PRIVATE RESIDENCE

DEAD HORSE POINT

VISITOR CENTER

EVAPORATION

DOLLAR BAR CAVEMAN RANCH

BASE CAMP LODGE

PONDS

COLORADO

1803

COTTONWOOD TREE
CATTLE GUARD
KM 9.5 (MILE 5.9)

HURRAH PASS & MOAB

WHITE RIM & ISLAND VISITOR CENTER
THELMA & LOUISE POINT

P 1250
KM 11.5 (MILE 7.2)

ROAD
OLD ROAD
TRACK

KM 2.6 (MILE 2.6)

POTASH

OIL WELL BOTTOM
GATE

CATTLE GUARD

1370

JH SHAFER WELL NO. 1
PET. LOGS
1354

1406

POND

CATACOMB ROCKS

PETRIFIED LOGS

HORSE BOTTOM

CHICKEN
CORNERS
ROAD

TUNNEL BOTTOM

KM 4.1 (MILE 2.6)
PYRAMIDE PEAK 1742

POND
POND

P

COWBOY CAMP

MAIN CANYON

DAY BAR

CHICKEN CORNER TRAIL
OLD PIPE

POND

1280

MILLING'S CABIN

PET

P

MILLINGS BOTTOM

MUSSELMAN
CANYON

WASH JOHNSON BOTTOM

MUD GRANARY

ALFALFA BOTTOM

DRIPPING SPRING

LOCHART BASIN & NEEDLES HIGHWAY

LOCKHART ROAD

VERY BAD 4WD ROAD

OLD URANIUM MINES

SCALE 0 1 2 3 4 5 **KMS**

On this bench today are the ruins of old boats (one is an old naval landing craft) along the river and a couple of buildings--which in 2012 were on the ground. Just to the south of the buildings are 3 metal shafts sticking up from the ground. All 3 were drilled later, after they had trouble with water getting into the first oil well--more on this later.

The Frank Shafer Well was started in the **winter of 1924-25**, then struck oil with a gusher on **December 8, 1925**. However, water problems plagued the drillers an entire year, then it was shut down. Over the years there were other attempts nearby to get at the original oil horizon.

This was an exciting period of time in Moab history, because the town prospered and the newspapers were full of stories about the oil drilling boom. In each of the weekly editions of ***The Times Independent***, there was an ***Oil Well Drilling Report*** on the front page, detailing progress on the wells in the region. It was also a time of boat building, and traffic increased greatly on the Colorado River between Moab and several downstream oil well drilling sites.

241

The **Frank Shafer Well No. 1**, later known as the **Discovery Well**, located 1 1/2 kms downriver from the Potash Boat Ramp. Later, this site was known to some locals as **MGM Bottom**. There's an old washed-out road leading down to it from the **old oil wells** on the bench above. See Map 24. This picture dates from 1925 or '26. (Glen Ruby foto & BYU foto archives)

In those early years of the oil boom, there was no road downstream along the Colorado River. The only way into that country was on a very long and rugged cattle trail--or in boats. So naturally all the oil wells drilled right on the river bank or nearby, were supplied by boat. Almost all drilling equipment was taken down on the river, and most of it was handled by a local freight hauling outfit called the **Moab Garage Company**. The only exception being, some of the very first equipment to be taken downriver was hauled by team & bobsled during the cold winter of 1924-25. All the old timers remember the river freezing over completely that winter and it literally became a road for sleds on the ice.

One of the best sources of information concerning these boats and the companies involved is from the testimonies of witnesses in the **Colorado River Bed Case hearings**, which were held in Los Angeles, Denver and Salt Lake City in the fall of 1929. That case involved the United States vs Utah, and they were trying to determine whether or not the Green & Colorado Rivers were navigable, and who owned the mineral rights under the river beds--in other words, who collected the taxes from these oil wells. A complete history of that court case is told in the author's other book, *River Guide to Canyonlands National Park and Vicinity, 2nd Edition*.

One of the witnesses testifying was **R.C. Clark**. He was part owner of the Moab Garage Company, along with the Baldwin brothers, Clarence and Virgil. Part of Clark's testimony went like this:

My company owns a scow which is operated on the Colorado River. It does not have a name but the words "Moab Garage" are written on the front of it. It was built in [February of] 1925. It is 15 feet wide and 75 feet long [roughly 5 x 25m]; 3 feet [1m] deep from the gunnel to the bottom; the sides are 4 inch [10 cm] plank, the bottom is two layers of 2 inch [5 cm] plank, pointed bow, stern wheel, and was first operated with a motor taken from an automobile but we later put in an industrial motor. The draft of the scow empty was 4 inches [10 cms]; with a load of 15 tons it drew about 20 inches [50 cms or half a meter]. The boat cost about $7000. Virgil Baldwin usually operated the boat and he had charge of the scow all the time.

*It was constructed to care for a contract between our company and the **Midwest Exploration Company**, which was drilling an oil well about 20 miles [32 kms] down the Colorado from Moab. We made a contract in writing with that company.*

The Midwest Exploration Company paid us $1.75 a hundred for transportation of their freight on the first contract from Thompson to Kane Creek No. I [Frank Shafer] well for the first 400 tons. For transportation between Thompson and Moab we usually charge fifty cents per hundred pounds [45 kg], a distance by truck of 37 miles [60 kms].

From the 2nd day of March, 1925, until June, 1929, I think 245 or 250 trips were made altogether. I think 8 trips were made during the year 1929. The scow has never been farther down the river than Lockhart Canyon, that is 40 miles [64 kms].

In addition to Clark's testimony, Clarence E. Baldwin also testified that aside from the big scow or barge generally known as the *Moab Garage*, they also ran several other boats, but not all during the same time period. One was the *Pumpkin or Punkin Seed*, another was the *Black Boat*, and the *Chandler*. They also operated 3 outboard motor boats at various times during the mid to late 1920's.

Clarence E. Baldwin went into detail describing 3 of these boats: *The first boat that I personally operated regularly was the **Pumpkin Seed**. It was a round-bottom boat, about 21 feet long and about 9 feet wide [7 x 3m]. It was used for hauling passengers and light freight. The boat had a model T Ford motor in it. The motor had been taken out of an old Ford car. It had about 22 horsepower. We would haul up to 10 passengers in the Punkin Seed. We carried as freight in the Punkin Seed, groceries for* the oil camps and fishing tools used in the drilling operation and small freight of that kind that they needed at the wells.

I operated the boat between Moab and the Shafer No. 1 well. I also went to Lockhart with it a few trips [near the mouth of Lockhart Canyon is another old oil well which will be discussed later]. I personally operated the Punkin Seed on these round-trips to Shafer No. 1 well and to Lockhart about three or four months. It took about four hours with that boat to go from Moab to Lockhart. It would take about 7 or 8 hours for the return journey from Lockhart to Moab. The speed depended somewhat on the amount of load. I would take loads both up and down in operating the boat. Going up I would take what ever there was to go. It would be the passengers coming back, tools that needed repairing, and there was quite a bit of up-freight of various kinds from the oil wells while the drilling was going on and while preparations were being made for drilling. Anything that was light, that was in a hurry to go out, and if the big boat was not available that day, I would take out on the Punkin Seed to hurry it up. The principal use of this boat was as a passenger boat.

There was a smaller boat. It was about 20 feet long and about 4 1/2 feet wide [6 x1 1/2m]. It had a Model T Ford motor in it which had been taken from a Ford car. That boat was at times called the **"Black Boat"**, because it was painted black. I personally operated the Black boat in regular service for about 7 or 8 months between Moab and Shafer No. 1 and 2 wells and Lockhart. Passengers mostly were carried on the Black boat. I generally took about four passengers on it. I have had as high as nine in it but it was over-loaded. Any small packages or items of freight I would carry on that boat also.

We had another boat equipped with a Chandler motor. It was known as the **"Chandler Boat"**. It was 26 feet long and 6 feet wide [8 x1 1/2m] at the top and 5 feet [1 1/2m] wide at the bottom. The motor was a 38 horsepower motor, I judge. The Chandler boat was used principally for hauling passengers, small freight and anything that could go on that boat. I have hauled as high as 10 passengers in it and as high as two tons. I operated the Chandler between Moab and Shafer No. 1 well and Shafer No. 2 well, Lockhart and the junction [The Confluence of the Green & Colorado Rivers].

In addition to our freight operations we have had quite a little passenger traffic on the river. We have taken parties up and down the river to The Confluence with the Green River. We have paid no attention to the Green River, confining our operations to the Colorado River. We have run advertisements for sightseers and have invited traffic in our boats from sightseers and there has been some response to that. Since 1925 our boats have made from 200 to 300 trips with passengers only.

We operated regular passenger service on the river. Our boats left on a schedule at a certain time every day. That was during the excitement after they struck oil down there. A lot of people came from all over the country and wanted to go down and see the wells, and others were interested in other structures there. That lasted 5 or 6 weeks, as long as the excitement kept up. It was in December, 1925, January and part of February, 1926. We had a little passenger transportation all the time up until our last shut-down. We carried passengers in the launches and some of them on the big boat. We had several excursions with the big boat recently.

Before leaving the site of the most famous oil well along the Colorado River, one last story has to be told. Almost every old timer interviewed on the subject of oil wells told the story, and it's truly become legendary in the folk history of the Moab area. It involved 2 rough-necks from Moab who were working on one of the wells at the site of the old Frank Shafer oil well. The late **Mitch Williams** probably remembered it better than anyone and claims to have been told the story by one of the participants:

There was a guy named Joe Watts. Joe Bally Watts they called him. And he was asleep one day taking a nap and he had his mouth open, and old Bart Stewart, who was a cut-up anyway, he got up there real close and opened his pants and he got right up by Joe's mouth, then somebody tickled Joe's nose with a feather and he woke up and he saw old Bart, and he come out of there just a roarin'. And old Joe said, "you dirty so-and-so", and he took after him and he chased Bart all over those cliffs. Now old Bart told me this himself, so I know! And Joe couldn't catch him, so he went on back to camp, and Bart he finally came down and went into the outhouse.

Now the outhouse was on two timbers stuck out over the river, so everything dropped right into the water. So Bart he went in there and he was takin' a crap. And by god, when old Joe Bally saw he was in there, he got a hammer and some nails and went and nailed the door shut. Bart heard him poundin' away out there, but didn't realize what he was up to. So Joe nailed that door completely shut. Then he came along with a long pole and push that damn toilet off into the river--with Bart in it! And Bart came out the hole! It was high water too! Bart could have died, but ol' Joe Bally didn't care. Bart said, "that hole wasn't very big but I come through it". That's a true story, that's just the way it happened!

Here's a little more oral history of this area and drilling oil wells. **Karl Tangren**, lifelong resident of Moab knows something about later events at the **Discovery Well site**:

All of my life, a guy named **Monte Mason** had those leases there at the site of the Discovery Well and others nearby. In 1925, some outfit hit oil and it seeped into the river for years. Finally somebody sued 'em and they come back and capped it but they left a 3/4" [2 cm] valve sticking out of the top. Well, when I was boating cattle up & down the river in the early 1950's, we had an old Model A [Ford] engine in the barge we run and we'd camp there and we'd open that valve at night and stick in a 50 gallon [188 liter] drum and the next morning we'd have 50 gallons of crude oil. Then we always had a 50 gallon drum of gas with us and we'd mix that 50/50 with that crude oil, and that old Model A engine would burn it! So we just doubled our fuel supply every time we got to that oil well.

I worked down there for Monte in 1951. That was the year I got married. My brother and I went down there, and the road leading down to that narrow bottom next to the river wasn't there then. When I was workin' there, everything went down by boat; the road to Potash didn't exist then. Then after I worked on that, Monte was down there another time and that's when he was drillin' up on the bench and I and my brother-in-law run the barge up and down the river haulin' all the material in and out. This was before I went to Anderson Bottom in 1957. Now Monte was in there several different times drilling. He drilled one hole up on the flats near the Potash Road [maps show several old drill sites there].

The Potash Road we know today was constructed in 1962-63 for the benefit of the Potash plant, so it was sometime between then and the late 1960's when Monte built that steep road down to the river next to the Discovery Well [it's totally washed out today].

Monte Mason got himself in trouble after he came here and got that Shafer lease. He'd go out and sell stock and come down there and open it up and go to drillin' until the money was gone, then he'd close 'er down--and ya couldn't get down there only by boat! So after a while the county would put all that equipment up for sale, a tax sale, and nobody could get down there to get it, and nobody wanted it, so ol' Monte would go in and buy it all for taxes, then start sellin' stock again and make another company, then go back to drillin'.

If you hike down to that bottom today, you'll find 3 metal poles sticking out of the ground marking the last 3 capped wells that were drilled. All 3 are dated *12-29-1969*, with one inscribed **Fed. Mason #1.**

Dollar Bar, Tangren's Dude Ranch & Tangrela, and now Caveman Ranch

About **3.4 kms (2.1 miles)** up the Potash Road from the turnoff to the Potash Boat Ramp, is a side-road running southeast. This road, with a locked gate near the start, runs down to what used to be the **Tangren's Dude Ranch or Tangrela** on the Colorado River. Karl Tangren of Moab tells a little of the story of this ranch and his brother Bud up to **1991** and for the **1st Edition** of this book:

I was all over this country before I went to Anderson Bottom [on the Green River]. When I went to Anderson Bottom, I pulled out of this country and took my cows there. I was here along the Colorado in the 1950's. When they kicked me out of Anderson Bottom in 1964, then I come back over on the Colorado River and bought them permits [to graze cattle] back in there.

My brother owns this ranch now, and all during the '70's, we fought with the BLM and the state. I had a lease on the biggest part of it. The upper end was state land. They withdrew this land for the Potash outfit. We were dealing with the state, and the BLM still owned the lower end of this big bottom; it was kind of a three way deal. I had a lease on the state's part for grazing; then we went back and got one for farming, and then we decided we'd better just get title to the thing, so we went to work and it took us 8 years to gain title to that land. We now have title to 136 acres [54 hectares].

In 1980, we finally got a deed from the bureaucrats and when my brother flew in there with the deed that day, then we started arguing--because he showed up with it all in his name. He left our names [Karl and his wife] off from it.

But before that, when I had it for lease, I went down and shot a hole in the rock--a hole 30 feet deep, 10 feet high and 12 feet wide [about 10 x 3 x 4m]. I put a front on it and a big steel door I could swing shut and made it into a camp. I had a propane frig and cook stove in there. This was made back in the 1960's, after I came back from Anderson Bottom.

I had a friend with a D-2 Cat and we built a road--more like a trail--down along the river bank. Then we drug a compressor in there and you could get a pickup over it, a 4WD. So we shot that hole out and made that camp and since then you can hardly get down that old trail, even on horseback. I took my brother down there, and showed him around, and he said we ought to make a ranch out of this, and that's when it all started. Then we went back up higher in the ledge where another horse trail went in and we built a road down through the rocks to the bottom. That's where the road is now.

*During the time when we were trying to gain title to the place, we were in there trying to build a dude ranch. There's a gravel knoll out in the middle of the bottom, and we went upon it and built a big **lodge**-two story. We scooped the gravel off down to the solid rock, then we shot down into the rock 8 feet [2 1/2m], and built the bottom part of the lodge. Then over in the ledge where I had that original hole, we shot out 9 more holes, and made a 10 unit motel right there in the rock. About the time we had those pretty well shot out, and the lodge was built, that's when we got to arguing and so me and my wife left there and sold our half of it to my brother. He's still got it and he's been there 10 years now [1991].*

He never did get it going, but he keeps workin' on it. He's got them cabins all finished now and with glass fronts in 'em, with big drapes and carpets--nice hole-in-the-rock cabins. He went in there last spring and put in a solar electric unit upon the rock, and he's got 12 volt lights in all those rock cabins, which are run off that solar outfit. Just this past winter [1990-91] he shot out 3 more holes in the rock, and he's going to make an equipment shed. Now he's got another guy down there drilling and says he's going to build him a home, just above the equipment shed. He still hasn't got the dude ranch going.

*This past winter, he went up town here and traded Southern Paving some land he had out on the flat, to go down there and gravel that mile and a half [2 1/2 kms] of road into the ranch and put culverts in it and made a nice road. We also had an airstrip down on the bottom and he had them also gravel the whole airstrip. You can land 6-place planes in there easy. His name is Richard, we call him **Bud--Tangren**. He built a pipe gate with a lock on it, where the country road is. And just before you get down into the ranch, he built another gate.*

As this book goes to press in early 2013, the Tangren Dude Ranch sometimes called **Tangrela**, has morphed into the **Caveman Ranch** and it now belongs to Bud's son Rodney Tangren. Here's some of what he told this writer in the fall of 2011 about the place since 1991:

After Dad and Karl split, then Dad basically did nothing with it. I told Dad I'd like to make this a lifelong project and in about 1992, I got a 99 year lease, and I kinda got Dad out that same year. He was around but he didn't really have any say about what went on around here. So from there, I proceeded to redo things and fix things that we should have done right from the git go. Clearn back on August 18, 1972 is when Karl and me and Dad actually walked down in here--there was no road then. I was just 12 years old. I've been with it along with Dad but my name's not mentioned much--I guess I'm too young.

In '92, when I got my lease, I had responsibilities in Vegas, I had a son in school and trying to hold down a household there. So I'd be there for a couple of weeks and come back to the ranch--I was haulin' in a lot of material as I was building different things. So I did that for many years until about a year and a half ago. Two years ago I finally got my son out of high school so I just decided to move over here full time with all my uncles. I've been mostly full time since May of 2010.

I had an aircraft and it was paid for, so I sold it and put the money into the ranch. Then we got into a family dispute; Father took me to task and threw me in the court system. He actually sued me and from 2000 to 2008 we were in court. In one case, the judges thought he was senile; that was back in about 2005. The judge at that time threw me out of the ranch and gave it back to him; and deemed my lease no good, so we appealed that and it took a couple or 3 years to go through and I beat him in the appeals court. Then he had his attorneys appeal that to the Supreme Court of Utah. I drove to Salt Lake and stood before 5 judges and they had questions about what went on. And I had 4 of 5 judges rule in my favor that my lease was good and we actually went down as case law for the state of Utah. Years earlier, Dad actually said you're the one who built it and you're the one that should have it.

My son is living here along with my wife; she used to work for one of the casinos in Las Vegas. We've jumped in on these projects I've got going, and got a lot of big plans, but the economy has everything shut down to the point that you can't do anything.

I cater to a lot of pilots; I don't really want mom & pop and the kids who are travelin' around the country lookin' at the national parks to come in for one night. As far as pilots comin' in, they are a slightly different breed of people and they have a little more invested in what they do so they take a little bit better care of what goes on. My main thing eventually will be catering to any kind of aviation.

Aerial view of the Tangren's **Caveman Ranch** as of 4/2011. The airstrip is near the river, while on the other side, the **Base Camp Lodge** can barely be seen to the upper left a little.

My airstrip is 3000 feet long [915m] and 50 feet wide [15m] and I have an elevation of 3950 feet [1204m]. I have water rights to water 50 acres [20 hectares]. In the early days we used to pump our tanks full, let'em settle for a couple of weeks, then pump 'em out of there through osmosis filters, but you have that talcum sand in the river and it eats all your fittings--showers and taps. So I cleaned the tank and I haul drinking water out of Moab. I just put it in a 10,000 gallon [37,500 L] tank then it goes into some pressure tanks for the lodge and the caves. I have my own truck to haul water. I built the trailer with a 750 gallon [2800 L] polyurethane tank and I just have it on the back of my truck and when I go to town once or twice a week to shop, see people and check my email, I go down to Moab City and fill it up there and they charge me anywhere's from $5 to $8 bucks.

I keep all the former fields clean; I've been reluctant to put any kind of produce in because that's a full-time job; it's like having animals. So I just plant watermelons, cantaloupe and pumpkins plus we have an orchard with about 50 fruit trees.

We're in the process of adding to my solar building with batteries, converter and panels. But we also have generators. And we're planning on putting in a big Wind Jammer windmill so we have the wind power. In the mornings the wind blows up the river, then in the afternoons, it blows downstream.

If you're curious about the Caveman Ranch, go to the website **cavemanranch.com.** Also remember **this is private land.**

Before the Tangrens settled there, this place was known as **Dollar Bar** by placer miners who worked there during the Great Depression years of the 1930's. On *August 15, 1935,* the *TI* of Moab gave a report of the workings there. Part of that article went like this:

C.C. Stewart and Judge M.S. Moran were in town this week with the results of another rich cleanup after a few days run of the gravel on the Dollar Bar about 20 miles [32 kms] south of Moab. The partners, with the placer crew left Tuesday for the camp with additional mining equipment, which is expected to increase production. The Grand Junction Sentinel has the following to say of the rich gold strike.

It's the gold rush of 1935, only the scene is laid, not in a frontier saloon, but in a fashionable jewelry store..... A pound [453 grams] of gold which was on display Friday at the A.C. Parsons Jewelry store. The precious metal, bought by Parsons for $401.00, was the result of placer diggings by C.C. Stewart and Judge M.F. Moran.

Stewart and Judge Moran have been operating a gravel bar down the Colorado river about 20 miles [32 kms] from Moab, Utah. During the past month their gravel bar has produced in excess of $1,000 worth of gold, their returns averaging about a pound [453 grams] of dust a week. They have a crew of five men at work, and are operating a hydraulic sluice outfit.

Clive C. Stewart is dead now, but his son **Buster Stewart** was interviewed in 1991 and he remembered a few things about Dollar Bar:

You see, I was born in 1934, so most of what I know is what Dad (Clive Stewart) told me. I was down there and saw the operations before the Tangrens ever made Tangrela. Dad had 5 men workin' for him there at that time. This was in the early and mid-1930's, but I think he was fiddling around down there as early as the late 1920's. His operation consisted of sluice boxes, and he had a team of horses to move things with. He used what they called a fresno scraper--that's what he drew his material up with. Then he had a man on the river running the pump with a gasoline engine. That was Rube Walker. Then what he had for a grizzly [grizzlys are built with pipes which takes out larger rocks, like a screen] was 2 men with pitchforks--for throwing out the big rocks. Then after the grizzly, the material went into his sluice box. The reason Dollar Bar got that name, it brought a dollar a yard. A dollars worth of gold in a cubic yard [nearly a c/meter] of gravel. He was paying his men $5 a day. That Dollar Bar was high

Left Looking south at part of the **trail** down to **Alfalfa Bottom**. More construction work was done here than on any other section. **Right** The old **cabin** built by Jack (Beans) Milling on **Alfalfa Bottom**. Most of it has collapsed under its own weight. Part of Hatch Point is seen in the background.

grade gravel. But when Dad was working, he was only getting about $20 an once [28 grams].

One thing I do remember, I was still trying to learn how to walk while Dad was down working on Dollar Bar. That would be 1935, and mother told me that I didn't learn to walk--I learned to run, and I'd run straight towards that river, and I had 'em all just scared to death. The placerin' was mostly a summer time deal and I think they mostly used tents as shelter. Dad, along with the placer mining, was also a bootlegger. He used to run it out of Bootlegger Canyon. He did a lot on Theof Bottom too [This would have all been before the repeal of Prohibition in 1933].

Buster's sister, **Beverly Stewart Guire**, remembered a few more things about the Colorado River:

Part of the time they lived on the Moab Garage boat. The barge had a kitchen and a bedroom, however we kids were sleepin' on the floor. I was about 13 years old when we were down there. The boat wasn't being used at the time, so Dad made some kind of arrangements to use it. Dad used to be a government trapper in the late 1930's, and game warden in the 1940's.

Hikes to Alfalfa, Tunnel, Oil Well, and Horse Bottoms

There are several river bottoms in this area you can reach by making short hikes. Each bottom also has some interesting history associated with it. From the turnoff to the Caveman Ranch, continue westward on the Potash Road. About **9.5 kms (5.9 miles)** up the Potash Road from the turnoff to the Potash Boat Ramp and the **cattle guard** (this is after you pass the **Potash evaporation ponds** and re-enter **public lands**), be looking for a minor track running south along the west side of **Pyramid Butte**. This is not well-used, but it's surface is as good as the Potash Road, so you can drive your car or mtn. bike for **4.1 kms (2.6 miles)** to the **Alfalfa Bottom Trailhead** marked **1280m** on this map. At that point, you'll be overlooking the Colorado River, with Pyramid Butte to the north. Park there where the hillside and the river gorge pinch together.

From the trailhead, follow a horse trail eastward through some large boulders, then veer northeast and cross a large flat area. About 1 km from the trailhead, you'll come to the head of a short little canyon which drains down onto Alfalfa Bottom. The beginning of a sandy horse trail angles down to the southeast into this drainage. Further along, you'll see one major place where the trail has been constructed. At the mouth of this little canyon, and just as you arrive at the river bottom, look to the right or west and you'll see the remains of a little **board cabin** and a **chicken coop** (but which is now under a boulder the size or a pickup truck with camper). **Karl Tangren** knew about this place and it's only resident:

Jack (Beans) Milling built them cabins there with some of the same lumber he'd got from those old oil wells. He also built a corral out of tamarisks he cut. He was working for Swanny Kerby in the early 1950's. Swanny had that country and the grazing permit that I've got now; that's my winter range. Swanny had hired him and he built some feed bunks and stuff and that's just after Kerby started into the rodeo contracting business. Jack Milling would boat grain down the river in that old boat he had, and he stayed there and fed those bulls. The old troughs he fed them in are still there, the old cabins are still there too. I've got cattle there now and have had for 30 something years [closer to 50 years in 2013!]. Milling spent a couple of winters there at Alfalfa Bottom working for Kerby.

*It got the name of **Alfalfa Bottom** because when Jack and Swanny first went in there it used to be just an old dry lake in the middle, and it had big cracks in the mud. And they just went out there and broadcast that alfalfa seed, and all the seeds which fell in them cracks where it was wet, sprouted. And that big old dry lake bed was covered with alfalfa. They never did any tilling or nothing--just grazed it.*

Didn't irrigate either, it just sub irrigated down to that clay under that old hard crust.

The late **Swanny Kerby** (who grew up in Moab and has a city park named after him) also remembered Jack (Beans) Milling: *We used to take Beans to Grand Junction to get his supplies--beans. He ate beans, corn flakes and raisins. The first time I saw him was on Alfalfa. He had this barge over against the river, and I had just come from town, and this was when I'd go down and stay for 2 or 3 weeks at a time. Just before this trip, I remember the song "Mockingbird Hill" was real popular [1951]; you heard it every where. So as I was riding down on Alfalfa Bottom looking around to see if there were any cattle, I could hear this song, and I thought it was ringing in my ears. So I went after the sounds-- over to the river and there was ol' Beans on this old barge and he had 'im a radio and listening to that song. And that's the first time I met Beans. After that, he started workin' for me some of the time. Later on we took him to Grand Junction and helped him buy a few calves that he took down on Milling's Bottom [further down river].*

At one time Beans was at **Lake Bottom** [about 5 kms north of Potash on the east side of the river; see Map 25], and he farmed it some and he had a pretty good little deal there at one time. He built the boat himself, and he lived on it most of the time. It was big enough to haul horses and cattle. He had a Model A Ford motor in it on the back end, and the horses would ride in the front in a little corral. He had kind of a little shelter on the boat too, then I think he took the cabin off when he was hauling cattle or the horses.

John (Sog) Shafer, who was interviewed in 1978 by a couple of BLM staffers, remembered Jack Milling as being a quarter-breed Indian from one of the southern reservations, perhaps from Arizona. Read more on Jack (Beans) Milling when he was on Tidwell Bottom on the Green River side in a separate chapter in the back of this book along with the story of Clyde Tidwell, Bill Tibbetts & John Jackson; and at Milling's & Hermit Bottoms further down the Colorado River.

From Milling's old cabin, walk west around a little point of rocks to see the remains of a small corral and the old **feed troughs** mentioned earlier. Also, about 1 km west of the cabin and right where the bottom pinches out and where the river and cliffs come together, is a little old Anasazi or Fremont Indian **granary** made out of red mud & rock. It's almost directly under the trailhead above.

Now back on the Potash Road. About 160m (.1 mile) west of the turnoff to Alfalfa Bottom, is another inconspicuous side-road running southeast. That old track is hard to see, but it runs out to several overlooks of Tunnel & Oil Well Bottoms. It's a good place for views looking downriver and toward Dead Horse Point; be there about mid-day. That track is rough in places, and not for cars, so why not walk.

If you're interested in getting to **Tunnel, Oil Well or Horse Bottoms**, stop and park at Km 11.5 (**Mile 7.2** from the cattle guard). There you'll be in a drainage bottom; park where you can. From there, walk south down this dry wash; or after about 300-400m, veer left or east and get up on a low bench to find an old vehicle **track** heading south into a canyon. About 500m from the Potash Road, the track has been blocked off to motorized travel, but continue walking south on the old vehicle track. After about 2 1/2 kms the track goes down through one ledge to the southeast, then it heads west 300-400m to where you'll be on another rim overlooking **Oil Well Bottom**. About 200m east of where you see some junk at the well site below, look for a **horse trail** dropping down through the last bench to Oil Well Bottom itself.

This last part of the trail ends near where the Midwest Exploration Company's **J.H. Shafer Well No. 1** was located. It's uncertain when this old trail or road was put in, because the entire drilling rig was taken downriver by the Moab Garage barge. It was likely first built by the Shafer brothers, but may have been improved by oil drillers while the well was being drilled so they could have a second way of communicating with the Frank Shafer Discovery Well No. 1, located just south of Potash.

Once on the river bottom, walk west 150m and you'll see where the old rig had been set up with junk, including cables, bricks once used to line a boiler (they used steam power) and boards lying around. Further to the east is where their camp was. It has one dugout, several footings of former buildings, and some old pipe, junk and a large metal wheel scattered about, but that's covered with tamarisks.

This J.H. Shafer Well No. 1 began drilling operations in March of 1926, on the apex of the Shafer Dome or Anticline. It's interesting to follow the *Moab Oil Field Drilling Reports* each week in the *TI* newspaper of Moab. After about 14 months of drilling, the well was shut down. In the *May 19, 1927* issue the report reads: *J.H. Shafer No. 1. Shafer Dome, section 17-27-20. Bottom at 5863 feet [1787m]. Due to caving of hole and its extreme depth, decision has been made to abandon it. Casing now being pulled and hole will be plugged. Rig and materials will remain on ground pending future developments in district. The bottom 270 feet [82m] of hole was drilled in shales, the drill passing out of the salt formation at 5592 feet [1704m]. This well drilled 3500 feet [1067m] of salt. Before drilling was stopped a 10-foot [3m] stratum of sandy lime was penetrated, carrying fresh water which arose 1500 feet [457m] in the hole.*

From the ledges above where the oil well was drilled, is the beginning of another interesting hike. This is on the ledges above the river and running downstream to **Horse Bottom**. To get there, just walk west along the 1st or widest bench you came to before actually dropping down to Oil Well Bottom. Soon the bench pinches down to just a narrow bench, and it's there you'll see for the first time an old **horse trail** emerge. Follow it southwest under **Thelma & Louise Point** to this isolated river bottom. Karl Tangren has ran horses down there since the 1950's; and others did the same before him. John Jackson may have been the first stockman to use this bottom, then the Shafer brothers, John (Sog) & Frank, began using it perhaps in the late 1910's or 20's (?).

The most interesting thing to see here is **petrified wood/logs**. Right at the upper east end of Horse Bottom, and at the lower end of a minor canyon, are many big chunks of logs lying around, but it's all over the area in the same formation. Once on the bottom, continue to where the mining symbol is on the map. Just north of that is one black petrified log about 20m long lying in a sea of red sandstone.

This bottom was also the scene of an attempt to do some placer gold mining. This appears to have been what used to be called **Day Bar**. A little history of that location is revealed in several articles in the *TI* in the fall of 1935. Part of one write-up on *September 19, 1935* went like this:

Clay Davis, local garage man, accompanied by Wayne Day and Frank Peterson, returned the first of the week from the Day bar, situated down the Colorado river about 30 miles [48 kms] from Moab. They were the possessors of approximately three ounces of gold dust which represented a test run of 11 hours at their placer camp. It is reported the Day bar contains a vast tonnage of gravel that carries exceptional values.

The discovery has revived interest in placer operations on river bars in the vicinity of Moab, and in richness it rivals if not overshadows the cleanups of the Stewart-Moran diggings on Dollar bar, 10 miles [16 kms] north of the new discovery. Several cleanups on the latter bar have netted the operators

Above The site of the **J.H. Shafer Well No. 1** on **Oil Well Bottom.** To the left, the pipe sticking up is the original drill hole which was capped long ago. There's also lumber, steel cables, and partially melted bricks on the ground as well. This is all just above the high water mark as seen in the background with all the brush & tamarisk.

Right Part of the trail leading down to the drill hole site on **Oil Well Bottom**. The top is marked with a little fence made out of stones. That's to keep livestock in or out of this bottom.

around a pound [453 grams] of nearly pure gold for a week's run..... A deal is under way whereby Judge M.F. Moran may purchase the interests of C.C. Stewart in the Dollar bar. Additional mining equipment of this camp will probably be obtained to speed up operations.

To see where this placer operation took place, walk south perhaps 100m from where the single big black petrified log is. Just down off this old higher river bank and maybe 40m from the river is a big pile of large gravel and pieces of lumber and metal junk. It appears the placer miners weren't there long as these tailings aren't that extensive.

If you'd like to take a short hike to **Tunnel Bottom**, then regress to the area of the overlook at Oil Well Bottom. Then walk north upcanyon toward your car to where the lower canyon flattens out, then cross the dry wash to the east just above where the lower canyon becomes entrenched. On the east-side bench, walk south then east. You'll see and can follow an old **horse trail** in places. After a ways the trail zig zags down over one ledge and runs along another narrow ledge between the cliffs and the river. Finally you'll reach Tunnel Bottom. When asked how it got that name, **Karl Tangren** said: *The first old timers who built that trail down there had to go under a big rock, so it was in through a kind of tunnel. But in 1984 the river was so high, that old limestone ledge caved in, and it caused that big rock to slide, and it slid off into the river, so there ain't no tunnel there any more.*

Karl didn't know who may have built it, but in 1978, Sog Shafer was interviewed by Steven A. Wing and David C. Minor of the BLM. In that interview, Sog stated he dug under a big rock that had slid down onto a ledge near the river. This created a tunnel which allowed him to take his cows down onto Tunnel Bottom for the first time. This must have happened sometime in the late 1910's or the 1920's.

Back on the Potash Road again. From the trailhead to Oil Well Bottom, continue west on the Potash Road. When you come to a narrow place between cliffs above and where it drops off to the Colorado River below, and where a **cattle guard** is located, drive a little ways beyond and park on the canyon rim at the point marked **1370m** on this map. That cattle guard is **14.1 kms (8.6 miles)** from the cattle guard and turnoff to the Potash Boat Ramp.

In the past, this area and the rock layer under the road, was always known as **Fossil Point** because you'll be walking on a grey limestone layer with lots of fossils. However, in recent years Moab residents have been calling it **Thelma & Louise Point**. **Karl Tangren** tells us about how he and other Moab people helped the movie industry and about the filming of the **1991 movie** *Thelma & Louise*:

I and Don Holyoak and Larry Campbell did 90% of the scouting for the movie people. They'd bring their story board and we'd see what kind of scenes they wanted. Then we knew where to take 'em to find what they wanted in the way of scenery.

They filmed about half of that movie around Moab. Some of it was filmed in Arches, and we was in some scenes that was shot over in Paradox Valley [in western Colorado near the Utah line] and around the town of Bedrock and that old store there. That was with Don Holyoak, Joe Taylor and I. We was the cowboys and they had about 50 head of cattle in one scene, and we was a wranglin'. They took a long shot of these girls comin' across Texas and they run into this herd of cattle in the middle of the road. Don, he got in the picture pretty good, the car came runnin' up there and they had Don whirl his horse around like the car was gonna run into 'im if he didn't get out of road. Then when they done the closeup, they had us bunch the cattle up, then they had the girls on a trailer in the hull of a car and it was up behind a ton truck with the camera mounted on the truck. Then they had us bring the cattle in, and then they started the wind machine and they were throwin' dirt in the air, and everything was really dusty. You can hear me hollerin' in there but the only thing you can see is guys on horses.

Here's what happened high above the Colorado River and shooting of the last scene in the film: *That point is right where the road comes out to the edge and makes a turn [about 250m west of the cattle guard], that's where they shot them cars going off in the movie. In the story, everywhere those 2 girls went [Susan Sarandon & Geena Davis], they got in trouble. They accidentally killed a man and the further they went, the deeper they got in trouble. So finally, 20 police cars had 'em surrounded, and they looked at one another, and said, "Well, looks like this is it", and they just stuck 'er in gear and off the ledge they went in their car. The end of the show was supposed to be in the Grand Canyon, but they couldn't film it there, so they shot the final scene up there below Dead Horse Point.*

*Old Ridley Scott was the director and he had a camera sittin' right out there on the edge; there's a little point runs out there [just west of **1370m** is on this map], and he was shootin' back this way [toward the northeast]. That first car went off and Ridley says, "Man that was good, but we got another car, so let's just run it off too". So they hooked up the second one and run it off. Ever since then, people have called that place Thelma & Louise Point. Before that, and during all my life, it was known as Fossil Point--there's a lot of fossils in that blue [limestone] ledge.*

Before they did that last scene, they brought in a stunt driver from Hollywood and he had a 2 ton truck. And they built an asphalt road that was 4-6 inches [10-15 cms] thick all down along that rim going southwest, and they drilled a hole in the rim and put a big peg in it and hung a chev on it and then hooked a cable to the car, they ran it through the chev and then back to this guy's truck. And I asked 'im afterwards, "How fast was you goin' when that car turned loose?" And he said, "60 miles per hour [100 kph]!" They built that good oiled road so his truck had good traction and it couldn't spin! I never did see what kind of a deal they had to turned that car loose, but something cut it loose when it got close to the rim. The car was shootin' straight out [southeast] toward the river, and the truck was runnin' southwest on the paved road along the rim. They never showed the car hittin' the water in the movie, it just showed 'em goin' out into space.

So after they shot the cars going into the river, they had 2 helicopters and some deep sea divers that they brought in from California, and in 10 minutes them guys went down, hooked onto them cars and had 'em sitting back up on the road.

When they cleaned up the area, they took ever bit of the asphalt. Afterwards, after they cleaned 'er up, you could never tell any asphalt had been there. There was a kid here in Moab who got the job to clean it up. He loaded up all that black top and brought it up here and stacked it in his yard and he used it around town for a lot of different things.

I've worked in the movies for 51 years and they never left any trash anywhere; anything they brought in, they cleaned it up and took it out.

From the cattle guard, drive southwest along the rim about 250m to the place where the car with Thelma & Louise flew into thin air--that's how and where the movie ended. About 200m beyond that is where the film crew had their camera placed on a point of rocks just a little lower than the actual rim. See the picture on the next page.

249

Left Part of the trail to **Tunnel Bottom**. It's in this section that a tunnel was formed by a large boulder falling across the way. **Right** The slope where the trail to **Horse Bottom** is located. In this area, it's quite visible. Almost directly above is **Thelma & Louise Point**, as shown on the opposite page.

This is the first place you'll come to where **petrified logs** are found on the trail to **Horse Bottom.** It's about 500m west (and below) **Thelma & Louise Point** and not far from the river.

Big Flat

Dead Horse Point

Potash Road

Thelma & Louise Point

Camera

Thelma & Louise Falling

Cattle Guard

Horse Trail

Pet. Wood

Top Aerial view of **Dead Horse Point** and points south including the Colorado River in the lower right hand corner of this picture. Also shown is **Thelma & Louise Point** and the route the 2 girls took on their way to the great beyond.

Bottom The finally 2-3 seconds of the movie, **Thelma & Louise**. This picture was literally taken with a camera of the last scene on a computer screen. Shown on the Top foto is where the camera was placed during the last shooting and the route the car took going to the river.

Moab Overlook Trails and Nearby River Bottoms, Jacksons Ladder Trail, Lower Pritchett & Hunters Canyons & Rock Art

Location & Access This map covers areas just to the west and southwest of Moab. All hikes and places to see are very easy and quick to get to from Moab and most access is along paved roads. To get to places on the **west side** of the Colorado River, drive north out of Moab on the main Highway 191. Cross the river bridge and head west. Near **mile post 130**, turn south onto the **Potash Road, State Highway 279**. It's paved all the way to the Potash complex.

To get to places on the **east side** of the river and to Pritchett, Hunters and Kane Creek Canyons, drive to the south end of Moab and at the corner where **McDonalds** is located, turn right or west onto the **Kane Creek Road**. Follow it northwest, then southwest right along the river. This road is paved all the way to the mouths of Pritchett and Kane Springs Canyons.

Elevations Visitor Center, Moab, 1227m; Potash, 1219m; top of Jackson's Ladder, 1390m; top of the Poison Spider Mesa (Sand Flats), 1599m; top of Moab Rim Trail, 1509m; Hurrah Pass, 1463m.

Water Take plenty with you, but there are springs with good water along lower Kane Creek & Spring Canyons, and in Hunters Canyon. Also, at some campgrounds along the Potash & Kane Creek Roads.

Maps USGS or BLM maps Moab & La Sal (1:100,000); Moab, Gold Bar Canyon, Shafer Basin & Trough Springs Canyon (1:24,000--7 1/2' quads); the plastic Trails Illustrated/National Geographic map, Moab South (1:70,000); or covering most of this area is the plastic Latitude 40° map Moab West (1:75,000).

Main Attractions A couple of short hikes to viewpoints high above Moab with the snowcapped La Sal Mountains in the background; several historic river bottoms; at least 6 good arches, many good mtn. biking routes; the historic & scenic Jackson's Ladder Trail; many campsites (all for a fee) close to Moab; and some of the highest concentrations of rock art (mostly petroglyphs) in the world.

West Side of the Colorado River

Theof Bottom and the Hinton Trail

At about mile post 12 on the Potash Road, you'll leave Spanish Valley, and enter a gorge which constricts the Colorado River. As you drive along, the river will be on your immediate left, while first the Wingate, then Kayenta, and finally the Navajo Sandstone cliffs will rise abruptly on your right. Driving downstream along this section, and at about where **mile post 11** should be, there's a very small narrow bottom on the north side of the road. This used to be called **Theof Bottom** (it now has a small campground called the **Jaycee Park Camping**) and there's an old stockman's trail which now begins there with a good parking place & toilet. The late **Swanny Kerby** tells us a little about the place:

*It was before and during World War II that I was grazing cattle down there along the Colorado River. Our range started right there at Theof Bottom. The **Hinton Trail** goes from Theof Bottom way up there on them ledges. It's one of the wildest trails down there. It goes up on **Poison Spider Mesa**, which we used to call the **Sand Flats**. Some of the sheepmen over there used it occasionally--not very often though because it was such a hazardous affair. We got acquainted with that country and used this trail before the Taylor Grazing Act came in [signed by FDR on 7/27/1934], that's when we first used that trail. Dad had helped Bill Hinton with some cattle there. We went down in there with a little bunch of cattle once, and then went up this Hinton Trail and across the Sand Flats, and then back down to the river at*

Looking southeast at Moab and the **La Sal Mountains** as seen from the top of the **Hinton Trail**.

Map 25, Moab Overlook Trails & Nearby River Bottoms, Jacksons Ladder Trail, L. Pritchett & Hunters Canyons & Rock Art

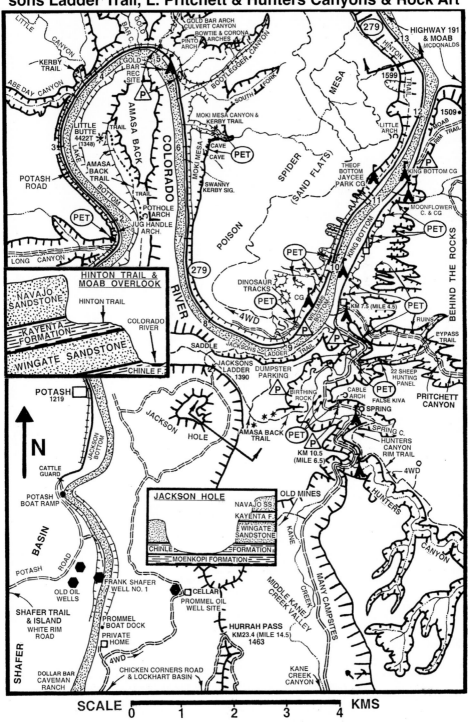

Left Doc Williams, later in life, in the 1930's or 40's (?). Many consider him to be the father of Arches National Monument. **Right** The ranch house built and owned by Doc Williams on **Williams Bottom**. In those days, the only way to reach this place was by boat on what was then the Grand River (renamed the Colorado on July 25, 1921). This picture was likely taken before about 1908 or 1910 (?) and before Hy Turner bought the place. (Mitch Williams Collection)

Williams Bottom.
    There used to be 2 different bottoms, Theof and Williams Bottoms. Williams Bottom was right across from where Kane Creek comes in. You go down the river and come to Theof Bottom first. And before Potash came to be, the river run to a ledge after you went past Theof. So in order to get to Williams Bottom you had to go way up over this Poison Spider Mesa then drop back down to Williams Bottom.
    There isn't much of a bottom at Theof. At that time there was a livin' spring there, and that's where all the bootleggers hung out and made [moonshine] whiskey because it was close to town. It was right across from the upper end of **King Bottom**. The river run under a ledge for about 100 yards [90m] and you could only get down to Williams Bottom by boat.
    Not a lot is known about Theof Bottom, except that it was first settled by a guy named Theof (?). There today you'll find a little walk-in campground, but for a fee (it's not so good, because it's right on a main road, and the campsites are close together). There used to be spring water coming out of a pipe--but that's nowhere to be found today--take your own water! There's also a good toilet & dumpster nearby, and the Hinton Trail begins at the Theof parking lot. This trail then heads northeast and actually parallels the road for about 500m, so you could park up the road a ways from Theof and save a little walking. After that flat section, the trail begins to climb up along the Kayenta bench which makes a natural route. The rock strata in this area is uplifted to the northeast, so this same bench rises at a good angle. The higher you climb the narrower the bench becomes. Finally, as you turn the corner to the left, the bench narrows to just a ledge. At that point and for the next 500m or so, you'll have some very fine views of Moab and the Spanish Valley, and usually the snow-capped La Sal Mountains beyond.
    When you reach the very top of the Hinton Trail, you'll come to the upper part of the Sand Flats or Poison Spider Mesa 4WD road. This old track begins further downriver at Williams Bottom and heads up on top of this sloping mesa. This road is especially popular with Jeepers, mtn. bikers & ATV's. Some bikers ride up the road, then head down the Hinton Trail, but that's a rugged place for mtn bikes. If you do try it, best to go down the trail, not up. Really though, this is a hikers trail, and maybe should be left that way. It's about 4 kms from Theof to the top of the Hinton Trail, so most people can walk it round-trip in 2-3 hours. Take lots of water on a hot summer day.
    In the area downstream from Theof, and on either side of **mile post 10**, be sure to observe the sheer walls carefully, because there are several good **petroglyph panels** along that stretch of road. There's also a sign pointing out the **Indian Writings**. These panels are some of the best you'll find anywhere. Park in designated parking places only, as the road is narrow at that point. In the past this is where the ledges came down right to the river. Just northeast of the rock art is a very popular place for rock climbing on the sheer Navajo Sandstone walls. Drive slow for about 1 km so you don't hit climbers.

Williams Bottom, Dinosaur Tracks and more Rock Art Panels

    Between **mile posts 9 & 10**, the space between the river and the cliff widens a little. This is called **Williams Bottom**. It got the name from a man named **John W. "Doc" Williams**. First a little history of Doc Williams and this bottom. Doc was born in 1853 in Missouri and crossed the plains to Colorado in 1875 as a cowboy. For 6 years he punched cows, then got into the drugstore business in Hugo, Colorado. He did that for 12 years before going to Denver to study medicine. Williams graduated from medical school in 1895 and set up practice at Ordway, Colorado. Sometime in 1896, J.N. Corbin, the owner and editor of **The Grand Valley Times (GVT)** newspaper of Moab, started a campaign to attract a doctor to town. Doc Williams heard about it and first visited Moab in December of 1896. He was to be the county physician and get paid $150 a year from Grand County **(12/11/1896--GVT)**. He soon opened his first office in Moab in January of 1897. In 1900, at age 47, he married a Utah girl named Lavina Larson and they had 5 children. He practiced medicine for 23 years before retiring in 1919. He died much later--in 1956, at the age of 103. Because of his interest in conservation, Doc Williams is considered by many to be the *"Father of Arches National Park"*.

The one person in Moab who knew more about Doc Williams & Bottom than anyone alive in 1991 was the now-late **Mitch Williams**, one of Doc's sons. Here's what he remembered about the place:

That's named after my dad, John W. "Doc" Williams. He had a ranch down there. It was before I was born. My sister Eda, she remembers going down there. You see, we had a ranch down in the lower end of this Moab Valley, 80 acres [32 hectares]. They'd go down there and get in a rowboat, then go down to Williams Bottom in that. There used to be a nice adobe house there and you can go down there today and see the old **root cellar**. *It's on the side of the hill and it looks like an old Indian ruin. There was a spring there which evidently produced more water than it does now. At one time they had some goats down there along with some cows. And my dad had a water wheel up there where there's a* **big rock** *in the river. He had a waterwheel between that rock and the bank. You couldn't go down there by land then--only by boat. That's all been filled in now to make the [Potash] road. The water went right up against the cliffs and it would turn the wheel and lift the water up, and part of the old ditch is still there.*

You know where that bear is, the petroglyph up on the wall? Near that, you might see a big rock that's separated from the bank a little bit, it's got an iron spike on top, which I think was put in later by boatmen, because they had a big paddlewheeled boat tied up there one time--and it sunk right there. I remember it, I was there and I saw the barge. And the river started droppin' and one edge of the barge was on the bank and it started tippin' down on the other side. And they hired some of the guys around here to go down and they told 'em if they could save the boat they'd give 'em a lot of money--$10 apiece or something like that. So they nailed 2 x 4's on the side, and they worked like beavers trying to build that side up, because they figured the river would stop dropping. But they lost it. This was in the late 1920's. It was the second boat the Moab Garage built. They built another paddlewheeler which people don't seem to know much about. I don't think they had it very long before they lost it. The rock where the paddlewheeler was lost at is the same place where my dad had his waterwheel.

One time my dad wanted to take a bull down there to Williams Bottom, and my uncle Roy Larson was helpin' him. They were going to row a boat down and let the bull swim. And papa said, "Roy you row the boat and I'll take care of the bull". And my dad got a great big long willow switch, and he had a halter on the bull, and they started out down the river and the bull was swimmin'. Of course that bull wanted to get in the boat, and Roy said he was just scared to death. He thought that damn bull was gonna get in that boat, and of course he would have sunk everything if he'd got one foot in. But every time the bull would get a little close, my dad would just whip'im on the end of his nose and he'd back up a little bit. And they went all the way down to Williams Bottom that way.

My dad first went down there in about 1900. I can only guess as to when they left but it must have been in about 1908 or 1910. I don't think my dad ever had a deed to the place. In those days what they would do is sell their improvements to the next guy. It was just like selling the ranch, but without a deed. I think it was Hy Turner who bought out my dad, and they called it Turner Bottom for a while. I remember vaguely when Hy Turner was down there when I was pretty small. Hy was a trapper, and he kind of lived off from the country. I think the place was abandoned after that. And of course, the old adobe house finally fell down and it was just laying there with the roof still there on the ground. Then when they built the Potash Road [1962-63], they bulldozed it out of existence. It's completely gone now. Only the root cellar is still there in the middle and just above the campground].

(Hy Turner is believed to be the brother of **Mel Turner**, the cattleman who built the cabin in House Park. Read more about Mel and that cabin in the chapter, ***Archaeological Sites--Beef Basin Country*** in the back of this book.)

In looking through the old Moab newspapers, several bits and pieces of the early history of Williams Bottom backs up what Mitch speaks about above. By ***February 1, 1901(GVT)***: *J.W. Williams received 3 fine angora goats which were placed on the Williams Ranch down the river.* (**Angora goats** were introduced into Utah in about 1895 near Kanab in Southern Utah. They were brought in for their fleece or **Mohair**, but the goats lasted only until World War II. Read that history in this writer's other book on the **Paria River**.)

The Friday, ***May 24, 1901,*** issue of *GVT* states: *Dr. J.W. Williams had the misfortune to have his irrigation waterwheel, which he had just succeeded in getting into successful operation on his ranch on the river, carried away by the high water last Sunday. He has just planted an orchard and other crops which is all likely to be lost.* By September of that year, Doc and Carl Lowmeyer went downriver about 40 miles [65 kms] in a rowboat to look for the waterwheel, but failed to find it. The need for water was acute so the next year Doc tried something else. In the ***February 7, 1902***, issue of the *GVT* it states: *Dr. Williams has received a 4 horse power gas engine which will be used to pump water onto his river ranch.*

The late **Swanny Kerby** formerly of Moab, remembered a little about **Hy Turner**, the man who lived on Williams Bottom from about 1910 until the early or mid-1930's:

Hy Turner was living at Williams Bottom at the time we built the trail in Moki Canyon. Dad and him had a little bunch of cattle, and we run our cattle with his. He was kind of the old river rat. He had a little canoe and he kinda moved us around the river bottoms. He also trapped up and down the river. When I remember him he was 80 some odd years old, and was active down there with the cattle. He knew more about that river than anybody alive. That river was his life.

When we first went to Williams Bottom, he had been there a long time. We'd take the cattle down there by way of the Sand Flats [Poison Spider Mesa], and he'd bring our supplies down by boat. That way we didn't have to pack so much up and over the top. We were there several years doing that.

Between the Potash Road and the cliffs on Williams Bottom, and between **mile posts 9 & 10**, are a number of campsites, all a part of the **Williams Bottom Recreation Site**. These are part of a fee use area and include a big dumpster and toilets.

In about the middle of Williams Bottom you can walk up a short trail on the hillside to see the tumbled-down **root cellar** built by Doc Williams. Also, at the southwestern end of this bottom there's a sign pointing out a place where you can climb up the hillside a ways to see impressions of **dinosaur tracks** in the rock. About 60m above these dino tracks to the north, are **5 good panel of petroglyphs**, some of the best around. This is in this same area where the old stock trail used to come down off Sand Flats or Poison Spider Mesa, the one Swanny Kerby mentioned above. Also, right at that sign, there's a good road running uphill about 100m to a large parking area. This is the **Poison Spider Trailhead**, complete

Near **mile post 10** on the Potash Road is one of the more unusual rock art panels around. It's simply called the **Bear** or **The Bear Panel**. The main figure is about a meter long.

One of 5 rock art panels seen about 60m above the **Dinosaur Tracks**. Near **mile post 9** on the **Potash Road**, turn right or north and drive about 100m uphill to the **Poison Spider Trailhead**. Park near the restroom and walk northeast uphill to see the dino tracks and the 5 panels above.

with **toilet,** where ATV and mtn. bikers park their cars or trucks and begin running up on the mesa. This mesa is a favorite playground for 4WD's, ATV's and mtn. bikers. This would be the preferred parking place if you want to see the dino tracks or the rock art panels. You can see all these sites in 10-15 minutes. Read a warning about sleeping in your car at this Poison Spider Trailhead on **page 15**.

Moki Mesa, Moki Mesa Canyon and the Kerby Trail

From Williams Bottom, continue along the Potash Road which gradually veers to the right and runs north. About 500m before you reach the mouth of **Bootlegger Canyon** (with the railroad tunnel) and near **mile post 6**, is a short little side-drainage coming down to the river from the east. This we'll call **Moki Mesa Canyon**. For an interesting hike, park on the east side of the road next to a fence across the mouth of this little drainage. There are some box elder trees there and a little shade. Hop over the fence and walk east upcanyon, staying on the south side of the canyon bottom. This place has many trees and other vegetation.

Near the upper end of the drainage, and about 500m from the highway, is an old **cattle trail** blasted out of solid Navajo Sandstone leading up on a bench to the south. Some of the old timers called this hidden benchland **Moki Mesa**. See picture below. This is a small grassy area above the river and canyon, but below a higher rim to the east. Upon this little triangular flat are 2 west-facing **caves** which were old Indian campsites and several small **petroglyph sites**. At one place, Swanny Kerby even left his lightly-scratched signature. See map. The only way the Fremont Indians could have gotten up there is from the area where the trail is now--this writer still hasn't figured that out. They must have used ladders or hacked hand and foot holds out of solid rock (?).

At the very upper end of Moki Mesa Canyon is usually a pool of water at the bottom of a very high dryfall coming off the top of the plateau above--and with no more cattle around, it's likely drinkable (?). From there, you can climb up the slickrock to the north and walk around, and with a little climbing, drop down into the south fork of Bootlegger Canyon.

Now for a little history of who built the trail in this little inconspicuous canyon as related by the late **Swanny Kerby:** *We put that trail up there and when we went up the first time we found a lot of moki [Fremont Indian] caves--I guess we called it Moki Mesa. We put our weaner calves up there when we were blasting the trail. It was kinda of a hard deal to get the cattle to take to that trail and so we didn't use it too many times. I was born in 1917, and I guess we put that up there when I was in high school, in about 1932, or maybe a year or two before that (?).*

I doubt if the Indians used that route up where the trail is now. They may have used some ladders or cut some steps in the rock (?). We looked and looked at that thing before we made that trail, because we knew it was quite a little mesa and it had never been grazed off. I don't think we ever got up there before we built that trail. I think we saw it from above--just looked down on it. I remember we had hell finding enough money to buy the powder to build it with. It was me and Hy Turner and my dad Ed Kerby who built that trail.

Corona and Bowtie Arches

Further north along the Potash Road and east of the BLM's **Gold Bar Recreation Site**, and about

Aerial view of **Moki Mesa**, so named by Swanny Kerby. No cattle and almost no people had ever been there until Ed & Swanny Kerby and Hy Turner built the trail up to it in about 1932.

Bowtie & Corona Arches. The hike to these natural arches is one of the more popular around Moab.

200m before you come to **mile post 5**, you'll see where the Denver & Rio Grande Western Railroad line comes out of Bootlegger Canyon (it runs through a tunnel under Poison Spider Mesa). From there, this railway runs next to the road all the way to Potash. It was built to take potash from the mines at Potash to the main railway line near Crescent Junction. From where the railroad reaches the Colorado River, and on down to Potash, there are a number of canyons entering the gorge; **Culvert, Gold Bar, Little, Abe Day and Long Canyons** have already been discussed along with **Map 17** page 181.

Right where you first see the railway line coming out of this canyon is a signposted parking place & **trailhead** on the east side of the highway. From the parking, follow a popular and well-used trail about 1 1/2 kms to the east. This takes you to 2 fotogenic arches almost side by side. On one map one of the arches is called **Little Rainbow Bridge**, but the sign on the road, and in most literature these days, they're called **Corona and Bowtie Arches**. Most people can do this round-trip in about an hour; or two at most. This short hike is one of the more popular places in the Moab area for anyone with a camera.

East Side of the Colorado River

Moab Rim Trail

The first hike here could be up the **Moab Rim Trail**, but it's shown & described better in the next chapter, under **Map 26**, so go there for this nice hike to an overlook of Moab. However, to reach this site, drive along the **Kane Creek Road** starting at **McDonalds** in the south end of Moab. Head westwards and into the Colorado River Gorge. After **4.3 kms (2.7 kms)** is a parking lot & trailhead with toilet on the left or south side of the road. This is the Moab Rim Trail TH.

King Bottom and Rock Art

From the Moab Rim Trailhead, continue southwest on the Kane Creek Road. You'll soon pass the riverside **King Bottom Campground**, then at **Km 5 (3.1 mile)** is the mouth of **Moonflower Canyon**, with a parking place, toilet, and a walk-in campground. Immediately west of the parking place will be a panel of **petroglyphs**.

A little further along, the flat land broadens and there are several trailer homes, tunnels and **private land** along the left or southeast side of the road. Near one tunnel, is a small boulder with **rock art**, plus there's more behind it on the main wall. This wide place is known as **King Bottom**. This name comes from a man named **Samuel N. King** who was in this area before 1900. The first we know of King being in Moab is from the *November 12, 1897*, issue of the *Grand Valley Times*. In it an article states: *Charles McPherson, of Green River, Wyo. has come to Moab to make his home for a few months, and will make his headquarters at the Times office. Mr. McPherson is the inventor of a waterwheel elevator that excels anything ever attempted in the way of a current wheel. One of the wheels will be erected at once on the river at the King ranch.....* A couple of years later McPherson ran an ad in the **GVT** advertising the McPherson Water Elevator. It took McPherson and crew until *4/21/1899* to complete the water wheel at King Bottom.

Some time in the fall of 1898, King won a bid to build a road from Moab up along the Colorado River to Richardson, which is/was located on the river just below Castleton. Later, King was operating the ferry and was postmaster at Dewey (which is further northeast along the Colorado River) in 1902, but he resigned as postmaster in January of that year. All this time he apparently still maintained his ranch on the river below Moab. In the **March 20, 1903** issue of the **GVT**, an article under *Realty Transfers* states: *Samuel N. King to **Edward Johnson**, Desert Claim on Grand River west of Moab, Consideration $700, January 2, 1903* (the Grand was renamed the Colorado River on July 25, 1921 because up to that time the state of Colorado didn't have this famous river within its boundaries and the Colorado State Legislature didn't want to be cheated out of the name Colorado!). Ed Johnson was apparently the 2nd owner of this river bottom.

King was involved in mining in the La Sal Mountains after that. The next thing we know about him came in the **8/7/1908 GVT**. One article states: *"Captain Samuel N. King has been notified by the war department that a special act of congress he will receive a pension of $25 a month"*, says Sunday's *Salt Lake Herald*. *"He served in a Pennsylvania regiment and was promoted from the ranks to first lieutenant for going twelve miles [20 kms] inside the rebel lines in Virginia and recovering the body of Colonel George H. Covode in 1868. He expects to sell his ranch in Moab and go back to his old home in Pennsylvania"*.

The late **Ray Holyoak** of Moab, who was born in 1914, wasn't sure who may have owned the King Bottom ranch after **Ed Johnson**, but he did remember a little about his own family being there and the old cattle route which is now known as the **Moab Rim Trail**:

It was my dad and uncle who bought it from someone else, and our family moved onto King Bottom way back when I was just a little bitty kid. This must have been in the late 1910's that we moved in there. I don't remember King himself, but he lived in a kind of a dugout. It was blocked up in the front. I never did find out if he had cattle down there. I never saw a waterwheel, but I've seen the ditch where water come to a little garden spot.

All we did on King Bottom was use it for winter grazing. We fenced it off at each end and kept the stock out in summer and let the vegetation grow and then grazed it in winter. This would be from about the first of November when we'd get down there. Our Forest permit run until the 15th of October and it'd usually take us about 2 weeks from the time we'd get 'em gathered up on the mountain, then cut out the ones we wanted to go down there. We'd sell the calves. The normal route we took getting our cattle there was to bring'em off the mountain and take the trail up above Moab on the rim, then down the trail along the Kayenta bench [Moab Rim Trail] to King Bottom. We didn't take 'em through town.

We never did live on King Bottom, we stayed right here in town and went down during the day and come back in the evening. We didn't have any road in there until Ralph Miller bought it.

*Much later our family sold King Bottom to **Ralph Miller**, and he made his egg ranch down there. He shot a room out of that solid rock and put chickens in there, and they really laid good. They was all in separate cages and 3 hens to a cage. And he had the water running through all the cages. They just ate and laid eggs. The temperature was good for layin' eggs.*

According to **Ray Tibbetts** of Moab (who married Ralph's daughter), Ralph Miller bought much of the private land at King Bottom in **1957 or '58**, just after he sold Anderson Bottom on the Green River to Karl Tangren. Ralph built and operated what everybody called the **Egg Ranch** for several years before selling it.

In about the middle of King Bottom, and just beyond a couple of trailer homes, you'll see a road running up and to the left going to another trailer house on a low intermittent bench. If you park near the highway, walk up this road, but then turn left or south, you can follow a right-of-way 4WD road up on another bench above King Bottom. There are some powerlines and an old gravel pit up there, but if you walk along the base of the Navajo Sandstone wall, you'll see more **rock art**, including one they call **The Elephant**.

Farther south along King Bottom and as you near the mouth of Pritchett Canyon, there are more **rock art** panels on your left; but nothing too spectacular there.

Kane Creek Canyon and lots of Rock Art

Continue driving southwest on Kane Creek Road. You'll know you're at the mouth of **Pritchett Canyon** when you see a house, then a little campground on the left, and just after that the pavement ends at a **cattle guard**, that's where the good graded gravel road begins. This will be at about Km 7.5 (**Mile 4.5**, from McDonalds).

Here's the situation as of late 2012. Since 1991, and after the first edition of this book came out, a home was built right at the mouth of Pritchett on a small piece of private land. With that came a fee to pass their property and into the canyon. Later came a small camping place. As of the last trip there, hikers and motorcycles had to pay $2 a day; 4WD's $3 per day. This of course will discourage most people, but there is a new route into Pritchett Canyon bypassing the private property and, pioneered, in-part, by this cheap-skate writer. Pritchett Canyon will be discussed in the next chapter with **Map 26**.

From the end of the paved road & cattle guard, drive west 200m or so to a large parking lot on the right. This is the **trailhead** for the hike to Jackson's Hole & Ladder--but we'll get to that later. Continue south and into Kane Springs Canyon. At **Km 8.2** (**Mile 5.1**) will be 2 metal posts painted **yellow & black**, and a 2-car parking place on the left or east. Park there and walk up a newly made hiker's path about 100m at the base of the Navajo Sandstone wall. Facing west, will be a really nice **petroglyph panel** sculptured in the *Barrier Canyon style*. That style is usually a pictograph, but not here.

Continue south, then west to **Km 8.6** (**Mile 5.3**), and on your right or north will be a large parking lot with a garbage bin; let's call this the **Dumpster Parking**. This is used often by base jumpers, or in this case, **cliff jumpers**, who start hiking there, and wind up on top of some cliffs--then jump off a perfectly good Navajo Dome! Beware: when their chutes open--it sounds like a cannon shot.

From the Dumpster Parking, walk south up a steep zig zag trail, the same one the jumpers use, and to the end of a sandstone fin above. There you'll see a kind of **false kiva** (a low walled Fremont Indian shelter) and about 300m of scattered **rock art**. Continue east on a good trail up through a short steep place where you climb using all-4's. Immediately above that, turn left or north, and on the wall maybe 75m away, will be a panel of **22 big horn sheep & 2 hunters** all in a straight line. Nice panel, one of the most interesting around.

Remember this panel and route getting to it. This is the free **Bypass Trail** into Pritchett Canyon and the Behind the Rocks area from the west. It will be covered in the next chapter with Map 26 along with the South or Main Fork of Mill Creek east of Moab.

Now back to the Dumpster Trailhead and driving west. Soon you'll pass the beginning of the **Amasa Back Trail** on the right or north at **Km 9.5** (**Mile 5.9**). This track is used mostly by **mtn. bikers**, then a few hikers, modified 4WD's, Rock Buggies, ATV's & motorcycles. Most of you won't wanna go there

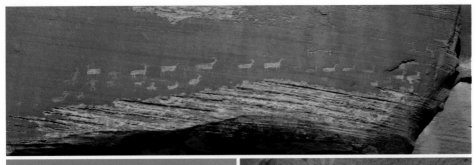

Top The **22 Sheep Hunting Panel** located along the **Bypass Trail** into lower **Pritchett Canyon**. **Left** It's only a short hike to **Cable Arch** which is on the rim of lower Kane Creek Canyon. **Right** This rock art is on a large boulder next to the Kane Creek Road and it's called the **Birthing Rock**.

with a vehicle--it's a terrible track! More on this hike below.

At **Km 9.8 (Mile 6.1)** will be a couple of small parking places on the right or west side of the road. Stop at the first, and walk 40m down a trail to a van-sized boulder called the **Birthing Rock**. You'll wanna go there! It has art on 4 sides, including an image of a woman giving birth--this is one piece of art we can all figure out. To the right of her is a guy who looks like the guilty one. From that parking place, look for a route up to the Navajo wall above. There's one small panel some are calling **The Map**; it has some lines pecked in, but calling it a map is a stretch! It's not worth the effort. This country is full of panels with doodlings like that.

About 150m up the road to the south is another smaller boulder right next to the road with art on one side. About 650m past the 1st Birthing Rock parking place, will be a parking place for about 5 cars on the left or north and at **Km 10.5 (Mile 6.5)**. It sits opposite to a sign of a truck going downhill & **10% grade**. From there climb north upon another level or bench and to the right a little to see some faint images on the lower Navajo Sandstone wall. From there, get into the obvious drainage and scramble north up a steep near-vertical chute using all-4's, then turn right or east into another minor drainage. After another 300-350m, will be **Cable Arch**.

From the Cable Arch parking, continue down the Kane Springs Canyon Road past a paved **S curve**, then to the mouths of **Spring and Hunters Canyons,** both with walk-in campsites nearby. Near the mouth of Spring Canyon is a good spring; fill your water bottles there. At the mouth of Hunters is a new toilet. Both of these canyons and some good hiking will be discussed in the next chapter along with **Map 26.**

Middle Kane Creek Valley, Hurrah Pass, and Wash Johnson's Cabin

The lower end of Kane Creek Canyon is deeply entrenched, then upstream to the southwest a ways, the canyon opens up into a broad but still deep valley. Let's call this **Middle Kane Creek Valley**. The road into this part is very good and used a lot by people in cars, on mtn. bikes, ATV's and motorcycles. There are lots of campsites here--all for a fee. In 2012, the BLM was in the process of installing toilets and picnic tables at some sites. Go online to **blm.gov/gov/ut/st/en/fo/moab**, then look for recreation and camping. There somewhere should be a map of the Moab area and the official campsites. They're calling these 2 main sections, **The Ledge Camping, Loop A & B**. It cost $8 a car in 2012, but you'll have to furnish your own water. This writer last saw the place on 10/20/2012, and with good weather, it was packed wall to wall, mostly with ATV enthusiasts! Look for changes in this valley in the future.

Just as the valley is beginning to widen, look to the west and you'll see running along one of the inclined beds of the Chinle Formation, an **old miner's track**. You can walk up there today for some good views to the east.

Toward the south end of this Middle Kane Creek Valley, the main road veers to the west at a junction **(Km 18.4/Mile 11.4)** and heads for **Hurrah Pass** at Km 23.4 **(Mile 14.5** from McDonalds). We'll call this road over Hurrah the **Lockhart Road**. Someone in Moab recorded the history of Hurrah Pass in the book, **Grand Memories, a History of Grand County**. They thought the name came from old cowboys who drove cattle across this pass, then hollered *"Hurrah"* as the last of their cows crossed over. But the late **Kent Johnson** had something else to say after reading that history in the author's other book, **River Guide to Canyonlands National Park and Vicinity**. Kent first went down there in about 1920 with his father Wash Johnson, and he said this:
*Hurrah Pass wasn't Hurrah Pass when we used it. The name Hurrah Pass came later. Ace Turner was prospecting down there in that country, and when they got back up to the pass they started calling it Hurrah Pass. This was in the early 1950's. When I was cowboyen down in there, nobody knew anything about Hurrah Pass; we just called it **The Notch**. You see, **Ace Turner** went over that pass and went down into what we called **Main Canyon** and to some mines he had up there. Main Canyon is where **Dripping Springs** is.* Read more on that area in the chapter with Map 27.

Dave Baker of Moab, came to this country in the early 1950's, and added a little more history to the Kane Creek Road: *We built the Kane Creek Road in 1956. Before that, the only way you could get down there was on horseback. I worked for an engineer, a surveyor, and he had to go down in there and flag a school section. The Bureau of Public Roads was buildin' it for the AEC [Atomic Energy Commission] because they was puttin' up the money, I suppose. The county never had anything to do with it when they first built it. Miner's built [the road] over Hurrah Pass [because they] was doin' some prospecting when we was down in there.*

Back in 1990-'91, the author's VW Rabbit with oversized tires had no problems getting to the top of Hurrah Pass, and some low slung cars did. On his last trip in the fall of 2012, it seemed worse than ever. But the good news is, the west side is now the better half, partly due to the 2 private residents who live down by the river. They're doing some maintenance on it. Most people driving cars park in the valley somewhere and bike up to the top and often times beyond. On top of Hurrah Pass, there are places to camp, but there's always a breeze too, so don't be there if a storm's rolling in. To have success on the west side of Hurrah Pass, better have a 4WD/AWD with lots more clearance than a car.

Near the bottom of Hurrah Pass on the west site, and as you go down into a dry wash and up the other side, look for a sign on the right or north; this is the entrance to the **Base Camp Lodge** and another private home beyond. However, along that road are 2 turnoffs to the left which go to these 2 places. If you stay on this **Jackson Hole Road** instead, then you can legally bypass the private land. This old track is in pretty good shape and will take you past the old **Prommel oil well** and into **Jackson Hole**. This would be another way to get to the bottom of Jacksons Ladder.

Back on the Lockhart Road again. A little nearer the river, one former branch of this main road runs west upon a bench overlooking Tangren's Caveman Ranch. That track has been blocked off for vehicles, but you can walk up there to view the river. From that point and just downhill to the north are the old ruins of **Wash Johnson's cabin** (It's about 100m north of the Base Camp Lodge, so if you want to see it you'll have to talk to the owner Tom Higginson first). Wash Johnson's son **Kent** formerly of Moab knew the history of this old cabin and how his father got it where it is today:
Ya see, the oil well company moved the lumber and stuff from the boat docks down on the river, up to the Prommel Well below Hurrah Pass. The hauling was done with these steel-wheeled Ford tractors. They pulled a trailer behind it to haul their stuff up there. One thing they had a problem with was the steel wheels--sometimes they'd catch in the rocks when they was pullin' hard and hell, the front end of that tractor would come right up over the driver! Anyway, they built cabins up at the Prommel Well for their crews. They drilled that in 1926, but then after they got through drilling and abandoned it, then my dad made a deal with them for that cabin. Then with horses, he went up there and skidded the one cabin down there to the river and set it up. He skidded it down in one piece, as a unit. This must have been around 1930 when he did this.
There was 2 guys that helped him. One of 'em was named Johnny May and the other was a guy named Woodruff. It was in The Depression and times was hard, and so they went down and helped my dad move that cabin. After that they lived in it and trapped foxes down there for 2 or 3 years, then they left the country. Those 2 guys used it more than anybody. My dad, Wash Johnson died in February, 1941, and it was never used after that.

Today this cabin is on the ground, having collapsed under it's own weight, plus tamarisks have grown up all around it so it's hard to see or get at. There's also some interesting junk lying around nearby; but it's on **private ground.**

Jacksons Ladder & Trail to Jackson Hole, and the Amasa Back Trail

One of the more interesting hikes in this area is to a place called **Jackson's Ladder**. There are about 3 ways you can get to this historic trail, but for most people, especially those with cars, the best way would be to stop at the large parking lot & **Jacksons Ladder Trailhead** just beyond the end of pavement & the cattle guard on Kane Creek Road. This is **7.6 kms (4.6 miles)** from McDonalds. At the south end of the parking, will be an information board and the beginning of the trail. It goes down to Kane Creek and up the other side heading downriver. In some places beside the trail will be a metal pipe. This is a **gas pipeline** running to **Potash**. It was built in 1961 or '62 when they started building the infrastructure for the Potash mining operation.

About 1 km past the trailhead, the path zig zags up to a higher bench, then it more or less contours part-way around a big bend of the river until it reaches a **saddle** between the Colorado and **Jackson Hole**. Jackson Hole is an old **abandoned meander** or rincon. When you get to this saddle, you'll find the very rough LR/HC/4WD/ATV/mtn. biking **Amasa Back Trail** which begins inside the lower end of Kane Creek Canyon. Once on top of the saddle, look for the gas pipeline and powerlines. Follow one or the other to where it drops down over the cliff to the south. There you'll find what is known as **Jacksons Ladder**. It starts down about halfway between the powerlines and the gas pipeline.

This is the best of several sites with rock art at **Km 8.2 (Mile 5.1** from McDonalds) along the **Kane Creek Road** (near the 2 yellow & black metal posts).   Look closely on the right side and you can just make out the biggest of these human-like figures.   These petroglyphs are similar to the Barrier Creek style of rock art; but usually that style comes in red painted forms.

Left This foto was taken from the high cliffs & lookout about 1 1/2 kms west of Jacksons Ladder. It shows the main facility at **Potash**, with Dead Horse Point on the high ground in the distance, and the Colorado River in the lower part of the picture. **Right** From the **Amasa Back Trail**, looking northwest at the **Jacksons Ladder Trail**. Notice power poles in the upper left; and the gas pipeline, right.

The trail zig zags straight down a steep ravine and rockslide. When you see it, you'll know how it got its name. About halfway down, the pipeline crosses the trail. At the bottom you'll come to the 4WD road inside Jackson Hole. This one originates on the lower west side of **Hurrah Pass** on the Lockhart Road. More on that track later.

Now the **Amasa Back Trail**, but first a little history of its building as told by **Karl Tangren** of Moab: *They built that road in there when they put the powerlines into Potash, this was back in about 1962. The power company built that road so they could put in the powerlines. The gas company, when they built that pipeline used helicopters to pack that pipe up there and held it there while them guys welded it. They both went in there in around 1962, it was all the while they was buildin' the Potash Plant. It was when they was puttin' in the road and the railroad, powerlines and everything; it all happened at the same time.*

Instructions on how to get to the **Amasa Back Trailhead** & parking are mentioned above. Right at the trailhead there's no place to park, but if you're doing this on a mtn. bike, leave your car at the **Dumpster Parking** and ride uphill to the beginning of the trail. Or perhaps for hikers, park about 150m uphill and around one corner to the west & south.

The first part of this track is perhaps the roughest of all the bad sections! You'll have to push a bike both ways! Beginners may not like this track (at least parts of), but the pros just love it. To start this trail, go downhill to Kane Creek, up the other side and in a prominent but shallow alcove, you'll find some painted images, and one petroglyph; but it's hardly worth the walk. From Kane Creek, the track climbs up to the southwest. Once on the divide between Kane Springs Canyon and Jackson Hole, you'll have some nice views to the east and of the Behind the Rocks with the La Sal Mountains in the background; and down into Jackson Hole with Dead Horse Point to the west.

Further along, you can veer northeast on another track and end up looking down on the Colorado River and Jacksons Trail; a detour worth taking. Further along the Amasa Back Trail and at the **saddle**, you'll come to Jacksons Trail and the powerlines & gas pipeline. From there, a sign points out the way to an overlook of Potash for motorized vehicles, and beyond to the **Pothole Arch Trail**. This writer walked to the arch and finally found it on the second trip. Only mtn.bikers & hikers on that trail--no motor vehicles. Toward the arch, the trail runs mostly across slickrock with an old faded painted red line marking the way in 2012, so follow that. The last part is easier riding than getting out of Kane Creek. In that area you'll have a nice look down on Jug Handle Arch, the Colorado and the mouth of Long Canyon.

If you continue north past Pothole Arch 300m or so, you'll come to the first of **4 constructed sections** of a **livestock trail**. These 4 parts are spread out over roughly 400m. Then it flattens a little and runs over the top of a low limestone-covered divide. About 1 km north of the first constructed part, you'll see a little pointed **little butte** down to the left or west sitting on an intermediate bench (the *Gold Bar Canyon 7 1/2' quad* shows its altitude is **4422T/1348m**). Immediately east of that, there's another section of a **man-made trail** going over the cliff to the west, then cuts back to the south on a narrow ledge. In that area, livestock used to pasture on some grassy flats but for water, would head to the north end of the Amasa Back peninsula and down to the Colorado. This writer didn't quite get that far north, but there must be another constructed trail immediately south and across the river from the mouth of Gold Bar Canyon. The river would provide the only water for livestock in that area.

This peninsula of land jutting north in a big bend of the Colorado River is named **Amasa Back**, after one of the early settlers of Moab called Amasi Larsen. No one this writer talked to could shed any light on how the place got its name, but Amasi was there doing something.

Before leaving the historic Jacksons Trail, a little history on cattle grazing in the Shafer Basin and Jackson Hole area should be discussed along with part of the story of one of Moab's most famous characters, **John Jackson**. It's not known who may have been the very first stockman in this part of the country, but it very well could have been John Jackson. From old newspaper articles, we know he was in Moab in 1896 & '97, when he got married and had some kind of flooding trouble at his Moab farm or ranch. By **November 30, 1900**, he placed an ad in the **GVT** that went like this: *John Jackson, has arranged a pasture on Grand river [renamed the Colorado in July of 1921] about 14 miles [22 kms] below Moab, and would like to get a number of horses to give personal care for during winter. Good feed and water, rates $1.50 for the winter. Horses delivered at any time.*

From the description in the ad, the horse pasture was somewhere beyond Jacksons Ladder and Trail, probably in Jackson Hole and Jackson Bottom along the river. He may have built this rough trail just prior to placing that ad (?).

Old newspaper articles say John was on jury duty for the county in 1905; apparently lived in Castleton in July of 1905; worked in the mines in the La Sal Mountains in February of 1907; and had cattle in the Blue (Abajo) Mountains & upper Indian Creek by July, 1907. It appears his wife and family were in Moab all the time from 1896 until 1917, but he was cow punchin' down here on the river and in Shafer Basin, and doing a little part-time mining in the mountains. In November of 1908, he brought the election returns to Moab from the mining camp of **Basin**.

By **1911, old maps** show Jackson owned property down on Indian Creek just south of Newspaper Rock at what most people before and since that time called the old **Kelly Place or Ranch**. Jackson and his wife rounded up stray cattle in that area and built up their herd, part of which roamed this Jackson Hole--Shafer Basin country. There was an interesting article in the **GVT** on **March 21, 1913**. It stated: *John Jackson, who returned last week from his cattle range states that wolves are playing havoc with the stock and that a number of cattle have been killed by the predatory beasts. Mr. Jackson states that he found eighteen head of cattle that had been killed and partly devoured by the wolves.*

It would appear the range spoken of above is on Indian Creek which is on the northwest slopes of the Blue (Abajo) Mountains and south of the Dugout Ranch. That part of the country became notorious for wolves at that time and big rewards were paid to trappers to hunt them down. Read more about the history of the extinction of wolves in southeastern Utah in the last part of this book on page 354.

Jackson had his cows on both sides of the Colorado River in those days between Jackson Hole, Hurrah Pass, Potash and the Shafer Trail area. He must have gotten his cattle into the Shafer Basin country west of the river by first taking them down Jacksons Ladder, then swimming them across the Colorado near where Potash is today. An article in the **March 28, 1913** edition of the **GVT** gives us a clue as to what he was doing there then and of a tragic event:

His wife and children standing on the banks of the stream and powerless to render him any assistance, Walter L. Clark was drowned in Grand river yesterday at eleven o'clock. His body is now somewhere in the river and his family are alone near the scene of the tragedy, their grief over his loss accentuated by the absence of anyone to comfort them and by the knowledge that his body may never be recovered.

The tragedy occurred about eighteen miles [29 kms] below Moab on the river. John Jackson, for whom Clark had been working, brought the news of the drowning to Moab.

Jackson and Clark had been fording a bunch of cattle. With a boat they had forced the cattle onto a sand bar in the middle of the river, from which they intended to push the herd to the other side. Fearing that the cattle would swim back to the shore from which they had come, Mr. Jackson left Clark with the boat at the lower end of the bar and started to go around the stock. At a distance of about 75 yards [70m] away he heard Clark cry, and turning around he saw the boat drifting down the stream. Clark was in the water a few feet from the boat, evidently trying to catch it and prevent it from floating away.

Mr. Jackson saw that the man was in trouble and he ran to help him. By the time he reached the lower end of the bar Clark had sunk beneath the surface of the water. He came up once further downstream, and immediately sank again. On account of the swift current and the depth of the water Jackson was unable to swim after the drowning man.

Jackson immediately rode a horse to Moab and a search party was organized to hunt for the body, but it was never found. Mrs. Clark and her 4 small children who witnessed it all stayed in the camp next to the scene for several more days, then they were all taken back to town.

It's believed this drowning took place right close to where Potash is today, because about halfway between Potash and the Potash Boat Ramp is a place called **Jackson Bottom**.

John Jackson stayed in these parts until the summer of 1917. Then he and his wife started divorce proceedings. They then sold much of what they had and headed for California to buy another ranch, apparently still trying to reconcile their differences (?). Later he got a divorce from his first wife (1921) while she was residing in California. Read more about some of John Jackson's earlier escapades in life in the back of this book under **Tidwell Bottom History & the Range War of 1924-25** page 368.

When Jackson pulled out of this country in 1917, two other families moved in. The Shafer brothers **John L. (Sog) and Frank Shafer**, had been running cattle up on Big Flat earlier, but when Jackson started getting a divorce and sold out, they started improving a natural trail down the cliffs and into what would later be called **Shafer Canyon**. It had been a natural route down through the Wingate Sandstone and had been used by the Indians. It was in the late 1910's when the Shafers started working on this trail and taking cows down into Shafer Basin. The trail became known as the **Shafer Trail**, after Sog Shafer. Since those early days, it's been upgraded (1952) to the **Shafer Trail Road**.

The other family was **Wash Johnson's**. They moved in on the east side of the river and into the Hurrah Pass area sometime in the late 1910's (?), probably at the time John Jackson moved out (?). Later, the Holyoaks took over the Shafer range in the early 1930's after the Shafer boys got big checks from the oil company. The Johnsons then traded Holyoaks grazing permits, so the Johnsons ended up on the west side of the Colorado, with the Holyoaks on the east.

Wash Johnson died in February of 1941. Shortly after that his widow and son Kent sold out to a guy from Colorado by the name of **Jim Brown**--shortly after that, he sold his permit to **Howard Lathrop** and **Herman Rowe**. For a while these 2 stockmen had all that country from Abe Day Canyon north of Potash, all the way down to The Confluence on the east side of Gray's Pasture (Island in the Sky) and on top of the White Rim. As it turned out, Rowe had cattle and he put them in the northern half of the range--in the Shafer Basin country; and Lathrop had everything south of there out on the White Rim. Lathrop ran sheep.

Later, **Swanny Kerby** and **Kent Johnson** bought Rowe's permit, then in about 1952, Kerby sold out to **Roy Holyoak** and got in the rodeo business full-time; and **Karl Tangren** bought Johnson's permit. In the 1960's Karl Tangren returned from Anderson Bottom and bought out Roy Holyoak and he still has the grazing permit for cattle and horses in the Shafer Basin country. The sheep range that **Howard Lathrop** had was bought by the French Basque sheepman **Martin Etchart** of Montrose, Colorado in 1955; in 1965, he bought out John Allise's permit for up on top of Big Flat; then on June 30, 1975, all grazing permits inside the park were terminated.

On the east side of the river, the Holyoaks eventually sold their grazing permit to the late **Melvin Dalton** of Monticello. His son **Val Dalton** took over his father's range rights for several years, then in the summer of 2012, sold all the Lockhart country south of Chicken Corners Road to Indian Creek to a guy named **Dicky Joe Ladner** who is presently living in Paradox, Colorado. Most of this grazing history comes from Kent Johnson, Martin Etchart and Karl Tangren.

The later history of Jacksons Ladder is remembered by **Karl Tangren** when he used to take horses over it: *It never was a good trail, but Holyoaks took horses up and down there all my life. I've seen a 100 head of horses on that trail. When Wash Johnson had cattle in there, they took 'em out over Hurrah Pass on that trail. No cattle in my life time ever went over the Jacksons Ladder, but horses did, every spring and every fall. I spent a lot of time taking horses up and down that sucker. Then when they put that gas pipeline in to Potash (1962-'63), it made it pretty hard to use after that.*

The **Kerby Trail** leading up to **Moki Mesa**. It was Ed Kerby and his son Swanny, plus Hy Turner who blasted this trail out of solid Navajo Sandstone in about 1932.

Jug Handle Arch

Above From the very top of **Jacksons Ladder (Trail)** looking straight down the big rockslide that covers the Wingate Sandstone. It's believed **John Jackson** built this trail in the year 1900 so he could take horses to pasture in Jackson Hole, which would be about 14 miles (22 kms) downriver; read more on page 263. Notice the gas pipeline in about the center of the picture; that was put in sometime in 1962-'63.

Left This is the 3rd section of the man-made parts of the horse trail running out onto **Amasa Back ridge**. In the far middle distance is **Potash**; while **Long Canyon** is seen coming down to the river in the upper right. **Jug Handle Arch** is barely visible on the point in the upper right and immediately left of the words on the picture.

Jackson

Hole

Hatch Point

Saddle   Amasa Back Trail

Jackson Trail

Above An aerial view looking south at the rincon or abandoned meander known as **Jackson Hole**. In the far distance is Hatch Point, which is shown on Map 27. Nearer the camera is the **Jackson & Amasa Back Trails,** and the **Saddle**--all shown on Map 25.

Right Looking north at the first of 4 places along the **Amasa Back Trail** that were man-made. The metal stakes drilled into the slickrock which are holding the logs, are made of **rebar**, which means it was built later in history--maybe the 1940's or '50's--or sometime after rebar was invented and began to be widely used (?).

266

Another aerial view looking northwest at the **Potash evaporation ponds**, with **Big Flat** in the distance. Dead Horse Point is to the left and just out of site.

A different look at **Corona Arch**, this time looking west at the east side. This shot was taken in the morning hours. Bowtie Arch is on the other side and to the right or north just a little. The hike to these arches is one of the more popular in the Moab area.

Behind the Rocks, Hidden Valley, and the
South Fork of Mill Creek Rock Art Sites

Location & Access Discussed on this map are 2 areas near Moab; one is called **Behind the Rocks.** This is a maze of narrow canyons and Navajo Sandstone slickrock fins the result of uplifted formations on the southwest side of Spanish Valley & Moab. That slow uplift caused faultline cracks in the Navajo resulting in an east-west tending line of drainages & fins. The other part of this map shows the main or **South Fork of Mill Creek** and a bunch of rock art. That area is southeast of downtown Moab.

Here are the main entry points into **Behind the Rocks.** To reach the beginning of the **Moab Rim Trail,** drive to the south end of Moab and to the signal light next to **McDonalds.** From there, drive westwards on the **Kane Creek Road** and into the Colorado River Gorge. After **4.3 kms (2.7 miles)** is a parking lot & trailhead with **toilet** on the left (south side) of the road. For the story of this trail along with King Bottom history, see the previous chapter & Map 25.

Next entry place will be at or near the mouth of **Pritchett Canyon,** so continue southwest on the Kane Creek Road. At **Km 7.5 (Mile 4.5** from McDonalds) you'll see a house, then a little campground & gate on the left, and just after that the pavement ends at a **cattle guard.** To enter at that point which is on private land, hikers will have to pay a fee of $2 a day. But for a free entry into Pritchett and Behind the Rocks, continue into Kane Springs Canyon until you reach the **Dumpster Parking** at **Km 8.6 (Mile 5.3).** This is a big parking lot on the right or north with a big dumpster trash bin. Park there.

To reach the mouth of **Spring Canyon** and the **Hunters Canyon Rim Trail,** continue southward into Kane Springs Canyon. At **Km 11.2 (Mile 6.9)** is a walk-in camping place; park there. Or continue southward to **Km 12.4 (Mile 7.7)** and park at another walk-in campground with toilet at the mouth of **Hunters Canyon.** One or both of these trailheads can be used to reach **Pritchett Arch.** More later.

Now to get to **Mill Creek Canyon.** From the middle of Moab, proceed to the signal light at 300 S. and turn east; proceed to 400 E. and turn right or south; after a short block, turn left or east again onto **Mill Creek Drive.** Continue east to a **4-way stop,** and turn right or south, again on Mill Creek Drive. After another 1 km (.6 mile), turn left or east onto **Power House Lane.** After another km you'll be at the **main trailhead** for both the North & South Forks of Mill Creek at 1298m altitude.

Here's another way to an upper section of the South Fork of Mill Creek. Head south out of Moab on Highway 191. Between **mile posts 121 & 122,** and at the **Shell Station,** turn eastward onto **Spanish Trail Road.** Proceed on this main road (best to get a city map of Moab at the visitor center for this drive) to a **round-about** and continue in the same direction on **Westwater Drive.** This road circles through a new sub-division and past the **golf course** (see the **petroglyphs** on the rock outcropping to the left behind a log fence), but continue east on that road toward a pass where the paved road veers left or north; but you veer right or eastward onto a rocky graveled road. Proceed over the **pass** and down into what used to be called by the old timers as **Hidden Valley** in the **South Fork of Mill Creek.** At the bottom, and where the road makes a 180° switchback, park right there beside some private farm land with a walk-through gate in front of you. Let's call this the **South Trailhead.**

Elevations Moab Rim Trailhead, 1210m; Hunters Canyon Trailhead, 1250m; Mill Creek Trailhead on Power House Lane, 1298m; the upper South Trailhead on upper Mill Creek, 1408m.

Water Take your own on all hikes, but there is good spring water at the mouth of Spring Canyon and in some parts of Hunters Canyon. Better treat Mill Creek water--skinny dippers are there in summer!

Maps USGS or BLM map Moab (1:100,000); Moab & Rill Creek (1:24,000--7 1/2' quads); the plastic Trails Illustrated/National Geographic map Moab South (1:70,000); or the pastic Latitude 40° map Moab West (1:75,000) for the Behind the Rocks only--it doesn't show Mill Creek.

Main Attractions Lots of **ROCK ART**, easy access on mostly paved roads and nice scenery.

Moab Rim Trail

The first hike or mtn. bike ride here could be up the **Moab Rim Trail.** This trail runs northeast up along the upturned Kayenta bench just below the Navajo Sandstone wall. There are 4WD's & ATV's doing this one, but it's so rugged few attempt it; along the way you'll see a smattering of oil stains running along the slickrock. Only those who enjoy punishing their vehicles try this one. It seems too steep for a mtn. bike, but of course you could push a bike part way up, ride around on some pretty good roads above, then coast back down. From the trailhead to the rim overlooking Moab and the La Sal Mountains beyond, is only about 2 kms, so walking seems the easiest all-around way to get up there. The author made the round-trip hike in 1 hour, 10 minutes once. Plan on at least a couple of hours. The view on top looking east is worth the effort, especially if the La Sals are snow-capped.

Here's an option for mtn. bikers; head for the Hidden Valley Trailhead discussed below, walk and carry your bike up the first part of that trail, then ride northwest on top and come down the Moab Rim Trail--or vise-versa. Either way you go, you'll be riding your bike through part of south Moab to get back to your car.

Pritchett Canyon Bypass Trail and the Big Snake Rock Art Panel

As mentioned earlier, if you walk up Pritchett Canyon from the mouth, you'll have to pay a $2 entry fee, but there's a new **bypass trail** around this private land. What you do is drive into Kane Springs Canyon and to the **Dumpster Parking** at **Km 8.6 (Mile 5.3** from McDonalds). From there, walk south up a well-used zig zag trail which takes you to the west end of a big Navajo Sandstone fin. Around that point are several rock art panels and some kind of Fremont or Archaic Indian shelter. From there, walk east into a minor canyon where you'll have to use all-4's to get up one short pitch. Immediately after that look left or north to see the **22 big horns (& 2 hunters) panel** about 75m away. From the hunters panel, continue due east between fins of Navajo SS. About 2 kms from the Dumpster, you'll downclimb over a ledge and into a short steep drainage. At the bottom will be the road going up Pritchett. From there, you could walk downcanyon about 300m and into a prominent canyon to the east. Up there a ways is an alcove and some kind of Fremont shelter. But forget that; instead walk up Pritchett to the southeast. After about 1 km, will be **winch site** (with lots of black rubber marks on the rocks) where Jeepsters can winch themselves up--or those with home-made rock buggies with huge tires with only 5 lbs of pressure just climb up!

From there, continue southeast upcanyon about another 600m and walk left or northeast into a prominent canyon along a now-blocked-off **old road.** After another 800m, the old road splits; continue left and to the northeast into another drainage. After another 300m, the road ends at some large **boul-**

Map 26, Behind the Rocks, Hidden Valley, and the South Fork of Mill Creek Rock Art Sites

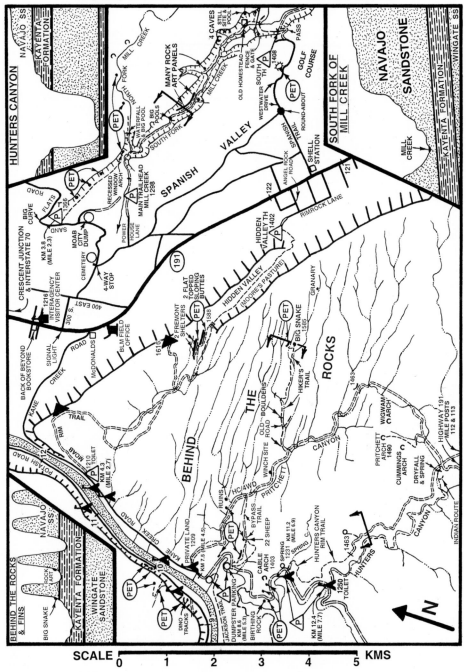

ders. From the end of that old road, continue east on an emerging hiker's trail for about 1 1/2 kms (1 mile). Near the end of that distance, be looking east for the western end of a prominent Navajo Sandstone fin. On the south side of that, and at the bottom of the Navajo SS part of the wall, will be the **Big Snake panel**. This is lighter in color (not as much desert varnish, therefore more recently made) than other **petroglyphs** in the area, but one BLM archaeologist says it's a real Indian-made panel. But this

From near the head of **Hidden Valley**, looking east across Spanish Valley at the snow-capped La Sal Mountains. The hike to the ruins and rock art in Hidden Valley is becoming very popular.

Looking north at the south side of **Pritchett Arch**. Two other arches are nearby; behind the camera a ways and next to the Pritchett Arch Trail is **Cummings Arch**; with **Wigwam Arch** to the right.

writer thinks there's about a 50/50 chance it could have been made more recently by some palefaced moki Indian. If you walk back down a few meters to the west then around the corner to the north, you'll find several more etchings on the next fin, and one pretty nice panel of older petroglyphs. These are genuine. If you were to continue east a little more than 1 km above the Big Snake, you should see a small **granary** under a thin ledge, but it's hardly worth the effort.

Pritchett Arch, Hunters & Spring Canyons, & the Hunters Canyon Rim Trail

Here's one of the better hikes in **Behind the Rocks**. Continue south into Kane Springs Canyon to **Spring Canyon** at **Km 11.2 (Mile 6.9** from McDonalds). Just before its mouth is a good spring on the left, and just below the mouth is a walk-in camping area (for a fee). Park at the mouth somewhere and head upcanyon on a trail. Higher up, you'll scramble to the right and up through some ledges and onto one of the Kayenta Formation benches. There's a pretty good trail there now and it's marked with cairns. This is called the **Hunters Canyon Rim Trail**. After about 2 1/2 kms of rim-walking with good views into lower Hunters Canyon, you'll come to the end of a vehicle track. Follow it south & southeast along the rim of upper Hunters. Eventually, you'll come to the Pritchett Canyon Road where it crosses upper Hunters Canyon drainage. From there road-walk northeast 1 km, then turn left onto a side-road. At the end of that track is the trailhead to **Pritchett Arch**. From there follow a cairned trail up on a bench then north to the arch. Along the way are 2 lesser-known arches; **Wigwam and Cummings**.

Another way to this arch is to continue southward up Kane Springs Canyon Road to **Km 12.4 (Mile 7.7)** and park at another walk-in campground with **toilet** at the mouth of **Hunters Canyon**. From there head up Hunters on a well-used trail. Hunters Canyon is deeply entrenched in the Wingate Sandstone, and depending on the time of year, or how long it's been since the last flood, you'll find some running water, especially in the upper end. In 1990, the upper end of Hunters was an easy walk, but on 9/15/2012, it was overgrown with willows & cattails making walking a little slow in places. At that time it was necessary to walk right in the stream. The reason for all the vegetation was there had not been a big flash flood in the drainage for several years.

Right at the upper end of Hunters is a big **dryfall** & **spring** and good water; but don't go quite that far. About 200m below the dryfall is an old **Indian route** up the south side to the Kayenta bench above. Part of that route has moki steps and it's the only place around where anyone has a chance to exit the canyon. Once on top, road-walk northeast to Pritchett Arch as discussed above.

Here's another option for someone who enjoys a day-hike without backtracking. Park at the mouth of either of these canyons, let's say Spring Canyon for now, then hike up the Hunters Canyon Rim Trail to Pritchett Arch, but return via Hunters Canyon. When you reach Kane Springs Canyon, road-walk about 1 1/2 kms back to your car (or plan ahead and leave a mtn. bike at one end to speed things along). On 9/15/2012, the author walked up Hunters Canyon to Pritchett Arch, and down Spring Canyon in a round-trip time of 5 1/4 hours.

You could even walk up (or down) Pritchett Canyon and use one of the above-mentioned routes to get back to the Kane Creek Road, but that would take 2-3 hours longer than the loop suggested above.

Hidden Valley (Formerly Moore's Pasture) Rock Art & Ruins

Jumping now to the other side of **Behind the Rocks** next to Moab. Here's how to reach some of the best **petroglyph panels** around. Drive the main Highway 191 south out of Moab. Just southeast of **mile post 122** look for **Angel Rock Road** on the west side; once on it drive uphill southwest to **Rimrock Lane** and turn right or northwest and follow the signs to the **Hidden Valley Trailhead** which is 1 km (.6 mile) from the highway. At the trailhead is an information board pointing out the Hidden Valley Trail. In the beginning, it zig zags up the steep rocky slope to the west, then heads northwest into what used to be called since the late 1800's, **Moore's Pasture** (after Eph Moore's father Joseph W. who was with

The **Big Snake panel**. Because it's so unusually large with less desert varnish than others in the neighborhood, some visitors have doubts to its authenticity. However, one BLM archaeologist claims it's for real and made by a Fremont Indian. One reason it may be real is that there are 2 other big snakes at different sites in the area; near **Moab Dump**, and near the panel shown on **page 262**.

the second group of pioneers to enter Salt Lake Valley just behind Brigham Young. He was sent by The Church to help colonize Moab in 1889. He was the ditch rider/water master, for years), but the newcomers to Moab in the late 1900's started calling it **Hidden Valley**.

After about 3 kms of easy walking, you'll come to a pass or low divide at **1588m** altitude. If you stay on the main trail you'll end up on the Moab Rim 4WD Trail not far beyond; but don't go down there. Instead, right at the divide, veer right or north and walk along an emerging hiker's trail that heads toward the southwestern face of another sandstone fin. Along that face and at the bottom of the Navajo SS wall, are about **14 panels** of rock art. At the lower end of that fin, circle around the end to the right and locate another trail going back southeast uphill, then you climb upon a bench to the left to find another **13 panels of art** on the southwest face of the next fin to the north. Walk northwest downhill observing the panels. At the end of that fin, climb or chimney-up a 5m-high crack to the top of a flat topped, but sloping mini **butte**, which is capped with a **limestone lens**. Once on top, walk southeast uphill to find **2 big circular Fremont Indian (?) shelters or ceremonial sites**--or something (?). Hopefully, they are real and not made by a bunch of palefaced mokis! This whole site is a must-see.

South Fork of Mill Creek, and more Rock Art

Now to the other side of **Spanish Valley**. You can start at either end but for now, let's start at the **Main Trailhead** for Mill Creek at the end of Power House Lane. From there walk east along a heavily-used trail; soon you'll pass an old cement dam that diverted water into a wooden pipeline that ran downhill to a former hydroelectric power station. Continue east upcanyon and soon you'll be at the confluence of the North and South Forks of Mill Creek Canyon. At that point, look up to the northeast and inside a kind of **recessed window arch** in the wall, will be a good panel of **rock art**. You'll need binoculars to see it from below, but if you wade the creek, you can route-find up to it.

Another option at the confluence is to head up the **North Fork**, but you will have to wade in a place or two before you get up to the bottom of a **waterfall & big pool**. This is extremely popular for locals and tourists alike in summertime. Some jump off the ledges into the pool; it's that deep. If you continue upcanyon, there are more pools and rock art; one panel is in a cave. After about 2 kms, the canyon is not as deep and less-interesting.

But for some, the better hike here is into the **South Fork** of Mill Creek. There's a good trail heading southeast upcanyon and if the water isn't too high, you can usually step across using stones or logs and keep you feet dry. After a little more than a km from the confluence, you'll be walking east as you pass an old fence. From there, veer left to find several **big pools** in the creek for bathing. Not too far after that, be watching for a trail going to the east side of the creek and to the first of many **rock art/petroglyph panels** in the next km or so. While there are 2-3 panels on the southwest side of the creek, most are on the northeast side. Just follow some newly emerging hiker's trails. Much further along, maybe 4-5 kms from the trailhead, will be **4 alcove caves** in a big bend of the canyon. Locals have camped & partied in these cave quite a bit recently, but the **soot** on the ceilings of 2 caves are from several thousand years of fires used by either Fremont and/or Archaic Indians, or likely both (?).

About a km beyond the 4 caves, you'll see the remains of an old **homestead**. From there if you pick your way east through oak brush, you'll come to the lower end of a drainage pouring off the slickrock. Most of the time you'll find a **pool** and water, and an old **still** used by someone during the 1920's by a moonshiner making illegal whiskey. If it's not there, it will hopefully be in the Moab Museum near the visitor center (?).

From that old still & pool, walk along a pretty good trail south along the west-facing eastern canyon wall to find another real good **panel** of petroglyphs. It too is under a kind of window or arch set back in the canyon wall. From there, walk a good trail west to find a group of **hitching posts** for people with horses. Just south of that, is an east-west running **fence** with **gate** across the canyon bottom. South of that it's private land. This is where you turn around and head back to your car. The author did this hike in 4 1/3 hours round-trip.

However, if you drive along Spanish Trail Road & Westwater Drive to the **South Trailhead**, you can **legally walk through that little gate** (but you can't take a vehicle in) north along an old road crossing private land to the gate & fence just mentioned. Using that trailhead would get you to that last rock art panel, the still site, and the 4 caves much quicker than coming up from Power House Lane. From the South Trailhead, the author walked up 2 forks a ways; one to the east and one along the road heading southeast and found nothing in the way of rock art.

Moab Dump Rock Art Sites

Here's another interesting hike located on this map. Start at the signal light on 300 S. in Moab (set odometer at 0) and drive to the **4-way stop** described earlier, but head east uphill past the **cemetery** on the paved **Sand Flats Road**. Along the way you'll pass the **Moab City Dump**. After **3.8 kms (2.3 miles)**, stop at a parking place on the right or east side of the road just below a **big curve**. From there, walk southeast on an old vehicle track; but which is now for hikers only. This path takes you along a west facing Navajo Sandstone wall which has at least 3 places with **rock art**. One panel has a big snake, but the 3rd one is the best; you'll have to climb up onto a bench to reach that one. At the end of this trail you can reach the panel in the **recessed window arch** described above at the confluence of the North & South Forks of Mill Creek.

Here's one last rock art site but which isn't shown on this map. Drive north out of Moab on Highway 191. Cross the Colorado River Bridge and after about 100m turn left into the parking for Moab by Night & Day (If someone gets mad about parking there, you may have to drive further west to the trailhead for **Lower Courthouse Wash** at **mile post 129**). From the parking lot, walk north across the highway until you're about 150m east of the bridge over Courthouse, then be looking for a trail heading eastward up to the cliffs which are about 150m away. Just follow a hikers trail. At the base of those cliffs are several places with petroglyphs and one pictograph panel which is protected by an overhang. This place is called the **Courthouse Wash site**.

One of the better single rock art panels located at the head of **Hidden Valley**. There are 2 lines of panels at the base of 2 fins. This writer counted 27 panels, similar to this, at the 2 sites.

Looking north at one of 2 unusual ruins located at the head of **Hidden Valley**. This one is located on top of the northern-most of 2 separate Navajo Sandstone fins. These stones are made of limestone which caps both fins. On the south side of both fins are the petroglyph panels.

One of many petroglyph or rock art panels in the **South Fork** of **Mill Creek**. Most of the panels are on the northeast side of the canyon, with just a few on the other side. Just follow the most-used trails in the area, and take a pair of binoculars to help locate them.

Left The waterfall at the **diversion dam** about 400m above the **Main Trailhead** on Mill Creek. This dam diverted water into a wooden pipeline which flowed downcanyon to a power plant. **Right** One of **4 caves** in the upper part of **South Fork of Mill Creek**. Notice the black **soot** on the ceiling; that's from thousands of campfires used by aborigines over what may be several thousand years.

One of 3 sites with rock art located just east of the **Moab City Dump**, and along the base of a south-west facing Navajo Sandstone wall.

This is the **Courthouse Wash Rock Art Site**. It's located about 300m east of the bridge over lower Courthouse Wash. The main pictograph panel here is under an overhang; but notice the petroglyphs on the boulder the author is standing on. There's other rock art to the right and left of this site.

Trough Springs Canyon, Viewpoints from Hatch Point, and Hikes from the Lockhart Road

Location & Access Featured here is a high mesa or plateau south and southwest of Moab called **Hatch Point**; plus some lower country between Hatch Point and the Colorado River. To get on top of Hatch Point, drive along Highway 191 between Monticello & Moab. Very near **mile post 93**, turn west onto **The Needles and Anticline Overlooks Highway**. This road passes Wind Whistle Campground, then at **Km 24.4 (Mile 15.2** from Highway 191) the main road turns left or west and runs to the **Needles Overlook**, a total distance of 36.5 kms (22.6 miles) from Highway 191. The road is paved all the way to the Needles Overlook.

To reach northern Hatch Point, continue north from the Needles Overlook turnoff & paved road on a very good gravelled county road which basically has an all-weather surface. At **Km 32.8 (Mile 20.4)**, pull off to the left at a viewing place. This is where you park a car if going to the **Redd's Sheep Trail**. Or, continue north to **Km 39.9 (Mile 24.8)** which is the turnoff to **Canyonlands Overlook**. At **Km 44.7 (Mile 27.8)** turn right onto a side-road sign-posted for **Trough Spring Canyon Trailhead**. Or, continue north **51.5 kms (32 miles)** from Highway 191 which is the end of the road at the **Anticline Overlook**. This site gives you a look down on the **Potash evaporation ponds, Hurrah Pass** and other places.

To get to the **Lockhart Road**, which runs north-south along the east side of the Colorado River below Hatch Point, begin in the south end of Moab next to **McDonalds** and drive westward along the **Kane Creek Road**, along the Colorado, then up **Kane Creek Canyon** and over **Hurrah Pass**, which is getting rougher by the day! The **Lockhart Road** begins at Hurrah Pass and heads generally south--but beware, about 8 kms (5 miles) beyond Hurrah, this road is for **LR/HC/4WD** vehicles only. On the map it's labelled **Very Bad Road**.

Or, drive along Highway 191 between Moab & Monticello and near **mile post 86** & **Church Rock**, turn west onto **The Needles Highway 211**, which runs westward to the **Needles District of Canyonlands NP**. About halfway between the Dugout Ranch and The Needles Visitor Center, turn north onto the southern end of the **Lockhart Road**. This is **47.1 kms (29.7 miles)** from Highway 191 and just west of **mile post 10**. This southern part of the Lockhart Road is pretty good and in normal conditions, cars can handle it up to **Km 24.9 (Mile 15.5** from the Needles Highway). At that point is a junction; turn left or northwest onto the road going down Lockhart Canyon; or veer right and continue on the Lockhart Road going in the direction of the **airplane tail section** and Hurrah Pass. That section or road stays pretty good to **Km 28.5 (Mile 17.7)**, then it's for LR/HC/4WD vehicles only. Lots of 4WD's turn back at that point. Driving the Lockhart Road from south to north is supposedly a little easier.

Elevations Needles Overlook, 1919m; Anticline Overlook, 1736m; Upper trailhead to Trough Spring Canyon, 1664m; Hatch Point CG, 1768m; the Colorado River, about 1210m.

Water Always carry plenty in your car, otherwise water can be found at Hatch Point Campground in the warmer half of the year (it's a fee-use BLM site); in lower Trough Spring Canyon; and in the Colorado River if you get that far; but purify it first.

Maps USGS or BLM map La Sal (1:100,000); Lockhart Basin, Shafer Basin, Trough Springs Canyon & Eightmile Rock (1:24,000--7 1/2' quads); the plastic Trails Illustrated/National Geographic map, Moab South (1:70,000); or the pastic Latitude 40° map Moab West (1:75,000).

Main Attractions Several nice viewpoints from the rim of Hatch Point, 2 interesting hikes down off the top, and several hikes down to the Colorado River.

Trough Springs Canyon from Kane Springs Canyon

One of the better hikes in this book is into a short but deep and impressive drainage called **Trough Springs Canyon**. You can get there from the top and Hatch Point **(the preferred way)**, or from Kane Springs (Creek) Canyon. First from the bottom. Drive westward out of Moab on the Kane Creek Road which starts at McDonalds, and head down along the Colorado. Continue into Kane Creek Canyon. At **Km 18.4 (Mile 11.4)** is the turnoff to **Hurrah Pass** and the Lockhart Road to the right. But, turn left onto a bumpy, never graded and less-used road. Continue along this rough 4WD-type road into Kane Creek Canyon. It's washed out in places but HC/4WD's, motorcycles & ATV's use it. About 6 kms (3.7 miles) past the Hurrah Pass turnoff, you'll see Trough Spring Canyon coming in on you right or west. Park your wheels somewhere near the mouth and look for a way through the jungle of tamarisks to the other side of Kane Creek and into the lower end of the canyon. The author came down this canyon from the top in 4/2012, and didn't make it past the tams and beaver ponds, so it's recommended you hike this canyon **from the top down**. The roads are better on top anyway.

But, if you go up from the bottom, you should find good running water throughout. About 2 kms from Kane Creek, you'll see a side-canyon coming in from the right or west; and an **old cattle trail** zig zags up (or down) a big rock slide to the top. This little side-canyon is along a faultline, with the north block having been thrust up. You can see this feature as you go up the trail, because it's the Wingate Sandstone which forms the big walls in the canyon bottom, then as you climb higher and look to the north, there's the Wingate again right in front of you.

Back to the old cattle trail mentioned above. It was originally built by **J.T. Loveridge** in about **1900**, but reconstructed for hikers in **1982**. JT was one of the first settlers to Moab, having arrived in a covered wagon in 1883. On thing the late **Kent Johnson** remembered about this place was when JT's son, Arthur (Corky) Loveridge was running cattle up & down this trail, wintering them in the middle part of Kane Creek Canyon, then summering them up on Hatch Point. This was in the late 1910's.

The late **Kenny Allred** of Moab had one strange experience out there as a young cowboy. He had this to say: *There was troughs there at the time we camped up on top, in the upper end of the canyon. That was back in about 1930 or '32. I suppose somebody put in some troughs--maybe an old timer, then the next person to come along hung that name Trough Springs Canyon on it.*

I was workin' for a guy named Ralph Estes who had 'im a bunch of horses and was trying to run a dude outfit--but there wasn't no dudes! Then these 3 guys come in and hired me to go help 'em. So we took these guys and went out there on Hatch Point with a machine that looked about like a television. It was a heavy ol' outfit, and we had a hard time balancing it on the packhorse. I don't have any idea what it was, but we heard later they was a huntin' gold and that was a gold machine. We went up Trough Spring Canyons Trail, then camped at the spring up above. Then we took 'em out there on top and took this machine out there for 'em, then we come back to camp and stayed. They didn't want us around. Then we'd go back out in the evening and get 'em. This went on for a couple of days, maybe three.

This drainage will be covered later, from the top down--the best way to see it.

Map 27, Trough Springs Canyon, Viewpoints from Hatch Point, and Hikes from the Lockhart Road

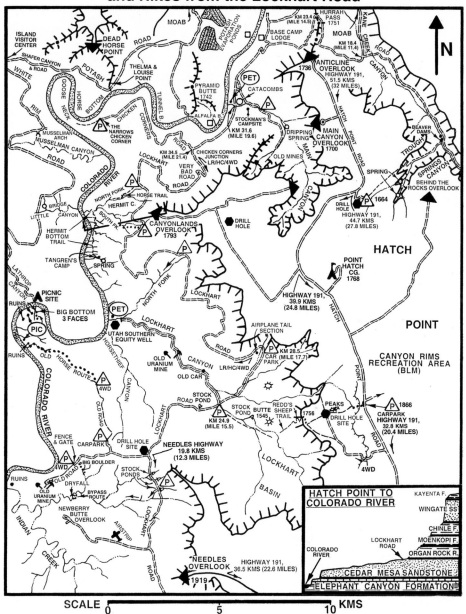

The Lockhart Road south from Hurrah Pass, and the Chicken Corners Road

From **Hurrah Pass**, which is **23.4 kms (14.5 miles** from McDonalds), you'll drive downhill (the west side of Hurrah was a better road than the east side as of 2012) to a junction at **Km 27.7 (Mile 17.2)**. For now let's leave the Lockhart Road and turn right or north toward the Base Camp Lodge and another private home nearby. That road running north crosses private land, but you'll have a right-of-way. Soon you'll come to a minor wash, but which the author's Jeep Patriot couldn't handle. It's mostly ATV's from there on toward **Jackson Hole**, but mtn. bikes do well over most of that road. In fact, there are 2 major rough places on that road. Along the way is one interesting place to see. It's the old **Prommel Oil Well site** as shown on **Map 25.** There you'll see an old oil well site on the left which was drilled in 1926, and

Left Looking southwest up **Trough Springs Canyon**. The trail zig zags up or down the drainage on the right. There should be water in the creek by the cottonwood trees on the left. **Right** From where the **Chicken Corners Road** ends and **The Narrows** begin, you'll have a good view of Dead Horse Point in the far background, and the upper end of Horse Bottom in the middle part of this foto.

a cellar on the right which is still in good condition even though it dates from 1926.

If you make it to Jackson Hole, you could walk up Jackson's Ladder to the rim and the Jackson and Amasa Back Trails. Or you can get to Jackson Hole from along either of those 2 trails, but the Jackson Trail is for hikers only, while the Amasa Back Trail is for anything that can handle it. It's popular with mtn. bikers.

Now back to the Lockhart Road and heading south. The first canyon you come to on the left was called **Main Canyon** by Wash Johnson's outfit, which dates back to the late 1910's; and it still has the same name. Where the Lockhart Road crosses this drainage it's **31.6 kms (19.6 miles)** from Moab. There are some cottonwood trees nearby which would make a good campsite. From there, if you walk west down the dry creek bed about 200m, you'll come to where some cliffs begin to rise on the right or north. There, you'll see a little trail climbing out of the wash bottom. Climb this 3m-high earthen bank and after another 50m or so, you'll find a small panel of **petroglyphs**. But this one is hardly worth the effort.

If you'd like to visit the upper part of Main Canyon and Dripping Spring, go back up the Lockhart Road 1 km and at the signed junction, turn right or southeast. This road passes a bunch of rocks called the **Catacombs** or The Caves on the east side--that place sounds interesting, but it's just another pile of rocks! From there, the road enters the dry wash bottom of Main Canyon, and shortly, you'll see a little drainage coming down from the right or south. This is a little box canyon **stockmen** have fenced off to create a holding pen and **campsite**.

The track running up **Main Canyon** gets rougher pretty quick, then it leaves the wash bottom on the right and runs along a bench. After that it gets a little better, but there are a couple of places where you'll need a **LR/HC/4WD** to get past. This old road runs up into a side-canyon to some **uranium mines** up under the Wingate wall. Some of these mine tunnels still have relics from the 1950's, and apparently haven't been closed off to the public.

Dripping Spring is out in the middle of the main drainage near some tamarisks and a green patch of salt grass. Water drips off a ledge in a couple of places, and if you could catch it using 2 wide pans, it would be enough to sustain at least one cowboy. But, it's really not worth the effort of going there.

Now back to the Lockhart Road. Further along and when you finally get to a point due south of Alfalfa Bottom, the road forks at **Km 34.5 (21.4 miles)**. The one going west is the **Chicken Corners Road**. It runs along a bench above the Colorado for about 7.2 kms (4.5 miles) and ends at an old **cattle trail** the 4WD/ATV crowd calls **Chicken Corners**. The late **Ray Holyoak** of Moab remembered the place:

It was made before we got out there. We called it The Narrows. I have an idea it was John Shafer who first used that pasture [but John Jackson was more likely the first one in that country]. He was on both sides of the river. Later on, Shafer sold out to Wash Johnson and he run cows down there for years. Then we put horses around there and they'd have to come back out the same way they went in. From that pasture, it slopes right down to the river and you can get right down to the river from there.

Karl Tangren of Moab remembered it too: *The old timers used to take horses around that trail, but it was narrow. When I was just a kid, second grade or so, Alvey Holyoak was running horses in that country. And I was down there with him one spring and we packed hand steel and stuff down there and drilled them holes in that ledge. If you notice, there's some pegs sticking up in that ledge. Maybe they've taken 'em out now, but we drilled those holes in there with hand tools, then went back along that rim* and cut cedar trees and laid them logs along on them pins that we stuck in them holes. So we built that up with logs, then cedar boughs and piled rocks on it, and built a pretty good trail so that livestock could trail around there on their own. But that thing was narrow--you had to take the saddle off your horse and lead 'im around. I was born in 1931, so that would have been about 1939 when we did that.

From the end of the road, that real narrow ledge on the trail is only about 100m away. If you walk around it, you can then hike out along the cliffs of the **Goose Neck** and above **California and Horse Bottoms.** All along Chicken Corners Road, you'll have some nice looks down on the Colorado River and to the place on the other side called **Thelma & Louise Point**; that's where the last scene of the movie of the same name was filmed. Read more about that in the part with **Map 24** on page 249.

Now back to the Lockhart Road. As you leave the river, you'll be running up the bottom of a short little canyon. This is by far the worst part of the Lockhart Road. Most 4WD's turn back; only specialized vehicles here! The best way to run this place would be to drive from south to north, then you'd be going down this terrible section. Once you get out of the drainage bottom, the road is closer to normal again. But a warning, the Lockhart Road between Chicken Corners Junction to the road running down Lockhart Canyon is a kind of no man's land and only for people who enjoy beating the crap out of 4WD's!

For most people to visit sections of the Lockhart Road beyond Chicken Corners, it's best to have a mtn. bike. Roughly **8.8 kms (5.5 miles)** past the Chicken Corners Junction, you'll come to a place just past a lone pinnacle on the right or west. As the road is beginning to veer southeast, park there somewhere if you want to hike down to the river and **Hermit Bottom** via **Hermit Canyon**. From the road, set your sights on the *Airport Tower* across the river on the White Rim, and walk about 1 km. There's an old **horse trail** running off the rim and into **Hermit Canyon's North Fork**; but there's no sign of the trail on top. At about where the actual trail begins there may be several stone cairns marking the upper end. This trail enters the North Fork about halfway between the road and the river in a little side-drainage running to the southeast. Once in the north fork, walk west down to the river. If you're coming back up from the river, the trail runs up the second little side-drainage on the left or north. By closely inspecting a good topo map you can just pick out this little side-canyon. A horse could probably be walked down this trail today.

You can also get down to Hermit Bottom by driving (or mtn. biking) another couple of kms south **(at about Km 11/Mile 7)** and parking somewhere near the upper end of the **South Fork of Hermit Canyon**. There's no trail, but in 1991, the author left a large cairn by the road marking a route down. It's an easy hike, but you'll have to route-find down past and around several minor ledges or dropoffs.

Now a little history on **Hermit Bottom**. Nothing much ever happened there until later in history. That's when **Jack (Beans) Milling** squatted there and tried to grow a garden. Milling had been on Tidwell Bottom along the Green River, then came directly from there to Hermit Bottom, and from here--and later in time--went further upriver to Alfalfa Bottom and worked for Swanny Kerby for a while. Still later, he settled on Milling's Bottom--the story of which has already been told. As for Hermit Bottom, here is more to what has already been stated under **Maps 23 & 24** in the interview with **Karl Tangren**:

This place never had a name until Jack Milling came along. He planted maybe 50 to 100 fruit trees on that bottom. I remember the year I first knew him. It was the year I was a freshman [in high school], because Efe Olivera, Kenny Allred and Jimmy Walker took their canoes to Green River and paddled them down the Green and up the Colorado River to Moab. That was in the fall of 1947, and Milling was there then. Them guys crawled out on the bank where he had watermelons growing. It was in the fall when they were ripe and those guys were late gettin' back for football practice. I remember old Efe a sayin', "man here's some watermelons"--he was hollerin' at old Jimmy down in the canoe, and about that time old Jack stepped out from under that ledge and says "them's my watermelons"! He packed water in buckets from the river to water that stuff--watermelons, fruit trees. The trees are gone now, but

This is part of the **Hermit Bottom Trail** that runs on top of a limestone bench next to the Colorado River south from **Hermit Bottom**. It runs south and into the lower end of Lockhart Canyon. In the far distance is Dead Horse Point.

Above Tangren's Camp
built by Karl Tangren in
the **1950's**. It likely hasn't
been used since then.
Notice the bed springs,
table, and bench, all rescued from the old oil
drillers camp at the mouth
of **Lockhart Canyon**.
There's still some canned
food in the metal box.

Right The **tail section**
from the T-33 Jet Trainer
which crashed in **Lock-
hart Basin** in September
of 1952. It's made of aluminum and should be
there for a long time.

they was right along the river bank.

There's nothing to see at Hermit Bottom, except maybe under the ledge where Jack lived. But when the author stopped there at the lower end of the bottom on 2 different boating trips, he found nothing that would indicate anyone had ever lived there. There's one place where the cliff has caved in, so maybe that's where he had his camp.

There's an interesting hike in the area running south from Hermit Bottom along on a bench above the river. From the lower end of Hermit, look for one of several routes up on the limestone bench just to the east. This is about 20m high. Get upon it and you'll find a horse trail heading south. Let's call it the **Hermit Bottom Trail**. It actually starts to the north a ways, but you can climb up over one little ledge to make a short-cut. Walk along this trail south as it follows the top of this limestone bench. You'll go into one little drainage, then the ledge narrows to almost nothing as it runs out across the face of a cliff directly above the river. Walking there will allow you some fine views and a place for taking fotos looking up or downriver. If you were to look at this cliff-face from the river you'd never think there could be a horse trail there.

If you continue south on the Hermit Bottom Trail, it goes in and out of several little drainages, always staying on top of this same level limestone bench. About 3 or 4 kms from the lower end of Hermit Bottom, you'll be heading east into a slightly larger canyon. Near the eastern end of this you'll pass a group of large boulders where cowboys built a rock fence to control livestock. This is where **Tangren's Camp** is located. Karl tells about when they set this camp up:

I built it in the 1950's, before I went to Anderson Bottom. That bed, we packed from them old oil well cabins down in Lockhart. We hoisted it up over that ledge with ropes; it and that table and that bench. That metal storage bin we took down the river in a boat and packed it up there on horses. We did that to store our stuff in to keep the mice out. That's one of those big ol' tin cases that used to be mounted on them old 1929 Chevy's or other old cars. It was used as a tool box and it used to be mounted across the back of them cars. The last time we ever used that camp was in about 1957. We just wintered our horses in that country in them days. There's parts to an old pack saddle there on the table too.

There's a little ol' seep in the draw just east of the camp. There's a wet spot there under the ledge and we dug back in there and got a little ol' spring of water comin' out--that was the first time we was there. So the next time we went there we took a pipe about 2-3 feet [about a meter] long and we shoved it back under that ledge and pretty soon the water come drippin' out of that pipe and we set a bucket under it. And it was good water; most of them little ol' seeps are alkali and you can't drink it. That little seep wasn't more than 300 feet [100m] to the east of the camp, just as you head that little canyon and just above the trail. The horses generally watered on the river, then we'd bring'em back up there at night and hobble'em out to feed on the bench. When we left the horses there to winter they always had to go to the river to water.

What you'll see there today, both under and beside a large boulder, is an old bed or cot, a table and bench, the metal storage box, a pick and several wooden boxes. The metal box is mostly full of paper towels, and some canned food maybe dating back to the 1950's (?). Don't try to eat any of it! It'll be poison! On top of the table are parts of an old pack saddle.

If you were to continue south on this Hermit Bottom Trail, you'd come out directly above the mouth of **Lockhart Canyon** and look down on the site where a cabin used to be when they were drilling for oil. More on this later. The trail remains on this same bench as it winds in and out of several more drainages and finally ends in the North Fork of Lockhart Canyon. That's where the trail actually begins.

The third parking symbol on the map is where it's believed this trail actually starts, in the **North Fork of Lockhart**. The late Mel Dalton formerly of Monticello, whose son Val ran cattle & horses there until 2012 (Dicky Joe Ladner of Paradox, Colorado now owes the grazing permit), mentioned it, but the author hasn't tried it yet. On a long day-hike, you might make a loop using the Hermit Canyon & Bottom and Hermit Bottom Trail, then the North Fork of Lockhart Canyon and finally a little road walking or biking back to your 4WD at the other trailhead. If you just go down to Hermit Bottom and back to the road, it'll only take maybe 3 hours at most. Once the author parked at Hurrah Pass, then biked to the North Fork Trailhead, hiked down to the river, then returned to Hurrah Pass, but with a side-trip into Main Canyon--all in just under 7 hours.

Next place of interest on the Lockhart Road,would be where an early model **Air Force training jet** crashed. Observe this map carefully and match it with a better one. It's rather easy to locate part of the wreckage. It sits in the middle of a sharp curve of the road on the north side of Lockhart Basin.

To find the crash site--or at least the **airplane tail section**, come in from the south on the southern end of the Lockhart Road as mentioned earlier; cars driven with care might get to the parking place shown on the map **(28.5 kms/17.7 miles** from The Needles Highway). From the car-park, first walk north along the road, then west and southwest. From the left-hand side of the road at the bottom of the steep part, look left and down 75-80m. In the gully just west of the main drainage is the 2m-high aluminum tail section. From where you see it, back up along the road 30m or so and where you see a large **cairn**, route-find down to the south a little. Details of the crash appeared in the *September 11, 1952* issue of *The Times-Independent (TI)* of Moab:

A T-33 Jet Trainer on routine flight from Larson Air Force Base, Washington to Biggs Field, Texas, crashed and burned in the rugged canyon area southwest of Moab Saturday, killing the student and injuring the pilot. Both men jumped from the flaming plane, but evidence exists that one parachute failed to open, probably because the flyer was too close to the ground when he jumped. The accident occurred when one engine flamed out and the occupants of the plane were forced to jump.

The dead man was listed as Lt. D. Wingert.... The other man was Lt. J. Harsh, pilot of the plane, who is now resting easily in the Hill A.F. Base hospital. Lt. Harsh is suffering from a leg injury received in his jump.

The ill-fated craft made a routine stop at Hill A.F. Base near Salt Lake City and then continued its flight. Some twenty minutes after the take-off, officials there and the Civil Aeronautics office at Grand Junction, intercepted a distress call from the plane as it started to crash. The distress call faded out and the officials were unable to regain contact. The search began with planes from Grand Junction, Hamilton A.F. Base, Calif.; Hill A.F. Base, Lowry Field and private planes from Moab participating. No trace of the crash was found the first day of the search.

The first break in the hunt came Saturday night when two Moab young men, Jim Walker and Kay Young, reported seeing black smoke rising out of the desolate area southwest of here. The word was transferred by Trooper Merlin Brown of the highway patrol to officials of Hill A.F. Base who concentrated their search efforts on Sunday in the area described by the young men. Mr. Young accompanied the searchers Sunday morning.

This picture from an old 1990 color slide shows the wooden cabin near the mouth of **Lockhart Canyon.** It was used by crews who were drilling the nearby oil well. It has since burned down.

Wreckage of the plane was finally sighted Sunday morning by a B-17 from Hamilton Base. One man was spotted wandering about a quarter of a mile from the plane. Then Jack Turner, Moab uranium operator and pilot, flew his light Taylorcraft into the river canyon during a heavy rainstorm, landed it and picked up the injured man..... Paramedics had previously been dropped into the crash site and they assisted Mr. Turner in getting the injured pilot aboard. The take-off was delayed for some time. Even after the storm had passed on and Turner had taken off, he had to fly in the canyon some time before he could gain enough altitude to "jump" over the canyon rim. The medics stayed in the area to be picked up later by a boat rescue crew which had gone downriver from Moab. The boat crew was headed by Sheriff Robert Burr. They were unable to bring out the body of the dead man and Fred Frazer, another local pilot flew in with his small plane and brought out the body, landing at a private Moab airport after dark Monday night.

Observers stated that the death craft was completely demolished in the crash. Intense heat from burning fuel caused most of the metal to melt. An explosion apparently occurred and pieces of the wreckage were scattered over a large portion of the area. This made it hard to locate from the air, and is probably the main reason the plane was not found on the day of the crash.

Now heading south again. When you reach the turnoff to **Lockhart Canyon (24.9 kms/15.5 miles** from the Needles Highway), the Lockhart Road at that point has been graded and is generally good for cars to travel (at least right after its been graded). But check on its condition with the NPS or BLM somewhere first if you can. The Needles Visitor Center is a good place for road reports because the lower end of Lockhart Canyon is NPS territory and they make patrols there occasionally.

Now for **Lockhart Canyon.** The first third of the way down is generally in good condition, and there's a seep a little ways into the drainage. It has a slightly mineral taste however. About a third the way down is an **old car** on the right. The middle third of the road is beginning to be sandy in places, and the last third of the distance has many sandy spots and would be for 4WD's or ATV's only--or mtn. bikes. But sometimes mtn. bikes aren't any better than a 2WD car! Just before reaching the river will be the site of a small board cabin (it burned down sometime after 1991) on the right, with an old cellar behind. This is where the old **Utah Southern--Equity Oil Company** did some drilling for oil in the late 1920's.

The history on this well began in the summer of 1926; that's when the Moab Garage began transporting equipment and men to the site by boat. They had hoped to get the drilling underway in August, but delays put the date back to September. In the ***September 9, 1926*** issue of *TI* under the *Moab Oil Field Drilling Reports,* it states: *UTAH SOUTHERN-EQUITY OIL, Hazelwood No. 1, Lockhart dome, section 16-29-20. Spudding in will start within a few days.*

By **October 21**, the drilling report stated: *Being drilled by Utah Southern. Depth under 200 feet [61m], operating daylight tower at present.* In the **January 27, 1927** paper it states: *Bottomed at 527 feet [161m] and temporarily closed down. Reported that drilling will be resumed within a month.* It was never mentioned in the paper again.

The former frame cabin mentioned above was apparently part of the camp where the men ate and slept. That cabin site is just east of where the **rock art panel** is shown on the map. The drilling occurred another 200-300m south across the dry wash and in a little alcove. The steel casing can still be seen sticking up out of the ground and there are odds and ends of junk lying around.

If you continue west down the road where the tamarisks begin, look to the right on a wall facing south, and you'll see a panel of **petroglyphs**. About halfway between this panel and the old cabin site, and up on the wall to the north, is where some of the oil drillers left their **signatures**.

About 500m downriver from the mouth of Lockhart is Horsethief Canyon. Someone might do some hiking up there, but it's a shallow drainage, and seems uninteresting. You can get into Horsethief by walking along a trail located on a bench about 15m above the river. You can get upon that bench by walking up Lockhart a ways, or by climbing upon it from near the oil well site.

Now back to the main Lockhart Road. If you're interested in hiking up to the top of Hatch Point via an **old sheep trail**, then drive south about 300m from the junction of the Lockhart Road and the Lockhart Canyon Road. There you'll see the remains of an old miner's or ranchers track heading southeast into upper **Lockhart Basin**. A 4WD can use it for a ways, but it's very faint and if we start using it, ATV's are sure to follow, so why not park on the main road. The walking distance isn't far.

From the Lockhart Road, walk southeast and set your sights on the little **butte** marked **1545m** in front of you but just to the left of the track and main drainage. Just after you pass this little former remnant of Hatch Point, turn left and walk east. Somewhere on that broken-down slope to the east is what's left of **Redd's Sheep Trail**. To actually find it you'll have to be up the slope a ways. This trail zig zags up the most-prominent talus slope to the top of Hatch Point as shown.

This trail is said to have been built by one of the Redds who had cattle and sheep on Hatch Point in the early 1900's. At the same time, Lockhart Basin below was winter range for the Indian Creek Cattle Company at the Dugout Ranch located to the south. As the story goes, when the Indian Creek cattle were on the mountain in their summer range, the Redds built this trail, and hid some of their buck sheep down in Lockhart Basin without permission. Then in the fall of the year would take them back up on top of the mesa. The Indian Creek cowboys apparently tried to blast this trail out of existence once, but it's still good enough today to walk a horse up or down. How to reach this trail from the top down is discussed below.

The Hike to Big Bottom

From the middle of Lockhart Basin, drive west, then south on the Lockhart Road. When you reach an **old drill site (19.8 kms/12.3 miles** from The Needles Highway) right under an extension of Hatch Point, drive a car **1.6 kms (1 mile)** west and turn north. After another 500m, is a parking place for cars, and the beginning of an old road, then cairned trail or route, heading north and northwest toward **Big Bottom** on the Colorado River. In 4/2012, the author rode a mtn. bike along this old track, but the dirt was soft in places. At the end of the road he walked northwest along a ridge-top marked with cairns, and down to Big Bottom. When you get close to the river, there is more than one way down off the rim. Once you reach the bottom, head north and circle around to the north side to find a place that's popular with boaters. They've cut a trail through the tamarisks which leads up to several Anasazi ruins or moki houses and at least 3 pictograph panels. The entire trip took 6 3/4 hours. A mtn. bike on this route doesn't help that much, unless it has really fat tires.

Just a brief comment on one of the pictographs on Big Bottom. One of those panels will now be called **3 Faces**. The reason is, the painted figures look surprisingly similar to those on other panels in The Needles District just to the south. Those include **4 Faces** in Upper Salt Creek; **5 Faces** in Davis Canyon just inside the park boundary; and the **9, 11 & 13 Faces** all in the upper end of Horse Canyon. Because these are all so close together, and have a similar look, this writer feels there's a chance they all could have done by the same painter, or clan. Maybe another Michelangelo (?).

The same thing could have happened in the western and northwestern part of the park because of similarities in other paintings in Horseshoe, Pictograph, Range, Clearwater and Hell Roaring Canyons and even upper Sevenmile Canyon. All these fall in the category of the Barrier Creek style, and could have been created by one person, or clan. If only someone could date all of these accurately.

Overlooks and the Redd's Sheep Trail hike from Hatch Point

Back on top of Hatch Point again. At **Km 32.8 (Mile 20.4)** on the Hatch Point Road, pull off to the left at a viewing place as mentioned earlier. From there, and with a compass & topo map in hand, head due west cross-country. Soon you'll come to some steep Navajo slickrock, so route-find down this heading in the direction of some Navajo Sandstone **peaks** in the middle of a big flat area. Walk on the south side of these peaks and west (there's an old drill hole there and with a good 4WD, you might be able to drive to that point?). When you reach the rim of Hatch Point, look for the biggest of several talus slopes running down to the southwest; then locate one of several cairns on the rim marking the beginning of **Redd's Sheep Trail**. The trail zig zags down and toward the south side of that little round **butte** shown. Return the same way. This access route via Hatch Point is the easiest and quickest way to reach this trail.

Further up the Hatch Point Road is a signed turnoff toward Canyonlands Overlook. In this same general area is the turnoff to **Hatch Point Campground**. This campground is operated by the BLM with a number of sites, plus pit toilets and running water. This is a fee-use campsite. Actually, you can camp anywhere you like on Hatch Point, but you're supposed to be 1 mile (1 1/2 kms) from the main road or highway.

Further along this Hatch Point Road will be the turnoff to **Trough Spring Canyon** which is **44.7 kms (27.8 miles)** from Highway 191. Turn right or south, then east and drive to another old **drill hole site**. That point is now the trailhead parking for hiking down into Trough Spring Canyon. You can camp there, which is near the upper springs. Look for a way down into the shallow canyon nearby for water. From this trailhead, follow the **trail** east. Part of it is along an old road which apparently went out near the beginning of the trail down into the lower part of the canyon. This trail is well-used and easy to find and follow. It took the author 3 1/2 hours to walk down to Kane Creek and back. There are lots of backpackers campsites down there with good running water. There may be cattle there in winter, so the higher in the canyon you are, the better the water will be.

Next stop on the Hatch Point Road would be the **Main Canyon Overlook**. This is on the eastern rim of **Main Canyon** and just above **Dripping Spring**. Still further along is the end of the road at the **Anticline Overlook**. This has a large shaded picnic site with toilets, and walkways around the point where you can look down on Hurrah Pass, the wide part of lower Kane Springs Canyon and the Cane Creek Anticline just south of Potash which is where the Frank Shafer Well No. 1 was drilled. Also seen will be the **evaporation ponds** of Potash; the only real sore spot in the scene.

If you're spending time on Hatch Point, remember it's on BLM and public land and you can camp about anywhere you like, but of course pick up after yourself and leave a clean campsite. The higher altitude of this plateau makes summer a little more bearable than down near the Colorado River.

Above From the **stock pond** on the Lockhart Road west of **Redd's Sheep Trail,** looking due east; in the upper right is the little round **butte** shown on the map. From there, the trail runs up and to the left along the obvious talus slope to the top of Hatch Point. The approximate location of the trail is shown on the foto. It's probably better for most people to reach the trail from Hatch Point. because the main road on Hatch Point is better than the Lockhart Road.

Right If you do the hike to **Big Bottom** on the Colorado, this is the 2nd ruin (which is a **small granary**) you'll pass as you walk north after reaching the river. It's not easy getting up to this one. There are at least 4 moki houses or granaries around Big Bottom, and there are at least 3 rock art panels as well; the **3 Faces Panel** is shown on the opposite page.

These dwellings or moki houses are located near the Colorado River at the mouth of **Indian Creek**. To the left and out of sight, is a well-preserved granary. These would have been built by what we call today the Anasazi Indians.

This is one of at least 3 rock art panels on **Big Bottom**. Let's call this the **3 Faces Panel**, and it has the same look as those sites in upper Salt Creek **(4 Faces)**, in Davis Canyon **(5 Faces)** and in Horse Canyon **(9, 11 & 13 Faces)**. After seeing all of these paintings, one has to think there's a pretty good chance all were painted by the same individual or clan.

Lower Indian Creek: Newberry Butte & Rincon, and Routes into Rustler Canyon, and Historic Oil Wells

Location & Access This map shows the lower or northern end of **Indian Creek**, that part below and west of the Needles Overlook on Hatch Point. It's also north of the Needles Visitors Center. You can get to these parts from the north via the Lockhart Road, but that route is for LR/HC/4WD's only. So the best way in is from the south and the **Needles Highway, State Road 211**. To get there, drive along Highway 191 between Moab & Monticello. At Church Rock and between **mile posts 86 & 87**, turn west and head for Newspaper Rock, the Dugout Ranch, and finally towards **The Needles District of Canyonlands**. About halfway between the Dugout Ranch and the Needles Visitor Center, and between **mile posts 10 & 11**, turn north onto the south end of the **Lockhart Road**. A sign there used to state: *Hurrah Pass--48 miles (77 kms), Lockhart Basin--15 miles (24 kms)*.

On the way to this area, there are 2 places along the southern end of the Lockhart Road which are popular for camping, mostly by the ATV & motorcycle crowd. The BLM has installed pit toilets at what are now called the **Indian Creek** and **Hamburger Rock Campsites** but these are now fee-use sites. Away from this area, you can camp where you like, but you're supposed to have in your vehicle, a **portable toilet**. Please leave a clean campsite for the next visitor.

From the paved highway, drive north **4.8 kms (3 miles)** to where the road crosses **Indian Creek**. Immediately below that ford is **Indian Creek Falls**, something you'll want to see if there's running water in the creek (usually in winter or spring). You can begin hiking downcanyon anywhere in that area, but a better trailhead might be to continue northward on the Lockhart Road to **K6 (Mile 3.7)** and park where the road is leaving the Indian Creek drainage. More driving directions below.

Elevations Needles Overlook on top of Hatch Point, 1919m; Lockhart Road near where it crosses Indian Creek, 1417; Indian Creek Trailhead, 1426m; Needles Visitor Center, 1500m; the Colorado River at the mouth of Indian Creek, about 1206m.

Water Always have a good supply of water in your car. Also, there's water coming out of the mountains and running down Indian Creek for about 4-6 of the months of the year. This is in the winter & spring months, or in times of flood. Many times it reaches the Colorado River. However, during the growing season, the Dugout Ranch uses the water to irrigate alfalfa. If there's running water in the canyon when you're there, better purify it first, because there are lots of cattle grazing in the mountains and drainage above. The water you might find in small seeps down in the canyon in the warmer half of the year, would likely be good to drink (?). Treat Colorado River water.

Maps USGS or BLM map La Sal (1:100,000); Monument Basin, The Loop & North Six Shooter Peak (1:24,000--7 1/2' quads); the plastic Trails Illustrated/National Geographic map Canyonlands National Park (1:70,000); or the pastic Latitude 40° map Moab West (1:75,000).

Main Attractions A long, or short, wilderness hike to the Colorado River; a fun hike to the top of Newberry Butte; 4 historic oil wells, 2 of which have interesting artifacts to see; and Anasazi ruins.

From the Lockhart Road & Indian Creek Falls to the Colorado River

Right where the road crosses Indian Creek find a parking place, then look for a way around Indian Creek Falls (in summer it will be a **dryfall**) and into the canyon bottom below. Or you could save walking about 1 1/2 km if you start at the trailhead suggested above at **1426m**. Right where a little side-drainage enters Indian Creek, route-find to the bottom into Indian Creek and simply walk downcanyon.

After about 5 kms, you'll come to where **2 huge piles of wood** once were. This wood was cut and stacked there for use in drilling the **Deseret Petroleum oil well**. More on the history of this below. However, in 3/2012, these stacks of wood were nowhere to be found; one was burned up, the other may have been washed away by the 10/2006 floods (?), or maybe it burned up too (?). Just to the south of where the first stack of wood was is a big sandslide coming down from the canyon rim. That's where the drillers brought all their equipment down into the canyon. You can still see part of the old road today, but motorcyclists and ATV's are using it as a test track.

Also, from the drill hole site, look up to the cliffs to the north to see **4 ruins**; either habitation sites or granaries (?). This site is about as far north as the Anasazi got. To the west a little is another granary. You can circle around to the north and crawl along a ledge that's made of the rottenest shalely rock this writer has seen--that's the reason he didn't get there. Or take a rope and rappel down, then jumar back up. Not many people have visited these moki houses.

Further downcanyon about 2 kms and on the bench to the right or north, will be another old **oil well drilling site**. This is perhaps the most interesting thing to see in this whole canyon. There's a bunch of old rope, boards, a couple of bull wheels, huge timbers, bricks which lined boilers and other junk from 1926. This well was drilled by **Western States Development**. More on this below.

There's also a short-cut route down to this site via a little **North Fork**. To do this, drive northward along the Lockhart Road to **Km 12 (Mile 7.5** from the Needles Highway). There you'll be in a minor drainage and if you look north less than 100m, you should see some tamarisks which have sprouted from a sediment-filled **stock pond** at 1447m altitude. From there walk south in the dry wash and after about an hour or less, you'll come to Western States Well. The author walked down this route, took a bunch of pictures using a tripod and returned in 1 2/3 hours.

From these oil well ruins on down, the canyon is deeper and it meanders a lot. There's at least one place under an overhang where a **Fremont Indian camp** was located, as shown on the map. There are likely more downcanyon. Other people have stated there's a granary down there some place. As you near the Colorado, Rustler Canyon will enter on your right. Let's stop here for a moment and discuss a shortcut route for this long hike to the Colorado River.

Rustler Canyon, and Climbing & History of Newberry Butte

Here are a couple of shortcuts down into lower Indian Creek via **Rustler Canyon**. First, you can park right on the **Lockhart Road** at the **1st** of **3 stock ponds** shown on the map (**18 kms/11.2 miles** from the Needles Highway). You'll know you're there when you actually drive across the dam of this sediment-filled pond. From there walk down the **main fork** heading west. This is easy hiking without dropoffs--until further downcanyon (read more below).

Or, an even shorter hike, but with a longer drive, would be to continue north to the **drill hole site** at **Km 19.9 (Mile 12.3)** shown on the map (altitude **1405m**), turn left or west, and drive a rough-in-places track out to one of several carparks or HC/4WD parking places north of Rustler Canyon. A HC/4WD

Map 28, Lower Indian Creek: Newberry Butte & Rincon, and Routes into Rustler Canyon and Historic Oil Wells

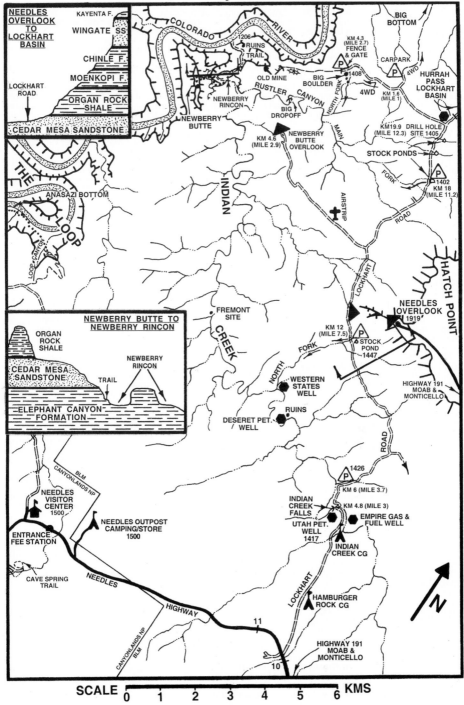

NEEDLES OVERLOOK TO LOCKHART BASIN

KAYENTA F.

WINGATE SS

CHINLE F.

MOENKOPI F.

ORGAN ROCK SHALE

LOCKHART ROAD

CEDAR MESA SANDSTONE

THE LOOP

ANASAZI BOTTOM

LOOP CANYON

COLORADO RIVER

1206

RUINS TRAIL

OLD MINE

RUSTLER CANYON

NEWBERRY RINCON

NEWBERRY BUTTE

BIG DROPOFF

BIG BOULDER

NORTH FORK

KM 4.6 (MILE 2.9)

NEWBERRY BUTTE OVERLOOK

BIG BOTTOM

KM 4.3 (MILE 2.7) FENCE & GATE

1408

CARPARK

4WD

HURRAH PASS LOCKHART BASIN

KM 1.6 (MILE 1)

4WD

KM19.9 DRILL HOLE (MILE 12.3) SITE 1405

STOCK PONDS

FORK

1402 KM 18 (MILE 11.2)

INDIAN

CREEK

AIRSTRIP

LOCKHART

HATCH POINT

FREMONT SITE

NEWBERRY BUTTE TO NEWBERRY RINCON

ORGAN ROCK SHALE

CEDAR MESA SANDSTONE

TRAIL

NEWBERRY RINCON

ELEPHANT CANYON FORMATION

NORTH FORK

NEEDLES OVERLOOK 1919

KM 12 (MILE 7.5)

STOCK POND 1447

HIGHWAY 191 MOAB & MONTICELLO

WESTERN STATES WELL

DESERET PET. WELL

RUINS

ROAD

BLM CANYONLANDS NP

NEEDLES VISITOR CENTER 1500

NEEDLES OUTPOST CAMPING/STORE 1500

ENTRANCE FEE STATION

CAVE SPRING TRAIL

NEEDLES HIGHWAY

CANYONLANDS NP BLM

1426

KM 6 (MILE 3.7)

INDIAN CREEK FALLS

KM 4.8 (MILE 3)

UTAH PET. WELL 1417

EMPIRE GAS & FUEL WELL

INDIAN CREEK CG

LOCKHART

HAMBURGER ROCK CG

11

10

HIGHWAY 191 MOAB & MONTICELLO

N

SCALE 0 1 2 3 4 5 6 **KMS**

can get you to the park boundary (**4.3 kms/2.7 miles** from the drill hole & Lockhart Road) where the road is blocked off (during the 1950's it went out to a uranium mine). From the parking & walk-through gate, head east (not through the gate) about 150m to the **big** mushroom-shaped **boulder**, the only place around with shade. Once there, walk over the nearby low rim and route-find southeast to the bottom of a major **North Fork** of Rustler Canyon. From there head westward downcanyon. About 3 kms from the trailhead, you'll meet the main fork of Rustler mentioned earlier; then after another km going westward, you'll come to a **big dropoff**. Veer left, walk along the north side of the rim less than 100m, and downclimb over a ledge. If you're alone take a 10m-long rope to tie to a rock or put your pack in a crack, with rope attached, to insure you get back up. Just one big step and you're back up. Then walk on down into lower Indian Creek.

About 1 km downstream from where Rustler enters Indian Creek, you'll come to **2 dry/waterfalls**, one right after another. You can't get down that way (unless you rappel), so you'll have to veer to the left or west, and look for a hikers trail up along the bench to the west and toward **Newberry Rincon** (abandoned meander). Look for a trail perhaps marked by cairns. About 350m from the dry/waterfalls, you'll come to the lip of the rincon. The trail heads down a little, then veers to the left and on the southwest side it drops off a minor ledge to the very bottom. From there just head downcanyon once again about 1 km to the river.

When you reach the river, you'll see some trails and a good campsite on the north side right at the mouth of Indian Creek. Boaters stop there because it's a good campsite. About 150m from the river, are at least **4 Anasazi ruins**, perhaps granaries, up against the south-facing wall.

To hike the entire length of Indian Creek from Indian Creek Falls will take at least 2 days, maybe a 3rd. It's just too far to go down and back on a one day-trip. If you're there and the canyon has running water (all winter long) prepare to wade some. Or if you use the shortcut route suggested above using Rustler Canyon, it can be done in 4-7 hours round-trip.

Here are some of this writer's experiences in these 2 canyons. Once in late March, he hiked down Indian Creek from the road to about the halfway point, and returned in about 7 1/2 hours. Another time he hiked up from the river about 1/3 of the way and back. Another time in 1991, he hiked down from the north to the Western States oil well to re-foto the place. That took a couple of hours round-trip. Another trip was down from the end of the road between the Colorado River and Rustler Canyon; that took 4 hours round-trip, but he turned back at Newberry Rincon. Another hike was down to the main fork from the **stock pond** mentioned earlier. That took a couple of hours.

Here's one more short hike beginning at the rincon. It's to the top of **Newberry Butte**. As you leave the river going back up Indian Creek, climb upon the intermediate bench in the rincon; then as you're about to climb out of the rincon through a dry wash coming down from the southeast, leave the little trail which bypasses the dryfalls on Indian Creek, and head about due south. At first stay in the drainage, then higher up near the big ledge or headwall, veer right while looking for a route up through it. It's not difficult to find a route up. Once on top of the bench made of Cedar Mesa SS (see geology cross section) then head northwest for 500m and turn left where there's a break in the cliff face. Scramble up the steep, but-easy-to-climb slope to the top of the butte which consists entirely of Organ Rock Shale. You'll have some fine views from there, particularly down on Newberry Rincon. On 2 river trips the author hiked from the river to the top of Newberry Butte and back in 2 1/2 hours.

Now some history about this place now called Newberry Butte. The best place to read about it is in the late F. A. Barnes' book, ***Hiking the Historic Route of the 1859 Macomb Expedition***. Briefly, here's a quote from that booklet, part of which comes from Crampton's book, ***Standing Up Country***:

In April 1859, Captain John N. Macomb, was ordered to take an expedition directly into the canyon country. He was to determine the course of the San Juan River, to fix the position of the confluence of the Green and Grand [renamed the Colorado River on 7/25/1921; but below the Confluence it's always been called the Colorado] rivers, and to find the best and most direct route between the Rio Grande and the southern settlements of Utah......

Macomb was in the field from mid-July to the end of September 1859. His party, which included John Strong Newberry, who had been the geologist with Ives the year before, followed the well-defined Spanish Trail past Mesa Verde, across the Sage Plain to the Ojo Verde, a spring on the route between the La Sal and Abajo mountains. Here they established a base camp and Macomb, Newberry and some of the others headed west to find the confluence of the Green and Grand....

From their base camp at Ojo Verde, they headed down a side-canyon of Hart Draw, then found and followed the lower part of Indian Creek all the way down to the dry/waterfalls just above the rincon discussed above. They were stopped there, and never did find a route down into the rincon and to the Colorado River. It is known however that geologist Newberry did climb up to the top of this butte to make some sketches. Thus the name Newberry Butte.

History of the Gibson Dome Oil Wells

There are 4 old oil well drill sites in the area where the Lockhart Road crosses Indian Creek. It seems that Indian Creek flows right over an old uplift or anticline called the **Gibson Dome**. Since oil is often found in such structures, early-day wildcatters decided to drill there.

Part of the following history is from **USGS Bulletin 841**, titled: ***Geology and Oil Possibilities of the Moab District, Grand and San Juan Counties, Utah, by A. A. Baker, 1933***.

In the southern part of the district five wells were started in 1926. Four were on the Gibson dome, in the valley of Indian Creek, and one on the Colorado River at the mouth of Lockhart Canyon. The well of the **Empire Gas & Fuel Co.**, which was spudded August 19, 1926, and drilled to a depth of 4163 feet [1269m] obtained small showings of oil and gas. It was abandoned in July, 1927.

The **Utah Petroleum Corporation** spudded a well September 1, 1926. After reaching a depth of 1643 feet [501m] drilling was suspended in April, 1927. The **Deseret Petroleum Co.** spudded a well June 30, 1926, and drilled it 514 feet [157m]. [According to Moab's **Times-Independent (TI)** newspaper it was closed down on March 10, 1927]. Another shallow well, reported to be 500 feet [152m] deep, was drilled by the **Western States Development Co.** This well was spudded July 30, 1926 [and according to the TI was closed down by October 21, 1926].

Some of the history of these old oil wells comes from newspaper accounts in the **TI**. On **April, 27, 1926**, one article mentions how far out the **Deseret Petroleum well** was and how hard it was to get equipment there: To reach the location it was necessary to spend a large sum of money on the construction of roads. The old wagon road leaving the Moab-Monticello highway at Church Rock and running to the Dugout ranch on Indian creek was followed, but before trucks could travel it, a large amount of road work was required. From the Dugout [Ranch] to the Gibson dome it was necessary to build about five miles [8 kms] of new road. M.W. Geer and Sons and M.L. Meeker had the trucking contract, and succeeded in placing the equipment at the location on contract time..... It was necessary to use horse freight outfits to move the heavy loads over some portions of the route.

Another article from the **October 21, 1926** issue of the *TI* gives some of the history of the first road built down Lockhart Canyon: *George W. [Wash] Johnson [Kent's father]....has the contract for building twelve miles [20 kms] of wagon road from the Utah Petroleum corporation well on Indian Creek to the mouth of Lockhart draw on the Colorado river..... When the road is completed Utah Petroleum will haul its supplies and equipment down the river by barge to Lockhart, and thence overland by wagon to the location on Indian Creek.* The road was under construction when this article was written, but it wasn't completed even by 1933, as shown on Baker's map.

Because the **Western States well** is much more isolated than the other 3, much of the old camp and derrick were left in place. At that site are a couple of big old wooden bull wheels, huge rope, square timbers half a meter thick, and other camp junk including a pile of bricks with the name, *The Denver Hi Fire Clay Co* on each. These were to line a boiler which was to heat water which ran a steam engine for drilling; but in 2012, none of the bricks looked like they'd ever been in a furnace. An interesting place to visit, but please leave everything there for others to discover.

Near the **Deseret Petroleum well** used to be 2 huge stacks of wood and other scattered relics; both are gone now, one pile was burned, the other perhaps taken away by floods (?). Much of that wood was cedar or rather Utah juniper. Anyone who has tried to cut down a cedar tree with an ax knows how much work went into cutting that much furnace wood! Apparently they were using steam boilers and decided to abandon drilling before the wood ran out.

What's left of the **Utah Petroleum well** is up on a little bench maybe 200m south of where the Lockhart Road crosses Indian Creek. There are a number of old relics on the ground at that site, but most of everything has been hauled away. The fourth well, and the one drilled the deepest, was that of the **Empire Gas & Fuel Company**. The author never did locate this one, but it's somewhere north of Indian Creek and east of the Lockhart Road as shown on Baker's old map. It's possible that if it was drilled in the bottom of the drainage, any remnant of the camp could have all been washed away by floods.

This picture was taken just up the road northwest from the old **stock pond at 1447m** located on the Lockhart Road. In the upper left is the **Needles Overlook** on top of Hatch Point. Most of that big cliff band is made of the **Wingate Sandstone** (but capped by the Kayenta Formation on top), but the maroon reddish layers closest to the camera are made of the **Organ Rock Formation**. As you round that point on the Lockhart Road, you'll have a number of foto opportunities like this one.

Above Part of what remains at the **Western States Well** site. Nearby are other huge timbers which were once part of the derrick, some huge rope about 6-7cms in diameter, and bricks that were to line a boiler which was the power source for drilling.

Right Looking east at **Indian Creek Falls.** About half the time, this is a dry-fall, but in April, 2012, it had running water making a nice dipping pool.

Above Looking eastward down on the **Newberry Rincon** or abandoned meander just east of Newberry Butte. In the middle distance is **Indian Creek** running from right to left. Newberry Butte is behind the camera.

Left This is the site of the **Deseret Petroleum Well** and what remains of a huge **stack of wood**. Sometime since 1991, the stack was torched and all that's left now are charred remains. On ledges behind and above the camera are several **moki houses** and/or granaries.

Big Spring & Lower Salt Creek Canyons, Colorado River Overlook, Loop Canyon & Anasazi Bottom & the Cave Spring Hike

Location & Access Featured on this map are portions of the northern **Needles District** of Canyonlands NP. Get to this region by driving along Highway 191 between Moab and Monticello. At **Church Rock** and between **mile posts 86 & 87**, turn west onto the **Needles Highway, State Road 211**. This paved road runs along parts of Indian Creek, past the Dugout Ranch, and finally to the Needles Outpost, Needles Visitor Center, Squaw Flat Campground and finally to the **Big Spring Canyon Overlook & Trailhead**. Also, in the bottom left part of this map roads are shown which take you to Elephant Hill & The Needles; and into the middle part of Salt Creek & Horse Canyons.

Shown on this map is the Needles Visitor Center, where you can get the latest information on trails & roads, and where water can be found. Also, the Squaw Flat Campground which is open year-round. Just as you arrive in the area will be the **Needles Outpost**, a little private outfit right on the park boundary. It got started back in about 1965 when the area became a national park. Needles Outpost is open from about March 1 until December 1 each year. Their website states: *Services include Gasoline, General store stocked with very low priced groceries, camping supplies, Southwest gifts, selection of books, maps on any subject, Western Grill featuring local cuisine (Breakfast & Lunch), 8:30-4:30, frozen meats for your own wood fire BBQ, Private Campground with flush toilets, showers. Reservations accepted.* Their website is **canyonlandsneedlesoutpost.com**, or Tele. 435-979-4007.

Elevations Needles Outpost & Visitor Center, 1500m; Big Spring Canyon/Confluence Overlook Trailhead, 1509m; Colorado River at Spanish Bottom (not shown on this map), about 1200m.

Water At the campground & visitor center. There are also several springs with some water in Big Spring and Little Spring Canyons, and at Cave Spring. Salt Creek below the Lower Jump (right in the middle of this map) always has running water in places, but it has a mineral taste. However, you could drink it in an emergency and live.

Maps USGS or BLM map La Sal (1:100,000); The Loop (1:24,000--7 1/2' quad); the plastic Trails Illustrated/National Geographic map Canyonlands National Park (1:70,000); or the Latitude 40° map, Moab West (1:75,000).

Main Attractions An old historic cowboy camp at Cave Spring, a good place to look down onto the Colorado River and The Loop, and 2 ways for experienced hikers to reach the Colorado.

Loop Canyon to the Colorado River and Anasazi Bottom

To do this almost unknown hike, stop at the Needles Visitor Center for last minute information about road conditions, then turn north on the west side of the visitor center; you'll soon be on a good sandy road signposted for the **Colorado River Overlook**. Normally, any car can be driven to as far as the **Lower Jump 4.3 kms (2.7 miles)** from the visitor center; stop there for a quick peek into the Lower Jump of Salt Creek. Then continue to the **carpark** at **Km 5.3 (Mile 3.3)**. At that point you'll need a HC/4WD, or mtn. bike, or walk. Beyond that, and at **Km 8.1 (Mile 5)**, park on slickrock to the right--and hopefully with a small cairn in sight. This parking is the beginning of an old bulldozer or **Cat track** running down into the upper and middle parts of what this author is calling **Loop Canyon**. This trailhead may not be easy to find, but it's at a point where the road begins to head west.

Once you get on this old track, it's fairly easy to follow until it ends down in the middle part of the drainage. Just before it ends, it cuts down a big steep dugway. Once down in, the old road vanishes and you simply walk northwest toward the river in the southern part a couple of big bends called **The Loop**. When you reach an overlook of the Colorado (**1st Limestone Bench**), you'll be on a rim made of limestone instead of sandstone. From there, bench-walk west for about 500m to some cairns marking the way over the 1st limestone bench and down to a **2nd limestone bench** near the Colorado. Once near the river, turn left again and you'll soon come to the boater's **Box Elder Campsite** in a little nook in the limestone rim.

If the river is low, go right down to the water's edge and walk **hunch-back** style through a tunnel-like cat walk about 60m to the bottom of a minor drainage. From there continue through willows & tamarisks to what this writer calls **Anasazi Bottom**. There you'll find parts of **9 man-made structures**, mostly granaries. About half are in pretty good condition, and most are at or near ground level. A couple are up high on a ledge that could only have been reached by a ladder. Others are in tiny natural cranny holes in the sandstone. Also, under an overhang facing downstream, in the lower end of the bottom, are the signatures of some of the early-day boaters on the Green & Colorado Rivers. They are: *E.T. Wolverton, R.C. Wheeler, W.E. Casaday and Walt Stork*, plus the dates *4/1/[19]05 & 4/17/[19]05*. Of the archaeology sites discussed in this book, and along either river, this is one of the more interesting.

If the water is too high for the hunch-back route, then stay on the rim just above the river and walk west from the Box Elder Campsite about 1 km to find a route down to the lower end of Anasazi Bottom.

Now back to the HC/4WD road above Loop Canyon; you might as well continue west to where the road ends at the **Colorado River Overlook**. The author rode a mtn. bike there once, then later took his VW Rabbit (with oversized tires) out there (1991). From along that point you'll have good views down onto the lower end of Salt Creek Canyon and the Colorado. In 2011, he attempted to drive his Jeep Patriot (only half a Jeep!) but only got to within 1 km of the end of the road. The last part of that track is now for LR/HC/4WD's only, so walk or bike the last part.

Roadside Ruin, Cave Spring and an Historic Cowboy Camp

About 500m west of the Needles Visitor Center and on the east side of the road will be a sign at a parking place stating **Roadside Ruin**. From there, a nature trail heads east about 200m to a low cliff. Tucked underneath will be one of the better preserved granaries around.

Almost due south of the Needles Visitor Center is an interesting relic of the old west; it's **Cave Spring** and nearby is an old **cowboy camp** which could date back as far as the 1890's (?). To get there drive west from the visitor center **1 km (.6 mile)** and turn south. At **Km 2.3 (Mile 1.4** from the visitor center) turn east and drive to **Km 3.9 (Mile 2.2)** on a graded & gravelled road to a parking place. From the parking spot, there's a short sign-posted loop-trail winding in and around the rocks, passing along the way, several overhangs and a place where cowboys once camped. Turn left at the trailhead if you just want to visit the spring and camp which are about 100m apart. At the cowboy camp are tables, benches, coffee pots, frying pans and kettles of various kinds, even some old tinned food. Also grub boxes (an oat box for horses is a little further along the trail) and other odds & ends. This place is now fenced off

Map 29, Big Spring & Lower Salt Creek Canyons, Colorado R. Overlook, Loop Canyon & Anasazi Bottom & Cave Spring Hike

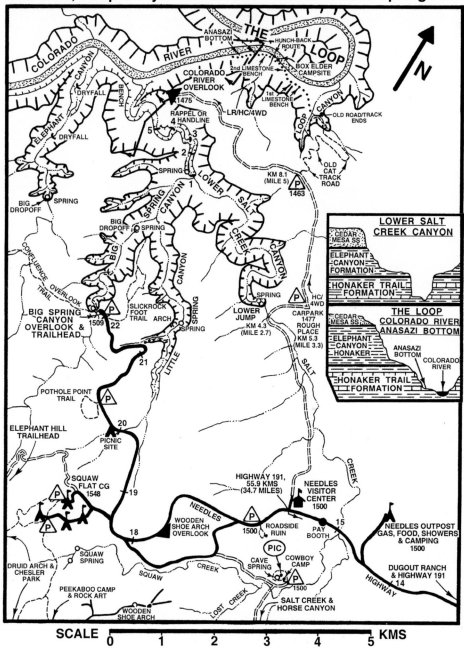

SCALE 0 1 2 3 4 5 KMS

so please leave all the old relics in place--it's the law, as this is an historic cowboy camp. At the spring are some red painted **pictographs**.

It's not known for sure who may have first camped at this site, but in the 1890's Dave Goudelock from Moab came into this country and joined other cowboys already on Indian Creek. They pooled together and created the **Indian Creek Cattle Company**. That outfit ranged cattle all over this country. They were in the mountains in summer and in these parts in winter. Later, Al & Jim Scorup and the

The **Hunched Back Route** to **Anasazi Bottom**. You can only use this shortcut when water levels in the Colorado River are low; otherwise, you'll have to go up and around to reach Anasazi Bottom.

Somervilles joined together and bought out the old timers in 1918. It was during the Scorup & Somerville Cattle Company era at the Dugout Ranch, this camp was used the most. The last time cowboys used the place was when the park came in (it may have been in 1978; that's when the permits were pulled from stockmen in the Island district). There's another old cowboy camp in Lost Creek Canyon, but that'll be discussed later. Read the full history of the Dugout Ranch along with **Map 33**.

Big & Little Spring Canyons, and Lower Salt Creek Gorge

Here are a couple of little-known canyons. It's down into Big & Little Spring drainages and into the lowest end of Salt Creek Canyon. To get to the trailhead, head west then north from the visitor center, pass the turnoff to Elephant Hill and the Squaw Flat Campground and to the end of the paved road to what the CNP calls the **Big Spring Canyon Overlook**. Park there which is the trailhead for the hike to **The Confluence Overlook**.

Once there, locate the beginning of the Confluence Overlook Trail heading west and use it to get started down into Big Spring Canyon. About 100m from the trailhead you'll be in the drainage bottom, with the **Confluence Overlook Trail heading upcanyon south, then west**. Just downcanyon from that point is a dropoff which is the beginning of the lower part of Big Spring Canyon. There should always be a spring and pool under that ledge. To hike down Big Spring Canyon, walk north along a faint trail on the east side of this dropoff until you come to 2 places to climb down in. The first such place is about 150m below the dropoff, but that's a difficult downclimb. The next place is a little easier. It's just around the corner another 50m. Most people who call themselves hikers won't have any trouble downclimbing this pitch which is done using all-4's, but a short rope will help some beginners.

Once in the bottom, just head downcanyon along the dry creek bed. Further downstream will be a **big dropoff** and good year-round water; pass it on the left or west side. You can easily walk down to the **1st Dropoff (shown as 1 on the map)** at the junction with **Salt Creek Canyon**; walk past that dropoff and continue down Salt Creek. After 400m or so will be the **2nd Dropoff**--downclimb it on the right. About 300m below that is the **3rd Dropoff** or cascade; sometimes wet, sometimes dry. When dry, it's an easy downclimb/upclimb; when wet, maybe you'll need a partner or two (?). About 400m below that is the **4th Dropoff**. This is a vertical climb with a little overhang, but with some steps or tiny ledges. Above are **2 bolts** & hangers and webbing with descent ring for a **6m rappel or handline**. Surely you'll be coming back this way, so what you need is a 10m-long rope, rappelling harness, and jumars/ascenders. Or, if you have pretty good upper body strength and low body fat, you could just tie off a large diameter rope and handline down, and later back up. Having knots 25 cms apart on your rope will help your grip coming back up.

This writer rappelled down, then handlined (hand over hand) back up. He was 69 at the time, so most of you should be able match that. Otherwise, you'll need jumars or ascenders.

After another 600m or so is the **5th Dropoff** and last problem in Lower Salt Creek Canyon. It's a 7-8m high dry/waterfall that has 11 limestone steps, just like a staircase. If there's running water this may be impossible to climb (it'll depend on how much water is flowing at the time), but if it's dry, it's an easy climb for anyone. One km below that is the Colorado.

If you're not into these downclimbs, another interesting hike in this area, would be to stay on the bench that begins at the confluence of Big Spring Canyon & Salt Creek. Simply bench-walk on this rim to view all the dropoffs mentioned; and you'll eventually come to another overlook of the Colorado at the mouth of Salt Creek Canyon. If you continue west on the same bench, you'll end up in the middle part of lower **Elephant Canyon**. The author tried to go up Elephant once, but it's impossible; however it's very likely possible to continue on the same bench all the way to **The Confluence**, and perhaps exit up the canyon wall from there.

To return to the trailhead, you could head up **Little Spring Canyon**. Higher up will be several little dryfalls and likely a waterfall or two in the wetter sections of the drainage; but with some brush and water loving vegetation! It's not the worst bushwhack in the world, but it's not fun either--especially with shorts! Wear long pants if you try this one. It's recommended you forget Little Spring Canyon.

If you do return up Little Spring Canyon, your first opportunity to get out will be on the right or west side just above a **natural arch**, but it's a climb (see map). After that, head south to the paved road. Actually, in the upper end of the drainage there are a number of different routes out to the west side and the paved road. Once out of the canyon, road-walk back to your car.

To hike down Big Spring and lower Salt Creek to the Colorado, then return via Little Spring Canyon and back to the trailhead, should take from 6-9 hours for most people. In 4/2012, the author walked down Big Spring Canyon to Salt Creek, down Salt Creek to the 3rd dropoff, then got on the bench and walked around into Elephant Canyon, attempted to get out, but couldn't, so he returned up Little Spring and back to his car in just under 9 hours--a long day. Later, he went down just below the 5th dropoff (he's been up to that point from the river a couple of times with running water) and returned in 4 3/4 hours.

NOTICE & COMMENTARY: Officially, Big Spring & Lower Salt Creek Canyons are closed to hikers from May 1 to September 1 to pamper the **big horn lambs**, but almost no one is aware of this. This writer wasn't! He was only told about it after returning from Lower Salt Creek in June, 2012. He asked why doesn't CNP put up a sign or notice of the closure at the trailhead? To that he was told by the backcountry specialist, *"If we did that, it would only attract more people to those canyons"*.

The control freaks in the CNP/NPS seem to think that hikers will spook big horn sheep in the lambing season causing great stress, or some kind of harm. However, coyotes are the lambs only real enemy in the park. In Utah, the Fish & Game Department (DWR) has been transplanting big horns, Rocky Mountain goats and other wildlife since the 1950's, and nowhere else in the state does anyone think hikers are a detriment in any way to big horns or any other wildlife. Besides, since everyone is addicted to AC--except this writer, there is no way that enough hikers will get out of their AC'ed cars to do that hike in the middle of summer.

Another short hike in this area is to an overlook of the confluence of Big & Little Spring Canyons. However the view is a little disappointing. It's a cairned trail beginning near the end of the paved highway and **mile post 22**. It's called the **Slickrock Foot Trail** and is an easy walk for beginners. It can be done in 1 1/2-2 hours. Also shown on the map is the **Pothole Point Trail**, but it doesn't seem interesting.

Left One of 9 granaries on **Anasazi Bottom**. This is one of the better preserved; and most are found in little cubby holes in the canyon wall. **Right** This is the pool just below the **3rd Dropoff** in **lower Salt Creek Canyon**. Water in lower Salt Creek has a mineral taste, thus the name.

Above The **Cowboy Camp** located near **Cave Spring**. It's almost due south of the visitor center. Notice the black soot or smoke on the ceiling in the upper left; this could have started with Indians, but cowboys may have used this place since about the 1890's (?).

Right The top of the **4th Dropoff** in lower **Salt Creek Canyon**. This is a rappel or handline down about 6-7m from a couple of bolts & hangers. This is the only real impediment in the canyon going all the way to the Colorado River.

Above Looking upcanyon at the **Big Dropoff in Big Spring Canyon.** Get around this obstacle by using a trail on the right side of this picture (if you're hiking downcanyon it will be on the left or west side). There's always good drinking water from this permanent spring.

Left This is the same **4th Dropoff** as seen on the opposite page, but this time from the bottom. Tie the rope to your pack and pull it up after you've handlined or jumarred back-up. Check the bolts & hangers carefully before putting your life on the line. Those bolts are put in a layer of limestone so they should last a few years (?). From here to the Colorado is about 2 kms with only the **5th Dropoff** to downclimb; but that's like going down a flight of 11 steps. In dry conditions that's an easy climb up or down.

The Confluence Overlook, Chesler Park, Druid Arch, and Red Lake & Lost Canyons

Location & Access Featured on this map is the heart of what is known as **The Needles (District)** of Canyonlands NP. This is the southeastern corner of CNP. To get there, drive along Highway 191 between Moab & Monticello. At Church Rock and between **mile posts 86 & 87**, turn west onto **The Needles Highway, State Road 211**. You'll drive west, then down along Indian Creek, past **Newspaper Rock** and the Dugout Ranch, and finally into **The Needles**. The first place you'll come to is the Needles Visitor Center. Be sure to stop there for updated information on trails, roads, weather forecasts, etc.

From the visitor center, drive westward on the paved road all the way to Squaw Flat Campground and/or the **Big Spring Canyon Overlook & Trailhead**. This last place could easily be called **The Confluence Overlook Trailhead**. Also, there's a good graveled road from the Squaw Flat Campground running west to the **Elephant Hill Trailhead**. All other roads in this part of the park are for HC/4WD's only. All locations on this map are within the national park.

Elevations Visitor center, 1500m; Elephant Hill Trailhead, 1512m; Big Spring Canyon Overlook & Trailhead, 1509m; Spanish Bottom on the Colorado River, about 1200m.

Water Drinking water is available at the visitor center and Squaw Flat Campground. Water is sometimes found in parts of Elephant, Squaw and Lost Canyons, but they dry up at times, so always carry your own drinking water on all hikes.

Maps USGS or BLM map La Sal (1:100,000); Spanish Bottom, The Loop, Druid Arch & Cross Canyon (1:24,000--7 1/2' quads); the plastic Trails Illustrated/National Geographic map Canyonlands National Park (1:70,000); or the plastic Latitude 40° map Moab West (1:75,000).

Main Attractions A number of hikes through The Needles--particularly interesting places are **Chesler Park**, the **Joint Trail**, and the walk to **Druid Arch**. Also, the overlook of **The Confluence** of the Green & Colorado Rivers, and a rugged hike down to it; a trail down to the head of Cataract Canyon and **Spanish Bottom**; and lots of spectacular geologic scenery. There's also another old cowboy camp in Lost Canyon that may be older than the one at Cave Spring.

The Confluence Overlook Trail

This hike begins at the end of the paved road and mile post 22 at the **Big Spring Canyon Overlook & Trailhead**. From the west end of the parking lot locate the trail. It immediately drops down into the shallow **Big Spring Canyon** drainage, then climbs out the other side and heads west for nearly 5 kms. This is a well-used and well-marked trail and you can't get lost. Near the end of the hike you'll cross one 4WD road, then walk on a footpath for 800m to another **4WD road**, walk that a ways to the **4WD Trailhead**, then continue another 800m to The Confluence Overlook. From there everybody walks another 800m to **The Confluence Overlook**. This is one of the more spectacular scenes around. This hike is along a flat track and easy but be sure to take lots of water in warmer weather. Just to hike to the overlook and back should take most people about half a day, maybe 4-5 hours, but it can be done in a fast 3 hours, round-trip. Arrive around mid-day for the best pictures.

Here's a long all-day hike and climb for the really fit and adventurous person. Start at the same trail-

An Aerial view of **The Confluence** of the Green (upper right) and Colorado Rivers (lower right) looking southwest. The Confluence Overlook is in the upper left, the 2nd Canyon lower left (see **Map 21**).

Map 30, The Confluence Overlook, Chesler Park, Druid Arch, and Red Lake & Lost Canyons

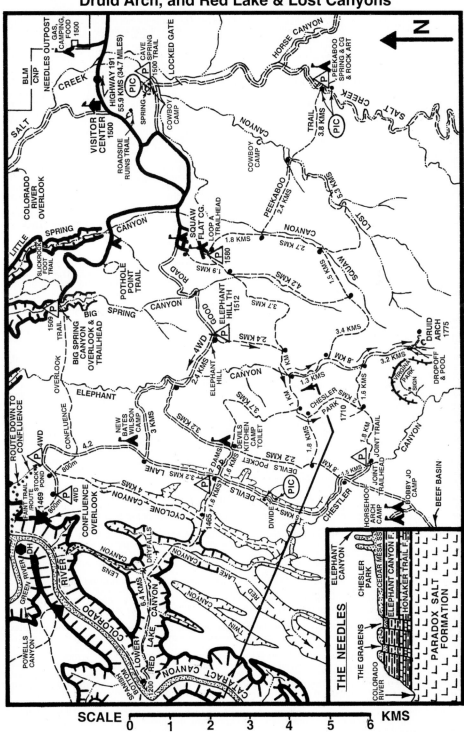

head and walk west on the same trail, but after you see The Confluence from above, return to the 4WD road and walk northeastward to the other **4WD** parking place shown on the map. From there head northwest down a shallow drainage east of The Confluence. You'll be walking along a partly-cairned route down to The Confluence itself (This route is shown a little better on **Map 21, page 219** than this one). Further on, there are some steep places, but if you stay on route it's not too difficult or dangerous. This former trail, now partly-cairned route, is shown on the *older 15' quads,* but it has never gotten popular with the public, and the CNP would never dream of making it into a real trail, or publicizing it any way. More people were using it in 1991 than in 2012, so you'll have to take a good topo map in hand and route-find along the lay of the canyon walls. Take along a more-rugged pair of boots or heavier shoes, plenty of water & lunch, and plan to make it a long all-day trip from Big Spring Canyon Trailhead.

When you reach The Confluence, you can return the same way, which would be faster, or try a different variation for the return trip. This would be for the toughest and most adventurous of hikers only! To do this, first head south along the east bank of the Colorado. About 1 1/2 kms from The Confluence, will be 2 minor drainages coming down from the east. At a point about halfway between the two, look up at the slope and visualize a route up through a series of ledges. Once you locate a way, climb up the route you've picked out, then veer right or south and go along a bench and into the most-southern of the 2 little canyons. From there, continue route-finding south into the upper end of **Lens Canyon**. After another 2 kms, you'll come to the upper end of **Lower Red Lake Canyon** where you'll find the good trail heading down to the river. Walk east on this well-used path to a former road, now just a foot trail in **Cyclone Canyon**, turn north along the former track till you reach the Confluence Overlook Trail, then walk east back to the carpark. This is a longer and more difficult hike than most people can handle in one day, so consider doing it in two. The author did the hike just suggested back in 1991 in just over 7 hours, but he was really moving. But that time couldn't be duplicated today because the route down to The Confluence now requires more time route-finding. Another alternate to this would be to walk along the river to where Red Lake Canyon enters the Colorado, then return via the good trail in that drainage. This would be a longer but easier hike, but you'd be near water where campsites would be easy to locate. If backpacking you're supposed to have a **permit**, which now costs **$30**--not exactly an incentive for backpacking.

History of the Confluence

Other than **Denis Julien** and other early-day trappers, members of the **Powell Expedition of 1869** may have been the first white men to see the junction of the Green and Colorado Rivers. That expedition camped at the north side of The Confluence from July 16 until July 20, 1869. They repaired boats, sifted flour which had become wet and musty, did some surveys, and on the 20th, Powell & Bradley climbed up on the east bank of the Colorado and managed to reach canyon rim and what is now The Needles. Powell's 1871 expedition also camped there for several days, from September 16 to 20. It was during this trip they climbed up and out of **Powells Canyon** to view The Confluence from the west.

Beginning in about the late 1880's, there have been numerous people or groups going down by boat to The Confluence. Many went on down the Colorado and into Cataract Canyon, but others went only this far, or to Spanish Bottom a little ways further down and still in quiet waters. The first steamboat made it to The Confluence and Spanish Bottom in April of 1892, but that's discussed in depth under **Map 10 on Spanish Bottom**. No one ever settled at The Confluence or built any permanent structures, but there was a big camp set up there once in the fall of 1914.

This was a government survey crew under the supervision of **John F. Richardson**. Perhaps the best place to locate information about this expedition is from the testimonies in the *Colorado River Bed Case hearings,* which took place in the fall of 1929. A number of those testifying made statements about their experience, including Richardson himself. Part of his statement went like this:

During the latter part of June, 1914, I went down the Green River in a boat from Greenriver, Utah, to the junction and back again to Greenriver on reconnaissance; that is, to look the country over and see whether the United States would be justified in making further examinations or surveys for a dam site at the junction or just below the junction. The purpose of making the surveys of those dam sites [there were half a dozen sites surveyed in that time period] was essentially for irrigation, with power as an incidental use. On this trip I had a launch that belonged to Captain Yokey. We afterwards had two launches there. One was named the "Belle of Shannon".

About the middle of July, I made a trip down the Green River, a part of the way with Mr. F.L. Salue, manager of the Yuma Project. Right after that I sent a drill outfit down. I had boats built at Greenriver on my plan and sent them down and I made a number of trips down there..... I built two drill scows and the drills were loaded on the scows at Wimmer's ranch at the mouth of the San Rafael..... [this is now known as the Ruby Ranch].

H.T. (Cap) Yokey, tells of his experience: *Mr. Richardson told me he had a party of 12 men coming in with ten tons of supplies to be taken down and wanted to know how I would get it there. I told him to make a barge and take it down, and I built a barge 32 feet long and 8 feet wide [10 x 2m] in ten days. No one made it clear who may have made the other scows, but they did have 2 or 3 powerless barges or scows on the river.*

Tom Wimmer also testified that: *In 1914, I had a government contract for hauling freight..... I made many round-trips down during that time from Greenriver or from my ranch [he owned the Ruby Ranch before Glen Ruby did]..... It was 8 to 12 trips to the Confluence..... We hauled coal from Floy [near Exit 175 on I-70], 16 miles [25 kms], to my ranch, where it would be stored for a while and then the boys would pick it up on the scows.*

The boat that did most of the work during this operation was Tom Wimmer's launch the **"Marguerite"**. It was this boat which pushed one of the barges or scows built by Cap Yokey. One of the scows was apparently called the **"Betsy Ann"**.

Lester A. Shaw stated: *I was on a salary and I also furnished boats. I furnished a motor boat about 14 or 16 feet long [4 or 5m]. It was named "Belle of Shannon". It had a two cylinder simple marine engine in it..... It was the Marguerite that pushed the equipment down. I think the Betsy Ann was made originally for the government. They may later have put some power on the Betsy Ann to come back up. The Marguerite was the power on the scow. The scow was ahead of it and the Marguerite pushed it.*

When everything was in place, including a camp, drilling outfit and a steam boiler which produced power for the drill, they commenced drilling, apparently on both sides of the river, to test the bedrock for a possible dam site. The drilling took place from sometime in September until well into November, around Thanksgiving time in 1914.

Lester A. Shaw tells the reason why they left the river: *I know why drilling at the junction ceased. The flood waters came down and destroyed the equipment that we were drilling with and the drill went down the river. It was high water, accompanied by heavy debris collecting against the cables and barges which anchored the drill, and the weight was so terrific that they finally gave way. After this occurrence the drilling outfit was taken out. The steam boiler was equipped on one of the barges with a paddle wheel geared to it from the rear and it came out under its own power. The Marguerite was used as power on the other barge. The other motor boat and my boat were attached to the other scow and we brought that out.*

While doing research for his *River Guide*, the author looked around on all 3 corners of The Confluence, and downstream a ways, but never saw anything that might indicate where Richardson's drilling camp was set up. After all his river trips were finished, someone suggested the old camp was along the lower Green River on the south side, about where the **DH** (drill hole) symbol is on the map. As yet this has not been confirmed. This would have to be checked out from the other side of the Colorado.

On the north side of The Confluence, between the Green & Colorado Rivers, you can see on a small rocky ledge, inscriptions left by several boaters. The oldest was left by the Kolb brothers in **1911**. You'd have to swim or float over to see that. Or be on a rafting trip--then fight through tamarisks!

Routes to the Colorado River via Elephant Hill

Another way of getting to **The Confluence Overlook**, **The Confluence** itself, or the lower end of **Red Lake Canyon**, would be to drive west on the good graveled road from the Squaw Flat Campground. It's about 5 kms to **Elephant Hill**, which is the beginning of LR/HC/4WD or Mountain Bike Land. The Elephant Hill Trailhead is also the beginning of a foot trail heading south into the heart of The Needles.

The road over Elephant Hill is very steep and rough, but in recent years the NPS has poured cement into some holes and made it just barely passable for LR/HC/4WD's. A 2WD hasn't a chance! People with cars can park at the trailhead and either walk or take a mtn. bike into the area to the west and south (but not on foot trails). To get down to the river, park your wheels at any of the three 4WD trailheads as shown on the map. With a bike or 4WD it's a hike of only about 800m to The Confluence Overlook from the end of the road. It's only a 3-4 km hike down to The Confluence from the most-northerly of the 3 trailheads, and this would take more than half a day for a strong hiker--if they returned the same way.

The 3rd 4WD or mtn. bike trailhead is in the middle of **Devils Lane**. The road getting there is pretty good after Elephant Hill, but it's sandy in spots which slows down mtn. bikes. If you park your wheels there, you can walk the remaining 8 kms to the Colorado River which is immediately across from Spanish Bottom. This is a very good trail and used often. Sorry, no mtn. bikes on this trail, or any other foot path in the park. This walk would take most people about 2 hours to reach the river, and maybe 5-6 hours round-trip from the Devils Lane Trailhead. If you ride a mtn. bike from Elephant Hill, park it in Devils Lane, walk to the river and return to Elephant Hill, plan on a long all-day trip. This same trip took the author 6 hours round-trip once at the end of March in 1990 (that was with firmer sand than later on, was with refreshing temperatures, and he parked in Cyclone Canyon--but you can't do that now).

Aerial view looking north down on the western part of **The Needles**. In the middle and far distance is The Confluence. Also, **Devils Lane** and the **Divide** & **rock art** are to the right; **Cyclone Canyon** middle, and upper **Red Lake Canyon** to the far left. These are all **graben valleys**; that is, faultlines on either side have caused each valley to drop in relation to the surrounding countryside.

Looking northward from just north of the **Divide** in the southern part of the **Devils Lane**. To the left and under the ledges in the shadows are several rock art panels. Part of one is shown below.

Rock art in **The Needles** region is mostly pictographs like these reverse hand print which are located in the southern part of **Devils Lane**. You'll find rock art like these just north & south of the **Divide**.

If you don't have a mtn. bike or 4WD, and must walk all the way to the river from Elephant Hill Trailhead, then it's about 14 kms (9 miles) one-way if you walk the first part along the main road in. That's about half a day to the river. Some people could do this in one very long day, but it's recommended you take a big pack, camp one night on the river and return the next day.

If you'd like to get into The Maze country on the other side of the river, you could walk from Elephant Hill down to the river, put your pack on an air mattress or inner tube and **swim** across to **Spanish Bottom**; but that's a mighty cold swim in the hiking season of spring or fall (Or better still, look into getting a **Alpaca packraft** designed for and used in the Grand Canyon. These weight about 1 1/2 kgs and you're in a small boat--not in the water!) For people driving a car only and don't have a mtn. bike, using this suggested route to get to the eastern parts of **The Maze**, would be easier than hiking down the North Trail (or down the Golden Stairs Trail--a HC/2WD pickup can get to that trailhead).

The author swam across the river on October 10, 1990, then walked down Cataract Canyon for a couple of days, then returned and swam back across. The swimming part came in the middle of the day each time, and it wasn't too bad, or too cold. You swim less than a 100m across while drifting maybe 150m downstream. This trick could be done in late summer until about October 1--unless you used a packraft, then you could do it anytime of year. A packraft is highly recommended.

You could also spend several days walking down the east bank of the Colorado River in **Cataract Canyon**. You can walk all the way to the upper end of Lake Powell, and probably all the way down to Hite if you wanted to bad enough and were willing to cross the river-lake occasionally. Cataract Canyon hiking is discussed in more detail with **Map 10.**

Now a little history on the trail in lower Red Lake Canyon. Before the white men came to this country, it was a regular Indian route from The Needles Country down to the river. Then it may have been used by Spaniards or perhaps Mexicans, but most researchers and historians don't buy this theory. Then it was allegedly used by cattle or horse thieves, and finally by stockmen who settled on Indian Creek as early as the late 1880's. However, if this canyon and trail was ever used on a regular basis by cattlemen, it would have to have been used mostly by Al Scorup & the Somervilles who bought the Dugout Ranch on Indian Creek in 1918.

Much later, and in the early 1940's, Al Scorup hired Angus (Puge) Stocks to take his bulldozer there and build some 4WD roads into The Needles area for the first time. That was when the first road was built over Elephant Hill and when the first stock ponds were dug. Before that, there couldn't have been too much grazing in this part of The Needles, because there was never any permanent water in those parts and could only have been grazed in winter when there was snow on the ground. Since the creation of Canyonlands NP, the trail down into lower Red Lake Canyon has been upgraded.

Hiking Trails in The Needles from Elephant Hill Trailhead

Probably the most-used trailhead for hiking into the heart of **The Needles** is at **Elephant Hill**. At that site are parking places, some of which are shaded by large piñon or cedar (juniper) trees, picnic tables and toilets. Besides the steep road going over Elephant Hill, there's also a trail heading south and into some of the best day-hiking areas of Canyonlands. There's a large information board at the beginning of the trail, then signs at each of the trail junctions. Be sure to have a better map than this before going into this country. The plastic Trails Illustrated/National Geographic map listed below may be the best; but the simple map they give you at the visitor center works well. Just follow this or that map carefully to the following places.

From Elephant Hill Trailhead to the northern part of **Chesler Park** is about 5 kms. This grass covered meadow surrounded by colorful walls or pinnacles of Cedar Mesa Sandstone is about as beautiful a scene as you'll see anywhere. Walk around to the south side of the park to have a better view looking back to the north. The rocks out in the middle make a nice viewpoint. Some of the trails inside are actually old 4WD roads, which have been blocked off and only hikers can use them now. The hike to and back from Chesler Park via the shortest way will take about half a day, if you don't linger too long.

You also can exit (or enter) on the eastern side of Chesler Park, which is further up **Elephant Canyon** than the route first described. In the upper end of Elephant Canyon there's another favorite place to visit, usually on a long half-day or short all-day hike. This is to **Druid Arch**, but first a short discussion on Virgina Park, one of the parks forbidden fruits. Maybe 700-800m upcanyon from where you leave Chesler Park on the east side is another little indistinguishable side-canyon coming down from the south. This is the north-side entrance to **Virginia Park**, another meadowland surrounded by colorful redrock pinnacles. But first here's an explanation of why the NPS has **officially closed this place**. This closure started sometime after the 1st Edition of this book came out in 1991.

Virginia Park was always impossible for cows to get into, therefore it was never grazed. The NPS considers this to be a special place because it was left more pristine than any other place in The Needles. Their main concern seems to be that hikers could carry **cheat grass seeds** in their socks and deposit them there; but no one ever mentions that birds can do the same! So can coyotes. And deer and big horn sheep. So, these control freaks have never promoted it in any way and will not mention it to you, unless you mention it first. They have never put it on any maps so few people know about it. The appearance of Virginia Park is the same as Chesler Park except there are no roads close to it. What grazing there was in Chesler never really had a negative effect on it because there has never been any permanent water nearby, therefore cattle could only graze there when snow was on the ground. So it was never overgrazed, which is the main reason invasive weeds overtake some areas.

Now back to the northern gateway to Virginia Park. Sometime in the 1990's, this writer got a letter from someone who stated that he went into Virginia Park from the north, and unbeknownst to him, they had a motion detector there and he ended up with a ticket. This may have been a big lie so this writer would mention it to scare tourists away, but who knows (?). Anyway, so forget the north entrance, but it is possible to reach a high point on the southwest rim where you can get a good look (and fotograph) into Virginia, without actually entering the place. This other route will be discussed later.

Another word on Virginia Park. The NPS has set up a ranger-guided hike into this meadow apparently once a year usually in September (?). They enter via the **Joint Trailhead** and the dry wash bottom west of the park. Also, in the middle of Virginia Park is now a research station powered by solar panels. CNP, BLM and The Nature Conservancy are doing research on grasses and drought conditions. For more info on that project, see *The Nature Conservancy magazine* for the **Winter of 2010**, the one with Heidi Redd's picture on the front cover.

Now back to the hike to **Druid Arch**. Continue to the upper end of Elephant Canyon to the south. Just before you arrive, notice the cairns on the left or east side; this is where the trail gets upon a bench

Aerial view of **Chesler Park** looking northeast; this is in the heart of **The Needles**. The **Joint Trail** is in the middle bottom part of this picture, while the **Elephant Hill Trailhead** is some place in the upper right-hand corner. All the rocks you see are part of the Cedar Mesa Sandstone Formation.

to bypass some willows, a dropoff & huge pool. Just follow the cairns & trail which eventually takes you to the east side of the arch. Or if it's afternoon, stay in the dry wash bottom above the dropoff until you can take fotos from the west or sunny side. This is the furthest you can get from the Elephant Canyon Trailhead. It's about 8 kms from the trailhead to this arch via the shortest route; but about 20 kms round-trip for the hike just described--passing through Chesler Park coming & going along the way. That's a long all-day hike for some, considering all the fotogenic scenery you'll be absorbing along the way.

Here's another way into Chesler, and to the south-side rim of Virginia Park. If you have a 4WD or mtn. bike, you can use the roads beginning at Elephant Hill to reach the parking place called the **Joint Trailhead** just southwest of Chesler Park (or you could hike directly from Elephant Hill, through Chesler and along the Joint Trail to this same trailhead). Follow the signs to this trailhead and the beginning of the **Joint Trail**. From the Joint Trail Trailhead into Chesler it's about 1 1/2 kms. This is a short hike but very scenic. As the name suggests, the Joint Trail runs along the bottom of a couple of joints or cracks in the Cedar Mesa Sandstone. Part of it is cave-like and dark, much like slot canyons found elsewhere on the Colorado Plateau.

From the same Joint Trailhead, you could head southeast into upper Chesler Canyon and to the southwest rim of Virginia Park from the south. Just follow the dry creek bed; or a hikers trail which is on either side of the dry wash--apparently quite a few people are going in that direction. Take a better map than this and be alert because it's easy to miss the right turnoff.

That turnoff would be a little drainage coming down from the north. Just follow other hikers tracks; you won't be the first. About halfway up this short side-drainage will be a little dropoff or jumpup. You may have to stand on some stones to get up over this. About 100m past it and as the canyon is con-stricting, get upon a little bench to the right or east side to see a **sign stating that the place is closed.** If you were to continue to the east you'd enter a hole in the wall. This is actually a tunnel. If you go up there, you would be guilty of entering Virginia Park. But, if you backup about 40m from the sign, then scramble up a little side-drainage to the west, you can climb out onto some small slickrock domes for a look into Virginia. There's no grass there, only slickrock, so there's no way you can pollute the forbidden sanctuary. Remember **Virginia Park is officially closed**, but getting to and staying on a southwest rim may seem alright for some people--but very likely not for CNP administrators. **Whether you go to this lookout or not will be your choice**; but in all honesty, **the scenery in Virginia is exactly the same as in Chesler Park--which is a lot easier to get to. Going to Virginia really isn't worth it!**

Once (1990 before Virginia was closed) the author left Elephant Hill with his mtn. bike, stopped at the Joint Trailhead, then hiked into both of these parks from the southwest, then returned to his car in about 7 1/2 hours.

Before leaving this part of The Needles, here's a little history of the building of the roads through this rugged country. The late **Angus (Puge) Stocks** formerly of Moab & La Sal, was a Cat Skinner (bulldozer driver) most of his life, and he worked out there for a while in the 1940's. He recalls a few events:

I worked down in there off and on for about 3 years. I was in there mostly in 1942; worked for Al Scorup. He was the owner of the Dugout Ranch. I lived at the Dugout one summer and one winter. I did an awful lot of work there with my Cat.

There was no roads at all [in the Needles] until I went in there; just trails. Scorup hired me first for piece-meal jobs. A ditch would go out, or something. One time I think I was down in there for about 3 weeks. We built a road over Elephant Hill and into Chesler Park. Then we went out from Chesler Park and into Butler Flats. That's south and a little bit west of Chesler Park. Then we went south across Beef Basin to the Dark Canyon Uplift there. We built a jeep road all the way. Cy Thornell was the guy who ran the cattle for Scorup at that time. We also built a lot of reservoirs down in there. It was public land but Al Scorup hired me to do the work because it was his allotted grazing area.

I used to fly in there all the time. I had one landing place right on top of Elephant Hill, believe it or not. If you look real close you'll see where it was. They used to have a small strip out there and used to fly an old T Craft in. You know where Chesler Park is (?), we landed right in there too, with a T Craft.

Cowboy Camp in Lost Canyon

From the end of the **Loop A Road in Squaw Flat Campground**, you could use trails heading south-east toward **Lost Canyon**. From this campground look for the trail signposted for **Peekaboo Campsite on Salt Creek**. It heads southeast and is well-cairned all the way. Follow the map carefully, then when you reach Lost Canyon, walk downstream or northeast. It's a shallow drainage and there are a few places that are swampy, with possible running water. About 1 1/2 kms below where the trail crosses the drainage, will be an **old cowboy camp** under an overhang facing south. It's behind a row of cot-tonwood trees and partially hidden. In the early days, it was used more than the camp at Cave Spring because there was always more water in Lost Canyon for the riding horses than at the Cave.

This site is similar to the camp at Cave Spring. There's an old table or two, a grub box which still has some baking powder and odds & ends--frying pans, kettles and a broom. On the wall behind and to the east a little, are a number of old cowboy signatures. The oldest ones are hard to read, but some go back to the 1920's, and probably earlier. There are several Spanish names, indicating that Mexicans or Basques were working for Al Scorup and the Indian Creek outfit.

The most interesting parts of The Needles have been described here, but there's still room to explore. The hike to **Peekaboo and the rock art** there is described in the next section and from the locked gate shown, but you could also get there from the Squaw Flat Campground. If you'd like to backpack into Salt Creek above Peekaboo, using this trail would be about the same distance as walking from the locked gate on the 4WD road.

Druid Arch from the west side. This foto was taken in the after-noon sun. If you arrive before about noon, then high-tail-it to the east side.

Above From the middle of **Chesler Park** looking northeast. The trail junction you see (lower left) is in the middle of this big meadow near the south end of the big line of pinnacles seen in the foto on page 304. This is one of the more fotogenic scenes in Canyonlands NP.

Right This tunnel-like crack is at the southern end of the **Joint Trail**. For whatever reason, kids have piled up rocks in this section.

The cowboy camp in **Lost Canyon**. Notice the upsidedown tin cans on the posts holding up both table tops; they were placed there to keep mice, chipmunks or squirrels from getting to the food.

This is a wide-angle view of the **Western States Well** featured on **Map 28**. Notice the huge square timbers that were part of the derrick, the bull wheel and the pile of bricks which were to line a boiler.

Middle Salt Creek and Horse Canyons

Location & Access This map shows upper Salt Creek, and Horse, Davis & Lavender Canyons; but discussed here will be the **middle section of Salt Creek**; that part above the confluence with **Horse Canyon**. Also Horse Canyon which got its name because the cowboys from the Indian Creek and/or the Scorup & Sommerville (S & S) Cattle Companies built a fence across the mouth somewhere and left their extra saddle horses there to graze. Both of these very scenic canyons are located due south of The Needles Visitor Center.

To get to The Needles District of Canyonlands, drive along Highway 191 between Moab & Monticello. At Church Rock, and from between **mile posts 86 & 87**, turn west onto **The Needles Highway, State Road 211**. Drive westward down along Indian Creek, past the Dugout Ranch and eventually to the visitor center which is **55.9 kms (34.7 miles)** from 191. From the visitor center, drive west toward the Squaw Flat Campground, but after **1 km (.6 mile)** turn south at the sign pointing out Cave Spring and/or Horse Canyon & Salt Creek. Just before you reach Cave Spring (which is discussed under **Map 29**) turn right or south and drive along a good graded dirt road another 500m to a parking place and a **locked gate (4.1 kms/2.6 miles** from the visitor center). See previous map, **Map 30**. To enter this area, you must first stop at the visitor center and pay **$10 for a permit to drive a 4WD vehicle** into Salt Creek up to Peekaboo Campsite; or into Horse Canyon **(But you can day-hike into either canyon without a permit--or backpack in and camp with a $30 backpacking permit)**. If you decide to drive in, along with the permit, they will give you the combination to the lock on the gate. If you're driving a 2WD car, park there; if you go any further you'll be stuck after 200-300m because of **Deep Sand!** Beyond the carpark it's **exclusively 4WD country!**

If you have a 4WD, then proceed into either canyon, but **lower the pressure in your tires**. For highway driving, this writer goes up to 38-40 lbs (warm tire pressure), but for this drive, he went down to 25 lbs. This puts more rubber to the road; and a softer tire somehow prevents getting stuck (?). Also, you'll want about 23cms (9") of clearance if you can. There shouldn't be too many problems after the first couple of kms with the deepest sand. Once into Horse Canyon, keep your momentum up and don't stop or slow down too much in deep sand. Without a 4WD, it's better to walk than take a mtn. bike.

Elevations Visitor center, Squaw Flat Campground & Cave Spring, about 1500m; the upper end of Horse Canyon, about 1600-1650m; and the benches above each, about 1950m.

Water In winter & spring there's usually a small stream and year-round running water in parts of Salt Creek. There are no more cattle in this drainage, but there are people, so it's best to treat this water. The higher up you go, the better the water quality should be. There may be a place or 2 in Horse Canyon with a little water too, but it varies greatly with the season; but don't bet your life on finding any! So take all the water you'll need for your trip; from the visitor center or the Squaw Flat Campground.

Maps USGS or BLM map La Sal (1:100,000), North Six Shooter Peak, The Loop, Druid Arch & South Six Shooter Peak (1:24,000--7 1/2' quads); the plastic Trails Illustrated/National Geographic map Canyonlands National Park (1:70,000); or the plastic Latitude 40° map Moab West (1:75,000).

Main Attractions Great scenery, especially in upper Horse Canyon and from the bench or rim above. There are also a several Anasazi Indian ruins in each canyon, plus the **13, 11 & 9 Faces Pictograph panels** in upper Horse--some of the best rock art around.

Horse Canyon

From the locked gate & carpark **(set you odometer at 0)** south of Cave Spring, drive or walk up the sandy road. The worst part of the road going to either canyon is in the first 2 kms from the locked gate. This is where the road runs along the dry creek bed and the sand is at it's deepest and worst; **at least in dry conditions**. A mtn. bike is useless in this part, so is a 2WD. Even 4WD's occasionally get stuck. Even with a 4WD, **lower the air pressure in your tires to about half of what is normal**, then just before you reach a section with deep sand, **gear down, rev up, and drive as fast as conditions allow**.

After the first 2 kms or so, you may find running water in places, or at least wet sand. Where the sand is wet, it'll be more firm and any vehicle can run it. Be observant in the area of the confluence of Salt Creek & Horse Canyon which is at **Km 3.6 (Mile 2.2** from the locked gate). It's sometimes easy to miss this turnoff.

In Horse Canyon, and at **Km 5.5 (Mile 3.4** from the locked gate) will be an arch up high in a corner called **Paul Bunyan's Potty**. When you see it, you'll know how it got the name--it looks just like a toilet seat. Just before you reach this arch, and at the sharp bend in the dry creek bed, will be one **Anasazi structure** under a ledge facing south. It's hidden behind some trees and is more often missed than seen. Just after this dwelling is the parking place for Paul Bunyan's Potty, and a **toilet**.

At **Km 7.2 (Mile 4.5)** and on the left or east, will be a side-road running northeast toward **Tower Ruins**. This road ends at a parking place after **1 km (.6 mile)**. This is one of the few Indian ruins in the park the NPS will discuss, mainly because it's up so high in an alcove and is unreachable without a tall ladder. However, at the end of the short little trail leading from the parking place to the base of that alcove, you can still get a good look at it from below.

The further up Horse Canyon you go, the more constricted the drainage becomes. The upper end is rather spectacular and is similar in appearance to the canyons west of The Confluence of the Green and Colorado Rivers in the areas known as The Maze and The Fins. The rocks are the same Cedar Mesa Sandstone.

At **Km 12.9 (Mile 8)** is the mouth of what this writer calls **Trail Fork** (In 1990 there was a trail up this drainage, but it's gone now; nobody goes there anymore partly because of NPS regulations). It's blocked off to vehicles with poles and there's no place to park, so proceed another 300m or so and park in a grove of **cottonwood trees**. But, while you're there at the mouth of Trail Fork, look northeast with binoculars and you'll see a **moki house** under a ledge part-way up the face. Just below it is a **log ladder** up against the wall.

One of the best hikes in this canyon will be up Trail Fork. About 1 km inside this canyon, be aware of a rounded drainage to your left or east. Inside it and facing southeast will be a large alcove with several **Anasazi ruins or moki houses**. This was once a campsite for the canyon's first aboriginals, then came the Anasazi who built at least **3 structures**. One is a **kiva**, the others aren't much to look at. In this alcove is some **rock art** on boulders, plus many **metate grooves** on top of large rocks. The presences of metates indicates they farmed the area and were grinding corn, and maybe some other seeds. If you continue east from the ruins, you'll be in a rounded bowl-shaped drainage; if you proceed to the southeast corner of this enclosure, you'll find a pictograph panel with **11 Faces** on it. See foto on page

Map 31, Middle Salt Creek and Horse Canyons

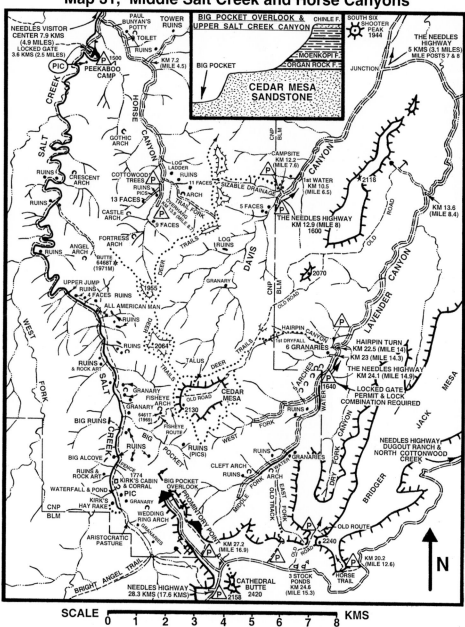

SCALE

0 1 2 3 4 5 6 7 8 KMS

311.

Continuing up Trail Fork now. Right at the end will be a steep drainage filled with rocks and boulders. There used to be a trail here but not today, so just scramble up to near the rim, then veer left or northwest and bench-walk 200m to a place where you can climb out of this Cedar Mesa Sandstone canyon and onto the benchland between the Cedar Mesa SS below, and the red clays of the Moenkopi/Organ Rock Formation immediately above. For good views down into all branches of Horse Canyon, walk cross-country near the rim in a southwest direction sometimes on deer trails; in fact, the old timers this writer spoke to in 1990, called this benchland above the canyons, **Deer Trails**. If you're backpacking long distance, you can later locate the **Fisheye Route** down into the **Big Pocket** of **Upper Salt Creek** making a long loop-hike. Read more in the next section which uses this same map. You'll need the 7 1/2' quads for this type of hike. Or just wander a couple of hours on the benchland or Deer Trails and return to

Above The kiva, and other features, located in the lower end of **Trail Fork**. On the map it's just labeled **Ruins**. This seems to be only one of 2 kivas in Horse Canyon; plus it's part of the largest habitation site as well. The other kiva is likely at **Tower Ruins**.

Right This is the little **moki house** or perhaps granary located 150m north of the toilet & parking place near **Paul Bunyan's Potty**. It's one of the better preserved structures around.

Horse Canyon and your vehicle.

About 300m south or upcanyon from the mouth of Trail Fork **(Km 13.1/Mile 8.1)**, is a side-drainage coming down from the southwest. This is in the southern part of that big grove of **cottonwoods** mentioned above. This is the 1st drainage north of, or below, Castle Arch. In the past, you could drive up this canyon a little but in 2012 it was blocked off to vehicles. Just park in the grove of **cottonwoods** and walk southwest up this side-canyon along a trail about 1 km. There on the right and up on a bench in the gamble oak will be the **13 Faces** pictograph panel (but there are only 10 there now; apparently 3 fell off in the dry wash according one park ranger?). This is one of the better rock art panels in The Needles, and in CNP. Also, from near the beginning of the hike to the 13 Faces, look left a little and at the north end of a ridge, point or buttress. There you'll see a pair of **granaries** (one might be a moki house?) and a **white painted panel** high in a horizontal seam. Be sure to have binoculars to view this well-preserved site because it's difficult to get to (walk around the corner to the east side).

Continue up the main canyon. At **Km 13.9 (Mile 8.7)**, you'll drive under an **overhang**, and have to make a sharp left turn while navigating through deep sand and around a big rock. The author parked there in the shade and walked. Beyond that ledge, the wash bottom gets rough & rocky quickly.

If you continue driving, and at about **Km 14.8 (Mile 9.2)**, is a small **hidden sign** on the right pointing out the way to **Castle Arch**. Hike west up that drainage a ways for a good look.

Continue upcanyon. From where Castle Arch Canyon enters the main drainage, continue southeast about 100m to the mouth of another sizable canyon coming in from the southeast. As the main dry creek bed veers right or south, you continue into this side-canyon another about 125m and behind a big flat boulder and under a sizable overhang is another panel called **9 Faces**, all painted white; as is most rock art in The Needles. Further south up the main drainage, and at about **Km 15.3 (Mile 9.5)** is another tiny hidden sign on the right and the beginning of the trail to **Fortress Arch**. After that, the stream channel has big rocks, marking the end of vehicle navigation.

Back in 1991, the author pushed a mtn. bike for about half the distance to Paul Bunyan's Potty, then locked it up and walked the rest of the way. He went up Trail Fork and out on top for a good look down in from the upper end of Horse Canyon, then returned to the carpark, all in 9 1/2 hours. A long and tiresome day! So forget taking a mtn. bike into this place! In 11/2004, he drove a Chevy Tracker up all the way to the end. He spent an entire day exploring the canyon. Then in 7/2012, he drove his Jeep Patriot up to the end and saw the arches. That trip lasted about 7 hours from the locked gate.

On 10/19/2012, he hiked from the **Sizable Drainage in Davis Canyon** up to then down Trail Fork. He visited the **11 & 9 Faces Panels** plus viewed the granaries mentioned, and returned in 6 3/4 hours. Going into the upper end of Horse Canyon from Davis is about 1/3 less distance to walk. Read the next section along with **Map 32** for more information on how to come in from Davis Canyon.

Here's something to speculate about regarding these Faces pictographs panels: On **Big Bottom** (see **Map 27**) there's one site with a **3 Faces**, and it has the same look as those sites in upper Salt Creek **(4 Faces)**, in Davis Canyon **(5 Faces)** and in Horse Canyon **(9, 11 & 13 Faces)**. After seeing all of these paintings, one has to think there's a chance all were painted by the same person; maybe another Michaelangelo (?). Only if we could date them accurately would we know for sure.

Salt Creek Canyon

Now back to the junction of Horse Canyon & Salt Creek. This time, veer right or southwest and you'll

This is the rock art panel simply called **11 Faces**. It's found in a little rounded drainage in the lower end of what this writer calls **Trail Fork**. It's located due east of the **Ruins** and in the southeastern corner of the rounded drainage, and faces north. Eight images are well-preserved; 3 are fading.

Left Fortress Arch, and **Right, Castle Arch.** Both are located in upper Horse Canyon; both are made from the Cedar Mesa Sandstone, and both are just beyond the end of the better track.

enter the middle part of **Salt Creek**. From this junction up to the present end of the road will be running water almost all the way--unless they're having a terrible drought at the time--like it was in the spring and early summer of 2012. Back in 1991 when the 1st Edition of this book came out, they allowed any-one & everyone to drive up Salt Creek a long ways; the road then ended at the Bates Wilson Campsite located just above where the road used to run up to Angel Arch. But the canyon was being torn up pretty bad, so they closed all that down and now you can only drive as far as **Peekaboo Campsite & Trailhead**.

One of the better things to see at or near Peekaboo, is only about 100m west of the campsite and very near the beginning of the **Peekaboo Trail** which runs northwest to the Squaw Flat Campground. These are white painted **pictographs** located just above the trail and just west of a **hole in the wall**. Some of these, the more faded red ones, the ones behind the white images, were put there up to 7600 years ago by what we now call the Archaic peoples. The white ones were done by the Fremonts; they occupied this canyon beginning about 2000 years ago--according to some researchers.

If you stand right in that hole in the wall and look south, you'll see high on the opposite wall, some white markings. Using a pair of binoculars, you can see more painted pictographs. Several of these are reverse hand prints--something that was very popular in The Needle. A good telefoto lens will get you there too; or climb up from the left or east side--a good climb. Also, on either side of the hole in the wall, and on the south side, will be a couple of other images, but they aren't worth your trouble.

From the Peekaboo Campsite & Trailhead where you'll have to park your wheels (mtn. bikes not rec-ommended), you can walk upcanyon on the old road, now hiker's trail, which runs up to Kirk's Cabin and beyond. Originally, this was a cow trail, but the cattle are now long gone.

Salt Creek gets better the further upcanyon you walk. Any of the side-canyons, which are seldom visited, may prove to be interesting. Further along, and in the area west of **Crescent Arch**, are 2 ruins on the west side. Higher up will be the **Angel Arch Campsite**, for backpackers only now, and up that side-canyon is **Angel Arch**. Both Bates Wilson, and the campsite named after him, are no longer with us; he was the first superintendent of Canyonlands National Park.

Near the former Bates Wilson Campsite, and just up the canyon running to Angel Arch, will be several more Anasazi structures. Remember, these will mostly be facing south and tucked in under a ledge or seam in the Cedar Mesa Sandstone (see geology cross section). There are several granaries and one large site with several dwellings. There are surely more sites than are shown in this map, including the West Fork (this writer has yet to check this out, so if you're backpacking check this drainage out. It's in the national park for a reason; read more below). There's one site just up Salt Creek from the mouth of the West Fork. Always carry a pair of binoculars into places like this.

In 1990, the author rode his mtn. bike from where the locked gate & carpark are now, to the end of the road at Bates Wilson Campsite, then hiked up another 3 kms or so before returning to his car. Round-trip took 6 1/2 hours. That included one stop for a broken bike chain. Therefore, in one long day, a strong hiker might be able to get as far as the Upper Jump and back to his/her vehicle at Peek-aboo; or the locked gate--but it would be a very long day. If you want to get any further than the old campsites, it would be best to backpack in. There's normally some water in places, depending on the season, but which most people would rather treat before drinking. Check at the visitor center about available water; and if the canyon is even open! In 2012, it was closed the entire summer except for one 2-week window. The upper end of Salt Creek will be discussed in the next section.

The Archaic, Fremont and Anasazi Indians

In 1966, Floyd W. Sharrock and C. Melvin Aikens of the University of Utah in Salt Lake City, did an archaeological survey of The Needles District of Canyonlands NP. Their report was published in the *University of Utah Anthropological Paper #83*. That report covers the entire national park, but most of the better sites visited were along Upper Salt Creek Canyon. The following is a summery of the important aspects of that report. Keep in mind, there's been a lot of research since then, so some conflicting information may have been refined since *Paper #83* was published

*Data previously accumulated from areas adjacent to Canyonlands N.P.--Beef Basin, Ruin Park, Indian Creek, Alkali Ridge, White Canyon, Upper Glen Canyon, the Fremont River drainage system and the desert north of Moab--indicated that the areas surrounding Canyonlands National Park were occupied during the Pueblo stage by **Fremont and Mesa Verde Anasazi** peoples. However, cultural distribution within the Park boundaries did not conform at all to what we had expected. No sites which are distinctively affiliated with the Fremont culture were recorded; no Fremont pottery or other portable artifacts; and no Fremont architectural styles or techniques were noted. But, petroglyph and pictographs--horned dancers, shield figures, and ghost figures--which have been considered part of the Fremont culture, occurred throughout the park at sites which otherwise show complete Mesa Verde affiliation.*

The cultural affiliation of the majority of sites, including chipping sites, camp sites, isolated granaries at which no pottery occurred, and isolated pictograph/petroglyph sites could not be reliably determined. However, all the large habitation sites (all in the Salt Creek drainage) with structures, pottery and numerous other portable artifacts were identifiable as Mesa Verde--other than the pictographs and petroglyphs. Hence, the anomalous situation of apparent Fremont--Mesa Verde associations is found at the major sites within the park.

The Fremont people were considered as poor relatives of the Anasazi, indigenous Great Basin Shoshoneans who incorporated, borrowed and modified Anasazi traits to create a marginal, peripheral Southwestern culture. Aikens suggests a linguistic barrier to account for lack of overlap. The Colorado River was also a barrier.

Pottery types indicate that all major sites date to the late Pueblo II--early Pueblo III periods, roughly 1075-1150 A.D. It is doubtful that significant occupation began much before 1050 A.D., but complete abandonment of the area may not have occurred until approximately 1200-1250 A.D.

Extensive alcove habitation sites are concentrated in the Salt Creek drainage system, and are particularly numerous in the Big Pocket of Salt Creek, the lower reaches of the West Fork of Salt Creek and Horse Creek drainage. Found in some ruins were corn cobs and stems from the common pumpkin or squash. These appear to be the only plants to have been cultivated by the Anasazi or Fremont Indians in this part of the Colorado Plateau.

These **metate grooves** are found in the big ruins in the lower part of **Trail Fork.** The kiva shown in the foto on **page 310** is just beyond the bush in the upper right-hand corner of this picture. In this same complex, are other metate grooves and petroglyphs found on top of boulders.

Above The **13 Faces Panel** found in a side-drainage of upper **Horse Canyon**. But there are only 10 faces here. One park ranger said the other 3 caved off in the dry wash; but there doesn't seem to be any evidence of that (?).

Right A close-up telefoto lenses look at **Tower Ruins**. The builders could only have gotten up there with ladders; and to have taken good sized logs there would have required a few strong men! If you look at these structures with binoculars, you'll see quite a few logs, indicating one building, the one on top, is likely a kiva.

Look closely and you'll see 9 white figures. This is the **9 Faces Panel** in the upper end of **Horse Canyon**. These are a little different than the other Faces Panels, but still could have been made by the same person or clan.

One of 2 well-built and well-preserved granaries located in upper **Horse Canyon**, and in between the main drainage and the dry wash coming down from **13 Faces**. Get to these from the left or east side of the north end of the point or buttress between the 2 drainages. Getting up over one ledge will require building a pile of rocks; or 2-3 people helping each other. Just to the left of this structure is the other smaller granary and to the left of that is a nice **pictograph** panel composed of white figures.

Davis, Lavender & Upper Salt Creek Canyons, Bridger Jack Mesa, Cathedral Butte, and the Lee Kirk Cabin & Hay Rake

Location & Access This map is a duplicate of the previous one, but the text and information concentrates on the upper ends of **Davis, Lavender and Salt Creek Canyons.** For access to Davis and Lavender, you'll have to use one of the maps below which shows the lower or northern ends of these 2 long drainages. The plastic **Latitude 40° map Moab West** is the best.

To get into this area, part of which is in The Needles District of CNP, drive along Highway 191 between Moab & Monticello. At **Church Rock** and between **mile posts 86 & 87**, turn west onto **The Needles Highway, State Road 211.** This paved road runs to, then down along Indian Creek to the Dugout Ranch, and beyond to The Needles.

To reach **Upper Salt Creek Canyon,** just northwest of the Dugout Ranch, and between camouflaged **mile posts 1 & 2** is the turnoff to (North) **Cottonwood Canyon**; that road takes you to **Cathedral Butte** and beyond, and to several routes into the upper ends of Lavender and Salt Creek Canyons. The main road shown at the bottom right-hand side of this map is called various names, but usually the **Cottonwood Canyon, Beef Basin or Elk Mountain Road.** This road starts on The Needles Highway, runs up Cottonwood, then southwest to Beef Basin and Ruin, Middle and House Parks. This road up to where it's shown on this map, is well-maintained and normally good for any car, but it does rise to moderate elevations. This means it's closed by snow and/or mud from sometime in November until sometime in March or April--but each year is different. You'll have to check with the BLM office (Tele. 435-587-1500) or San Juan County roads (Tele. 435-587-3230) in Monticello, or The Needles Visitor Center (Tele. 435--259-4711) about its condition. From The Needles Highway to Cathedral Butte and the **Upper Salt Creek Canyon Trailhead** is **28.3 kms (17.6 miles)**.

To get into **Davis and Lavender Canyons** from the lower northern end, drive northwest from the Dugout Ranch on The Needles Highway. Just west of where you cross **Indian Creek, between mile posts 7 & 8**, and **42.7 kms (26.5 miles)** from Highway 191, will be a sign on the left or south side of the road pointing out the public access road into Davis & Lavender. Immediately, you'll go through a gate--close it behind you--and **set your odometer at 0**. In the first km, you'll now find a rough spot or two, cross a dry wash and head south along the west side of an **old log corral** with one **gate** to open & close. For the next km, it's big dirt holes and dust in dry weather--or muddy after rains--terrible road! Later you'll be in a wide open valley and traveling along the lower end of Davis Canyons meandering dry creek bed. At **Km 5 (Mile 3.1)** is a **junction**; if you turn left or east, you'll end up in Lavender, but for now continue straight ahead into **Davis Canyon.** Heading south you'll be driving exclusively in the dry wash of Davis. In extra **dry conditions**, you'll be in **deep sandy gravel** all the way. You **must have 4WD** here with a little **more clearance** than an ordinary car. Also, be sure to keep up **a little speed and RPM's** and don't stop in deep soft stuff! Or, if there's been a flood or rain storm in the previous month or so, this may be a pleasant drive in a 2WD car (In 1990, the author drove his VW Rabbit up to Eightmile Spring in better-than-average conditions).

At about **Km 9.3 (Mile 5.8)** will be the first cottonwood trees. At **Km 10.5 (Mile 6.5)** you'll be entering a 2 km-long section called **Eightmile Spring** and will likely see some running water and lots of big cottonwood trees. You'll also be just starting to enter a canyon, but with low walls. At about **Km 12.2 (Mile 7.6)** is a side-road to the right or north and into a **sizable drainage** with a good **campsite** 150m away. This area will be the beginning of a hike to the **Deer Trails** above the canyon bottoms and into **Trail Fork** of Horse Canyon. At about **Km 12.9 (Mile 8)** is the end of the road and **park boundary & fence.**

Davis Canyon is named for one of the cowboys who came into southeastern Utah in about 1885 and settled on Indian Creek. Lavender Canyon is presumably named after David Lavender, the author of the book, *One Man's West,* first published in 1943. He grew up in western Colorado and later had dealings with Al Scorup at the Indian Creek Dugout Ranch. Read more history of the Dugout Ranch in the next chapter and Map 33.

To get into **Lavender Canyon**, go back to the **junction at Km 5 (Mile 3.1)**, and head east around the north end of a long ridge. Soon you'll be in the creek bed of **lower Lavender**, the first part of which may have running water and rough sections so be sure to take a shovel. Further along, it's a dry wash just like in Davis Canyon and you'll need a 4WD and keep up some speed in the deeper softer sandier parts; especially when conditions are dry.

Finally you'll enter an area with the canyon walls starting to rise. Soon after you notice this, you'll come to a prominent **hairpin turn** and an unnamed drainage entering from the west. This is at **Km 22.5 (Mile 14)**; and for lack of a better name let's call this **Hairpin Canyon.** This will be the beginning of an important hike. At **Km 23 (Mile 14.3)** is another drainage coming in from the right or west; this is where the **6 Granaries** are located. Continue upcanyon with running water in places. Both the **locked gate** and **park boundary** are at **Km 24.1 (Mile 14.9** from The Needles Highway). If you've paid $10 at the Needles Visitor Center for a permit & combination to the lock, you can proceed with your vehicle into the park. Otherwise, just walk in for free, and without a permit.

Elevations Park boundary at Davis & Lavender, 1600 & 1640m; trailhead to upper Salt Creek, 2158m; top of Bridger Jack Mesa, 2240m; and Cathedral Butte, 2420m.

Water Regardless of where you're going, take all the water you'll need in your vehicle. There's also a year-round spring and running water beginning just south (upcanyon) of Kirk's Cabin in Aristocratic Pasture. It seeps out of a meadow area. The author once drank it as it was; but better purify it first. Take it from the waterfall north of the meadow. There's plenty of good running water in upper Lavender, but none in upper Davis (maybe in a few scattered wet weather seeps after floods). There will likely be some water, perhaps just in pools, in the Eightmile Spring area of Davis, but don't bet your life on it!

Maps USGS or BLM map La Sal (1:100,000); South Six Shooter Peak, Hart Point South, Cathedral Butte & Shay Mountain (1:24,000--7 1/2' quads); the plastic Trails Illustrated/National Geographic map Canyonlands National Park (1:70,000); or the plastic Latitude 40° map Moab West (1:75,000).

Main Attractions Many Anasazi ruins in all canyons; but more in Salt Creek, fewer in Davis. Pictographs, petroglyphs, and the historic Kirk Cabin and hay rake. Also, some of the best scenery around in the upper ends of each canyon.

Davis and Lavender Canyons

In **Davis Canyon**, most people camp in the **Eightmile Spring** area where there are several sites with cottonwood trees for shade. It's also on BLM land where you don't need reservations or permit for anything! But leave a clean campsite, otherwise the control freaks will soon follow.

Map 32, Davis, Lavender & Upper Salt Creek Canyons, Bridger Jack Mesa, Cathedral Butte & the Lee Kirk Cabin & Hay Rake

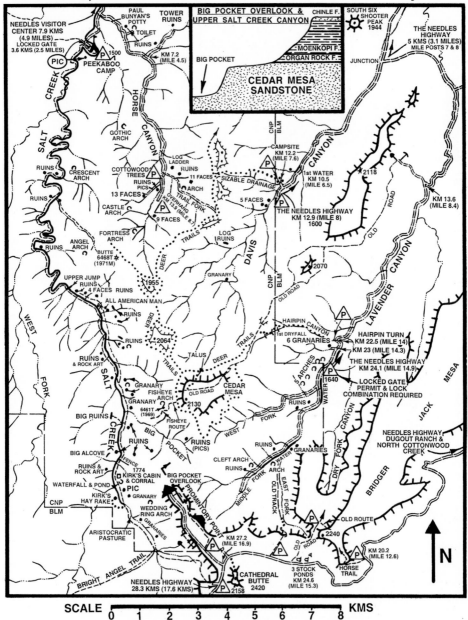

SCALE
0 1 2 3 4 5 6 7 8 KMS

The park boundary is marked with a fence & information board, and no vehicles are allowed to enter. For Davis, it's walking all the way and no permit of any kind is needed for **day-trips**. On the other hand, you're supposed to have a permit if backpacking. If backpacking, carry all your water just to be sure.

The first thing to see in Davis would be a dwelling, maybe a granary, on your right or west in a small alcove only about 200m inside the park boundary. Just beyond that and around a corner going west, and again on your right, will be another minor drainage with a couple of small ruins, then the **5 Faces panel**. Just follow all the foot prints and trails; everybody goes there to see this panel and little else. This place is on the Moab outfitter's trail.

Further up, and in a side-canyon coming in from the west, there's one group of dwellings high on a

Looking northeast into the upper end of **Horse Canyon**. Just behind the camera is the **butte** labeled **6468T (1971m)** on Map 32. All the rocks you see (up close) are made of the Cedar Mesa Sandstone.

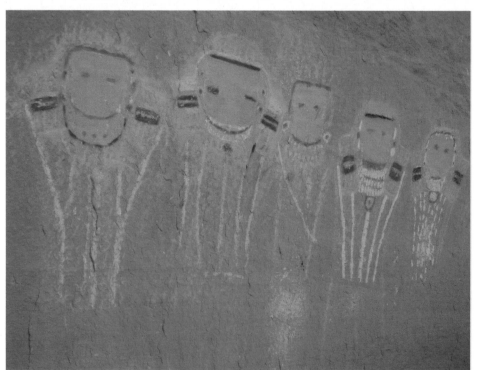

The **5 Faces Panel** located just inside the boundaries of CNP in **Davis Canyon**. Notice the similarities between this and the other **Faces panels** located in The Needles, and on Big Bottom.

ledge that's very difficult to get to without a tall ladder. Maybe the world's best rock climbers could get there using hand & arm chokes in a crack--but probably not you and I! However, from high on the opposite wall, and using binoculars (or a telefoto lens), you can see a pile of logs; it appears that their planned structure had not been completed (?). Because of these logs, this writer is calling it the **Log Ruins**. Right near ground level are several other structures or moki houses in a seam in the wall.

In 10/2012, the author walked well into all the major drainages of Davis and found only one other granary in a tiny alcove. The reason for so few habitation sites is due to lack of alcoves fit to make a home, and very little water. Within a month or so after a flood, you'll find pools and maybe minor seeps, but no real springs. Expect these to dry up after long dry spells.

There's no way out of the upper end of the Davis Canyon, but if you route-find west from the area of Eightmile Spring and the **campsite** shown on the map, you can find a way up to the bench above (there are several minor ruins just west of Eightmile Spring, and a couple of **moki houses** just above the **campsite**). Once out of Davis, walk west along the bench immediately north of the **sizable drainage** mentioned earlier and shown on the map. This will be along the contact point between the Cedar Mesa Sandstone below, and the red Moenkopi/Organ Rock clay beds above. It's easy walking on that bench or apron which rises to the west. At the head of that drainage, cross over a divide going west and turn left or south. Soon you'll be at the head of **Trail Fork** of Horse Canyon. Back in 1990, the old timers who knew this region told this writer, they called the area of narrow flat-topped ridges above the canyons, **Deer Trails**--apparently because of all the deer (and trails) there in winter. At one time there used to be a few hikers who came up out of Trail Fork, but in recent years, and with all the fees the CNP now has (not to mention the regulations!), almost no one uses this trail or the Deer Trails ridges anymore. There was no trail in Trail Fork in 10/2012.

Using this suggested route, on 10/1/2012, it took the author less than 1 1/2 hours to reach the head of Trail Fork, so you could visit all the cool places in upper Horse Canyon on a day-hike, bypassing the CNP fees & regs. On that day, the author continued westward around the head of Horse Canyon to the little **butte** marked **6468T (1971m)** (6436T on the Latitude 40° map) and back in 5 hours. The best views of these Cedar Mesa Sandstone canyons making up this part of The Needles is best seen from this high ground called **Deer Trails**. There are at least 2 ways in & out of Lavender and a route out of Big Pocket in Upper Salt Creek as well. These will be discussed below. This writer made a 2nd trip on 10/19/2012 into upper Horse Canyon; read about that adventure in the previous chapter and the previous map of Horse Canyon.

Lavender Canyon is about as close to being a twin to Davis as any 2 canyons can be; but there are more Anasazi ruins, arches and water in Lavender. There is a fence & locked gate at the park boundary, so if you want to drive into Lavender, get a permit, the combination to the lock and pay $10 at the Needles Visitor Center. Otherwise, if you **just walk in, no permit is needed.**

First, the **6 Granaries ruins** which are outside the park boundaries. There is now a 300m-long track up to that alcove from the main road, and some people have been there camping and using ropes to get into the alcove (notice the rope burns). The author climbed into it in 2004, but chickened-out in 6/2012! It's not an easy climb, even with the small moki steps over steep slickrock. The ruins--granaries or moki houses--in that alcove are very well-preserved.

On the map this is labeled **Log Ruins** and it's in the upper middle part of **Davis Canyon**. Notice the logs & moki houses to the upper left, a single log (maybe an original?) just right of center, and another dwelling to the far right just above the shadows. That's where you'd climb up--if you're good!

Looking northwest down into the upper end of **Horse Canyon** from what old timers told this writer were called **Deer Trails**. That's the high ridge-tops between the upper ends of Horse, Davis, Lavender and Salt Creek Canyons. Deer apparently sometimes roam these ridge-tops in winter. This drainage is what this writer calls **Trail Fork** which makes an easy way into Horse Canyon.

Beginning at the park boundary, you'll find **5 arches** on the west side in the 1st km, then **Cleft Arch** up near the head of the canyon. **Cleft Arch Ruins** are in the first tiny drainage just upcanyon or south from Cleft, but there are at least half a dozen ruins in this canyon as shown on the map. There's always drinkable water inside the park, and for a ways below. There are many bear tracks as well.

In areas where there's water or wet sand, a mtn. bike may do some good, otherwise you'll still have to push a bike in most parts of this upper canyon, so taking a bike isn't recommended. Another thing about Lavender is, you can get in or out of the **East Fork** from the high country to the south. This is good news for people with cars, because they can get into this drainage from the Cottonwood Canyon or Beef Basin Road without a 4WD vehicle. That route in from above is discussed below.

In both Davis and Lavender Canyons the geology is the same. All the high walls made of pink, white and sometimes purplish smooth massive sandstone is part of the Cedar Mesa Sandstone Formation. This is the same formation that makes up Salt Creek and Horse Canyon, The Needles and all the scenic canyons in The Maze on the west side of the Colorado River. On top of that are the red clays with some sandstone beds making the Moenkopi Formation (in some areas the Organ Rock Formation appears). Immediately above that, and on **Cedar Mesa** and a few other high points, is the **Moss Back Member** of the **Chinle Formation**; that's where the uranium is mined in this part of the country.

Here's another hike that begins outside the park boundaries and takes you up to the flat-topped ridges separating the canyons discussed here. It begins at the **hairpin turn** and goes up what this writer is calling **Hairpin Canyon**. You can drive up this entrenched drainage about 300-350m and camp. From there walk west upcanyon. About 2/3's the way through Hairpin, will be a dryfall few can climb, so veer to the right or north about 75m and climb upon some large boulders next to the canyon wall. There you'll find where previous hikers have piled up rocks to help get up a **3m-high pitch**. There are plenty of hand & foot holds, but take a short rope to help less-experienced hikers up the last step. Or just help each other with a push or pull; it's easy.

Just above this **1st dryfall** is a **2nd**, but you boulder-hop through it. Shortly after that is a **3rd dryfall**, but when you get there, turn right or north and scramble up the slope and out; again easy. Once in the upper part of this drainage, be looking for a route up through a couple of cliff bands to your right or northwest; there are several ways. After that, and after you arrive on the obvious ridgetop running northeast to southwest, you'll find an old **mining track or road**. This relic from the 1950's, begins about **13.6 kms (8.4 miles)** from The Needles Highway on the road to Lavender Canyon. It runs upon the lowest part of the Chinle Formation, which is the Moss Back Member, then follows this upsloping course sandstone band to the southwest and ends on top of Cedar Mesa. It hasn't been used in a long time, but you can walk along it in these parts.

If you follow this track to **Cedar Mesa**, you'll have some nice views down on parts of Lavender, Davis and Upper Salt Creek Canyons. Just south of the end of that old road is a small NPS solar powered communication tower. From there, if you want to get down onto the flat land around the rim of any of the canyons, either walk back to the northeast a couple of kms, or walk to the north side of the mesa to find at least one easy route down a **talus** slope to the head of the main fork of Davis Canyon. Once on

Above The alcove holding the **6 Granaries** in **Lavender Canyon** just outside the CNP boundaries. These are some of the best built & preserved **Anasazi Ruins** found anywhere. The author climbed into this alcove in 2004, but didn't quite make it in 2012! Those moki steps seem to be getting smaller by the year!

Left This is the **1st Dryfall** in what this writer calls **Hairpin Canyon.** The actual dryfall is to the left about 75m, but this is the easiest way to the high country above. This is quite an easy climb, but the hand-hold for the last step is a little small and the rocks downsloping. Just help each other up & down. If you're alone, have a short rope to loop over part of a big rock when coming down.

that little rim, you can visit the heads of any of these drainages as shown on the map.

Here's one way you can get into the **Big Pocket** of Salt Creek from above. From the west side of Cedar Mesa, and at the narrow ridge separating Big Pocket and another small basin just to the north, walk west toward **Fisheye Arch**. You can't see this arch from the east or south, but it's on the *South Six-Shooter 7 1/2' quad*--which you must have to do this trek! You'll start by going west, then curl left of an unclimbable buttress, then veer south, drop down a little via slickrock, continue south, then west across the south face of a buttress. From there, head south down fairly steep slickrock and route-find in a westerly direction down to the bottom of Big Pocket. Let's call this the **Fisheye Route**. While the author came back up this route, he left about a dozen cairns which will help. It's an easy way, but you must have a map in hand and use your eyes and brains to sort things out. In 10/2012, this writer walked up Hairpin Canyon, and did the route just described, but came back via the south side of Cedar Mesa. That took 9 1/3 hours--which included lots of exploring and picture taking.

There are lots of options for hiking along the flat-topped ridges above these canyons. One groups trek from 5/2008, was featured in **Backpacker Magazine**. They started at the Upper Salt Creek Trailhead, went down Salt Creek, into Big Pocket, up the Fisheye Route, around the north side of Cedar Mesa, along the old mining track to Hairpin Canyon, down it and up the East Fork of Lavender and up to the same Moss Back Bench surrounding Cathedral Butte and back to the same trailhead. They took 4 days. Most of the ridgetops shown on this map can be explored on day trips from Davis & Lavender, or Trail Fork & Salt Creek. Read more under upper Lavender and Salt Creek Canyons below.

Climbing Bridger Jack Mesa and Cathedral Butte

To get to the upper parts of Salt Creek and Lavender Canyons, and to Bridger Jack Mesa and Cathedral Butte, turn southwest from The Needles Highway and onto the (North) Cottonwood Canyon Road as mentioned earlier in the introduction. Follow your USGS or **Moab West Latitude 40°** map carefully, and when you arrive at the southern-most part of **Bridger Jack Mesa**, stop and park at the beginning of the trail as shown on the map in this book. Look on the right or west side of the road for a parking place marked by a large cairn in front of a log. This is beside a minor drainage and is **20.2 kms (12.6 miles)** from The Needles Highway.

The trail shown is an old **horse trail**. It's a little difficult to locate in its beginning so just head west and look for cairns running up a little small ridge to the left of a minor drainage. In 7/2012, it was soon easy to find as hikers or maybe the BLM have erected lots of cairns along the way. In that area is some kind of fault which has allowed a corner of the mesa to slip which created a ramp or dugway. The constructed part of this horse trail zig zags up this dugway to the west and to the top of the shattered Wingate Sandstone, then it contours at the same level back to the east, then turns the corner and heads northwest. This bench is formed by the Kayenta Formation. At the end of the constructed part, is a large cairn. At that point which is level ground, it disappears, but there are deer trails everywhere.

There's another **old route** which seems to be a series of deer or perhaps horse trails, running off a north-facing ramp of Bridger Jack Mesa. It's about due north from the south-side constructed trail. This one's on the north, is very steep and may have been enhanced by cowboys at one time (?). To get there, as you drive from the western end of Bridger Jack Mesa in the direction of Cathedral Butte, you'll drive past **3 small stock ponds** on your right or north. Within 100m or so after the 3rd pond, turn right or north onto a side-road at **Km 24.6 (Mile 15.3)**. Any vehicle can be driven along this old track about 1 1/2 kms then it deteriorates, and you'll need a HCV. But soon after that, look to the right or south to

A good look at **Cathedral Butte** as seen from the northeastern side of that **promontory point** running northwest from the base of this butte. The normal route up is on the left or north side.

Above From the south looking north at **Cleft Arch**. Just behind the camera a short distance is a short drainage coming down from the west. Inside it are some pretty good ruins of dwellings or moki houses as seen in the foto on the left.

Left This is part of ruins located just upcanyon from **Cleft Arch**, and in a little side-drainage of **Lavender**.

see the pine covered slope or ramp. At that point leave the road and route-find up the only possible route to the top.

This mesa got it's name from a Ute Indian by the name of **Bridger Jack**. A little of his story is told in the book, ***Grand Memories:***

As F.G. Murphy and his son William [the man most responsible for builting the Murphy Trail] were returning to Moab, darkness overtook them and they camped at Cane Springs [just north of today's Hole in the Rock between Moab & Monticello]. Mr. Murphy noticed the faint glimmer of a fire to the north on a big mesa. He told Will to wait quietly while he investigated. Upon his return he informed Will there was going to be an Indian fight. His assessment proved to be correct. It involved Wash and Posey, who fought against Bridger Jack. Bridger Jack was a medicine man and had attempted to cure Posey's sick boy, but he failed and the boy died. On that fateful night Bridger Jack was shot and killed. Since then the mesa just north of the Hole in the Rock has been known as Bridger Jack Mesa [The mesa discussed here is southwest of that, but is also named after the same medicine man].

It's hard to get any kind of personal history on the Dugout Ranch and the Indian Creek country (which includes Bridger Jack Mesa) today, because all the old timers of the area have died (this is from 1990). However, **Doyle Perkins** of Monticello did work at the Dugout Ranch from 1956 to about 1962. He had this to say about grazing upon Bridger Jack Mesa: *I remember when they put 50 head of horses up there. It was mostly a horse pasture in winter. We put some cattle up there one year, but it didn't do no good. They just put 'em up when there was snow because there wasn't any water.*

As you turn the corner of Bridger Jack, you'll see to the west and rising high in the sky, the unmistakable landmark known as **Cathedral Butte**. This is the highest point in the immediate area, rising to 2420m and there's an easy route to the top for some fine views. To do this, stop at a point due north of the butte where a short road runs north to a good campsite in the cedars and to a stock pond, then start walking south. First, walk up a ridge in the middle of the north face, then once on a bench, veer left and walk along the same level to the east side of the summit block. Route-find to the very summit.

From the top you'll have a good overall view of the entire area, but the best views down into Upper Lavender Canyon and the Big Pocket of Salt Creek is from the end of a finger of land or a **promontory point** running northwest from the base of Cathedral Butte. There's a very rough 4WD track running out to the end of this point which is called **Big Pocket Overlook**. That track begins **27.2 kms (16.9 miles)** from The Needles Highway. On the northeast side of this finger of land is a good place to look down into Upper Lavender. You could walk out to the end of that point, but this would also be a good place to use your mtn. bike. There's an ATV trail on both sides of this promontory point.

Upper Lavender Canyon

Here's how to get into the upper end of **Lavender Canyon** from the south and the plateau above. As you drive from the western end of Bridger Jack Mesa in the direction of Cathedral Butte, you'll pass **3 stock ponds** on your right or north. Just after that, you'll pass the road that runs around to the west side of Bridger Jack; and not far after that you'll come to a large open sagebrush flat. Near the western side of that flat and just before you reenter the piñon-junipers on the western side, stop where you see a metal post maybe 30m from the road. This will be roughly 400m (.3 mile) past the side-road you just passed. Leave your car on the road then walk north about 1 km to the rim of Lavender's **East Fork**. There you'll find an old **miners road** blasted out of the top part of the rim which is the Moss Back Member of the Chinle; it stops after about 250m. From there on down there seems to be just deer trails until you get to the bottom of the steep slope. Where it begins to level off, look for a very faint **vehicle track** heading north on the west side in the main drainage. After a couple of kms the track disappears, but just continue down the drainage to the 4WD track coming up the canyon from the gate below.

There may be (?) another route down in to the bottom of the upper **Middle Fork** of Lavender which is the next drainage west of the one just described. The author hasn't hiked this, but it appears to be possible (?).

The author once walked down into the East Fork and hiked almost to the park boundary, then to the upper end of the Middle and West Forks of Lavender, and returned the same way. Round-trip was just over 7 hours. So if you don't have a 4WD, but can walk fast, you can see most of Lavender Canyon in the park from this entry to the East Fork in one long day.

Upper Salt Creek

Probably the best hike on this map and one of the best hikes in Canyonlands NP, is down the **Upper Salt Creek Trail** and into the upper third of **Salt Creek**. To get there, drive to the western side of **Cathedral Butte** to where there's a fork in the road and a sign on the right stating **Bright Angel Trail** and **Salt Creek**. This is **28.3 kms (17.6 miles)** from The Needles Highway. Pull off to the right to camp and/or park. Or you could camp & park on the other side of the road to the east. There are several good camping places in the area under big piñon-juniper (cedar) trees. This is a fairly popular trailhead parking place and since it's outside the national park, you can camp for free, without a permit, and where you like--but please leave a clean campsite. For this hike it's strongly recommended you take a pair of **binoculars**, because there are many **Anasazi ruins** and rock art to be seen, most of which are up high in alcoves and difficult or impossible to reach unless you have a ladder.

The top of the constructed Salt Creek Trail heads down over the Moss Back Rim to the north. Further down it veers to the west. At the bottom of the steep drainage there's a fork in the trail right at the park boundary. From there the **Bright Angel Trail** heads west and comes out near the main road heading into the Beef Basin country. But that's another hike, and on a trail that may be hard to find & follow; and which hasn't been used much since 1975 when cows were in the area.

From there head northwest on the Salt Creek Trail. About 2 kms from the park boundary, you'll come to a meadow area once called **Aristocratic Pasture**. About 600-700m into this meadow and on the west side under an overhang, will be an **old hay rake** dating from the years just around 1900. The location is about 1 km almost due west of Wedding Ring Arch. It was taken there and used by **Lee Kirk**.

The best way to reach the hay rake is to stay on the trail (which is on the west side of the drainage at that point) until it veers right and dives into the meadow with cattails & willows; at that point, turn left or west instead, and walk up over some slickrock ledges in **white** sandstone. When you reach a **red band**, contour around to the west, north, then back to the east and to the end of a little point and overhang. From there, downclimb the ledge to find the hay rake; the reason for this slickrock detour is to avoid a jungle of stickery rose bushes and other brush. In 1991 & 2012, this hay rake was covered by wild roses and half of it was under an overhang and pretty well-preserved; but the other half was

The **Lee Kirk hay rake** located in **Aristocratic Pasture** in the upper end of **Salt Creek**. Because of all the stickery bushes around, the author used his mosquito pants and long sleaved shirt to get to it. It's partially under a ledge and half is better preserved than the other less-protected half. If you make it here, and have a couple of strong bodies, please pick up both wheels and move it 2m west. That would help, because the NPS will do nothing to preserve this relic of the Old West.

more exposed to the elements and rusting away. Both times, the author stomped down a lot of brush for a foto. There's a pictograph just above the rake high on the wall. After each trip in 1991 & 2012, the author reported the hay rake's location to the Needles Visitor Center, hoping they'll put it totally under the ledge, or get it out and place it in a museum or somehow preserve it, but so far nothing's happened. Read more on the history of Lee Kirk and this hay rake below.

Now out in the pasture again, and walking north. The trail at this point is sometimes hard to see so look for 3 posts or ribbons on bushes. Also, look closely on the ledges on the east side and you may see a small **granary** up in a seam. Continue north and you'll soon come to willows and tamarisks where the trail runs along the low canyon wall on the east side of the pasture. In that area, look up to see some white **paintings** under an overhang. Finally you'll come to a **waterfall** and **pond** where the water leaves Aristocratic Pasture. It's normally a nice stream at that point. During the years pryor to about 1900, or maybe 1910, there was over-grazing in upper Salt Creek and the area below this waterfall, then erosion began. The creek has since downcut about 6-8m leaving the former banks below the waterfall and Salt Creek high & dry. The bottom is now full of tamarisk and other brush.

A short distance beyond the waterfall is the old **Lee Kirk Cabin**. Next to it is a **wagon & corral**. They're all in deteriorating condition (and the NPS does nothing to preserve them!) which is a rather interesting site. Its history is discussed below. From the cabin look WNW across the entrenched stream to see ruins & colorful rock art with binoculars--unfortunately, there's no easy way to get there; but plenty of bushwhacking! Not far beyond the Kirk Cabin, you'll pass another real old all-wooden **fence**. Take note of its construction; notably the holes in the posts, and wooden cross bars.

Not far beyond the fence, and as you walk through cactus fields which produce edible cactus fruit by October, you'll come to the first good group of Anasazi dwellings or moki houses. It's in an alcove to the right or east, facing southwest. The trail now veers that way, then heads north. Across the way on the west side are more ruins tucked under overhangs; one is in a **big alcove**. Use your binoculars here; or bushwhack across the gulch! A couple of kms past these dwellings will be **Big Pocket** to the right or southeast. This is an interesting place. There are several major habitation sites in the lower and middle parts of this big meadow or park, but which are impossible to reach for ordinary hikers. You'll have to have a ladder to get into a couple of these. One faces southeast and is on the southwest side of Big Pocket. The other is in the middle east side and faces south.

If you want to exit Big Pocket and get upon the bench above the four major canyons on this sketch map, then walk to the northeast part of Big Pocket while using the *South Six-Shooter & Cathedral Butte 7 1/2' quads*. You may not get there using just this sketch map. On the quads, look for **Fisheye Arch**, which is not visible from the southwest, south or east; apparently you can see it only from the north (?). Anyway, this **Fisheye Route** starts about 1 km SSW of the arch on some ground-level slickrock. You'll first head east about 300m; part way along this section you should begin to see cairns this writer and others have left. After the 300m or so, route-find zig zag fashion north through some steep pitches of slickrock aiming for the highest dome around with the elevation **6461T** (1969m). As you near this dome, turn right or east a short distance, then head north again. Soon after that veer left and climb a little, then turn right or east and walk along the top of a narrow ridge toward **Cedar Mesa**.

Once on top of this flat-topped ridge or bench which is the contact point between the Cedar Mesa Sandstone below and the red Moenkopi (maybe a touch of Organ Rock Shale, but no White Rim Sandstone east of the Colorado River) clay beds above, you can walk northward to find some really great overlooks to canyons, or routes down into Lavender, Davis and Trail Fork of upper Horse Canyon. These have been discussed earlier.

Also discussed earlier is the geologic makeup of Cedar Mesa. The bulk of it is made of red clays mixed with sandstone which is the Moenkopi/Organ Rock (?). Above that is a capstone made of the Moss Back Member of the Chinle Formation. It consists of coarse sandstone and is the primary strata from which uranium in southeastern Utah was derived. That old mining track running from lower Lavender Canyon to the top of Cedar Mesa runs atop the Moss Back almost all the way.

Years ago, the author was told of a second route out of Big Pocket which begins somewhere near the big **ruins** with pictographs (**pics**) on the east side of Big Pocket, but hasn't seen it in 22 years. This writer was last there on 10/3/2012. He came down the trail in upper Salt Creek, walked the perimeter of Big Pocket, saw the lower end of the Fisheye Route and returned in 6 3/4 hours.

Now back to looking for Anasazi ruins. Across Salt Creek and west of the mouth of Big Pocket is what's called the **Big Ruins**. Look for one of several trails going that way. These ruins are up high in a long alcove facing east. There must be 15 or 20 mud and stone structures, but you can't get up there without a long ladder. North of Big Ruins are more dwellings or granaries, mostly on the east side of Salt Creek, but one or two on the west as well. Binoculars are real handy here.

Further north and maybe 2-3 kms south of the **Upper Jump**, and in a crack in a west-facing wall on the east side of Salt Creek, will be a dwelling and a pictograph called the **All American Man**. It gets its name because it's painted in red, white and blue colors. About 1 km north of this and again on the east side, will be more ruins facing south and another pictograph panel on the wall behind known as **4 Faces**. It's a painting with 4 distinct faces. Look for other habitation sites in the area.

The next point of interest will be the **Upper Jump**. This is an exposed sandstone ledge which has created a waterfall, but which you can get around easily. Before the white men brought their cattle into this country and overgrazed it, there was no Upper Jump (or the waterfall & duck pond). It was only after overgrazing and subsequent flooding made deep cuts in the alluvial banks, that this ledge was exposed. The flooding and downcutting must have started sometime around 1900, or a little later (?).

Three or 4 kms below the Upper Jump, the **West Fork** enters on the left or west. There used to be old cow trails in that drainage but they're long gone. The national park was created in 1964 and the grazing permits expired in 1975, so there haven't been cattle there for years either. So far, the author hasn't been in the drainage, but since there are some Anasazi ruins nearby, there must be some there too; if there's water. This is so far from any trailhead, to do any serious exploring, you'll have to backpack in--which means **a $30 permit!** Best to enter the West Fork from the bottom end. The adventurous hiker could stop at the Needles Visitor Center and ask about water and ruins there, but they won't reveal secrets to the public. They will discuss the Big Ruins and the All American Man; only because they're already known to all.

History of Lee Kirk, and the Kirk Cabin & Hay Rake

Rensselaer Lee Kirk was born in Michigan in 1859 and as a young man drove a freight wagon to Durango, Colorado. While in southwest Colorado he became interested in the cattle business. Some time between about 1885 & 1887, he purchased a small herd of cattle and drove them into southeastern Utah and landed on Indian Creek. No one alive today knows where he first settled, but Indian Creek below Newspaper Rock was a popular place because it was in between summer and winter ranges. He may have squatted on Indian Creek, but sometime later, perhaps in the 1890's, he found and settled on upper Salt Creek where his cabin is today. He squatted or made a Desert Claim on 80 acres, or about 32 hectares.

The cabin you see today must have been built in those early years. It's condition is good (except for the roof) considering its age. Kirk used to take his young family out there in summer but returned to Moab in the fall so his children could attend school. In those days, almost everyone having a ranch out in the wilderness, also had a home in town where their family stayed. Lee used to come into Moab for supplies at least twice a year. Old timers today (in 1990 interviews) tell of him driving his wagon (rumors persist that the wagon next to the cabin was brought in from elsewhere after the national park was established?) down Salt Creek, then up along Indian Creek and into Moab for supplies. On each trip he would have to take his wagon apart to get it over the Upper Jump, but this would only have been in later years, after all the erosion had taken place.

During the summers he cut hay in the meadow south of the cabin, to feed cows in the winter months. Then, according to the **April 7, 1905** issue of the **Grand Valley Times** of Moab, Kirk sold at least some of his cattle and range rights to the Indian Creek Cattle Company. If he left around 1905, that makes the cabin, corral, fences, and the hay rake pretty old. From other short articles in the local newspaper, we know that Kirk later got into the sheep business and by 1916 had sheep ranging around Castleton east of Moab. By 1917, he had a herd of sheep in the Book Mountains (or Cliffs) north of Thompson. He was involved with sheep in that region with a son for the rest of his life. He died in 1945.

When the Scorups and Sommervilles bought out the Indian Creek Cattle Company and the Dugout Ranch in April of 1918, they ended up with the Salt Creek pasture. The late **Rusty Musselman** who was born in 1915 and used to live on the brow of the hill north of Monticello, recalled a few things about when he worked for Al Scorup at the Dugout:

I worked for Scorup before I was married, and after [as early as the 1930's]. In fact, I worked down there off and on throughout my life, and up until 4 or 5 years ago. We used to call that grassy area above Kirk's Cabin **Aristocratic Pasture** *because that's where Scorup used to keep his good-blooded bulls. They also called it* **The Meadows**. *I think there used to be another cabin in there and a cow camp. There's some little caves along there and that* **hay rake** *is under one. It's an old hand dump rake and it seemed to me just below that was another old cabin. That hay rake was old the first time I saw it.*

My uncle Roy Musselman the trapper, used to stay up there at the Kirk Cabin a lot. He was trapping mostly coyotes then. In fact there's a cave with a lot of his traps buried in the sand up there somewhere near where that hay rake is.

In those early days anyone could squat on the land, perhaps improve it a little by building a cabin, then if they sold it, they could, but without a deed. Officially they were called Desert Claims. That's

Above The **Lee Kirk Cabin** in upper **Salt Creek**. This cabin is well-built, but no one will put a better roof on it. With a good roof, the logs would last a 1000 years or more. But the CNP/NPS refuses to rehab such things. In the foreground is what remains of an old horse-drawn carriage. One CNP ranger told this writer one reason they haven't tried to preserve it is because early in the parks history, they brought it from Capitol Reef NP and planted it here. A 2nd opinion wasn't found. So there it sits and rots away in the elements.

Left Looking west, this is the little **waterfall & pond** just above Lee Kirk's Cabin, and at the northern end of **Aristocratic Pasture.** The reason the water is flowing here is because a layer of rock has forced water closer to the surface--that's what makes a spring in a valley like this. Then came cattle and overgrazing and downcutting. Below this, the creek bed is 5-7m below the original banks.

what Kirk did, he just squatted on the land & lived there. He never did officially homestead it or buy it.

The first time anyone had title to this 80 acres (32 hectares) was in January 1942, when the Scorup & Sommerville (S & S) Cattle Company official bought it from the state of Utah for $200. Sounds like a tax sale (?)

The **S & S cattle outfit** had it until November 20, 1965, then the entire ranch and grazing rights were sold to the Charley Redd family. That sale included the old Lee Kirk place and Aristocratic Pasture. **Robert B. Redd** (former husband of Heidi Redd of the Dugout Ranch), one of Charley's boys, remembered what happened next:

When they established the park in 1964, one of the things they agreed to--to get the support of the local people--was a 10 year grazing phase-out. That was done just before the Redds actually bought the ranch. So for that first 10 years we were just grazing it. We continued to use it as it had always been used, and we always went in from the bottom end of the canyon along Salt Creek. While I was there we never did put cattle in or out of that Bright Angel Trail. It was a lot easier to take 'em out through the park (Documents from CNP HQ in Moab indicate all grazing permits expired **June 30, 1975?**).

After the 10 year phase-out period, the NPS wanted to obtain the land and we weren't averse to that, but they offered us only $132 a acre, I think. We didn't like that so we suggested that we trade land-- allow us to select 80 acres someplace else. But they were in too big a hurry to do that.

So they said they'd condemn the land, and they started condemnation proceedings. That must have been on December 2, 1976. We went to Salt Lake for the 2 day trial. Judge Ritter heard it, and Robert Campbell was our attorney. The final settlement was for I think $1400 an acre.

By 1977, Kirk's old ranch was in public hands and part of Canyonlands National Park, and that's where it stands today. You'd think the remains of Kirk's ranch would be in good hands, but the CNP/NPS does nothing to preserve the cabin, wagon or hay rake. It's now NPS policy to not restore or reconstruct anything--so there they sit and rot away in the elements! If a new roof were put on (and maintained) the cabin and the wagon and hay rake put inside, they would all last several hundred years, maybe a 1000 years (?).

Part of the **corral** built by **Lee Kirk** as early as perhaps the 1890's (?). Notice the holes in these fence posts. Kirk must have had lots of time to drill these holes and install wooden cross bars, because otherwise he would have used wire. Apparently wire was in short supply, and expensive at the time. The same type of fencing is seen at the corral at the John Jackson or Kelly Place on Indian Creek just above or south of Newspaper Rock.

This is most of what is called the **Big Ruins** located in upper **Salt Creek**. Access to these moki houses was done with log ladders. Unseen here are other ruins at the base of this ledge, along with lots of pottery fragments or potsherds indicating this was a well-know & long-used habitation site.

High in a little hole in the wall, and in red, white & blue colors, is the **All American Man** pictograph panel. Next to it and on both sides are several moki houses or dwellings. On the next page is a close-up showing hand prints, a favorite form of expression in **The Needles** region.

The **4 Faces Panel** in upper **Salt Creek**. They're found just above, and in a complex of several moki houses. These have the same look as the **3, 5, 9,11 & 13 Faces panels** found not too far from here.

This long panel of rock art is located only about 100m from the end of the road in **Salt Creek** and the **Peekaboo Campsite**. There are older red colored paintings behind, and newer white images over the top. There are other white paintings, with lots of hand prints, through the hole in the wall and in the next bend south of here. See the map.

Left This is a closeup of the painting known as the **All American Man** pictograph panel. Look on the right side, and above, to see some hand prints. **Right** Only 60-70m from the All American Man panel is this little alcove with a couple of **moki houses**. It's a good climb getting up to this one.

This picture was taken from the end of the **promontory point** northwest of Cathedral Butte and at the **Big Pocket Overlook**. The sizeable little mesa in the upper right part of this picture is **Cedar Mesa**. Below is **Big Pocket**. The Fisheye Route is in the upper left side of this foto.

History of the Indian & Cottonwood Creek Ranches, and Newspaper Rock & other Indian Creek Rock Art

Location & Access The 2 major canyons on this map, **Indian Creek and Cottonwood Creek** (officially it's called North Cottonwood Creek), are located about halfway between Highway 191 and The Needles. To get there, drive along Highway 191 about halfway between Moab & Monticello. At **Church Rock** and between **mile posts 86 & 87,** turn west onto **The Needles Highway, State Road 211,** and proceed to points along Indian Creek including the Dugout Ranch and beyond.
Elevations Newspaper Rock, 1878m; Hart Point, roughly 2000m; Dugout Ranch, 1633m.
Water Bring all the water you'll need into this area. Only in an absolute emergency would you want to beg water from the Dugout--which is a working cattle ranch--not a dude ranch. You could also get water at the Needles Visitor Center and the nearby Squaw Flat Campground. Cottonwood and Indian Creeks run year-round--in places, but the Dugout Ranch uses the water from both for irrigation, so the lower part of Indian Creek is dry during the warmer half of each year. In the cooler part of the year, you could probably drink right from the upper part of Indian Creek, but in summer there are lots of cattle upstream. Same with Cottonwood Creek.
Maps USGS or BLM maps La Sal & Blanding (1:100,000); Shay Mountain, Harts Point South & Cathedral Butte (1:24,000--7 1/2' quads); and the plastic Latitude 40° map Moab West & Moab East (1:75,000).
Main Attractions Featured here is Newspaper Rock, one of the best single petroglyph panels in the world, a world class rock climbing area along Indian Creek, a short hike from Indian Creek up to the top of Hart Point, and 7 historic ranch sites dating back to as early as the mid-1880's. Also shown here are about a dozen really good rock art sites (all petroglyphs) along Indian Creek between mile posts 3 & 7.

History of the Ranches on Indian and Cottonwood Creeks

One of the oldest and best known ranches in Utah lies along Indian Creek about halfway between Highway 191 and The Needles District of Canyonlands. Today the place is known as the **Dugout Ranch,** but in the early days there were a number of small family ranches strung out along both Indian and the lower end of Cottonwood Creeks. Some of the very earliest history of this region is told in the writings of **Frank Silvey** who once lived in the La Sal area. His family moved there as some of the first settlers in southeastern Utah:

During the fall of 1885, D.M. Cooper and Mel Turner settled with small bunches of cattle, on Indian Creek near the mouth of Cottonwood at the Dugout [Ranch]. A trapper and prospector by the name of George Johnson Wilbourne (the original Indian Creek Johnson), had trapped some there, but had made very little attempt at any permanent improvement, so Cooper and Turner were the first to attempt a bonifide settlement. Shortly after this, came V.P. Martin, Brewster, Davis, Wilson, Harry Green, Lee Kirk, Henry Goodman and others [like Mark Darrow, Joe Titus, Tom Trout, Bob Kelly & John Jackson].
*In 1887 John E. Brown settled here, planted a fine orchard at once, built good cabins and corral, with good fence surrounding his crop. The second year he had considerable hay ground and soon after had big hay stacks for the winter months. After 1895 Dave Goudelock settled on the head of Cottonwood where he made a very good ranch. After a number of years **Goudelock, Cooper and Martin** fused all their interests together and formed what was called the **Indian Creek Cattle Company.***

In 1887, some local Mormons contemplated starting a settlement on Indian Creek. Several men from Bluff, Utah, plus John E. and William Rogerson from Mancos, Colorado, went to Indian Creek to have a look around. They met a handful of cowboys and could have bought the whole valley, but the rest of the group failed to show up, and the settlement attempts failed before it really began.

The reason the main ranch in this country got the name *"Dugout"* was because the first one to attempt to settle at that site built a dugout and lived in it for a while. It was in December of 1898, when Dave Goudelock joined forces with V.H. Martin and D.M. Cooper to create a new company. The **December 30, 1898** issue of the **Grand Valley Times (GVT)** states: *Mr. Goudelock is a partner in the new firm of Cooper, Martin & Co., who bought the mercantile business of Wilson Brothers.* This may have been the beginning of the Indian Creek Cattle Company as well (?).

Dave Goudelock's daughter, the late **Helen Goudelock Taylor,** remembered 3 of the 4 men starting the new company: *Mr. Cooper was a Yale graduate and was a pharmacist, and he started a drug store. Mr. Green was from Texas and had some banking knowledge and started the bank; and Dad ran the livestock end of the company on Indian Creek. All 4 of them [including Martin] had a lot do with the beginning of this town. None of these men were LDS, so Moab has always been a different kind of town.*

As one looks through the oldest Moab newspapers, it's interesting to note that all these ranches and the entire region were referred to as *"Indian Creek"*. It seems this must have included Lee Kirk's Ranch in upper Salt Creek as well. It was in April of 1905 that Kirk sold his cattle & grazing rights to the Indian Creek Cattle Company.

Not a lot is known of the exact history of each of the **7 original ranches** in this immediate area. In those early days, no one bothered to gain official title or a deed from the government. If someone built a cabin on a piece of land, and later wanted to leave, they simple sold it just like we do today, but without any kind of title or deed from the government. The first officially recognized ownership of these ranches came late in history, in the late 1910's, 1920's and 1930's. However, we do get some clues of the original habitation from the first maps of the region. Some government surveys were made in **May and June of 1911,** but the maps they created weren't published until **March of 1914.** Here's a rundown on the history of each ranch from many different sources.

The **Goudelock Ranch** on upper **Cottonwood Creek** was there and known by that name in 1911. The 2 cabins there were likely built in the mid or late 1890's, then after consolidation of the Indian Creek Cattle Company, it was likely used as a cowboy line camp rather than a family dwelling. According to Goudelock's daughter Helen G. Taylor, Dave kept that ranch as his own private land even after the Indian Creek Cattle Co. was formed. It was most likely sold to the Scorups in 1918. The first official title to this ranch came when the S & S Cattle Company bought it from the State of Utah in 1935. More on the S & S outfit later.

The **Wilson Ranch** on **Cottonwood Creek** was apparently first settled in the late 1880's by Hy Wilson. At some point in time William Keller bought the place from Wilson. Keller was Moab's mayor in 1908. The 1911 maps shows it as the **William Keller Ranch,** but he didn't get title until October 1915, then sold it to the Indian Creek outfit in January, 1916. But it's always been known as the Wilson Ranch.

Now the **Kelly Ranch** on **Indian Creek** which is just **south (upcanyon)** of Newspaper Rock. The only Kelly anyone remembers was a Bob Kelly, who apparently first settled this site, but no evidence

Map 33, History of the Indian & Cottonwood Creek Ranches, and Newspaper Rock & other Indian Creek Rock Art (Map 33B)

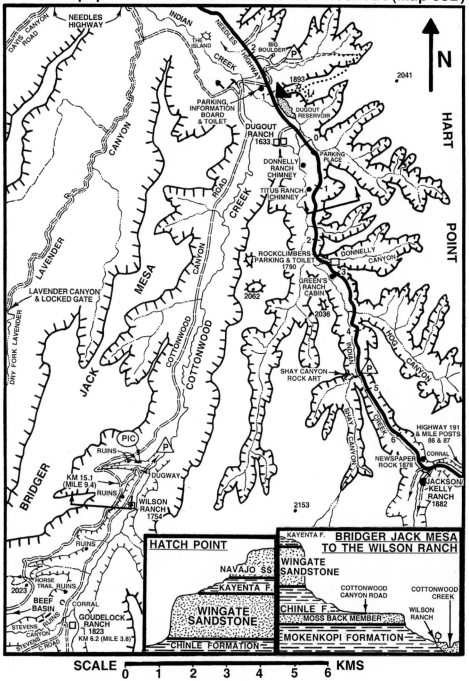

NEEDLES HIGHWAY

DAVIS CANYON ROAD

THE ISLAND

INDIAN CREEK

BIG BOULDER

P

1893

2041

N

HART

PARKING, INFORMATION BOARD & TOILET

DUGOUT RESERVOIR

DUGOUT RANCH 1633

PARKING PLACE

0

CANYON

DONNELLY RANCH CHIMNEY

TITUS RANCH CHIMNEY

1

POINT

LAVENDER MESA

ROAD

CREEK

ROCKCLIMBERS PARKING & TOILET 1790

2

DONNELLY CANYON

3

GREEN'S RANCH CABIN

2062

LAVENDER CANYON & LOCKED GATE

2036

4

HOG CANYON

DRY FORK LAVENDER

JACK

COTTONWOOD CANYON

COTTONWOOD

SHAY CANYON ROCK ART

INDIAN

P

CREEK

5

SHAY CANYON

6

HIGHWAY 191 & MILE POSTS 86 & 87

CORRAL

PIC

P

NEWSPAPER ROCK 1878

RUINS

7

DUGWAY

JACKSON/ KELLY RANCH 1882

BRIDGER

KM 15.1 (MILE 9.4)

RUINS

WILSON RANCH 1754

2153

RUINS

HORSE TRAIL RUINS

2023

HATCH POINT

KAYENTA F.

BRIDGER JACK MESA TO THE WILSON RANCH

BEEF BASIN

CORRAL

NAVAJO SS

WINGATE SANDSTONE

STEVENS RUINS

GOUDELOCK RANCH 1823 KM 6.2 (MILE 3.8)

KAYENTA F.

COTTONWOOD CANYON ROAD

COTTONWOOD CREEK

STEVENS CANYON

C ROAD

WINGATE SANDSTONE

CHINLE F.

MOSS BACK MEMBER

WILSON RANCH

CHINLE FORMATION

MOKENKOPI FORMATION

SCALE 0 1 2 3 4 5 6 KMS

333

Looking almost due south toward the **Dugout Ranch**; the buildings are there in the cottonwood trees. The date of this picture was October 20, 2012 and the leaves are just staring to turn yellow. The big cliff band above the Dugout is the **Wingate Sandstone**; above it is the Kayenta Formation; below the Wingate is the Chinle Formation.

From the **Dugout Ranch Overlook** looking south at the **Dugout Ranch**, left; and (North) **Cottonwood Creek** coming in from the middle distance; and the Dugout Reservoir below (with low water).

could be found to indicate when it occurred. It was surely before 1900, because on the map with 1911 information, it shows it belonging to **John Jackson**. Read the full story on John Jackson in the back of this book, along with what's written with **Map 25** on Jackson Hole, Jacksons Ladder and Jackson Bottom. Jackson likely sold or traded this place in 1917 when his first wife started divorce proceedings. The Indian Creek outfit likely got it at that time (?). The first official title came in September of 1941 when the S & S Cattle Co. bought it from the State of Utah. In 2012, there was the foundation of a house, plus really old log corrals & fencing and parts of a barn or granary still there.

The first ranch below, or north of, the Kelly/Jackson place was the **Harry G. Green Ranch**. Harry Green was mayor of Moab as early as 1903 and was one of the original Texans who were the cornerstones of Moab in those early days. He was also instrumental in creating Moab's first bank in the mid-1910's. This ranch dates back to the mid or late 1880's. It's shown as the Green Ranch on the 1911 survey maps but official title didn't come until February of 1919, when Joe Titus officially got the patent deed from the United States. Titus sold it to Scorup in 1922, then according to courthouse documents, title was transferred to the S & S Cattle Company in 1927. In 2012, there was still one **cabin** and a **chimney** from another marking the place.

The next place downstream to the north was the old **Joe Titus Ranch**. Joseph M. Titus was born and raised in Illinois, but migrated west in 1893, and worked as a cowboy in southeastern Utah. He was married in 1894 in Monticello, then he and his wife moved down onto Indian Creek the last of September, 1899. After he began a family, he built a home in Moab, where the children could go to school. Joe became partners in the Indian Creek Cattle Company, then when it was bought out by the Scorups and Somervilles in 1918, he continued on with the new co-owners as a ranch foreman. In about 1922, he moved to Richardson, which is northeast of Moab about 30 kms near the Colorado River, but he still retained some land on Indian Creek. He lived at Richardson until 1942, then sold that ranch and moved back Moab where he died in May, 1945.

The next place to the north has always been known as the **Donnelly Ranch**, but on the original survey plats of 1911, this place is called the **Joseph James Davis Ranch**. This must have been the original Davis fellow who came into this country in the mid-1880's, and for whom **Davis** Canyon is named (?).

The only person to know anything about **Joe Donnelly** was the late **Pearl Bliss Buttes** of Monticello, who was born in 1894--and was still alive and kicking in 1991 when this writer found her. She worked at the Dugout Ranch in 1912 as a young girl of 18. Here's what she had to say about Donnelly:

Joe Donnelly was a boy who came into Moab with a young man named Myron Lance who had been on a mission back east somewhere, in Ohio I think. This missionary brought Joe back with him. He made his home along Indian Creek for several years and had some cattle and a place of his own.

Pearl didn't know when he first arrived in this country, but thought is was around 1910. She dated him as a girl of 16. Newspaper accounts state he made a trip to Kansas City with a shipment of cattle in November, 1910. Then it appears he bought the old Davis Ranch sometime after June, 1911, and before he took some cows to Thompson in November, 1914. Joe was one of the only early ranchers on Indian Creek to take advantage of the Homestead Act and officially get title to the land. He got the patented deed from the USA in June, 1921, which meant he must have first applied for it 5 years previous, in about 1916. Courthouse records show that by November, 1921, he sold it to Al Scorup who was part owner of the S & S Cattle Company at the time.

Before getting into the history of the 7th and most important settlement site on Indian Creek called the **Dugout Ranch**, it must be noted that this was a fairly populated region in those early years. According to the book, *Saga of San Juan: Under the name of Carlisle, Indian Creek received a post office March 8, 1898, with Mrs. Lizzie Trout postmaster. Sixteen years later, March 31, 1914, the office was discontinued. Joseph Titus was postmaster at the time.*

By September of 1910, they completed a telefone line from the Dugout Ranch to Carlisle [Ranch], which was near present-day Monticello. The 1911 survey maps show this telefone line ending at the Dugout Ranch, which had **David M. Cooper's** name on it.

For some reason the original land that D.M. Cooper settled on must have been the very best site, because today it's the only ranch still occupied on Indian Creek. There's supposed to be a good spring nearby, perhaps that's the reason. It's also at the junction of 2 important year-round flowing streams (but both can dry up in the driest of times) with lots of flat agriculture-type land around.

Years after the place was originally settled, **Pearl Bliss Buttes** worked there during the summer of 1912. Here's what she remembered about the Dugout Ranch at that time:

*I worked there in the summer of 1912. I was workin' for Goudelock, **Dave Goudelock's** wife, just to help out with the house work. Mrs. Goudelock had 3 children and I cared for them. Goudelock had his home in Moab, but his family lived at the ranch in the summer time. All the owners of the Dugout Ranch lived in Moab. They had about 3 cowboys working there at the time. The cowboys had their own bunkhouse.* She also remembered that John Jackson and Joe Titus had their families there on Indian Creek that summer. John Jackson must have been living at what some ranchers have called the Kelly Ranch.

The first time David M. Cooper got around to getting title to the land he had squatted on for nearly 30 years on a desert entry, was in October of 1915. He apparently got it as part of the Homestead Act from the USA and had the **patent deed** (first official deed from the USA). By January, 1916, he turned around and deeded it to the Indian Creek Cattle Company, of which he was a major owner.

In **April 1918**, one of the biggest land swaps in Utah history took place. That's when **Al & Jim Scorup**, and **Bill & Andrew Somerville** bought the Indian Creek Cattle Company. But before getting into this deal, a brief history of the Scorup brothers is necessary.

Al Scorup first got into the cattle business in southeastern Utah when he left Salina alone and headed for White Canyon near Hite on the Colorado River. He was sent there in 1891 to roundup some cows for another man. Later he and his brother Jim got more involved and eventually built up their herd. Still later they joined forces with the **Bluff Mormons** and after a while had about all the range between the Colorado and San Juan Rivers, to as far east as the Blanding area, and south of Elk Ridge and the Blue (Abajo) Mountains. By **March of 1918**, they were tired of being so far from home, which for Al was Provo (246 E. Center Street and still standing in 2013), so they sold out to **John E. and Jacob Adams**. They sold 2500-3000 cattle and range rights for $252,700. which included lots of real estate in the Bluff area. With this deal completed, and Jim Scorup handling the Scorup property at Loss Creek near Salina, Utah, Al went looking for bigger challenges.

Now back to the Dugout Ranch. Some of the events leading up to the sale of the Indian Creek outfit are told in the *April 26, 1918 issue of GVT*, but Al Scorup tells it in his own words in the little self-published book, *J.A. Scorup--A Utah Cattleman*, by his sister Stena Scorup. He states:

Al Scorup somewhere near the Dugout Ranch in the late 1940's (?). From Stena Scorup's book, *J.A. Scorup--A Utah Cattleman*.

We paid $426,000 for Indian Creek, which was far too much; but we bought [it] in 1918 during World War I when prices were out of sight. But we got fine prices for what we sold; unfortunately the people to whom we sold [our Bluff property] were not as good at paying their debts as we were. We got a good contract; and then $50,000 for the next ten years. I planned from the beginning that Jim and I should have the controlling interest. We paid $33,000 of the down payment, and the Somervilles and Joe Titus paid the remainder or $17,000. The Somervilles put $100,000 into the company, Joe Titus $50,000 and Jim and I $276,000. Later we had to take over Joe Titus' interest. Fortunately for all of us we made a fine sale of cattle that spring and were able to pay Titus another $50,000 in June, 1918.

Things started out well for the new owners, but in the fall of 1919 just after the Armistice was signed ending World War I, the price of cattle began to drop. The price went from $50 or $60 a steer, down to $30 or $40. But this was just the beginning of a terrible year for everyone, especially for the Scorups. On Thanksgiving Day, 1919, one of the biggest early season snow storms to ever hit southeastern Utah laid down nearly a meter of snow on Monticello and the high country, with lesser amounts down on Indian Creek.

Every spear of feed was buried, and we hadn't even planned on feeding the cattle--couldn't have fed them because we didn't have the feed. The snow was up to the horses' bellies. Three hundred cattle died right in our feed yards. I paid Roy Musselman, a trapper, $1.50 each to skin them and then sold their hides for 28 cents a pound..... By spring there were 1500 starved, frozen dead cattle dotting the range.

In February, just when conditions at Indian Creek were as bad as they could be, I received a telegram from Salina telling me Jim was seriously ill with pneumonia. I dropped everything and on horseback bucked that terrific snow and went back to Salina. But I was too late to cheer him up,.... for he was dead even before I got to Thompson [nearest railway station].

Things were rough throughout the 1920's, but the prices for cattle gradually increased. Then: *In 1926, the Adamses had failed to pay their interest for two years. That was the year we had to take over what was left of the T.Y.'s and my real estate in Bluff. I sold my home to Freeman Nielsen, who paid me for it...... On **October 26, 1926,** we got together and formed the **Scorup & Sommerville Corporation**. W.G. Sommerville, Andrew Somerville, Frank J. Adams, Emma [Al's wife], and I were the incorporators..... In 1927, Harve Williams, an Oklahoma man, came into the company.*

In 1928, we sold 4,400 head of cattle, as I planned we must finish paying our debt to Goudelock and got rid of all that interest. For those cattle we received $194,000, and paid Goudelock $100,000, the last payment we ever had to give him.

By 1928, the **S & S Cattle Company** had grazing rights (mostly on public lands) of all the land north of the San Juan River, east of the Colorado River, south of Lockhart Basin and east of Dry Valley and the Blue or Abajo Mountains. It may have covered more territory than any other ranch in the United States.

The late **Rusty Musselman** formerly of Monticello was about the oldest ex-cowboy alive in 1992 who worked at the Dugout Ranch for Scorup. He remembered a few things about the ranch and his personal experiences:

I was down there workin' for Scorup in about 1934 or '35. I worked several times for the S & S Cattle Company but not as a cowboy all the time. I sometimes worked at puttin' up hay right at the ranch.

*I remember some of the differences between the old time cattlemen. **Al Scorup** wouldn't allow a bull whip or a dog on the ranch. He didn't want them cattle riled up. But **David Lavender** was the other way around, he liked a big long bull whip a poppin' and dogs a barkin'. Those 2 men had different concepts about how to handle cattle. In fact, I was sleeping down at Scorup's house one night, and Lavender was there and them 2 old buggers sat up all night arguing about how to run cattle. Old Lavender was a very colorful cowboy; he'd wear a bandana and special ridin' pants; he was a kind of dude-looking sort of a guy.*

*David Lavender used to buy a lot of cows from Scorup. That's how **Lavender Canyon** got it's name. He was a lawyer or somethin'; he never was much when it came to cowboyen. I remember when we used to drive cows out to Colorado when there used to be about 2500 to 3000 head in a herd. We had cattle drives twice a year. One drive would go to Colorado this way; over here at Coalbeds [on the Utah--Colorado state line south of the La Sal Mountains on the way to Paradox]. Scorup's cowboys would take 'em to the state line, then 12 or 14 of Lavender's boys would take them on from there. The* other herd would go to the trains up at Thompson. Lavender would buy 'em and put 'em on the mountains in Colorado in the summer; fatten 'em up and ship 'em on to Kansas.

All of Lavender's cowboys each had a dog and a bull whip; and us cowboys over here would have to ease those cattle along 'till they got to Coalbeds, then it was a hullabaloo! Lavender's cowboys would whistle at their dogs and crack their whips, and say, "come on you Mormon sons-a-bitches, you're gentile cattle now". Then it took 3 days to gather 'em up!

Now we all camped together, and they were friendly--they were just puttin' on a show. But that was the kind of reception we got. We would just ease 'em along and keep as much meat on 'em as possible. This was back in the 1930's, and earlier, when David Lavender would buy Scorup's cattle.

But now the cattle drives are finished and the trucks have taken over. You can truck 'em so much easier and it saves so much flesh. It used to take about 6 weeks to drive from the Elk Mountains to the railroad up at Thompson. We'd first have to gather that White and Red Canyon country [south and east of Hite on Lake Powell], then they'd cut'em out and take the ones he wanted to ship. Then it took 7 or 8 days to drive 'em out from the Dugout to Thompson after we had the herd gathered up. Along the way you'd have to drive to water, and with that many cattle it was a problem. After the Colorado River, it was on to Valley City Reservoir. He [Burdick?] used to sell water to Scorup, then they could make it on up to Thompson and the railroad.

On one drive they put the cattle in the stock pen at Thompson, then everybody went to town to the bar, except for one guard. Sometime during the night an engine pulled out and let off a bunch of that cold steam into the pen and it scared them cows so bad, they just laid that fence flat, and it took another 3 days to gather'em again. I wasn't there then, but I heard about it.

By 1939 & '40, business was good at the Dugout Ranch. It was in those years Scorup built four new cabins for the hired hands. They also installed electric lights and piped water from the spring and had running water and showers. They also had a fine orchard of peaches, pears, grapes, apples, etc. In 1940, they built line cabins out on the range; 2 cabins at Mormon Pasture on Elk Mountain, and another at Big Flat on Horse Mountain. These areas are south of the upper end of Salt Creek Canyon.

For many years not a lot of things happened. But in about 1952, at the age of 80, Al Scorup had to quit riding the range. After that **Harve Williams**, his son-in-law, took over as range manager. Al suffered a stroke in the early part of 1959, and by October died at age 87.

By November of 1965, the ranch, range and grazing rights were sold to the **Charley Redd** family of La Sal. Later, one of Charley's sons, **Robert B. Redd** inherited the Dugout Ranch part of what was a huge livestock raising operation. As of the early 1990's, Robert's ex-wife **Heidi** and their 2 sons, **Matt & Adam** were operating the Dugout Ranch. The name of the outfit was still the **Indian Creek Cattle Company**, under the management of Heidi Redd & Sons.

Here's the situation on the Dugout Ranch as this book goes to press in 2013. One source of information comes from **The Nature Conservancy** magazine for the **Winter, 2010**. It's the one with Heidi Redd's picture on the front cover. In it is an article about the ranch. Part of it states: *In 1997 the [Nature] Conservancy negotiated a deal and raised enough money to purchase the ranch for $4.6 million. Heidi negotiated a lifetime lease on the ranch house and 25 acres, as well as a 10-year lease to continue running the ranch. The deal hinged on the Conservancy's commitment to partner with Heidi to continue the historical use of the cattle ranch. "We pretty much made a promise to Heidi and to this community that the Dugout Ranch will always be a cattle ranch",....* This means it will never be sold to developers for the purpose of making condos or golf courses.

The grazing permits for Indian Creek Cattle Co. on the public domain now belong to The Nature Conservancy, and they own the private land at the Dugout Ranch. Matt & Adam Redd are wrangling the cows which are now owned by the Conservancy--which is now in the cattle business. They can work for the Conservancy as long as everyone is happy. As long as Heidi Redd is alive she will own the 25 acres--when she dies it will revert back to the Conservancy. The Conservancy and others, are involved with doing research on the range in regards to the effects of grazing cattle in this region. The number of cows they own and graze will depend on range conditions just like all other permit holders.

The Indian and Cottonwood Creek Ranches Today

Here's what you'll find at these old ranches today. First, the 2 on **(North) Cottonwood Creek**. About 1 1/2 kms northwest of **The Dugout Ranch**, and about 300m northwest of **mile post 1**, turn left or southwest and onto a good graded county road. After about 40m with are a parking place, an information board & toilet. From there, head southwest on what's called the **Cottonwood Canyon Road**. This is the same one you take if going to Upper Salt Creek, Beef Basin and Dark Canyon. Drive to a point **15.1 kms (9.4 miles)** from **The Needles Highway**, and veer left or east. Set your **odometer at 0**. Drive down another graded road along a **dugway**. About halfway down this little side-canyon, look north to see on the opposite side, some pretty good **Anasazi ruins & rock art** facing south. We'll come back to these ruins, but for now continue downhill to the road along Cottonwood Creek and turn south. As you make this drive to these 2 old ranches, be watching the cliffs on the right or west side of this valley and you can see at least 7 different ruins. Be sure to take a pair of **binoculars** for this part.

At **Km 2.1 (Mile 1.3 from the Cottonwood Canyon Road)** stop and park--or drive east toward the house just to the east. That house was headquarters for the **Wilson Ranch**. At the Wilson Ranch, you'll find a couple of big cottonwood trees and an **old cabin**. Part of this cabin is made from logs and very old; while a newer addition appears to have been built as late as the 1940's (?). In between these parts is an open but roofed part which could be called a breeze-way, perhaps a place to hangout in hot summer weather. One interesting thing about this building is, someone tore the roof off the old log cabin then put one new roof covering both cabins and the breeze-way--an interesting combination. Nearby is Cottonwood Creek (official name is North Cottonwood Creek), but it's cut down 7-8m or so to bedrock leaving the ranch high and dry. This downcutting probably started sometime around 1900 after the area had been overgrazed for about 15 years.

From the Wilson place, continue southwest along the western side of Cottonwood Creek. At or just before **Km 6.2 (Mile 3.8)**, is a fork in the road; veer left or east off the graded **Stevens Canyon Road** and drive another 150m or so and you'll come to **2 cabins** at the **Dave Goudelock Ranch**. One structure is made of rock and well-built, but its log roof is gone and it apparently never had a fireplace (?). The other one is made of logs and it's out in the meadow 50m away. It has 3 rooms with a veranda or breeze-way facing west. At one time there must have been a big flood come down Cottonwood Creek which deposited nearly a meter of silt inside this cabin. Maybe that was the same flood which started all the downcutting in the creek (?). There used to be some odds and ends of old horse-drawn farm

Looking west at the **Wilson Ranch** house. At the left end is an old log cabin, perhaps built in the late 1800's (?). To the right is a more recently made frame structure. In the middle is a kind of breeze-way; and the whole thing is covered with one roof, perhaps dating from the 1940's (?).

Looking east at the 2 cabins at the old **Dave Goudelock Ranch**. The cabin in the foreground is made of stone; behind it is a 3-part log cabin that has a meter of dirt inside. In the distance running from right to left is the (North) Cottonwood Creek which is downcut because of overgrazing.

Above Looking northwest at part of the old **Jackson/Kelly Place**, which is just south of **Newspaper Rock**. John Jackson owned it and lived here for a while in the early 1900's. What's left of an old barn or granary & corral is in the background.

Left. Part of an old corral at the **Jackson/Kelly Place**. Notice the post on the left; it has 3 holes which were drilled out and cross members installed to hold up poles. This indicates it was build way back before 1900 (?).

machinery lying around, but they were nowhere to be found in 2012. Both of these ranches on Cottonwood Creek are on small plots of private ground, but surely it's OK to look around as long as you don't disturb anything. This writer didn't see any *"No Trespassing"* signs at either.

Now back to those **ruins** you saw on the way in. Instead of going back up the dugway, continue north a short distance and turn west for 200m or so. There's a parking and/or camping place there. Walk up to the ruins and some **pictographs** which have been painted using something white.

Now to **Indian Creek**. Just south, or upcanyon from Newspaper Rock, is the old **Jackson/Kelly Ranch**. Just west of **mile post 7** and where the highway meets Indian Creek for the first time, is where a little side-road turns off to the south. Pass through a wire gate, but close it behind you. About 200-300m from the highway will by a **log corral** and a **log shed.** The cabins shown on the 1911 map seem to have burned down; the foundation is just south of the log shed. This too is on a small plot of private land, but just south of the corrals is a nice meadow where deer hunters sometimes camp. If you do camp there, please leave a clean site and don't bother anything.

Near **mile post 3** on The Needles Highway will be the site of the **Harry Green Ranch**. It's off to the south and under some big cottonwood trees. You'll have to park at a little spot on the south side of the highway and walk about 100m to reach it. At this place is one **log cabin**, a nearby **chimney**, and an old fruit tree or two. That cabin surely dates back to around 1900.

Further down (north) along Indian Creek and roughly 300-350m south of **mile post 1,** will be the **Joe Titus Ranch** off to the west. This is the hardest one to find. Look for some large boulders just to the east & northeast of the actual ranch site. You'll have to cross an old ditch, then look for a single **chimney** standing out in a grove of gamble oak brush. You can see it from the highway, but you have to be in just the right spot.

Top The old cabin and a 2nd chimney located at the **Harry Green Ranch** near mile post 3 along Indian Creek. **Left** This chimney is the only thing left at the **Joe Titus Ranch**. It's hard to see, but from the right place on the highway you can see it. **Right** This chimney is the only thing left of the **Donnelly Ranch**; this one is easily visible from The Needles Highway.

A little further to the north and in a large open field on the west side of the road, and between **mile post 0 & 1,** look for another old chimney standing out in the open down near the creek about 350m away. This is all that's left of the old **Davis and/or Joe Donnelly Ranch.** So you won't have to walk across this field, which is private land (in 2012, there didn't seem to be any *"no trespassing"* signs around--Utahns tend to be a little more laid-back about such matters as long as nothing is disturbed), use a pair or binoculars. There's not much to see there anyway--just a chimney.

(Immediately east of the **Dugout Ranch** is a fence & cattle guard and **mile post 0.** From that point going in the direction of Highway 191 is one set of mile posts and put there by the State of Utah; it's a state road. From there going into The Needles District of CNP, is another set of mile post markers, all camouflaged on brown fiberglass posts--so you can't see them--influenced by the NPS no doubt)

When asked what may have happened to cabins at these last 2 ranches, Rusty Musselman stated: *There were cabins at all those places along Indian Creek in the 1930's where I first started working for Scorup. But here a few years ago, we had a couple of bachelor brothers burned down every cabin in the country; but not intentionally. They just moved into those old cabins, built too hot of a fire and went off and left 'em. There used to be old corrals and bunkhouses along in there too.*

Hike to Hart Point and to an Overlook of the Dugout Ranch

In the area of Hog and Donnelly Canyons, and right along The Needles Highway, are a number of places where **rock climbers** are scaling big walls made of **Wingate Sandstone.** If it's big wall climbing you want, this is one of the most accessible sites anywhere. At the mouth of Donnelly Canyon, they now have a new paved parking place with toilet. This was built in 2011.

There are probably routes up and out of Hog and Donnelly Canyons to Hart Point, but the big walls there aren't as impressive as they are downcanyon in the vicinity of the Dugout Ranch. There's one un-named canyon just east of the old Joe Donnelly place that likely has a route out the top end, but the author has not explored that drainage.

If you're interested in a hike to an **overlook of the Dugout Ranch,** here's how to get there. Just northwest of **mile post 1** along the Needles Highway, and on the left or southwest, is the turnoff to North Cottonwood Creek and Beef Basin. There's a toilet, information board and parking place there. If you continue toward The Needles less than 1 1/2 kms and just a little ways before **mile post 2,** is a turnoff to the right or east. That point is beyond the private land of the Dugout Ranch, so drive through that gate but always close it behind you. Drive east on a good road for just less than 1 km and park and/or camp (there's another track branching off to the left going to a **big boulder,** and campsite). From there, walk up this valley which is almost due east. You may see and can use an old vehicle track, or use horse trails. Higher up, veer right and into the right-hand drainage; at that point it's likely best to stay in the dry wash bottom, at least for a ways. Further along, route-find upcanyon on the right-hand side; that's where it gets rugged and the route is up through boulders--but walking is still quite easy. Once on top of the Wingate, make a hard right turn and bench-walk west on one of the Kayenta ledges, then route-find up through the last of the ledges and continue west on top of this point (see map). At the far west end of this big point, you'll be directly above the **Dugout Reservoir** with a great view looking down and to the south at the Dugout Ranch. The author did this climb twice in 2012 in 3 & 3 1/4 hours round-trip. The Dugout Ranch is covered with cottonwood trees so late October would be a good time for taking fotos from this viewpoint.

From where you turn east going to the hike to the Dugout Ranch Overlook, continue northwest along the Needles Highway. Between mile posts 2 & 3, is another drainage or valley coming down from the northeast (not shown on this map). This land is also public and you can drive through a gate and into the valley a ways. When the track gets too rough, walk northeast and into the longest part of this unnamed canyon. There's no trail, but the climbing is easy. When you get above the Wingate part of the drainage, turn left 180° and ledge-walk west along one of the Kayenta benches on the north side. After about 500m, work your way up through the remaining Kayenta ledges then turn northeast and route-find up through the Navajo. You'll eventually come to an old vehicle track which leads to a **windmill and storage tank** on top of Hart Point. This hike should take the average person 4-5 hours (depending on where you park) to walk to the windmill and back.

Indian Creek Rock Art: Newspaper Rock, Shay Canyon and other sites

Indian Creek has one of the better concentrations of rock art found anywhere. The line stretches for about 7 kms **between mile posts 3 & 7.** Once you make it down to Indian Creek from the east, and just west of **mile post 7,** is an overhang on the right or north. Under that are some old and nearly faded cowboy signatures and several small panels of Indian rock art. One non-Indian date goes back to **Mar 23 1885** along with **Jack Cottrell** and **J.D. Powers;**

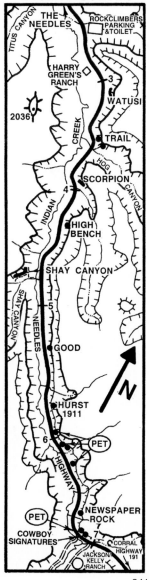

Map 33B, Indian Creek Rock Art

these seem genuine and this was the first year settlement began on Indian Creek.

About 300m around the corner from there and on the right will be **Newspaper Rock**, one of the single best petroglyph panels in the world. To get the best fotos, be there in the morning hours when it's totally in shadows; or later in the afternoon when it's all in sun. This site has a parking lot & restrooms.

Just north and south of **mile post 6** are several small panels of rock art. To see those, you'll have to walk along the road, preferable with binoculars. One nearly hidden panel has several cowboy signatures; one is that of **Ralph Hurst, 1911**. About 350m south of **mile post 5** is a **good** panel you'll have to climb up to. Then roughly 400m north of **mile post 5** and next to 2 boulders on the left, **Shay Canyon** enters Indian Creek from the left or west. Park there, and use a hiker's trail down just a few meters to where Shay Canyon dry wash enters Indian Creek. Walk west up Shay about 200m and turn right or north and get out of the drainage bottom and onto a good hiker's path. From there, you'll be on a good trail, so just follow it up to the corner of the 2 canyons. There on the lower part of the Wingate Sandstone wall, will be about 200m of separate, but closely spaced, rock art panels, all petroglyphs. This is the best rock art site in the valley.

Going north again. Just less than 1 km north of Shay Canyon is another site that's up on a **high bench** to the east. About 750m north of that, and immediately north of **mile post 4**, are several other panels, one of which has a **scorpion**, snakes & a centipede. This is a good one, so walk north to the south facing wall; the best panel is to the west a little in a corner.

Just north of the mouth of **Hog Canyon** are a couple of minor panels that won't be worth your trouble; get up to them via a constructed **trail**. Further north and about 150m south of **mile post 3**, will be another good concentration. Park where you can on the right or east side of the highway, then with binoculars, scan the west side of a large bulge in the canyon wall. By the time you get there, there may be a trail of sorts going straight upslope. One of these half dozen panels stretching for about 150m, has what looks like a drawing of the head of an African or **Watusi bull** with large curled horns.

There doesn't seem to be any more rock art north of mile post 3, because it's a pretty good climb to get up to the base of the Wingate Sandstone cliffs which is the only place along Indian Creek where petroglyphs are found. If you have time, you might explore the west side of the valley, but there seems to be some bushwhacking getting there, and not too many possible sites--at least when viewed from the highway with binoculars.

Right A small part of the **Scorpion Panel** which is very old. Notice how dark these images are compared to Newspaper Rock below; and the perfect scorpion just to the left of center.
Below Newspaper Rock, maybe the best single petroglyph panel in the world.

Top Part of the **Good** panel shown on the small map **(page 341)**. **Middle** The better part of the several panels at the **Watusi** site near mile post 3. **Bottom** Lots of doodling at the **Shay Canyon** site. There are maybe a dozen different panels in this large complex of petroglyphs.

343

Driving Tour and Hiking to Archaeological Sites
in the Beef Basin Country

Location & Access Featured on this map is the greater **Beef Basin Country** which lies due south of The Needles Districts of Canyonlands NP. It's also due west of Cathedral Butte and the upper end of Salt Creek Canyon. What we have here is a driving tour of a number of open parks or meadows with Anasazi ruins scattered about. Hikes here are mostly short walks from your car to dwellings or moki houses, and to rock art sites.

Before going into this area, be sure you have a good running vehicle with good tires and lots of extra water, food, fuel, tools and anything else that might come in handy in case of a breakdown or any kind of emergency. It's a long way in & out Beef Basin mostly on dirt roads. Parts of this map are at least 90 kms (55 miles) from the nearest paved road, The Needles Highway.

You could drive into this country from the area to the south and from around Natural Bridges National Monument and the Bears Ears, but that's the longest way. The best way to get to **Beef Basin** is to drive **Highway 191** between Moab & Monticello. Between **mile posts 86 & 87**, and immediately next to **Church Rock**, turn west onto **State Road 211, The Needles Highway**, and head toward The Needles District. After **33 kms (20.5 miles)**, and just beyond the historic **Dugout Ranch**, turn southwesterly onto the North **Cottonwood Canyon Road (set odometer at 0)**. Drive past Cathedral Butte and finally to the **Beef Basin Turnoff** which is **41.7 kms (25.3 miles)** from The Needles Highway. This is at a cool **2507m** altitude. It's hard to miss this junction because it has several signs, but you'll have to have a better map than this to see the whole route. The plastic **Latitude 40° map Moab West** listed below is the best one to have because it shows the entire route into this country from The Needles Highway. When you arrive, the first meadowland you come to will be **House Park.** From there you branch out in different directions as detailed below.

Before starting out on this trip, stop at the BLM headquarters field office on Dogwood Street in Moab; or the visitor center, in Moab; or The Needles Visitor Center (Tele. 435--259-4711) ; or the BLM office in Monticello (Tele. 435-587-1500), to get the latest information on road conditions into this region. Or call San Juan County roads in Monticello, Tele. 435-587-3230 for road updates. Getting into Beef Basin requires driving a **HC/4WD** over some moderately high altitude dirt roads that are closed by snow in winter. Snow and mud generally makes access impossible from sometime in November until about the end of March or the first part of April. Each year is different.

When roads are dry and in good condition, stock SUV's (some cars with a little clearance-maybe?) can get to and along all the main roads shown on this map, but having a shovel and doing a little road work may be necessary in one or 2 places; depending on the vehicle, and how long it's been since the road was last graded. Once you get into any of the parks or meadows, the roads are generally good even for cars, but a little sandy in a place or two, which means if they're a little wet, driving is made easier. Once down in the basin, there's only one **rough place** where you will need a little clearance & 4WD; or do a little road work by hand.

Here's a short history on **cattle grazing in Beef Basin**. This region was, since the introduction of cattle into San Juan County, the grazing territory for those who owned the Dugout & Indian Creek Ranches. During World War I days, Al Scorup and the Sommervilles of Moab, bought out several little ranchers on Indian Creek, and put together the Scorup & Sommerville (S & S) Cattle Company. When Al died in 1959, it went to the Redds, another prominent family in the ranching business in southeastern Utah. Finally, in 1997, an agreement was reached between the Redds and The Nature Conservancy. All the grazing rights formerly owned by Scorup, Sommervilles and the Redds now are owned by the Conservancy, and it's their cattle which graze there during the winter & spring seasons. Heidi Redd's 2 sons now manage the wrangling end of the business for The Conservancy.

Here's one more little interesting feature about Beef Basin. In 1975 plans started for the Redds & BLM to put in a rain catchment or guzzler facility along the boundary between Ruin & Middle Parks but it wasn't until 1982 that it was constructed. The catchment is made of aluminum siding laid out on the ground surrounded by a tall fence. Rain is caught on the catchment and funnelled/piped into 2 steel tanks, then water gravity-flows down into Middle and Ruin Parks and into 7 watering troughs for the cattle. To install the plumbing system, a bulldozer with a special plow-like implement was used to put plastic pipe underground and covered, all in one operation. Spreading out the water troughs spreads out the grazing more evenly. There are several fenced grazing pastures in the greater Beef Basin and cows are moved from pasture to pasture depending on rainfall and feed availability. In summer and fall the cattle are moved to higher mountain meadows to the east.

Elevations Ruin, Middle, House Parks & Pappys Pasture are between 1950-2000m altitude, while the lower part of Beef Basin is around 1900m. Higher buttes or ridges in the area are over 2250m.

Water Take plenty of drinking water into this country. Even though maps show a number of springs, most could go dry in a long dry spell; or they may be hard to get a safe drink from. The only guaranteed place to find water on this map is from springs in upper Gypsum Canyon on the west side of Beef Basin; and at Stanley, Beef Basin (?) and Homewater Springs.

Maps USGS or BLM maps La Sal & Blanding (1:100,000); Druid Arch, Cross Canyon, Fable Valley & House Park Butte (1:24,000--7 1/2' quads); the plastic Trails Illustrated/National Geographic map Canyonlands National Park (1:70,000); or the **best** is the plastic Latitude 40° map Moab West (1:75,000).

Main Attractions Lots of Anasazi ruins to see. It's also outside the national park, so you can camp anywhere you like--but please leave a clean campsite and keep all vehicles on existing roadways--or the control freaks are sure to come here too! Plus, it's a nice quiet place to visit.

House Park

As you enter the Beef Basin Country, you'll come downhill from the **Beef Basin Turnoff (reset odometer at Km & Mile 0)** with a rocky place or two (no real problem), then will enter the first of 4 major parks or meadows. This will be **House Park.** Like all the others, it's flat with a sandy meadow in the middle surrounded by buttes or sandstone mountains of various sizes. On the south side of House Park are 2 sites to visit. The first will be **12.6 kms (7.8 miles)** from the Beef Basin Turnoff. Park where a road used to take off to the south but which was washed out 2012 (another track may develop?), then walk about 300m to a **north facing ruins** (Anasazi habitation site) under a cliff just south and uphill from an old **stock pond**. This is unusual because it faces north, while almost all others face south to get warmth from the low winter sun. Therefore, it's assumed this site was used more in summer when they were looking for shade more than sun.

Map 34, Driving Tour and Hiking to Archaeological Sites in the Beef Basin Country

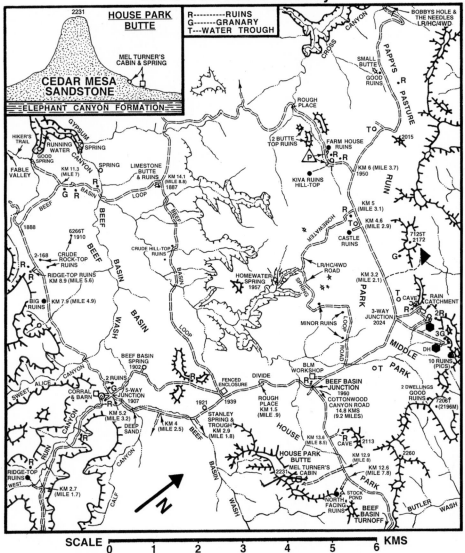

The next site is **Mel Turner's Cabin**. At **Km 12.9 (Mile 8)**, and only about 350m past the parking place for the north facing ruins, turn left and drive south. After about 1 1/2 kms, the road is washed out. Park there and walk a short distance west to the cabin. The unusual thing about this cabin is that part of it was built with large pine logs in the usual way, while the other half was built with shorter cedar (juniper) posts in stockade fashion, or upright. Inside this part are willows nailed to the walls horizontally to help seal it. Only part of the roof on the regular log cabin is still on (9/2012), but the roof over the stockade part has collapsed along with all 4 walls. About 10m south of the cabin is a small **corral**; probably for riding horses, and up the drainage a ways to the south is **Turner's Spring** that seeps out from under a ledge. Just above it is some **rock art**.

The late **Reed Wilson** of Monticello told the author he asked all of the old timers in that country, *"who made that cabin in House Park?"* He was told Mel Turner built it. Now **Mel Turner**, along with David M. Cooper, settled on Indian Creek in the fall of 1885. This date is a little different than the one given in Mel's obituary which was in the *September 15, 1932* issue of *The Time Independent* newspaper of Moab. Part of his obituary went like this:

Mr. Turner was 80 years of age. He was born in Lincoln, Maine, February 19, 1853, and came west

This is the **North Facing Ruins** in the eastern part of **House Park**. Look closely on this wall and you'll see finger prints in the mud that are between 800-950 years old.

The 2nd place to see in **House Park** is the **Mel Turner Cabin**. The tumbled-down part of this cabin on the right is the part that was built stockade-style using upright cedar posts. Inside the main cabin is a 55 gallon drum that was a stove--a fireplace was in the tumbled-down part. A corral is to the right.

Above This is probably a habitation dwelling which is just around the corner from the **granaries** shown in the foto to the left.

Left These **granaries** are found just above the good parking place near the one drill hole (DH) in **Middle Park**. The 10 Ruins site is about 500m east of these and the parking place.

about 1875. In about 1880 he moved to Indian Creek, south of Moab, where he was engaged in the cattle business for 30 years. He accumulated large cattle holdings and was one of the leading stockmen of this section of the west. When he first went into the Indian creek and Beef basin district, Mr. Turner lived alone for six years in a cave, taking care of his cattle. About 20 years ago [1912?] he moved his cattle to Paradox, Colorado and established a large ranch there. He was one of the pioneers in the uranium mining industry of western Colorado, being one of the original locaters of many valuable mines in the Paradox district. (We think (?) Mel had a brother named **Hy Turner**, who lived on Williams Bottom west of Moab for 25-30 years in the early 1900's.)

Now to finish the story about Mel Turner in this part of the country. Turner built up his herd to about 800 head, then must have sold his range or grazing rights to Dave Goudelock, Harry Green and D.M. Cooper. This, after the Indian Creek Cattle Company was apparently organized in 1898 (?), and according to Mel's obituary, around 1910 or '12. This cabin then would have been built some time between 1885 and about 1910, although it was more likely built sometime between the late 1890's and early 1900's. The western half of the cabin is in surprisingly good condition considering its age.

Now back on the main House Park Road. If you continue west to **Km 13.6 (Mile 8.5)**, you'll come to a side-road heading north. Drive this for 350-400m to a campsite. Immediately north of that is a small cave with soot on the ceiling (made by campfires), and a partially rocked-up front. Not much to look at there, but the author saw a couple of pottery fragments nearby.

Continue west to **Beef Basin Junction** which is **14.8 kms (9.2 miles)** from the **Beef Basin Turnoff**. Right at this junction is an information board and a road running southeast to a good campsite in the piñon/junipers (P/J's). If you park there and walk west about 100m, you'll find a couple of **Anasazi structures or ruins** (labeled R on this map) right out in the open; but they're not much to look at. West of those and just over the hill, is a BLM workshop.

Middle Park

From this **Beef Basin Junction**, let's first head north toward Middle & Ruin Parks (reset odometer to **Km & Mile 0**). At **Km .8 (Mile .5)**, the southern end of the **Homewater Spring Loop Road** begins to the left or west. This is a pretty good road until you get close to the middle of the loop and the turnoff to Homewater Spring, then it's for a LR/HC/4WD (along the way are **3 minor ruins**). If you're coming in via the north approach you'll encounter the same 400m section in the middle of the loop that's very rough. But you can walk from either end and down into a little canyon to the south to visit the spring. **Homewater Spring** has 2 parts; in 9/2012, the first part, on the left going down into the drainage, needed repairs to get water into a single trough next to the old road; while the second and main spring further down and on the far right end, on the east side, has 2 troughs full of good water (cows are grazing there in winter/spring, so at that time better treat the water).

Middle Park has a number of Anasazi sites. Best way to these places to proceed north to the center of Middle Park and to a **3-Way Junction** at **Km 2.6 (Mile 1.6 & 2024m altitude)**. To start, take the road heading northeast. Drive it for **1.4 kms (.9 mile)** to near an old drill hole (**DH**) site. From there, which is a popular campsite, walk the trail heading north. Be observant. In those cliffs are **3 granaries facing** southeast, and under a larger ledge is what appears to be a **dwelling** or **moki house** that's in good condition.

From that campsite near the end of the road, walk east along the base of the cliffs for about 500m to find **10 ruins**, with some white **pictographs** above, and a small collection of pottery fragments. It's just south of elevation **7038T (2145m)** on the appropriate **7 1/2' quad**. From there, walk south about 750m and around some ledges, then another 750m to the southeast, where you'll come to a couple of dwellings at ground level. These are 400m west of elevation **7206T (2196m)**.

Now back to the 3 granaries & campsite. About 500m west of that is another **drill hole** site, but the road leading to it is now too obscure to see or use, so to see the next interesting site, either walk west about 750m along the base of the cliffs; or better, go back to the **3-way junction** & main road. From there, take a second side-road heading north for about 500m to the **BLM rain catchment facility**. At this site is a tall fenced enclosure protecting a section of aluminum siding about 60 x 100m. Read more about the history of this facility above.

So, from the east side of this catchment, you can drive a short distance to one of the water troughs & stock pond, and park. From there, walk northeast about 500m, while looking for a west-facing cave with **2 Anasazi dwellings (2R)** inside. This is an interesting place. The cave has lots of black soot on its ceiling; this comes from thousands of campfires, either Fremont or Archaic, then at a later time, the Anasazi built the granaries. See foto on opposite page. There are still some pottery fragments around too--but leave them there, it's against the law to take them! Take pictures instead.

Or, you can drive to the northwest corner of the catchment and park next to a **small butte** detached from the main line of cliffs. On top of it is another cave (facing east) with a moki house, and on the south side is another **cave** with soot on the ceiling and a little rock art nearby.

Ruin Park

Now use the **3-Way Junction** again. Everything west of there would be considered **Ruin Park**. Head west to **Km 3.2 (Mile 2.1** from Beef Basin Junction) and stop at what was the beginning of a road running north (it's now blocked off). Park there and walk north with binoculars. After a ways, you can see another dwelling or granary on the south side of another mountain of sandstone. It's about 400m due south of elevation **7125T (2172m)**. Not a lot to look at there but up the old road is an overlook.

Continue driving west. At **Km 4.6 (Mile 2.9)**, turn left or south and drive about 300m to the base of some cliffs. On top of a ledge is **Castle Ruins**, a 2-3 story ridge-top lookout from Anasazi days. It's one of the bigger and more-unique sites in these parts.

Going west again. At **Km 5 (Mile 3.1)** is the northern end of the Homewater Spring Loop-Road. At **Km 6 (Mile 3.7** and altitude **1950m)** is a road heading left or west, then south (**reset odometer at 0)**. After 500m, and as the road veers left, look straight ahead (west) to see a lone structure out in the open. At **Km .7 (Mile .4)** will be another watering trough on a corner. If you park there, you can walk along an old blocked-off road running due south to some **hill-top** structures which includes what appears to be ruins of a **kiva**. These are rather large too, having a 2-3 story complex.

If you continue west to **Km .8 (Mile .5)** there's a short side-road running northwest; park & walk 150m to the biggest ruins in the area. This is called the **Farm House Ruins**. It too was 2 or 3 stories high, and several timbers are still there, out in the open, after all these years (at least they appear to be original?). These are definitely related to the hill-top ruins. From the Farm House Ruins parking, walk

The place this writer calls **10 Ruins** and it's located in the northeastern corner of **Middle Park**. There are ruins of 10 moki houses or granaries here, plus a line of white images painted on above. This is the kind of pictographs you find along Salt Creek and other locations in The Needles.

These are the **2 Ruins** shown on the map just east of the **Rain Catchment**. The soot on the ceiling was there before the dwellings were put in place. There are some pottery fragments here too, but please leave them there for others to discover.

southwest to the top of a small **butte** and a couple of minor ruins. Continue driving west from Farm House on this side-road. At about **Km 1.6 (Mile 1)**, will be a campsite on the right or north. From there look south to see another small **butte** with a **moki house** on the north side and one level down from the top.

Now back to the main Ruin Park Road at Km 6 (Mile 3.7). Head northwest and drop down into **Pappys Pasture**. At Km 8.6 (Mile 5.3) look north about 300m to see some kind of **ruins** at ground level. Continue west another 300m and on the left or south will be a **small butte**. At the eastern base of that will be some pretty **good ruins** with several rooms at ground level.

Further west is **Bobbys Hole**--but there's one place on that road that stops even Jeeps--so you don't want to go there. You must have a **LR/HCV/4WD** to do that. If you were to take that road north, you'd have to go over Elephant Hill to get back home. Not many vehicles can do that.

Beef Basin's Southern Park

Let's go back to **Beef Basin Junction** and head south into Beef Basin itself, the largest of all the parks or meadowlands in this part of the country. Set your **odometer at 0**. Drive south nearly 1 1/2 kms and over a **divide** and down the other side. On the south or downhill side and at **Km 1.5 (Mile .9)** is a steep, **rough place** that require anyone with a lower slung vehicle to do some road work, maybe with a shovel, and/or move a few rocks around--this part is definitely for HC/4WD's. Coming back up on the way out will be more challenging. Most 4WD/SUV's won't have any trouble. This is the worst place on this whole trip.

At **Km 2.3 (Mile 1.4)** & **1939m** altitude is a road coming in from the right or west. This will be the end (or beginning) of the **Beef Basin Loop Road**. This tour will go in a clockwise direction, so this will be the end of the loop. Continue south. At **Km 2.9 (Mile 1.8)** and on the right will be **Stanley Spring**. It's been developed by cattlemen & the BLM. There you'll see 3 watering toughs, apparently with water year-round. On 7/4/2012 and in the middle of a long dry spell, the author found water in each.

Just south of Stanley Spring, and at **Km 3 (Mile 1.9)** will be a side-road heading to the left or east. This is the upper part of Beef Basin Wash. The author drove up there for a couple of kms to some rough roads, and returned. He didn't see anything interesting. Continue southwest on the Loop Road. **At Km 4 (Mile 2.5)** is another side-road heading left or east into **Calf Canyon**. Roughly halfway between there and the 5-way Junction, and where Ruin & Calf Canyon dry washes enter Beef Basin Wash, expect to find some deep sand; so drive fast and don't stop until you reach the other side.

At **Km 5.2 (Mile 3.2)** is the **5-Way Junction**. This is the southern end of the Beef Basin Spring Loop Road (discussed below), and the beginning of the **Ruin Canyon Road**. Let's go south from the **5-Way Junction** first. Take the road going straight ahead (the left track goes to some ruins 150m away) which leads directly to a **corral & granary or barn**; you have to drive right through the corral to reach the canyon beyond. After driving **2.7 kms (1.7 miles)** from the 5-Junction, turn right into the **West Fork** of Ruin Canyon. Continue another 600m and park. From there walk west on a trail to find some big **ridge-top ruins** that are 3 stories high, and one of the best sites in the area. There are other ruins further up Ruin Canyon, but walking is best to find these, which are about 1 km south of the bottom of this map.

Now back to the 5-Way Junction and driving west on the Beef Basin Loop Road. After about 300m and on the right will be a **granary** in the ledges to the north. Around the corner and at **Km 5.5 (Mile 3.4)** turn to the right for just a few meters then walk 50m to **2 ruins** or moki houses under a soot-covered overhang (see foto on page 353). The Anasazi apparently built their shelter where for thousands of years other nomadic people had camped and built campfires.

Moving west and at **Km 7.9 (Mile 4.9)** look left or south and just into the trees will be a line of dwellings (labeled **Big Ruins**) stretching east-west. There were 6-8 rooms here. Down the road west 1 km and at **Km 8.9 (Mile 5.6)** is a side-road to the left or south. Drive 100m to find several little **ridge-top ruins**. And from that same area, look north to see some low hills and/or ridges. On the east end of the closest little ridge, are signs of a rock-top dwelling of some kind. A little to the west, and to the north near elevation **6266T (1910m)** and **2-168**, are the remains of 2 other **crude rock-top ruins**.

Moving west, then north. At **Km 11.3 (Mile 7)** will be a road heading west. This will get you onto the **hiker's trail** going toward **Fable Valley** and upper Gypsum Canyon. That hike is covered in the author's other book, **Non-Technical Canyon Guide to the Colorado Plateau, 6th Ed.,** or later. About 150m north of that junction, look right or east up through the trees to see a well-preserved **granary (G)**.

Down the road north at **Km 11.9 (Mile 7.4)** is a small butte on the right or east. On the east side of that butte is a **dwelling** (labeled **R**) with a couple of pottery fragments lying around. Further along and at **Km 12.2 (Mile 7.6)** will be some crude low rock walls **(R)** to the left or west and just off the road 15m. From there you'll go down and cross Beef Basin Wash. Continue north. At **Km 14.1 (Mile 8.8)** will be the southern end of the road that connects Ruin Park and the Farm House Ruins, with Beef Basin. The author hasn't seen all that road, but it doesn't go through any meadows, so don't expect to find any ruins; but likely some rough roads. Anyway, right at that junction and just to the east is a small flat-topped **butte** capped with a **limestone** lens. On the east side of that are a couple of crude low-walled shelters made of limestone rocks. Who knows if this was built by Anasazi or earlier aborigines (?).

Continue east now. At **Kms 15.6 & 16 (Miles 9.7 & 9.9)** will be 2 little hills, both of which have **crude hill-top shelters** or man-made ruins of some kind. From there on, there's not much to see until you reach the beginning or end of the Beef Basin Loop Road at **Km 19.6 (Mile 12.2)**. Near the end of that loop road is the fenced enclosure shown on the map. From that junction back up to the west about 200m and turn left or southwest and onto the **Beef Basin Spring Road**. After **800m (.5 mile)** look right or west and on one of the ledges will be the remains of another shelter or dwelling **(R)**. On down the good road at **Km 2.1 (Mile 1.3)** will be a good campsite just 35-40m from **Beef Basin Spring**. There you'll find a trough, and perhaps water year-round, but purify or filter it first. If you continue to the south and to **Km 3.1 (Mile 1.9)**, you'll come to the **5-Way Junction** and the end of this loop-road. This is a good road all the way, as is the Beef Basin Loop Road.

Looking southeast at the **Rain Catchment**, otherwise known as a *guzzler*. The 2 steel storage tanks are to the left and just out of sight. From there, rain water flows by pipeline into **Ruin & Middle Parks** and into 7 watering troughs. In the far upper right-hand side of this picture is **House Park Butte**.

Perhaps the tallest ruins in the Beef Basin country is **The Castle**; it's located in about the middle of Ruin Park. It appears to have been a 3-story structure when it was built.

The **Hill-Top Ruins** located just southeast of the Farm House Ruins in the western end of Ruin Park. The depression in the foreground may have been a kiva; in the background may be a watch tower (?), and another dwelling or living quarters.

This is one corner of the **Farm House Ruins**. This may be the largest Anasazi site in the Beef Basin country. The logs stuck in the wall which created at least a 2nd story appear to be the originals; but after 800-900 hundred years it seems they would have rotted away being out in the open like this.

This structure is labeled **2 Ruins** on the map. It's located in the southern part of Beef Basin just west of the **5-Way Junction**. It appears the soot on the ceiling was there before the moki house was built.

In the southeast corner of Beef Basin and in **Ruin Canyon**, is what this writer calls the **Ridge-Top Ruins**. It's another 2-3 story affair and in pretty good condition. There are several more small granaries or moki houses in Ruin Canyon, located just off this map in the upper end of the canyon.

The Extinction of Wolves in Canyonlands & Southeastern Utah, and Trapper Roy Musselman

In the earliest days of cattle ranching in southeastern Utah, there were few if any wolves that anyone can remember. Then in 1908, according to Albert Lyman's story on **Big Foot** in the book, **L.D.S. Adventure Stories**, some cowboys in western Colorado chased a pack of 10 wolves across the Dolores River and into Utah in the vicinity of the La Sal Mountains. It was after that time that wolves began to cause problems for stockmen in Southeastern Utah.

That pack of 10 gradually increased and spread out. Some went south into Dry Valley (halfway between Moab & Monticello), others took up the greater Blue or Abajo Mountain range, and others roamed to the south almost to the San Juan River. It was in 1913 that we read the first of many wolf stories in the **Grand Valley Times** of Moab. Part of an article in the **March 21, 1913** issue went like this:

*A large gray wolf well known to the Monticello cattlemen because of the absence of one of its feet and whose tracks have many a time revealed the identity of the perpetrator of numberless slaughters of cattle, will no longer be a cause of worry.... **John Jones** brought in his hide yesterday which measured seven feet [2.1m] from tip to tip to the country clerk for bounty. He also brought the story of his experience chasing the wolf..... Two weeks ago Mr. Jones and other cowboys were in the East canyon country [just northeast of Monticello in Dry Valley] riding after their stock when they noticed the tracks of wolves..... One afternoon as Jones was riding into camp he saw two wolves some distance away. He galloped toward them and saw that because of the slightly crusted snow they could make small headway and he rapidly gained on the animals.*

Taking down his rope, for he had no gun, he evolved the scheme of roping one of the wolves, but a wolf is a wily creature and is not easily captured. Five times the cowboy threw his rope over the wolf but each time the animal freed himself with his hair standing on end and made for the man. Had it not been for the splendid horse Jones rode there might have been a different story to tell. After a fifth unsuccessful attempt to capture the animal, the man evaded the wolf's rush and made a smaller loop with his rope and threw it over the head of the beast. Swiftly turning his rope before the wolf could get out, he started to camp, on the run, dragging the animal and choking him to death.

In the very same issue of the paper (3/21/1913) another article went like this: **John Jackson,** who returned last week from his cattle range, states that wolves are playing havoc with the stock and that a number of cattle have been killed by the predatory beasts. Mr. Jackson states that he found eighteen head of cattle that had been killed and partly devoured by the wolves.

Part of John Jackson's range at the time was on the northwest slope of the Blue or Abajo Mountains and in the upper Indian Creek country.

At about this time period the cattle & sheepmen began to offer bounties on wolves and some even hired their own trappers. Originally the bounties ranged from $75 to $100 for each wolf hide. In 1915, a J.M. Redd Jr. collected bounty on 8 wolf hides.

In this same time period, Al & Jim Scorup had their cattle range in the country north of the San Juan River, east of the Colorado River, south of the Dark Canyon country and west of Comb Ridge and the Blue or Abajo Mountains. The **Scorups & Jacob Adams** decided to hire a trapper of their own, so they wrote letters to **Roy Musselman**, who at the time was trapping in the northwest (either Oregon or Washington?). Now in all the literature on the subject, there are 3 different dates given as to when Musselman and another guy named Sesson Sitton, arrived in Utah. An article in the **February 17, 1927** issue of **The Times Independent** (the Grand Valley Times ran to 1919, then renamed The Times Independent) states it was 1912; Rusty Musselman and the **Fall 1989** issue of **Blue Mountain Shadows** states 1914, and Albert Lyman thought is was 1916.

Besides tracking down and eliminating all wolves in the Scorup Brothers & Adams range, another reason for hiring Roy was to catch what people at the time thought was the biggest wolf of them all. This legendary wolf made a big circle and never stayed in one place very long. For this reason he was known by various names; the Big Wolf, Big Foot, Lobo, Peavine Wolf, Slickhorn Wolf, and the Comb Wash Wolf. The name **Big Foot** is the most common name.

Most accounts state that Big Foot had once put his toes in a trap. Fighting to escape, he ran downhill with the trap and stake bouncing behind him. As he came to a fork in the trail, he jumped over a small tree instead of going around it. The trap got caught jerking two of his toes off. When his foot healed, it was larger and deformed, so he was dubbed **"Big Foot"** from then on.

During the late 1910's, the government offered bounties for wolves and it eventually went up to $300 apiece, but local stockmen added another $1000 on top of that for Big Foot. With those kinds of rewards, there must have been trappers everywhere! They included salaried government trappers, as well as bounty hunters. One reason for the large bounties was the perception that a wolf will kill for the fun of it and will make a killing every night, leaving the rest of the carcass to the coyotes and other vermin. Since almost everybody in southeastern Utah was involved in the livestock business, everybody wanted to exterminate the wolves.

After several years, Big Foot's fateful day came on **March 24, 1920**. That's when he stepped into one of Roy Musselman's #9 traps and couldn't get loose. He fought the trap which was chained to a large stake for some time before pulling it out, then dragged the trap from Elk Ridge (somewhere around Natural Bridges?) all the way to the Slickhorn Canyon country on Cedar Mesa northwest of Mexican Hat. Musselman followed and 5 days later found him dead. The **April 15, 1920** issue of the **TI** ran the story:

Old Big Foot known as the "Peavine wolf" and the "Outlaw" which, during the past ten years has inflicted so much damage on stockmen in San Juan country, has at last been captured and the pelt has been delivered to the commissioners of San Juan county for bounty. In addition to the bounty paid by the state there has long been a standing offer by stockmen of a reward of $1000 for the capture of "Big Foot".

The animal was captured last week by Roy Musselman, a trapper on the south side of the Elk Mountains in San Juan county. The pelt measured eight feet [2.4m] from tip to tip. The wolf is supposed to be 12 years old, his fur is light, and when in life and seen at a distance appeared almost white.

Big Foot has ranged a circle of 100 miles [160 kms], according to stockmen, and was always followed by a pack of coyotes who fed upon the carcasses which the wolf left. Cowmen and Indians in the region in which the animal ranged say that his hoarse howl could be heard a distance of five miles [8 kms]. During the ravages among the livestock he has slain thousands of dollars worth of cattle, sheep and horses.

From other accounts, Big Foot may have been 16 years old, according to some who examined the condition of his teeth. His hide was left hanging on the wall of the Morgan Barton barn in Monticello, but some time later it burned down, destroying the famous hide.

With the passing of Big Foot, the threat to cattlemen from the wolves still didn't end. When the Scorup brothers sold out in March of 1918, they turned right around and a month later bought the Indian Creek company which was the cattle outfit immediately north of their former range. The move from south of Dark Canyon to the country north of there didn't change things because Big Foot had been in the Indian Creek country too. When the Scorups moved, Musselman moved with them because there were still wolves in the Indian Creek range as well.

Another article in the *TI* for **April 28, 1921** stated: *.....Already this spring [trappers] have killed fourteen wolves, exterminating a den in Hart draw and another on Island mesa. They are now laying their plans toward cleaning out four more wolves which are believed to inhabit that region.*

Hart Draw is just east of Hart Point and the Dugout Ranch. It runs north draining into Indian Creek just north of Dugout. It appears the last wolves taken in the Indian Creek country were taken on Hart Point. An article in the **March 30, 1922,** issue of the *TI* states:

Roy Musselman, the veteran trapper of the Indian creek country, has finally captured the last of a pack of wolves which he had been hunting in that neighborhood for the past year. He made gradual progress towards cleaning out the wolves, until finally there remained only one pair. Two months ago he caught the female, and then set out to get the remaining lobo. He at last succeeded in catching the wolf on Hart point, about a mile [1 1/2 kms] from the place where he trapped the female. The big wolf had made off with the trap and had jumped over a ledge of rock, but the trap caught in a crevice, suspending the lobo in the air where he was found stone dead by the trapper. The outlaw wolf measured eight feet [2.4m] from tip to tip.

By about the mid-1920's the wolves seemed to have been wiped out--at least they weren't causing as much damage to area stockmen. And the man mostly responsible for the extinction, or near extinction, of wolves in southeastern Utah was **Roy Musselman**. The **February 17, 1927,** issue of the *TI* ran a story about Roy written by a supporter who had known him for 11 years. It went like this:

The cattlemen and sheepmen of San Juan county declare that Roy Musselman, a county trapper of the Elk and Blue mountains, has no peer in the west as a trapper. Eleven years of close acquaintance with this mountaineer has established a confidence that cannot be shaken, in fact these stockmen of San Juan go as far as to say that no government trapper can be classed as his competitor.

Roy, as he is familiarly called by all the stockmen of this section, has trapped on Indian creek cattle range and Redd, Bayles and Nielson sheep range eleven years. During this time he has caught 2100 lynx or bob cats, 6000 coyotes, 1500 foxes, 6000 skunks, 43 wolves and 4 lions. This does not include innumerable badgers, civet cats, crows, etc. He has turned loose thousands of skunks caught during the summer because their furs are not valuable at that season.

Three of the wolves caught by this expert were puzzlers to the stockmen, to government trappers and to other bounty trappers for years before the advent of Mr. Musselman. These animals were so well known that they were christened Big Foot (also called Pea Vine and Slick Horn), Beef Basin, and Black Mesa. Despite the strenuous efforts of trappers and stockmen, these crafty wolves killed all the cattle and sheep they wanted. Mr. Musselman proved to be craftier, however, and was handsomely rewarded by the stockmen when he displayed before them the beautiful skins of these troublesome wolves.

Mr. Musselman apparently lives a lonely life for his only companions are Jack and Old Blue. Jack is a large grizzly dog of the Airedale breed and Old Blue is his faithful horse. These friends never desert him on his long hunts nor at his lonely cabin at **Mormon pasture** *[about 15 kms due south of upper Salt Creek]. He always carries a revolver in his pocket and a gun [rifle] on his saddle. He has become noted as a marksman as well as a trapper. His evenings are spent in his crude cabin which is artistically decorated with his trophies--the skins of all kinds of animals. His winters are spent at the Dugout, the capital ranch of the great Indian creek range, which is owned by J.A. Scorup and W.G. Somerville. Roy's honesty has become proverbial among his acquaintances.*

Mr. Musselman is a hard worker. He rides all day and in the evening he and his two companions return covered with fur and their booty. Other trappers may work as long and as hard as Roy does, but he seems to have discovered a secret unknown to others, for he is always successful. Some maintain that secret is in his bait; others declare it lies in his intense interest in the work; Roy says nothing, but he knowns. He has 200 traps out all the time and has little time to discuss his methods.

This trapper is a native of Pittsburgh, Pennsylvania. He has trapped in Utah fifteen years [since 1912?]. He has a large farm east of Monticello but he gives his entire time to trapping. Although he is congenial and friendly, he always attends strictly to his business.

Roy had a couple of brothers, one of which came to Utah. That was **Ross Musselman**, the dude wrangler, after which the **Musselman Arch** is named. Ross had a son named **Rusty** who was born in 1915. The now late Rusty Musselman came west with his father in 1929, and here's some of what he remembered about his Uncle Roy and the trapping of wolves:

Roy and his other brother named **Riff** *came west from Fairfield, Pennsylvania, and they were involved in that Oklahoma Strip when they had that land rush there. They were in that and they staked claims there but they weren't there too long. From there they went to Washington state. They were having problems up around Walla Walla, so he went up there and trapped until the wolf population down here was cleanin' these guys out--I mean they were killin' $600 or $800 worth of beef a night! You see, wolves would kill for the fun of it--and more than they can eat. Then the coyotes, foxes and badgers and everything else would follow and clean up after 'em.*

So finally the Scorups and Jacob Adams hired him to come down from Washington to take care of the wolves. That must have been in about 1914 or so. So he came down and followed one pack of wolves for nearly a year before he ever set a trap for 'em. When he started trappin', then he caught 'em fast. There was 14 of 'em that he caught; actually, a cowboy shot one of 'em, and he trapped 13 of 'em. But it was just a matter of weeks 'till he caught 'em all. He was quite a trapper.

I guess he was pretty lucky on Big Foot, because he caught the mate first. After he caught her, then Big Foot hung around. In a few days he caught him. But then he got loose with the trap and he trailed him clearn down to Slickhorn before he found it.

Now Ross Musselman was my dad, and we came later. We came in 1929. Roy and Riff were my uncles. Ross was Roy's younger brother. Ross had run a boys camp in east New Jersey for several years and was director of the camp. It handled about 400 boys. So his work had been with young people, and since he had poor health, he came out here for that reason. Then he decided to start a boys ranch out here. He built the Musselman Lodge, which is about 6 miles [10 kms] east and 2 miles [3 kms] south of Monticello. But all that got to be farmin' country and wasn't much of a ranch. We used to run dudes down in The Needles country too.

I trapped with Roy Musselman when I was young, in fact I think I trapped the last wolf in the county. Back in **1938**, I caught a wolf out by Vegi, out east of Monticello near the city dump. That was the year I was married. I used to have a foto of that--it showed my mother holding onto it as high as she could reach and the tail was draggin' on the ground. That was the last one that I know of that was trapped in the county. That ones fur was nearly white, a real pale yellow. Another time I saw a wolf running right across the mouth of Arch Canyon. This must have been in the 1950's.

As far as Roy Musselman is concerned, he never did get married, he remained a batchelor all his life. Most of his time was spent in the backwoods. In the summer of 1948 he had a stroke and was left semi-invalid. After that he stayed with his nephew Rusty Musselman in Monticello. He died at Rusty's home on September 5, 1948 at the age of 69. He was buried in the **Lockerby or Mountain View Cemetery** which is about 20 kms (12 miles) east of Monticello and just east of the small farming community of **Eastland**.

To add a personal touch to this story of wolves, this writer's father, Roland Kelsey worked as a lumberjack on the south slope of the Uinta Mountains in the summers of 1947 & '49. It was after one of those summers, he told us he was wandering through the timber one afternoon and saw a big lobo wolf on the other side of a little meadow. That could have been the last wolf in Utah until the 2000's, when they seem to have wandered down from the Yellowstone Park area and into extreme northern Utah.

Jim (Left) and **Al Scorup** (Right). This picture was taken sometime when these 2 brothers occupied the range just north of the San Juan River and before they bought the Dugout Ranch & the Indian Creek Cattle Company. (Steena Scorup Collection)

Roy Musselman the trapper and $8000 worth of wolf and coyote hides-- probably in the early 1920's (?). (Rusty Musselman Collection)

Swanny Kerby and Professional Rodeos

Back in 1990 & '91, the author talked to an old cowboy named **Swanny Kerby** on a couple of occasions about his life as a rancher growing up in Moab. He was familiar with local history and events beginning in the late 1920's and into the 1930's & '40's. He is quoted in at least half a dozen places throughout this book regarding the naming of such places as Musselman Arch; who made the trail up to Moki Mesa; and who built the trail in lower Little Canyon.

In the 1940's, he got into the rodeo business, and furnishing buckin' broncs and bulls for the local rodeos and became a well-known figure, so it was decided to include a story of his life in this 2nd Edition. Much of the information here about Swanny Kerby comes from his daughter **Vonna "Tiss" McDougall**, and his obituary.

Swanny Kerby was born in Moab, Utah on January 23, 1917. He was raised in Moab and graduated from Grand County High School in 1935. He married Verda Burdick in 1938. His father Ed Kerby helped him get into the cattle business. They were running cows and building trails in the canyons around Moab marking the beginning of his cowboy days.

According to Vonna, his daughter: *Dad's name was DeVaughn Arthur Kerby. He never used the middle name, but he used DeVaughn when growing up. That seemed to change, when, while he was in a high school production, he sang "Swanee River" and the name "Swanny" stuck. After he graduated and went on with his life, he was known as D.A. Swanny Kerby or just Swanny Kerby.*

*He had a history of being a jockey, but when he outgrew the opportunity to ride race horses due to his size, he decided he wanted to create something involving livestock and resembling a **wild west show**. Not sure where to begin; his employment at the time [1930's] provided him with a direction on how to get started. One of his jobs required him to "rid" the desert of the "wild horses". He was to kill the wild horses that he and Kenny Allred gathered for the Grazing Service [today's BLM]; bring back the ears and they would pay them per head. But, because of his love of horses, that wasn't a feasible way of doing business. So he and Kenny Allred began gathering the wild horses, but instead of shooting them, they brought them to his place where Swanny Park is today in [northeast] Moab. He broke the ones he could break, and the ones that were not breakable, became the first of his rodeo stock. This was the beginning of the **Bar T Rodeo Company**. All the horses he broke, he gave to every kid who wanted a horse; and the kids in Moab knew they could get a horse from Swanny. So the ones that didn't buck, he gave to the kids. We might say, this was the beginning of a horse adoption program like the BLM operates today.*

Swanny's first rodeo bulls came from wild cows he gathered along the river bottoms of the Colorado River. They were cross-bred with Brahma bulls. In the late '40's he went to Louisiana and brought back the first Brahma bull to this area. That first bull's name was Ferdinand,. His horns are displayed in the Dan O' Laurie Canyon Country Museum in Moab. Swanny began to cross-breed the Brahma bulls with wild hereford cows, and this was the start of his bucking bull program.

His first out of town rodeo was in 1945. Because he didn't own a livestock truck, he trailed his stock to Monticello. Future rodeos were held in Grand Junction, Colorado, and he would "trail" his livestock from Moab to the railroad in Thompson, Utah, and transport them to Colorado by train. He built the first rodeo grounds in Moab where Swanny Park now stands. During this time, he was still running cattle down along the rims and river bottoms of the Colorado, while putting together a rodeo company.

He left Moab in about 1952 and we moved to Grand Junction, [Colorado]. He and his family were there for a couple of years, then they bought the place in Salt Lake--but spent some winters at the Kinsley Ranch in Arizona--that was in the mid-50's. All the family went with him. It was a guest ranch between Tucson and Nogales. There, he produced rodeos through the winter months, then came back to Moab in the summertime. He produced rodeos in Utah, Colorado, Idaho and Wyoming until late in the fall each year. In 1954, they purchased a home and 10 acres of land at 3450 South 900 West in South Salt Lake, which became their home for 40 years.

Swanny & Verda, along with their son Bud, traveled all over the western part of the United States producing rodeos. They and their livestock participated in every National Finals Rodeo since it began in 1959. In 1995, Swanny & Verda purchased a ranch and built a new home near Mt. Pleasant in Sanpete County, Utah. Their son Bud, purchased their rodeo business in 1995, upon Swanny's retirement.

In 1997, he was one of only 2 men from the state of Utah to be inducted into the **Pro Rodeo Cowboy Hall of Fame**. The other one was Lewis Feild who lives near Payson in northern Utah. In 1999, his hometown of Moab gave him, what he often referred to as his greatest honor, as they re-named the local city park, **"Swanny City Park".** The seven acre park is part of his original ranch which once housed his famous horses & bulls.

Swanny passed away at 88, at his home in Mt. Pleasant, Utah, on December 15, 2005. He's buried in the Sunset Memorial Cemetery in his hometown of Moab, Utah.

See pictures of Swanny on the next page.

Church Rock If you're driving from Monticello to Moab on Highway 191, this is what you'll see just as you come to the turnoff to the Needles Highway. The La Sal Mountains are in the background to the north.

357

Above Left Swanny **Kerby** on the horse he called "Socks" at Canyonlands Rodeo in Moab in 1973.

Above Right Swanny again with some of his bulls that he cross-bred using Brahma bulls and wild Hereford cows.

Right The sign at the southeast corner of the park in Moab that's named after Swanny Kerby. The land where this park now sits once belonged to the Kerby family.

Moonshining in the Canyons & The John Romjue Story

Here's a brief summery of the laws which created, then ended, the **Prohibition Era** or the **Noble Experiment** as it was sometimes called: *The United States Senate proposed the 18th Amendment on December 18, 1917. Having been approved by 36 states, the 18th Amendment was ratified on January 16, 1919; it was certified on January 29, 1919; and went into effect on **January 17, 1920**.*

On **March 22, 1933**, President Franklin D. Roosevelt [FDR] signed into law an amendment to the Volstead Act known as the Cullen-Harrison Act, allowing the manufacture and sale of certain kinds of alcoholic beverages. On **December 5, 1933**, the ratification of the 21st Amendment repealed the 18th Amendment.

While interviewing many old timers and gathering information for this book, it seemed that everyone had a story to tell about some of the goings-on during the Prohibition days of the 1920's and early '30's. It seems everyone knew of, or had relatives, who had engaged in the moonshining or bootlegging business. Much of these activities took place out in the canyons and along the Green and Colorado Rivers.

Later on, and after hearing about the locations of so many of the stills, it was decided to use parts of a short chapter in a book written by the late **Pearl Biddlecome Marsing Baker**. This book is titled, ***Rim Flying Canyonlands, with Jim Hurst***. It was the Green River airport manager and pilot Jim Hurst telling his story to Pearl B. Baker. In it, Pearl includes one chapter on moonshining that was so interesting and amusing, the author has Pearl's permission to duplicate part of it.

For those who aren't up to date on terminology, the word **moonshining** means to illegally make home-brew whiskey; many times at night in the moonlight. ***bootlegging*** means to conceal illegally-made whiskey, sometimes in their cowboy boots, while delivering it to market. Here then is part of the story by Jim Hurst as told to Pearl B. Baker:

*There was some awful rotgut popskull stuff made and sold but it is my understanding that there were two "producers" who put out a product equal to and sometimes superior to refinery liquor. These were the **Frenchmen** at the old **Joe Nougier ranch** on the San Rafael [River], and **John Romjue**, who had relatives on the Spur [his sister Eva was Clyde, Leland and Delbert Tidwell's mother]. Both of these made really excellent potables when such was hard to come by.*

*John's still was in the little canyon coming into Horseshoe from the Spur, just above where the road crossed the canyon below the Indian Paintings [In an alcove just north of Water Canyon called **John's Hole**--but he had other stills in different locations over the years]. There used to be a spring in the head of it, and John often "ran a batch" there, concealing his equipment in the brush between operations.*

There were lots of these locations, out by springs in the canyons of Canyonlands and in the San Rafael Reef, along the San Rafael River and on down along the Green. I know of one rather major location on Junes Bottom, and on Nigger Bill Bottom [now Bull Bottom, which is more politically correct] there is an old dugout which once housed a still. A dugout was a good setup, I was told, because it kept the mash at an even temperature for better fermenting--the man pronounced this "fomenting". It was also somewhat concealing, although the locations were mostly so isolated that there wasn't much danger of their being discovered.

I have heard that W.F. Asimus, one of the early day merchants of Green River remarked one time that it just amazed him how much sugar and kegs it took to run a small cow outfit in this country. Having a few head of cattle out in the canyons seemed to be the standard excuse for spending so much time out there.

The livestock men had used five and ten gallon [19 & 38 liter] kegs to carry water from the springs out to the camps on the ranges for years. These containers were in much use long before the day of the moonshiner, and were still being used. They were common, but the thing that seemed to be in short supply was bottles. Gallon jugs, both glass and the old demijohns, stone jars of one, two or three gallons were not too hard to get, but the smaller deliveries sometimes had to go in fruit jars, which were easy to buy but had their drawbacks. Their weakness was getting the lid to seal down tightly enough to keep the contents safe, and besides leaking they were awkward to carry and easy to break. When you got hold of a few flasks, you just tried to hang onto them, and most everyone had his own.

There was an old joke in the country that you were eligible for your bootlegger's license when you could pour whiskey into a flask from a five-gallon [19 liter] keg and not spill a drop. If you have ever poured anything out of the bung-hole on the side of a keg, you know how funny this is--god! you can't pour it into a tub without spilling it, especially if the keg is almost full. It just sheets down the side of the keg, then it gets a big bubble of air and gushes out. That may have been a joke, but I doubt anyone ever wasted good liquor in the test.

Another Volstead (the Puritan who wrote & sponsored the bill for Prohibition) joke that had considerable validity, I understand, was the one about the tight nosepiece in the eyeglasses of the time. Drinking out of a fruit jar put the upper edge of the bottle at about the bridge of the nose, and it was said that at one time most everyone in the area had a deep crease between his eyes which he attributed to the tight nosepiece of his spectacles.

Leland Tidwell and I had been good friends for a long time, and from things he had said, I thought he might know something about this business. So the other day I ran onto him at the Oasis Café at lunch, and started questioning him. He told me right off that that's where he learned to weld and solder--making stills. He said that when he was just a young man he could earn $250 to $300 building a still. He'd put a roll of copper tubing and some oxygen and acetylene on a pack mule with various other essentials and take off across the desert some place, or go down the river in a boat. The Green River was one of the favorite places for a still, there was plenty of water to cool the "coils" and it was so damn inaccessible that the law just couldn't get there.

"Lee," I said, kidding him along a bit, "How much liquor could you make out of a hundred pounds [45 kgs] of sugar?"

"Oh," he laughed, "I didn't make any. I just knew where it was being made--most of it. But I imagine five to seven gallons [19 to 26 liters]."

"How about corn? Did it take some corn or grain?"

"Let me remember." He thought a moment. "You take an 800-gallon [3000 liter] vat--which is what most of them used--and put 50 pounds [22 kgs] of yeast and about 80 pounds [36 kgs] of corn and 1,000 pounds [450 kgs] of sugar in it and fill it up to about four to six inches [10 to 15 cms] from the top with water, then let it work."

"How long?"

"About ten days or two weeks. It will just boil and churn away in there, and when it stops you have to cook it off right away. You put the mash into a cooker, similar to a pressure cooker, only of course

you don't put any pressure on it, and heat it to a boil, just a simmer. It don't do any good to get it to a rolling boil, you just want it to cook slow. Simmer it along. The steam from this goes through your condensing coil, that copper tubing it took to make a still. You want to keep the coils cool, so that's the reason it was nice to have the still near a spring or somewhere you could run cold water over the coils."

"You just keep it cooking that way, and you can keep a stream about as big as the end of your little finger just running damn near all the time. Out of a vat of mash, you would get about 50 gallons [190 liters] of grain alcohol."

I already knew that they added water to this. They called it "cutting" instead of blending; and they brought it down to about 80 proof on a tester. I've heard they colored it with tobacco juice, although I have heard, too, that whiskey properly aged in a charred keg had the right color. Thus, they had about seventy or eighty gallons [265-300 liters] of drinking liquor worth about ten to fifteen dollars a gallon [3.75 liters] wholesale, out of a vat of mash.

Before the alcohol was cut, it was aged; that is, it was aged by the better moonshiners. Sometimes all the aging it got was running through a felt hat full of charcoal, which was supposed to take the fusel oil out of it. This was an undesirable, almost poisonous, combination of alcohols and fatty acids that gave the whiskey a bad taste and smell, and produced hangovers of epic proportions. The better product was buried for a few months in a charred keg.

Lee said one time he was coming to town horseback and met the Deputy Sheriff, Harry Bennett, who stopped him. "Say, Kid, would you like to earn a little money?" When Lee answered in the affirmative, the sheriff said, "Well, I understand that the Federal Agents are coming down in a few days to raid a still down there on the San Rafael. You can make yourself a little money just to go out there and move it out of the way."

Lee told me that he didn't know exactly where the still was, but he knew who owned it. As he remembered, he got in touch with another young fellow, Doyle Stilson, who thought, who knew where it was and they moved it. Lee told how he had to fix up a packsaddle on a burro to hold this great big old vat. Luckily everything was empty when they got there. He just chuckled when he told how they got this 800 gallon vat loaded on a burro and headed it out across the desert. You couldn't even see the burro, it looked like the vat was walking.

They moved it eight or ten miles [13 to 16 kms]. When the Federal Agents came down, all they could find was some ashes from the fires with which the mash had been cooked off. I heard that the owner of this still became a Mormon Bishop a few years ago, so you can see that moonshining was not a profession to be looked down on in those "dry" days.

Lee told me about one time he was coming to town horseback, and he saw a part of a keg sticking out of the sand. He had heard there was a keg buried there somewhere, and he was about half looking for it. He rode over and sure enough, that's what it was. The owner had buried it to age, and could never find it after the spring winds had wiped out all his markers.

Leland dug the keg out and took it to camp on his way back from town. It had been there three or four years, or maybe more, and had concentrated down a little bit; it was like syrup. He couldn't explain why it had gone thick like that, and I don't know why either.

A few days later George Franz came past the camp and being quite a judge of good liquor, Lee poured him out about half a water glass of this. He sat there sipping it and bragging about how good it was. Finally he said he had to go, and started to get up. He was just damn near paralyzed sitting right there in the chair.

"What the hell was that you gave me?" he demanded. Lee told him about digging up the keg. "It's the best tasting whiskey I ever drank," George said, "but it sure is powerful."

Not all of the old caches in this country were buried by Butch Cassidy and the Wild Bunch. Men who know, tell me that if a person could find some of this old whiskey, especially the kind that was good in the beginning, he would have something worth waiting for. They say that the whiskey buried in kegs would undoubtedly be evaporated by this time, but if you could come upon a gallon jug, with a tight cork, you would have a treasure indeed.

As you're wandering around Canyonlands, be aware of some of the still locations mentioned, and be on the lookout for a keg buried in the sand.

Here's another short story about John Romjue and **June Marsing**, the man who later settled on Wiley's Bottom (since then it's been known as **Junes Bottom**) with his family in the spring of 1933. In fact, it was in March, 1933, that Prohibition came to an end. Telling this story is the late **Bob Marsing**, the only son of June Marsing. Here's what Bob remembered:

Dad and many others did some moonshining out on The Spur. John Romjue was one and he lived out there. We called him Uncle John. He made the best moonshine liquor in the country. Dad would go out there and get that moonshine and bring it back and sell it [this was before he took the family to Willy's/Junes Bottom]. Uncle John made most of it and Dad sold it You had to be good at that. You had to know what you were doing. Dad and Uncle Harv [Marsing], and I imagine a dozen other guys that was starvin' to death [because of the Depression], would take it out and sell it.

I've talked to the rest of the family since that time including my father, and he did make whiskey. In fact, he and John Romjue worked together during Prohibition days. Some of my uncles know where some of the stills were located. They were probably on some of the river bars and possibly even down Horsethief Canyon. I've heard my dad talk about a still at Keg Springs.

My dad told me he and John Romjue had their still rigged to where they could tear it down and haul it on 3 pack horses. They would run off a batch and I think they had to cook it down for about 24 hours. This would kick off a lot of smoke, so they would start at night when the smoke couldn't be seen, and they'd cook it all that night, and then the next day would hide the whiskey and tear down the still and put it on the pack horses and be gone.

Here was one way to sell bootleg whiskey: Dad would take it out in the desert and bury it, then he'd go to town and if somebody wanted to buy it, he'd tell them where it was buried. Then the buyer would have to go out and get it. That way Dad wasn't involved. For Dad, the bootlegging was all over and done with before we got to Junes Bottom. On Junes Bottom, it was strictly ranching and farming, but as a farm, it was a losing proposition, but people had to make a living. It was during the beginning of the Great Depression they was doing most of the bootlegging. Then Roosevelt came in, put in the WPA and helped people to make a living. And he abolished Prohibition.

The John Romjue Story

Here's a brief life story of one of the best moonshiners in southeastern Utah, **John Romjue**. Most of this information comes from La Var Wells of Hanksville, and Ila Mae & Frank, Delbert Tidwell's daughter & son:

John Henry Romjue was born in Days Creek, Oregon, August 10, 1865. In April 1901 he married Minnie Celestela Shick. At that time he was 36 years old, she was only 17. Soon, they had one daughter named **Rose Hazel Romjue**; she was born July 8, 1902 in Hefner, Oregon. About 3 years later, Minnie took Hazel and left John for a younger man. When John found out where they were, he went after them and took his daughter. Hazel was about 3 years old at the time and she remembered when this all happened. She told me (La Var Wells) about it. She remembered the ferry trip she was on--apparently they were on an island (?).

John raised Hazel with the help of his parents who had settled in Wellington, Utah. No one knows when John's parents came to Utah.

John had 2 sisters; one was Evaline or **Eva Romjue** and her first husband's last name was Loughery. They had one son named **Clyde**. When Loughery died of an accidental shooting, Eva married Frank Tidwell; and together they had 2 sons, **Delbert and Leland**. Clyde took the name Tidwell (willingly or not) after his stepfather, Frank Tidwell, died of the flu on Christmas Eve, 1918. (This is the same Clyde Tidwell **Pearl B. Baker** almost married, and may have been murdered on Tidwell Bottom. Read more in the chapter about the Range War, etc. starting on page 368)

John's other sister was **Lina** Romjue. Lina married a guy name Missmer and they lived in Rifle, Colorado for a while, then they divorced and she high-tailed-it to Watsonville, California near Ft. Ord with one daughter. According to Frank Tidwell, in 1939, Lina visited the Uncle John & Eva and the Tidwells when they were on The Spur. The Tidwells have many pictures of the 3 Romjue siblings together, some of which may have been taken during Lina's visit that summer as they all looked like they were in their 70's.

As John got older, he lived in Wellington for several years after the Tidwells left The Spur in 1945.

Now back to John's daughter Hazel. Later, and as a young adult, she married Ernest Prettyman. They had 6 children and all of them are dead now. No one left a written family history, but they all told stories. Ernest Prettyman died of a heart attack at age 48.

After that Hazel, married David Smithson and they lived up on Gordon Creek which is west of Price and Carbonville. Smithson had a little 35 acre farm but after a few years, they moved down to Carbonville, which is halfway between Price and Helper. In John's last years, he lived with his daughter Hazel, and he died in her home in Carbonville. John Romjue died October 22, 1956 at 91 years of age, and he was buried in the Wellington, Utah Cemetery on October 25, 1956.

Left Romjue Family L to R Lina Romjue, John Romjue, Eva Romjue Loughery Tidwell and family friend, Marvel Chinn. This foto was taken sometime in the late 1930's or early '40's (?). (Ila Mae Tidwell Clark Collection)

Below L to R Eva Romjue Loughery Tidwell, Mary & Delbert Tidwell and June Marsing, somewhere on **The Spur** in 1930. (Ned Chaffin Collection)

Native Americans in Canyonlands National Park and Vicinity

Some archaeological sites in Canyonlands National Park are along the Green and Colorado Rivers. Along the Green River the best places to see ruins of granaries, dwellings or moki houses are at **Fort & Valentine Bottoms** (and just across the river near the mouth of **Deer Canyon**), **Turks Head Bottom**, and at the mouth of **Jasper Canyon**. On the Colorado River side, the best places are at **Big Bottom** (across the river from the mouth of Lathrop Canyon), at the mouth of **Indian Creek**, and on what this author calls **Anasazi Bottom**, located on the southern part of The Loop. One main reason these people found the river bottoms better was the rich soils which allowed them to grow corn, beans and squash. Being next to the rivers made watering their crops easy as well.

There are other scattered locations in areas back from the rivers as well. These include **rock art panels**, mostly pictographs, in **Horseshoe, Clearwater, Range & Pictograph Fork of Horse Canyons** in the Robbers Roost & Maze Country west of The Confluence. Rock art which includes petroglyphs are scattered everywhere. The most favorable sites for dwellings in The Needles Country is in **Horse, Davis, Lavender** and especially along **upper Salt Creek** below or north of Cathedral Butte.

There are several different ancient cultures represented in the area of Canyonlands National Park. To the south are the various **Anasazi Cultures**. Most of these are in Arizona and New Mexico, but the **Mesa Verde Anasazi**, which covered the Four Corners region, extended north to include the southern half of Canyonlands NP. They were mostly on the east side of the Colorado River and south of The Confluence, but some made the crossing and went up the Green River a ways. Fort Bottom seems to be as far north as they got.

To the north and west were the **Fremont Indians**, believed to be a Shoshoni speaking group. They were scattered throughout Canyonlands, and extended their range to the Abajo Mountains just south of this map. To the west was the **Sevier Culture**, sometimes called the **Sevier Fremont or Great Basin Fremont**. No one as yet has completely standardized these various names. They were west of both the Green and Colorado Rivers.

The cultures above were all in this region from roughly 2000 years ago up to 1250 AD, or shortly thereafter. But covering this entire region was an even older culture which most archaeologists call the **Archaic Culture**. They entered as early as 8000 to 9000 years ago, but not a lot is known about them; except they were the ones who created the mostly-red colored paintings seen at the Great Gallery in Horseshoe Canyon and other nearby areas as mentioned above.

Concerning the main sites along the river, one study done by William A. Lucius of the University of Utah Anthropology Department, stated: *Of the 55 sites recorded along the Green River, 45 could be securely attributed to Anasazi horticulturists. Over half--28--were storage sites or habitation and rock shelter sites with storage facilities. It seems that the Fremonts were more scattered, and since they did less in the way of agriculture, didn't depend on water in the same way the Anasazi did.*

As for dating some of the sites, the same study further stated: *Pottery found at the river sites indicated that the great bulk of the occupation is traceable--as in The Needles District--to the Pueblo II/Early Pueblo III Anasazi expansion that occurred at about 1075 to 1150 A.D.(Sharrock 1966). The lack of large habitation sites and midden material also indicates that the majority of the occupation occurred within a short time span--perhaps 50 years--and involved small groups, possibly inhabiting the sites only seasonally to plant and harvest their crops.*

For more information on these ancient cultures and their ruins & rock art, consult some of the literature listed under **Further Reading** in the back of this book. Also, read the chapter on Salt Creek, and Horse, Davis & Lavender Canyons, **Maps 31 & 32**, for more information on the sites in that region.

These are the ruins labeled **2 Dwellings** on **Map 34**, and they're in the northeast part of **Middle Park**. One of these is a moki house with soot inside; the other a granary. Pottery fragments are there too.

Native Americans in Canyonlands National Park and Vicinity

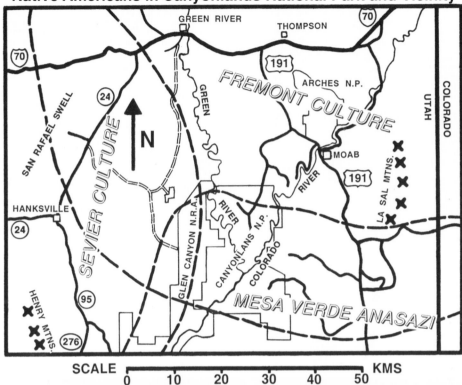

Below one of the Anasazi Ruins in **Big Pocket** in the upper end of **Salt Creek**, is this collection of potsherds or pottery fragments. Take pictures but please leave them for others to enjoy. Besides, it's against the law to walk away with stuff like this.

Geology of Canyonlands National Park and Vicinity

Observe the geology cross-section on the opposite page. At the top is the Mancos Shale Formation. This is seen in the blue-gray clay hills surrounding and just to the north of the town of Green River and Interstate Highway 70. If you were to follow the Green River down to The Confluence & Spanish Bottom, you would see all of the formations shown here. As you travel, each area map will have a small geology cross-section insert or two. They show the local formations along the way.

As you observe the formations listed, and compare them with other geology maps, you may find some differences. Some older maps of this region show the Rico Formation as being part of the lower Cutler or as being separate from and below the Cutler. The geology maps shown in the latest edition of the book, *Geology of Utah's Parks and Monuments* published by the Utah Geological Association, shows these same beds as **Elephant Canyon Formation** and/or **Halgaito Shale**. Some maps also show an Upper Member of the Hermosa Group, while newer map shows the same beds as the **Honaker Trail Formation**. The Rico has been taken out and thrown to the east into Colorado where it belongs.

In this region, there are still other changes in some local geology maps. Throughout the Colorado Plateau, the formation where most of the uranium mining took place was in the middle part of the Chinle. During the 1950's Uranium Boom around Moab, apparently most miners called this thin layer the Shinarump Member of the Chinle Formation. However, in recent years geologists have had a pow wow on the subject and now call this uranium hot bed north of White Canyon (which drains into northern Lake Powell from the east) the **Moss Back Member**. South of White Canyon and Highway 95, they call a very similar bed the **Shinarump Member**. The apparent reason for this renaming is a slight difference in age and it's situated in a different place or layer within the Chinle.

Also, in most parts of the Colorado Plateau especially south and west of this area, geologists have found another distinct layer immediately above the Navajo; that is now called the **Page Sandstone**. Almost no maps have it because it's newly named, it comes and goes in different regions, and is a thin layer even where it does exist. It's only found on newer and smaller scale geology maps. But nothing has really changed for 180 million years, except for some names.

The **Mi Vida Mine** which is where **Charley Steen** struck it rich on **July 6, 1952**. Just barely visible on the right is a little train with ore cars coming out of a tunnel (unseen). The tracks lead to the red structure where the ore was dumped into trucks which hauled it to Moab and the former Atlas Mill for processing. The rock formation of the cliffs above is the Wingate Sandstone and below that the Chinle. The mine is found in the Moss Back Member of the Chinle Formation. (David Bagshaw Collection)

Geology Cross Section: Canyonlands National Park & Vicinity

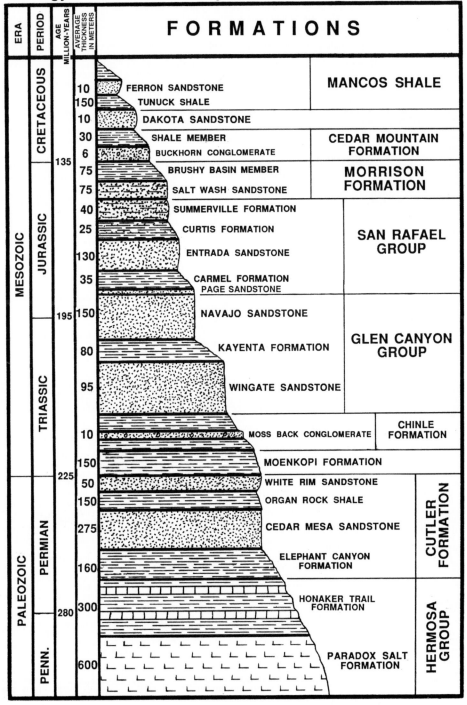

ERA	PERIOD	AGE MILLION-YEARS	AVERAGE THICKNESS IN METERS	FORMATIONS	
MESOZOIC	CRETACEOUS		10	FERRON SANDSTONE	MANCOS SHALE
			150	TUNUCK SHALE	
			10	DAKOTA SANDSTONE	
		135	30	SHALE MEMBER	CEDAR MOUNTAIN FORMATION
			6	BUCKHORN CONGLOMERATE	
			75	BRUSHY BASIN MEMBER	MORRISON FORMATION
			75	SALT WASH SANDSTONE	
	JURASSIC		40	SUMMERVILLE FORMATION	SAN RAFAEL GROUP
			25	CURTIS FORMATION	
			130	ENTRADA SANDSTONE	
			35	CARMEL FORMATION / PAGE SANDSTONE	
		195	150	NAVAJO SANDSTONE	GLEN CANYON GROUP
			80	KAYENTA FORMATION	
	TRIASSIC		95	WINGATE SANDSTONE	
			10	MOSS BACK CONGLOMERATE	CHINLE FORMATION
		225	150	MOENKOPI FORMATION	
PALEOZOIC	PERMIAN		50	WHITE RIM SANDSTONE	CUTLER FORMATION
			150	ORGAN ROCK SHALE	
			275	CEDAR MESA SANDSTONE	
			160	ELEPHANT CANYON FORMATION	
		280	300	HONAKER TRAIL FORMATION	HERMOSA GROUP
	PENN.		600	PARADOX SALT FORMATION	

Charley Steen and the Uranium Boom in Southeastern Utah

Most people who come to Moab and Canyonlands and who have been hiking, biking or 4-wheeling, will have seen a maze of old roads running along the talus slopes below the big walls formed by the Wingate Sandstone. These are all old mining roads and for the most part ran to uranium mines in the Moss Back Member of the Chinle Formation.

The history of uranium mining in southeastern Utah is too long to tell here, but there's room for a few highlights. Much of this information comes from 3 issues of **Canyon Legacy**, which is the *Journal of the Dan O'Laurie Museum of Moab*. They are the Spring, Summer and Fall/Winter of 2006. Some information comes from the internet, but some of that must be taken with a little caution.

One starting point would be that the United State needed to develop a domestic source for uranium after World War II which would be used not only for atomic bombs, but in nuclear power plants as well. Here's part of one quote from the **Spring, 2006** issue of **Canyon Legacy:**

The Atomic Energy Commission (AEC) announced a domestic procurement program designed to stimulate prospecting and to build a domestic uranium mining industry in April 1948. Private industry would be tasked with finding, mining, and processing uranium ores. The AEC would assist by making geologic surveys, furnishing free testing and assaying services, and, most important, guaranteeing the market.

In other words the AEC would subsidize the price of uranium. This is what got the ball rolling and there were hundreds of prospectors crawling all over the mesas and canyons of southeastern Utah using **geiger counters** which detect radioactive material. There was a lot of low grade uranium found and claims made, but then came Charley Steen.

Charles A. Steen was born in Texas in 1919, entered college in 1940, and ended up with a degree in geology from what would later be the U. of Texas at El Paso (UTEP) in 1943. Poor eyesight kept him out of World War II, so he worked as a geologist in Bolivia and Peru before returning to Texas in 1945.

He spent one year at the U. of Chicago, then spent 2 years working for Standard Oil Company of Indiana before being fired for insubordination--he then had trouble getting a job in the oil industry. In the late 1940's, and with the coming of the AEC and its effort to end buying uranium from Canada and the Belgian Congo, Charley borrowed $1000 from his mother and headed for the Colorado Plateau.

Charley didn't use a geiger counter, he had different ideas; that was the reason he didn't get on well with other geologists or companies. Instead he used a second-hand drilling rig and drilled for radioactive stuff similar to how they did it in the oil industry. He started in Dove Creek, Colorado, then moved into a tarpaper shack in Cisco, Utah (south of I-70 near the Colorado state line).

Ray Tibbetts of Moab remembered a few things about the big strike and Charley Steen like this: *They were hole'n up at Cisco, they had a cabin out there and they was poor as church mice, him and his wife and 3 kids. They was tryin' to find ore down in Yellow Cat [east of Arches NM], then he went south to the Big Indian Mining District south of the La Sal Mountains......*

One day he came back to Cisco and he had some drill cores in the back of his truck--I talked to the old boy that was there and he said, "What have you got in there", and Charley said, "I got some cores I drilled and I don't know if they're any good", and the guy said, "Let me check", and when he got his geiger counter, they were hotter'n hell; they were almost pitchblende (uraninite)! That's when he first hit it, and he wasn't even sure what he had it.

That was on **July 6, 1952**. Steen had found a massive, high grade uranium deposit near the Big Indian Wash of Lisbon Valley. He named it the *Mi Vida Mine* (My Life), and it was the first big strike of the Uranium Boom. Steen organized a company to mine it himself, instead of selling it to some big mining company--and made millions! This of course started a real "Uranium Rush or Boom" of prospectors in the region similar to the Gold Rush of 1849 in California.

With all the attention on prospecting and mining, the AEC's procurement program was almost too successful, so on **May 24, 1956**, they made the announcement to alter its policy of subsidizing uranium. By **late 1957**, another announcement stated; *it no longer is in the interest of the government to expand production of uranium concentrate.* Then, on **November 24, 1958**, *in order to prevent further expansion of production under its essentially unlimited purchase commitment, the AEC redefined its procurement program by withdrawing portions of the program announced in May 1956..... That announcement effectively shut down exploration activities in the industry.* And the "Uranium Boom" was history.

But there was still some mining and milling going on after that. During the 'Boom, there were uranium mills built at Monticello, White Canyon (now under the waters of Lake Powell and near today's Hite), Mexican Hat and the mill just north of Moab on the north bank of the Colorado River (the tailings of which they're cleaning up today--2013). The Moab mill started operations in **October, 1956**, but on August 1, 1962, a change in ownership began and it was then called the **Atlas Mill**. Years later and due to low prices of uranium, Atlas Minerals closed all of its remaining mines, as well as its Moab mill, in **March 1984**. It was about that time tourism started booming.

Now to finish hard-headed Charley Steen's story. Once his wealth started coming, he built a then-$250,000 house (more like a million $ today!) to replace his rented tarpaper shack. He had big parties in the airport hanger and invited the whole town to come. He gave a lot of money for the building of a new hospital, in addition to giving land to churches & schools. In 1958, he was elected to the Utah State Senate, but quickly became disillusioned with politics; he resigned in 1961 and moved to a ranch near Reno, Nevada.

By then the Uranium Boom was over and the prices for uranium dropped, so he sold his mining interests and reinvested it in a marble quarry, airplane factory and real estate, but he somehow had misfortunes, maybe mismanagement, and according to one internet source, declared bankruptcy in 1968 after the IRS grabbed his assets to pay back taxes. In 1971, he suffered a head injury in a copper prospect. Toward the end, he had Alzheimer's and died basically penniless January 1, 2006 in Loveland, Colorado.

Charley Steen's legacy still lives on in Moab. In the north end of town next to the main highway, and on a high outcropping to the east, you can still see his home. It's now used as a kind of museum and a restaurant called the **Sunset Grill;** and of course the public is invited to drive up there. Inside are many pictures of Charley, his family and some of his mines on the walls. Outside is the same Jeep he had when he struck it rich in 1952. The house is still owned by one of his sons but other people are running the restaurant which is open in the evenings only.

Left The former **home of Charley Steen** perched on a hill in the north end of Moab at 900 N. Highway 191. It's still owned by a member of the Steen family, but it's being leased to someone using it as a restaurant, the **Sunset Grill**. It's only open in the evenings after 5pm. **Right Charley Steen** near his **Mi Vida Mine** in the 1950's (snapped from a picture on a wall of Charley's home/restaurant).

Immediately behind the former home of Charley Steen on the hill in north Moab, is this 1940's genuine **Jeep**. It's the one Charley was using when he struck it rich on **July 6, 1952**. That first bore hole into a mining claim was later named the **Mi Vida Mine**.

History of Tidwell Bottom: Range War of 1924-25, & the Stories of Clyde Tidwell, Bill Tibbetts, John Jackson & Bill Hinton

Tidwell Bottom

Directly across the river from the boat ramp near the mouth of **Mineral Canyon** is what everyone now calls **Tidwell Bottom**. This particular place has some of the most interesting history of any bottom along the Green River. A total of 5 different individuals made attempts to settle on it. Here's some of the history of this place which includes a number of interesting characters.

It appears the first name that was attached to this place was either **Foot** or **Phil Foote Bottom**. Probably the best source for some of this early history is from testimonies at the **Colorado River Bed Case hearings** in the fall of 1929. The USA and the state of Utah were in court trying to determine who owned the river bottoms, if the rivers were navigable and who owned the mineral rights below, and who could collect taxes. One of those testifying was a **Henry E. Blake**. Part of his testimony went like this:

.....*The place I have referred to as Woodruff is at* **Foot Bottom**, *some six or eight miles [10 to 13 kms] above Fort Bottom. It was a large bottom that had been squatted on by a surveyor named Robert Foot, who expected to make a fruit ranch there and built a two story frame house, the lumber for which was rafted down the river from the town of Green River or from the [Wimmer] ranch [Ruby Ranch].*

It appears from this testimony that the name Foot was applied first, then Woodruff Bottom. It's also possible that Blake may have some last names mixed-up, because his testimony fits a surveyor named **Robert Woodruff** perfectly (?). Blake had landed there in about 1909 while traveling the river with his 13 year-old son.

Another man named **William (Bill) F. Reeder** also testified and spoke of going downriver with E.T. Wolverton and returning: *The purpose of that trip was to take some people from Indiana down the river to show them the land down there. The idea was to show them the river and raise stock on it. There are several large bottoms down there, one called the Townsite [now Anderson] Bottom, and one called the* **Phil Foote Bottom**. *The Phil Foote Bottom contains several hundred acres.*

He took this trip sometime in 1905 or '06, just when the land was being sold around Green River, Elgin and Little Valley which started the peach boom there. During this time period, many people from the mid-west were lured to Utah by promoters. When they arrived in Green River, many went downriver looking for places to settle and homestead.

It's easy to assume that both the Foot and Phil Foote Bottoms spoken of here are the same (?). However, in the book by the Kolb Brothers who duplicated J.W. Powell's trip in 1911, they tell a story about a Phil Foote who was a stagecoach robber and gambler who broke out of jail in Salt Lake City and headed down the river. Along with a partner, they stole a rowboat in Green River and got to Cataract Canyon, only to lose everything in the rapids. They eventually made it to Hite, part way by raft--partly on foot. At a later date, this Phil Foote was killed in Nevada. No date was given on this story, but it must have been long before the 1911 expedition. This Phil Foote certainly could have tried to settle on this bottom, but no evidences exists that he did.

Sometime later, another man entered the picture. This was **Robert Woodruff** the surveyor who lived in Green River from sometime just after the turn of the century (1900) until his death in December, 1915. His name keeps popping up in the old newspapers articles in conjunction with some of the early-day rivermen like Wolverton, Oppenheimer and Wimmer. The story presented by Blake above, fits Robert Woodruff more than a Robert Foot (?).

Woodruff was a well-known surveyor who had something to do with the building of the first bridges over the rivers at Green River and Moab and some of the roads between these 2 towns. And since his name is mentioned so often in the Moab newspaper, one is led to believe that maybe it was Woodruff instead of Foot who may have built the house and tried to make a fruit farm on this bottom. In an interview with Leland Tidwell of Green River in 1973, he stated: *It is sometimes called Tidwell Bottom, but we called it Woodruff. Old man Woodruff had built a house back a little from the river, but [later] we built a cabin right on the bank.......* It seems that Woodruff would have tried to settle the place sometime between about 1905 and 1908 or '09, because most of the promoting of the Green River area was in those 3 or 4 years. It was in 1919 or '20, when the Tidwells first arrived on the river bottoms and The Spur.

Now when Milton Oppenheimer's boat the **Paddy Ross**, was launched and made its maiden voyage down the Green River in mid-November, 1907, a Robert Woodruff hired it to take 1 1/2 tons of supplies downriver to what the **Grand Valley Times, November 22, 1907** issue called **Fort Bottom**. This is 11 miles/18 kms below today's Tidwell Bottom. It sounds as though Woodruff either got off at what is now Tidwell Bottom, or he may have gone on down to Fort Bottom as the paper suggests (?). However, no one the author talked to ever thought Fort Bottom was ever settled. Besides, the log cabin on Fort Bottom was built by Mark Walker, and used only as a line cabin for cowboys while running cows in the area.

There are many conflicting stories about this bottom, making its early history very confusing, but it appears that someone with the name of either Phil Foote or Robert Foot, first made an attempt to live there. Then sometime later, Robert Woodruff the surveyor was involved, then the Tidwells were living there on 2 different occasions. The last person there was a guy named Jack "Beans" Milling, but that will be discussed later. The Tidwells were probably the most important people to have tried to settle this bottom, therefore it carries their name. The following section is part of their history.

The Death/Murder of Clyde Tidwell

One of the most interesting and almost forgotten events to have happened on **Tidwell Bottom** and perhaps this whole section of river, occurred in December, 1925. It involves the death, and perhaps murder, of **Clyde (Loughery) Tidwell**.

In the fall of 1991, about a month after the 1st Edition of this writers book, *River Guide to Canyonlands National Park & Vicinity* came out, the author got a letter from Mr. and Mrs. **Alex Tidwell** who were working on the Dunham (Ruby) Ranch at the time (winter of 1991-92). Alex is a nephew of the Tidwells involved in this story. The author paid them a visit, and Alex stated that the ending to this chapter has yet to be written and that I should see his mother, Crystal. At the end of this part on Clyde Tidwell will be Crystal Tidwell's statement of what *may have happened* to him.

Clyde was born on May 2, 1891 in Craig, Colorado, to William and Eva Romjue Loughery. The rest of his life story is filled in below. This was so long ago that few people alive today ever heard of him, much less can recall any accurate details to his story. But there was one person who remembered well and had a very good account of at least part of the event. This is the late **Pearl Biddlecome Marsing**

Baker who passed away on December 19, 1992. Pearl was born in 1907 and grew up on the Robbers Roost (now Ekker) Ranch east of Hanksville in the middle of the Roost Country. She wrote several books about her life in the Roost and the region including ***The Wild Bunch at Robbers Roost***, ***Robbers Roost Recollections***, **Rim Flying Canyonlands with Jim Hurst**, and **Trail on the Water** (Some of the history of the Robbers Roost Ranch is told in the new 3rd Edition of this writer's book, **Hiking & Exploring Utah's Henry Mountains & Robbers Roost**). When asked to relate all she knew about Clyde, she decided to think it over and write a letter, rather than being interviewed on tape. Here is her thoughtful letter:

Dear Mike,   *May 30, 1990*
You asked me about Clyde Tidwell, since his mysterious death is part of your book on the Green River. You indicated that this might be a personal sidelight that would enhance the book's general interest. And, of course, the personal element is what makes it so difficult for me to tell you the story.
Probably I knew Clyde Tidwell (his real name was Loughery) better than anyone outside his immediate family; we were close in my late teens and had planned to be married as soon as I finished school. My family liked him--everybody liked him. Their only objection was that he was older than I and they wanted me to have a girlhood before I was married. But my girlhood wasn't panning out all that well; from the time I was fourteen or fifteen life was pretty rough for me, but that is another story.
I really don't know too much of Clyde's background. When he was a baby his parents came west in a covered wagon. Near Wellington [Utah, near Price] his father pulled a rifle from the wagon; it discharged and he was badly wounded. He lived only a few days, and Clyde's mother [Eva Romjue] had no choice but to stay where she was. She was well educated, and began teaching school until she married Frank Tidwell. Their eldest son and his father [Frank] died in the flu epidemic [1918-19] while Clyde was in service in WW I. Delbert, Leland and Dolphie were younger, and when Clyde returned home, he sort of took over the family to raise [Eva Loughery Tidwell was a sister to John Romjue the moonshiner].
Clyde rarely talked about his service, but it left a deep mark on him. He was an orderly, caring for the wounded, and his experiences seemed to have left him over-compassionate and caring. He was very much of a loner, and when the Tidwells moved their cattle to The Spur shortly after he came home, he always stayed with the cattle.
Chaffins took their cattle Under the Ledge about the same time, and the Chaffin boys and the Tidwells spent a good deal of time at our place at Robbers Roost. It was sort of central, and the latch string was always out [In other words, the door was always unlocked].
As near as I can remember--this was almost 70 years ago!--Clyde and I became close at Dolphie's funeral. Dolphie [Tidwell] was at our ranch late in the fall when he became sick. He was in too much pain to ride, so my father brought him to town in the wagon. He put Dolphie on the train at Green River, and the Tidwells got on at Wellington. Dolphie had a ruptured appendix, and although he lived a day or two after he reached the hospital in Salt Lake City, there was no way in those days to save him.
My mother, sister and I went to his funeral, staying at the Tidwells and I was with Clyde most of the time. From then on we were together whenever we could be, and he was the only one I knew who treated me as grown up, and we planned to be married as soon as we could. From time to time, during the summer, Clyde would ride over and stay a day or two and then go back to The Spur. We never wrote, I never had a letter from him, and I can't ever remember writing one; we just enjoyed what time together we could manage.
I remember one time when I was about 17, we were camped at the Point of Rocks on Twin Corral

Clyde (Loughery) Tidwell age 15 in 1906 (Ila Mae Tidwell Foto); and **Pearl Biddlecome Marsing Baker** in about 1932 at age 25 while living and managing the old Joe Biddlecome or Robbers Roost Ranch (Pearl B. M. Baker Collection)

Clyde (Loughery) Tidwell (right) in Green River in about 1922 at the age 31 (Ila Mae Tidwell Clark Collection)

[Flat] and Clyde rode in for a visit. He joined the crew for a day or two, along with me. One morning my father said someone would have to check the water at the Roost Spring. Most of his stock ran in the Roost Flats, and if a cow broke through the fence around the spring and trampled the head box and flume out, a few days would almost put him out of business. I suggested that Clyde and I check it since it would give me a chance to ride a colt I was breaking for an easier day for the horse than on circle.

It had rained early that morning, and the world was fresh and cool. There was no hurry, and we loafed along all day, riding slowly through a fresh-washed rangeland, chatting and enjoying the freedom and companionship.

I was graduated from St. Mary's of the Wasatch [boarding school in Salt Lake City] in **1925**, at age 18, and was to go on to college that fall. I had reached home just in time to deliver steers, and Clyde must have sold some with ours, as both he and I had horses in the yard at Green River. He stayed at our house, and when he was ready to leave the next morning, asked if I would ride a ways with him as he had something he wanted to say to me.

We saddled up and rode south toward Little Valley but I was doing most of the talking, as I remember. We had not been so close since the affair in Thompson, and I didn't understand why. No one thought he was much involved in that, but he was completely thrown by it. He would not go to town, or associate with people unless he knew them well, and he acted like a wanted criminal. He trusted us, but very few others.

We stopped at the ridge four or five miles from town, pulled up and I guessed I had better go back because I had to get ready to go to the Roost that day, and this looked like a good place to say goodbye. He agreed and then said: "For the last time. This is where we part, probably never to meet again."

I was stunned, and started to protest, but he cut me off. "You have grown into a fine woman, Pearl, but we have come to the parting of the ways. I have nothing to offer you any more, and you have your whole life before you." When I asked if our dreams and promises had meant nothing to him, he said, "More than anyone will ever know. You shared many a lonely campfire with me, and I had hoped at one time you would actually be there. But that is over. If you feel you owe me any promises, you are entirely free. You have grown up now, and can make your own decisions. Don't look back, keep moving ahead and my love go with you. Do this much for me." And he put his hand over mine on the saddle swell, kissed me gently on the lips and picked up his reins. His horse (the horse that was to have been mine) moved down the rocky road, In a few moments they were out of sight. Clyde never looked back. I never saw him again, he was killed that next winter [**12/14/1925**, see tombstone, next page. This happened at the end of the **Range War of 1924-25**, but could well have been a related event].

My horse moved restlessly, and I turned him and started back to town. After a mile or so, I knew I had to sort things out, and turned aside and rode up on a knoll, where I dismounted and changed my whole life directions. Clyde had always been right, he was my knight in shining armor; we had never disagreed about anything. It wasn't easy to make a new start, but at last I came to understand that again he was right--it was over, but far from feeling cast off, I felt whole and free, ready to begin a new life with a solid base to build on. I realized to the fullest there on that rocky knoll, that I had known well the finest man that ever lived.

Thanks, Mike, not only for giving me the hardest writing assignment I ever had, but also for a chance to experience in memory the beauty and joy of that first love which has lain in my heart all these years.

Sincerely   Pearl B. Baker

The Shooting of Little Joe Miller

Before going on, one thing in Pearl's letter must be cleared up. She mentions the incident in Thompson (east of Crescent Junction and just north of 1-70), which Clyde was supposedly involved with. That was the shooting of **Joseph P. Miller Jr.** on Wednesday, January 30, 1924 at Thompson. The following information comes from a number of issues of **The Times-Independent (TI)** newspaper of Moab. Also, keep this date in mind, because it was right in the middle of the Range War mentioned above, and below.

Little Joe Miller as he was called, was a 21 year-old college student and the son of a prominent Moab citizen. He had bought a pool hall in Thompson the year before to help make money to attend the University of Utah. He had closed a deal to sell the place and had enrolled in classes not long before the shooting. But then he had to return to Thompson in late January and re-negotiate the sale of his business to another individual.

On Tuesday, January 29, 1924, Ed Cottrell, Leslie Tomlinson and Clyde Tidwell arrived in town on horseback. The next morning, these men were joined by others, and they started drinking from a jug of moonshine whiskey. About noon, Clyde Tidwell left and headed back to his cattle--either on The Spur or along the Green River where he had a cabin at **Tidwell Bottom** (this had to be the cabin built by Foote or Woodruff, as mentioned above). Being half drunk, 3 men by the names of Watt, Jim Warner and Tomlinson went to Joe Miller's pool hall with the jug. It was Prohibition days, and of course, booze

Above **Tidwell Bottom** on the Green River. The author is standing on stones that is part of a foundation to a former cabin which is likely the remains of Leland & Helen Tidwell's cabin. **Left** is part of an old stove; **Right** is part of an old bedstead.

Left Clyde Loughery Tidwell's tombstone in the Wellington, Utah Cemetery. Apparently he, or his mother and uncle--the ones who buried him--decided he wanted to retain his birth name at least in death. In life he was always known to others as Clyde Tidwell.

couldn't legally be sold at the pool hall. They got pretty drunk, then a Mexican sheep herder came in and he and Cottrell started arguing, apparently over an insulting remark about the Mexican. When things started to get out of hand, Joe Miller stepped in and told them to go outside. He helped them out, then closed the door and locked it. But **Ed Cottrell**, being totally smashed, pulled out a .45 and emptied it into the door. One of the bullets hit Miller in the head and he died later.

Being a small town, something like this was big time news, and the local Moab newspaper was dominated by the story. The newspapers for the next 2 weeks after the shooting, did mention that Clyde Tidwell had brought the moonshine whiskey to Thompson, but that he had left town and had nothing to do with later events or the shooting. As it turned out, Ed Cottrell was held on a murder charge and the trial was held on April 28, 1924 in Moab. The jury ended up dead-locked. After that trial, Jim Warner was rounded up and held for complicity in the murder as well.

Cottrell's re-trial was held on November 15, 1924, in Price, and he pleaded guilty to manslaughter and was given a 2 1/2 year sentence. During the next April of 1925, the charges against Jim Warner were dropped for lack of evidence. In August, 1925, Ed Cottrell was paroled after serving 8 months. Counting his time in jail before the trial, he had been incarcerated a total of about 18 months. Remember the name **Ed Cottrell**--he once shared a jail cell with **Bill Tibbetts** in **July, 1924**--that story is told later.

The newspapers never mentioned Clyde Tidwell's name during the trial, but according to Pearl, it had troubled him greatly and according to other old timers this writer talked to, he was laying low.

The Tidwell's range included The Spur, which was in between upper Horseshoe Canyon and Fort Bottom on the Green River. Also, they were down in Horsethief Canyon and on the river bottoms between The Frog at the mouth of Horseshoe Canyon, and Fort Bottom. This included Tidwell Bottom.

The Tidwells used that cabin or house on Tidwell Bottom which they lived in at that time while punchin' cows along the river. No one knows for sure, but this structure, which they all called a cabin, must have been the house built by either Foote or Robert Woodruff (?).

Anyway, Clyde was there on the river bottom in December, 1925. The next part of this story is best told by **Frank Tidwell**, presently of Farmington, Utah. He is the son of Delbert Tidwell, a half brother to Clyde. Frank wasn't even born (May 1, 1930) at the time, but Delbert had talked to him often about the event. Here is what Frank remembered:

On New Year's day, 1926, they [Tidwell family] were sitting down to have dinner in Wellington and the Sheriff came in and gave a message that said Clyde was overdue. Uncle John Romjue [of moonshining fame] had sent the message. John was out on The Spur and he was getting nervous because Uncle Clyde hadn't shown up. Clyde was down on the river; now we called it Woodruff Bottom. It's been renamed Tidwell Bottom now.

So Uncle John went into Green River and got a message to the Sheriff in Wellington. Then Dad [Delbert] and Uncle Leland drove down there and borrowed some horses, I think it was from Gillies [Ranch on the San Rafael River]. And they went down onto the river from Keg Knoll, probably down the Frog Trail. Once they got on the river, they went down to Woodruff Bottom and that's when they saw the cabin had been burned. As I understand, it was burned right down to the old ashes, and Clyde was pretty well burned up too. I never did know what part of him was left but he was almost ashes and they packed him out in a saddle bag or gunny sack. Dad never talked about it much; it was kind of painful.

I remember Dad telling about one fellow who was supposed to be a key witness and he later decided he didn't want to testify. There was a Judge Keller down in Price, and Dad talked like they had a good case and he was doing all they could to help solve the thing. They performed an autopsy on Clyde and they were sure that it was going to show cyanide, but it didn't prove out. Something was supposed to have been sent to the state chemist or somewhere. That was the thing they were banking on and when they sent the evidence to the state they hoped it would prove it was cyanide [that had killed Clyde]. It was 2 or 3 years after Clyde's death that his body was exhumed and examined. When the report came back it showed no poison.

The late **Albert Thayne** of Price, who was 87 years old in 1990, was an uncle to the Tidwells. He had a story very similar to Frank's, but adds and we quote: *His boots were outside the cabin, and there was a note in the boots. "Pretty sick today, if it don't change can't take it much longer," or something like that. That's what the note said..... Leland [Delberts brother] told me later, a few years later, there was a guy drunk at a bar, two or three years after Clyde died, and he told that he put arsenic in Clyde's flour out there..... I knew that guy who was supposed to have told this. He grew up in Wellington. He associated with Clyde, in fact he had stayed with Clyde out there on the desert. It was a guy named Jack Brace. Jack said he put arsenic in Clyde's flour..... Clyde at the time was going with one of them Biddlecome girls [Pearl]. She blamed Uncle John Romjue for Clyde's death. He was out there moonshining with Clyde; that was the story. She said Clyde would never have been moonshining if it hadn't been for Uncle John.*

It must be noted here that the newspapers had almost nothing to say about this event. The only article that could be found was in the **January 7, 1926** issue of the Moab **TI**. In the *Green River News* section it stated: *The body of Clyde Tidwell was brought to Green River Wednesday. A mystery surrounds his death, as his body was found partly burned in his cabin in the San Rafael Country.*

The story about Jack Brace poisoning Clyde's flour was only one of about 4 that are usually told by the citizens of Green River and Moab. Jack had grown up in Wellington and had married one of the Burdick girls from Valley City (about 10 kms south to Crescent Junction) and lived there for a number of years. It must be pointed out that there were no arrests in this case and no trial, so the stories about Jack or all the others accused in this case, have to be placed in the category of *"rumors"* only, of which there are many in this story.

Read more about the rest of the mystery of Clyde Tidwell's death after the Range War on page 376.

The Bill Tibbetts Story and The Range War of 1924-25

Before going further into the story about how Clyde may have met his demise, it's best to stop and do a background check on events in that part of the country at the time, which was in 1924 & '25.

During the years prior to the passing of the **Taylor Grazing Act** (signed on June 27, 1934), which created the Grazing Service--which was the forerunner to the Bureau of Land Management (BLM), the range lands of the west had no controls whatsoever on grazing. Whoever got to an area first, and was determined and tough, got grazing rights. Nobody patrolled the country then or set any kind of grazing regulations or quotas like we have today. In the very earliest days in this part of the country, grazing regulations weren't needed, because there was plenty of room for everyone; but later on, after all the range was taken, fights broke out everywhere. All over the west there were range wars and killings in the several years leading up to when the Roosevelt Administration came into power on March 4, 1933.

Now a brief summery of the life of Bill Tibbetts and friends. It all started with a cowboy named **James William (Bill) Tibbetts, Senior**. He was raised in Illinois, and later went to Oregon, got married, had a daughter, but things didn't work out, so he landed in Southeastern Utah. He ended up running cows for a big cattle outfit south of the La Sal Mountains. He later met and married a girl named **Amy Moore** from Moab. Amy had 2 brothers, **Bill "Pegleg"Moore**, as he was known later in life, and **Ephraim (Eph) Moore**, one of the more important characters in this story.

Bill and Amy settled into a homestead south of the La Sal area and built a log cabin. A year or two later they had a son they named **James William Tibbetts, Junior**. Everybody just called him **Bill Tibbetts** and he was born on March 23, 1898. Everything was going well at La Sal until 4 years later. In March of 1902, 17-year-old Mary Bothe, one of the Tibbetts neighbors, was having troubles with her husband and had ran away to the Tibbetts place. **Charles Bothe** had been beating her while drinking. On the night of March 19, 1902, Charles went to the Tibbetts cabin and ended up shooting through the window and killing Bill Tibbetts, Sr. Bothe then grabbed his wife, took her outside and shot her dead too (**March 28, 1902** issue of **The Grand Valley Times** of Moab). Bothe was rounded up, put on trial and later executed for the double murder.

Fast forward. Amy then moved from La Sal to a place closer to Moab called **Browns Hole** and bought another place. Not long after that she met and later married a man named Wilfred W. **(Winny) Allred** of Moab. Winny wasn't the cowboy type, instead he liked to play in bands and was more of a city kid. The Allreds had 6 children, 4 boys and 2 girls. The youngest boy was **Kenny Allred**, another important character in this story who was born in 1915, and was a half brother to Bill Tibbetts. Bill was a lot older than Kenny but they got along well.

Later on, Winny and Amy were either divorced or separated, then came tragedy. On January 13, 1923, Winny and J.V. Ellis, a farmer from La Sal, were drinking in Winny's cabin in Brown's Hole. They got into a fight, and Ellis, a much larger man, was beating the hell out of Winny. To stay alive, Winny grabbed a rifle and shot Ellis dead--in self defense, then waited till the next day to be taken into custody in Moab **(1/18/1923 issue of The Times Independent (TI) newspaper of Moab)**. He was held

Amy Moore Tibbetts Allred and her brother **Eph Moore** in about 1900. And **Bill Tibbetts** in the army, 1917-'18. (Ray Tibbetts Collection)

The man on the far right is Jack Brace, probably in the 1920's (?). (Bob Marsing Collection)

in jail, but in May was taken out on a work release with Deputy Sheriff Wilson onto a farm in Dry Valley between Moab & Monticello. At one point, Winny was separated from the other workers and the Sheriff, went back to camp, found a .22 rifle and shot himself *(4/5/1923, TI)*.

Now back to Bill Tibbetts, Jr, and to June, 1915. Bill and Carlisle Dalton rounded up 9 horses in the Moab area and drove them west to Hanksville, where they sold some of them, and ended up in Parowan where they sold the rest of the herd *(9/10/1915, GVT)*. They were later captured and Bill was tried in Manti and was sent to reform school in Ogden *(9/24/1915, GVT)*. After 18 months there, he returned home and later enlisted in the Army *(4/19/1918, GVT)*. About a year later he returned home *(7/4/1919, GVT)*. It was then that Bill and his uncle Eph Moore decided to go into the cattle business. Bill started with his mother's (Eph's sister Amy) cows and his own brand and he would join them with Eph's cows.

In the late summer of 1919 and with all the high ground Between the Rivers such as Big Flat, Dubinky and Grey's Pasture (Island in the Sky) and Horsethief Point taken up by other Moab cowmen, the decision was made to head for hopefully greener pastures in the region west of the Green River & The Confluence, and the Colorado River in Cataract Canyon. This was known as the **Under the Ledge Country**, but not a lot was known of it, it being so isolated. So they took their cows down the Horsethief Trail, eventually crossed the Green River and ended up in the area of **Elaterite Basin** sometimes called **Big Water** country. They left their cows there and headed south to scout the north end of Waterhole Flat where they met **Lou Chaffin** and sons in their camp. Neither group wanted to see each other, but a deal was made for grazing areas. Chaffins would take Waterhole Flat and points south; and Bill and Eph would have Elaterite Basin and north along the Green River to as far as Tidwell Bottom.

These 2 groups were some of the first to take cattle into parts of the Under the Ledge country, but sheepmen preceeded them in the 1890's as told by **Pearl Biddlecome Marsing Baker**; *The earliest were Andy Miller and John Boline. Also, there were other Frenchmen or perhaps French Basques like big Henry Dusseir and Pete Maziet who had sheep.* Also a man named Ezra Huntsman who was a herder for the Hyrum Seely family out of Castle Dale, Utah, had a sheep herd somewhere in that region during the 1910's, according to the book, *Seely History,* published in 1988.

For about 3 years, things went well for Bill and Eph and they would take turns going back to Moab for supplies and a little R & R. Later on, Bill and a 1st cousin named **Tom Perkins** began running a trap line along the river. This supplemented their income and Tom was an extra hand when it came to moving cows. In the summer of 1923, Bill lost his stepfather Winny Allred, as mentioned above.

It was about this time, the fall of 1923, that range lands in southeastern Utah suffered from lack of rainfall. The cows were grazing grass off faster than it would grow. Normally when drought conditions come, stockmen sell part of their herds to compensate. Bill and Eph pondered what to do. It was decided that since this was a kind of an emergency, they had the right to move their cows up to higher and greener pastures Between the Rivers to keep them from starving to death. But also into country that was already occupied!

In the winter of 1923-24 and on the east side of the Green River, from about Tenmile Canyon south to about Taylor and Upheaval Canyons, and to the east to include Dubinky, Big Flat and Grays Pasture is where a number of prominent Moab citizens were running cows. And since they had been there first, they felt it was rightfully theirs. Some of their names were Patterson, Owen Riordan & Snyders, John Jackson, Albert Beach, Deb Taylor and others in that large family, and the Murphys. We'll call these cattlemen the *Moab Establishment.*

So Bill and Eph moved their cows up to the **Horsethief Point** area, which is immediately south of Mineral Canyon. That of course raised hell with the Moab Establishment, even though it was public domain. They had some arguments and everybody was pretty upset, but they tolerated the situation. In the spring of 1924, Bill and 9-year-Kenny Allred discovered and helped to develop the Horsethief Spring (later this would become a 5-acre ranch that both would later own at different times). It was at this time, Eph Moore took his and his sister's cows off Horsethief Point and back to the river bottoms they were using before, but hardheaded Bill kept his own branded cows in the higher country.

Later on, in June of 1924, Tibbetts and Perkins killed one of their own calves for camp meat leaving the hide and entrails half buried. One of the Taylors found this, and thinking it belonged to him, rode to Moab and brought back Deputized Sheriff Beach, Jackson, Riordan and others to have a showdown with the intruders. Years later, one of the Murphys who was there told **Ray Tibbetts**, Bills son, that they smashed the ear markings off the hide which showed that it was really Bill's calf. They were trying to frame Tibbetts for anything to get him out of there. While in the area this posse of vigilantes, discovered 13 head of young cows belonging to Snyder & Riordan, the Jacksons and the Beaches *(7/10/1924, TI)* had been taken down the Horsethief Trail and were in willows by the river. No brands had been altered and none wore Bill's brand, but the posse rode back to Moab and filed a complaint. Years later, Ray Tibbetts, remembered the story his dad and Kenny Allred had told him about the arrest:

They sent a crew down, and Kenny Allred was with Dad at that time. They were down in Taylor Canyon workin' some cows when the posse showed up. Kenny was just a young boy and he said they come in there and said, "Bill, we got a warrant for your arrest". And Bill said, "For what", and they said "For rustlin'." And he said, "I certainly wasn't rustlin'." And they said, "We want you to come to town", and he said, "Well I'll be to town, but I can't come today, I've got work to do, and I'll be in Thursday". And they said, "No, that's not good enough". And this one guy--whoever he was, got off his horse, and said, "Well damn Bill we'll fight". And Kenny says, "Bill got off his horse and said by god we'll fight too". And ol' Kenny said, "I looked around and there was just two of us"--and he was like 9 years old, just a real young kid. But anyway, the posse finally decided they didn't want to take him on and they all went back to town, and Dad did go in on Thursday and turned himself in.

So Tibbetts and Perkins were jailed, but hired Knox Patterson as their attorney. Knox was the brother of one of the other Moab cattlemen who had cows in the area. As it turned out, Knox met them in jail and said, *"You better break out, they're gonna hang you."*

So they did, and **Ed Cottrell** was the eyewitness. He was in the same jail cell as Bill and Tom and he was being held for the shooting of Little Joe Miller out at Thompson. Here's what Ed Cottrell told Ray Tibbetts years later about the *July 30, 1924* jailbreak: *All of a sudden this one night we were awakened by some noise outside. There was 3 guys out there and they pried the bars a little wider and they got'em spread out and they were puttin' Tom Perkins through the window, but he was heavier than your dad. And he got hung up there, so Dad had to pull him back inside and then Dad scooted out, as he was more of a thin willowy guy. They had a great big heavy crowbar and when they started, they had 2 guys as lookouts and only one guy on the bar. So with Bill outside, the two of them pried it open enough so that Tom could get out.*

Then your Dad said to Ed, "Ed aren't you going to go"? And Ed said, "No, no, I'm not goin', I'm innocent". And Dad said, "I'm innocent too but I'm not going to hang around for this neck tie party". So Ed told me all about it--that was old Ed Cottrell, he's dead now.

There's some speculation as to who the 3 men were who helped 'em make a jailbreak. I think Uncle Eph put'em up to it. I think one was Joe Tibbetts, my dad's full brother, then Sog and Gib Allred, 2 of Kenny's oldest brothers. And they got that great big bar, like a crow bar, from the road department or somewhere. That jail was made out of adobe brick but the bars were in pretty solid.

There was an old boy down in the lower end of the valley and his name was Rocky Steward. And he had a rowboat, and he thought the world of Dad, and when they contacted him--Uncle Eph probably--he turned his rowboat over to 'em and that's what they took off with going down the river. Then of course, Ross Thompson told me about it too. He knew all about it; they got him out of bed to come and get that damn big boat to run down the river. The Sheriff got'im out of bed. This was in the middle of the night that they had a merry chase down the Colorado.

Ross Thompson told Ray what happened next: *Now what the Sheriff done was he took over the barge from the Moab Garage and said I need it, we're goin' down the river. So Ross was the only one who knew how to run it. Later they overtook Bill and Tom down at Standing Rock Canyon [This is the canyon coming out of Monument Basin. Old cattlemen in Moab called that Standing Rock Basin]. And that's where Dad shot around 'em [the posse] and tryin' to scare 'em. He could have killed any one of 'em. Ross said, "I wasn't afraid of that, but what really made me mad at 'im was in the night, Dad snuck down to the boat and got some supplies out of the boats and poured water in our gas tank". He said, "I didn't know that until I was goin' up the river and the motor started missin", and he said, "god what's wrong"--then it dawned on 'im that Dad had fouled up his gas. They only got halfway up the river, and none of the other newspaper reports told about that. And he said, "The posse and everybody had to bailout and walk into town" which took about 3 days.*

After the boat chase, Bill and Tom made their way to the west side of the Green River apparently via the Shafer Trail and were able to find supplies they had cached during their days of running a trap line

374

Top The signature of **Bill Tibbetts** on the ceiling of a cave he and **Tom Perkins** stayed in just south of **Keg Knoll**. It reads: *My Home Bill Tibbetts Sept. 15 1924.* Tom also left a similar inscription. **Left Bill Tibbetts** and wife **Betty Jewell Agens**, most likely taken in Santa Fe, New Mexico in the late 1920's (?). They were married on December 31, 1925 in Bessie, Washita, Oklahoma. **Right Bill Tibbetts** in Moab and in the 1940's (?). (Both from Ray Tibbetts Collection)

and herding cows, but at one point they ate grasshoppers for about a week. Also, Eph Moore helped them with supplies. They also managed to come up with horses and left Elaterite Basin via the North Trail. Once in the Roost Country, they found a south-facing cave (probably one of many) overlooking the middle part of Horseshoe Canyon and carved their initials. Bill wrote, *My Home Bill Tibbetts Sept. 15, 1924.* That cave is less than 1 km south of Keg Knoll. Tom Perkins left his name there too.

In the fall of 1924, Bill and Tom stayed in the Roost Country west of the Green River and helped Eph gather steers for market. After they had gathered a herd, they drove them up the North Trail and eventually to Green River where they were left in the stock yards to be shipped. All 3 men then returned to the Roost and Eph volunteered to gather some of Bill's steers and take them to Thompson to be shipped. (It was about that time, *October 16, 1924,* that the *TI* published a letter that Bill and Tom sent to the editor explaining why they broke out of jail and about that merry chase down the river.) So Eph went up to the Big Flat Country and found most of Bill's cows had been shot by what must have been members of the Moab Establishment. But he did gather about 100 head and pushed them down on the river and out of harms way.

It was then in December and January of 1924-'25, that Bill (and probably Tom Perkins) headed for the Big Flat Country and quietly gathered small herds of the other stockmen's cows and drove them down the Horsethief Trail. Once on the bottom, they pushed the cows into the river at a location where they couldn't get back out. So many of them drowned. A while after this started, people at Hite Ferry

375

began to notice dead cows floating downriver. That's when the Moab Establishment got wind of what was happening to their cows. Normally, if there's snow, therefore water, and feed out on the range, stockmen didn't bother to check the herds too often in the middle of winter.

It wasn't long before the Moab stockmen either gathered their herds and trailed them closer to town and safer pastures; or they hired armed guards to go after the hoof prints going off the rim following cows. By the spring of 1925, all the high ground around Big Flat was all but empty of livestock.

It was sometime in late 1924 or the first half of 1925 (but not between mid-February and mid-May when Eph and cousin Joe Perkins were in jail--couldn't afford bail--for stealing cows of the Moab Establishment; at trial the case was thrown out. Read more below), Eph got back to the boys and told them the happening's of the previous winter wasn't written-up in the paper and he thought the stockmen and the authorities were out to shoot first and ask questions later. Soon after that, Eph, Bill and Tom made it to a railroad siding in Thompson in the middle of the night and the 2 young cowpokes hopped a freight train heading east toward Kansas. Eph took their horses and ditched the saddles.

In Kansas, Bill changed his name to **James Lee**. After doing some farm work in Kansas, they went to Watonga, Oklahoma where he met **Betty Jewel Agens** and later got married in Bessie, Washita, Oklahoma on December 31, 1925. In about 1927, all 3 of them went on to Santa Fe for several years.

In the late 1920's, Bill and Tom Perkins worked for the governor of New Mexico breaking horses; just one of many different jobs they had. In 1930, Bill's mother Amy got a letter from James Lee, their first contact in 5 years. Then in the summer of 1930, Amy and her brother Eph Moore went to Santa Fe for a visit. Eph told them what happened to the Moab Establishment after that range war. **Albert Beach** sold out and left town, maybe for Arizona. **John Jackson** had a few cows in the Ten Mile Canyon country and lived at Upper Courthouse, and at a home in Moab (?). Jackson spent most of a year gathering a few of his strays from along the river. But by that time he was also in the money lending business. **Taylors** quit and sold all or most of their cows. **Patterson** apparently gathered what stock he had left and moved to Lisbon Valley which is south of the La Sal Mountains. The **Snyder-Riordan** outfit sold most of their livestock in November, 1925 (the rest a couple of weeks later), flew the coop and landed in Colorado. The **Murphys** were hangin' around, but with fewer cows. **Uncle Eph Moore** had sold out to a guy named **Art Murray** in 1929 and Art's stock was up on Big Flat and Horsethief Point. Bill's mother **Amy Moore Tibbetts Allred** also sold most of her cows, but some were being cared for by her youngest son **Kenny Allred** along with his own small herd which were running in the same area as Art Murray's stock. Eph also brought a tidy sum of money from the sale of what was left of Bill's cows.

Then, as one story goes, 2 days after Amy and Eph got to Santa Fe, Bill & Jewel got married for the 2nd time; this time Jewel married James William (Bill) Tibbetts. This 2nd marriage doesn't show up on the LDS Church's genealogy website, likely because if was just a formality to make Jewel happy.

Sometime in the summer of 1930, Bill and Jewell moved back to Moab with 2 young boys. That's where Jewell had their 3rd child, **Rodney Gail on August 13, 1930**. He was born in the little house where the Jailhouse Cafe is now. After they came back to Moab, Bill got into a knock-down-drag-out fist fight with John Jackson in the Moab Garage waiting room. But not long after that he barrowed money from Jackson, bought a few sheep and ran sheep and cattle in the Big Flat area for about a year, then returned to New Mexico. That's where Jewell had their 4th son, **Ray Tibbetts on April 22, 1932**. Bill worked odd jobs throughout the Great Depression, including being a carpenter, and for a real estate company.

In about 1939, Bill again moved his family back to Utah and to Hanksville and the Henry Mountains. An attempt at homesteading the Starr Ranch didn't pan out partly because, as Ray explained, *Those hard-shelled Mormons over there wouldn't accept Mother because she was a Baptist.* So it was back to Moab sometime around 1941. Bill again became a home builder--building a home, then selling it and moving--and selling real estate. In August, 1944, Tibbetts was appointed city marshal by the Moab city council. After several years of this, he was back in the home building trade. In 1959, Bill and Jewell also bought the Horsethief Ranch from Kenny Allred, who had in turn bought if from Art Murray in 1953. They lived there for 6 years and ran a few cows, then it was back to Moab. Finally on the evening of August 9, 1969, he and his wife went for a ride and near what is now the bowling alley at the south end of Moab, their VW bus was hit by another car and Bill and Jewell were both killed. For a more detailed account of the life of Bill Tibbetts read the book, *Last of the Robbers Roost Outlaws: Moab's Bill Tibbetts* (as mostly told by his son Ray Tibbetts, and others), by Tom McCourt; or *Horse Thief Ranch*, by H. Michael Behrendt who bought the Horsethief Ranch in 1985, and still owns it.

Now back to the **Clyde Tidwell story** and the **Range War of 1924-25**. In the same time period-- **February, 1925**, Eph Moore and cousin **Joe Perkins** (Tom Perkin's brother), who were running cattle on the west side of the Green River, were arrested for stealing 18 head of Deb Taylor's cows. They had gone to Upheaval Bottom and taken some of their own stray cattle back across the river to the west side on the ice, but that herd included some of Taylor's cows. They were arrested and held--because they couldn't pay the $1000 bail--so they sat in jail until their trial. Finally after several hearings, their trial was held in **May of 1925** in Castle Dale, Utah. At the end of the trial, the judge instructed the jury to return a verdict of **not guilty**, on account of lack of evidence. As any old cowpoke will tell you, it's very difficult to separate cows on the open range, so Eph and Joe were merely trying to put the cows in a box canyon so they could separate the different brands. It must be noted here, that the sheriff's posse who rounded up Moore and Perkins included; Sheriff Murphy and deputy Albert Beach--also Deb Taylor, Owen Riordan and John Jackson, all of whom were part of the Moab Establishment.

This was the situation in the 2 years or so leading up to Clyde Tidwell's death. Now one of the other stories about who may have had something to do with Clyde's death. Keep in mind that Clyde supposedly died on **December 14, 1925**, just months after the men of the Moab Establishment were having their cows run into the river by Bill Tibbetts. Now the late **Chad Moore** of Green River, who was working in Moab in the early 1950's when the Uranium Boom was first getting started, told this writer that all the cowboys in town then were aware of an *alleged death-bed confession* of John Jackson who died not long before in May, 1950. The alleged confession was that he somehow had intimate knowledge of the death of Clyde Tidwell, and somebody burned the cabin down to hide the evidence. Clyde had been accused of having done a little cattle rustlin' or **mavericking** (rounding up unbranded calves or cows from the open range and putting your brand on them) himself, which may have helped perpetuate this particular rumor. Also, in Pearl B. Baker's letter to this writer, she stated that *he acted like a wanted criminal*, so maybe Clyde was guilty of something too (?).

Pearl B. Baker told this writer that one of the men who worked for John Jackson, once told her that John told him that he admitted to killing Clyde. Pearl also stated that Delbert Tidwell, Clyde's half brother, had told her that he *believed* John Jackson had done it. There are several other versions of how John

The Tidwell Clan: The young boy in the forefront is **Delbert Tidwell** who was about 3 years of age (born in 1898); that would mean this is in about 1901 or '02. Ila & brother Frank, believe it was taken in Sunnyside, Utah. The woman on the left holding the baby is believed to be Mary Grundig, wife of Hyrum Tidwell--who is behind her holding a towel. There's a good chance that most of the 6 Tidwell brothers; Orange, Lon, Dos, Hyrum (Alex's grandfather), William and Frank (Delbert and Leland's father) are in this picture. One or more of these brothers may have gone to Mexico looking for gold, and claim to have met Clyde Tidwell there. No proof of that though and that's just one story. This is a typical home for people living in rural Utah in that time period. (Ila Mae Tidwell Clark Collection)

Jackson may have had intimate knowledge of Clyde's alleged death. Everything is hearsay of course.

The third or maybe fourth version of how Clyde died was that John Jackson and Clyde Tidwell were there in the cabin drinking. They both got pretty drunk and since they were both carrying firearms, one thing led to another. Anything can happen when two men start drinking!

In October, 1987, Delbert Tidwell was taken down on The Spur by Gary Cox and others, as the National Park Service was trying to gather information on the history of the Tidwell Ranch (Delbert died in 1989). Part of Delbert's statement at that time went like this, which only adds to the confusion and perpetuates a bad rumor even more: *We're sure he was murdered and even know who it was, problem was no real evidence [existed] against the man. Clyde apparently was poisoned by cyanide in his bread or flapjacks, although they found a note about his being sick. The coroner never found any poison. It was 2 months from the time Clyde was last seen alive until we found the body. There wasn't much left of him by then. The cabin burned down; real hot fire.*

It must be noted here that never once did any of the local newspapers have any story about any kind of police investigation of Clyde's death. As Delbert has stated above, there was no evidence of any kind--and so if there was an investigation, nothing turned up in the newspapers and no charges were ever filed on anyone. No one was ever arrested and there was never any trial. In all fairness to John Jackson, and for that matter to Jack Brace, and especially their living relatives, there was no evidence on them or anyone else in connection with the death of Clyde Tidwell.

As for John Jackson, his wild & woolley younger days followed him throughout his life and is a likely reason for some to suspect him. John was also part of the Moab Establishment whose cows were being run into the Green River not long before Clyde died. All of these factors made Jackson an easy target. This writer has attempted to report stories and statements made about events at Tidwell Bottom as unbiased as possible because a history of the area would not be complete without this story.

Now, as stated at the beginning of this part on Clyde Tidwell, an **Alex Tidwell**, a nephew to Delbert and Leland, stated the story was not quite complete. He made a statement to the author, then his mother the late **Crystal Tidwell** was interviewed in Wellington. It seems that Crystal had married **Dick Tidwell**, another uncle to Delbert and Leland, in the spring of 1933. They ran cows down along the east side of the Green River on Upheaval Bottom and up on Gray's Pasture until the fall of 1936, when the Grazing Service forced them to head back to the Wellington area near their home base. Sometime before Dick died in 1945, he told her what really happened to Clyde Tidwell--or at least one last version of what happened. Here then is his story as told by Crystal Tidwell half a century later:

The note Clyde Tidwell wrote and placed in his boots outside the cabin said that he'd been bitten by a rattlesnake and he didn't want 'em to see what a mess his body would be in when they came down. So he was going to shoot himself and burn the cabin down. This was in the note--that he was committing suicide (?).

Now Frank Tidwell (Senior), who was the father of Delbert and Leland, and stepfather to Clyde, was in some way a close relative to a man named Bill Chinn. He [and some of the other Tidwells] went down into Mexico and when he came back he told 'em that Clyde was alive. He was down in Mexico and that he had told him that he [Clyde] had owed a big gambling debt, and the guy kept riding him to pay the bill. This was wherever he'd been gambling--probably in Thompson (?). Anyway, this man came down to the river bottom where the cabin was, to make him pay the bill whether he wanted to or not. I guess he was going to take it out of his hide if he didn't pay. So they got in a fight and he [Clyde] ended up shooting this other guy. So he just took this guy's body and put it in the cabin, set it on fire, and took the other guy's boots and left his own boots there with the note in it, and left the country.... The guy who was killed was apparently never reported missing.

This all happened before I met Dick and married him in the spring of 1933. But nobody ever said anything to people outside the family, I guess because they were protecting Clyde who must have been alive for a long time. Bill Chinn was a relative of Delbert and Leland, so I'm sure he told them. They all talked about it. I didn't hear this from Bill Chinn, because he had told 'em that before I married into the family.

It seems that in the period of time from about January 1926 until the spring of 1933, several of the older Tidwell brothers had gone to Mexico hoping to get involved in gold mining. That's how Bill Chinn fits in. In the Tidwell family, which was largely responsible for the settlement of Wellington, Utah, there were 6 brothers; Orange, Lon, Dos, Hyrum (Alex's grandfather), William and Frank (Delbert and Leland's father). See a picture of the Tidwell clan on page 377.

Joe Tidwell from Vernal, whose father was Dos, confirmed that some of these brothers had been to Mexico and were involved in looking for gold: *My dad told me several times about going down to old Mexico with my Uncle Orange [Hyrum also went down there]. I don't remember him telling me how old he was or when he went. Hubert told me before he died, now he was another of Hyrum's sons, and a brother to Dick, that they went down there and they were involved in gold mining, or just looked at it. They went down there several times, so I know they went down there to old Mexico.*

Uncle Orange and my dad were old bachelors until they were both around 60 years old, then they got married. Dos, my dad, was married in about 1932, at 60 years of age.

This pretty well confirms that some of the older Tidwells had indeed gone to Mexico hunting for gold, but no one alive in the early 1990's seemed to know exactly when or where. Joe seemed to think the old bachelors, Orange and Dos, were down there on several different occasions.

The late **Harold Halverson** of Green River also confirmed that some of the Tidwells were at least planning to go to Mexico: *The Tidwells, they're shirtale relations of mine, on my mother's side, they was here in this house, Orange, Lon & Dos, talkin' to Dad and they wanted him to put in some money for a mine or something down in Mexico. I was a teenager then [born in 1911], must have been in the late 1920's. He didn't give'em any money--he didn't have any money to give! I told Delbert here a year or two before he died, "By golly I remember when them old Tidwells was over home and they was wantin' Dad to invest in that". And Delbert said, "Ya, they went south with the money, then some guy went and blowed it".*

Crystal's son Alex, further states that some of the Tidwells sold a bunch of sheep and cattle to get the money to go to Mexico. He also had this to say about a conversation he had with Delbert before he died:

I know Delbert knew this story, because I talked to him about it. But Delbert didn't want it known that Clyde was still alive. He was really reserved about it. When I talked to him he didn't want me to know anything about it. I was the one who brought up the subject. This was in about the mid-1980's. Yes, he confirmed this story but he said, "Well I didn't want anybody to know about it". He was trying to protect Clyde. "Anyway it was self defense, and it wasn't murder".

No one seems to know where Clyde went after Mexico--if indeed he left the cabin alive and went to Mexico, but Albert Thayne was told by one of these old Tidwells that he saw Clyde somewhere in Nevada, but Albert didn't consider that person a reliable source, and didn't think anything more about it. Pearl B. Baker, when told about this new twist to the story, stated that Mary, Delbert's first wife, had once told her this, but Pearl just brushed it off as a rumor without credibility.

If you go to Wellington (southeast of Price) and the cemetery just north of town, you'll see a headstone in the Tidwell plot (northeast corner of the cemetery next to the north fence) which reads: *Clyde E. Loughery, Utah, PVT. 51 Regt. C.A.G., December 14, 1925.* See a foto of his headstone, page 371.

This still leaves us with the question, who is in Clyde Tidwell's grave? The only way to know for sure would be to dig up Clyde for the 2nd time, and his mother, or perhaps some living relative, and test their DNA. But after all these years there may not be enough DNA in that grave to test.

The John Jackson & Bill Hinton Story

With all the excitement of the Range War of the mid-1920's, sheriff's posses chasing all over the country after various cattle rustlers, and with all the allegations, rumors and stories about the alleged death/murder of Clyde Tidwell, this introduces us to yet another interesting story about one of Moab's most legendary characters. He was a prominent cattleman in these parts at the time and was a member of the Sheriff's posse on more than one occasion. It's the life and times of **John Jackson**, and to a lesser extent, his brother **Bill (William D.) Hinton**. They were certainly a couple of the most colorful and wildest cowboys in the history of southeastern Utah. So a story of part of their lives must be told.

John and brother Bill were both born as Hintons, and had grown up in Texas using that name. Bill was born on **December 18, 1868** (1867 on his tombstone) ; younger John was born **June 22, 1871**; both in Llano, Texas. In 1878 their father died; in 1882, their mother died--leaving both as orphans. They then lived with an uncle for a while, but John being rather young was knocked around a lot. John was red-headed and freckle-faced--which didn't help his chances much. But they both somehow survived, and ended up as cowboys for various outfits in Texas. Somewhere along the line one or both got into trouble with the law, but no one knows for sure what really happened. There are lots of rumors about that part of their lives. One story is told that because they were so beloved in Texas, that one of the Sheriffs followed them all the way to the state line trying to talk them into coming back. It must have been when they left Texas in a hurry they both changed their last names to Jackson.

In about 1886, both brothers were in Roswell, New Mexico, working on a cattle ranch, but both went to Arizona in 1888. **Bill** married Annie L. Bowen from Fruitland, New Mexico on **December 10, 1892**. But before the wedding, Annie insisted he change his name back to Hinton, which he did. John always kept the name Jackson. Later, and in the early 1890's, both brothers landed in southeastern Utah. By 1894 or '95, they were in Moab, and **John** married Lillian Webb on **March 5, 1896**. John Jackson had 7 children by his first wife, another 7 by his second wife (one died young at age 2); Bill had 5.

It's been said that both men were heavy drinkers, and this led to many of their later troubles and to their wild & woolly times. Sometime in the late 1890's or early 1900's, Bill moved to southwestern Colorado, where he had an altercation and shot a man. The *June 21, 1907* issue of the *GVT* ran one story, then on the *28th* another: *The following item, taken from the Dolores Star, indicated that the shooting of Morrison by Bill Jackson alias Hinton which was reported in last week's Times was more serious than at first supposed.*

"George Morrison was shot in the right arm last Friday by Bill Hinton. The shooting occurred near Dove Creek in Dolores county about forty miles [64 kms] from this place. Medical aid was summoned from this place and Dr. Rentz went out Saturday, returning with the wounded man Sunday morning. He was taken to the Oshner (?) hospital at Durango Tuesday where he died at 1:15 Wednesday morning. The doctor says that death was caused by internal injures probably received in falling from his horse after being shot. We have not learned the particulars regarding the cause of the shooting, but understand that Mr. Morrison and Mr. Hinton have had more or less trouble for some time past. The sheriff of Dolores county has Hinton in custody. Mr. Morrison was ?6 years of age and leaves a wife and five children......"

About 2 weeks later Hinton was let out of jail on $2500 bond. By February of 1908, he was visiting relatives in Moab and had sold all of his range cattle and was to invest in other parts of western Colorado. Finally, at his trial in Rico, Colorado (halfway between Cortez and Telluride), in March of 1908, he was acquitted. He insisted he shot in self-defense, and it took the jury only 1 1/2 hours to bring a verdict of not guilty. Sometime after Hinton's trial, according to Bill's son **Clay Hinton** (interviewed by telefone in 1992 from Yuma, Arizona): *A couple of Morrison's brothers caught Pa there in a store and gunwhipped 'em--beat the hell out of him!* This encouraged Hinton to move out of that part of the country.

After getting married, John Jackson settled down with Lillian in Moab and began raising a family. From one-line captions in the *GVT* we know he had flood damage to his home in October of 1897, and in the **11/30/1900** issue of *GVT*, he ran an advertisement stating: *John Jackson, has arranged a pasture on Grand river [now the Colorado] about 14 miles [23 kms] below Moab, and would like to get a number of horses to give personal care for during the winter. Good feed and water, rates $1.50 for the winter. Horses delivered at any time.* This sounds like the **Jackson Hole** country, indicating he may have built the **Jackson's Ladder Trail** at about that time (Read more on John in that part of the country in the chapter covered by **Map 25**, starting on page 261).

From tiny articles in the Moab newspaper, we know in 1903 & '05, John was on jury duty, but apparently was living part time in Castle Valley northeast of Moab. By 1907, he was working in the mines in the La Sal Mountains, at least part time, and delivering steers to miners. In the summer of 1907 he was in the Blue (Abajo) Mountains, probably taking care of his cattle on upper Indian Creek, but his family was living in Moab so there kids could go to school. By 1907 they had 4 children.

By about 1910, life must have been getting down on Jackson, for in January, 1910, while living in Moab, he was involved in a drunken brawl and was fined $25. Bill Hinton migrated back to Moab in August, 1911, but got into a fight in May, 1912, and was arrested and fined. In October, 1912, John was arrested for disturbing the peace, along with Morgan Stewart, and fined $50. In June, 1913, John got into a fight with a W.F. Gordon, and each was fined $15. In October, 1913, Bill was charged with an assault on Deb Taylor, and fined $20.

About this time the town must have been getting tired of all the fighting because in February, 1914, a complaint was issued from the county attorney's office charging both Bill and John with threatening to do bodily harm to the person of County Attorney F.B. Hammond, Jr., who asked that they be placed under bonds of $3000 each to keep the peace. As it turned out, within a month or so, both men were required to put up $1000 worth of personal securities to cover the *"peace bonds"* levied against them.

But the story doesn't end there. On July 4, 1914, both brothers got drunk again and tried to beat up Frank Randall, and were charged with assault. At Hinton's trial which was held in Elgin (across the river east of Green River), a jury found him not guilty. The main contention of the defense was that Hinton assaulted Randall to save the life of his brother John--who the defense contended, was receiving a severe and unmerciful beating at the hands of Randall. What Bill actually did was to whack Randall over the head with a beer bottle!

Jackson was found guilty in his first trial, but made an appeal in the district court. At the second trial in November of 1914, the case was *dismissed upon motion of District Attorney J.W. Cherry, who stated that the chief witnesses for the prosecution had left the county and could not be found (**GVT-- 11/13/1914**).* Putting 2 & 2 together, it's not difficult to figure out why the witnesses may have left the county! Had either of these brothers been found guilty of assault, they would have lost their $1000 peace bond. In those days, that wasn't exactly pocket change.

After that, the boys seemed to have cooled their heels a bit. In **June, 1915**, Jackson became a director in a new bank, the **Moab State Bank**, but this is still not the end of the story. In October, 1915, Jackson was charged with disturbing the peace and fined $15. A month later, John was again charged with disturbing the peace and made another $50 contribution to Moab City. In July, 1916, John got into still another fight, this time with Walter Wood. According to the paper, this was his 9th arrest for disturbing the peace or fighting. This time John chose jail to paying the fine, so he got a 50 day jail sentence. After 11 days in the stockade, he gave up peacefully and handed Justice D.A. Johnson a $50 check. But this still wasn't the end. In September of 1916, John and brother Bill got into fisticuffs in Jackson's home, and both made another $15 contribution to Moab City.

By this time John Jackson's marriage was on the rocks, for on **June 8, 1917**, Lillian Jackson filed for divorce. The charge was: *the defendant had for the last 5 years.... been a habitual drunkard, indulging to excessive intoxicating liquors frequently; that under the influence of intoxicating liquor defendants conduct is vile and reprehensible, rendering married life with said defendant unbearable....*(Divorce records, Moab courthouse)

Before proceeding further, another event must be mentioned. It's another interesting side-story-- with no less than a dozen variations--about how a big slickrock outcropping with a big pothole right on top in **Dry Valley** between Moab and Monticello, got the name **Jail or Jailhouse Rock**. If indeed this event ever did take place, it was before 1917, and probably a lot earlier. It's about John and his wife Lillian and is best told by the late **Mitch Williams** (son of Dr. Williams) of Moab:

John and his wife were going south from Moab to Monticello. Now the campers and wagons used to stop there to get water, and you have to climb way up and there's one hell of a big pothole up there. And I've seen a tremendous amount of water in it. I don't know how many gallons it holds, but in the wet season it gets a lot of water. Anyway, they would climb up and let buckets down with ropes, but if the water was real low, you couldn't get your bucket to the water. So they would let somebody down and he would have to walk over a ways and then put the bucket in the water and carry it back and hoist it up. Well, of course this is all rumor with me too, I mean hell, I wasn't there, but these are stories that are told around here since Christ was a pup!

Well anyway, John and his wife had been arguing and fightin' all day, and they got up there and he let his wife down in there to fill the bucket. And she had some hell to say to him and he got mad and just throw the rope down in the hole; and you can't get out of there by god, I'll tell you for sure. You can-

Both of these fotos are of **Jail Rock**; that's how it's written on USGS maps, but some people call it Jailhouse Rock. From just the right viewpoint, you'll see the **La Sal Mountains** in the far background (they are the mountains east of Moab). Or you can climb to the top and have a good look down into the huge pothole on the south side. It would take a good storm to put much water in this natural tank. Also, there are some old signatures just below the pothole, but almost none are readable today because of natural erosion. Those lost signatures dated from the late 1800's and early 1900's.

not get out of there! So then ol' John went down and got in the wagon and went on to Monticello. Then he got in with some guys, probably at Mons Peterson's store, and they got drunker than skunks.

So there his wife was, she had water but she couldn't get out. And finally some other people came along to get water, and they got'er out. But they were headed the other way, they were headed for Moab, and they offered to take her to Moab, but she said, "No sir, I'm going to go find that damn John Jackson and I'm going to kill that son-of-a-bee". So she started out for Monticello on foot, and as the story was, she walked all the way. And when she went in there ol' John saw her comin' in the front door, and he went out the back door. I guess she didn't kill 'im, cause he was around for a long time after that! So that's the story of how Jail or Jailhouse Rock got it's name.

(If you're interested in seeing Jailhouse Rock, drive along Highway 191 about halfway between Moab & Monticello. Near **mile post 93**, turn west and northwest onto the **Needles Overlook Highway**. Drive northwest **4 kms (2.5 miles)** and turn left or south onto a graded dirt road. From there drive south for **1.6 kms (1 mile)** and turn right or west and head straight for **Jail Rock**. Continue west for 300m, then just before the 'Rock, veer left and drive to the south side and park. Climb steep slickrock to the pothole halfway up. Along the south face of this huge rock outcropping were many old signatures of people who had been to this famous landmark, but most were worn away and unreadable in 2012.)

After the divorce proceedings got underway, the Jacksons started selling things, including their grazing rights down in the Shafer Basin and Jackson Hole country, and John went to Arizona for a while. Lillian went to California. Details are lacking, as most of this information comes from 3-line captions in the local newspaper, and from divorce papers. By May, 1918, John had acquired an 80 acre (32 hectare) farm in Orland, California, but it's not certain whether John and Lillian were still living together at that time (?). Perhaps they were, and trying reconcile with each other. John continued to have some business ties in the Moab area, because for at least 3 years, John made periodic trips to this country on business, sometimes with one of his sons. In March of 1920, John was working as a government trapper in the Book Mountains (Book Cliffs) north of Thompson.

The problem they had in getting a divorce, was the settlement of their property. Apparently the divorce proceedings were suspended because they couldn't come to terms on the settlement of their estate. Finally they did agree on some kind of arrangements with each getting 50/50, or about $24,000 each. Then on December 20, 1919, a second divorce hearing was held in Glenn County, California. The divorce was finalized on **January 22, 1921.**

In October, 1921, John married **Sinda Cordova** of **Thompson**, who was just 19 years old at the time. John was 31 years older at age 50. They eventually had 7 more children, 2 of which were still alive in 2012. John's youngest daughter by this second marriage, the late **Alice Jackson Olson** of Price, remembers her mother telling about the first time she met John:

The first time my mother saw my dad, was when he rode into their camp. He knew Grandpa Cordova and he brought in half a cow on a pack mule. That's the first time she saw this tall, straight guy. She said he belonged on the horse and that he was the best rider she ever saw. And she said when she saw those big blue eyes, she fell in love with him right there. That was when she was 19 years old, and they were married not too long after that. He had cattle in the Thompson area at that time.

By this time Jackson was older and wiser and had apparently mellowed, for the newspapers never did mention him being in any more drunken brawls or disturbing the peace. Later on, both John Jackson and Bill Hinton were part-time deputy sheriffs at various times. Jackson and Sinda lived first in Thompson where they had one daughter which died young and is buried there. They then moved down to the old Upper Courthouse Station (located at mile post 141 on Highway 191, 3 kms northwest of the Dalton Wells CCC Camp) after 2 or 3 years.

In scanning the old Moab newspapers, an interesting story about John Jackson was found in the **April 16, 1925** issue. It tells us where he lived at the time and where he was running cattle. This was during the Range War, and while Eph Moore & Bill Perkins were in jail. Part of that article went like this:

*John Jackson of Court House, a well known cattleman, underwent a harrowing experience Saturday which he will not soon forget. Mr. Jackson was riding after cattle in the Big Flat country, southwest of Moab. His horse fell with him, breaking his left leg between the knee and ankle. Mr. Jackson bound the injured leg as best he could, climbed back on his horse, and rode to the Colorado river, some ten or twelve miles [16 to 19 kms] distance. The trail, leading down rimrocks and through almost impassable canyons, was not a pleasant one to follow, but Mr. Jackson knew that it led to the nearest help. He struck the river just opposite **Pritchett's wash**, six miles [10 kms] below Moab, and as luck would have it, Al Holman was fishing there. Mr. Jackson called across the river to Mr. Holman, advising him of his condition, and the latter left at once for Moab to summon help.*

The Moab Garage company boat was secured to bring Mr. Jackson to town, Dr. I.W. Allen going along to attend to the injury. The fracture was reduced and Mr. Jackson was brought to Moab.

The route John Jackson took was east from **Big Flat** (on top where the road to Dead Horse Point leaves Highway 313), then east across **Arth's Pasture** and the heads of **Little** and **Gold Bar Canyons**. Then he curled around to the southeast and south across what was then called the **Sand Flats** (it's now called **Poison Spider Mesa**). Finally he got on the trail leading down to **Williams Bottom**. Al Holman was fishing at the mouth of Pritchett Canyon.

By September 10, 1925 we know the Jackson's were still living there near the Courthouse Station, which by that time was close to being shut down. The Jacksons were running cattle in the area to the west and the Range War was winding down. That was the time when Mrs. Evelyn Standford's car rolled over right at the station and she was killed (that was first car wreck to cause a death in southeast Utah). It was John's wife Sinda Jackson who helped pull her and others from the car.

There's a funny story told about John which took place while they were living at Upper Courthouse. **Mitch Williams** told it like this: *When he was out there at Courthouse they tell another story. When the first cars started comin' in, some guy came in and stopped and went up to ol' John and he said, "I'm having carburetor trouble here, do you think you could fix it?" and ol' John said, "You damn rights I can fix it". And he went to the blacksmith shop and got a great big old hammer and a chisel and great big pair of these horse nippers, and he come out and said, "Where is the son-of-a-bee, I'll fix'er." And the guy said, "No, no, no, no, leave it alone, it's alright". At that time, he didn't have any more idea than the man in the moon about what a carburetor was.*

From Upper Courthouse Wash the Jacksons moved back to Thompson for several years. That move must have been in the late 1920's, when their oldest children were old enough to attend school. In the 3 or 4 years they lived there, John had another experience that has become legendary throughout the county--at least with the old timers. The late (?) **Kenny Davis** of Thompson knew John personally and he tells the story about how John tipped over an outhouse with somebody in it, and got sued:

Above John Jackson and his 2nd wife **Sinda Cordova Jackson**. John is at his ranch & corral at what is today the south end of Moab; and likely in the mid or late 1940's. Karl Tangren says it was Harry Reid who took this picture of John.

Above John Jackson and his oldest son **Jim Jackson** by his 2nd wife Sinda. Jim was born in 1924, so this foto was taken in about 1926.   **Left John Jackson Jr.**, the 3rd child in John Jackson's 1st family with Lillian. He was born in 1902, so this picture must have been in about 1920 while in the Navy. This is the son that was in a California mental hospital for a while, but spent time with his Dad and 2nd family in Moab in the 1940's. (All fotos from Ellesa Jackson Day Ekker)

Well, it happened on the road goin' south just out of Thompson. Ol' John came along and he said he was going to take a shortcut, instead of going around by this old road, so he went straight across this yard, and he hit a clothes line that went from the corner of this building to the shithouse. and he took that shithouse for a ride. But Edith Dubois was in it at the time! It just rolled her and the toilet down the flat a ways. And she sued him--she got some money. He was driving an old Hudson car at the time and it tore the roof off and took the windshield too. This must have happened sometime between 1930 and 1932, because I moved here in 1930. (Court records don't show Dubois suing John Jackson, so they may have settled out of court?)

Alice Jackson Olson remembered part of the outhouse story too: *She wasn't hurt, except for her dignity, but she took Dad to court, and she won. And right after he paid her the money, she bought a brand new car. Years later, my sisters and mother were telling me that Dad would always point to that car as they were driving around and say, "There goes my new car."*

It must have been in about 1931 or '32 when the Jacksons moved to Moab. They lived in town a while then in 1934, repossessed **Bert Allred's ranch** south of Moab near the present-day bowling alley and across the road southwest from the Alco store, and that's where they lived until John died in 1950.

Beginning in about 1915, when he became a director of the Moab State Bank, and extending through the rest of his life, John made part of his living by loaning money to people and lived off the interest. **Mitch Williams** of Moab had another story to tell of a time when he and his brother Dudley wanted to borrow money from ol' John Jackson. Part of that conversation went like this:

We wanted to build a gas station down there on the corner of Center and Main [in Moab], but we didn't have the money to do it with, and we didn't have the collateral to cover a loan. At that time there was only one place to get the money and that was from John Jackson. He had it and in this country he was the only guy who could come up with large sums of money. We needed $10,000--which is about like a million dollars nowadays.

So my brother Dudley [Le Duc] decided he was going to get that money out of John Jackson. And my father was quite old at the time and he ran a state liquor store downtown. So Dudley went down there and got a gallon [3.75 liters] of whiskey and he hunted up ol' John, and they started drinking it. And they drove around and you'd see 'em going down the street and then you wouldn't see 'em for a while, and then they'd come back. And when they'd run out of whiskey, Dud, he'd go back and get another gallon--I mean a gallon jug! Not 4 quarts! As long as it was being furnished, ol' John would drink it. Dudley said later it god damn near killed him after he stayed drunk all that time with ol' John. You couldn't drink him under the table!

And finally old John put his arm around Dudley and they staggered into the First National Bank, which was on the corner where First Security [Wells Fargo] Bank is now, and he went up to Harry Green who was the banker, and said, "Harry, give this boy $10,000 dollars; come on Dudley let's go have another drink", and that's all there was to it. Then Dudley got away from 'im as soon as he could. But the money was there, and John never signed anything.

When you'd borrow money from John, the bank would write up the promissory note, and it was old Harry Green who took care of all the notes and paperwork. So Dudley went in and signed for it. And the bank put the money into our account. But John never did draw up any papers. The bank handled everything. You see, the big depositors always have something to say about how the bank is run--and John was on the board of directors.

Even though John couldn't read or write very well, he did learn how to sign his signature [and read the newspaper]. You see, I was in high school at the time and I'd come home and tend the store, which also meant I tended the liquor store, and everybody had to sign a card in those days; these were state liquor stores. And old John would come in and he was so damn drunk sometimes that I'd have to sign his name for him--because he wasn't going to leave 'till he got the booze! But he would sign his name when he wasn't too drunk--and he would sign it real slooooow.

Another story the late **Mitch Williams** tells is about John, Sinda and Niva Kirk, Buck Kirk's wife (Buck was the son of Lee Kirk, the guy who built the cabin up in Salt Creek in The Needles District):

The Kirk's had a ranch up at Brown's Hole [southwest of Moab] and ol' John Jackson was saying he went up there one time, and he had some business with Buck--maybe a cattle deal or something, and they were talkin', and in those days you never asked anyone to dinner, you just assumed they were going to have dinner--and you just went ahead and prepared for them. I never heard anybody ask, "Won't you stay for dinner"?--that's the way they do it nowadays.

Anyway, Niva was rolling out the biscuit dough, and she had a rolling pin, and was rollin' it, and Sinda was watchin'. And Sinda said, "Oh I wished I had one of those". And Niva said, "A what"? And Sinda said, "A rollin' pin, John always makes me use a beer bottle". So when they left, Niva gave her the rollin' pin, and said, "Now Sinda, you've got yourself a rolling pin". And Sinda was as proud of that rolling pin as any they ever saw.

All the old timers around Moab knew John Jackson and everyone had a story to tell. Some weren't all that flattering, but most were rather amusing. **Ray Tibbetts** (Bill Tibbetts son) tells a story about another fight John and his brother Bill Hinton got into sometime in about the early 1940's:

I was quite a young kid, and John Jackson came down to our farm one day. And he was standing there talkin' to Dad; by this time they were pretty good friends. John had quite a little blood around his mouth, and some cuts on his lip, and he was spittin' blood. And Dad said, "My god John, what's wrong with you". And John opened his mouth and stuck his tongue out, and it and his cheek was cut real bad. Then he said that he and his brother Bill had got into a real ruckus. John had been driving the car across the old one-lane bridge across the Colorado River [north of Moab], and when you'd come out of it on this side, on the south side of the river, the road turned to the right and made quite a steep climb over a hill. And as they was goin' around there, they was also hot and heavy into an argument about what they was going to do about a piece of property they owned together over there about where the Atlas Mill is [was] today. And Bill got so infuriated with John, that he reached over with this real sharp pocket knife and stuck it in John's mouth and went around and around and around with it. And it cut his lips up, the roof of his mouth, and his tongue was just in shreds.

The car motor had died at the top of the hill and then it rolled back down this steep embankment and down into the willows by the river. They finally had to have somebody with a truck come and pull 'em out of there. Ol' John was a real character, no doubt about it.

Ray Tibbetts tells another story about John Jackson and his family fishing on the Colorado River perhaps in the late 1930's or early '40's:

At that time everybody fished on the Colorado River. The prime game fish was channel catfish. There's a few carp and a few suckers, and a few of these squawfish, I guess, or Colorado minnows they call 'em. But everybody fished on the river. And John and his family spent quite a little time fishin' there too. Anyway, this game warden stopped there one time--Moab didn't have a game warden, so this guy came down from Price. He'd come down and had observed different people along the river fishin'. He stopped to check licences, and of course nobody had a licence, because nobody enforced the law. Afterwards the warden had stopped down here at Cord Bowen's Motel, and was tellin' old Cord, "Well I come down to see what was happening and I observed all these people fishin' without licences, and I wrote 'em all tickets". And he went on to say, "I shook this one old boy and his family down but I didn't have the heart to write him a ticket--he looked so broke and looked like he needed the fish so bad to feed his family--because he had a bunch of kids with him".

Now John always wore his pants very low on his hips, and when he'd bend over, you could always see far down his lower backside. And also, John used to wear long handled underwear all summer, as well as all winter. He used to say, "What keeps the cold out also keeps the heat out too". But anyway, Cord asked the warden who the guy was, and he said, "I don't know what his name was, but he wore a black hat and when he bent over, his pants about fell off". And of course he was describing John Jackson. And ol' Cord says, "He was probably the only one of the bunch who could afford to pay a fine"! At that time John was probably the richest guy in the county.

An earlier version of the story of John Jackson was published in the 1st Edition of this writer's other book, *River Guide to Canyonlands*, but since then more information has surfaced, and finally 3 of John's daughters by the second marriage spoke to the author about their father. One was the late Alice Jackson Olson of Price. She was born in 1935, and quite close to her mother. She remembered things a little different than some of the real old timers of Moab because her father John was a vastly different man in later life with his second wife than when he was a wild young cowboy. Here's a few things she recalls, including another funny story or two:

Dad and Mom lived in tents when they first got married, that must have been up at Thompson, but up at our ranch just south of Moab, we had a big beautiful house, and nice beds and a big round table in the dining room. But we didn't have electricity or a toilet in the house. We had an outhouse. Dad didn't believe in indoor toilets.

Sometimes he would bring people who was goin' through town broke and hungry and starvin', up to our house and feed 'em and give 'em a bed. Then he'd give 'em a bus ticket to where ever they had to go. Some of 'em would scare my mother half to death.

My dad would not carry insurance--on the car or the house. He'd say, "Because, if I wrecked the car or the house burned down, they'll say that old so and so burned it down for the insurance money."

He got the ranch south of town because he had loaned money to the people who lived there, and they pulled out and left it [it was **Bert Allred**]. They didn't pay the debt. So he got it--he had no choice. He didn't really want it. It must have been a couple of hundred acres.

We lived there in the ranch house for approximately one year after Dad died. Half of it burned down only 3 days before he died, but he never knew about it. We lived in the back part afterwards. But the first thing Mom did after Dad died, was to put electricity up there. Dad didn't want electricity either. He'd say, "What was good enough for my mom and dad is good enough for you". Mom owned the ranch, but my oldest brother farmed it. Then she bought a house downtown in Moab, and we moved there.

Most of the money we got from Dad was in the way of bonds, and we drew interest on them throughout the years. Harry Green used to tell us kids, "Your dad had the most mathematically minded brain I ever saw. He could figure up money and amounts faster than they can on the adding machine". I remember when he loaned money for 8% interest. It may have gone up to 10% in later years?

My dad was a practical joker. He loved to play jokes on people and loved to tease. One game he liked to play with kids especially was called, "snatch the penny". He would always play this game in the barnyard somewhere and with a bunch of pennies. He always had everything ready beforehand--a flat rock, a bunch of pennies and a shovel full of cow manure nearby. He would put a blindfold on someone, then he'd have 'em reach out for the flat rock and try to grab pennies. The first time you grabbed, you always got pennies, and you got to keep them. Then he'd say, grab with both hands. Then he'd take the shovel of manure and tip it out on the rock before you grabbed the second time. Then you'd grab and there'd be nothing but cow manure on the rock! He even played this trick on some grown-ups. I remember the first time he pulled it on me. I was mad! Later, I pulled that one on of my girl friends too, and she came loose. That was Diane Kerby, Ed Kerby's daughter, and my best friend. She chased me, and we had that crap on both of us from one ear to the other. Dad was a prankster, so as far as leaving his first wife down there in that hole at Jailhouse Rock, it wouldn't surprise me. But I think he would have checked on her before too long.

Here's another story. Dad used to butcher pigs, and he'd cut the pigs up in the 2 pieces. One day he took some of these pigs from the ranch down to the Tony Meader's Cafe. He had 'em wrapped up in sheets in the back end of the truck. Well, when he got down there, somebody hit him in the back of the head and knocked him out. When he come to, $40 was gone from his pocket and he was in the back of the truck with the pigs!

Christmas was real big around our house and we always had all new clothes, shoes and coats. Depending on how old we were, we always had some toys. But most of all I remember Christmas as a time we always had a big box of oranges. Dad always used to send away to Montgomery Ward and Sears for 2 big cans of candy. The candy came in five gallon buckets, then we'd use 'em for milking after we ate the candy. Also, Dad would always go out near the ranch and cut a Christmas tree--usually a cedar tree. We always had a good Christmas with lots of good memories. Dad was the most loving father with his children. He was kind to us, and set us on his lap and told us stories.

Another guy who remembered the brighter and mellower side of John Jackson was **Fred Newman** of Moab. He too knew John when he was an older, wiser man:

Don Taylor recited another story to me once, and this happened long ago. John had these cattle down on King Bottom, which is the first bottom down the river from Moab on the east side. Don was comin' up along the river one day and lookin' for some of his stock, and he saw John a walkin'--he didn't even have a horse. And it was a cold blustery day and John's lips was blue he was so cold, but he was goin' down the river to check on his cattle. And Don Taylor said, "I had an old coat, it was pretty well worn, but it was warm, and I felt sorry for him and I just untied it from behind my saddle and give it to John". And John thanked him, and went on. He was a man of few words. Don Taylor said it was probably 3 years later that he was eatin' breakfast one morning, and a knock came on his door and it was John Jackson. He said, "Tied up out in front of his house was the prettiest paint horse that he'd ever seen". And John said, "There's the pay for that coat you gave me 3 years ago". There was a lot of wild horses in the country at that time and John had caught this paint horse and broke 'im and give 'im to

Don Taylor as a gift to pay for that coat he had given him about 3 years before.

John came to this country as a boy and had some pretty hard times. The old timers said he used to live down there under a big cottonwood tree by the Helen M. Knight School, and everybody had a wood pile and burned wood, and butchered their own beef and mutton, etc. And John would stand there all day and chop wood for a dollar a day. Or he would butcher a beef or a mutton for the hide and the heart and liver. He lived in a tent at that time.

John told me when he sold out his stock in the late 1920's [after the Range War], [John's daughter Ellesa thought it was in 1934?] he delivered cattle to Thompson and got $32 a head for everything from yearlings and up, and just throwd in the calves. He said he rounded up 989 head the first gather, so he had built up his herd to well over a 1000 head of cattle in the time he was out on the desert. Of course he had quite a lot of help; there never was a finer woman than Sinda Jackson. She was with 'im a lot and worked with him side by side. One time John told me that Sinda was ridin' with him when she was 8 months pregnant with Jim [their first boy] and stayin' out there in those cow camps. So they had a pretty tough life, but it paid off.

I know he was not only a good stockman but a good farmer too. I remember 3 or 4 years in my time, when I was a boy, he took the Blue Ribbon for field corn in the State Fair in Salt Lake. He done that for quite a few years. Ol' John, was hard and tough, but he survived in a tough world.

In 2012, this writer spent a little time on several occasions visiting with John's only surviving daughter, **Ellesa Jackson Day Ekker** in Moab. She recalled a few more things about her father:

We didn't know Dad's first family very well, but I remember Bill lived in Nevada, Josephine lived in California, Bud lived in California, and John (Kiddle) was in a mental hospital in California, I think (?). Then there was Belle who came to visit her father several times, and Fanny who had died. Those kids used to came to see us and their Dad sometimes, and Kiddle lived with us for several months, or maybe a year once [In John's divorce papers filed on June 7, 1917, it lists 7 children: Belle, age 20; Jesse, 18; John, 15; Fannie, 12; Eldiva, 9; Glen, 5; and Josephine, 2 years old].

In my family, Mom and Dad were married in [October] 1921, and they had one daughter named Georgia, who was born, then died in Thompson at age 2. She's buried in Thompson. Then there's Jim the oldest, then Opel and me Ellesa [born 1930], then Alice, Joe and Jack. The only ones alive now [2013] are Jack and myself.

The Alco store [in south Moab] was almost sitting on our ranch. Everything on the west side of the highway from Alco was my dad's land and we had some land down by the creek south of Alco. We raised everything we ate, and everything we fed to the horses and cows and pigs.

Dad died of cancer of the throat. He smoked some, but he rolled his own cigarettes and they would fall apart, so he didn't smoke a lot!

I believed he sold his cows in about 1934 and we moved up to the ranch that he had repossessed, and I was 2 years old then. After that he just loaned money--he was just like a bank.

A couple of more things Ellesa told this writer. She stated that he never talked about his earlier life at all, and that she only learned about that from reading the first edition of this book. She also had heard about Jackson's Ladder & Trail and Jackson Bottom & Hole, but had never been down there; she now has some pictures.

The story of John Jackson ends when he died on **May 1, 1950** in Moab. It was cancer of the throat that got him. He left a significant sum of money to both his families, most of which was in the form of

Left L to R **Bill Hinton** (John Jackson's Brother), Bill Sperry & **Mark Walker**, the man who built the "Outlaw Cabin" on Fort Bottom. This picture was taken before March of 1942; that's when Mark Walker died. (Connie Murphy Skelton Collection) **Right Bill Hinton**, probably in the 1910's or '20's. (Alice Jackson Olson Collection)

Right L to R **Helen & Leland Tidwell, Eva Romjue Loughery Tidwell, and Bobby Tidwell**, the only child of Helen & Leland. It was these 3 who went down on Woodrufff (later known as Tidwell) Bottom, trying to homestead it in the early 1930's. This picture was taken in about 1937 or '38, and likely in the town Green River. (Ila Mae Tidwell Clark Collection)

Below L to R Pearl Biddlecome (later Marsing Baker), Clyde (Loughery) Tidwell, Unknown, Joe Biddlecome, and Hazel Biddlecome (later Ekker). This picture was taken at branding time in **Twin Corral** which is West Southwest of the Hans Flat (Maze) Ranger Station and not too far south of the Maze Road. This picture was taken in about 1920-'21 (Pearl was born in 1907), soon after Clyde got home from WWI. Twin Corral was made by dragging a bunch of old logs and cedar (juniper) trees together and just stacking them to make an enclosure. Both teenage girls are wearing bibb overalls and working along side the men! (Pearl B. M. Baker Collection)

Pearl   Clyde Tidwell   Joe   Hazel

at Twin Corral

promissory notes, or loans he had made. As of 2013, only one of John's daughters was still alive, that was 80-year-old Ellesa Jackson Day Ekker who was living with a daughter in Moab. One son, Jack Jackson, born in 1941, was still alive and living in Lincoln, Nebraska.

Read a little more about John Jackson's life as a stockmen in the Shafer Basin and Jackson Hole country near Potash in the chapter with **Map 25**.

The end of Bill Hinton's Story

In the early 1920's, Bill went to Winthrop, Washington, and bought a large dairy farm. That was in August of 1923, but he didn't move his family until sometime the next winter. He sold most of his cattle to his brother John Jackson. Bill's son Clay Hinton remembered what happened from then on: *We lived there until my mother got quite sick with some kind of emphysema, and we had to sell the cows. So we left there and bought a place over at Granite Falls. This was just 2 or 3 years after we first went to Washington, in about 1925 or '26. Then we got rid of that place and moved to Everett. Dad went back and forth between Washington and Moab, then finally he moved back down to Utah. I think it was in about 1928 or '29 they moved back to Moab. Finally, in 1951 he moved back up to Washington, then he'd stay a month with my brother and a month with me--like that [he was in Moab with his brother when John Jackson died on May 1, 1950]. On November 1, 1958, he finally died. The family didn't have the money to ship his body back to Moab for burial, so he was buried in Hoquiam, Washington.*

Leland Tidwell on Tidwell Bottom

Now back to the history of **Tidwell Bottom**. About 6 years after Clyde Tidwell's death, **Leland Tidwell**, his half brother, went down to Tidwell Bottom and tried to set up a ranch. The late **Bobby Tidwell**, Leland's only son, remembered a few things about the place on Tidwell Bottom:

My father Leland and his wife Helen, tried to homestead Woodruff [now Tidwell] Bottom beginning before I was born or shortly thereafter, but I don't know anything about it other than my dad mentioned once or twice that he tried to homestead it. I was born on November 27,1932.

I do remember the log cabin; one room, as near as I can remember. Afterwards, the thing they always laughed about when we were down there was, I spent about half my time pounding nails into the bottom log--that would be the door sill. And sure enough, years later [when we visited the place] there were still a bunch of rusty nails in it. I can only remember parts of it, so I must have been 2 or 3 years old, somewhere along in there. That would have been in the mid-1930's I did that.

I don't remember when it was, but my mother had a miscarriage down there, and they buried it not too far from the cabin. It was a boy and was born before I was, so he would have been an older brother. He [the miscarriage] must have been born in 1931 or in early '32. So they must have been down there trying to homestead it at that same time. We had used the Woodruff [Tidwell] Bottom all along while in the country and up until we packed up and sold out [in 1945].

The late **Kenny Allred** remembered Leland & Helen Tidwell, and one miscarriage: *Now I was the one who named it Tidwell Bottom. The old timers had a different name for that. They [Tidwells] used to camp there. They talked about comin' down and farming it. After the Clyde Tidwell thing, I remember another old cabin being there [which had been built by the Tidwells].*

I knew Leland pretty well. I met him quite a few times. They had a little old row boat they left over there, and they'd come around and down that Horsethief Trail sometimes. Then one time Leland and his wife was down there on the river and had a miscarriage, and I know he come up and got my wife to go down there. We lived there at Murray's Horsethief Ranch at the time [this miscarriage must have been a 2nd one because Kenny was born on 7/8/1915 and wasn't married to his first wife Babe until November 24,1933--he was 18, Hazel C. Stevens was 22]. My wife went down there and stayed a couple of days and helped 'em out until she got to feeling better. That's how we kinda got acquainted with 'em. That was where the Tidwells stayed, where the stone foundations are now.

See a picture of part of the foundation to the cabin apparently built by Leland Tidwell on page 371.

Jack (Beans) Milling on Tidwell Bottom

It seems the next time anyone tried to live on **Tidwell Bottom** was in the early 1940's. It was a guy who everybody thought was a draft dodger, because he was there during World War II. **Kenny Allred** was the best source on this fellow named **Jack (Beans) Milling** and his stay on Tidwell Bottom:

He didn't live in a cabin, just a dugout; out there in those sand flats where there's trees and tamaracks [tamarisks] now. He made 'im a dugout down in the ground and covered it over with brush and dirt and pert near level, and his old hair was full of sand every time you'd see him. He was quite a guy. Stories got out that he was dodging the law, and a draft dodger, and this, that, and the other. It had to have been during the war when he first went there. I went in the Army in 1943, and Beans was there before that. Art Murray was still out there at Horsethief at that time.

Art Murray was with me the day we first talked with him across the river, and he asked Art to bring them beans down for him. I don't know to this day how he got hooked up down there, but we packed him in 500 lbs [230 kgs] of beans. So that's how we hung that name of "Beans" on 'im. I never did know his real name until later. He must have cooked those beans on a campfire; he couldn't have cooked them in that dugout--oh I guess he could have cooked them there in the winter time. When we first met him it was way early in the spring, and the river was just startin' to raise. He had a little old boat made out of barrels--but I don't think he had it at that time. If he did, he had it pulled back in the brush, because I never seen it for quite a while. He got to where he'd cross the river in that boat.

*He showed up with that little boat, and he hauled 'em [the beans] across. We packed 'em down on horseback for 'im. There wasn't any road down there then, just the **Horsethief Trail** itself. We heard that he had somebody on the other side packin' 'im in some beans too. But later, after the burn, I found this one barrel and it was damn near full of beans. It would still be there somewhere if it wasn't rusted away, but it wouldn't all rust away. There should still be a little evidence left there.*

I'll bet those horses you [MRK] saw down there in the summer of 1990 were grazing illegally, because I had the last [BLM] permit down there.

Jack (Beans) Milling was there a year or two, then he packed up and went over on the Colorado River to what Karl Tangren later called **Hermit, Jack Milling's and Alfalfa Bottoms**. Read more on that part of the Jack Milling's story on the Colorado River side.

There's not much to see on **Tidwell Bottom today**. The **house** that **Robert Woodruff** seems to have built (?) was likely the same cabin that Clyde Tidwell was staying in when it burned down in December, 1925 with a human body inside. No one today can say for sure, but that house may have been located in about the middle of the bottom. In 1990, the author found **2 old stoves** in that area. But these weren't seen in 2011--in part because the author was there during the high waters of 2011, and there was a lake covering the bottom, which created the worst mosquito breeding grounds in the country so he really didn't have a chance to search the place as planned. No one this writer talked to could come up with an answer as to who these old stoves belonged to, or in what cabin they may have come out of. Seems likely they were in the Woodruff cabin (?) and the one Clyde was using in 1925.

However, in the northeast part of the bottom and at the south end of a little ridge coming down from the north, you'll find some **flat stones** which were part of a cabin's foundation, and part of an old **bedstead & stove** half buried in the red Moenkopi dirt. About 100m north of that is what remains of an old **log fence** running up the steep hillside to the west, and some cottonwood trees to the east of the house site. The high water mark of the floods of 2011, came very close to this cabin site.

After the Clyde Tidwell thing, and in about 1931 or '32, **Leland Tidwell**, Clydes half brother, built another **cabin** that his son Bobby Tidwell claims was right on the bank of the river, so it's possible this foundation could be from Leland's cabin since tamarisks are pretty close by. All areas near the river bank and below the high water mark today are covered with tamarisks and willows. Kenny Allred had a permit to graze cows there sometime in the 1950's, and got a BLM permit to burn off the bottom to allow grasses to come back. He seemed to remember the ruins of Leland's old cabin still there at the time, but it would be gone now, probably finished off by that fire.

The author never did find the dugout that Jack "Beans" Milling built, but if you put on long pants and wander around through the tamarisks, you might locate it, and the remains of that barrel of beans. Best to look at areas just above the high water mark and the tamarisks.

Backpacking to Tidwell Bottom

It's a lot easier for boaters to reach **Tidwell Bottom**, but if you're the adventurous type you can get there on **foot by backpacking** down the **Angel Trail in Lower Horseshoe Canyon**. Or better still, drive to the trailhead for the nearby **Frog Trail**, which can be done with a car, then walk southward along what used to be an old cattle trail along the west bank of the Green River all the way to Tidwell.

Another option would be to come down **Horsethief Canyon** to the Green River, then walk northward along the west bank to this bottom. Some cattle used to be driven along that old horsethief trail too, but be warned, you'll have to walk along the river bank above the high water mark which is above the jungle of tamarisks. For this trek, better have a pair of light weight hiking boots for walking on some steeper slopes and probably along some big game trails.

If you try this, there's no need to get a permit of any kind because it's outside the boundaries of Canyonlands National Park.

Left Art Murray, and John Jackson's only surviving daughter in 2013, **Ellesa Jackson Day Ekker**. This picture was taken in 1977 or '78. (Ellesa Jackson Day Ekker Collection). **Right Kenny Allred** at age 10 or 11 (born in 1915), and we believe **Bill "Peg Leg" Moore**, Eph & Amy Moore's older brother (born in 1872). Not long after this foto was taken, a horse fell with him on it near Dubinky (north of Big Flat) breaking his right foot. He had to crawl several miles for help, then had to have the foot amphutated below the knee; thus the name Peg Leg in his later years. According to Pearl B. M. Baker and Kenny Allred, Bill Moore was the one who introduced the burros into Millard and Horseshoe Canyons in the Robbers Roost country. (Connie Murphy Skelton Collection)

A Moore-Allred-Tibbetts Family Reunion in Moab. From the left, and adults: Aunt Lona Moore, Kenny Allred, Bill Tibbetts, Eph Moore, Agatha & Evelyn Allred (Kenny's sisters), and Amy Moore Tibbetts Allred--the mother of both Kenny and Bill, and the sister of Eph & Lona Moore. Bill & wife Jewell were married on December 31, 1925. The 3 young children belonged to Bill Tibbetts--oldest is Bob born April 12, 1927 in Santa Fe; then Jim on the ground was born October 27, 1928 in Santa Fe; and Gail in Kenny's arms, born August 13, 1930 in Moab. This picture must have been taken in the fall of 1930 or the spring of 1931 (with leaves still on the trees) in Moab and it was taken by Bill Tibbett's wife Jewell. The Tibbetts moved to Moab in the summer of 1930 and were there for a year or two, then moved back to Santa Fe where their 4th son Ray was born on April 22, 1932. In about 1939, Tibbetts moved his family back to Utah for good. (Kenny Allred Collection, and Tom McCourt researched these dates from an LDS genealogy site; *familysearch.org*)

Left The late, great **Pearl Biddlecome Marsing Baker** in the Castle Country Care Center in Price, Utah in 1990. (MRK foto) **Right** This appears to be a genuine **still** for making moonshine whiskey during the 1920's located in the South Fork of Mill Creek Canyon. Good thing it's too heavy to carry!

Left Looking west from the top of what this writer calls, **Halfdome**; some maps call it Shaft (Peak). In the far distance upper left, is **Candlestick Tower.** You can walk the narrow bench in the middle of this picture for some interesting views. **Right** A boulder covered with grooves in the Alcove in lower **West Fork of Sevenmile Canyon** 300m west of **Intestine Man.** See **Map 16.**

Looking northeast from the middle of **Chesler Park**. This is one of the more popular destinations in The Needles, and one of the more fotogenic places in Canyonlands NP.

Further Reading

Area History

A Canyon Voyage--The Narrative of the Second Powell Expedition, Frederick S. Dellenbaugh, University of Arizona Press, Tucson, Arizona, 1908 and 1984 (or later printing).

Archaeological Investigations in the Maze District, Canyonlands National Park, Utah, Lucius and others, *Antiquities Section, Selected Paper, #11*, Department of Anthropology, University of Utah, Salt Lake City, Utah.

Colorado River Bed Case, testimonies of many witnesses, Utah State Historical Society, Salt Lake City, Utah, 1929-1931.

Canyonlands National Park--Early History and First Descriptions, F.A. Barnes, Canyon Country Publications, Moab, Utah, 1988.

Geological Survey Bulletin #841, *Geology and Oil Possibilities of the Moab District*, A.A. Baker.

Geological Survey Professional Paper #491-A, *Introduction, Spread and Areal Extent of Saltcedar (Tamarix) in the Western States*, T.W. Robinson, 1965.

Grand Canyon Rapids--Running the Green and Colorado Rivers, Muriel W. Smith, Carlton Press, Inc., New York, or from Muriel W. Smith (?), Green River, Utah, 1990.

Grand Memories, Daughters of Utah Pioneers, Grand County, Utah Printing Company, Salt Lake City, Utah, 1972.

Historical Sites in Cataract and Narrow Canyons, and in Glen Canyon to California Bar, C. Gregory Crampton, *Anthropological Papers, #72*, University of Utah, August, 1964.

Horsethief Ranch--an Oral History, H. Michael Behrendt, Self Published, 1985.

In Search of Butch Cassidy, Larry Pointer, University of Oklahoma Press, Norman, Oklahoma, 1978.

Last of the Robbers Roost Outlaws: Moab's Bill Tibbetts, Tom McCourt, Canyonlands Natural History Association, Moab, Utah, 2010.

Look to the Mountains, Charles S. Peterson, Brigham University Press, Provo, Utah, 1975.

Monticello Journal--A History of Monticello until 1937, Harold and Fay Muhlestein, Self Published, Monticello, Utah, 1988.

My Canyonlands, Kent Frost, Abelard-Schuman, New York, 1971.

Nature Conservancy, Winter 2010, Article about Heidi Redd and the Dugout Ranch.

Old Spanish Trail, Santa Fe to Los Angeles, LeRoy and Ann Hafen, Author H. Clark Company, Glendale, California, 1954.

One Man's West, David Lavender, University of Nebraska Press, Lincoln, Nebraska, 1977.

Rim Flying Canyonlands, with Jim Hurst, Pearl Biddlecome Marsing Baker, A-to-Z Printing, Inc., Riverside, California, 1973.

Robbers Roost Recollections, Pearl Biddlecome Marsing Baker, Utah State University Press, Logan, Utah, 1991 (or later printing).

Saga of San Juan, C.A. Perkins, N.G. Nielson & L.B. Jones, San Juan County Daughters of Utah Pioneers, Monticello, Utah, 1968.

Seely Family Newsletter: A Legacy of Love, *An Under the Ledge Diary* by Edwin MG Seely for October, 1945; May 2008, Vol. 19 #2, Edited by Montel & Katherine Seely, Castle Dale, Utah.

Steamboats on the Colorado River--1852 to 1916, Richard E. Lingenfelter, University of Arizona Press, Tucson, Arizona, 1978.

The Bandit Invincible (Butch Cassidy), William T. Phillips, Carbon County Historical Society, Price, Utah, 1991 (?).

The Exploration of the Colorado River and its Canyons, John W. Powell, Dover Publications, Inc., New York, 1895 and 1961 (or later printing).

The Wild Bunch at Robbers Roost, Pearl Biddlecome Marsing Baker, University of Nebraska Press, Lincoln, Nebraska, 1989.

The Grand Valley Times (5/30/1896 to 9/5/1919) and **The Times-Independent** (9/12/1919 to Present), Moab, Utah. For this book, the papers read were from 1896 until about 1950

Trail on the Water, Pearl Biddlecome Marsing Baker, Pruett Publishing Company, Boulder, Colorado.

Utah Historical Quarterly, Autumn 2010, *The Origins of Chesler Park*, Clyde L. Denis (origin of the name, old cowboy signatures, snowfall and the history of grazing in The Needles).

Utah Historical Quarterly, Fall 2012, Clyde L. Denis, *Departure of the Late Nineteenth Century Cattle Companies from Southeastern Utah: A Reassessment*.

Guide Books

Arches National Park, John R. Hoffman, Western Recreational Publications, San Diego, California, 1985.

Canyonlands River Guide, Bill & Buzz Belknap, Westwater Books, All New Edition of 2010.

Guidebook (Geology) to the Colorado River--Part 3, Moab to Hite, Utah, Rigby, Hamblin, Matheny & Welsh, Department of Geology, Brigham Young University, Provo, Utah, 1972.

Hiking, Biking and Exploring Canyonlands National Park and Vicinity, 2nd Edition, Michael R. Kelsey, Kelsey Publishing, Provo, Utah, 2013.

Hiking and Exploring Utah's Henry Mountains and Robbers Roost: *Including The Life and Legend of Butch Cassidy*, 3rd Edition and in Color, 2009, Michael R. Kelsey, Kelsey Publishing, Provo, Utah.

Hiking the Historic Route of the 1859 Macomb Expedition, F.A. Barnes, Canyon Country Publications, Moab, Utah, 1989.

Non-Technical Canyon Guide to the Colorado Plateau, 6th Edition, 2011, Michael R. Kelsey, Kelsey Publishing, Provo, Utah.

River Runners Guide to Canyonlands National Park and Vicinity (with Emphasis on Geologic Features), Felix E. Mutschler, Powell Society Ltd., Denver, Colorado, 1969.

Other Guidebooks by the Author

Books listed in the order they were first published. Some are momentarily out-of-print; some may never be reprinted. Go to **kelseyguidebooks.com** for a list of his books currently in print (Prices as of April, 2013, but may change without notice).

Climber's and Hiker's Guide to the World's Mountains & Volcanos (4th Edition), 1248 pages, 584 maps, 652 B+W fotos, ISBN 0-944510-18-3. **SALE PRICE US$19.95 (Mail Orders US$23).**
Utah Mountaineering Guide (3rd Edition), 208 pages, 143 fotos, 54 hikes, ISBN 0-944510-14-0. US$10.95 (Mail Orders US$13).
China on Your Own and *Guide to China's Nine Sacred Mountains,* **Out of Print.**
Non-Technical Canyon Hiking Guide to the Colorado Plateau (6th Edition), 416 pages, 135 hiking maps, **385 color fotos,** ISBN 978-0-944510-27-8. US$19.95 (Mail Orders US$22).
Hiking and Exploring Utah's San Rafael Swell (3rd Edition) **Out of Print** until the new color & 4th edition which should come out in **March of 2014.**
Hiking and Exploring Utah's Henry Mountains and Robbers Roost, *Including The Life and Legend of Butch Cassidy* (3rd Edition), 288 pages, 38 hiking or climbing areas, **311 mostly color fotos,** ISBN 978-0-944510-25-4. US$15.95 (Mail Orders US$18).
Hiking and Exploring the Paria River, *Including: The Story of John D. Lee & the Mountain Meadows Massacre* (5th Edition), 384 pages, 41 mapped hiking areas from Bryce Canyon to Lee's Ferry, **523 mostly color fotos,** ISBN 978-0-944510-26-1. US$19.95 (Mail Orders US$22).
Hiking and Climbing in the Great Basin National Park--*A Guide to Nevada's Wheeler Peak, Mt. Moriah, and the Snake Range,* **Out of Print.**
Boater's Guide to Lake Powell, *Featuring: Hiking, Camping, Geology, History & Archaeology* (5th Edition), 288 pages, **263 color fotos,** ISBN 978-0-944510-24-7. US$19.95 (Mail Orders US$22).
Climbing and Exploring Utah's Mt. Timpanogos, 208 pages, 170 fotos. **Out of Print, but will be updated in a few years.**
River Guide to Canyonlands National Park & Vicinity, *Featuring: Hiking, Camping, Geology, Archaeology, and Steamboating, Cowboy, Ranching & Trail Building History,* **2nd Edition,** 272 pages, **282 mostly color fotos,** ISBN 978-944510-28-5. US$17.95 (Mail Orders US$20).
Hiking, Biking and Exploring Canyonlands National Park & Vicinity, *Featuring: Hiking, Biking, Geology, Archaeology, and Cowboy, Ranching & Trail Building History,* 2nd Edition, 392 pages, 35 Mapped Areas, over **400 mostly color fotos,** ISBN 978-0-944510-29-2, US$19.95 (Mail Orders US$22).
Life on the Black Rock Desert: A History of Clear Lake, Utah, Venetta B. Kelsey, 192 pages, 123 fotos. **Out of Print, but will be reprinted & updated when time is available.**
The Story of Black Rock, Utah, 160 pages, 142 fotos, ISBN 0-944510-12-4. US$9.95 (Mail Orders US$12).
Hiking, Climbing & Exploring Western Utah's Jack Watson's Ibex Country, 272 pages, 224 fotos, ISBN 0-944510-13-2. US$9.95 (Mail Orders US$12).
Technical Slot Canyon Guide to the Colorado Plateau (2nd Edition), 336 pages, **341 color fotos,** ISBN 978-0-944510-23-0. US$19.95 (Mail Orders US$22).

Distributors for Kelsey Publishing

Primary Distributor All of Michael R. Kelsey's books are sold by this distributor. A list of Kelsey's titles is shown above. Or go to *kelseyguidebooks.com* for the latest list of distributors and what books are presently in print.
Brigham Distributing, 110 South, 800 West, Brigham City, Utah, 84302, Tele. 435-723-6611, Fax 435-723-6644, Website *brighamdistributing.com,* Email *brigdist@sisna.com.*

Many of Kelsey's books are sold by these distributors.
Partners West, 1901 Raymond Avenue SW, Renton, WA, 98057, Tele. 425-227-8486, Fax 425-204-1448, Email *orders@partners-west.com.*
Books West, 18101 East Colfax Avenue, Aurora, Colorado, USA, 80011, Tele. 303-449-5995, or 800-378-4188, Fax 303-449-5951, Website *bookswest.com.*
Treasure Chest Books (Owners of Canyonlands Publications), 451 North, Bonita Avenue, Tucson, Arizona, USA, 85745, Tele. 520-623-9558, or 800-969-9558, Website *treasurechestbooks.com,* Email *info@rionuevo.com.*

Some of Kelsey's books are sold by the following distributors.
Liberty Mountain, 4375 West 1980 South, Suite 100, Salt Lake City, Utah, 84104, Tele. 800-578-2705 or 801-954-0741, Fax 801-954-0766, Website *libertymountain.com,* Email *sales@libertymountain.com.*
Rincon Publishing, 1913 North Skyline Drive, Orem, Utah, 84097, Tele. 801-377-7657, Fax 801-356-2733, Website *rinconpub@utahtrails.com.*
Recreational Equipment, Inc. (R.E.I.), 1700 45th Street East, Sumner, Washington, USA, 98390, Website *rei.com,* Mail Orders Tele. 800-426-4840 (or check at any of their local stores).
Online--Internet: *amazon.com;* btol.com ; Ingrams.com; Bdaltons.com; BarnesandNoble.com.

For the **UK and Europe,** and the world contact: **Cordee,** 3a De Montfort Street, Leicester, England, UK, LE1 7HD, Tele. Inter+44-116-254-3579, Fax Inter+44-116-247-1176, Website *cordee.co.uk.*